Elizabeth Gaskell

SYLVIA'S LOVERS

Edited and introduced by
NANCY HENRY
State University of New York, Binghamton

Other critical material by
GRAHAM HANDLEY

EVERYMAN
J. M. DENT · LONDON
CHARLES E. TUTTLE
VERMONT

Series Editor for the Everyman Elizabeth Gaskell
Graham Handley

Introduction and other critical material
© J. M. Dent 1997

Sylvia's Lovers first published by Everyman in 1964
This edition first published by Everyman Paperbacks
in 1997

J. M. Dent
Orion Publishing Group
Orion House
5 Upper St Martin's Lane
London WC2H 9EA
and
Charles E. Tuttle Co. Inc.
28 South Main Street
Rutland, Vermont 05701, USA

Typeset by CentraCet Ltd, Cambridge
Printed in Great Britain by
The Guernsey Press Co. Ltd, Guernsey, C. I.

British Library Cataloguing-in-Publication Data
is available upon request.

ISBN 0 460 87783 6

CONTENTS

NOTE ON THE AUTHOR

ELIZABETH CLEGHORN GASKELL was born in Chelsea, London, on 29 September 1810. Her father William Stevenson, who had been a Unitarian preacher, was a clerk and also a journalist at this time. After the death of her mother, when Elizabeth was a year old, she was sent to Knutsford in Cheshire (the town upon which Cranford is modelled) where she was brought up by her aunt, Hannah Lumb, and where she attended the Misses Byerleys' school in Warwickshire 1821–6. In 1832 she married William Gaskell, a minister at Cross Street Unitarian Chapel, Manchester. The Gaskells had five children, the only son William dying before he was a year old in 1845. To alleviate her grief Mrs Gaskell began writing fiction: her first stories appeared in Howitt's Journal in 1847, and Mary Barton, her novel about industrial life in Manchester, in 1848. Despite these being published anonymously, her name became known. She contributed stories and then Cranford to Charles Dickens's magazine Household Words from 1850 onwards. Ruth (1853) boldly dealt with the controversial subject of the unmarried mother, while North and South was serialised in Household Words in 1854–5. Her next major undertaking, at the suggestion of Patrick Brontë, was The Life of Charlotte Brontë (1857). Mrs Gaskell was an untiring worker in support of her husband in Manchester, but she also found time for much travel in Europe. She produced a remarkable number of stories which reflect her talent. Sylvia's Lovers (1863) is a major historical novel, while her masterpiece, Wives and Daughters (1864–5), was unfinished at her death from a heart attack at Alton, Hampshire, on 12 November 1865.

NOTE ON THE EDITORS

GRAHAM HANDLEY has written widely on nineteenth-century literature, particularly on George Eliot and Anthony Trollope. His books include *George Eliot: The State of the Art* (1990), *George Eliot's Midlands: Passion in Exile* (1991) and *Trollope the Traveller* (1993).

NANCY HENRY, who is Assistant Professor of English at the State University of New York, Binghamton, has edited George Eliot's *Impressions of Theophrastus Such* (1994).

ACKNOWLEDGEMENTS

The editor and publishers wish to thank the following for permission to use copyright material:

Faber & Faber Ltd for material from Jenny Uglow, *Elizabeth Gaskell: A Habit of Stories* (1993), pp. 513–15;

Oxford University Press for material from Winifred Gerin, *Elizabeth Gaskell: A Biography* (Clarendon Press, 1976), pp. 212–15;

Prentice Hall for material from Patsy Stoneman, *Elizabeth Gaskell* (Harvester, 1987), pp. 149–53;

Routledge for material from Angus Easson, *Elizabeth Gaskell* (Routledge & Kegan Paul, 1979), pp. 170–73; and Wendy A. Craik, *Elizabeth Gaskell and the Provincial Novel* (Methuen & Co., 1975), pp. 147–51.

Every effort has been made to trace the copyright holders but if any have been inadvertently overlooked the publishers will be pleased to make the necessary arrangement at the first opportunity.

CHRONOLOGY OF
ELIZABETH GASKELL'S LIFE

Year	Age	Life
1810		Born 29 September, second surviving child of William and Elizabeth Stevenson, in Chelsea, London. (An older brother, John)
1811	1	October. Her mother dies. In November Elizabeth is taken to Knutsford, Cheshire, where she will be brought up by her aunt, Hannah Lumb
1821	10	Goes to the Misses Byerleys' school at Barford, Warwickshire

CHRONOLOGY OF
HER TIMES

Year	Literary Context	Historical Events
1812	Birth of Charles Dickens Crabbe, *Tales* Byron, *Childe Harold's Pilgrimage*	
1813	Jane Austen, *Pride and Prejudice*	Wellington defeats French at Vittoria, Spain
1814	Scott, *Waverley* Wordsworth, *Excursion*	
1815		Battle of Waterloo, Napoleon banished to St Helena
1816	Birth of Charlotte Brontë	
1817	Death of Jane Austen Ricardo, *Principles of Political Economy and Taxation*	
1818	Mary Shelley, *Frankenstein* Scott, *Heart of Midlothian*	Frontier between USA and Canada agreed
1819	Birth of George Eliot (Mary Ann Evans) Byron, *Don Juan*	'Peterloo massacre': troops fire on workers in Manchester
1820		George III dies, succeeded by George IV
1821	Death of Keats	Napoleon dies on St Helena

Year	Age	Life
1824	14	The school moves to 'Avonbank', Stratford-upon-Avon
1826	16	June. Leaves school
1827	17	Knutsford, holiday in Wales
1828	18	Her brother John disappears on a voyage to India. Elizabeth goes to Chelsea to live with her father and stepmother
1829	19	March. William Stevenson dies. Elizabeth goes to stay with Revd William Turner, Newcastle upon Tyne
1830	20	Spent in Knutsford and Newcastle
1831	21	Visits Edinburgh with Anne Turner. Summer in Liverpool then Knutsford. In Manchester meets Revd William Gaskell, junior minister at Cross Street Unitarian Chapel
1832	22	30 August. Marries William Gaskell, moves to Manchester
1833	23	Birth of a still-born daughter
1834	24	12 September. Her daughter Marianne is born
1837	27	January. 'Sketches among the Poor' (with William), in *Blackwood's Edinburgh Magazine* 5 February. Margaret Emily (Meta) born May. Aunt Lumb dies

Year	Literary Context	Historical Events
1822	Shelley drowns at Lerici Beethoven, *Missa Solemnis*	
1823	Lamb, *Essays of Elia*	
1824	Death of Byron at Missolonghi	
1826	Fenimore Cooper, *Last of the Mohicans*	
1827	Keble, *Christian Year* Manzoni, *I promessi sposi*	Treaty between Britain, Russia and France to assure independence of Greece (confirmed 1830)
1830	Tennyson, *Poems, chiefly Lyrical* Charles Lyell, *Principles of Geology*	George IV dies, succeeded by William IV Revolutionary uprisings in Germany, Poland, Belgium, France (abdication of Charles IX; election of Louis Philippe as King)
1831	Ebenezer Elliot, *Corn Law Rhymes*	Russell introduces first Reform Bill
1832	Deaths of Sir Walter Scott and Goethe	First Reform Act passed
1833	Carlyle, *Sartor Resartus*	Factory inspection introduced in England
1834		Slavery ended in British possessions
1836	Dickens, *Pickwick Papers*	
1837	Dickens, *Oliver Twist*	William IV dies, succeeded by Queen Victoria

Year	Age	Life
1840	30	'Clopton Hall' included in William Howitt, *Visits to Remarkable Places*
1841	31	Visits Germany with William
1842	32	7 October. Florence Elizabeth (Flossy) born
1844	34	23 October. Birth of her son, William
1845	34	10 August. William dies, aged ten months, in North Wales
1846	36	3 September. Fourth daughter, Julia Margaret Bradford, born
1847–8	37	'Libbie Marsh's Three Eras', 'The Sexton's Hero', 'Christmas Storms and Sunshine', in *Howitt's Journal*

Year	Literary Context	Historical Events
1838		Anti-Corn-Law League founded in Manchester
1839	Carlyle, *Chartism*	Chartist petition presented to Parliament Opium war with China: Hong Kong taken New Zealand declared a British colony
1840	Browning, *Sordello*	Marriage of Queen Victoria to Prince Albert of Saxe-Coburg-Gotha
1841		Peel succeeds Melbourne as British Prime Minister
1842	Comte, *Cours de la philosophie positive* Macaulay, *Lays of Ancient Rome*	Hong Kong ceded to Britain Widespread Chartist riots
1843	Carlyle, *Past and Present* Ruskin, *Modern Painters*, I	
1844	Disraeli, *Coningsby*	
1845	Disraeli, *Sybil*	Texas made USA state, Mexico loses Arizona, California, New Mexico join USA in 1847 Beginning of potato famine in Ireland
1846	Edward Lear, *Book of Nonsense*	Pius IX elected Pope Repeal of Corn Laws in Britain
1847	Tennyson, *The Princess* Charlotte Brontë, *Jane Eyre* Emily Brontë, *Wuthering Heights*	Poland made a Russian province

Year	Age	Life
1848	38	November. *Mary Barton*
1849	39	Visits London: meets Dickens, Carlyle, Forster
1850	40–41	Begins to write for Dickens's *Household Words*: 'Lizzie Leigh', 'The Well of Pen Morfa', 'The Heart of John Middleton' The Gaskells move to 84 Plymouth Grove, Manchester August. First meeting with Charlotte Brontë December. *The Moorland Cottage*
1851	41	July. Visits Great Exhibition December–May 1853. *Cranford* episodes in *Household Words*
1852	42	'The Old Nurse's Story'
1853	42	January. *Ruth* May. Visit to Paris July. Holiday in Normandy 19–23 September. Visit to Haworth
1854	43–4	February. Visits Paris September–January 1855. *North and South* in *Household Words*
1855	44	February. Visits Paris 31 March. Death of Charlotte Brontë June. Patrick Brontë asks her to write Charlotte's *Life*

Year	Literary Context	Historical Events
1848	Thackeray, *Vanity Fair* J. S. Mill, *Principles of Political Economy*	Revolutions in Sicily, Austria (Emperor Ferdinand abdicates in favour of nephew, Francis Joseph), and France (Republic proclaimed: Louis Napoleon elected President). Uprisings against Austria in Italy Lord Dalhousie appointed Governor-General of India First Women's Rights Convention, Seneca Falls, USA Pre-Raphaelite Brotherhood formed
1849	Charlotte Brontë, *Shirley*	Garibaldi enters Rome Britain annexes Punjab
1850	Dickens, *David Copperfield* *Household Words* founded Tennyson, *In Memoriam* Death of Wordsworth; Tennyson becomes Poet Laureate	Australian Constitution Act
1851	Ruskin, *The Stones of Venice* Melville, *Moby-Dick*	Great Exhibition in London Gold found in New South Wales and Victoria First women's suffrage petition presented to House of Commons
1852	Harriet Beecher Stowe, *Uncle Tom's Cabin*	South African Republic established at Sand River Convention
1853	Charlotte Brontë, *Villette* Dickens, *Bleak House*	France: Napoleon III proclaimed Emperor Russian army enters Turkey: Turkey declares war
1854	Thoreau, *Walden*	France and Britain declare war on Russia: armies land in Crimea
1855	Death of Charlotte Brontë Browning, *Men and Women*	Paris World Exhibition

Year	Literary Context	Historical Events
1856		Paris Peace Congress ends Crimean War
1857	Dickens, *Little Dorrit* Trollope, *Barchester Towers* George Eliot, *Scenes of Clerical Life* Barrett Browning, *Aurora Leigh* Flaubert, *Madame Bovary* Baudelaire, *Les fleurs du mal*	'Indian Mutiny': Massacre of Cawnpore, loss of Delhi
1858	Tennyson, *Idylls of the King*	Ottawa declared capital of Canada
1859	Charles Darwin, *The Origin of Species* J. S. Mill, *On Liberty* George Eliot, *Adam Bede* Dickens, *A Tale of Two Cities*	Revolutions against Austrian rule in Parma, Modena and Tuscany USA: John Brown's raid on Harper's Ferry De Lesseps begins Suez Canal
1860	George Eliot, *The Mill on the Floss*	Plebiscites in favour of Italian unification, Garibaldi enters Naples Abraham Lincoln elected President of USA
1861	George Eliot, *Silas Marner* Dickens, *Great Expectations*	Confederation of Southern States proclaimed: American Civil War Victor Emanuel King of Italy Prince Consort dies
1862		Bismarck appointed Prussian Premier
1863	Death of Thackeray Tolstoy begins *War and Peace* (published 1868–9)	
1864	Browning, *Dramatis Personae* J. H. Newman, *Apologia pro Vita Sua*	

Year	Age	Life
1865	54–5	August. *Wives and Daughters* begins in the *Cornhill* (concluded January 1866) 12 November. Elizabeth dies of a heart attack at her newly bought house, 'The Lawn', Holybourne, Hampshire

Year	Literary Context	Historical Events
1865	Lewis Carroll, *Alice in Wonderland* Dickens, *Our Mutual Friend*	Lincoln assassinated: Confederate army surrender Palmerston dies: Russell Prime Minister; Gladstone Leader of the House

INTRODUCTION

In the autumn of 1859, Elizabeth Gaskell and her daughters Meta and Julia visited Whitby in Yorkshire, on England's north-east coast. The trip was planned as a holiday from Manchester for the benefit of Julia's health (she had 'outgrown her strength'). Whitby soon became more than a restful escape for Gaskell; it was an encounter with an unfamiliar and romantic part of England and an inspiration for her fifth novel, *Sylvia's Lovers*. In particular, the town's history – its whaling trade, its 1793 riot in response to press-gang activities, and the hanging for treason of the riot's instigator, William Atkinson – interested her as potential material for fiction. Having published *Mary Barton* (1848), *Cranford* (1851–3), *Ruth* (1853), *North and South* (1854–5), and *The Life of Charlotte Brontë* (1857), 'Mrs Gaskell' (the name under which she published) was a major literary figure, known for realistic presentations of areas such as Knutsford, where she spent part of her childhood, and Manchester, where she had moved in 1832 with her husband William, a Unitarian minister. *Sylvia's Lovers*, however, combined the strict realism of Gaskell's previous novels with an element of the strange and uncanny, more evident in some of her short stories. Whitby became 'Monkshaven', its outlines filled in by Gaskell after numerous informal conversations with residents and a more systematic investigation of the town's past, particularly the once-thriving whaling industry. She relied on such texts as Scoresby's *Account of the Arctic Regions* and George Young's *A History of Whitby* (1817). For her research on the period of the French Revolutionary War (1793–1802), she read some of the Annual Registers of the 1790s. George Eliot's *Scenes of Clerical Life* (1857), *Adam Bede* (1859) and *The Mill on the Floss* (1860) provided recent literary precedents for writing historical romances as realistic novels, which stressed the everyday life of the poor and uneducated classes. Prior to 1863, both of these influential experimenters in the regional novel had written primarily about areas familiar to them, but now each began to move in a different direction. As Eliot was researching *Romola*, her novel of fifteenth-century Florence, Gaskell was turning to her no less exotic historical romance. While most of the action in *Sylvia's Lovers* takes place within England, the work nonetheless retains the sense of foreignness that Gaskell experienced at Whitby. The question of how those people living on the national margins (the Yorkshire coast) saw themselves in relation to the centre (London), and ultimately of what constituted a coherent sense of Englishness at the turn of the century, pervades this tragic narrative of unforeseen encroachments of national events on individual lives.

Sylvia's Lovers begins with a carefully balanced travelogue account of Monkshaven, its place in history, and its geographical, economic and social characteristics. As the narrator focuses on a period in the region's history when the coasts were terrorized by the Navy's press-gang, she recasts the north/south distinction of Gaskell's earlier fiction: 'it is certain that the southerners took the oppression of the press-warrants more submissively than the wild north-eastern people.' Whereas in *North and South* the lives of northerners are dominated by the effects of industrialization, in *Sylvia's Lovers* the northerners are seaward-looking, isolated, superstitiously afraid of the city and its temptations. Part of the reason for their resistance to government authority is the sheer distance of their lives from London, the centre of politics and news. *Sylvia's Lovers* presents the sheltered domestic existence of a family that has never been to London. Daniel Robson, a former whaler running Haytersbank farm outside Monkshaven, lives quietly with his wife Bell and daughter Sylvia. His connection to the world is limited, news filtering in by word of mouth and by weekly newspaper from York. Daniel's political opinions are simple. He believes in the primacy of individual rights and asserts his views in contrast to those of his better-educated nephew Philip Hepburn. Philip, unlike his relatives, lives in the town proper and works in a shop owned by the Foster brothers, Quakers who have trained him in the skills of their trade. His commercial and political values differ significantly from his uncle's, for Philip contends that 'laws is made for the good of the nation, not for your good or mine' (p. 38). Their argument concerns the war and the press-gangs, which Daniel confronted in his youth, during the war with 'Ameriky'; he has no doubt about the immorality of their practices, and so dismisses Philip's conservative views: 'Nation here! nation theere! I'm a man and yo're another, but nation's nowheere' (p. 39).

While this might seem like a refusal to acknowledge the abstract idea of 'nation,' Gaskell has complicated Daniel's relationship to his country by showing that he is a patriot as well as a sceptic and is necessarily committed to the *idea* of being English: 'he had a true John Bullish interest in the war without very well knowing what the English were fighting for' (p. 87). He almost instinctively kicks against interference from the Crown or its representatives, but the vague knowledge that England is fighting an enemy rouses his English pride. Independent-minded men like Daniel would die to protect their individual rights, but they feel no less loyal to king and government, no less English for hating English laws. Daniel's temper leads him beyond the dismissal of 'nation', and to damn it on the grounds of its obscurity: 'I can make out King George, and Measter Pitt, and yo' and me, but nation! nation go hang!' (p. 39). This curse turns into an ironic prophecy when, as punishment for his impulse to fight the local press-gang, the nation hangs him. The riot scene, based on the Whitby riot and the hanging of William Atkinson, transforms the life of a simple but obstinate man into a tragedy of misapplied justice and state discipline. Daniel is not a leader, nor even a political rebel. He is like other Yorkshire men in his general support for the war: 'The great body of the people gloried in being Tories and haters of the French, with whom they were on tenter-hooks to fight' (p. 153). True to his own characterization of 'nation' as 'nowheer', Daniel's executioners are faceless. His speedy trial and quick execution are carried out by an impersonal mechanism, strengthening the novel's sense of an ominous public authority cruelly reaching its hand into the lives of people who must be terrorized for the sake of maintaining an army to defend England.

Sylvia herself is like her father in temper and stubbornness. Her hostile, even vengeful, spirit is channelled into the confined space of her controlled but passionate life. For the local women, who could not vote, fight, or even read about the war, national issues were irrelevant. Sylvia's body is not threatened directly by the press-gang, but her sympathy with the men who are physically restrained and abducted is painfully felt. She responds hysterically, with an impulse to act that anticipates her father's: 'Let us go into t' thick of it and do a bit of help; I can't stand quiet and see 't!'. This scene, early in the novel, looks forward to Daniel's fatal attempt to 'go into t' thick of it'. The depth of her feeling about the press-gang is tragic because her own life will be ruined when her lover, Charley Kinraid, is abducted by the gang, and also ironic because she will not witness that abduction, or even know about it. More subtly, Sylvia's passionate objection to men capturing other men anticipates her own physical and psychological entrapment by Philip, whose persistent authority she is unable to fight. Just as Philip believes that the good of the nation requires some sacrifice of personal liberty, and that king and government know what is best for England, he also supposes that he knows what is best for Sylvia. He assumes the responsibility, seizes it by chance, of protecting her from Charley Kinraid, rationalizing her suffering as a necessary sacrifice for her ultimate good. *Sylvia's Lovers* suggests that, in both political and domestic relationships, the line between paternalism and tyranny is easily crossed. The temporal and geographical distance between Gaskell's audience and the world of the barely literate Sylvia emphasizes the complexities of defining Englishness during this chaotic period in European history. Obscure people like Sylvia are marginal to the making of political decisions and the fighting of national battles, but Gaskell represents their experiences as central to English history.

Language, class, location and time distance these characters from the novel's presumably educated, urban, middle-class audience. Gaskell makes regional life seem almost foreign, for example by reproducing the local dialect to contrast with her narrator's clear, literate, standardized English. Not only language differs, but, Gaskell implies, modes of thought as well. Speaking of Daniel, Bell, Sylvia and Philip, her narrator observes: 'In the agricultural counties, and among the class to which these four persons belonged, there is little analysis of motive or comparison of characters and actions, even at this present day of enlightenment' (p. 69). The Robsons' hearth is rustic, warm, inviting, but the narrator creates a coolness and distance by articulating and analysing a fundamental difference between her characters, and contemporary readers:

taken as a general rule, it may be said that few knew what manner of men they were, compared to the numbers now who are conscious of their virtues, qualities, failings, and weaknesses, and who go about comparing others with themselves – not in a spirit of Pharisaism and arrogance, but with a vivid self-consciousness that more than anything else deprives characters of freshness and originality. (p. 69)

The domestic circle at Haytersbank farm is composed of characters who reflect neither on themselves nor on their place in the world; they are too involved in the chores, pleasures and sorrows of everyday life, and it would appear, from the narrator's comments, that Gaskell believes this lack of self-consciousness improves the spontaneity – the freshness and originality – of her characters.

For Sylvia and Philip, only pain and loss bring self-awareness. The suffering begins with the disappearance of Kinraid, but the plot turns on the hanging of Daniel, who is as innocent of any real crime as was Gaskell's Lois in 'Lois the Witch' (1859). And after the vigil in York, Monkshaven seems as darkly gothic as that novella's seventeenth-century Salem. The state has made an example of Daniel, who has been sacrificed to instil a fear of disloyalty in the people, and the tactic seems to work in Monkshaven, as no mention is made of local resistance to the press-gang after Daniel's death. Sylvia and her mother have little choice but to rely on a man, and Philip, with his long-harboured desire for Sylvia, gets his chance to step in. By contrast to Kinraid, to Daniel, and to Sylvia herself, Philip aspires to a conventional and, significantly, an urban life. He wants success in business, a respectable family and a pew in church. His drive to possess Sylvia, however, is the sign of a more intense desire and a less balanced ambition. To have her, he betrays her and his own conscience, setting in motion a parallel tragedy to that of Daniel's execution. His instantaneous decision not to tell Sylvia that Kinraid was taken by the press-gang, rather than drowned as she believes, hardens into a rationalized resolve to marry and protect her, not only from Kinraid, but from herself. Gaskell is analysing public and private tyranny, internal and external prisons. Philip marries Sylvia in bad faith, and his lie creates a prison both for himself and for her.

Philip's various attempts to discipline Sylvia are compared to physical torture. When he tries to teach her to read, she complains: 'Well! if I mun be taught, I mun; but I'd rayther be whipped and ha' done with it'. He teaches her to spell, but she quits in disgust and protest, mocking him: 'Abednego! Abednego! Abednego!'. Sylvia's mechanical and resistant repeating of the word 'Abednego' suggests that the teaching has left her ignorant of or indifferent to its biblical associations of rebellion and captivity. However well-intended, Philip's teaching, like his reading, is wooden and lifeless. Much later, having given birth to Philip's child in the prison of their marriage, Sylvia dreams of Kinraid, calling out passionately for 'Charley' in the presence of her husband. Philip reproaches her in language that recurs in her mind, repeated oppressively like the spelling lesson. Remembering his words of rebuke, 'she used to shudder as if cold steel had been plunged into her warm, living body'.

Whereas Philip tries to confine her mind, Kinraid had set it free with tales of travel and adventure. What Philip takes from Sylvia is the freedom she loves – the outdoors, the sea and Kinraid. No one, least of all the reader, is sure about what Kinraid is – a trifler and heartbreaker, or just the kind of man who invites such rumours. Gaskell leaves his moral character in question. He is a likeable but dubious outsider, whose reputation precedes his appearance in Monkshaven, and whose absence throughout the novel is more consequential than his presence. Philip was wrong about Kinraid; the specksioneer did return to claim his love, having become an officer in the Royal Navy. But he recovers from the blow of Philip's betrayal and Sylvia's marriage and soon finds a new wife whose social position fits his own ambitions.

A provisional title for *Sylvia's Lovers* was *Philip's Idol*. Philip worshipped Sylvia, as he comes to recognize on his deathbed, more than he loved God, and this was his downfall as well as hers. Both Sylvia and Philip are Christianized in the final stages of the novel. It is important to remember that Gaskell was a Unitarian and believed her form of Christianity to be an enlightened one. The unevenness of the narrative, often noted by critics, is caused by a breakdown of realism and by Gaskell's apparent desire, nourished perhaps by religious feeling, to soften the emotions of characters driven by love, betrayal, vengeance and death. As if condensing in one lifetime a series of historical changes, the action becomes mythical, fateful, symbolic. Philip moves from pagan idol-worship to personal crusade and virtual martyrdom, emerging finally with a new self-consciousness. The execution of innocents, the will to possess that denies women their freedom, and the modern siege of a Crusader fort are succeeded by a gentler, more inward form of Christianity which can only be viewed as conversion. Sylvia vows she will never forgive, but in the end she does. Philip journeys to Saint-Jean d'Acre, where he fights the French – the modern infidels. With heroism, physical suffering, penitence – a general humbling of his formerly ambitious self – Philip becomes the kind of Christian (the novel suggests) he should have been all along. Philip's ordeal, the erasure of Kinraid except as a passing presence, and Sylvia's eventual ability to forgive suggest that in the course of the narrative Gaskell's sympathies moved towards the elevation of a steadfast love, even one leading to destruction.

Philip's last act is to save his daughter Bella from drowning. Her improbable rescue – as improbable as his saving of Kinraid at Acre – marks the reconciliation of her estranged parents, but her immersion in the sea also symbolizes the birth of a new generation, one closer to Victorian readers. *Sylvia's Lovers* is an historical novel less in the sense of showing its readers something about political events which actually occurred than in its registering of psychological differences between one generation and the next. The weariness of the characters at the novel's end emphasizes by contrast all the fresh hopefulness of life in Monkshaven before the war. This has been a story about how one town adapted to rapid external changes, about the psychological responses to crisis, and finally about how individual lives are part of a diverse national history. Nation is both nowhere and everywhere in *Sylvia's Lovers*, because those who have the least to say about its operation, and who are perhaps the least conscious of themselves as English, are revealed to be invisibly but inextricably tied to its fate. Local history is the medium in which characters move, but the novel also measures imperceptible changes in perspectives and social movements. 'Tis sixty years since', and although the past informs the present, that present is itself informed with the past. From the Victorian point of view, this is one account of how the present came to be the present.

Sylvia's Lovers is a tragic story about the interrelated lives of a few people and the war in which their country is engaged.

That war is not merely 'background', but, rather, creates the conditions within which one young woman's happiness is destroyed. As the novel ends, the narrator takes a revealing interest in posterity – in the way Philip and Sylvia's story came to be told. Sylvia could not run away with Kinraid upon his return: for all her fiery defiance, she felt tied by the conventions of her marriage to Philip. Gaskell could not leave Sylvia hate-filled and unforgiving; nor could she leave Philip unredeemed. In George Eliot's *Romola*, the heroine is betrayed by her husband Tito. Like Sylvia, Romola smoothes over the transgressions of her husband after his death. Gaskell's choice of the title *Sylvia's Lovers*, rather than *Philip's Idol*, or *The Specksioneer*, places Sylvia at the centre. As the narrator tells the story, she revises a version that had been passed on verbally to her. Sylvia's story stands beside that of yet another George Eliot heroine, Dorothea Brooke. Just as the finale to *Middlemarch* (1872) shows that history was not kind to Dorothea, so the final pages of *Sylvia's Lovers* show that history has judged Sylvia harshly, in fact has written her out of Philip Hepburn's story. The narrator observes that 'the memory of man fades away', and it is an ironic comment on the writing of history that Philip and the self-sacrificing Hester Rose, who silently loved him, became legends. Gaskell called this novel the 'saddest' story she ever wrote. It is the novel's final sadness that a stone outside the alms-house founded by Hester reads: 'This building is erected in memory of P.H.' (p. 451), while Sylvia, victimized by circumstances as well as by Philip, lies, we fear, in an unvisited tomb.

NANCY HENRY

NOTE ON THE TEXT

Sylvia's Lovers was published in three volumes early in 1863. A second and third edition in the same format followed later in the year. Gaskell made a number of corrections and alterations to the second, and in December 1863 a single volume edition, illustrated by George Du Maurier, and incorporating her revisions, was published; it was later reprinted as Volume III of *Novels and Tales by Mrs Gaskell*. The 1906 reprint has been used for this edition, and is preferred to the Knutsford Edition (ed. A. W. Ward) of 1906, which contains a number of errors.

SYLVIA'S LOVERS

Oh for thy voice to soothe and bless!
What hope of answer or redress?
Behind the veil! Behind the veil!
TENNYSON*

This book is dedicated to
My Dear Husband
by her who best knows his value

On the nor
Monkshave
thousand in
at the end o
events narra
  Monkshav
England, and
throneless qu
had been a
which was n
even earlier d
the most anci
stood on tho

shipowners – to his own father, possi
other boys, or, it might be, even
months he and his fellow appr
Greenland seas, returning with
and employing the winter m
of the oil from the blubb
navigation from some
schoolmaster, half
stirring narration
house of the sh
home and th
October
accordi
of

...ocean that blended with the distant sky. Monkshaven itself was built by the side of the Dee,* just where the river falls into the German Ocean.* The principal street of the town ran parallel to the stream, and smaller lanes branched out of this, and straggled up the sides of the steep hill, between which and the river the houses were pent in. There was a bridge across the Dee, and consequently a Bridge Street running at right angles to the High Street; and on the south side of the stream there were a few houses of more pretension, around which lay gardens and fields. It was on this side of the town that the local aristocracy lived. And who were the great people of this small town? Not the younger branches of the county families that held hereditary state in their manor-houses on the wild bleak moors, that shut in Monkshaven almost as effectually on the land side as ever the waters did on the sea-board. No; these old families kept aloof from the unsavoury yet adventurous trade which brought wealth to generation after generation of certain families in Monkshaven.

The magnates of Monkshaven were those who had the largest number of ships engaged in the whaling-trade. Something like the following was the course of life with a Monkshaven lad of this class: – He was apprenticed as a sailor to one of the great

ly – along with twenty
more. During the summer
entices made voyages to the
their cargoes in the early autumn;
months in watching the preparation
ber in the melting-sheds, and learning
quaint but experienced teacher, half
sailor, who seasoned his instructions by
s of the wild adventures of his youth. The
ip-owner to whom he was apprenticed was his
at of his companions during the idle season between
nd March. The domestic position of these boys varied
ng to the premium paid; some took rank with the sons
the family, others were considered as little better than
ervants. Yet once on board an equality prevailed, in which, if
any claimed superiority, it was the bravest and brightest. After
a certain number of voyages the Monkshaven lad would rise by
degrees to be captain, and as such would have a share in the
venture; all these profits, as well as all his savings, would go
towards building a whaling vessel of his own, if he was not so
fortunate as to be the child of a ship-owner. At the time of
which I write, there was but little division of labour in the
Monkshaven whale fishery. The same man might be the owner
of six or seven ships, any one of which he himself was fitted by
education and experience to command; the master of a score of
apprentices, each of whom paid a pretty sufficient premium; and
the proprietor of the melting-sheds into which his cargoes of
blubber and whalebone* were conveyed to be fitted for sale. It
was no wonder that large fortunes were acquired by these ship-
owners, nor that their houses on the south side of the river Dee
were stately mansions, full of handsome and substantial furniture. It was also not surprising that the whole town had an
amphibious appearance, to a degree unusual even in a seaport.
Every one depended on the whale fishery, and almost every male
inhabitant had been, or hoped to be, a sailor. Down by the river
the smell was almost intolerable to any but Monkshaven people
during certain seasons of the year; but on these unsavoury
'staithes'* the old men and children lounged for hours, almost
as if they revelled in the odours of train-oil.*

This is, perhaps, enough of a description of the town itself. I
have said that the country for miles all around was moorland;

high above the level of the sea towered the purple crags, whose summits were crowned with greensward that stole down the sides of the scaur* a little way in grassy veins. Here and there a brook forced its way from the heights down to the sea, making its channel into a valley more or less broad in long process of time. And in the moorland hollows, as in these valleys, trees and underwood grew and flourished; so that, while on the bare swells of the high land you shivered at the waste desolation of the scenery, when you dropped into these wooded 'bottoms' you were charmed with the nestling shelter which they gave. But above and around these rare and fertile vales there were moors for many a mile, here and there bleak enough, with the red freestone cropping out above the scanty herbage; then, perhaps, there was a brown tract of peat and bog, uncertain footing for the pedestrian who tried to make a short cut to his destination; then on the higher sandy soil there was the purple ling, or commonest species of heather growing in beautiful wild luxuriance. Tufts of fine elastic grass were occasionally to be found, on which the little black-faced sheep* browsed, but either the scanty food, or their goat-like agility, kept them in a lean condition that did not promise much for the butcher, nor yet was their wool of a quality fine enough to make them profitable in that way to their owners. In such districts there is little population at the present day; there was much less in the last century, before agriculture was sufficiently scientific to have a chance of contending with such natural disqualifications as the moors presented, and when there were no facilities of railroads to bring sportsmen from a distance to enjoy the shooting season, and make an annual demand for accommodation.

There were old stone halls in the valleys; there were bare farmhouses to be seen on the moors at long distances apart, with small stacks of coarse poor hay, and almost larger stacks of turf for winter fuel in their farmyards. The cattle in the pasture fields belonging to these farms looked half starved; but somehow there was an odd, intelligent expression in their faces, as well as in those of the black-visaged sheep, which is seldom seen in the placidly stupid countenances of well-fed animals. All the fences were turf banks, with loose stones piled into walls on the top of these.

There was comparative fertility and luxuriance down below in the rare green dales. The narrow meadows stretching along

the brookside seemed as though the cows could really satisfy
their hunger in the deep rich grass; whereas on the higher lands
the scanty herbage was hardly worth the fatigue of moving
about in search of it. Even in these 'bottoms' the piping sea-
winds, following the current of the stream, stunted and cut low
any trees; but still there was rich thick underwood, tangled and
tied together with brambles, and briar-rose, and honeysuckle;
and if the farmer in these comparatively happy valleys had had
wife or daughter who cared for gardening, many a flower would
have grown on the western or southern side of the rough stone
house. But at that time gardening was not a popular art in any
part of England; in the north it is not yet. Noblemen and
gentlemen may have beautiful gardens; but farmers and day-
labourers care little for them north of the Trent, which is all I
can answer for. A few 'berry' bushes, a black currant tree or
two (the leaves to be used in heightening the flavour of tea, the
fruit as medicinal for colds and sore throats), a potato ground
(and this was not so common at the close of the last century as
it is now), a cabbage bed, a bush of sage, and balm, and thyme,
and marjoram, with possibly a rose tree, and 'old man'* growing
in the midst; a little plot of small strong coarse onions, and
perhaps some marigolds, the petals of which flavoured the salt-
beef broth; such plants made up a well-furnished garden to a
farmhouse at the time and place to which my story belongs. But
for twenty miles inland there was no forgetting the sea, nor the
sea-trade; refuse shell-fish, sea-weed, the offal of the melting-
houses, were the staple manure of the district; great ghastly
whalejaws, bleached bare and white, were the arches over the
gate-posts to many a field or moorland stretch. Out of every
family of several sons, however agricultural their position might
be, one had gone to sea, and the mother looked wistfully
seaward at the changes of the keen piping moorland winds. The
holiday rambles were to the coast; no one cared to go inland to
see aught, unless indeed it might be to the great annual horse-
fairs held where the dreary land broke into habitation and
cultivation.

Somehow in this country, sea thoughts followed the thinker
far inland; whereas in most other parts of the island, at five
miles from the ocean, he has all but forgotten the existence of
such an element as salt water. The great Greenland trade of the
coasting towns was the main and primary cause of this, no

doubt. But there was also a dread and an irritation in every one's mind, at the time of which I write, in connection with the neighbouring sea.

Since the termination of the American war,* there had been nothing to call for any unusual energy in manning the navy; and the grants required by Government for this purpose diminished with every year of peace. In 1792 this grant touched its minimum for many years. In 1793 the proceedings of the French had set Europe on fire,* and the English were raging with anti-Gallican excitement, fomented into action by every expedient of the Crown and its Ministers. We had our ships; but where were our men?* The Admiralty had, however, a ready remedy at hand, with ample precedent for its use, and with common (if not statute) law to sanction its application. They issued 'press warrants',* calling upon the civil power throughout the country to support their officers in the discharge of their duty. The sea-coast was divided into districts, under the charge of a captain in the navy, who again delegated sub-districts to lieutenants; and in this manner all homeward-bound vessels were watched and waited for, all ports were under supervision; and in a day, if need were, a large number of men could be added to the forces of his Majesty's navy. But if the Admiralty became urgent in their demands, they were also willing to be unscrupulous. Landsmen, if able-bodied, might soon be trained into good sailors; and once in the hold of the tender,* which always awaited the success of the operations of the press-gang, it was difficult for such prisoners to bring evidence of the nature of their former occupations, especially when none had leisure to listen to such evidence, or were willing to believe it if they did listen, or would act upon it for the release of the captive if they had by possibility both listened and believed. Men were kidnapped, literally disappeared, and nothing was ever heard of them again. The street of a busy town was not safe from such press-gang captures, as Lord Thurlow could have told, after a certain walk he took about this time on Tower Hill, when he, the attorney-general* of England, was impressed, when the Admiralty had its own peculiar ways of getting rid of tiresome besiegers and petitioners. Nor yet were lonely inland dwellers more secure; many a rustic went to a statute fair or 'mop',* and never came home to tell of his hiring; many a stout young farmer vanished from his place by the hearth of his father, and was no more heard of by mother or lover; so great was the press for men to serve in the navy during the early years of the war with France, and after every great naval victory of that war.

The servants of the Admiralty lay in wait for all merchantmen and traders; there were many instances of vessels returning home after long absence, and laden with rich cargo, being boarded within a day's distance of land, and so many men pressed and carried off, that the ship, with her cargo, became unmanageable from the loss of her crew, drifted out again into the wild wide ocean, and was sometimes found in the helpless guidance of one or two infirm or ignorant sailors; sometimes such vessels were never heard of more. The men thus pressed were taken from the near grasp of parents or wives, and were often deprived of the hard earnings of years, which remained in the hands of the masters of the merchantman in which they had served, subject to all the chances of honesty or dishonesty, life or death. Now all this tyranny (for I can use no other word) is marvellous to us; we cannot imagine how it is that a nation submitted to it for so long, even under any warlike enthusiasm, any panic of invasion, any amount of loyal subservience to the governing powers. When we read of the military being called in to assist the civil power in backing up the press-gang, of parties of soldiers patrolling the streets, and sentries with screwed bayonets placed at every door while the press-gang entered and searched each hole and corner of the dwelling; when we hear of churches being surrounded during divine service by troops, while the press-gang stood ready at the door to seize men as they came out from attending public worship, and take these instances as merely types of what was constantly going on in different forms, we do not wonder at Lord Mayors, and other civic authorities in large towns, complaining that a stop was put to business by the danger which the tradesmen and their servants incurred in leaving their houses and going into the streets, infested by press-gangs.

Whether it was that living in closer neighbourhood to the metropolis – the centre of politics and news – inspired the inhabitants of the southern counties with a strong feeling of that kind of patriotism which consists in hating all other nations; or whether it was that the chances of capture were so much greater at all the southern ports that the merchant sailors became inured to the danger; or whether it was that serving in the navy, to those familiar with such towns as Portsmouth and Plymouth, had an attraction to most men from the dash and brilliancy of the adventurous employment – it is certain that the southerners took the oppression of press-warrants more submissively than the wild north-eastern people. For with them the chances of profit beyond their wages in the whaling or Greenland trade extended to the lowest description of sailor. He might rise by daring and saving to be a shipowner himself. Numbers around him had done so; and this very fact made the distinction between class and class less apparent; and the common ventures and dangers, the universal interest felt in one pursuit, bound the inhabitants of that line of coast together with a strong tie, the severance of which by any violent extraneous measure, gave rise to passionate anger and thirst for vengeance. A Yorkshireman once said to me, 'My county folk are all alike. Their first thought is how to resist. Why I myself, if I hear a man say it is a fine day, catch myself trying to find out that it is no such thing. It is so in thought; it is so in word; it is so in deed.'

So you may imagine the press-gang had no easy time of it on the Yorkshire coast. In other places they inspired fear, but here rage and hatred. The Lord Mayor of York was warned on 20 January 1777, by an anonymous letter, that 'if those men were not sent from the city on or before the following Tuesday, his lordship's own dwelling, and the Mansion-house also, should be burned to the ground.'

Perhaps something of the ill-feeling that prevailed on the subject was owing to the fact which I have noticed in other places similarly situated. Where the landed possessions of gentlemen of ancient family but limited income surround a centre of any kind of profitable trade or manufacture, there is a sort of latent ill-will on the part of the squires to the tradesman, be he manufacturer, merchant, or shipowner, in whose hands is held a power of money-making, which no hereditary pride, or gentlemanly love of doing nothing, prevents him from using. This ill-will, to be sure, is mostly of a negative kind; its most common form of manifestation is in absence of speech or action, a sort of torpid and genteel ignoring all unpleasant neighbours, but really the whale-fisheries of Monkshaven had become so impertinently and obtrusively prosperous of late years at the time of which I write, the Monkshaven shipowners were growing so wealthy and consequential, that the squires, who lived at home at ease in the old stone manor-houses scattered up and down the surrounding moorland, felt that the check upon the Monkshaven trade likely to be inflicted by the press-gang, was wisely ordained by the higher powers (how high they placed these powers I will not venture to say), to prevent overhaste in getting rich,* which was a scriptural fault, and they also thought that they were only doing their duty in backing up the Admiralty warrants by all the civil power at their disposal, whenever they were called upon, and whenever they could do so without taking too much trouble in affairs which did not after all much concern themselves.

There was just another motive in the minds of some provident parents of many daughters. The captains and lieutenants employed on this service were mostly agreeable bachelors, brought up to a genteel profession, at the least they were very pleasant visitors, when they had a day to spare; who knew what might come of it?

Indeed, these brave officers were not unpopular in Monk-shaven itself, except at the time when they were brought into actual collision with the people. They had the frank manners of their profession; they were known to have served in those engagements, the very narrative of which at this day will warm the heart of a Quaker,* and they themselves did not come prominently forward in the dirty work which, nevertheless, was permitted and quietly sanctioned by them. So while few Monks-haven people passed the low public-house over which the navy blue-flag streamed, as a sign that it was the rendezvous of the press-gang, without spitting towards it in sign of abhorrence, yet, perhaps, the very same persons would give some rough token of respect to Lieutenant Atkinson* if they met him in High Street. Touching their hats was an unknown gesture in those parts, but they would move their heads in a droll, familiar kind of way, neither a wag nor a nod, but meant all the same to imply friendly regard. The ship-owners, too, invited him to an occasional dinner or supper, all the time looking forward to the chances of his turning out an active enemy, and not by any means inclined to give him 'the run of the house', however many unmarried daughters might grace their table. Still as he could tell a rattling story, drink hard, and was seldom too busy to come at short notice, he got on better than any one could have expected with the Monkshaven folk. And the principal share of the odium of his business fell on his subordinates, who were one and all regarded in the light of mean kidnappers and spies – 'varmint',* as the common people esteemed them: and as such they were ready at the first provocation to hunt and to worry them, and little cared the press-gang for this. Whatever else they were, they were brave and daring. They had law to back them, therefore their business was lawful. They were serving their king and country. They were using all their faculties, and that is always pleasant. There was plenty of scope for the glory and triumph of outwitting; plenty of adventure in their life. It was a lawful and loyal employment, requiring sense, readiness, courage, and besides it called out that strange love of the chase inherent in every man. Fourteen or fifteen miles at sea lay the *Aurora*,* good man-of-war; and to her were conveyed the living cargoes of several tenders, which were stationed at likely places along the sea-coast. One, the *Lively Lady*, might be seen from the cliffs above Monkshaven, not so far away, but hidden by the angle of the high lands from the constant sight of the townspeople; and there was always the Randyvow-house* (as the public-house with the navy blue-flag was called thereabouts) for the crew of the *Lively Lady* to lounge about, and there to offer drink to unwary passers-by. At present this was all that the press-gang had done at Monkshaven.

CHAPTER 2

Home from Greenland

One hot day, early in October of the year 1796,* two girls set off from their country homes to Monkshaven to sell their butter and eggs, for they were both farmers' daughters, though rather in different circumstances; for Molly Corney was one of a large family of children, and had to rough it accordingly; Sylvia Robson was an only child, and was much made of in more people's estimation than Mary's by her elderly parents. They had each purchases to make after their sales were effected, as sales of butter and eggs were effected in those days by the market women sitting on the steps of the great old mutilated cross till a certain hour in the afternoon, after which, if all their goods were not disposed of, they took them unwillingly to the shops and sold them at a lower price. But good housewives did not despise coming themselves to the Butter Cross, and, smelling and depreciating the articles they wanted, kept up a perpetual struggle of words, trying, often in vain, to beat down prices. A housekeeper of the last century would have thought that she did not know her business, if she had not gone through this preliminary process; and the farmers' wives and daughters treated it all as a matter of course, replying with a good deal of independent humour to the customer, who, once having discovered where good butter and fresh eggs were to be sold, came time after time to depreciate the articles she always ended in taking. There was leisure for all this kind of work in those days.

Molly had tied a knot on her pink-spotted handkerchief for each of the various purchases she had to make; dull but important articles needed for the week's consumption at home; if she forgot any one of them she knew she was sure of a good 'rating'* from her mother. The number of them made her pocket-handkerchief look like one of the nine-tails of a 'cat';* but not a single thing was for herself, nor, indeed, for any one individual of her numerous family. There was neither much thought nor much money to spend for any but collective wants in the Corney family.

It was different with Sylvia. She was going to choose her first cloak, not to have an old one of her mother's, that had gone down through two sisters, dyed for the fourth time (and Molly would have been glad had even this chance been hers), but to buy a bran-new duffle cloak all for herself, with not even an elder authority to curb her as to price, only Molly to give her admiring counsel, and as much sympathy as was consistent with a little patient envy of Sylvia's happier circumstances. Every now and then they wandered off from the one grand subject of thought, but Sylvia, with unconscious art, soon brought the conversation round to the fresh consideration of the respective merits of grey and scarlet. These girls were walking bare-foot and carrying their shoes and stockings in their hands during the first part of their way; but as they were drawing near Monkshaven they stopped, and turned aside along a foot-path that led from the main-road down to the banks of the Dee. There were great stones in the river about here, round which the waters gathered and eddied and formed deep pools. Molly sat down on the grassy bank to wash her feet; but Sylvia, more active (or perhaps lighter-hearted with the notion of the cloak in the distance), placed her basket on a gravelly bit of shore, and, giving a long spring, seated herself on a stone almost in the middle of the stream. Then she began dipping her little rosy toes in the cool rushing water and whisking them out with childish glee.

'Be quiet, wi' the', Sylvia? Thou'st splashing me all ower, and my feyther'll noane be so keen o' giving me a new cloak as thine is, seemingly.'

Sylvia was quiet, not to say penitent, in a moment. She drew up her feet instantly; and, as if to take herself out of temptation, she turned away from Molly to that side of her stony seat on which the current ran shallow, and broken by pebbles. But once disturbed in her play, her thoughts reverted to the great subject of the cloak. She was now as still as a minute before she had been full of frolic and gambolling life. She had tucked herself up on the stone, as if it had been a cushion, and she a little sultana.*

Molly was deliberately washing her feet and drawing on her stockings, when she heard a sudden sigh, and her companion turned round so as to face her, and said, 'I wish mother hadn't spoken up for t'gray.'

'Why, Sylvia, thou wert saying as we topped t'brow,* as she did nought but bid thee think twice afore settling on scarlet.'

'Ay! but mother's words are scarce, and weigh heavy. Feyther's liker me, and we talk a deal o' rubble;* but mother's words are liker to hewn stone. She puts a deal o' meaning in 'em. And then,' said Sylvia, as if she was put out by the suggestion, 'she bid me ask cousin Philip for his opinion. I hate a man as has getten an opinion on such-like things.'

'Well! we shall niver get to Monkshaven this day, either for to sell our eggs and stuff; or to buy thy cloak, if we're sittin' here much longer. T' sun's for slanting low, so come along, lass, and let's be going.'

'But if I put on my stockings and shoon here, and jump back into yon wet gravel, I'se not be fit to be seen,' said Sylvia, in a pathetic tone of bewilderment, that was funnily childlike. She stood up, her bare feet curved round the curving surface of the stone, her slight figure balancing as if in act to spring.

'Thou knows thou'll have just to jump back barefoot, and

wash thy feet afresh, without making all that ado; thou shouldst ha' done it at first, like me, and all other sensible folk. But thou'st getten no gumption.'

Molly's mouth was stopped by Sylvia's hand. She was already on the river bank by her friend's side.

'Now dunnot lecture me; I'm none for a sermon hung on every peg o' words.* I'm going to have a new cloak, lass, and I cannot heed thee if thou dost lecture. Thou shall have all the gumption, and I'll have my cloak.'

It may be doubted whether Molly thought this an equal division.

Each girl wore tightly-fitting stockings, knit by her own hands, of the blue worsted common in that country; they had on neat high-heeled black leather shoes, coming well over the instep, and fastened as well as ornamented with bright steel buckles. They did not walk so lightly and freely now as they did before they were shod, but their steps were still springy with the buoyancy of early youth; for neither of them was twenty, indeed I believe Sylvia was not more than seventeen at this time.

They clambered up the steep grassy path, with brambles catching at their kilted petticoats, through the copse-wood, till they regained the high road; and then they 'settled themselves', as they called it; that is to say, they took off their black felt hats, and tied up their clustering hair afresh; they shook off every speck of wayside dust; straightened the little shawls (or large neck-kerchiefs, call them which you will) that were spread over their shoulders, pinned below the throat, and confined at the waist by their apron-strings; and then putting on their hats again, and picking up their baskets, they prepared to walk decorously into the town of Monkshaven.

The next turn of the road showed them the red peaked roofs of the closely packed houses lying almost directly below the hill on which they were. The full autumn sun brought out the ruddy colour of the tiled gables, and deepened the shadows in the narrow streets. The narrow harbour at the mouth of the river was crowded with small vessels of all descriptions, making an intricate forest of masts. Beyond lay the sea, like a flat pavement of sapphire, scarcely a ripple varying its sunny surface, that stretched out leagues away till it blended with the softened azure of the sky. On this blue trackless water floated scores of white-sailed fishing boats, apparently motionless, unless you measured their progress by some land-mark; but still, and silent, and distant as they seemed, the consciousness that there were men on board, each going forth into the great deep, added unspeakably to the interest felt in watching them. Close to the bar of the river Dee* a larger vessel lay to. Sylvia, who had only recently come into the neighbourhood, looked at this with the same quiet interest as she did at all the others; but Molly, as soon as her eye caught the build of it, cried out aloud –

'She's a whaler! she's a whaler home from t'Greenland seas! T' first this season! God bless her!' and she turned round and shook both Sylvia's hands in the fulness of her excitement. Sylvia's colour rose, and her eyes sparkled out of sympathy.

'Is ta* sure?' she asked, breathless in her turn; for though she did not know by the aspect of the different ships on what trade they were bound, yet she was well aware of the paramount interest attached to whaling vessels.

'Three o'clock! and it's not high water till five!' said Molly. 'If we're sharp we can sell our eggs, and be down to the staithes before she comes into port. Be sharp, lass!'

And down the steep long hill they went at a pace that was almost a run. A run they dared not make it; and as it was, the rate at which they walked would have caused destruction among eggs less carefully packed. When the descent was ended, there was yet the long narrow street before them, bending and swerving from the straight line, as it followed the course of the river. The girls felt as if they should never come to the market-place, which was situated at the crossing of Bridge Street and High Street. There the old stone cross was raised by the monks long ago; now worn and mutilated, no one esteemed it as a holy symbol, but only as the Butter Cross, where market-women clustered on Wednesday, and whence the town crier made all his proclamations of household sales, things lost or found, beginning with 'Oh! yes, oh! yes, oh! yes!' and ending with 'God bless the king and the lord of this manor', and a very brisk 'Amen', before he went on his way and took off the livery-coat, the colours of which marked him as a servant of the Burnabys, the family who held manorial rights over Monkshaven.

Of course the much frequented space surrounding the Butter Cross was the favourite centre for shops; and on this day, a fine market day, just when good housewives begin to look over their winter store of blankets and flannels, and discover their needs

betimes* these shops ought to have had plenty of customers.
But they were empty and of even quieter aspect than their every-
day wont. The three-legged creepie-stools* that were hired out
at a penny an hour to such market-women as came too late to
find room on the steps were unoccupied; knocked over here and
there, as if people had passed by in haste.

Molly took in all at a glance, and interpreted the signs, though
she had no time to explain their meaning, and her consequent
course of action, to Sylvia, but darted into a corner shop.

'T' whalers is coming home! There's one lying outside t' bar!'

This was put in the form of an assertion; but the tone was
that of eager cross-questioning.

'Ay!' said a lame man, mending fishing-nets behind a rough
deal counter. 'She's come back airly, and she's brought good
news o' t' others, as I've heered say. Time was I should ha' been
on th' staithes throwing up my cap wit' t' best on 'em; but now
it pleases t' Lord to keep me at home, and set me to mind other
folks' gear. See thee, wench, there's a vast o' folk ha' left their
skeps* o' things wi' me while they're away down to t' quay side.
Leave me your eggs and be off wi' ye for t' see t' fun, for mebbe
ye'll live to be palsied yet, and then ye'll be fretting ower spilt
milk, and that ye didn't tak' all chances when ye was young. Ay,
well! they're out o' hearin' o' my moralities; I'd better find a
lamiter* like mysen to preach to, for it's not iverybody has t'
luck t' clargy has of saying their say out whether folks likes it or
not.'

He put the baskets carefully away with much of such talk as
this addressed to himself while he did so. Then he sighed once
or twice; and then he took the better course and began to sing
over his tarry work.

Molly and Sylvia were far along the staithes by the time he
got to this point of cheerfulness. They ran on, regardless of
stitches and pains in the side; on along the river bank to where
the concourse of people was gathered. There was no great length
of way between the Butter Cross and the harbour; in five
minutes the breathless girls were close together in the best place
they could get for seeing, on the outside of the crowd; and in as
short a time longer they were pressed inwards, by fresh arrivals,
into the very midst of the throng. All eyes were directed to the
ship, beating her anchor* just outside the bar, not a quarter of
a mile away. The custom-house officer was just gone aboard of

her to receive the captain's report of his cargo, and make due examination. The men who had taken him out in his boat were rowing back to the shore, and brought small fragments of news when they landed a little distance from the crowd, which moved as one man to hear what was to be told. Sylvia took a hard grasp of the hand of the older and more experienced Molly, and listened open-mouthed to the answers she was extracting from a gruff old sailor she happened to find near her.

'What ship is she?'

'T' *Resolution** of Monkshaven!' said he, indignantly, as if any goose might have known that.

'An' a good *Resolution*, and a blessed ship she's been to me,' piped out an old woman, close at Mary's elbow. 'She's brought me home my ae' lad – for he shouted to yon boatman to bid him tell me he was well. "Tell Peggy Christison" says he (my name is Margaret Christison) – "tell Peggy Christison as her son Hezekiah is come back safe and sound." The Lord's name be praised! An' me a widow as never thought to see my lad again!'

It seemed as if everybody relied on every one else's sympathy in that hour of great joy.

'I ax pardon, but if you'd gie me just a bit of elbow-room for a minute like, I'd hold my babby up, so that he might see daddy's ship, and happen,* my master might see him. He's four months old last Tuesday se'nnight, and his feyther's never clapt eyne on him yet, and he wi' a tooth through, an' another just breaking, bless him!'

One or two of the better end of the Monkshaven inhabitants stood a little before Molly and Sylvia, and as they moved in compliance with the young mother's request, they overheard some of the information these ship-owners had received from the boatmen.

'Haynes says they'll send the manifest* of the cargo ashore in twenty minutes, as soon as Fishburn*has looked over the casks. Only eight whales, according to what he says.'

'No one can tell,' said the other, 'till the manifest comes to hand.'

'I'm afraid he's right. But he brings a good report of the *Good Fortune*. She's off St Abb's Head,* with something like fifteen whales to her share.'

'We shall see how much is true, when she comes in.'

'That'll be by the afternoon-tide to-morrow.'

'That's my cousin's ship,' said Molly to Sylvia. 'He's specksi-oneer* on board the *Good Fortune*.'

An old man touched her as she spoke –

'I humbly make my manners, missus, but I'm stone blind; my lad's aboard yon vessel outside t' bar; and my old woman is bed-fast. Will she be long, think ye, in making t' harbour? Because, if so be as she were, I'd just make my way back, and speak a word or two to my missus, who'll be boiling o'er into some mak o' mischief* now she knows he's so near. May I be so bold as to ax if t' Crooked Negro is covered yet?'

Molly stood on tip-toe to try and see the black stone thus named; but Sylvia, stooping and peeping through the glimpses afforded between the arms of the moving people, saw it first, and told the blind old man it was still above water.

'A watched pot,' said he, 'ne'er boils, I reckon. It's ta'en a vast o' watter t' cover that stone to-day. Anyhow, I'll have time to go home and rate my missus for worritin' hersen, as I'll be bound she's done, for all as I bade her not, but to keep easy and content.'

'We'd better be off too,' said Molly, as an opening was made through the press* to let out the groping old man. 'Eggs and butter is yet to sell, and tha' cloak to be bought.'

'Well, I suppose we had!' said Sylvia, rather regretfully; for, though all the way into Monkshaven her head had been full of the purchase of this cloak, yet she was of that impressible nature that takes the tone of feeling from those surrounding; and though she knew no one on board the *Resolution*, she was just as anxious for the moment to see her come into harbour as any one in the crowd who had a dear relation on board. So she turned reluctantly to follow the more prudent Molly along the quay back to the Butter Cross.

It was a pretty scene, though it was too familiar to the eyes of all who then saw it for them to notice its beauty. The sun was low enough in the west to turn the mist that filled the distant valley of the river into golden haze. Above, on either bank of the Dee, there lay the moorland heights swelling one behind the other; the nearer, russet brown with the tints of the fading bracken; the more distant, grey and dim against the rich autumnal sky. The red and fluted tiles of the gabled houses rose in crowded irregularity on one side of the river, while the newer suburb was built in more orderly and less picturesque fashion on the opposite cliff. The river itself was swelling and chafing with the incoming tide till its vexed waters rushed over the very feet of the watching crowd on the staithes, as the great sea waves encroached more and more every minute. The quay side was unsavourily ornamented with glittering fish-scales, for the hauls of fish were cleansed in the open air, and no sanitary arrangements existed tor sweeping away any of the relics of this operation.

The fresh salt breeze was bringing up the lashing, leaping tide from the blue sea beyond the bar. Behind the returning girls there rocked the white-sailed ship, as if she were all alive with eagerness for her anchors to be heaved.

How impatient her crew of beating hearts were for that moment, how those on land sickened at the suspense, may be imagined, when you remember that for six long summer months those sailors had been as if dead from all news of those they loved; shut up in terrible, dreary Arctic seas from the hungry sight of sweethearts and friends, wives and mothers. No one knew what might have happened. The crowd on shore grew silent and solemn before the dread of the possible news of death that might toll in upon their hearts with this uprushing tide. The whalers went out into the Greenland seas full of strong, hopeful men; but the whalers never returned as they sailed forth. On land there are deaths among two or three hundred men to be mourned over in every half-year's space of time. Whose bones had been left to blacken on the grey and terrible icebergs? Who lay still until the sea should give up its dead? Who were those who should come back to Monkshaven never, no, never more?

Many a heart swelled with passionate, unspoken fear, as the first whaler lay off the bar on her return voyage.

Molly and Sylvia had left the crowd in this hushed suspense. But fifty yards along the staithe they passed five or six girls with flushed faces and careless attire, who had mounted a pile of timber, placed there to season for ship-building, from which, as from the steps of a ladder or staircase, they could command the harbour. They were wild and free in their gestures, and held each other by the hand, and swayed from side to side, stamping their feet in time, as they sang –

> Weel may the keel row, the keel row, the keel row,
> Weel may the keel row that my laddie's in!*

'What for are ye going off, now?' they called out to our two girls. 'She'll be in in ten minutes!' and without waiting for the answer which never came, they resumed their song.

Old sailors stood about in little groups, too proud to show their interest in the adventures they could no longer share, but quite unable to keep up any semblance of talk on indifferent subjects.

The town seemed very quiet and deserted as Molly and Sylvia entered the dark, irregular Bridge Street, and the market-place was as empty of people as before. But the skeps and baskets and three-legged stools were all cleared away.

'Market's over for to-day,' said Molly Corney, in disappointed surprise. 'We mun make the best on't, and sell to t' huxters,* and a hard bargain they'll be for driving. I doubt mother'll be vexed.'

She and Sylvia went to the corner shop to reclaim their baskets. The man had his joke at them for their delay.

'Ay, ay! lasses as has sweethearts a-coming home don't care much what price they get for butter and eggs! I dare say, now, there's some un in yon ship that 'ud give as much as a shilling a pound for this butter if he only knowed who churned it!' This was to Sylvia, as he handed her back her property.

The fancy-free Sylvia reddened, pouted, tossed back her head, and hardly deigned a farewell word of thanks or civility to the lame man; she was at an age to be affronted by any jokes on such a subject. Molly took the joke without disclaimer and without offence. She rather liked the unfounded idea of her having a sweetheart, and was rather surprised to think how devoid of foundation the notion was. If she could have a new cloak as Sylvia was going to have, then, indeed, there might be a chance! Until some such good luck, it was as well to laugh and blush as if the surmise of her having a lover was not very far from the truth, and so she replied in something of the same strain as the lame net-maker to his joke about the butter.

'He'll need it all, and more too, to grease his tongue, if iver he reckons to win me for his wife!'

When they were out of the shop, Sylvia said, in a coaxing tone, –

'Molly, who is it? Whose tongue'll need greasing? Just tell me, and I'll never tell!'

She was so much in earnest that Molly was perplexed. She did not quite like saying that she had alluded to no one in particular, only to a possible sweetheart, so she began to think what young man had made the most civil speeches to her in her life; the list was not a long one to go over, for her father was not so well off as to make her sought after for her money, and her face was rather of the homeliest. But she suddenly remembered her cousin, the specksioneer, who had given her two large shells, and taken a kiss from her half-willing lips before he went to sea the last time. So she smiled a little, and then said, –

'Well! I dunno. It's ill talking o' these things afore one has made up one's mind. And perhaps if Charley Kinraid behaves hissen, I might be brought to listen.'

'Charley Kinraid! who's he?'

'Yon specksioneer cousin o' mine, as I was talking on.'

'And do yo' think he cares for yo'?' asked Sylvia, in a low, tender tone, as if touching on a great mystery.

Molly only said, 'Be quiet wi' yo',' and Sylvia could not make out whether she cut the conversation so short because she was offended, or because they had come to the shop where they had to sell their butter and eggs.

'Now, Sylvia, if thou'll leave me thy basket, I'll make as good a bargain as iver I can on 'em; and thou can be off to choose this grand new cloak as is to be, afore it gets any darker. Where is ta going to?'

'Mother said I'd better go to Foster's,' answered Sylvia, with a shade of annoyance in her face. 'Feyther said just anywhere.'

'Foster's is t' best place; thou canst try anywhere afterwards. I'll be at Foster's in five minutes, for I reckon we mun hasten a bit now. It'll be near five o'clock.'

Sylvia hung her head and looked very demure as she walked off by herself to Foster's shop in the market place.

CHAPTER 3

Buying a New Cloak

Foster's shop* was the shop of Monkshaven. It was kept by two Quaker brothers, who were now old men; and their father had kept it before them; probably his father before that. People remembered it as an old-fashioned dwelling-house, with a sort of supplementary shop with unglazed windows projecting from the lower story. These openings had long been filled with panes of glass that at the present day would be accounted very small, but which seventy years ago were much admired for their size. I can best make you understand the appearance of the place by bidding you think of the long openings in a butcher's shop, and then to fill them up in your imagination with panes about eight inches by six, in a heavy wooden frame. There was one of these windows on each side the door-place, which was kept partially closed through the day by a low gate about a yard high. Half the shop was appropriated to grocery; the other half to drapery, and a little mercery.* The good old brothers gave all their known customers a kindly welcome; shaking hands with many of them, and asking all after their families and domestic circumstances before proceeding to business. They would not for the world have had any sign of festivity at Christmas, and scrupulously kept their shop open at that holy festival, ready themselves to serve sooner than tax the consciences of any of their assistants, only nobody ever came. But on New Year's Day they had a great cake, and wine, ready in the parlour behind the shop, of which all who came in to buy anything were asked to partake. Yet, though scrupulous in most things, it did not go against the consciences of these good brothers to purchase smuggled articles. There was a back way from the river side, up a covered entry, to the yard-door of the Fosters, and a peculiar kind of knock at this door always brought out either John or Jeremiah, or if not them, their shopman, Philip Hepburn; and the same cake and wine that the excise officer's wife might just have been tasting, was brought out in the back parlour to treat the smuggler. There was a little locking of doors, and drawing of the green silk curtain that was supposed to shut out the shop, but really all this was done very much for form's sake. Everybody in Monkshaven smuggled who could, and every one wore smuggled goods who could, and great reliance was placed on the excise officer's neighbourly feelings.

The story went that John and Jeremiah Foster were so rich that they could buy up all the new town across the bridge. They had certainly begun to have a kind of primitive bank in connection with their shop, receiving and taking care of such money as people did not wish to retain in their houses for fear of burglars. No one asked them for interest on the money thus deposited, nor did they give any; but, on the other hand, if any of their customers, on whose character they could depend, wanted a little advance, the Fosters, after due inquiries made, and in some cases due security given, were not unwilling to lend a moderate sum without charging a penny for the use of their money. All the articles they sold were as good as they knew how to choose, and for them they expected and obtained ready money. It was said that they only kept on shop for their amusement. Others averred that there was some plan of a marriage running in the brothers' heads – a marriage between William Coulson,* Mr Jeremiah's wife's nephew (Mr Jeremiah was a widower), and Hester Rose, whose mother was some kind of distant relation, and who served in the shop along with William Coulson and Philip Hepburn. Again, this was denied by those who averred that Coulson was no blood relation, and that if the Fosters had intended to do anything considerable for Hester, they would never have allowed her and her mother to live in such a sparing way, ekeing out their small income by having Coulson and Hepburn for lodgers. No; John and Jeremiah would leave all their money to some hospital or to some charitable institution. But, of course, there was a reply to this; when are there not many sides to an argument about a possibility concerning which no facts are known? Part of the reply turned on this: the old gentlemen had, probably, some deep plan in their heads in permitting their cousin to take Coulson and Hepburn as lodgers, the one a kind of nephew, the other, though so young, the head man in the shop; if either of them took a fancy to Hester, how agreeably matters could be arranged!

All this time Hester is patiently waiting to serve Sylvia, who is standing before her a little shy, a little perplexed and distracted, by the sight of so many pretty things.

Hester was a tall young woman, sparely yet largely formed,

of a grave aspect, which made her look older than she really was. Her thick brown hair was smoothly taken off her broad forehead, and put in a very orderly fashion, under her linen cap; her face was a little square, and her complexion sallow, though the texture of her skin was fine. Her grey eyes were very pleasant, because they looked at you so honestly and kindly; her mouth was slightly compressed, as most have it who are in the habit of restraining their feelings; but when she spoke you did not perceive this, and her rare smile slowly breaking forth showed her white even teeth, and when accompanied, as it generally was, by a sudden uplifting of her soft eyes, it made her countenance very winning. She was dressed in stuff of sober colours, both in accordance with her own taste, and in unasked compliance with the religious customs of the Fosters; but Hester herself was not a Friend.

Sylvia, standing opposite, not looking at Hester, but gazing at the ribbons in the shop window,* as if hardly conscious that any one awaited the expression of her wishes, was a great contrast; ready to smile or to pout, or to show her feelings in any way, with a character as undeveloped as a child's, affectionate, wilful, naughty, tiresome, charming, anything, in fact, at present that the chances of an hour called out. Hester thought her customer the prettiest creature ever seen, in the moment she had for admiration before Sylvia turned round and, recalled to herself, began, –

'Oh, I beg your pardon, miss; I was thinking what may the price of yon crimson ribbon be?'

Hester said nothing, but went to examine the shop-mark.

'Oh! I did not mean that I wanted any, I only want some stuff for a cloak. Thank you, miss, but I am very sorry – some duffle, please.'

Hester silently replaced the ribbon and went in search of the duffle. While she was gone Sylvia was addressed by the very person she most wished to avoid, and whose absence she had rejoiced over on first entering the shop, her cousin Philip Hepburn.

He was a serious-looking young man, tall, but with a slight stoop in his shoulders, brought on by his occupation. He had thick hair standing off from his forehead in a peculiar but not unpleasing manner; a long face, with a slightly aquiline nose, dark eyes, and a long upper lip, which gave a disagreeable aspect to a face that might otherwise have been good-looking.

'Good day, Sylvie,' he said; 'what are you wanting? How are all at home? Let me help you!'

Sylvia pursed up her red lips, and did not look at him as she replied,

'I'm very well, and so is mother; feyther's got a touch of rheumatiz, and there's a young woman getting what I want.'

She turned a little away from him when she had ended this sentence, as if it had comprised all she could possibly have to say to him. But he exclaimed,

'You won't know how to choose,' and, seating himself on the counter, he swung himself over after the fashion of shopmen.

Sylvia took no notice of him, but pretended to be counting over her money.

'What do you want, Sylvie? 'asked he, at last annoyed at her silence.

'I don't like to be called "Sylvie"; my name is Sylvia; and I'm wanting duffle for a cloak, if you must know.'

Hester now returned, with a shop-boy helping her to drag along the great rolls of scarlet and grey cloth.

'Not that,' said Philip, kicking the red duffle with his foot, and speaking to the lad. 'It's the grey you want, is it not, Sylvie?' He used the name he had had the cousin's right to call her by since her childhood, without remembering her words on the subject not five minutes before; but she did, and was vexed.

'Please, miss, it is the scarlet duffle I want; don't let him take it away.'

Hester looked up at both their countenances, a little wondering what was their position with regard to each other; for this, then, was the beautiful little cousin about whom Philip had talked to her mother, as sadly spoilt, and shamefully ignorant; a lovely little dunce, and so forth. Hester had pictured Sylvia Robson, somehow, as very different from what she was: younger, more stupid, not half so bright and charming (for, though she was now both pouting and cross, it was evident that this was not her accustomed mood). Sylvia devoted her attention to the red cloth, pushing aside the grey.

Philip Hepburn was vexed at his advice being slighted; and yet he urged it afresh.

'This is a respectable, quiet-looking article that will go well

with any colour; you niver will be so foolish as to take what will
mark with every drop of rain.'

'I'm sorry you sell such good-for-nothing things,' replied
Sylvia, conscious of her advantage, and relaxing a little (as little
as she possibly could) of her gravity.

Hester came in now.

'He means to say that this cloth will lose its first brightness in
wet or damp; but it will always be a good article, and the colour
will stand a deal of wear. Mr Foster would not have had it in
his shop else.'

Philip did not like that even a reasonable peace-making
interpreter should come between him and Sylvia, so he held his
tongue in indignant silence.

Hester went on:

'To be sure, this grey is the closer make, and would wear the
longest.'

'I don't care,' said Sylvia, still rejecting the dull grey, 'I like
this best. Eight yards, if you please, miss.'

'A cloak takes nine yards, at least,' said Philip, decisively.

'Mother told me eight,' said Sylvia, secretly conscious that her
mother would have preferred the more sober colour; and feeling
that as she had had her own way in that respect, she was bound
to keep to the directions she had received as to the quantity.
But, indeed, she would not have yielded to Philip in anything
that she could help.

There was a sound of children's feet running up the street
from the river-side, shouting with excitement. At the noise,
Sylvia forgot her cloak and her little spirit of vexation, and ran
to the half-door of the shop. Philip followed because she went.
Hester looked on with passive, kindly interest, as soon as she
had completed her duty of measuring. One of those girls whom
Sylvia had seen as she and Molly left the crowd on the quay,
came quickly up the street. Her face, which was handsome
enough as to feature, was whitened with excess of passionate
emotion, her dress untidy and flying, her movements heavy and
free. She belonged to the lowest class of seaport inhabitants. As
she came near, Sylvia saw that the tears were streaming down
her cheeks, quite unconsciously to herself. She recognized Sylvia's face, full of interest as it was, and stopped her clumsy run
to speak to the pretty, sympathetic creature.

'She's o'er t' bar! She's o'er t' bar! I'm boun' to tell mother!'

She caught at Sylvia's hand, and shook it, and went on breathless and gasping.

'Sylvia, how came you to know that girl?' asked Philip, sternly. 'She's not one for you to be shaking hands with. She's known all down t' quay-side as "Newcastle Bess".'

'I can't help it,' said Sylvia, half inclined to cry at his manner even more than his words. 'When folk are glad I can't help being glad too, and I just put out my hand, and she put out hers. To think o' yon ship come in at last! And if yo'd been down seeing all t' folk looking and looking their eyes out,* as if they feared they should die afore she came in and brought home the lads they loved, yo'd ha' shaken hands wi' that lass too, and no great harm done. I never set eyne upon her till half an hour ago on th' staithes, and maybe I'll niver see her again.'

Hester was still behind the counter, but had moved so as to be near the window; so she heard what they were saying, and now put in her word:

'She can't be altogether bad, for she thought o' telling her mother first thing, according to what she said.'

Sylvia gave Hester a quick, grateful look. But Hester had resumed her gaze out of the window, and did not see the glance.

And now Molly Corney joined them, hastily bursting into the shop.

'Hech!' said she. 'Hearken! how they're crying and shouting down on t' quay. T' gang's among 'em like t' day of judgment. Hark!'

No one spoke, no one breathed, I had almost said no heart beat for listening. Not long; in an instant there rose the sharp simultaneous cry of many people in rage and despair. Inarticulate at that distance, it was yet an intelligible curse, and the roll, and the roar, and the irregular tramp came nearer and nearer.

'They're taking 'em to t' Randyvowse,' said Molly. 'Eh! I wish I'd King George* here just to tell him my mind.'

The girl clenched her hands, and set her teeth.

'It's terrible hard!' said Hester; 'there's mothers, and wives, looking out for 'em, as if they were stars dropt out o' t' lift.'*

'But can we do nothing for 'em? 'cried Sylvia. 'Let us go into t' thick of it and do a bit of help; I can't stand quiet and see 't!' Half crying, she pushed forwards to the door; but Philip held her back.

'Sylvie! you must not. Don't be silly; it's the law, and no one can do aught against it, least of all women and lasses.'

By this time the vanguard of the crowd came pressing up Bridge Street, past the windows of Foster's shop. It consisted of wild, half-amphibious boys, slowly moving backwards, as they were compelled by the pressure of the coming multitude to go on, and yet anxious to defy and annoy the gang by insults, and curses half choked with their indignant passion, doubling their fists in the very faces of the gang who came on with measured movement, armed to the teeth, their faces showing white with repressed and determined energy against the bronzed counten-ances of the half-dozen sailors, who were all they had thought it wise to pick out of the whaler's crew, this being the first time an Admiralty warrant had been used in Monkshaven for many years; not since the close of the American war, in fact. One of the men was addressing to his townspeople, in a high pitched voice, an exhortation which few could hear, for, pressing around this nucleus of cruel wrong, were women crying aloud, throwing up their arms in imprecation, showering down abuse as hearty and rapid as if they had been a Greek chorus.* Their wild, famished eyes were strained on faces they might not kiss, their cheeks were flushed to purple with anger or else livid with impotent craving for revenge. Some of them looked scarce human; and yet an hour ago these lips, now tightly drawn back so as to show the teeth with the unconscious action of an enraged wild animal, had been soft and gracious with the smile of hope; eyes, that were fiery and bloodshot now, had been loving and bright; hearts, never to recover from the sense of injustice and cruelty, had been trustful and glad only one short hour ago.

There were men there, too, sullen and silent, brooding on remedial revenge; but not many, the greater proportion of this class being away in the absent whalers.

The stormy multitude swelled into the market-place and formed a solid crowd there, while the press-gang steadily forged their way on into High Street, and on to the rendezvous. A low, deep growl went up from the dense mass, as some had to wait for space to follow the others – now and then going up, as a lion's growl goes up, into a shriek of rage.

A woman forced her way up from the bridge. She lived some little way in the country, and had been late in hearing of the return of the whaler after her six months' absence; and on rushing down to the quay-side, she had been told by a score of busy, sympathizing voices, that her husband was kidnapped for the service of the Government.

She had need pause in the market-place, the outlet of which was crammed up. Then she gave tongue for the first time in such a fearful shriek, you could hardly catch the words she said.

'Jamie! Jamie! will they not let you to me?'

Those were the last words Sylvia heard before her own hysterical burst of tears called every one's attention to her.

She had been very busy about household work in the morning; and much agitated by all she had seen and heard since coming into Monkshaven, and so it ended in this.

Molly and Hester took her through the shop into the parlour beyond – John Foster's parlour, for Jeremiah, the elder brother, lived in a house of his own on the other side of the water. It was a low, comfortable room, with great beams running across the ceiling, and papered with the same paper as the walls – a piece of elegant luxury which took Molly's fancy mightily! This parlour looked out on the dark courtyard in which there grew two or three poplars, straining upwards to the light; and through an open door between the backs of two houses could be seen a glimpse of the dancing, heaving river, with such ships or fishing cobles* as happened to be moored in the waters above the bridge.

They placed Sylvia on the broad, old-fashioned sofa, and gave her water to drink, and tried to still her sobbing and choking. They loosed her hat, and copiously splashed her face and clustering chestnut hair, till at length she came to herself; restored, but dripping wet. She sat up and looked at them, smoothing back her tangled curls off her brow, as if to clear both her eyes and her intellect.

'Where am I? – oh, I know! Thank you. It was very silly, but somehow it seemed so sad!'

And here she was nearly going off again, but Hester said –

'Ay, it were sad, my poor lass – if I may call you so, for I don't rightly know your name – but it's best not think on it, for we can do no mak' o' good, and it'll mebbe set you off again. Yo're Philip Hepburn's cousin, I reckon, and yo' bide at Haytersbank Farm?'

'Yes; she's Sylvia Robson,' put in Molly, not seeing that

Foster's purpose was to make Sylvia speak, and so to divert her attention from the subject which had set her off into hysterics. 'And we came in for market,' continued Molly, 'and for t' buy t' new cloak as her feyther's going to give her; and, for sure, I thought we was i' luck's way when we saw t' first whaler, and niver dreaming as t' press-gang 'ud be so marred.'*

She, too, began to cry, but her little whimper was stopped by the sound of the opening door behind her. It was Philip, asking Hester by a silent gesture if he might come in.

Sylvia turned her face round from the light, and shut her eyes. Her cousin came close up to her on tip-toe, and looked enviously at what he could see of her averted face, then he passed his hand so slightly over her hair that he could scarcely be said to touch it, and murmured –

'Poor lassie! it's a pity she came to-day, for it's a long walk in this heat!'

But Sylvia started to her feet, almost pushing him along. Her quickened senses heard an approaching step through the court-yard before any of the others were aware of the sound. In a minute afterwards, the glass-door at one corner of the parlour was opened from the outside, and Mr John stood looking in with some surprise at the group collected in his usually empty parlour.

'It's my cousin,' said Philip, reddening a little; 'she came wi' her friend in to market, and to make purchases; and she's got a turn* wi' seeing the press-gang go past carrying some of the crew of the whaler to the Randyvowse.'

'Ay, ay,' said Mr John, quickly passing on into the shop on tip-toe, as if he were afraid he were intruding in his own premises, and beckoning Philip to follow him there. 'Out of strife cometh strife. I guessed something of the sort was up from what I heard on t' bridge as I came across fra' brother Jere-miah's.' Here he softly shut the door between the parlour and the shop. 'It beareth hard on th' expectant women and childer; nor is it to be wondered at that they, being unconverted, rage together (poor creatures!) like the very heathen.* Philip,' he said, coming nearer to his 'head young man', 'keep Nicholas and Henry at work in the ware-room upstairs until this riot be over, for it would grieve me if they were misled into violence.'

Philip hesitated.

'Speak out, man! Always ease an uneasy heart, and never let it get hidebound.'

'I had thought to convoy my cousin and the other young woman home, for the town is like to be rough, and it's getting dark.'

'And thou shalt, my lad,' said the good old man; 'and I myself will try and restrain the natural inclinations of Nicholas and Henry.'

But when he went to find the shopboys with a gentle homily on his lips, those to whom it should have been addressed were absent. In consequence of the riotous state of things, all the other shops in the market-place had put their shutters up; and Nicholas and Henry, in the absence of their superiors, had followed the example of their neighbours, and, as business was over, they had hardly waited to put the goods away, but had hurried off to help their townsmen in any struggle that might ensue.

There was no remedy for it, but Mr John looked rather discomfited. The state of the counters, and of the disarranged goods, was such also as would have irritated any man as orderly but less sweet-tempered. All he said on the subject was: 'The old Adam! the old Adam!'* but he shook his head long after he had finished speaking.

'Where is William Coulson?' he next asked. 'Oh! I remember. He was not to come back from York till the night closed in.'

Philip and his master arranged the shop in the exact order the old man loved. Then he recollected the wish of his subordinate, and turned round and said –

'Now go with thy cousin and her friend. Hester is here, and old Hannah. I myself will take Hester home, if need be. But for the present I think she had best tarry here, as it isn't many steps to her mother's house, and we may need her help if any of those poor creatures fall into suffering wi' their violence.'

With this, Mr John knocked at the door of the parlour, and waited for permission to enter. With old-fashioned courtesy he told the two strangers how glad he was that his room had been of service to them; that he would never have made so bold as to pass through it, if he had been aware how it was occupied. And then going to a corner cupboard, high up in the wall, he pulled a key out of his pocket and unlocked his little store of wine, and cake, and spirits; and insisted that they should eat and drink while waiting for Philip, who was taking some last measures for the security of the shop during the night.

Sylvia declined everything, with less courtesy than she ought to have shown to the offers of the hospitable old man. Molly took wine and cake, leaving a good half of both, according to the code of manners in that part of the country; and also because Sylvia was continually urging her to make haste. For the latter disliked the idea of her cousin's esteeming it necessary to accompany them home, and wanted to escape from him by setting off before he returned. But any such plans were frustrated by Philip's coming back into the parlour, full of grave content, which brimmed over from his eyes, with the parcel of Sylvia's obnoxious red duffle under his arm; anticipating so keenly the pleasure awaiting him in the walk, that he was almost surprised by the gravity of his companions as they prepared for it. Sylvia was a little penitent for her rejection of Mr John's hospitality, now she found out how unavailing for its purpose such rejection had been, and tried to make up by a modest sweetness of farewell, which quite won his heart, and made him praise her up to Hester in a way to which she, observant of all, could not bring herself fully to respond. What business had the pretty little creature to reject kindly-meant hospitality in the pettish way she did, thought Hester. And, oh! what business had she to be so ungrateful and to try and thwart Philip in his thoughtful wish of escorting them through the streets of the rough, riotous town? What did it all mean?

CHAPTER 4

Philip Hepburn

The coast on that part of the island to which this story refers is bordered by rocks and cliffs. The inland country immediately adjacent to the coast is level, flat, and bleak; it is only where the long stretch of dyke-enclosed fields terminates abruptly in a sheer descent, and the stranger sees the ocean creeping up the sands far below him, that he is aware on how great an elevation he has been. Here and there, as I have said, a cleft in the level land (thus running out into the sea in steep promontories) occurs – what they would call a 'chine'* in the Isle of Wight; but instead of the soft south wind stealing up the woody ravine, as it does there, the eastern breeze comes piping shrill and clear along these northern chasms, keeping the trees that venture to grow on the sides down to the mere height of scrubby brushwood. The descent to the shore through these 'bottoms' is in most cases very abrupt, too much so for a cartway, or even a bridle-path; but people can pass up and down without difficulty, by the help of a few rude steps hewn here and there out of the rock.

Sixty or seventy years ago (not to speak of much later times) the farmers who owned or hired the land which lay directly on the summit of these cliffs were smugglers to the extent of their power, only partially checked by the coastguard distributed, at pretty nearly equal interspaces of eight miles, all along the north-eastern seaboard. Still sea-wrack* was a good manure, and there was no law against carrying it up in great osier baskets* for the purposes of tillage, and many a secret thing was lodged in hidden crevices in the rocks till the farmer sent trusty people down to the shore for a good supply of sand and seaweed for his land.

One of the farms on the cliff had lately been taken by Sylvia's father. He was a man who had roamed about a good deal – been sailor, smuggler, horse-dealer, and farmer in turns; a sort of fellow possessed by a spirit of adventure and love of change, which did him and his own family more harm than anybody else. He was just the kind of man that all his neighbours found fault with, and all his neighbours liked. Late in life (for such an imprudent man as he was, one of a class who generally wed, trusting to chance and luck for the provision for a family), Farmer Robson married a woman whose only want of practical wisdom consisted in taking him for a husband. She was Philip Hepburn's aunt, and had had the charge of him until she married from her widowed brother's house. He it was who had let her know when Haytersbank Farm had been to let; esteeming it a likely piece of land for his uncle to settle down upon, after a somewhat unprosperous career of horse-dealing. The farmhouse lay in the shelter of a very slight green hollow scarcely scooped out of the pasture field by which it was surrounded; the short crisp turf came creeping up to the very door and windows, without any attempt at a yard or garden, or any nearer enclosure of the buildings than the stone dyke that formed the boundary of the field itself. The buildings were long and low, in order to avoid the rough violence of the winds that swept over that wild, bleak spot, both in winter and summer. It was well for the inhabitants of that house that coal was extremely cheap; otherwise a southerner might have imagined that they could never have survived the cutting of the bitter gales that piped all round, and seemed to seek out every crevice for admission into the house.

But the interior was warm enough when once you had mounted the long bleak lane, full of round rough stones, enough to lame any horse unaccustomed to such roads, and had crossed the field by the little dry, hard footpath, which tacked about so as to keep from directly facing the prevailing wind. Mrs Robson was a Cumberland woman, and, as such, was a cleaner housewife than the farmers' wives of that north-eastern coast, and was often shocked at their ways, showing it more by her looks than by her words, for she was not a great talker. This fastidiousness in such matters made her own house extremely comfortable, but did not tend to render her popular among her neighbours. Indeed, Bell Robson piqued herself on her housekeeping generally, and once indoors in the gray, bare stone house, there were plenty of comforts to be had besides cleanliness and warmth. The great rack of clap-bread* hung overhead, and Bell Robson's preference of this kind of oat-cake over the leavened and partly sour kind used in Yorkshire was another source of her unpopularity. Flitches of bacon and 'hands' (i.e., shoulders of cured pork, the legs or hams being sold, as fetching a better price) abounded; and for any visitor who could stay, neither cream nor finest wheaten flour was wanting for 'turf cakes'* and 'singing hinnies',* with which it is the delight of the northern housewives to regale the honoured guest, as he sips their high-priced tea, sweetened with dainty sugar.

This night Farmer Robson was fidgeting in and out of his house door, climbing the little eminence in the field, and coming down disappointed in a state of fretful impatience. His quiet, taciturn wife was a little put out by Sylvia's non-appearance too; but she showed her anxiety by being shorter than usual in her replies to his perpetual wonders as to where the lass could have been tarrying, and by knitting away with extra diligence.

'I've a vast o' mind to go down to Monkshaven mysen, and see after t' child. It's well on for seven.'

'No, Dannel,' said his wife; 'thou'd best not. Thy leg has been paining thee this week past, and thou'rt not up to such a walk. I'll rouse Kester, and send him off, if thou think'st there's need on it.'

'A'll noan ha' Kester roused. Who's to go afield betimes after t' sheep in t' morn, if he's ca'ed up to-neet? He'd miss t' lass, and find a public-house, a reckon,' said Daniel, querulously.

'I'm not afeard o' Kester,' replied Bell. 'He's a good one for knowing folk i' th' dark. But if thou'd rather, I'll put on my hood and cloak and just go to th' end o' th' lane, if thou'lt have an eye to th' milk, and see as it does na' boil o'er, for she canna stomach it if it's bishopped* e'er so little.'

Before Mrs Robson, however, had put away her knitting, voices were heard at a good distance down the lane, but coming nearer every moment, and once more Daniel climbed the little brow to look and to listen.

'It's a' reet!'* said he, hobbling quickly down. 'Niver fidget theesel' wi' gettin' ready to go search for her. I'll tak' thee a bet it's Philip Hepburn's voice, convoying her home, just as I said he would, an hour sin'.'

Bell did not answer, as she might have done, that this probability of Philip's bringing Sylvia home had been her own suggestion, set aside by her husband as utterly unlikely. Another minute and the countenances of both parents imperceptibly and unconsciously relaxed into pleasure as Sylvia came in.

She looked very rosy from the walk, and the October air, which began to be frosty in the evenings; there was a little cloud over her face at first, but it was quickly dispersed as she met the loving eyes of home. Philip, who followed her, had an excited, but not altogether pleased look about him. He received a hearty greeting from Daniel, and a quiet one from his aunt.

'Tak' off thy pan o' milk, missus, and set on t' kettle. Milk may do for wenches, but Philip and me is for a drop o' good Hollands* and watter this cold night. I'm a'most chilled to t' marrow wi' looking out for thee, lass, for t' mother was in a peck o' troubles* about thy none coming home i' t' dayleet, and I'd to keep hearkening out on t' browhead.'*

This was entirely untrue, and Bell knew it to be so; but her husband did not. He had persuaded himself now, as he had done often before, that what he had in reality done for his own pleasure or satisfaction, he had done in order to gratify some one else.

'The town was rough with a riot between the press-gang and the whaling folk; and I thought I'd best see Sylvia home.'

'Ay, ay, lad; always welcome, if it's only as an excuse for t' liquor. But t' whalers, say'st ta? Why, is t' whalers in? There was none i' sight yesterday, when I were down on t' shore. It's early days for 'em as yet. And t' cursed old press-gang's agate* again, doing its devil's work!'

His face changed as he ended his speech, and showed a steady passion of old hatred.

'Ay, missus, yo' may look. I wunnot pick and choose my words, noather for yo' nor for nobody, when I speak o' that damned gang. I'm none ashamed o' my words. They're true, and I'm ready to prove 'em. Where's my forefinger? Ay! and as good a top-joint of a thumb as iver a man had? I wish I'd kept 'em i' sperits, as they done things at t' 'potticary's,* just to show t' lass what flesh and bone I made away wi' to get free. I ups wi' a hatchet when I saw as I were fast a-board a man-o'-war standing out for sea – it were in t' time o' the war wi' Amerikay, an' I could na' stomach the thought o' being murdered i' my own language – so I ups wi' a hatchet, and I says to Bill Watson, says I, "Now, my lad, if thou'll do me a kindness, I'll pay thee back, niver fear, and they'll be glad enough to get shut on us,* and send us to old England again. Just come down with a will." Now, missus, why can't ye sit still and listen to me, 'stead o' pottering* after pans and what not?' said he, speaking crossly to his wife, who had heard the story scores of times, and, it must be confessed, was making some noise in preparing bread and milk for Sylvia's supper.

Bell did not say a word in reply, but Sylvia tapped his shoulder with a pretty little authoritative air.

'It's for me, feyther. I'm just keen-set* for my supper. Once let me get quickly set down to it, and Philip there to his glass o' grog,* and you'll never have such listeners in your life, and mother's mind will be at ease too.'

'Eh! thou's a wilfu' wench,' said the proud father, giving her a great slap on her back. 'Well! set thee down to thy victual, and be quiet wi' thee, for I want to finish my tale to Philip. But, perhaps, I've telled it yo' afore?' said he, turning round to question Hepburn.

Hepburn could not say that he had not heard it, for he piqued himself on his truthfulness. But instead of frankly and directly owning this, he tried to frame a formal little speech, which would soothe Daniel's mortified vanity; and, of course, it had the directly opposite effect. Daniel resented being treated like a child, and yet turned his back on Philip with all the wilfulness of one. Sylvia did not care for her cousin, but hated the discomfort of having her father displeased; so she took up her tale of adventure, and told her father and mother of her afternoon's proceedings. Daniel pretended not to listen at first, and made ostentatious noises with his spoon and glass; but by-and-by he got quite warm and excited about the doings of the press-gang, and scolded both Philip and Sylvia for not having learnt more particulars as to what was the termination of the riot.

'I've been whaling mysel',' said he; 'and I've heerd tell as whalers wear knives, and I'd ha' gi'en t' gang a taste o' my whittle,* I'd been cotched up* just as I'd set my foot a-shore.'

'I don't know,' said Philip; 'we're at war wi' the French,* and we shouldn't like to be beaten; and yet if our numbers are not equal to theirs, we stand a strong chance of it.'

'Not a bit on't – so be d – d!' said Daniel Robson, bringing down his fist with such violence on the round deal table, that the glasses and earthenware shook again. 'Yo'd not strike a child or a woman, for sure! yet it 'ud be like it, if we did na' give the Frenchies some 'vantages – if we took 'em wi' equal numbers. It's not fair play, and that's one place where t' shoe pinches.* It's not fair play two ways. It's not fair play to cotch up men as has no call for fightin' at another man's biddin', though they've no objection to fight a bit on their own account, and who are just landed, all keen after bread i'stead o' biscuit, and flesh meat i'stead o' junk,* and beds i'stead o' hammocks. (I make naught o' t' sentiment side, for I were niver gi'en up to such carnal-mindedness and poesies.)* It's noane fair to cotch 'em up and put 'em in a stifling hole, all lined with metal for fear they should whittle* their way out, and send 'em off to sea for years an' years to come. And again it's no fair play to t' French. Four o' them is rightly matched wi' one o' us; and if we go an' fight 'em four to four it's like as if yo' fell to beatin' Sylvie there, or little Billy Croxton, as isn't breeched.* And that's my mind. Missus, where's t' pipe?'

Philip did not smoke, so took his turn at talking, a chance he seldom had with Daniel, unless the latter had his pipe between his lips. So after Daniel had filled it, and used Sylvia's little finger as a stopper to ram down the tobacco – a habit of his to which she was so accustomed that she laid her hand on the table by him, as naturally as she would have fetched him his spittoon when he began to smoke – Philip arranged his arguments, and began –

'I'm for fair play wi' the French as much as any man, as long as we can be sure o' beating them; but, I say, make sure o' that, and then give them ivery advantage. Now I reckon Government is not sure as yet, for i' the papers it said as half th' ships i' th' Channel hadn't got their proper complement o' men; and all as I say is, let Government judge a bit for us; and if they say they're hampered for want o' men, why we must make it up somehow. John and Jeremiah Foster pay in taxes, and Militiaman pays in person;* and if sailors cannot pay in taxes, and will not pay in person, why they must be made to pay; and that's what th' press-gang is for, I reckon. For my part, when I read o' the way those French chaps are going on, I'm thankful to be governed by King George and a British Constitution.'

Daniel took his pipe out of his mouth at this.

'And when did I say a word again King George and the Constitution? I only ax 'em to govern me as I judge best, and that's what I call representation. When I gived my vote to Measter Cholmley* to go up to t' Parliament House,* I as good as said, "Now yo' go up theer, sir, and tell 'em what I, Dannel Robson, think right, and what I, Dannel Robson, wish to have done." Else I'd be darned if I'd ha' gi'en my vote to him or any other man. And div* yo' think I want Seth Robson (as is my own brother's son, and mate to a collier) to be cotched up by a press-gang, and ten to one his wages all unpaid? Div yo' think I'd send up Measter Cholmley to speak up for that piece o' work?* Not I.' He took up his pipe again, shook out the ashes, puffed it into a spark, and shut his eyes, preparatory to listening.

'But, asking pardon, laws is made for the good of the nation, not for your good or mine.'

Daniel could not stand this. He laid down his pipe, opened

his eyes, stared straight at Philip before speaking, in order to enforce his words, and then said slowly –

'Nation here! nation theere! I'm a man and yo're another, but nation's nowheere.* If Measter Cholmley talked to me i' that fashion, he'd look long for another vote frae me. I can make out King George, and Measter Pitt,* and yo' and me, but nation! nation, go hang!'

Philip, who sometimes pursued an argument longer than was politic for himself, especially when he felt sure of being on the conquering side, did not see that Daniel Robson was passing out of the indifference of conscious wisdom into that state of anger which ensues when a question becomes personal in some unspoken way. Robson had contested this subject once or twice before, and had the remembrance of former disputes to add to his present vehemence. So it was well for the harmony of the evening that Bell and Sylvia returned from the kitchen to sit in the house-place. They had been to wash up the pans and basins used for supper; Sylvia had privately shown off her cloak, and got over her mother's shake of the head at its colour with a coaxing kiss, at the end of which her mother had adjusted her cap with a 'There! there! ha' done wi' thee,' but had no more heart to show her disapprobation; and now they came back to their usual occupations until it should please their visitor to go, then they would rake the fire and be off to bed; for neither Sylvia's spinning nor Bell's knitting was worth candle-light, and morning hours are precious in a dairy.

People speak of the way in which harp-playing sets off a graceful figure; spinning is almost as becoming an employment. A woman stands at the great wool-wheel, one arm extended, the other holding the thread, her head thrown back to take in all the scope of her occupation; or if it is the lesser spinning-wheel for flax – and it was this that Sylvia moved forwards to-night – the pretty sound of the buzzing, whirring motion, the attitude of the spinner, foot and hand alike engaged in the business – the bunch of gay coloured ribbon that ties the bundle of flax on the rock – all make it into a picturesque piece of domestic business that may rival harp-playing any day for the amount of softness and grace which it calls out.

Sylvia's cheeks were rather flushed by the warmth of the room after the frosty air. The blue ribbon with which she had thought it necessary to tie back her hair before putting on her hat to go

to market had got rather loose, and allowed her disarranged
curls to stray in a manner which would have annoyed her
extremely, if she had been upstairs to look at herself in the glass;
but although they were not set in the exact fashion which Sylvia
esteemed as correct, they looked very pretty and luxuriant. Her
little foot, placed on the 'traddle', * was still encased in its
smartly buckled shoe – not slightly to her discomfort, as she was
unaccustomed to be shod in walking far; only as Philip had
accompanied them home, neither she nor Molly had liked to go
barefoot. Her round, mottled arm and ruddy, taper hand drew
out the flax with nimble, agile motion, keeping time to the
movement of the wheel. All this Philip could see; the greater
part of her face was lost to him as she half averted it, with a shy
dislike to the way in which she knew from past experience that
cousin Philip always stared at her. And avert it as she would she
heard with silent petulance the harsh screech of Philip's chair as
he heavily dragged it on the stone floor, sitting on it all the
while, and felt that he was moving round so as to look at her as
much as was in his power, without absolutely turning his back
on either her father or mother. She got herself ready for the first
opportunity of contradiction or opposition.

'Well, wench! and has ta bought this grand new cloak?'

'Yes, feyther. It's a scarlet one.'

'Ay, ay! and what does mother say?'

'Oh, mother's content,' said Sylvia, a little doubting in her
heart, but determined to defy Philip at all hazards.

'Mother'll put up with it if it does na' spot would be nearer
fact, I'm thinking,' said Bell, quietly.

'I wanted Sylvia to take the gray,' said Philip.

'And I chose the red; it's so much gayer, and folk can see me
the farther off. Feyther likes to see me at first turn o' t' lane,
don't yo', feyther and I'll niver turn out when it's boun' for to
rain, so it shall niver get a spot* near it, mammy.'

'I reckoned it were to wear i' bad weather,' said Bell.
'Leastways that were the pretext for coaxing feyther out o' it.'

She said it in a kindly tone, though the words became a
prudent rather than a fond mother. But Sylvia understood her
better than Daniel did, as it appeared.

'Hou'd thy tongue, mother. She niver spoke a pretext at all.'

He did not rightly know what a 'pretext' was: Bell was a
touch better educated than her husband, but he did not acknowl-

edge this, and made a particular point of differing from her whenever she used a word beyond his comprehension.

'She's a good lass at times; and if she liked to wear a yellow-orange cloak she should have it. Here's Philip here, as stands up for laws and press-gangs, I'll set him to find us a law again* pleasing our lass, and she our only one. Thou dostn't think on that, mother!'

Bell did think of that often; oftener than her husband, perhaps, for she remembered every day, and many times a day, the little one that had been born and had died while its father was away on some long voyage. But it was not her way to make replies.

Sylvia, who had more insight into her mother's heart than Daniel, broke in with a new subject.

'Oh! as for Philip, he's been preaching up laws all t' way home. I said naught, but let Molly hold her own; or else I could ha' told a tale about silks an' lace an' things.'

Philip's face flushed. Not because of the smuggling; every one did that, only it was considered polite to ignore it; but he was annoyed to perceive how quickly his little cousin had discovered that his practice did not agree with his preaching, and vexed, too, to see how delighted she was to bring out the fact. He had some little idea, too, that his uncle might make use of his practice as an argument against the preaching he had lately been indulging in, in opposition to Daniel; but Daniel was too far gone in his Hollands-and-water to do more than enunciate his own opinions, which he did with hesitating and laboured distinctness in the following sentence:

'What I think and say is this. Laws is made for to keep some folks fra' harming others. Press-gangs and coast-guards harm me i' my business, and keep me fra' getting what I want. Theerefore, what I think and say is this: Measter Cholmley should put down press-gangs and coast-guards. If that theere isn't reason I ax yo' to tell me what is? an' if Measter Cholmley dont do what I ax him, he may go whistle for my vote,* he may.'

At this period in his conversation, Bell Robson interfered; not in the least from any feeling of disgust or annoyance, or dread of what he might say or do if he went on drinking, but simply as a matter of health. Sylvia, too, was in no way annoyed; not only with her father, but with every man whom she knew, excepting her cousin Philip, was it a matter of course to drink till their ideas became confused. So she simply put her wheel aside, as preparatory to going to bed, when her mother said, in a more decided tone than that which she had used on any other occasion but this, and similar ones –

'Come, measter, you've had as much as is good for you.'

'Let a' be!* Let a' be,' said he, clutching at the bottle of spirits, but perhaps rather more good-humoured with what he had drunk than he was before; he jerked a little more into his glass before his wife carried it off, and locked it up in the cupboard, putting the key in her pocket, and then he said, winking at Philip –

'Eh! my man. Niver gie a woman t' whip hand o'er yo'! Yo' seen what it brings a man to; but for a' that I'll vote for Cholmley, an' d— t' press-gang!'

He had to shout out the last after Philip, for Hepburn, really anxious to please his aunt, and disliking drinking habits himself by constitution, was already at the door, and setting out on his return home, thinking, it must be confessed, far more of the character of Sylvia's shake of the hand than of the parting words of either his uncle or aunt.

CHAPTER 5

Story of the Press-Gang

For a few days after the evening mentioned in the last chapter the weather was dull. Not in quick, sudden showers did the rain come down, but in constant drizzle, blotting out all colour from the surrounding landscape, and filling the air with fine grey mist, until people breathed more water than air. At such times the consciousness of the nearness of the vast unseen sea acted as a dreary depression to the spirits; but besides acting on the nerves of the excitable, such weather affected the sensitive or ailing in material ways. Daniel Robson's fit of rheumatism incapacitated him from stirring abroad; and to a man of his active habits, and somewhat inactive mind, this was a great hardship. He was not ill-tempered naturally, but this state of confinement made him more ill-tempered than he had ever been before in his life. He sat in the chimney-corner, abusing the weather and doubting the wisdom or desirableness of all his wife saw fit to do in the usual daily household matters. The 'chimney-corner' was really a corner at Haytersbank. There were two projecting walls on each side of the fire-place, running about six feet into the room, and a stout wooden settle was placed against one of these, while opposite was the circular-backed 'master's chair', the seat of which was composed of a square piece of wood judiciously hollowed out, and placed with one corner to the front. Here, in full view of all the operations going on over the fire, sat Daniel Robson for four live long days, advising and directing his wife in all such minor matters as the boiling of potatoes, the making of porridge, all the work on which she specially piqued herself, and on which she would have taken advice – no! not from the most skilled housewife in all the three Ridings.* But, somehow, she managed to keep her tongue quiet from telling him, as she would have done any woman, and any other man, to mind his own business, or she would pin a dish-clout to his tail.* She even checked Sylvia when the latter proposed, as much for fun as for anything else, that his ignorant directions should be followed, and the consequences brought before his eyes and his nose.

'Na, na!' said Bell, 'th' feyther's feyther, and we mun respect him. But it's dree work havin' a man i' th' house, nursing th' fire,* an' such weather too, and not a soul coming near us, not even to fall out wi' him; for thee and me must na' do that, for th' Bible's sake, dear; and a good stand-up wordy quarrel would do him a power of good; stir his blood like. I wish Philip would turn up.'

Bell sighed, for in these four days she had experienced somewhat of Madame de Maintenon's difficulty* (and with fewer resources to meet it) of trying to amuse a man who was not amusable. For Bell, good and sensible as she was, was not a woman of resources. Sylvia's plan, undutiful as it was in her mother's eyes, would have done Daniel more good, even though it might have made him angry, than his wife's quiet, careful monotony of action, which, however it might conduce to her husband's comfort when he was absent, did not amuse him when present.

Sylvia scouted* the notion of cousin Philip coming into their

household in the character of an amusing or entertaining person,
till she nearly made her mother angry at her ridicule of the good
steady young fellow, to whom Bell looked up as the pattern of
all that early manhood should be. But the moment Sylvia saw
she had been giving her mother pain, she left off her wilful little
jokes, and kissed her, and told her she would manage all
famously, and ran out of the back-kitchen, in which mother and
daughter had been scrubbing the churn and all the wooden
implements of butter-making. Bell looked at the pretty figure of
her little daughter, as, running past with her apron thrown over
her head, she darkened the window beneath which her mother
was doing her work. She paused just for a moment, and then
said, almost unawares to herself, 'Bless thee, lass,' before
resuming her scouring of what already looked almost snow-
white.

Sylvia scampered across the rough farmyard in the wetting,
drizzling rain to the place where she expected to find Kester; but
he was not there, so she had to retrace her steps to the cow-
house, and, making her way up a rough kind of ladder-staircase
fixed straight against the wall, she surprised Kester as he sat in
the wool-loft, looking over the fleeces reserved for the home-
spinning, by popping her bright face, swathed round with her
blue woollen apron, up through the trap-door, and thus, her
head the only visible part, she addressed the farm servant, who
was almost like one of the family.

'Kester, feyther's just tiring hissel' wi' weariness an' vexation,
sitting by t' fireside wi' his hands afore him, an' nought to do.
An' mother and me can't think on aught as'll rouse him up to a
bit of a laugh, or aught more cheerful than a scolding. Now,
Kester, thou mun just be off, and find Harry Donkin th' tailor,
and bring him here; it's gettin' on for Martinmas,* an' he'll be
coming his rounds, and he may as well come here first as last,
and feyther's clothes want a deal o' mending up, and Harry's
always full of his news, and anyhow he'll do for feyther to scold,
an' be a new person too, and that's somewhat for all on us.
Now go, like a good old Kester as yo' are.'

Kester looked at her with loving, faithful admiration. He had
set himself his day's work in his master's absence, and was very
desirous of finishing it, but, somehow, he never dreamed of
resisting Sylvia, so he only stated the case.

'T' 'ool's a vast o' muck in 't, an' a thowt as a'd fettle it, an'
do it up;* but a reckon a mun do yo'r biddin'.'

'There's a good old Kester,' said she, smiling, and nodding
her muffled head at him; then she dipped down out of his sight,
then rose up again (he had never taken his slow, mooney* eyes
from the spot where she had disappeared) to say – 'Now, Kester,
be wary and deep – thou mun tell Harry Donkin not to let on as
we've sent for him, but just to come in as if he were on his
round, and took us first; and he mun ask feyther if there is any
work for him to do; and I'll answer for 't, he'll have a welcome
and a half. Now, be deep and fause,* mind thee!'

'A'se deep an' fause enow wi' simple folk; but what can a do
i' Donkin be as fause as me – as happen he may be?'

'Ga way wi' thee! I' Donkin be Solomon, thou mun be t'
Queen o' Sheba;* and I'se bound for to say she outwitted him
at last!'

Kester laughed so long at the idea of his being the Queen of
Sheba, that Sylvia was back by her mother's side before the
cachinnation* ended.

That night, just as Sylvia was preparing to go to bed in her
little closet of a room, she heard some shot* rattling at her
window. She opened the little casement, and saw Kester standing
below. He recommenced where he left off, with a laugh –

'He, he, he! A's been t' queen! A'se ta'en Donkin on t' reet
side,* an' he'll coom in to-morrow, just permiskus,* an' ax for
work, like as if 't were a favour; t' oud felley* were a bit cross-
grained at startin', for he were workin' at farmer Crosskey's up
at t' other side o' t' town, wheer they puts a strike an' a half o'
maut* intil t' beer, when most folk put nobbut a strike, an 't
made him ill to convince: but he'll coom, niver fear!'

The honest fellow never said a word of the shilling he had
paid out of his own pocket to forward Sylvia's wishes, and to
persuade the tailor to leave the good beer. All his anxiety now
was to know if he had been missed, and if it was likely that a
scolding awaited him in the morning.

'T' oud measter didn't set up his back,* 'cause a didn't coom
in t' supper?'

'He questioned a bit as to what thou were about, but mother
didn't know, an' I held my peace. Mother carried thy supper in
t' loft for thee.'

'A'll gang after 't, then, for a'm like a pair o' bellowses wi' t' wind out; just two flat sides wi' nowt betwixt.'

The next morning, Sylvia's face was a little redder than usual when Harry Donkin's bow-legs were seen circling down the path to the house door.

'Here's Donkin, for sure!' exclaimed Bell, when she caught sight of him a minute after her daughter. 'Well, I just call that lucky! for he'll be company for thee while Sylvia and me has to turn th' cheeses.'

This was too original a remark for a wife to make in Daniel's opinion, on this especial morning, when his rheumatism was twinging him more than usual, so he replied with severity –

'That's all t' women know about it. Wi' them it's "coompany, coompany, coompany", an' they think a man's no better than theirsels. A'd have yo' to know a've a vast o' thoughts in mysel', as I'm noane willing to lay out for t' benefit o' every man. A've niver gotten time for meditation sin' a were married; leastways, sin' a left t' sea. Aboard ship, wi' niver a woman wi'in leagues o' hail,* and upo' t' masthead, in special, a could.'

'Then I'd better tell Donkin as we've no work for him,' said Sylvia, instinctively managing her father by agreeing with him, instead of reasoning with or contradicting him.

'Now, theere you go!' wrenching himself round, for fear Sylvia should carry her meekly made threat into execution. 'Ugh! ugh!' as his limb hurt him. 'Come in, Harry, come in, and talk a bit o' sense to me, for a've been shut up wi' women these four days, and a'm a'most a nateral* by this time. A'se bound for 't, they'll find yo' some wark, if 't's nought but for to save their own fingers.'

So Harry took off his coat, and seated himself professional-wise* on the hastily-cleared dresser, so that he might have all the light afforded by the long, low casement window. Then he blew in his thimble, sucked his finger, so that they might adhere tightly together, and looked about for a subject for opening conversation, while Sylvia and her mother might be heard opening and shutting drawers and box-lids before they could find the articles that needed repair, or that were required to mend each other.*

'Women's well enough i' their way,' said Daniel, in a philo-sophizing tone, 'but a man may have too much on 'em. Now there's me, leg-fast these four days, and a'll make free to say to yo', a'd rather a deal ha' been loading dung i' t' wettest weather; an' a reckon it's th' being wi' nought but women as tires me so: they talk so foolish it gets int' t' bones like. Now thou know'st thou'rt not called much of a man oather, but bless yo', t' ninth part's* summut to be thankful for, after nought but women. An yet, yo' seen, they were for sending yo' away i' their foolishness! Well! missus, and who's to pay for t' fettling of all them clothes?' as Bell came down with her arms full. She was going to answer her husband meekly and literally according to her wont, but Sylvia, already detecting the increased cheerfulness of his tone, called out from behind her mother, –

'I am, feyther. I'm going for to sell my new cloak as I bought Thursday, for the mending on your old coats and waistcoats.'

'Hearken till her,' said Daniel, chuckling. 'She's a true wench. Three days sin' noane so full as she o' t' new cloak that now she's fain t' sell.'

'Ay, Harry. If feyther won't pay yo' for making all these old clothes as good as new, I'll sell my new red cloak sooner than yo' shall go unpaid.'

'A reckon it's a bargain,' said Harry, casting sharp, professional eyes on the heap before him, and singling out the best article as to texture for examination and comment.

'They're all again these metal buttons,' said he. 'Silk weavers has been petitioning Ministers t' make a law to favour silk buttons; and I did hear tell as there were informers goin' about spyin' after metal buttons, and as how they could haul yo' before a justice for wearing on 'em.'

'A were wed in 'em, and a'll wear 'em to my dyin' day, or a'll wear noane at a'. They're for making such a pack o' laws, they'll be for meddling wi' my fashion o' sleeping next, and taxing me for ivery snore a give. They've been after t' winders,* and after t' vittle, and after t' very saut to 't; it's dearer by hauf an' more nor it were when a were a boy: they're a meddlesome set o' folks, law-makers is, an' a'll niver believe King George has ought t' do wi' 't. But mark my words; I were wed wi' brass buttons, and brass buttons a'll wear to my death, an' if they moither* me about it, a'll wear brass buttons i' my coffin!'

By this time Harry had arranged a certain course of action with Mrs Robson, conducting the consultation and agreement by signs. His thread was flying fast already, and the mother and daughter felt more free to pursue their own business than they had done for several days; for it was a good sign that Daniel had taken his pipe out of the square hollow in the fireside wall, where he usually kept it, and was preparing to diversify his remarks with satisfying interludes of puffing.

'Why, look ye; this very baccy had a run for 't.* It came ashore sewed up neatly enough i' a woman's stays, as was wife to a fishing-smack down at 't bay yonder. She were a lean thing as iver you saw, when she went for t' see her husband aboard t' vessel; but she coom back lustier by a deal,* an' wi' many a thing on her, here and theere, beside baccy. An' that were i' t'face o' coast-guard and yon tender, an' a'. But she made as though she were tipsy, an' so they did nought but curse her, an' get out on her way.'

'Speaking of t' tender, there's been a piece o' wark i' Monkshaven this week wi' t' press-gang,' said Harry.

'Ay! ay! our lass was telling about 't; but, Lord bless ye! there's no gettin' t' rights on a story out on a woman – though a will say this for our Sylvie, she's as bright a lass as iver a man looked at.'

Now the truth was, that Daniel had not liked to demean himself, at the time when Sylvia came back so full of what she had seen at Monkshaven, by evincing any curiosity on the subject. He had then thought that the next day he would find some business that should take him down to the town, when he could learn all that was to be learnt, without flattering his womankind by asking questions, as if anything they might say could interest him. He had a strong notion of being a kind of domestic Jupiter.*

'It's made a deal o' wark* i' Monkshaven. Folk had gotten to think nought o' t' tender, she lay so still, an' t' leftenant paid such a good price for all he wanted for t' ship. But o' Thursday t' *Resolution*, first whaler back this season, came in port, and t' press-gang showed their teeth, and carried off four as good able-bodied seamen as iver I made trousers for; and t' place were all up like a nest o' wasps, when yo've set your foot in t' midst. They were so mad, they were ready for t' fight t' very pavin' stones.'

'A wish a'd been theere! A just wish a had! A've a score for t' reckon up wi' t' press-gang!'

And the old man lifted up his right hand – his hand on which the forefinger and thumb were maimed and useless – partly in denunciation, and partly as a witness of what he had endured to escape from the service, abhorred because it was forced. His face became a totally different countenance with the expression of settled and unrelenting indignation, which his words called out.

'G'on, man, g'on,' said Daniel, impatient with Donkin for the little delay occasioned by the necessity of arranging his work more fully.

'Ay! ay! all in good time; for a've a long tale to tell yet; an' a mun have some 'un to iron me out my seams, and look me out my bits, for there's none here fit for my purpose.'

'Dang thy bits! Here, Sylvie! Sylvie! come and be tailor's man, and let t' chap get settled sharp, for a'm fain t' hear his story.'

Sylvia took her directions, and placed her irons in the fire, and ran upstairs for the bundle which had been put aside by her careful mother for occasions like the present. It consisted of small pieces of various coloured cloth, cut out of old coats and waistcoats, and similar garments, when the whole had become too much worn for use, yet when part had been good enough to be treasured by a thrifty housewife. Daniel grew angry before Donkin had selected his patterns and settled the work to his own mind.

'Well,' said he at last; 'a mought* be a young man a-goin' a wooin', by t' pains thou'st taken for t' match my oud clothes. I don't care if they're patched wi' scarlet, a tell thee; so as thou'lt work away at thy tale wi' thy tongue, same time as thou works at thy needle wi' thy fingers.'

'Then, as a were saying, all Monkshaven were like a nest o' wasps, flyin' hither and thither, and makin' sich a buzzin' and a talkin' as niver were; and each wi' his sting out, ready for t' vent his venom o' rage and revenge. And women cryin' and sobbin' i' t' streets – when, Lord help us! o' Saturday came a worse time than iver! for all Friday there had been a kind o' expectation an' dismay about t' *Good Fortune*, as t' mariners had said was off St Abb's Head o' Thursday, when t' *Resolution* came in; and there was wives and maids wi' husbands an' sweethearts aboard t' *Good Fortune* ready to throw their eyes out on their heads wi' gazin', gazin' nor'ards over t' sea, as were all one haze o' blankness wi' t' rain; and when t' afternoon tide comed in, an' niver a line on her to be seen, folk were oncertain as t' whether she were holding off for fear o' t' tender – as were out o' sight, too – or what were her mak' o' goin' on.* An' t' poor wet draggled women folk came up t' town, some slowly cryin', as if their hearts was sick, an' others just bent their heads to t' wind, and went straight to their homes, nother looking nor speaking to ony one; but barred their doors, and stiffened theirsels up for a night o' waiting. Saturday morn – yo'll mind Saturday morn, it were stormy and gusty, downreet dirty weather – theere stood t' folk again by daylight, a watching an' a straining, and by that tide t' *Good Fortune* came o'er t' bar. But t' excisemen had sent back her news by t' boat as took 'em there. They'd a deal of oil, and a vast o' blubber. But for all that her flag was drooping i' t' rain, half mast high, for mourning and sorrow, an' they'd a dead man aboard – a dead man as was living and strong last sunrise. An' there was another as lay between life an' death, and there was seven more as should ha' been theere as wasn't, but was carried off by t' gang. T' frigate as we 'n a' heard tell on, as lying off Hartlepool, got tidings fra' t' tender as captured t' seamen o' Thursday: and t' *Aurora*, as they ca'ed her, made off for t' nor'ard; and nine leagues off St Abb's Head, t' *Resolution* thinks she were, she see'd t' frigate, and knowed by her build she were a man-o'-war, and guessed she were bound on king's kidnapping. I seen t' wounded man mysen wi' my own eyes; and he'll live! he'll live! Niver a man died yet, wi' such a strong purpose o' vengeance in him. He could barely speak, for he were badly shot, but his colour coome and went, as t' master's mate an' t' captain telled me and some others how t' *Aurora* fired at 'em, and how t' innocent whaler hoisted her colours, but afore they were fairly run up, another shot coome close in t' shrouds, and then t' Greenland ship being t' windward, bore down on t' frigate; but as they knew she were an oud fox, and bent on mischief, Kinraid (that's he who lies a-dying, only he'll noane die, a'se bound), the specksioneer, bade t'men go down between decks, and fasten t' hatches well, an he'd stand guard, he an' captain, and t' oud master's mate, being left upo' deck for t' give a welcome just skin-deep to t' boat's crew fra' t' *Aurora*, as they could see coming t'wards them o'er t' watter, wi' their reg'lar man-o-war's rowing – '

'Damn 'em!' said Daniel, in soliloquy, and under his breath.

Sylvia stood, poising her iron, and listening eagerly, afraid to give Donkin the hot iron for fear of interrupting the narrative, unwilling to put it into the fire again, because that action would perchance remind him of his work, which now the tailor had forgotten, so eager was he in telling his story.

'Well! they coome on over t'watters wi' great bounds, and up t' sides they coome like locusts, all armed men; an' t' captain says he saw Kinraid hide away his whaling knife under some tarpaulin', and he knew he meant mischief, an' he would no more ha' stopped him wi' a word nor he would ha' stopped him fra' killing a whale. And when t' *Aurora*'s men were aboard, one on 'em runs to t' helm; and at that t' captain says, he felt as if his wife were kissed afore his face; but says he, "I bethought me on t' men as were shut up below hatches, an' I remembered t' folk at Monkshaven as were looking out for us even then; an' I said to mysel', I would speak fair as long as I could, more by token o' the whaling-knife, as I could see glinting bright under t' black tarpaulin'." So he spoke quite fair and civil, though he see'd they was nearing t' *Aurora*, and t' *Aurora* was nearing them. Then t' navy captain hailed him thro' t' trumpet, wi' a great rough blast, and, says he, "Order your men to come on deck." And t' captain of t' whaler says, his men cried up from under t' hatches as they'd niver be gi'en up wi'out bloodshed, and he sees Kinraid take out his pistol, and look well to t' priming; so he says to t' navy captain, "We're protected Greenlandmen, and you have no right t' meddle wi' us." But t' navy captain only bellows t' more, "Order your men t' come on deck. If they won't obey you, and you have lost the command of your vessel, I reckon you're in a state of mutiny, and you may come aboard t' *Aurora* and such men as are willing t' follow you, and I'll fire int' the rest." Yo' see, that were t' depth o' the man: he were for pretending and pretexting as t' captain could na manage his own ship, and as he'd help him. But our Greenland captain were noane so poor-spirited, and says he, "She's full of oil, and I ware* you of consequences if you fire into her. Anyhow, pirate, or no pirate' (for t' word pirate stuck in his gizzard), "I'm a honest Monkshaven man, an' I come fra' a land where there's great icebergs and many a deadly danger, but niver a press-gang, thank God! and that's what you are, I reckon." Them's the words he told me, but whether he spoke 'em out so bold at t' time, I'se not so sure; they were in his mind for t' speak, only maybe prudence got t' better on him, for he said he prayed i' his heart to bring his cargo safe to t' owners, come what might. Well, t' *Aurora*'s men aboard t' *Good Fortune*

cried out "might they fire down t' hatches, and bring t' men out
that a way?" and then t' specksioneer, he speaks, an' he says he
stands ower t' hatches, and he has two good pistols, and summut
besides, and he don't care for his life, bein' a bachelor, but all
below are married men, yo' see, and he'll put an end to t' first
two chaps as come near t' hatches. An' they say he picked two
off as made for t' come near, and then, just as he were stooping
for t' whaling knife, an' it's as big as a sickle—'

'Teach folk as don't know a whaling knife,' cried Daniel. 'I
were a Greenland-man mysel'.'

'They shot him through t' side, and dizzied him, and kicked
him aside for dead; and fired down t' hatches, and killed one
man, and disabled two, and then t' rest cried for quarter,* for
life is sweet, e'en aboard a king's ship; and t' *Aurora* carried 'em
off, wounded men, an' able men, an' all: leaving Kinraid for
dead, as wasn't dead, and Darley for dead, as was dead, an' t'
captain and master's mate as were too old for work; and t'
captain, as loves Kinraid like a brother, poured rum down his
throat, and bandaged him up, and has sent for t' first doctor in
Monkshaven for to get t' slugs out; for they say there's niver
such a harpooner in a' t' Greenland seas; an' I can speak fra my
own seeing he's a fine young fellow where he lies theere, all
stark and wan for weakness and loss o' blood. But Darley's dead
as a door-nail; and there's to be such a burying of him as niver
was seen afore i' Monkshaven, come Sunday. And now gi' us t'
iron, wench, and let's lose no more time a-talking.'

'It's noane loss o' time,' said Daniel, moving himself heavily
in his chair, to feel how helpless he was once more. 'If a were as
young as once a were – nay, lad, if a had na these sore
rheumatics, now – a reckon as t'press-gang 'ud find out as 't
shouldn't do such things for nothing. Bless thee, man! it's waur*
nor i' my youth i' th' Ameriky war, and then 't were bad
enough.'

'And Kinraid?' said Sylvia, drawing a long breath, after the
effort of realizing it all; her cheeks had flushed up, and her eyes
had glittered during the progress of the tale.

'Oh! he'll do. He'll not die. Life's stuff is in him yet.'

'He'll be Molly Corney's cousin, I reckon,' said Sylvia,
bethinking her with a blush of Molly Corney's implication that
he was more than a cousin to her, and immediately longing to
go off and see Molly, and hear all the little details which women

do not think it beneath them to give to women. From that time Sylvia's little heart was bent on this purpose. But it was not one to be openly avowed even to herself. She only wanted sadly to see Molly, and she almost believed herself that it was to consult her about the fashion of her cloak; which Donkin was to cut out, and which she was to make under his directions; at any rate, this was the reason she gave to her mother when the day's work was done, and a fine gleam came out upon the pale and watery sky towards evening.

CHAPTER 6

The Sailor's Funeral

Moss Brow, the Corneys' house, was but a disorderly, comfortless place. You had to cross a dirty farmyard, all puddles and dungheaps, on stepping-stones, to get to the door of the houseplace. That great room itself was sure to have clothes hanging to dry at the fire, whatever day of the week it was; some one of the large irregular family having had what is called in the district a 'dab-wash'* of a few articles, forgotten on the regular day. And sometimes these articles lay in their dirty state in the untidy kitchen, out of which a room, half parlour, half bedroom, opened on one side, and a dairy, the only clean place in the house, at the opposite. In face of you, as you entered the door, was the entrance to the working-kitchen, or scullery. Still, in spite of disorder like this, there was a well-to-do aspect about the place; the Corneys were rich in their way, in flocks and herds as well as in children; and to them neither dirt nor the perpetual bustle arising from ill-ordered work detracted from comfort. They were all of an easy, good-tempered nature; Mrs Corney and her daughters gave every one a welcome at whatever time of the day they came, and would just as soon sit down for a gossip at ten o' clock in the morning, as at five in the evening, though at the former time the house-place was full of work of various kinds which ought to be got out of hand and done with: while the latter hour was towards the end of the day, when farmers' wives and daughters were usually – 'cleaned' was the

word then, 'dressed' is that in vogue now. Of course in such a
household as this Sylvia was sure to be gladly received. She was
young, and pretty, and bright, and brought a fresh breeze of
pleasant air about her as her appropriate atmosphere. And
besides, Bell Robson held her head so high that visits from her
daughter were rather esteemed as a favour, for it was not
everywhere that Sylvia was allowed to go.

'Sit yo' down, sit yo' down!' cried Dame Corney, dusting a
chair with her apron; 'a reckon Molly'll be in i' no time. She's
nobbut gone int' t' orchard, to see if she can find windfalls
enough for t' make a pie or two for t' lads. They like nowt so
weel*for supper as apple-pies sweetened wi' treacle, crust stout
and leathery, as stands chewing, and we hannot getten in our
apples yet.'

'If Molly is in t' orchard, I'll go find her,' said Sylvia.

'Well! yo' lasses will have your conks' (private talks), 'a know;
secrets 'bout sweethearts and such like,' said Mrs Corney, with
a knowing look, which made Sylvia hate her for the moment.
'A've not forgotten as a were young mysen. Tak' care; there's a
pool o' mucky watter just outside t' back-door.'

But Sylvia was half-way across the back-yard – worse, if
possible, than the front as to the condition in which it was kept
– and had passed through the little gate into the orchard. It was
full of old gnarled apple-trees, their trunks covered with grey
lichen, in which the cunning chaffinch built her nest in spring-
time. The cankered branches remained on the trees, and added
to the knotted interweaving overhead, if they did not to the
productiveness; the grass grew in long tufts, and was wet and
tangled under foot. There was a tolerable crop of rosy apples
still hanging on the grey old trees, and here and there they
showed ruddy in the green bosses of untrimmed grass. Why the
fruit was not gathered, as it was evidently ripe, would have
puzzled any one not acquainted with the Corney family to say;
but to them it was always a maxim in practice, if not in precept,
'Do nothing to-day that you can put off till to-morrow,' and
accordingly the apples dropped from the trees at any little gust
of wind, and lay rotting on the ground until the 'lads' wanted a
supply of pies for supper.

Molly saw Sylvia, and came quickly across the orchard to
meet her, catching her feet in knots of grass as she hurried along.

'Well, lass!' said she, 'who'd ha' thought o' seeing yo' such a day as it has been?'

'But it's cleared up now beautiful,' said Sylvia, looking up at the soft evening sky, to be seen through the apple boughs. It was of a tender, delicate gray, with the faint warmth of a promising sunset tinging it with a pink atmosphere. 'Rain is over and gone,* and I wanted to know how my cloak is to be made; for Donkin's working at our house, and I wanted to know all about – the news, yo' know.'

'What news?' asked Molly, for she had heard of the affair between the *Good Fortune* and the *Aurora* some days before; and, to tell the truth, it had rather passed out of her head just at this moment.

'Hannot yo' heard all about t' press-gang and t' whaler, and t' great fight, and Kinraid, as is your cousin, acting so brave and grand, and lying on his death-bed now?'

'Oh!' said Molly, enlightened as to Sylvia's 'news', and half surprised at the vehemence with which the little creature spoke; 'yes; a heerd that days ago. But Charley's noane on his death-bed, he's a deal better; an' mother says as he's to be moved up here next week for nursin' and better air nor he gets i' t' town yonder.'

'Oh! I am so glad,' said Sylvia, with all her heart. 'I thought he'd maybe die, and I should niver see him.'

'A'll promise yo' shall see him; that's t' say if a' goes on well, for he's getten an ugly hurt. Mother says as there's four blue marks on his side as'll last him his life, an' t' doctor fears bleeding i' his inside; and then he'll drop down dead when no one looks for 't.'

'But you said he was better,' said Sylvia, blanching a little at this account.

'Ay, he's better, but life's uncertain, special after gun-shot wounds.'

'He acted very fine,' said Sylvia, meditating.

'A allays knowed he would. Many's the time a've heerd him say "honour bright," and now he's shown how bright his is.'

Molly did not speak sentimentally, but with a kind of proprietorship in Kinraid's honour, which confirmed Sylvia in her previous idea of a mutual attachment between her and her cousin. Considering this notion, she was a little surprised at Molly's next speech.

'An' about yer cloak, are you for a hood or a cape? a reckon that's the question.'

'Oh, I don't care! tell me more about Kinraid. Do yo' really think he'll get better?'

'Dear! how t' lass takes on about him. A'll tell him what a deal of interest a young woman taks i' him!'

From that time Sylvia never asked another question about him. In a somewhat dry and altered tone, she said, after a little pause –

'I think on a hood. What do you say to it?'

'Well; hoods is a bit old-fashioned, to my mind. If 't were mine, I'd have a cape cut i' three points, one to tie on each shoulder, and one to dip down handsome behind. But let yo' an' me go to Monkshaven church o' Sunday, and see Measter Fishburns' daughters, as has their things made i' York, and notice a bit how they're made. We needn't do it i' church, but just scan 'em o'er i' t' churchyard, and there'll be no harm done. Besides, there's to be this grand burryin' o' t' man t' press-gang shot, and 't will be like killing two birds at once.'

'I should like to go,' said Sylvia. 'I feel so sorry like for the poor sailors shot down and kidnapped just as they was coming home, as we see'd 'em o' Thursday last. I'll ask mother if she'll let me go.'

'Ay, do. I know my mother'll let me, if she doesn't go hersen; for it'll be a sight to see and to speak on for many a long year, after what I've heerd. And Miss Fishburns is sure to be theere, so I'd just get Donkin to cut out cloak itsel', and keep back yer mind fra' fixing o' either cape or hood till Sunday's turn'd.'

'Will yo' set me* part o' t' way home?' said Sylvia, seeing the dying daylight become more and more crimson through the blackening trees.

'No; I can't. A should like it well enough, but somehow, there's a deal o' work to be done yet, for t' hours slip through one's fingers so as there's no knowing. Mind yo', then, o' Sunday. A'll be at t' stile one o'clock punctual; and we'll go slowly into t' town, and look about us as we go, and see folk's dresses; and go to t' church, and say wer* prayers, and come out and have a look at t' funeral.'

And with this programme of proceedings settled for the following Sunday, the girls whom neighbourhood and parity of age had forced into some measure of friendship parted for the time.

Sylvia hastened home, feeling as if she had been absent long; her mother stood on the little knoll at the side of the house watching for her, with her hand shading her eyes from the low rays of the setting sun: but as soon as she saw her daughter in the distance, she returned to her work, whatever that might be. She was not a woman of many words, or of much demonstration; few observers would have guessed how much she loved her child; but Sylvia, without any reasoning or observation, instinctively knew that her mother's heart was bound up in her.

Her father and Donkin were going on much as when she had left them; talking and disputing, the one compelled to be idle, the other stitching away as fast as he talked. They seemed as if they had never missed Sylvia; no more did her mother for that matter, for she was busy and absorbed in her afternoon dairy-work to all appearance. But Sylvia had noted the watching not three minutes before, and many a time in her after life, when no one cared much for her out-goings and in-comings, the straight, upright figure of her mother, fronting the setting sun, but searching through its blinding rays for a sight of her child, rose up like a sudden-seen picture, the remembrance of which smote Sylvia to the heart with a sense of a lost blessing, not duly valued while possessed.

'Well, feyther, and how's a' wi' you?' asked Sylvia, going to the side of his chair, and laying her hand on his shoulder.

'Eh! harkee till this lass o' mine. She thinks as because she's gone galraverging,* I maun ha' missed her and be ailing. Why, lass, Donkin and me has had t' most sensible talk a've had this many a day. A've gi'en him a vast o' knowledge, and he's done me a power o' good. Please God, to-morrow a'll tak' a start at walking, if t' weather holds up.'

'Ay!' said Donkin, with a touch of sarcasm in his voice; 'feyther and me has settled many puzzles; it's been a loss to Government as they hannot been here for profiting by our wisdom. We've done away wi' taxes and press-gangs, and many a plague, and beaten t' French – i' our own minds, that's to say.'

'It's a wonder t' me as those Lunnon folks can't see things clear,' said Daniel, all in good faith.

Sylvia did not quite understand the state of things as regarded politics and taxes – and politics and taxes were all one in her mind, it must be confessed – but she saw that her innocent little scheme of giving her father the change of society afforded by Donkin's coming had answered;* and in the gladness of her heart she went out and ran round the corner of the house to find Kester, and obtain from him that sympathy in her success which she dared not ask from her mother.

'Kester, Kester, lad!' said she, in a loud whisper; but Kester was suppering the horses, and in the clamp of their feet on the round stable pavement, he did not hear her at first. She went a little farther into the stable. 'Kester! he's a vast better, he'll go out to-morrow; it's all Donkin's doing. I'm beholden to thee for fetching him, and I'll try and spare thee waistcoat fronts out o' t' stuff for my new red cloak. Thou'll like that, Kester, won't ta?'

Kester took the notion in slowly, and weighed it.

'Na, lass,' said he, deliberately, after a pause. 'A could na' bear to see thee wi' thy cloak scrimpit.* A like t' see a wench look bonny and smart, an' a tak' a kind o' pride in thee, an' should be a'most as much hurt i' my mind to see thee i' a pinched cloak as if old Moll's tail here were docked too short. Na, lass, a'se niver got a mirroring glass for t' see mysen in, so what's waistcoats to me? Keep thy stuff to thysen, theere's a good wench; but a'se main* and glad about t' measter. Place isn't like itsen when he's shut up and cranky.'

He took up a wisp of straw and began rubbing down the old mare, and hissing over his work as if he wished to consider the conversation as ended. And Sylvia, who had strung herself up in a momentary fervour of gratitude to make the generous offer, was not sorry to have it refused, and went back planning what kindness she could show to Kester without its involving so much sacrifice to herself. For giving waistcoat fronts to him would deprive her of the pleasant power of selecting a fashionable pattern in Monkshaven churchyard next Sunday.

That wished-for day seemed long a-coming, as wished-for days most frequently do. Her father got better by slow degrees, and her mother was pleased by the tailor's good pieces of work; showing the neatly placed patches with as much pride as many matrons take in new clothes now-a-days. And the weather cleared up into a dim kind of autumnal fineness, into anything but an Indian summer as far as regarded gorgeousness of

colouring, for on that coast the mists and sea fogs early spoil
the brilliancy of the foliage. Yet, perhaps, the more did the
silvery grays and browns of the inland scenery conduce to the
tranquillity of the time, – the time of peace and rest before the
fierce and stormy winter comes on. It seems a time for gathering
up human forces to encounter the coming severity, as well as of
storing up the produce of harvest for the needs of winter. Old
people turn out and sun themselves in that calm St Martin's
summer,* without fear of 'the heat o' th' sun, or the coming
winter's rages',* and we may read in their pensive, dreamy eyes
that they are weaning themselves away from the earth, which
probably many may never see dressed in her summer glory
again.

Many such old people set out betimes, on the Sunday afternoon to which Sylvia had been so looking forward, to scale the
long flights of stone steps – worn by the feet of many generations
– which led up to the parish church, placed on a height above
the town, on a great green area at the summit of the cliff, which
was the angle where the river and the sea met, and so overlook-
ing both the busy crowded little town, the port, the shipping,
and the bar on the one hand, and the wide illimitable tranquil
sea on the other – types of life and eternity. It was a good
situation for that church. Homeward-bound sailors caught sight
of the tower of St Nicholas, the first land object of all. They
who went forth upon the great deep might carry solemn
thoughts with them of the words they had heard there; not
conscious thoughts, perhaps – rather a distinct if dim conviction
that buying and selling, eating and marrying, even life and
death, were not all the realities in existence. Nor were the words
that came up to their remembrance words of sermons preached
there, however impressive. The sailors mostly slept through the
sermons; unless, indeed, there were incidents such as were
involved in what were called 'funeral discourses' to be narrated.
They did not recognize their daily faults or temptations under
the grand aliases befitting their appearance from a preacher's
mouth. But they knew the old, oft-repeated words praying for
deliverance from the familiar dangers of lightning and tempest;
from battle, murder, and sudden death; and nearly every man
was aware that he left behind him some one who would watch
for the prayer for the preservation of those who travel by land

or by water, and think of him, as God-protected the more for the earnestness of the response then given.

There, too, lay the dead of many generations; for St Nicholas* had been the parish church ever since Monkshaven was a town, and the large churchyard was rich in the dead. Masters, mariners, ship-owners, seamen: it seemed strange how few other trades were represented in that great plain so full of upright gravestones. Here and there was a memorial stone, placed by some survivor of a large family, most of whom perished at sea:– 'Supposed to have perished in the Greenland seas', 'Shipwrecked in the Baltic', 'Drowned off the coast of Iceland'. There was a strange sensation, as if the cold sea-winds must bring with them the dim phantoms of those lost sailors, who had died far from their homes, and from the hallowed ground where their fathers lay.

Each flight of steps up to this churchyard ended in a small flat space, on which a wooden seat was placed. On this particular Sunday, all these seats were filled by aged people, breathless with the unusual exertion of climbing. You could see the church stair, as it was called, from nearly every part of the town, and the figures of the numerous climbers, diminished by distance, looked like a busy ant-hill, long before the bell began to ring for afternoon service. All who could manage it had put on a bit of black in token of mourning; it might be very little; an old ribbon, a rusty piece of crepe; but some sign of mourning was shown by every one down to the little child in its mother's arms, that innocently clutched the piece of rosemary to be thrown into the grave 'for remembrance'.* Darley, the seaman shot by the press-gang, nine leagues off St Abb's Head, was to be buried to-day, at the accustomed time for the funerals of the poorer classes, directly after evening service, and there were only the sick and their nursetenders who did not come forth to show their feeling for the man whom they looked upon as murdered. The crowd of vessels in harbour bore their flags half-mast high; and the crews were making their way through the High Street. The gentlefolk of Monkshaven, full of indignation at this interference with their ships, full of sympathy with the family who had lost their son and brother almost within sight of his home, came in unusual numbers – no lack of patterns for Sylvia; but her thoughts were far otherwise and more suitably occupied. The unwonted sternness and solemnity visible on the countenances of all whom she met awed and affected her. She did not speak in reply to Molly's remarks on the dress or appearance of those who struck her. She felt as if these speeches jarred on her, and annoyed her almost to irritation; yet Molly had come all the way to Monkshaven Church in her service and deserved forbearance accordingly. The two mounted the steps alongside of many people; few words were exchanged, even at the breathing places, so often the little centres of gossip. Looking over the sea there was not a sail to be seen; it seemed bared of life, as if to be in serious harmony with what was going on inland.

The church was of old Norman architecture; low and massive outside: inside, of vast space, only a quarter of which was filled on ordinary Sundays. The walls were disfigured by numerous tablets of black and white marble intermixed, and the usual ornamentation of that style of memorial as erected in the last century, of weeping willows, urns, and drooping figures, with here and there a ship in full sail, or an anchor, where the seafaring idea prevalent through the place had launched out into a little originality. There was no woodwork, the church had been stripped of that, most probably when the neighbouring monastery had been destroyed. There were large square pews, lined with green baize, with the names of the families of the most flourishing ship-owners painted white on the doors; there were pews, not so large, and not lined at all, for the farmers and shopkeepers of the parish; and numerous heavy oaken benches which, by the united efforts of several men, might be brought within earshot of the pulpit. These were being removed into the most convenient situations when Molly and Sylvia entered the church, and after two or three whispered sentences they took their seats on one of these.

The vicar of Monkshaven was a kindly, peaceable old man, hating strife and troubled waters above everything. He was a vehement Tory in theory, as became his cloth in those days. He had two bugbears to fear – the French and the Dissenters. It was difficult to say of which he had the worst opinion and the most intense dread. Perhaps he hated the Dissenters most, because they came nearer in contact with him than the French; besides, the French had the excuse of being Papists, while the Dissenters might have belonged to the Church of England if they had not been utterly depraved. Yet in practice Dr Wilson did not object to dine with Mr Fishburn, who was a personal friend and follower of Wesley, but then, as the doctor would say, 'Wesley was an Oxford man,* and that makes him a gentleman; and he was an ordained minister of the Church of England, so that grace can never depart from him.' But I do not know what excuse he would have alleged for sending broth and vegetables to old Ralph Thompson, a rabid Independent,* who had been given to abusing the Church and the vicar, from a Dissenting pulpit, as long as ever he could mount the stairs. However, that inconsistency between Dr Wilson's theories and practice was not generally known in Monkshaven, so we have nothing to do with it.

Dr Wilson had had a very difficult part to play, and a still more difficult sermon to write, during this last week. The Darley who had been killed was the son of the vicar's gardener, and Dr Wilson's sympathies as a man had been all on the bereaved father's side. But then he had received, as the oldest magistrate in the neighbourhood, a letter from the captain of the *Aurora*, explanatory and exculpatory. Darley had been resisting the orders of an officer in his Majesty's service. What would become of due subordination and loyalty, and the interests of the service, and the chances of beating those confounded French, if such conduct as Darley's was to be encouraged? (Poor Darley! he was past all evil effects of human encouragement now!)

So the vicar mumbled hastily over a sermon on the text, 'In the midst of life we are in death';* which might have done as well for a baby cut off in a convulsion-fit as for the strong man shot down with all his eager blood hot within him, by men as hot-blooded as himself. But once, when the old doctor's eye caught the up-turned, straining gaze of the father Darley, seeking with all his soul to find a grain of holy comfort in the chaff of words, his conscience smote him. Had he nothing to say that should calm anger and revenge with spiritual power? no breath of the comforter to soothe repining into resignation? But again the discord between the laws of man and the laws of Christ stood before him; and he gave up the attempt to do more than he was doing, as beyond his power. Though the hearers went away as full of anger as they had entered the church, and some with a dull feeling of disappointment as to what they had got there, yet no one felt anything but kindly towards the old vicar. His simple, happy life led amongst them for forty years, and open to all men in its daily course; his sweet-tempered, cordial ways; his practical kindness, made him beloved by all; and neither he nor they thought much or cared much for admiration of his talents. Respect for his office was all the respect he thought of; and that was conceded to him from old traditional and hereditary association. In looking back to the last century, it appears curious to see how little our ancestors had the power of putting two things together, and perceiving either the discord or harmony thus produced. Is it because we are farther off from those times, and have, consequently, a greater range of vision? Will our descendants have a wonder about us, such as we have about the inconsistency of our forefathers, or a surprise at our blindness that we do not perceive that, holding such and such opinions, our course of action must be so and so, or that the logical consequence of particular opinions must be convictions which at present we hold in abhorrence? It seems puzzling to look back on men such as our vicar, who almost held the doctrine that the King could do no wrong, yet were ever ready to talk of the glorious Revolution,* and to abuse the Stuarts for having entertained the same doctrine, and tried to put it in practice. But such discrepancies ran through good men's lives in those days. It is well for us that we live at the present time, when everybody is logical and consistent. This little discussion must be taken in place of Dr Wilson's sermon, of which no one could remember more than the text half an hour after it was delivered. Even the doctor himself had the recollection of the words he had uttered swept out of his mind, as, having doffed his gown and donned his surplice, he came out of the dusk of his vestry and went to the church-door, looking into the broad light which came upon the plain of the churchyard on the cliffs; for the sun had not yet set, and the pale moon was slowly rising through the silvery mist that obscured the distant moors. There was a thick, dense crowd, all still and silent, looking away from the church and the vicar, who awaited the bringing of the dead. They were watching the slow black line winding up the long steps, resting their heavy burden here and there, standing in silent groups at each landing-place; now lost to sight as a piece of broken, overhanging ground intervened, now emerging sud-denly nearer; and overhead the great church bell, with its mediæval inscription, familiar to the vicar, if to no one else who heard it,

I to the grave do summon all,

kept on its heavy booming monotone, with which no other
sound from land or sea, near or distant, intermingled, except
the cackle of the geese on some far-away farm on the moors, as
they were coming home to roost; and that one noise from so
great a distance seemed only to deepen the stillness. Then there
was a little movement in the crowd; a little pushing from side to
side, to make a path for the corpse and its bearers – an aggregate
of the fragments of room.

With bent heads and spent strength, those who carried the
coffin moved on; behind came the poor old gardener, a brown-
black funeral cloak thrown over his homely dress, and supporting his wife with steps scarcely less feeble than her own. He had
come to church that afternoon, with a promise to her that he
would return to lead her to the funeral of her firstborn; for he
felt, in his sore perplexed heart, full of indignation and dumb
anger, as if he must go and hear something which should
exorcise the unwonted longing for revenge that disturbed his
grief, and made him conscious of that great blank of consolation, which faithlessness produces. And for the time he was
faithless. How came God to permit such cruel injustice of man?
Permitting it, He could not be good. Then what was life, and
what was death, but woe and despair? The beautiful solemn
words of the ritual had done him good, and restored much of
his faith. Though he could not understand why such sorrow had
befallen him any more than before, he had come back to
something of his childlike trust; he kept saying to himself in a
whisper, as he mounted the weary steps, 'It is the Lord's doing';*
and the repetition soothed him unspeakably. Behind this old
couple followed their children, grown men and women, come
from distant place or farmhouse service; the servants at the
vicarage, and many a neighbour, anxious to show their sympathy, and most of the sailors from the crews of the vessels in
port, joined in procession, and followed the dead body into the
church.

There was too great a crowd immediately within the door for
Sylvia and Molly to go in again, and they accordingly betook
themselves to the place where the deep grave was waiting, wide
and hungry, to receive its dead. There, leaning against the
headstones all around, were many standing – looking over the

broad and placid sea, and turned to the soft salt air which blew on their hot eyes and rigid faces; for no one spoke of all that number. They were thinking of the violent death of him over whom the solemn words were now being said in the gray old church, scarcely out of their hearing, had not the sound been broken by the measured lapping of the tide far beneath.

Suddenly every one looked round towards the path from the churchyard steps. Two sailors were supporting a ghastly figure that, with feeble motions, was drawing near the open grave.

'It's t' specksioneer as tried to save him! It's him as was left for dead!' the people murmured round.

'It's Charley Kinraid, as I'm a sinner!' said Molly, starting forward to greet her cousin.

But as he came on, she saw that all his strength was needed for the mere action of walking. The sailors, in their strong sympathy, had yielded to his earnest entreaty, and carried him up the steps, in order that he might see the last of his messmate. They placed him near the grave, resting against a stone; and he was hardly there before the vicar came forth, and the great crowd poured out of the church, following the body to the grave.

Sylvia was so much wrapt up in the solemnity of the occasion, that she had no thought to spare at the first moment for the pale and haggard figure opposite; much less was she aware of her cousin Philip, who now singling her out for the first time from among the crowd, pressed to her side, with an intention of companionship and protection.

As the service went on, ill-checked sobs rose from behind the two girls, who were among the foremost in the crowd, and by-and-by the cry and the wail became general. Sylvia's tears rained down her face, and her distress became so evident that it attracted the attention of many in that inner circle. Among others who noticed it, the specksioneer's hollow eyes were caught by the sight of the innocent blooming childlike face opposite to him, and he wondered if she were a relation; yet, seeing that she bore no badge of mourning, he rather concluded that she must have been a sweetheart of the dead man.

And now all was over: the rattle of the gravel on the coffin; the last long, lingering look* of friends and lovers; the rosemary sprigs had been cast down by all who were fortunate enough to have brought them – and oh! how much Sylvia wished she had remembered this last act of respect – and slowly the outer rim of the crowd began to slacken and disappear.

Now Philip spoke to Sylvia.

'I never dreamt of seeing you here. I thought my aunt always went to Kirk Moorside.'

'I came with Molly Corney,' said Sylvia. 'Mother is staying at home with feyther.'

'How's his rheumatics?' asked Philip.

But at the same moment Molly took hold of Sylvia's hand, and said –

'A want t' get round and speak to Charley. Mother'll be main and glad to hear as he's getten out; though, for sure, he looks as though he'd ha' been better in 's bed. Come, Sylvia.'

And Philip, fain to keep with Sylvia, had to follow the two girls close up to the specksioneer, who was preparing for his slow laborious walk back to his lodgings. He stopped on seeing his cousin.

'Well, Molly,' said he, faintly, putting out his hand, but his eye passing her face to look at Sylvia in the background, her tear-stained face full of shy admiration of the nearest approach to a hero she had ever seen.

'Well, Charley, a niver was so taken aback as when a saw yo' theere, like a ghost, a-standin' agin a gravestone. How white and wan yo' do look!'

'Ay! 'said he, wearily, 'wan and weak enough.'

'But I hope you're getting better, sir,' said Sylvia, in a low voice, longing to speak to him, and yet wondering at her own temerity.

'Thank you, my lass. I'm o'er th' worst.'

He sighed heavily.

Philip now spoke.

'We're doing him no kindness a-keeping him standing here i' t' night-fall, and him so tired.' And he made as though he would turn away. Kinraid's two sailor friends backed up Philip's words with such urgency, that, somehow, Sylvia thought they had been to blame in speaking to him, and blushed excessively with the idea.

'Yo'll come and be nursed at Moss Brow, Charley,' said Molly; and Sylvia dropped her little maidenly curtsey, and said, 'Good-by'; and went away, wondering how Molly could talk so freely to such a hero; but then, to be sure, he was a cousin, and probably a sweetheart, and that would make a great deal of difference, of course.

Meanwhile her own cousin kept close by her side.

CHAPTER 7

Tête-À-Tête – The Will

'And now tell me all about t' folk at home,' said Philip, evidently preparing to walk back with the girls. He generally came to Haytersbank every Sunday afternoon, so Sylvia knew what she had to expect the moment she became aware of his neighbourhood in the churchyard.

'My feyther's been sadly troubled with his rheumatics this week past; but he's a vast better now, thank you kindly.' Then, addressing herself to Molly, she asked, 'Has your cousin a doctor to look after him? '

'Ay, for sure!' said Molly, quickly; for though she knew nothing about the matter, she was determined to suppose that her cousin had everything becoming an invalid as well as a hero. 'He's well-to-do, and can afford iverything as he needs,' continued she. 'His feyther's left him money, and he were a farmer out up i' Northumberland, and he's reckoned such a specksioneer as niver, niver was, and gets what wage he asks for and a share on every whale he harpoons beside.'

'I reckon he'll have to make himself scarce on this coast for awhile, at any rate,' said Philip.

'An' what for should he?' asked Molly, who never liked Philip at the best of times, and now, if he was going to disparage her cousin in any way, was ready to take up arms and do battle.

'Why, they do say as he fired the shot as has killed some o' the men-o'-war's men, and, of course, if he has, he'll have to stand his trial* if he's caught.'

'What lies people do say!' exclaimed Molly. 'He niver killed nought but whales, a'll be bound; or, if he did, it were all right and proper as he should, when they were for stealing him an' all t' others, and did kill poor Darley as we come fra' seein' buried. A suppose, now yo're such a Quaker that, if some one was to break through fra' t' other side o' this dyke, and offer for to murder Sylvia and me, yo'd look on wi' yo'r hands hanging by yo'r side.'*

'But t' press-gang had law on their side, and were doing nought but what they'd warrant for.'

'Th' tender's gone away, as if she were ashamed o' what she'd done,' said Sylvia, 'and t' flag's down* fra' o'er the Randyvowse. There'll be no more press-ganging here awhile.'

'No; feyther says,' continued Molly, 'as they've made t' place too hot t' hold 'em, coming so strong* afore people had getten used to their ways o' catchin' up poor lads just come fra' t' Greenland seas. T' folks ha' their blood so up they'd think no harm o' fighting 'em i' t' streets – ay, and o' killing 'em, too, if they were for using fire-arms, as t' *Aurora*'s men did.'

'Women is so fond o' bloodshed,' said Philip; 'for t' hear you talk, who'd ha' thought you'd just come fra' crying ower the grave of a man who was killed by violence? I should ha' thought you'd seen enough of what sorrow comes o' fighting. Why, them lads o' t' *Aurora* as they say Kinraid shot down had fathers and mothers, maybe, a looking out for them to come home.'

'I don't think he could ha' killed them,' said Sylvia; 'he looked so gentle.'

But Molly did not like this half-and-half view of the case.

'A dare say he did kill 'em dead; he's not one to do things by halves. And a think he served 'em reet, that's what a do.'

'Is na' this Hester, as serves in Foster's shop?' asked Sylvia, in a low voice, as a young woman came through a stile in the stone wall by the roadside, and suddenly appeared before them.

'Yes,' said Philip. 'Why, Hester, where have you been?' he asked, as they drew near.

Hester reddened a little, and then replied, in her slow, quiet way –

'I've been sitting with Betsy Darley – her that is bedridden. It were lonesome for her when the others were away at the burying.'

And she made as though she would have passed; but Sylvia, all her sympathies alive for the relations of the murdered man, wanted to ask more questions, and put her hand on Hester's arm to detain her a moment. Hester suddenly drew back a little, reddened still more, and then replied fully and quietly to all Sylvia asked.

In the agricultural counties, and among the class to which these four persons belonged, there is little analysis of motive or comparison of characters and actions, even at this present day of enlightenment. Sixty or seventy years ago there was still less. I do not mean that amongst thoughtful and serious people there was not much reading of such books as *Mason on Self-Knowledge*, and *Law's Serious Call*,* or that there were not the experiences of the Wesleyans, that were related at class-meeting for the edification of the hearers. But, taken as a general rule, it may be said that few knew what manner of men they were, compared to the numbers now who are fully conscious of their virtues, qualities, failings, and weaknesses, and who go about comparing others with themselves – not in a spirit of Pharisaism* and arrogance, but with a vivid self-consciousness that more than anything else deprives characters of freshness and originality.

To return to the party we left standing on the high-raised footway that ran alongside of the bridle-road to Haytersbank. Sylvia had leisure in her heart to think 'how good Hester is for sitting with the poor bed-ridden sister of Darley!' without having a pang of self-depreciation in the comparison of her own conduct with that she was capable of so fully appreciating. She had gone to church for the ends of vanity, and remained to the funeral for curiosity and the pleasure of the excitement. In this way a modern young lady would have condemned herself, and therefore lost the simple, purifying pleasure of admiration of another.

Hester passed onwards, going down the hill towards the town. The other three walked slowly on. All were silent for a few moments, then Sylvia said –

'How good she is!'

And Philip replied with ready warmth, –

'Yes, she is; no one knows how good but us, who live in the same house wi' her.'

'Her mother is an old Quakeress, bean't she?' Molly inquired.

'Alice Rose is a Friend,* if that is what you mean,' said Philip.

'Well, well! some folk's so particular. Is William Coulson a Quaker, by which a mean a Friend?'

'Yes; they're all on 'em right-down good folk.'

'Deary me! What a wonder yo' can speak to such sinners as Sylvia and me, after keepin' company with so much goodness,' said Molly, who had not yet forgiven Philip for doubting Kinraid's power of killing men. 'Is na' it, Sylvia?'

But Sylvia was too highly strung for banter. If she had not been one of those who went to mock, but remained to pray,* she had gone to church with the thought of the cloak-that-was-to-be uppermost in her mind, and she had come down the long church stair with life and death suddenly become real to her mind, the enduring sea and hills forming a contrasting background to the vanishing away of man. She was full of a solemn wonder as to the abiding-place of the souls of the dead, and a childlike dread lest the number of the elect should be accomplished before she was included therein. How people could ever be merry again after they had been at a funeral, she could not imagine; so she answered gravely, and slightly beside the question:

'I wonder if I was a Friend if I should be good?'

'Gi' me your red cloak, that's all, when yo' turn Quaker; they'll none let thee wear scarlet, so it'll be of no use t' thee.'

'I think thou'rt good enough as thou art,' said Philip, tenderly – at least as tenderly as he durst, for he knew by experience that it did not do to alarm her girlish coyness. Either one speech or the other made Sylvia silent; neither was accordant to her mood of mind, so perhaps both contributed to her quietness.

'Folk say William Coulson looks sweet on Hester Rose,' said Molly, always up in Monkshaven gossip. It was in the form of an assertion, but was said in the tone of a question, and as such Philip replied to it.

'Yes, I think he likes her a good deal; but he's so quiet, I never feel sure. John and Jeremiah would like the match, I've a notion.'

And now they came to the stile which had filled Philip's eye for some minutes past, though neither of the others had perceived they were so near it; the stile which led to Moss Brow from the road into the fields that sloped down to Haytersbank. Here they would leave Molly, and now would begin the delicious *tête-à-tête* walk, which Philip always tried to make as lingering as possible. To-day he was anxious to show his sympathy with Sylvia, as far as he could read what was passing in her mind; but how was he to guess the multitude of tangled thoughts in that unseen receptacle? A resolution to be good, if she could, and always to be thinking on death, so that what seemed to her now as simply impossible, might come true – that

she might 'dread the grave as little as her bed';* a wish that
Philip were not coming home with her; a wonder if the specksioneer really had killed a man, an idea which made her shudder;
yet from the awful fascination about it, her imagination was
compelled to dwell on the tall, gaunt figure, and try to recall the
wan countenance; a hatred and desire of revenge on the press-
gang, so vehement that it sadly militated against her intention
of trying to be good; all these notions, and wonders, and fancies,
were whirling about in Sylvia's brain, and at one of their
promptings she spoke, –

'How many miles away is t' Greenland seas? – I mean, how
long do they take to reach?'

'I don't know; ten days or a fortnight, or more, maybe. I'll
ask.'

'Oh! feyther'll tell me all about it. He's been there many a
time.'

'I say, Sylvia! My aunt said I were to give you lessons this
winter i' writing and ciphering. I can begin to come up now,
two evenings, maybe, a week. T' shop closes early after November comes in.'

Sylvia did not like learning, and did not want him for her
teacher; so she answered, in a dry little tone, –

'It'll use a deal o' candle-light; mother 'll not like that. I can't
see to spell wi'out a candle close at my elbow.'

'Niver mind about candles. I can bring up a candle wi' me,
for I should be burning one at Alice Rose's.'

So that excuse would not do. Sylvia beat her brains for
another.

'Writing cramps my hand so, I can't do any sewing for a day
after; and feyther wants his shirts very bad.'

'But, Sylvia, I'll teach you geography, and ever such a vast o'
fine things about t' countries, on t' map.'

'Is t' Arctic seas down on t' map?' she asked, in a tone of
greater interest.

'Yes! Arctics, and tropics, and equator, and equinoctial line;
we'll take 'em turn and turn about; we'll do writing and
ciphering one night, and geography t' other.'

Philip spoke with pleasure at the prospect, but Sylvia relaxed
into indifference.

'I'm no scholard; it's like throwing away labour to teach me,
I'm such a dunce at my book. Now there's Betsy Corney, third

girl, her as is younger than Molly, she'd be a credit to you. There niver was such a lass for pottering ower books.'

If Philip had had his wits about him, he would have pretended to listen to this proposition of a change of pupils, and then possibly Sylvia might have repented making it. But he was too much mortified to be diplomatic.

'My aunt asked me to teach *you* a bit, not any neighbour's lass.'

'Well! if I mun be taught, I mun; but I'd rayther be whipped and ha' done with it,' was Sylvia's ungracious reply.

A moment afterwards, she repented of her little spirit of unkindness, and thought that she should not like to die that night without making friends. Sudden death was very present in her thoughts since the funeral. So she instinctively chose the best method of making friends again, and slipped her hand into his, as he walked a little sullenly at her side. She was half afraid, however, when she found it firmly held, and that she could not draw it away again without making what she called in her own mind a 'fuss'. So, hand in hand, they slowly and silently came up to the door of Haytersbank Farm; not unseen by Bell Robson, who sat in the window-seat, with her Bible open upon her knee. She had read her chapter aloud to herself, and now she could see no longer, even if she had wished to read more; but she gazed out into the darkening air, and a dim look of contentment came like moonshine over her face when she saw the cousins approach.

'That's my prayer day and night,' said she to herself.

But there was no unusual aspect of gladness on her face, as she lighted the candle to give them a more cheerful welcome.

'Wheere's feyther?' said Sylvia, looking round the room for Daniel.

'He's been to Kirk Moorside Church, for t' see a bit o' th' world, as he ca's it. And sin' then he's gone out to th' cattle; for Kester 's ta'en his turn of playing hissel', now that father's better.'

'I've been talking to Sylvia,' said Philip, his head still full of his pleasant plan, his hand still tingling from the touch of hers, 'about turning schoolmaster, and coming up here two nights a week for t' teach her a bit o' writing and ciphering.'

'And geography,' put in Sylvia; 'for,' thought she, 'if I'm to learn them things I don't care a pin about, anyhow I'll learn what I do care to know, if it 'll tell me about t' Greenland seas, and how far they're off.'

That same evening, a trio alike in many outward circumstances sat in a small neat room in a house opening out of a confined court on the hilly side of the High Street of Monkshaven – a mother, her only child, and the young man who silently loved that daughter, and was favoured by Alice Rose, though not by Hester.

When the latter returned from her afternoon's absence, she stood for a minute or two on the little flight of steep steps, whitened to a snowy whiteness; the aspect of the whole house partook of the same character of irreproachable cleanliness. It was wedged up into a space which necessitated all sorts of odd projections and irregularities in order to obtain sufficient light for the interior; and if ever the being situated in a dusky, confined corner might have been made an excuse for dirt, Alice Rose's house had that apology. Yet the small diamond panes of glass in the casement window were kept so bright and clear that a great sweet-scented-leaved geranium grew and flourished, though it did not flower profusely. The leaves seemed to fill the air with fragrance as soon as Hester summoned up energy enough to open the door. Perhaps that was because the young Quaker, William Coulson, was crushing one between his finger and thumb, while waiting to set down Alice's next words. For the old woman, who looked as if many years of life remained in her yet, was solemnly dictating her last will and testament.

It had been on her mind for many months; for she had something to leave beyond the mere furniture of the house. Something – a few pounds – in the hands of John and Jeremiah Foster, her cousins: and it was they who had suggested the duty on which she was engaged. She had asked William Coulson to write down her wishes, and he had consented, though with some fear and trepidation; for he had an idea that he was infringing on a lawyer's prerogative, and that, for aught he knew, he might be prosecuted for making a will without a licence, just as a man might be punished for selling wine and spirits without going through the preliminary legal forms that give permission for such a sale. But to his suggestion that Alice should employ a lawyer, she had replied –

'That would cost me five pounds sterling; and thee canst do it as well, if thee'll but attend to my words.'

So he had bought, at her desire, a black-edged sheet of finewove paper, and a couple of good pens, on the previous Saturday; and while waiting for her to begin her dictation, and full of serious thought himself, he had almost unconsciously made the grand flourish at the top of the paper which he had learnt at school, and which was there called a spread-eagle.*

'What art thee doing there?' asked Alice, suddenly alive to his proceedings.

Without a word he showed her his handiwork.

'It's a vanity,' said she, 'and 't may make t' will not stand. Folk may think I were na' in my right mind, if they see such fly-legs and cob-webs* a-top. Write, "This is my doing, William Coulson, and none of Alice Rose's, she being in her sound mind."'

'I don't think it's needed,' said William. Nevertheless he wrote down the words.

'Hast thee put that I'm in my sound mind and seven senses? Then make the sign of the Trinity, and write, "In the name of the Father, the Son, and the Holy Ghost."'*

'Is that the right way o' beginning a will?' said Coulson, a little startled.

'My father, and my father's father, and my husband had it a-top of theirs, and I'm noane going for to cease fra' following after them, for they were godly men, though my husband were o' t' episcopal persuasion.'*

'It's done,' said William.

'Hast thee dated it?' asked Alice.

'Nay.'

'Then date it third day, ninth month.* Now, art ready?'

Coulson nodded.

'I, Alice Rose, do leave my furniture (that is, my bed and chest o' drawers, for thy bed and things is thine, and not mine), and settle, and saucepans, and dresser, and table, and kettle, and all the rest of my furniture, to my lawful and only daughter, Hester Rose. I think that's safe for her to have all, is 't not, William?'

'I think so, too,' said he, writing on all the time.

'And thee shalt have t' roller and paste-board, because thee's so fond o' puddings and cakes. It 'll serve thy wife after I'm gone, and I trust she'll boil her paste* long enough, for that's been t' secret o' mine, and thee'll noane be so easy t' please.'

'I din't reckon on marriage,' said William.

'Thee'll marry,' said Alice. 'Thee likes to have thy victuals hot and comfortable; and there's noane many but a wife as'll look after that for t' please thee.'

'I know who could please me,' sighed forth William, 'but I can't please her.'

Alice looked sharply at him from over her spectacles, which she had put on the better to think about the disposal of her property.

'Thee art thinking on our Hester,' said she, plainly out.

He started a little, but looked up at her and met her eye.

'Hester cares noane for me,' said he, dejectedly.

'Bide a while, my lad,' said Alice, kindly. 'Young women don't always know their own minds. Thee and her would make a marriage after my own heart; and the Lord has been very good to me hitherto, and I think He'll bring it t' pass. But don't thee let on as thee cares for her so much. I sometimes think she wearies o' thy looks and thy ways. Show up thy manly heart, and make as though thee had much else to think on, and no leisure for to dawdle after her, and she'll think a deal more on thee. And now mend thy pen for a fresh start. I give and bequeath – did thee put "give and bequeath", at th' beginning?'

'Nay,' said William, looking back. 'Thee didst not tell me "give and bequeath"!'

'Then it won't be legal, and my bit o' furniture 'll be taken to London, and put into chancery,* and Hester will have noane on it.'

'I can write it over,' said William.

'Well, write it clear then, and put a line under it to show those are my special words. Hast thee done it? Then now start afresh. I give and bequeath my book o' sermons, as is bound in good calfskin, and lies on the third shelf o' corner cupboard at the right hand o' t' fire-place, to Philip Hepburn; for I reckon he's as fond o' reading sermons as thee art o' light, well-boiled paste, and I'd be glad for each on ye to have somewhat ye like for to remember me by. Is that down? There; now for my cousins John and Jeremiah. They are rich i' world's gear,* but they'll prize what I leave 'em if I could only onbethink me what they would like. Hearken! Is na' that our Hester's step? Put it away, quick!

I'm noane for grieving her wi' telling her what I've been about. We'll take a turn at t' will next First Day;* it will serve us for several Sabbaths to come, and maybe I can think on something as will suit cousin John and cousin Jeremiah afore then.'

Hester, as was mentioned, paused a minute or two before lifting the latch of the door. When she entered there was no unusual sign of writing about; only Will Coulson looking very red, and crushing and smelling at the geranium leaf.

Hester came in briskly, with the little stock of enforced cheerfulness she had stopped at the door to acquire. But it faded away along with the faint flush of colour in her cheeks; and the mother's quick eye immediately noted the wan heavy look of care.

'I have kept t' pot in t' oven; it'll have a'most got a' t' goodness out of t' tea by now, for it'll be an hour since I made it. Poor lass, thou look'st as if thou needed a good cup o' tea. It were dree work sitting wi' Betsy Darley, were it? And how does she look on her affliction?'

'She takes it sore to heart,' said Hester, taking off her hat, and folding and smoothing away her cloak, before putting them in the great oak chest (or 'ark', as it was called), in which they were laid from Sunday to Sunday.

As she opened the lid a sweet scent of dried lavender and rose-leaves came out. William stepped hastily forwards to hold up the heavy lid for her. She lifted up her head, looked at him full with her serene eyes, and thanked him for his little service. Then she took a creepie-stool and sate down on the side of the fire-place, having her back to the window.

The hearth was of the same spotless whiteness as the steps; all that was black about the grate was polished to the utmost extent; all that was of brass, like the handle of the oven, was burnished bright. Her mother placed the little black earthenware teapot, in which the tea had been stewing, on the table, where cups and saucers were already set for four, and a large plate of bread and butter cut. Then they sate round the table, bowed their heads, and kept silence for a minute or two.

When this grace was ended, and they were about to begin, Alice said, as if without premeditation, but in reality with a keen shrinking of heart out of sympathy with her child –

'Philip would have been in to his tea by now, I reckon, if he'd been coming.'

William looked up suddenly at Hester; her mother carefully turned her head another way. But she answered quite quietly –

'He'll be gone to his aunt's at Haytersbank. I met him at t' top o' t' Brow, with his cousin and Molly Corney.'

'He's a deal there,' said William.

'Yes,' said Hester. 'It's likely, him and his aunt come from Carlisle-way, and must needs cling together in these strange parts.'

'I saw him at the burying of yon Darley,' said William.

'It were a vast o' people went past th' entry end,' said Alice. 'It were a'most like election time; I were just come back fra' meeting when they were all going up th' church steps. I met yon sailor as, they say, used violence and did murder; he looked like a ghost, though whether it were his bodily wounds, or the sense of his sins stirring within him, it's not for me to say. And by t' time I was back here and settled to my Bible, t' folk were returning, and it were tramp, tramp, past th' entry end for better nor a quarter of an hour.'

'They say Kinraid has getten slugs and gun-shot in his side,' said Hester.

'He's niver one Charley Kinraid, for sure, as I knowed at Newcastle,' said William Coulson, roused to sudden and energetic curiosity.

'I don't know,' replied Hester; 'they call him just Kinraid; and Betsy Darley says he's t' most daring specksioneer of all that go off this coast to t' Greenland seas. But he's been in Newcastle, for I mind me she said her poor brother met with him there.'

'How didst thee come to know him?' inquired Alice.

'I cannot abide him if it is Charley,' said William. 'He kept company with my poor sister as is dead for better nor two year, and then he left off coming to see her and went wi' another girl, and it just broke her heart.'

'He don't look now as if he iver could play at that game again,' said Alice; 'he has had a warning fra' the Lord. Whether it be a call no one can tell. But to my eyne he looks as if he had been called,* and was going.'

'Then he'll meet my sister, said William, solemnly; 'and I hope the Lord will make it clear to him, then, how he killed her, as sure as he shot down yon sailors; an' if there's a gnashing o' teeth* for murder i' that other place, I reckon he'll have his share on't. He's a bad man yon.'

'Betsy said he were such a friend to her brother as niver was; and he's sent her word and promised to go and see her, first place he goes out to.'

But William only shook his head, and repeated his last words, –

'He's a bad man, he is.'

When Philip came home that Sunday night, he found only Alice up to receive him. The usual bedtime in the household was nine o'clock, and it was but ten minutes past the hour; but Alice looked displeased and stern.

'Thee art late, lad,' said she, shortly.

'I'm sorry; it's a long way from my uncle's, and I think clocks are different,' said he, taking out his watch to compare it with the round moon's face that told the time to Alice.

'I know nought about thy uncle's, but thee art late. Take thy candle, and begone.'

If Alice made any reply to Philip's 'good-night', he did not hear it.

CHAPTER 8

Attraction and Repulsion

A fortnight had passed over and winter was advancing with rapid strides. In bleak northern farmsteads there was much to be done before November weather should make the roads too heavy for half-fed horses to pull carts through. There was the turf, pared up* on the distant moors, and left out to dry, to be carried home and stacked; the brown fern was to be stored up for winter bedding for the cattle; for straw was scarce and dear in those parts; even for thatching, heather (or rather ling) was used. Then there was meat to salt while it could be had; for, in default of turnips and mangold-wurzel, there was a great slaughtering of barren cows as soon as the summer herbage failed; and good housewives stored up their Christmas piece of beef in pickle before Martinmas was over. Corn was to be ground while yet it could be carried to the distant mill; the great racks for oat-cake, that swung at the top of the kitchen, had to be filled. And last of all came the pig-killing, when the second frost set in. For up in the north there is an idea that the ice stored in the first frost will melt, and the meat cured then taint; the first frost is good for nothing but to be thrown away, as they express it.

There came a breathing-time after this last event. The house had had its last autumn cleaning, and was neat and bright from top to bottom, from one end to another. The turf was led; the coal carted up from Monkshaven; the wood stored; the corn ground; the pig killed, and the hams and head and hands lying in salt. The butcher had been glad to take the best parts of a pig of Dame Robson's careful feeding; but there was unusual plenty in the Haytersbank pantry; and as Bell surveyed it one morning, she said to her husband –

'I wonder if yon poor sick chap at Moss Brow would fancy some o' my sausages. They're something to crack on,* for they are made fra' an old Cumberland receipt, as is not known i' Yorkshire yet.'

'Thou's allays so set upo' Cumberland ways!' said her husband, not displeased with the suggestion, however. 'Still, when folk's sick they han their fancies, and maybe Kinraid 'll be glad o' thy sausages. I ha' known sick folk tak' t' eating quails.'

This was not complimentary, perhaps. But Daniel went on to say that he did not mind if he stepped over with the sausages himself, when it was too late to do anything else. Sylvia longed to offer to accompany her father; but, somehow, she did not like to propose it. Towards dusk she came to her mother to ask for the key of the great bureau that stood in the house-place as a state piece of furniture, although its use was to contain the family's best wearing apparel, and stores of linen, such as might be supposed to be more needed upstairs.

'What for do yo' want my keys?' asked Bell.

'Only just to get out one of t' damask napkins.'

'The best napkins, as my mother span?'

'Yes!' said Sylvia, her colour heightening. 'I thought as how it would set off t' sausages.'

'A good clean homespun cloth will serve them better,' said Bell, wondering in her own mind what was come over the girl, to be thinking of setting off sausages that were to be eaten, not to be looked at like a picture-book. She might have wondered still more, if she had seen Sylvia steal round to the little flower border she had persuaded Kester to make under the wall at the sunny side of the house, and gather the two or three Michaelmas daisies, and the one bud of the China rose, that, growing against the kitchen chimney, had escaped the frost; and then, when her mother was not looking, softly open the cloth inside of the little basket that contained the sausages and a fresh egg or two, and lay her autumn blossoms in one of the folds of the towel.

After Daniel, now pretty clear of his rheumatism, had had his afternoon meal (tea was a Sunday treat), he prepared to set out on his walk to Moss Brow; but as he was taking his stick he caught the look on Sylvia's face, and unconsciously interpreted its dumb wistfulness.

'Missus,' said he, 't' wench has nought more t' do, has she? She may as well put on her cloak and step down wi' me, and see Molly a bit; she'll be company like.'

Bell considered.

'There's t' yarn for thy stockings as is yet to spin; but she can go, for I'll do a bit at 't mysel', and there's nought else agate.'

'Put on thy things in a jiffy, then, and let's be off,' said Daniel.

And Sylvia did not need another word. Down she came in a twinkling, dressed in her new red cloak and hood, her face peeping out of the folds of the latter, bright and blushing.

'Thou should'st na' ha' put on thy new cloak for a night walk to Moss Brow,' said Bell, shaking her head.

'Shall I go take it off, and put on my shawl?' asked Sylvia, a little dolefully.

'Na, na, come along! a'm noane goin' for t' wait o' women's chops and changes.* Come along; come, Lassie!' (this last to his dog).

So Sylvia set off with a dancing heart and a dancing step, that had to be restrained to the sober gait her father chose. The sky above was bright and clear with the light of a thousand stars, the grass was crisping under their feet with the coming hoar frost; and as they mounted to the higher ground they could see the dark sea stretching away far below them. The night was very still, though now and then crisp sounds in the distant air sounded very near in the silence. Sylvia carried the basket, and looked like Little Red Riding Hood.* Her father had nothing to say, and did not care to make himself agreeable; but Sylvia enjoyed her own thoughts, and any conversation would have been a disturbance to her. The long monotonous roll of the distant waves, as the tide bore them in, the multitudinous rush at last, and then the retreating rattle and trickle, as the baffled waters fell back over the shingle that skirted the sands, and divided them from the cliffs; her father's measured tread, and slow, even movement; Lassie's pattering – all lulled Sylvia into a reverie, of which she could not have given herself any definite account. But at length they arrived at Moss Brow, and with a sudden sigh she quitted the subjects of her dreamy meditations, and followed her father into the great house-place. It had a more comfortable aspect by night than by day. The fire was always kept up to a wasteful size, and the dancing blaze and the partial light of candles left much in shadow that was best ignored in such a disorderly family. But there was always a warm welcome to friends, however roughly given; and after the words of this were spoken, the next rose up equally naturally in the mind of Mrs Corney.

'And what will ye tak'? Eh! but t' measter 'll be fine and vexed* at your comin' when he's away. He's off to Horncastle t' sell some colts, and he'll not be back till to-morrow's neet. But here's Charley Kinraid as we've getten to nurse up a bit, an' t' lads 'll be back fra' Monkshaven in a crack o' no time.'*

All this was addressed to Daniel, to whom she knew that none but masculine company would be acceptable. Amongst uneducated people – whose range of subjects and interest do not extend beyond their daily life – it is natural that when the first blush and hurry of youth is over, there should be no great pleasure in the conversation of the other sex. Men have plenty to say to men, which in their estimation (gained from tradition and experience) women cannot understand; and farmers of a much later date than the one of which I am writing, would have contemptuously considered it as a loss of time to talk to women; indeed, they were often more communicative to the sheep-dog that accompanied them through all the day's work, and frequently became a sort of dumb confidant. Farmer Robson's Lassie now lay down at her master's feet, placed her nose between her paws, and watched with attentive eyes the preparations going on for refreshments – preparations which, to the disappointment of her canine heart, consisted entirely of tumblers and sugar.

'Where's t' wench?' said Robson, after he had shaken hands with Kinraid, and spoken a few words to him and to Mrs

Corney. 'She's getten' a basket wi' sausages in 'em, as my missus has made, and she's a rare hand at sausages; there's noane like her in a' t' three Ridings, I'll be bound!'

For Daniel could praise his wife's powers in her absence, though he did not often express himself in an appreciative manner when she was by to hear. But Sylvia's quick sense caught up the manner in which Mrs Corney would apply the way in which her mother's housewifery had been exalted, and, stepping forwards out of the shadow, she said, –

'Mother thought, maybe, you hadn't killed a pig yet, and sausages is always a bit savoury for any one who is na' well, and –

She might have gone on but that she caught Kinraid's eyes looking at her with kindly admiration. She stopped speaking, and Mrs Corney took up the word –

'As for sausages, I ha' niver had a chance this year, else I stand again any one for t' making of 'em. Yorkshire hams 's a vast thought on, and I'll niver let another county woman say as she can make better sausages nor me. But, as I'm saying, I'd niver a chance; for our pig, as I were sa fond on, and fed mysel', and as would ha' been fourteen stone by now if he were an ounce, and as knew me as well as any Christian, and a pig, as I may say, that I just idolized, went and took a fit a week after Michaelmas Day,* and died, as if it had been to spite me; and t' next is na' ready for killing, nor wunnot be this six week. So I'm much beholden to your missus, and so's Charley, I'm sure; though he's ta'en a turn to betterin'* sin' he came out here to be nursed.'

'I'm a deal better,' said Kinraid; 'a'most ready for t' press-gang to give chase to again.'

'But folk say they're gone off this coast for one while,' added Daniel.

'They're gone down towards Hull, as I've been told,' said Kinraid. 'But they're a deep set;* 'they'll be here before we know where we are, some of these days.'

'See thee here!' said Daniel, exhibiting his maimed hand; 'a reckon a served 'em out time o' t' Ameriky war.' And he began the story Sylvia knew so well; for her father never made a new acquaintance but what he told him of his self-mutilation to escape the press-gang. It had been done, as he would himself have owned, to spite himself as well as them; for it had obliged him to leave a sea-life, to which, in comparison, all life spent on shore was worse than nothing for dulness. For Robson had never reached that rank aboard ship which made his being unable to run up the rigging, or to throw a harpoon, or to fire off a gun, of no great consequence; so he had to be thankful that an opportune legacy enabled him to turn farmer, a great degradation in his opinion. But his blood warmed, as he told the specksioneer, towards a sailor, and he pressed Kinraid to beguile the time when he was compelled to be ashore, by coming over to see him at Haytersbank, whenever he felt inclined.

Sylvia, appearing to listen to Molly's confidences, was hearkening in reality to all this conversation between her father and the specksioneer; and at this invitation she became especially attentive.

Kinraid replied, – 'I'm much obliged to ye, I'm sure; maybe I can come and spend an ev'ning wi' you; but as soon as I'm got round a bit, I must see my own people as live at Cullercoats, near Newcastle-upo'-Tyne.'

'Well, well!' said Daniel, rising to take leave, with unusual prudence as to the amount of his drink. 'Thou'lt see, thou'lt see! I shall be main glad to see thee, if thou'lt come. But I've na' lads to keep thee company, only one sprig of a wench. Sylvia, come here, an' let's show thee to this young fellow!'

Sylvia came forwards, ruddy as any rose, and in a moment Kinraid recognized her as the pretty little girl he had seen crying so bitterly over Darley's grave. He rose up out of true sailor's gallantry, as she shyly approached and stood by her father's side, scarcely daring to lift her great soft eyes, to have one fair gaze at his face. He had to support himself by one hand rested on the dresser, but she saw he was looking far better – younger, less haggard – than he had seemed to her before. His face was short and expressive; his complexion had been weatherbeaten and bronzed, though now he looked so pale; his eyes and hair were dark, – the former quick, deep-set, and penetrating; the latter curly, and almost in ringlets. His teeth gleamed white as he smiled at her, a pleasant friendly smile of recognition; but she only blushed the deeper, and hung her head.

'I'll come, sir, and be thankful. I daresay a turn'll do me good, if the weather holds up, an' th' frost keeps on.'

'That's right, my lad,' said Robson, shaking him by the hand,

and then Kinraid's hand was held out to Sylvia, and she could not avoid the same friendly action.

Molly Corney followed her to the door, and when they were fairly outside, she held Sylvia back for an instant to say, –

'Is na' he a fine likely* man? I'm so glad as yo've seen him, for he's to be off next week to Newcastle and that neighbourhood.'

'But he said he'd come to us some night?' asked Sylvia, half in a fright.

'Ay, I'll see as he does; never fear. For I should like yo' for to know him a bit. He's a rare talker. I'll mind him o' coming to yo'.'

Somehow, Sylvia felt as if this repeated promise of reminding Kinraid of his promise to come and see her father took away part of the pleasure she had anticipated from his visit. Yet what could be more natural than that Molly Corney should wish her friend to be acquainted with the man whom Sylvia believed to be all but Molly's engaged lover?

Pondering these thoughts, the walk home was as silent as that going to Moss Brow had been. The only change seemed to be that now they faced the brilliant northern lights* flashing up the sky, and that either this appearance or some of the whaling narrations of Kinraid had stirred up Daniel Robson's recollections of a sea ditty, which he kept singing to himself in a low, unmusical voice, the burden of which was, 'for I loves the tossin' say!'* Bell met them at the door.

'Well, and here ye are at home again! and Philip has been, Sylvie, to give thee thy ciphering lesson; and he stayed awhile, thinking thou'd be coming back.'

'I'm very sorry,' said Sylvia, more out of deference to her mother's tone of annoyance, than because she herself cared either for her lesson or her cousin's disappointment.

'He'll come again to-morrow night, he says. But thou must take care, and mind the nights he says he'll come, for it's a long way to come for nought.'

Sylvia might have repeated her 'I'm very sorry' at this announcement of Philip's intentions; but she restrained herself, inwardly and fervently hoping that Molly would not urge the fulfilment of the specksioneer's promise for to-morrow night, for Philip's being there would spoil all; and besides, if she sat at the dresser at her lesson, and Kinraid at the table with her father, he might hear all, and find out what a dunce she was.

She need not have been afraid. With the next night Hepburn came; and Kinraid did not. After a few words to her mother, Philip produced the candles he had promised, and some books and a quill or two.

'What for hast thou brought candles?' asked Bell, in a half-affronted tone.

Hepburn smiled.

'Sylvia thought it would take a deal of candlelight, and was for making it into a reason not to learn. I should ha' used t' candles if I'd stayed at home, so I just brought them wi' me.'

'Then thou may'st just take them back again,' said Bell, shortly, blowing out that which he had lighted, and placing one of her own on the dresser instead.

Sylvia caught her mother's look of displeasure, and it made her docile for the evening, although she owed her cousin a grudge for her enforced good behaviour.

'Now, Sylvia, here's a copy-book wi' t' Tower o' London on it, and we'll fill it wi' as pretty writing as any in t' North Riding.'

Sylvia sat quite still, unenlivened by this prospect.

'Here's a pen as 'll nearly write of itsel',' continued Philip, still trying to coax her out of her sullenness of manner.

Then he arranged her in the right position.

'Don't lay your head down on your left arm, you'll ne'er see to write straight.'

The attitude was changed, but not a word was spoken. Philip began to grow angry at such determined dumbness.

'Are you tired?' asked he, with a strange mixture of crossness and tenderness.

'Yes, very,' was her reply.

'But thou ought'st not to be tired,' said Bell, who had not yet got over the offence to her hospitality; who, moreover, liked her nephew, and had, to boot,* great respect for the learning she had never acquired.

'Mother!' said Sylvia, bursting out, 'what's the use on my writing "Abednego, Abednego, Abednego",* all down a page? If I could see t' use on 't, I'd ha' axed father to send me t' school; but I'm none wanting to have learning.'

'It's a fine thing, tho', is learning. My mother and my grandmother had it: but th' family came down i' the world, and

Philip's mother and me, we had none of it; but I ha' set my heart on thy having it, child.'

'My fingers is stiff,' pleaded Sylvia, holding up her little hand and shaking it.

'Let us take a turn at spelling, then,' said Philip.

'What's t' use on't?' asked captious Sylvia.

'Why, it helps one i' reading an' writing.'

'And what does reading and writing do for one?'

Her mother gave her another of the severe looks that, quiet woman as she was, she could occasionally bestow upon the refractory, and Sylvia took her book and glanced down the column Philip pointed out to her; but, as she justly considered, one man might point out the task, but twenty could not make her learn it, if she did not choose; and she sat herself down on the edge of the dresser, and idly gazed into the fire. But her mother came round to look for something in the drawers of the dresser, and as she passed her daughter she said in a low voice –

'Sylvie, be a good lass. I set a deal o' store by learning, and father 'ud never send thee to school, as has stuck by me sore.'*

If Philip, sitting with his back to them, heard these words, he was discreet enough not to show that he heard. And he had his reward; for in a very short time, Sylvia stood before him with her book in her hand, prepared to say her spelling. At which he also stood up by instinct, and listened to her slow succeeding letters; helping her out, when she looked up at him with a sweet childlike perplexity in her face: for a dunce as to book-learning poor Sylvia was and was likely to remain; and, in spite of his assumed office of schoolmaster, Philip Hepburn could almost have echoed the words of the lover of Jess MacFarlane –

> I sent my love a letter,
> But, alas! she canna read,
> And I lo'e her a' the better.*

Still he knew his aunt's strong wish on the subject, and it was very delightful to stand in the relation of teacher to so dear and pretty, if so wilful, a pupil.

Perhaps it was not very flattering to notice Sylvia's great joy when her lessons were over, sadly shortened as they were by Philip's desire not to be too hard upon her. Sylvia danced round to her mother, bent her head back, and kissed her face, and then said defyingly to Philip, –

'If iver I write thee a letter it shall just be full of nothing but "Abednego! Abednego! Abednego!"'

But at this moment her father came in from a distant expedition on the moors with Kester to look after the sheep he had pasturing there before the winter set fairly in. He was tired, and so was Lassie, and so, too, was Kester, who, lifting his heavy legs one after the other, and smoothing down his hair, followed his master into the house-place, and seating himself on a bench at the farther end of the dresser, patiently awaited the supper of porridge and milk which he shared with his master. Sylvia, meanwhile, coaxed Lassie – poor footsore dog – to her side, and gave her some food, which the creature was almost too tired to eat. Philip made as though he would be going, but Daniel motioned to him to be quiet.

'Sit thee down, lad. As soon as I've had my victual, I want t' hear a bit o' news.'

Sylvia took her sewing and sat at the little round table by her mother, sharing the light of the scanty dip-candle.* No one spoke. Every one was absorbed in what they were doing. What Philip was doing was, gazing at Sylvia – learning her face off by heart.

When every scrap of porridge was cleared out of the mighty bowl, Kester yawned, and wishing good-night, withdrew to his loft over the cowhouse. Then Philip pulled out the weekly York paper, and began to read the latest accounts of the war then raging. This was giving Daniel one of his greatest pleasures; for though he could read pretty well, yet the double effort of reading and understanding what he read was almost too much for him. He could read, or he could understand what was read aloud to him; reading was no pleasure, but listening was.

Besides, he had a true John Bullish* interest in the war, without very well knowing what the English were fighting for. But in those days, so long as they fought the French for any cause, or for no cause at all, every true patriot was satisfied. Sylvia and her mother did not care for any such far-extended interests; a little bit of York news, the stealing of a few apples out of a Scarborough garden that they knew, was of far more interest to them than all the battles of Nelson and the North.*

Philip read in a high-pitched and unnatural tone of voice,

which deprived the words of their reality; for even familiar expressions can become unfamiliar and convey no ideas, if the utterance is forced or affected. Philip was somewhat of a pedant; yet there was a simplicity in his pedantry not always to be met with in those who are self-taught, and which might have interested any one who cared to know with what labour and difficulty he had acquired the knowledge which now he prized so highly; reading out Latin quotations as easily as if they were English, and taking a pleasure in rolling polysyllables, until all at once looking askance at Sylvia, he saw that her head had fallen back, her pretty rosy lips open, her eyes fast shut; in short, she was asleep.

'Ay,' said Farmer Robson, 'and t' reading has a'most sent me off. Mother'd look angry now if I was to tell yo' yo' had a right to a kiss; but when I was a young man I'd ha' kissed a pretty girl as I saw asleep, afore yo'd said Jack Robison.'

Philip trembled at these words, and looked at his aunt. She gave him no encouragement, standing up, and making as though she had never heard her husband's speech, by extending her hand, and wishing him 'good-night'. At the noise of the chairs moving over the flag floor, Sylvia started up, confused and annoyed at her father's laughter.

'Ay, lass; it's iver a good time t' fall asleep when a young fellow is by. Here's Philip here as thou'rt bound t' give a pair o' gloves* to.'

Sylvia went like fire; she turned to her mother to read her face.

'It's only father's joke, lass,' said she. 'Philip knows manners too well.'

'He'd better,' said Sylvia, flaming round at him. 'If he'd a touched me, I'd niver ha' spoken to him no more.' And she looked even as it was as if she was far from forgiving him.

'Hoots, lass! wenches are brought up sa mim,* now-a-days; i' my time they'd ha' thought na' such great harm of a kiss.'

'Good-night, Philip,' said Bell Robson, thinking the conversation unseemly.

'Good-night, aunt; good-night, Sylvie!' But Sylvia turned her back on him, and he could hardly say 'good-night' to Daniel, who had caused such an unpleasant end to an evening that had at one time been going on so well.

CHAPTER 9

The Specksioneer

A few days after, Farmer Robson left Haytersbank betimes on a longish day's journey, to purchase a horse. Sylvia and her mother were busied with a hundred household things, and the early winter's evening closed in upon them almost before they were aware. The consequences of darkness in the country even now are to gather the members of a family together into one room, and to make them settle to some sedentary employment; and it was much more the case at the period of my story, when candles were far dearer than they are at present, and when one was often made to suffice for a large family.

The mother and daughter hardly spoke at all when they sat down at last. The cheerful click of the knitting-needles made a pleasant home-sound; and in the occasional snatches of slumber that overcame her mother, Sylvia could hear the long-rushing boom of the waves, down below the rocks, for the Haytersbank gulley allowed the sullen roar to come up so far inland. It might have been about eight o'clock – though from the monotonous course of the evening it seemed much later – when Sylvia heard her father's heavy step cranching* down the pebbly path. More unusual, she heard his voice talking to some companion.

Curious to see who it could be, with a lively instinctive advance towards any event which might break the monotony she had begun to find somewhat dull, she sprang up to open the door. Half a glance into the grey darkness outside made her suddenly timid, and she drew back behind the door as she opened it wide to admit her father and Kinraid.

Daniel Robson came in bright and boisterous. He was pleased with his purchase, and had had some drink to celebrate his bargain. He had ridden the new mare into Monkshaven, and left her at the smithy there until morning, to have her feet looked at, and to be new shod. On his way from the town he had met Kinraid wandering about in search of Haytersbank Farm itself, so he had just brought him along with him; and here they were, ready for bread and cheese, and aught else the mistress would set before them.

To Sylvia the sudden change into brightness and bustle

occasioned by the entrance of her father and the specksioneer was like that which you may effect any winter's night, when you come into a room where a great lump of coal lies hot and slumbering on the fire; just break it up with a judicious blow from the poker, and the room, late so dark, and dusk, and lone, is full of life, and light, and warmth.

She moved about with pretty household briskness, attending to all her father's wants. Kinraid's eye watched her as she went backwards and forwards, to and fro, into the pantry, the back-kitchen, out of light into shade, out of the shadow into the broad firelight where he could see and note her appearance. She wore the high-crowned linen cap of that day, surmounting her lovely masses of golden brown hair, rather than concealing them, and tied firm to her head by a broad blue ribbon. A long curl hung down on each side of her neck – her throat rather, for her neck was concealed by a little spotted handkerchief carefully pinned across at the waist of her brown stuff gown.

How well it was, thought the young girl, that she had doffed her bed-gown and linsey-woolsey petticoat, her working-dress, and made herself smart in her stuff gown, when she sat down to work with her mother.

By the time she could sit down again, her father and Kinraid had their glasses filled, and were talking of the relative merits of various kinds of spirits; that led on to tales of smuggling, and the different contrivances by which they or their friends had eluded the preventive service; the nightly relays of men to carry the goods inland; the kegs of brandy found by certain farmers whose horses had gone so far in the night, that they could do no work the next day; the clever way in which certain women managed to bring in prohibited goods; in fact, that when a woman did give her mind to smuggling, she was more full of resources, and tricks, and impudence, and energy than any man. There was no question of the morality of the affair; one of the greatest signs of the real progress we have made since those times seems to be that our daily concerns of buying and selling, eating and drinking, whatsoever we do, are more tested by the real practical standard of our religion than they were in the days of our grandfathers. Neither Sylvia nor her mother was in advance of their age. Both listened with admiration to the ingenious devices, and acted as well as spoken lies, that were talked about as fine and spirited things. Yet if Sylvia had attempted one tithe of this deceit in her every-day life, it would have half broken her mother's heart. But when the duty on salt* was strictly and cruelly enforced, making it penal to pick up rough dirty lumps containing small quantities that might be thrown out with the ashes of the brine-houses on the high-roads; when the price of this necessary was so increased by the tax upon it as to make it an expensive, sometimes an unattainable, luxury to the working man, Government did more to demoralize the popular sense of rectitude and uprightness than heaps of sermons could undo. And the same, though in smaller measure, was the consequence of many other taxes. It may seem curious to trace up the popular standard of truth to taxation;* but I do not think the idea would be so very far-fetched.

From smuggling adventures it was easy to pass on to stories of what had happened to Robson, in his youth a sailor in the Greenland seas, and to Kinraid, now one of the best harpooners in any whaler that sailed off the coast.

'There's three things to be afeared on,' said Robson, authoritatively: 'there's t' ice, that's bad; there's dirty weather, that's worse; and there's whales theirselves, as is t' worst of all; leastways, they was i' my days; t' darned brutes may ha' larnt better manners sin'. When I were young, they could niver be got to let theirsels be harpooned wi'out flounderin' and makin' play* wi' their tales and their fins, till t' say were all in a foam, and t' boats' crews was all o'er wi' spray, which i' them latitudes is a kind o' shower-bath not needed.'

'Th' whales hasn't mended their manners, as you call it,' said Kinraid; 'but th' ice is not to be spoken lightly on. I were once in th' ship *John*, of Hull, and we were in good green water, and were keen after whales; and ne'er thought harm of a great grey iceberg as were on our lee-bow, a mile or so off; it looked as if it had been there from the days of Adam, and were likely to see th' last man out,* and it ne'er a bit bigger nor smaller in all them thousands and thousands o' years. Well, the fast-boats were out after a fish, and I were specksioneer in one; and we were so keen after capturing our whale, that none on us ever saw that we were drifting away from them right into deep shadow o' th' iceberg. But we were set upon our whale, and I harpooned it; and as soon as it were dead we lashed its fins together, and fastened its tail to our boat; and then we took breath and looked about us, and away from us a little space were th' other boats, wi' two other fish making play,* and as likely as not to break loose, for I may say as I were th' best harpooner on board the *John*, wi'out saying great things o' mysel'. So I says, "My lads, one o' you stay i' th' boat by this fish,' – the fins o' which, as I said, I'd reeved* a rope through mysel', and which was as dead as Noah's grandfather* – 'and th' rest on us shall go off and help th' other boats wi' their fish." For, you see, we had another boat close by in order to sweep th' fish.* (I suppose they swept fish i' your time, master?)'

'Ay, ay!' said Robson; 'one boat lies still holding t' end o' t' line; t' other makes a circuit round t' fish.'

'Well! luckily for us we had our second boat, for we all got into it, ne'er a man on us was left i' th' fast-boat. And says I, "But who's to stay by t' dead fish?" And no man answered, for they were all as keen as me for to go and help our mates; and we thought as we could come back to our dead fish, as had a boat for a buoy, once we had helped our mate. So off we rowed, every man Jack on us, out o' the black shadow o' th' iceberg, as looked as steady as th' pole-star. Well! we had na' been a dozen fathoms away fra' th' boat as we had left, when crash! down wi' a roaring noise, and then a gulp of the deep waters, and then a shower o' blinding spray; and when we had wiped our eyes clear, and getten our hearts down agen fra' our mouths, there were never a boat nor a glittering belly o' e'er a great whale to be seen, but th' iceberg were there, still and grim, as if a hundred ton or more had fallen off all in a mass, and crushed down boat, and fish, and all, into th' deep water, as goes half through the earth in them latitudes. Th' coal-miners round about Newcastle way may come upon our good boat if they mine deep enough, else ne'er another man will see her. And I left as good a clasp-knife in her as ever I clapt eyes on.'

'But what a mercy no man stayed in her,' said Bell.

'Why, mistress, I reckon we a' must die some way; and I'd as soon go down into the deep waters as be choked up wi' moulds.'*

'But it must be so cold,' said Sylvia, shuddering and giving a little poke to the fire to warm her fancy.

'Cold!' said her father, 'what do ye stay-at-homes know about cold, a should like to know? If yo'd been where a were once, north latitude 81, in such a frost as ye ha' niver known, no, not i' deep winter, and it were June i' them seas, and a whale i' sight, and a were off in a boat after her: an' t' ill-mannered brute, as soon as she were harpooned, ups wi' her big awkward tail, and struck t' boat i' her stern, and chucks me out into t' watter. That were cold, a can tell the! First, I smarted all ower me, as if my skin were suddenly stript off me: and next, ivery bone i' my body had getten t' toothache, and there were a great roar i' my ears, an' a great dizziness i' my eyes; an' t' boat's crew kept throwin' out their oars, an' a kept clutchin' at 'em, but a could na' make out where they was, my eyes dazzle, so wi' t' cold, an' I thought I were bound for "kingdom come", an' a tried to remember t' Creed, as a might die a Christian. But all a could think on was, "What is your name, M or N?"* an' just as a were giving up both words and life, they heaved me aboard. But, bless ye, they had but one oar; for they'd thrown a' t' others after me; so yo' may reckon, it were some time afore we could reach t' ship; an', a've heerd tell, a were a precious sight to look on, for my clothes was just hard frozen to me, an' my hair atmost as big a lump o' ice as yon iceberg he was a-telling us on; they rubbed me as missus theere were rubbing t' hams yesterday, and gav' me brandy; an' a've niver getten t' frost out o' my bones for a' their rubbin', and a deal o' brandy as I 'ave ta'en sin'. Talk o' cold! it's little yo' women known o' cold!'

'But there's heat, too, i' some places,' said Kinraid. 'I was once a voyage i' an American. They goes for th' most part south, to where you come round to t' cold again; and they'll stay there for three year at a time, if need be, going into winter harbour i' some o' th' Pacific Islands. Well, we were i' th' southern seas, a-seeking for good whaling-ground; and, close on our larboard beam, there were a great wall o' ice, as much as sixty feet high. And says our captain – as were a dare-devil, if ever a man were – "There'll be an opening in yon dark grey wall, and into that opening I'll sail, if I coast along it till th' day o' judgment." But, for all our sailing, we never seemed to come nearer to th' opening. The waters were rocking beneath us, and the sky were steady above us; and th' ice rose out o' the waters, and seemed to reach up into the sky. We sailed on, and we sailed on, for more days nor I could count. Our captain were a strange, wild man, but once he looked a little pale when he came upo' deck after his turn-in,* and saw the green-grey ice going straight up on our beam. Many on us thought as the ship were bewitched for th' captain's words; and we got to speak low, and to say our prayers o' nights, and a kind o' dull silence came into th' very air; our voices did na' rightly seem our own. And we sailed on, and we sailed on. All at once, th' man as were on watch gave a cry: he saw a break in the ice, as we'd begun to think were everlasting; and we all gathered towards the bows, and the captain called to th' man at the helm to keep her course, and cocked his head, and began to walk the quarter-deck jaunty again. And we came to a great cleft in th' long weary rock of ice; and the sides o' th' cleft were not jagged, but went straight sharp down into th' foaming waters. But we took but one look at what lay inside, for our captain, with a loud cry to God, bade the helmsman steer nor'ards away fra' th' mouth o' Hell.* We all saw wi' our own eyes, inside that fearsome wall o' ice – seventy mile long, as we could swear to – inside that gray, cold ice, came leaping flames, all red and yellow wi' heat o' some unearthly kind out o' th' very waters o' the sea; making our eyes dazzle wi' their scarlet blaze, that shot up as high, nay, higher than th' ice around, yet never so much as a shred on 't was melted. They did say that some beside our captain saw the black devils dart hither and thither, quicker than the very flames themselves; anyhow, *he* saw them. And as he knew it were his own daring as had led him to have that peep at terrors forbidden to any on us afore our time, he just dwined* away, and we hadn't taken but one whale afore our captain died, and first mate took th' command. It were a prosperous voyage; but, for all that, I'll never sail those seas again, nor ever take wage aboard an American again.'

'Eh, dear but it's awful t' think o' sitting wi' a man that has seen th' doorway into Hell,' said Bell, aghast.

Sylvia had dropped her work, and sat gazing at Kinraid with fascinated wonder.

Daniel was just a little annoyed at the admiration which his own wife and daughter were bestowing on the specksioneer's wonderful stories, and he said –

'Ay, ay. If a'd been a talker, ye'd ha' thought a deal more on me nor ye've iver done yet. A've seen such things, and done such things.'

'Tell us, father 'said Sylvia, greedy and breathless.

'Some on 'em is past telling,' he replied, 'an' some is not to be had for t' asking, seeing as how they might bring a man into trouble. But, as a said, if a had a fancy to reveal all as is on my

mind a could make t' hair on your heads lift up your caps –
well, we'll say an inch, at least. Thy mother, lass, has heerd one
or two on 'em. Thou minds the story o' my ride on a whale's
back, Bell? That'll maybe be within this young fellow's comprehension o' t' danger; thou's heard me tell it, hastn't ta?'

'Yes,' said Bell; 'but it's a long time ago; when we was
courting.'

'An' that's afore this young lass were born, as is a'most up to
woman's estate. But sin' those days a ha' been o'er busy to tell
stories to my wife, an' as a'll warrant she's forgotten it; an' as
Sylvia here niver heerd it, if yo'll fill your glass, Kinraid, yo'
shall ha' t' benefit o't.

'A were a specksioneer mysel, though, after that, a rayther
directed my talents int' t' smuggling branch o' my profession;
but a were once a whaling aboord t' *Aimwell* of Whitby.'* An'
we was anchored off t' coast o' Greenland one season; an' we'd
getten a cargo o' seven whale; but our captain he were a keen-
eyed chap, an' niver above doin' any man's work; an' once seein'
a whale he throws himself int' a boat an' goes off to it, makin'
signals to me, an' another specksioneer as were off for diversion
i' another boat, for to come after him sharp. Well, afore we
comes alongside, captain had harpooned t' fish; an' says he,
"Now, Robson, all ready! give into her again when she comes
to t' top;" an' I stands up, right leg foremost, harpoon all ready,
as soon as iver I cotched* a sight o' t' whale, but niver a fin
could a see. 'Twere no wonder, for she were right below t' boat
in which a were; and when she wanted to rise, what does t' great
ugly brute do but come wi' her head, as is like cast iron, up bang
again t' bottom o' t' boat. I were thrown up in t' air like a
shuttlecock, me an' my line an' my harpoon – up we goes, an'
many a good piece o' timber wi' us an' many a good fellow too;
but a had t' look after mysel', an' a were up high i' t' air, afore I
could say Jack Robison, an' a thowt a were safe for another dive
int' saut water; but i'stead a comes down plump on t' back o' t'
whale. Ay! yo' may stare, master, but theere a were, an' main
an' slippery it were, only a sticks my harpoon intil her an'
steadies mysel', an' looks abroad o'er t' vast o' waves, and gets
sea-sick in a manner, an' puts up a prayer as she mayn't dive,
and it were as good a prayer for wishin' it might come true as
iver t' clargyman an' t' clerk too puts up i' Monkshaven church.
Well, a reckon it were heerd, for all a were i' them north

latitudes, for she keeps steady, an' a does my best for t' keep steady; an' 'deed a was too steady, for a was fast wi' t' harpoon line, all knotted and tangled about me. T' captain, he sings out for me to cut it; but it's easy singin' out, and it's noane so easy fumblin' for your knife i' t' pocket o' your drawers, when yo've t' hold hard wi' t' other hand on t' back of a whale, swimmin' fourteen knots an hour. At last a thinks to mysel' a can't get free o' t' line, and t' line is fast to t' harpoon, and t' harpoon is fast to t' whale; and t' whale may go down fathoms deep wheniver t' maggot stirs i' her head,* an' t' watter's cold, an' noane good for drownin' in; a can't get free o' t' line, and a connot get my knife out o' my breeches pocket though t' captain should ca' it mutiny to disobey orders, and t' line's fast to t' harpoon – let's see if t' harpoon's fast to t' whale. So a tugged, and a lugged, and t' whale didn't mistake it for ticklin', but she cocks up her tail, and throws out showers o' water as were ice or iver* it touched me; but a pulls on at t' shank, an' a were only afeard as she wouldn't keep at t' top wi' it sticking in her; but at last t' harpoon broke, an' just i' time, for a reckon she was near as tired o' me as a were on her, and down she went; an' a had hard work to make for t' boats as was near enough to catch me; for what wi' t' whale's being but slippery an' t' watter being cold, an' me hampered wi' t' line an' t' piece o' harpoon, it's a chance, missus, as thou had stopped an oud maid.'*

'Eh dear a' me!' said Bell, 'how well I mind yo'r telling me that tale! It were twenty-four year ago come October. I thought I never could think enough on a man as had rode on a whale's back!'

'Yo' may learn t' way of winnin' t' women,' said Daniel, winking at the specksioneer.

And Kinraid immediately looked at Sylvia. It was no pre-meditated action; it came as naturally as wakening in the morning when his sleep was ended; but Sylvia coloured as red as any rose at his sudden glance, – coloured so deeply that he looked away until he thought she had recovered her composure, and then he sat gazing at her again. But not for long, for Bell, suddenly starting up, did all but turn him out of the house. It was late, she said, and her master was tired, and they had a hard day before them next day; and it was keeping Ellen Corney up; and they had had enough to drink, – more than was good for them, she was sure, for they had both been taking her in with their stories, which she had been foolish enough to believe. No one saw the real motive of all this almost inhospitable haste to dismiss her guest, how the sudden fear had taken possession of her that he and Sylvia were 'fancying each other'. Kinraid had said early in the evening that he had come to thank her for her kindness in sending the sausages, as he was off to his own home near Newcastle in a day or two. But now he said, in reply to Daniel Robson, that he would step in another night before long and hear some more of the old man's yarns.

Daniel had just had enough drink to make him very good-tempered, or else his wife would not have dared to have acted as she did; and this maudlin amiability took the shape of hospitable urgency that Kinraid should come as often as he liked to Haytersbank; come and make it his home when he was in these parts; stay there altogether, and so on, till Bell fairly shut the outer door to, and locked it before the specksioneer had well got out of the shadow of their roof.

All night long Sylvia dreamed of burning volcanoes* springing out of icy southern seas. But, as in the specksioneer's tale the flames were peopled with demons, there was no human interest for her in the wondrous scene in which she was no actor, only a spectator. With daylight came wakening and little homely every-day wonders. Did Kinraid mean that he was going away really and entirely, or did he not? Was he Molly Corney's sweetheart, or was he not? When she had argued herself into certainty on one side, she suddenly wheeled about, and was just of the opposite opinion. At length she settled that it could not be settled until she saw Molly again; so, by a strong gulping effort, she resolutely determined to think no more about him, only about the marvels he had told. She might think a little about them when she sat at night, spinning in silence by the household fire, or when she went out in the gloaming to call the cattle home to be milked, and sauntered back behind the patient, slow-gaited creatures; and at times on future summer days, when, as in the past, she took her knitting out for the sake of the freshness of the faint seabreeze, and dropping down from ledge to ledge of the rocks that faced the blue ocean, established herself in a perilous nook that had been her haunt ever since her parents had come to Haytersbank Farm. From thence she had often seen the distant ships pass to and fro, with a certain sort of lazy pleasure in watching their swift tranquillity of motion, but no thought as to where they were bound to, or what strange places they would penetrate to before they turned again, home-ward bound.

CHAPTER 10

A Refractory Pupil

Sylvia was still full of the specksioneer and his stories, when Hepburn came up to give her the next lesson. But the prospect of a little sensible commendation for writing a whole page full of flourishing 'Abednegos', had lost all the slight charm it had ever possessed. She was much more inclined to try and elicit some sympathy in her interest in the perils and adventures of the northern seas, than to bend and control her mind to the right formation of letters. Unwisely enough, she endeavoured to repeat one of the narratives that she had heard from Kinraid; and when she found that Hepburn (if, indeed, he did not look upon the whole as a silly invention) considered it only as an interruption to the real business in hand, to which he would try to listen as patiently as he could, in the hope of Sylvia's applying herself diligently to her copy-book when she had cleared her mind, she contracted her pretty lips as if to check them from making any further appeals for sympathy, and set about her writing-lesson in a very rebellious frame of mind, only restrained by her mother's presence from spoken mutiny.

'After all,' said she, throwing down her pen, and opening and shutting her weary, cramped hand, 'I see no good in tiring myself wi' learning for t' write letters when I'se never got one in a' my life. What for should I write answers, when there's niver a one writes to me? and if I had one, I couldn't read it; it's bad enough wi' a book o' print as I've niver seen afore, for there's sure to be new-fangled words in 't. I'm sure I wish the man were farred* who plagues his brains wi' striking out new words. Why can't folks just ha' a set on 'em* for good and a'?'

'Why! you'll be after using two or three hundred yoursel' every day as you live, Sylvie; and yet I must use a great many as you never think on about t' shop; and t' folks in t' fields want their set, let alone the high English that parsons and lawyers speak.'

'Well, it's weary work is reading and writing. Cannot you learn me something else, if we mun do lessons?'

'There's sums – and geography,' said Hepburn, slowly and gravely.

'Geography!' said Sylvia, brightening, and perhaps not pronouncing the word quite correctly, 'I'd like yo' to learn me geography. There's a deal o' places I want to hear all about.'

'Well, I'll bring up a book and a map next time. But I can tell you something now. There's four quarters in the globe.'

'What's that?' asked Sylvia.

'The globe is the earth; the place we live on.'

'Go on. Which quarter is Greenland?'

'Greenland is no quarter. It is only a part of one.'

'Maybe it's a half quarter.'

'No, not so much as that.'

'Half again? '

'No!' he replied, smiling a little.

She thought he was making it into a very small place in order to tease her; so she pouted a little, and then said, –

'Greenland is all t' geography I want to know. Except, perhaps, York. I'd like to learn about York, because of t' races, and London, because King George lives there.'

'But if you learn geography at all, you must learn 'bout all places: which of them is hot, and which is cold, and how many inhabitants is in each, and what's the rivers, and which is the principal towns.'

'I'm sure, Sylvie, if Philip will learn thee all that, thou'lt be such a sight o' knowledge as ne'er a one o' th' Prestons has been sin' my great-grandfather lost his property. I should be main proud o' thee; 'twould seem as if we was Prestons o' Slaideburn once more.'

'I'd do a deal to pleasure yo', mammy; but weary befa' riches and land, if folks that has 'em is to write "Abednegos" by t' score, and to get hard words int' their brains, till they work like barm,* and end wi' cracking 'em.'

This seemed to be Sylvia's last protest against learning for the night, for after this she turned docile, and really took pains to understand all that Philip could teach her, by means of the not unskilful, though rude, map which he drew for her with a piece

of charred wood on his aunt's dresser. He had asked his aunt's
leave before beginning what Sylvia called his 'dirty work'; but
by-and-by even she became a little interested in starting from a
great black spot called Monkshaven, and in the shaping of land
and sea around that one centre. Sylvia held her round chin in
the palms of her hands, supporting her elbows on the dresser;
looking down at the progress of the rough drawing in general,
but now and then glancing up at him with sudden inquiry. All
along he was not so much absorbed in his teaching as to be
unconscious of her sweet proximity. She was in her best mood
towards him; neither mutinous nor saucy; and he was striving
with all his might to retain her interest, speaking better than
ever he had done before (such brightness did love call forth!) –
understanding what she would care to hear and to know; when,
in the middle of an attempt at explaining the cause of the long
polar days, of which she had heard from her childhood, he felt
that her attention was no longer his; that a discord had come in
between their minds; that she had passed out of his power. This
certainty of intuition lasted but for an instant; he had no time to
wonder or to speculate as to what had affected her so adversely
to his wishes before the door opened and Kinraid came in. Then
Hepburn knew that she must have heard his coming footsteps,
and recognized them.

He angrily stiffened himself up into coldness of demeanour.
Almost to his surprise, Sylvia's greeting to the new corner was
as cold as his own. She stood rather behind him; so perhaps she
did not see the hand which Kinraid stretched out towards her,
for she did not place her own little palm in it, as she had done
to Philip an hour ago. And she hardly spoke, but began to pore
over the rough black map, as if seized with strong geographical
curiosity, or determined to impress Philip's lesson deep on her
memory.

Still Philip was dismayed by seeing the warm welcome which
Kinraid received from the master of the house, who came in
from the back premises almost at the same time as the specksioneer entered at the front. Hepburn was uneasy, too, at finding
Kinraid take his seat by the fireside, like one accustomed to the
ways of the house. Pipes were soon produced. Philip disliked
smoking. Possibly Kinraid did so too, but, he took a pipe at any
rate, and lighted it, though he hardly used it at all, but kept
talking to farmer Robson on sea affairs. He had the conversation

pretty much to himself. Philip sat gloomily by; Sylvia and his aunt were silent, and old Robson smoked his long clay pipe, from time to time taking it out of his mouth to spit into the bright copper spittoon, and to shake the white ashes out of the bowl. Before he replaced it, he would give a short laugh of relishing interest in Kinraid's conversation; and now and then he put in a remark. Sylvia perched herself sideways on the end of the dresser, and made pretence to sew; but Philip could see how often she paused in her work to listen.

By-and-by, his aunt spoke to him, and they kept up a little side conversation, more because Bell Robson felt that her nephew, her own flesh and blood, was put out, than for any special interest they either of them felt in what they were saying. Perhaps, also, they neither of them disliked showing that they had no great faith in the stories Kinraid was telling. Mrs Robson, at any rate, knew so little as to be afraid of believing too much.

Philip was sitting on that side of the fire which was nearest to the window and to Sylvia, and opposite to the specksioneer. At length he turned to his cousin and said in a low voice –

'I suppose we can't go on with our spell at geography till that fellow's gone?'

The colour came into Sylvia's cheek at the words 'that fellow;' but she only replied with a careless air –

'Well, I'm one as thinks enough is as good as a feast; and I've had enough of geography this one night, thank you kindly all the same.'

Philip took refuge in offended silence. He was maliciously pleased when his aunt made so much noise with her preparation for supper as quite to prevent the sound of the sailor's words from reaching Sylvia's ears. She saw that he was glad to perceive that her efforts to reach the remainder of the story were baulked; this nettled her, and, determined not to let him have his malicious triumph, and still more to put a stop to an attempt at private conversation, she began to sing to herself as she sat at her work; till, suddenly seized with a desire to help her mother, she dextrously slipped down from her seat, passed Hepburn, and was on her knees toasting cakes right in front of the fire, and just close to her father and Kinraid. And now the noise that Hepburn had so rejoiced in proved his foe. He could not hear the little merry speeches that darted backwards and forwards as the specksioneer tried to take the toasting-fork out of Sylvia's hand.

'How comes that sailor chap here?' asked Hepburn of his aunt. 'He's none fit to be where Sylvia is.'

'Nay, I dunnot know,' said she; 'the Corneys made us acquaint first, and my master is quite fain of his company.'

'And do you like him, too, aunt?' asked Hepburn, almost wistfully; he had followed Mrs Robson into the dairy on pretence of helping her.

'I'm none fond on him; I think he tells us traveller's tales, by way o' seeing how much we can swallow. But the master and Sylvia think that there never was such a one.'

'I could show them a score as good as he down on the quay side.'

'Well, laddie, keep a calm sough.* Some folk like some folk and others don't. Wherever I am there'll allays be a welcome for thee.'

For the good woman thought that he had been hurt by the evident absorption of her husband and daughter with their new friend, and wished to make all easy and straight. But do what she would, he did not recover his temper all the evening: he was uncomfortable, put out, not enjoying himself, and yet he would not go. He was determined to assert his greater intimacy in that house by outstaying Kinraid. At length the latter got up to go; but before he went, he must needs bend over Sylvia and say something to her in so low a tone that Philip could not hear it; and she, seized with a sudden fit of diligence, never looked up from her sewing; only nodded her head by way of reply. At last he took his departure, after many a little delay, and many a quick return, which to the suspicious Philip seemed only pretences for taking stolen glances at Sylvia. As soon as he was decidedly gone, she folded up her work, and declared that she was so much tired that she must go to bed there and then. Her mother, too, had been dozing for the last half-hour, and was only too glad to see signs that she might betake herself to her natural place of slumber.

'Take another glass, Philip,' said farmer Robson.

But Hepburn refused the offer rather abruptly. He drew near to Sylvia instead. He wanted to make her speak to him, and he saw that she wished to avoid it. He took up the readiest pretext.

It was an unwise one as it proved, for it deprived him of his chances of occasionally obtaining her undivided attention.

'I don't think you care much for learning geography, Sylvie? '

'Not much to-night,' said she, making a pretence to yawn yet looking timidly up at his countenance of displeasure.

'Nor at any time,' said he, with growing anger, 'nor for any kind of learning. I did bring some books last time I came, meaning to teach you many a thing – but now I'll just trouble you for my books; I put them on yon shelf by the Bible.'

He had a mind that she should bring them to him; that, at any rate, he should have the pleasure of receiving them out of her hands.

Sylvia did not reply, but went and took down the books with a languid, indifferent air.

'And so you won't learn any more geography,' said Hepburn.

Something in his tone struck her, and she looked up in his face. There were marks of stern offence upon his countenance, and yet in it there was also an air of wistful regret and sadness that touched her.

'Yo're niver angry with me, Philip? Sooner than vex yo', I'll try and learn. Only, I'm just stupid; and it mun be such a trouble to you.'

Hepburn would fain have snatched at this half proposal that the lessons should be continued, but he was too stubborn and proud to say anything. He turned away from the sweet, pleading face without a word, to wrap up his books in a piece of paper. He knew that she was standing quite still by his side, though he made as if he did not perceive her. When he had done he abruptly wished them all 'good-night', and took his leave.

There were tears in Sylvia's eyes, although the feeling in her heart was rather one of relief. She had made a fair offer, and it had been treated with silent contempt. A few days afterwards, her father came in from Monkshaven market, and dropped out, among other pieces of news, that he had met Kinraid, who was bound for his own home at Cullercoats. He had desired his respects to Mrs Robson and her daughter; and had bid Robson say that he would have come up to Haytersbank to wish them good-bye, but that as he was pressed for time, he hoped they would excuse him. But Robson did not think it worth while to give this long message of mere politeness. Indeed, as it did not relate to business, and was only sent to women, Robson forgot

all about it, pretty nearly as soon as it was uttered. So Sylvia
went about fretting herself for one or two days, at her hero's
apparent carelessness of those who had at any rate treated him
more like a friend than an acquaintance of only a few weeks'
standing; and then, her anger quenching her incipient regard,
she went about her daily business pretty much as though he had
never been. He had gone sway out of her sight into the thick
mist of unseen life from which he had emerged – gone away
without a word, and she might never see him again. But still
there was a chance of her seeing him when he came to marry
Molly Corney. Perhaps she should be bridesmaid, and then what
a pleasant merry time the wedding-day would be! The Corneys
were all such kind people, and in their family there never seemed
to be the checks and restraints by which her own mother hedged
her round. Then there came an overwhelming self-reproaching
burst of love for that 'own mother'; a humiliation before her
slightest wish, as penance for the moment's unspoken treason;
and thus Sylvia was led to request her cousin Philip to resume
his lessons in so meek a manner, that he slowly and graciously
acceded to a request which he was yearning to fulfil all the time.

During the ensuing winter, all went on in monotonous
regularity at Haytersbank Farm for many weeks. Hepburn came
and went, and thought Sylvia wonderfully improved in docility
and sobriety; and perhaps also he noticed the improvement in
her appearance. For she was at that age when a girl changes
rapidly, and generally for the better. Sylvia shot up into a tall
young woman; her eyes deepened in colour, her face increased
in expression, and a sort of consciousness of unusual good looks
gave her a slight tinge of coquettish shyness with the few
strangers whom she ever saw. Philip hailed her interest in
geography as another sign of improvement. He had brought
back his book of maps to the farm; and there he sat on many an
evening teaching his cousin, who had strange fancies respecting
the places about which she wished to learn, and was coolly
indifferent to the very existence of other towns, and countries,
and seas far more famous in story. She was occasionally wilful,
and at times very contemptuous as to the superior knowledge of
her instructor; but, in spite of it all, Philip went regularly on the
appointed evenings to Haytersbank – through keen black east
wind, or driving snow, or slushing thaw; for he liked dearly to
sit a little behind her, with his arm on the back of her chair, she

stooping over the outspread map, with her eyes, – could he have seen them, – a good deal fixed on one spot in the map, not Northumberland, where Kinraid was spending the winter, but those wild northern seas about which he had told them such wonders.

One day towards spring, she saw Molly Corney coming towards the farm. The companions had not met for many weeks, for Molly had been from home visiting her relations in the north. Sylvia opened the door, and stood smiling and shivering on the threshold, glad to see her friend again. Molly called out, when a few paces off, –

'Why, Sylvia, is that thee? Why, how thou'rt growed, to be sure! What a bonny lass thou is!'

'Dunnot talk nonsense to my lass,' said Bell Robson, hospitably leaving her ironing and coming to the door; but though the mother tried to look; as if she thought it nonsense, she could hardly keep down the smile that shone out of her eyes, as she put her hand on Sylvia's shoulder, with a fond sense of proprietorship in what was being praised.

'Oh! but she is,' persisted Molly. 'She's grown quite a beauty sin' I saw her. And if I don't tell her so, the men will.'

'Be quiet wi' thee,' said Sylvia, more than half offended, and turning away in a huff at the open barefaced admiration.

'Ay; but they will,' persevered Molly. 'Yo'll not keep her long, Mistress Robson. And as mother says, feel it a deal more to have yer daughters left on hand.'*

'Thy mother has many, I have but this one,' said Mrs Robson, with severe sadness; for now Molly was getting to talk as she disliked. But Molly's purpose was to bring the conversation round to her own affairs, of which she was very full.

'Yes! I tell mother that wi' so many as she has, she ought to be thankful to t' one as gets off quickest.'*

'Who? which is it?' asked Sylvia, a little eagerly, seeing that there was news of a wedding behind the talk.

'Why! who should it be but me?' said Molly, laughing a good deal, and reddening a little. 'I've not gone fra' home for nought; I'se picked up a measter on my travels, leastways one as is to be.'

'Charley Kinraid,' said Sylvia, smiling, as she found that now she might reveal Molly's secret, which hitherto she had kept sacred.

'Charley Kinraid be hung!'* said Molly, with a toss of her head. 'Whatten good's a husband who's at sea half t' year? Ha, ha, my measter is a canny Newcassel shopkeeper, on t' Side.'* A reckon a've done pretty well for mysel', and a'll wish yo' as good luck, Sylvia. For yo' see,' (turning to Bell Robson, who, perhaps, she thought would more appreciate the substantial advantages of her engagement than Sylvia,) 'though Measter Brunton is near upon forty if he's a day, yet he turns over * a matter of two hundred pound every year; an' he's a good-looking man of his years too, an' a kind, good-tempered feller int' t' bargain. He's been married once, to be sure; but his childer are dead a' 'cept one; an' I don't mislike childer either; an' a'll feed 'em well, an' get 'em to bed early, out o' t' road.*

Mrs Robson gave her her grave good wishes; but Sylvia was silent. She was disappointed; it was a coming down from the romance with the specksioneer for its hero. Molly laughed awkwardly, understanding Sylvia's thoughts better than the latter imagined.

'Sylvia's noane so well pleased. Why, lass! it's a' t' better for thee. There's Charley to t' fore now, which if a'd married him, he'd not ha' been, and he's said more nor once what a pretty lass yo'd grow into by-and-by.'

Molly's prosperity was giving her an independence and fear-lessness of talk such as had seldom appeared hitherto, and certainly never before Mrs Robson. Sylvia was annoyed at Molly's whole tone and manner, which were loud, laughing, and boisterous; but to her mother they were positively repug-nant. She said shortly and gravely, –

'Sylvia's none so set upo' matrimony; she's content to bide wi' me and her father. Let a be such talking, it's not i' my way.'

Molly was a little subdued; but still her elation at the prospect of being so well married kept cropping out of* all the other subjects which were introduced; and when she went away, Mrs Robson broke out in an unwonted strain of depreciation.

'That's the way wi' some lasses. They're like a cock on a dunghill, when they've teased a silly chap into wedding 'em. It's cock-a-doodle-doo, I've cotched a husband, cock-a doodle-doo, wi' 'em. I've no patience wi' such like; I beg, Sylvie, thou'lt not get too thick wi' Molly. She's not pretty behaved, making such an ado about men-kind, as if they were two-headed calves to be run after.'

'But Molly's a good-hearted lass, mother. Only I never dreamt but what she was troth-plighted wi' Charley Kinraid,' said Sylvia, meditatively.

'That wench 'll be troth-plight to th' first man as 'll wed her and keep her i' plenty; that's a' she thinks about,' replied Bell, scornfully.

CHAPTER 11

Visions of the Future

Before May was out, Molly Corney was married and had left the neighbourhood for Newcastle. Although Charley Kinraid was not the bridegroom, Sylvia's promise to be bridesmaid was claimed. But the friendship brought on by the circumstances of neighbourhood and parity of age had become very much weakened in the time that elapsed between Molly's engagement and wedding. In the first place, she herself was so absorbed in her preparations, so elated by her good fortune in getting married, and married, too, before her elder sister, that all her faults blossomed out full and strong. Sylvia felt her to be selfish; Mrs Robson thought her not maidenly. A year before she would have been far more missed and regretted by Sylvia; now it was almost a relief to the latter to be freed from the perpetual calls upon her sympathy, from the constant demands upon her congratulations, made by one who had no thought or feeling to bestow on others; at least, not in these weeks of 'cock-a-doodle-dooing', as Mrs Robson persisted in calling it. It was seldom that Bell was taken with a humorous idea; but this once having hatched a solitary joke, she was always clucking it into notice – to go on with her own poultry simile.

Every time during that summer that Philip saw his cousin, he thought her prettier than she had ever been before; some new touch of colour, some fresh sweet charm, seemed to have been added, just as every summer day calls out new beauty in the flowers. And this was not the addition of Philip's fancy. Hester Rose, who met Sylvia on rare occasions, came back each time with a candid, sad acknowledgment in her heart that it was no wonder that Sylvia was so much admired and loved.

One day Hester had seen her sitting near her mother in the market-place; there was a basket by her, and over the clean cloth that covered the yellow pounds of butter, she had laid the hedge-roses and honeysuckles she had gathered on the way into Monkshaven; her straw hat was on her knee, and she was busy placing some of the flowers in the ribbon that went round it. Then she held it on her hand, and turned it round about, putting her head on one side, the better to view the effect; and all this time, Hester, peeping at her through the folds of the stuffs displayed in Foster's windows, saw her with admiring, wistful eyes; wondering, too, if Philip, at the other counter, were aware of his cousin's being there, so near to him. Then Sylvia put on her hat, and, looking up at Foster's windows, caught Hester's face of interest, and smiled and blushed at the consciousness of having been watched over her little vanities, and Hester smiled back, but rather sadly. Then a customer came in, and she had to attend to her business, which, on this as on all market days, was great. In the midst she was aware of Philip rushing bare-headed out of the shop, eager and delighted at something he saw outside. There was a little looking-glass hung against the wall on Hester's side, placed in that retired corner, in order that the good women who came to purchase head-gear of any kind might see the effect thereof before they concluded their bargain. In a pause of custom, Hester, half ashamed, stole into this corner, and looked at herself in the glass. What did she see? a colourless face, dark soft hair with no light gleams in it, eyes that were melancholy instead of smiling, a mouth compressed with a sense of dissatisfaction. This was what she had to compare with the bright bonny face in the sunlight outside. She gave a gulp to check the sigh that was rising, and came back, even more patient than she had been before this disheartening peep, to serve all the whims and fancies of purchasers.

Sylvia herself had been rather put out by Philip's way of coming to her. 'It made her look so silly,' she thought; and 'what for must he make a sight of himself, coming among the market folk in that-a-way;' and when he took to admiring her hat, she pulled out the flowers in a pet,* and threw them down, and trampled them under foot.

'What for art thou doing that, Sylvie?' said her mother. 'The flowers is well enough, though may be thy hat might ha' been stained.'

'I don't like Philip to speak to me so,' said Sylvia, pouting.

'How?' asked her mother.

But Sylvia could not repeat his words. She hung her head, and looked red and pre-occupied, anything but pleased. Philip had addressed his first expression of personal admiration at an unfortunate time.

It just shows what different views different men and women take of their fellow-creatures, when I say that Hester looked upon Philip as the best and most agreeable man she had ever known. He was not one to speak of himself without being questioned on the subject, so his Haytersbank relations, only come into the neighbourhood in the last year or two, knew nothing of the trials he had surmounted, or the difficult duties he had performed. His aunt, indeed, had strong faith in him, both from partial knowledge of his character, and because he was of her own tribe and kin; but she had never learnt the small details of his past life. Sylvia respected him as her mother's friend, and treated him tolerably well as long as he preserved his usual self-restraint of demeanour, but hardly ever thought of him when he was absent.

Now Hester, who had watched him daily for all the years since he had first come as an errand-boy into Foster's shop – watching with quiet, modest, yet observant eyes – had seen how devoted he was to his master's interests, had known of his careful and punctual ministration to his absent mother's comforts, as long as she was living to benefit by his silent, frugal self-denial.

His methodical appropriation of the few hours he could call his own was not without its charms to the equally methodical Hester; the way in which he reproduced any lately acquired piece of knowledge – knowledge so wearisome to Sylvia – was delightfully instructive to Hester – although, as she was habitually silent, it would have required an observer more interested in discovering her feelings than Philip was to have perceived the little flush on the pale cheek, and the brightness in the half-veiled eyes whenever he was talking. She had not thought of love on either side. Love was a vanity, a worldliness not to be spoken about, or even thought about. Once or twice before the Robsons came into the neighbourhood, an idea had crossed her

mind that possibly the quiet, habitual way in which she and
Philip lived together, might drift them into matrimony at some
distant period; and she could not bear the humble advances
which Coulson, Philip's fellow-lodger, sometimes made. They
seemed to disgust her with him.

But after the Robsons settled at Haytersbank, Philip's evenings were so often spent there that any unconscious hopes
Hester might, unawares, have entertained, died away. At first
she had felt a pang akin to jealousy when she heard of Sylvia,
the little cousin, who was passing out of childhood into womanhood. Once – early in those days – she had ventured to ask
Philip what Sylvia was like. Philip had not warmed up at the
question, and had given rather a dry catalogue of her features,
hair, and height, but Hester, almost to her own surprise,
persevered, and jerked out the final question.

'Is she pretty?'

Philip's sallow cheek grew deeper by two or three shades; but
he answered with a tone of indifference, –

'I believe some folks think her so.'

'But do you?' persevered Hester, in spite of her being aware
that he somehow disliked the question.

'There's no need for talking o' such things,' he answered, with
abrupt displeasure.

Hester silenced her curiosity from that time. But her heart
was not quite at ease, and she kept on wondering whether Philip
thought his little cousin pretty until she saw her and him
together, on that occasion of which we have spoken, when
Sylvia came to the shop to buy her new cloak; and after that
Hester never wondered whether Philip thought his cousin pretty
or no, for she knew quite well. Bell Robson had her own
anxieties on the subject of her daughter's increasing attractions.
She apprehended the dangers consequent upon certain facts, by
a mental process more akin to intuition than reason. She was
uncomfortable, even while her motherly vanity was flattered, at
the admiration Sylvia received from the other sex. This admiration was made evident to her mother in many ways. When
Sylvia was with her at market, it might have been thought that
the doctors had prescribed a diet of butter and eggs to all the
men under forty in Monkshaven. At first it seemed to Mrs
Robson but a natural tribute to the superior merit of her farm
produce; but by degrees she perceived that if Sylvia remained at

home, she stood no better chance than her neighbours of an early sale. There were more customers than formerly for the fleeces stored in the wool-loft; comely young butchers came after the calf almost before it had been decided to sell it; in short, excuses were seldom wanting to those who wished to see the beauty of Haytersbank Farm. All this made Bell uncomfortable, though she could hardly have told what she dreaded. Sylvia herself seemed unspoilt by it as far as her home relations were concerned. A little thoughtless she had always been, and thoughtless she was still; but, as her mother had often said, 'Yo' canna put old heads on young shoulders'; and if blamed for her carelessness by her parents, Sylvia was always as penitent as she could be for the time being. To be sure, it was only to her father and mother that she remained the same as she had been when an awkward lassie of thirteen. Out of the house there were the most contradictory opinions of her, especially if the voices of women were to be listened to. She was 'an ill-favoured, overgrown thing'; 'just as bonny as the first rose i' June, and as sweet i' her nature as t' honeysuckle a-climbing round it'; she was 'a vixen, with a tongue sharp enough to make yer very heart bleed'; she was 'just a bit o' sunshine wheriver she went'; she was sulky, lively, witty, silent, affectionate, or cold-hearted, according to the person who spoke about her. In fact, her peculiarity seemed to be this – that every one who knew her talked about her either in praise or blame; in church, or in market, she unconsciously attracted attention; they could not forget her presence, as they could that of other girls perhaps more personally attractive. Now all this was a cause of anxiety to her mother, who began to feel as if she would rather have had her child passed by in silence than so much noticed. Bell's opinion was, that it was creditable to a woman to go through life in the shadow of obscurity, – never named except in connection with good housewifery, husband, or children. Too much talking about a girl, even in the way of praise, disturbed Mrs Robson's opinion of her; and when her neighbours told her how her own daughter was admired, she would reply coldly, 'She's just well enough,' and change the subject of conversation. But it was quite different with her husband. To his looser, less-restrained mind, it was agreeable to hear of, and still more to see, the attention which his daughter's beauty received. He felt it as reflecting consequence on himself. He had never troubled his mind with speculations as to whether he himself was popular, still less whether he was respected. He was pretty welcome wherever he went, as a jovial good-natured man, who had done adventurous and illegal things in his youth, which in some measure entitled him to speak out his opinions on life in general in the authoritative manner he generally used; but, of the two, he preferred consorting with younger men, to taking a sober stand of respectability with the elders of the place; and he perceived, without reasoning upon it, that the gay daring spirits were more desirous of his company when Sylvia was by his side than at any other time. One or two of these would saunter up to Haytersbank on a Sunday afternoon, and lounge round his fields with the old farmer. Bell kept herself from the nap which had been her weekly solace for years, in order to look after Sylvia, and on such occasions she always turned as cold a shoulder to the visitors as her sense of hospitality and of duty to her husband would permit. But if they did not enter the house, old Robson would always have Sylvia with him when he went the round of his land. Bell could see them from the upper window: the young men standing in the attitudes of listeners, while Daniel laid down the law on some point, enforcing his words by pantomimic actions with his thick stick; and Sylvia, half turning away as if from some too admiring gaze, was possibly picking flowers out of the hedgebank. These Sunday afternoon strolls were the plague of Bell's life that whole summer. Then it took as much of artifice as was in the simple woman's nature to keep Daniel from insisting on having Sylvia's company every time he went down to Monkshaven. And here, again, came a perplexity, the acknowledgment of which in distinct thought would have been an act of disloyalty, according to Bell's conscience. If Sylvia went with her father, he never drank to excess; and that was a good gain to health at any rate (drinking was hardly a sin against morals in those days, and in that place); so, occasionally, she was allowed to accompany him to Monkshaven as a check upon his folly; for he was too fond and proud of his daughter to disgrace her by any open excess. But one Sunday afternoon early in November, Philip came up before the time at which he usually paid his visits. He looked grave and pale; and his aunt began, –

'Why, lad! what's been ado? Thou'rt looking as peaked and pined as a Methody preacher after a love-feast,* when he's talked hisself to Death's door. Thee dost na' get good milk enow, that's what it is, – such stuff as Monkshaven folks put up wi'!'

'No, aunt; I'm quite well. Only I'm a bit put out – vexed like at what I've heerd about Sylvie.'

His aunt's face changed immediately.

'And whatten folk say of her, next thing?'*

'Oh,' said Philip, struck by the difference of look and manner in his aunt, and subdued by seeing how instantly she took alarm. 'It were only my uncle; – he should na' take a girl like her to a public. She were wi' him at t' Admiral's Head upo' All Souls' Day* – that were all. There were many a one there beside, – it were statute fair; but such a one as our Sylvie ought not to be cheapened wi' t' rest.'

'And he took her there, did he?' said Bell, in severe meditation. 'I had never no opinion o' th' wenches as 'll set theirselves to be hired for servants i' th' fair; they're a bad lot, as cannot find places for theirselves – 'bout going and stannin' to be stared at by folk, and grinnin' wi' th' ploughlads when no one's looking; it's a bad look-out for t' missus as takes one o' these wenches for a servant; and dost ta mean to say as my Sylvie went and demeaned hersel' to dance and marlock* wi' a' th' fair-folk at th' Admiral's Head?'

'No, no, she did na' dance; she barely set foot i' th' room; but it were her own pride as saved her; uncle would niver ha' kept her from it, for he had fallen in wi' Hayley o' Seaburn and one or two others, and they were having a glass i' t' bar, and Mrs Lawson, t' landlady, knew how there was them who would come and dance among parish 'prentices if need were, just to get a word or a look wi' Sylvie! So she tempts her in, saying that the room were all smartened and fine wi' flags; and there was them in the room as told me that they never were so startled as when they saw our Sylvie's face peeping in among all t' flustered maids and men, rough and red wi' weather and drink; and Jem Macbean, he said she were just like a bit o' apple-blossom among peonies; and some man, he didn't know who, went up and spoke to her; an' either at that, or at some o' t' words she heard – for they'd got a good way on afore that time – she went quite white and mad, as if fire were coming out of her eyes, and then she turned red and left the room, for all t' landlady tried to laugh it off and keep her in.'

'I'll be down to Monkshaven before I'm a day older, and tell

Margaret Lawson some on my mind as she'll not forget in a hurry.'

Bell moved as though she would put on her cloak and hood there and then.

'Nay, it's not in reason as a woman i' that line o' life shouldn't try to make her house agreeable,' said Philip.

'Not wi' my wench,' said Bell, in a determined voice.

Philip's information had made a deeper impression on his aunt than he intended. He himself had been annoyed more at the idea that Sylvia would be spoken of as having been at a rough piece of rustic gaiety – a yearly festival for the lower classes of Yorkshire servants, out-door as well as in-door – than at the affair itself, for he had learnt from his informant how instantaneous her appearance had been. He stood watching his aunt's troubled face, and almost wishing that he had not spoken. At last she heaved a deep sigh, and stirring the fire, as if by this little household occupation to compose her mind, she said –

'It's a pity as wenches aren't lads, or married folk. I could ha' wished – but it were the Lord's will—It would ha' been summut to look to, if she'd had a brother. My master is so full on his own thoughts, yo' see, he's no mind left for thinking on her, what wi' th' oats, and th' wool, and th' young colt, and his venture* i' th' *Lucky Mary*.'

She really believed her husband to have the serious and important occupation for his mind that she had been taught to consider befitting the superior intellect of the masculine gender; she would have taxed herself severely if, even in thought, she had blamed him, and Philip respected her feelings too much to say that Sylvia's father ought to look after her more closely if he made such a pretty creature so constantly his companion; yet some such speech was only just pent within Philip's closed lips. Again his aunt spoke –

'I used to think as she and yo' might fancy one another, but thou'rt too old-fashioned like for her; ye would na' suit; and it's as well, for now I can say to thee, that I would take it very kindly if thou would'st look after her a bit.'

Philip's countenance fell into gloom. He had to gulp down certain feelings before he could make answer with discretion.

'How can I look after her, and me tied to the shop more and more every day?'

'I could send her on a bit of an errand to Foster's, and then, for sure, yo' might keep an eye upon her when she's in th' town; and just walk a bit way with her when she's in th' street, and keep t' other fellows off her – Ned Simpson, t' butcher, in 'special, for folks do say he means no good by any girl he goes wi' – and I'll ask father to leave her a bit more wi' me. They're coming down th' brow, and Ned Simpson wi' them. Now, Philip, I look to thee to do a brother's part by my wench, and warn off all as isn't fit.'

The door opened, and the coarse strong voice of Simpson made itself heard. He was a stout man, comely enough, as to form and feature, but with a depth of colour in his face that betokened the coming on of the habits of the sot. His Sunday hat was in his hand, and he smoothed the long nap of it, as he said, with a mixture of shyness and familiarity –

'Sarvant,* missus. Yo'r measter is fain that I should come in an' have a drop; no offence, I hope?'

Sylvia passed quickly through the house-place, and went upstairs without speaking to her cousin Philip or to any one. He sat on, disliking the visitor, and almost disliking his hospitable uncle for having brought Simpson into the house, sympathizing with his aunt in the spirit which prompted her curt answers, and in the intervals of all these feelings wondering what ground she had for speaking as if she had now given up all thought of Sylvia and him ever being married, and in what way he was too 'old-fashioned'.

Robson would gladly have persuaded Philip to join him and Simpson in their drink, but Philip was in no sociable mood, and sat a little aloof, watching the staircase down which sooner or later Sylvia must come, for, as perhaps has been already said, the stairs went up straight out of the kitchen. And at length his yearning watch was rewarded; first, the little pointed toe came daintily in sight, then the trim ankle in the tight blue stocking, the wool of which was spun and the web of which was knitted by her mother's careful hands; then the full brown stuff petticoat, the arm holding the petticoat back in decent folds, so as not to encumber the descending feet; the slender neck and shoulders hidden under the folded square of fresh white muslin; the crowning beauty of the soft innocent face radiant in colour, and with the light brown curls clustering around. She made her way quickly to Philip's side; how his heart beat at her approach! and even more when she entered into a low-voiced *tête-à-tête*.

'Isn't he gone yet?' said she. 'I cannot abide him; I could ha' pinched father when he asked him for t' come in.'

'Maybe, he'll not stay long,' said Philip, hardly understanding the meaning of what he said, so sweet was it to have her making her whispered confidences to him.

But Simpson was not going to let her alone in the dark corner between the door and the window. He began paying her some coarse country compliments – too strong in their direct flattery for even her father's taste, more especially as he saw by his wife's set lips and frowning brow how much she disapproved of their visitor's style of conversation.

'Come, measter, leave t' lass alone; she's set up* enough a'ready, her mother makes such a deal on her. Yo' an' me's men for sensible talk at our time o' life. An', as I was saying, t' horse was a weaver* if iver one was, as any one could ha' told as had come within a mile on him.'

And in this way the old farmer and the bluff butcher chatted on about horses, while Philip and Sylvia sat together, he turning over all manner of hopes and projects for the future, in spite of his aunt's opinion that he was too 'old-fashioned' for her dainty, blooming daughter. Perhaps, too, Mrs Robson saw some reason for changing her mind on this head as she watched Sylvia this night, for she accompanied Philip to the door, when the time came for him to start homewards, and bade him 'good-night' with unusual fervour, adding –

'Thou'st been a deal o' comfort to me, lad – a'most as one as if thou wert a child o' my own, as at times I could welly think thou art to be. Anyways, I trust to thee to look after the lile* lass, as has no brother to guide her among men – and men's very kittle* for a woman to deal wi'; but if thou'lt have an eye on whom she consorts wi', my mind 'll be easier.'

Philip's heart beat fast, but his voice was as calm as usual when he replied –

'I'd just keep her a bit aloof from Monkshaven folks; a lass is always the more thought on for being chary of herself;* and as for t' rest, I'll have an eye to the folks she goes among, and if I see that they don't befit her, I'll just give her a warning, for she's not one to like such chaps as yon Simpson there; she can see what's becoming in a man to say to a lass, and what's not.'

Philip set out on his two-mile walk home with a tumult of happiness in his heart. He was not often carried away by delusions of his own creating; to-night he thought he had good ground for believing that by patient self-restraint he might win Sylvia's love. A year ago he had nearly earned her dislike by obtruding upon her looks and words betokening his passionate love. He alarmed her girlish coyness, as well as wearied her with the wish he had then felt that she should take an interest in his pursuits. But, with unusual wisdom, he had perceived his mistake; it was many months now since he had betrayed, by word or look, that she was anything more to him than a little cousin to be cared for and protected when need was. The consequence was that she had become tamed, just as a wild animal is tamed; he had remained tranquil and impassive, almost as if he did not perceive her shy advances towards friendliness. These advances were made by her after the lessons had ceased. She was afraid lest he was displeased with her behaviour in rejecting his instructions, and was not easy till she was at peace with him; and now, to all appearance, he and she were perfect friends, but nothing more. In his absence she would not allow her young companions to laugh at his grave sobriety of character, and somewhat prim demeanour; she would even go against her conscience, and deny that she perceived any peculiarity. When she wanted it, she sought his advice on such small subjects as came up in her daily life; and she tried not to show signs of weariness when he used more words – and more difficult words – than were necessary to convey his ideas. But her ideal husband was different from Philip in every point, the two images never for an instant merged into one. To Philip she was the only woman in the world; it was the one subject on which he dared not consider, for fear that both conscience and judgment should decide against him, and that he should be convinced against his will that she was an unfit mate for him, that she never would be his, and that it was waste of time and life to keep her shrined in the dearest sanctuary of his being,* to the exclusion of all the serious and religious aims which, in any other case, he would have been the first to acknowledge as the object he ought to pursue. For he had been brought up among the Quakers, and shared in their austere distrust of a self-seeking spirit; yet what else but self-seeking was his passionate prayer, 'Give me Sylvia, or else I die'?* No other vision had ever crossed his masculine fancy for a moment; his was a rare and constant love that deserved a better fate than it met with. At this time his hopes were high, as I have said, not merely as to the growth of Sylvia's feelings towards him, but as to the probability of his soon being in a position to place her in such comfort, as his wife, as she had never enjoyed before.

For the brothers Foster were thinking of retiring from business, and relinquishing the shop to their two shopmen, Philip Hepburn and William Coulson. To be sure, it was only by looking back for a few months, and noticing chance expressions and small indications, that this intention of theirs could be discovered. But every step they took tended this way, and Philip knew their usual practice of deliberation too well to feel in the least impatient for the quicker progress of the end which he saw steadily approaching. The whole atmosphere of life among the Friends at this date partook of this character of self-repression, and both Coulson and Hepburn shared in it. Coulson was just as much aware of the prospect opening before him as Hepburn; but they never spoke together on the subject, although their mutual knowledge might be occasionally implied in their conversation on their future lives. Meanwhile the Fosters were imparting more of the background of their business to their successors. For the present, at least, the brothers meant to retain an interest in the shop, even after they had given up the active management; and they sometimes thought of setting up a separate establishment as bankers. The separation of the business, – the introduction of their shopmen to the distant manufacturers who furnished their goods (in those days the system of 'travellers' was not so widely organized as it is at present), – all these steps were in gradual progress; and already Philip saw himself in imagination in the dignified position of joint master of the principal shop in Monkshaven, with Sylvia installed as his wife, with certainly a silk gown, and possibly a gig* at her disposal. In all Philip's visions of future prosperity, it was Sylvia who was to be aggrandized by them; his own life was to be spent as it was now, pretty much between the four shop walls.

CHAPTER 12

New Year's Fête

All this enlargement of interest in the shop occupied Philip fully for some months after the period referred to in the preceding chapter. Remembering his last conversation with his aunt, he might have been uneasy at his inability to perform his promise and look after his pretty cousin, but that about the middle of November Bell Robson had fallen ill of a rheumatic fever, and that her daughter had been entirely absorbed in nursing her. No thought of company or gaiety was in Sylvia's mind as long as her mother's illness lasted; vehement in all her feelings, she discovered in the dread of losing her mother how passionately she was attached to her. Hitherto she had supposed, as children so often do, that her parents would live for ever; and now when it was a question of days, whether by that time the following week her mother might not be buried out of her sight for ever, she clung to every semblance of service to be rendered, or affection shown, as if she hoped to condense the love and care of years into the few days only that might remain. Mrs Robson lingered on, began slowly to recover, and before Christmas was again sitting by the fireside in the house-place, wan and pulled down, muffled up with shawls and blankets, but still there once more, where not long before Sylvia had scarcely expected to see her again. Philip came up that evening and found Sylvia in wild spirits. She thought that everything was done, now that her mother had once come downstairs again; she laughed with glee; she kissed her mother; she shook hands with Philip, she almost submitted to a speech of more than usual tenderness from him; but, in the midst of his words, her mother's pillows wanted arranging and she went to her chair, paying no more heed to his words than if they had been addressed to the cat, that lying on the invalid's knee was purring out her welcome to the weak hand feebly stroking her back. Robson himself soon came in, looking older and more subdued since Philip had seen him last. He was very urgent that his wife should have some spirits and water; but on her refusal, almost as if she loathed the thought of the smell, he contented himself with sharing her tea, though he kept abusing the beverage as 'washing the heart out of a man', and attributing all the degeneracy of the world, growing up about him in his old age, to the drinking of such slop. At the same time, his little self-sacrifice put him in an unusually good temper; and, mingled with his real gladness at having his wife once more on the way to recovery, brought back some of the old charm of tenderness combined with light-heartedness, which had won the sober Isabella Preston long ago. He sat by her side, holding her hand, and talking of old times to the young couple opposite; of his adventures and escapes, and how he had won his wife. She, faintly smiling at the remembrance of those days, yet half-ashamed at having the little details of her courtship revealed, from time to time kept saying, –

'For shame wi' thee, Dannel – I never did,' and faint denials of a similar kind.

'Niver believe her, Sylvie. She were a woman, and there's niver a woman but likes to have a sweetheart, and can tell when a chap's castin' sheep's-eyes at her; ay, an' afore he knows what he's about hissen.* She were a pretty one then, was my old 'ooman, an' liked them as thought her so, though she did cock her head high, as bein' a Preston, which were a family o' standin' and means i' those parts aforetime. There's Philip there, I'll warrant, is as proud o' bein' Preston by t' mother's side, for it runs i' t' blood, lass. A can tell when a child of a Preston tak's to being proud o' their kin, by t' cut o' their nose. Now Philip's and my missus's has a turn beyond common i' their nostrils, as if they was sniffin' at t' rest of us world, an' seein' if we was good enough for 'em to consort wi'. Thee n' me, lass, is Robsons – oat-cake folk, while they's pie-crust.* Lord! how Bell used to speak to me, as short as though a was'nt a Christian, an' a' t' time she loved me as her very life, an' well a knew it, tho' a'd to mak' as tho' a didn't. Philip, when thou goes courtin', come t' me, and a'll give thee many a wrinkle.* A've shown, too, as a know well how t' choose a good wife by tokens an' signs, hannot a, missus? Come t' me, my lad, and show me t' lass, an' a'll just tak' a squint at her, an' tell yo' if she'll do or not; an' if she'll do, a'll teach yo' how to win her.'

'They say another o' yon Corney girls is going to be married,' said Mrs Robson, in her faint deliberate tones.

'By gosh, an' it's well thou'st spoke on 'em; a was as clean forgettin' it as iver could be. A met Nanny Corney i' Monkshaven last neet, and she axed me for t' let our Sylvia come o'

New-Year's Eve, an' see Molly an' her man, that'n as is wed beyond Newcassel, they'll be over at her feyther's, for t' New-Year, an' there's to be a merry-making.'

Sylvia's colour came, her eyes brightened, she would have liked to go; but the thought of her mother came across her, and her features fell. Her mother's eye caught the look and the change, and knew what both meant as well as if Sylvia had spoken out.

'Thursday se'nnight,' said she. 'I'll be rare and strong by then, and Sylvie shall go play hersen: she's been nurse-tending long enough.'

'You're but weakly yet,' said Philip shortly; he did not intend to say it, but the words seemed to come out in spite of himself.

'A said as our lass should come, God willin', if she only came and went, an' thee goin' on sprightly, old 'ooman. An' a'll turn nurse-tender mysen for t' occasion, 'special if thou can stand t' good honest smell o' whisky by then. So, my lass, get up thy smart clothes, and cut t' best on 'em out,* as becomes a Preston. Maybe, a'll fetch thee home, an' maybe Philip will convoy thee, for Nanny Corney bade thee to t' merry-making, as well. She said her measter would be seein' thee about t' wool afore then.'

'I don't think as I can go,' said Philip, secretly pleased to know that he had the opportunity in his power; 'I'm half bound to go wi' Hester Rose and her mother to t' watch-night.'*

'Is Hester a Methodee?' asked Sylvia in surprise.

'No she's neither a Methodee, nor a Friend, nor a Church person; but she's a turn for serious things, choose wherever they're found.'

'Well, then,' said good-natured farmer Robson, only seeing the surface of things, 'a'll make shift* to fetch Sylvie back fra' t' merry-making, an' thee an' thy young woman can go to t' prayer-makin'; it's every man to his taste, say I.'

But in spite of his half-promise, nay against his natural inclination, Philip was lured to the Corneys' by the thought of meeting Sylvia, of watching her and exulting in her superiority in pretty looks and ways to all the other girls likely to be assembled. Besides (he told his conscience) he was pledged to his aunt to watch over Sylvia like a brother. So in the interval before New-Year's Eve, he silently revelled as much as any young girl in the anticipation of the happy coming time.

At this hour, all the actors in this story having played out their parts and gone to their rest, there is something touching in recording the futile efforts made by Philip to win from Sylvia the love he yearned for. But, at the time, any one who had watched him might have been amused to see the grave, awkward, plain young man studying patterns and colours for a new waistcoat, with his head a little on one side, after the meditative manner common to those who are choosing a new article of dress. They might have smiled could they have read in his imagination the frequent rehearsals of the coming evening, when he and she should each be dressed in their gala attire, to spend a few hours under a bright, festive aspect, among people whose company would oblige them to assume a new demeanour towards each other, not so familiar as their everyday manner, but allowing more scope for the expression of rustic gallantry. Philip had so seldom been to anything of the kind, that, even had Sylvia not been going, he would have felt a kind of shy excitement at the prospect of anything so unusual. But, indeed, if Sylvia had not been going, it is very probable that Philip's rigid conscience might have been aroused to the question whether such parties did not savour too much of the world for him to form one in them.

As it was, however, the facts to him were simply these. He was going and she was going. The day before, he had hurried off to Haytersbank Farm with a small paper parcel in his pocket – a ribbon with a little briar-rose pattern running upon it for Sylvia. It was the first thing he had ever ventured to give her – the first thing of the kind would, perhaps, be more accurate; for when he had first begun to teach her any lessons, he had given her Mavor's Spelling-book,* but that he might have done, out of zeal for knowledge, to any dunce of a little girl of his acquaintance. This ribbon was quite a different kind of present; he touched it tenderly, as if he were caressing it, when he thought of her wearing it; the briar-rose (sweetness and thorns) seemed to be the very flower for her; the soft, green ground on which the pink and brown pattern ran, was just the colour to show off her complexion. And she would in a way belong to him: her cousin, her mentor,* her chaperone, her lover! While others only admired, he might hope to appropriate; for of late they had been such happy friends! Her mother approved of him, her father liked him. A few months, perhaps only a few weeks more of self-restraint, and then he might go and speak openly of his wishes, and what he had to offer. For he had resolved, with the quiet force of his character, to wait until all was finally settled between him and his masters, before he declared himself to either Sylvia or her parents. The interval was spent in patient, silent endeavours to recommend himself to her.

He had to give his ribbon to his aunt in charge for Sylvia, and that was a disappointment to his fancy, although he tried to reason himself into thinking that it was better so. He had not time to wait for her return from some errand on which she had gone, for he was daily more and more occupied with the affairs of the shop.

Sylvia made many a promise to her mother, and more to herself, that she would not stay late at the party, but she might go as early as she liked; and before the December daylight had faded away, Sylvia presented herself at the Corneys'. She was to come early in order to help to set out the supper, which was arranged in the large old flagged parlour, which served as best bed-room as well. It opened out of the house-place, and was the sacred room of the house, as chambers of a similar description are still considered in retired farm-houses in the north of England. They are used on occasions like the one now described for purposes of hospitality; but in the state bed, overshadowing so large a portion of the floor, the births and, as far as may be, the deaths, of the household take place. At the Corneys', the united efforts of some former generation of the family had produced patchwork curtains and coverlet; and patchwork was patchwork in those days, before the early Yates and Peels* had found out the secret of printing the parsley-leaf. Scraps of costly Indian chintzes and palempours* were intermixed with commoner black and red calico in minute hexagons; and the variety of patterns served for the useful purpose of promoting conversation as well as the more obvious one of displaying the workwoman's taste. Sylvia, for instance, began at once to her old friend, Molly Brunton, who had accompanied her into this chamber to take off her hat and cloak, with a remark on one of the chintzes. Stooping over the counterpane, with a face into which the flush would come whether or no, she said to Molly, –

'Dear! I never seed this one afore – this – for all t' world like th' eyes in a peacock's tail.'

'Thou's seen it many a time and oft, lass. But weren't thou surprised to find Charley here? We picked him up at Shields, quite by surprise like; and when Brunton and me said as we was comin' here, nought would serve him but comin' with us, for t' see t' new year in. It's a pity as your mother's ta'en this time for t' fall ill and want yo' back so early.'

Sylvia had taken off her hat and cloak by this time, and began to help Molly and a younger unmarried sister in laying out the substantial supper.

'Here,' continued Mrs Brunton; 'stick a bit o' holly i' yon pig's mouth, that's the way we do things i' Newcassel; but folks is so behindhand in Monkshaven. It's a fine thing to live in a large town, Sylvia; an' if yo're looking out for a husband, I'd advise yo' to tak' one as lives in a town. I feel as if I were buried alive comin' back here, such an out-o'-t'-way place after t' Side, wheere there's many a hundred carts and carriages goes past in a day. I've a great mind for t' tak yo two lassies back wi' me, and let yo' see a bit o' t' world; maybe, I may yet.'

Her sister Bessy looked much pleased with this plan, but Sylvia was rather inclined to take offence at Molly's patronizing ways, and replied, –

'I'm none so fond o' noise and bustle; why, yo'll not be able to hear yoursels speak wi' all them carts and carriages. I'd rayther bide at home; let alone that mother can't spare me.'

It was, perhaps, a rather ungracious way of answering Molly Brunton's speech, and so she felt it to be, although her invitation had been none of the most courteously worded. She irritated Sylvia still further by repeating her last words, –

'"Mother can't spare me;" why, mother'll have to spare thee sometime, when t' time for wedding comes.'

'I'm none going to be wed,' said Sylvia; 'and if I were, I'd niver go far fra' mother.'

'Eh! what a spoilt darling it is. How Brunton will laugh when I tell him about yo'; Brunton's a rare one for laughin'. It's a great thing to have got such a merry man for a husband. Why! he has his joke for every one as comes into t' shop; and he'll ha' somethin' funny to say to everything this evenin'.'

Bessy saw that Sylvia was annoyed, and, with more delicacy than her sister, she tried to turn the conversation.

'That's a pretty ribbon in thy hair, Sylvia; I'd like to have one o' t' same pattern. Feyther likes pickled walnuts stuck about t' round o' beef, Molly.'

'I know what I'm about,' replied Mrs Brunton with a toss of her married head.

Bessy resumed her inquiry.

'Is there any more to be had wheere that come fra', Sylvia?'

'I don't know,' replied Sylvia. 'It come fra' Foster's, and yo' can ask.'

'What might it cost?' said Bessy, fingering an end of it to test its quality.

'I can't tell,' said Sylvia, 'it were a present.'

'Niver mak' ado about t' price,' said Molly; 'I'll gi'e thee enough on 't to tie up thy hair, just like Sylvia's. Only thou hastn't such wealth o' curls as she has; it'll niver look t' same i' thy straight locks. And who might it be as give it thee, Sylvia?' asked the unscrupulous, if good-natured Molly.

'My cousin Philip, him as is shopman at Foster's,' said Sylvia, innocently. But it was far too good an opportunity for the exercise of Molly's kind of wit for her to pass over.

'Oh, oh! our cousin Philip, is it? and he'll not be living so far away from your mother? I've no need be a witch to put two and two together. He's a coming here to-night, isn't he, Bessy?'

'I wish yo' wouldn't talk so, Molly,' said Sylvia; 'me and Philip is good enough friends, but we niver think on each other in that way; leastways, I don't—'

'(Sweet butter! now that's my mother's old-fashioned way; as if folks must eat sweet butter now-a-days, because her mother did!) That way,' continued Molly, in the manner that annoyed Sylvia so much, repeating her words as if for the purpose of laughing at them. "That way?" and pray what is t' way yo're speaking on? I niver said nought about marrying, did I, that yo' need look so red and shamefaced about yo'r cousin Philip? But, as Brunton says, if t' cap fits yo', put it on. I'm glad he's comin' to-night tho', for as I'm done makin' love and courtin', it's next best t' watch other folks; an' yo'r face, Sylvia, has letten me into a secret, as I'd some glimpses on afore I was wed.'

Sylvia secretly determined not to speak a word more to Philip than she could help, and wondered how she could ever have liked Molly at all, much less have made a companion of her. The table was now laid out, and nothing remained but to criticise the arrangement a little.

Bessy was full of admiration.

'Theere, Molly!' said she. 'Yo' niver seed more vittle brought together i' Newcassel, I'll be bound; there'll be above half a hundredweight o' butcher's meat, beside pies and custards. I've eaten no dinner these two days for thinking on 't; it's been a weary burden on my mind, but it's off now I see how well it looks. I told mother not to come near it till we'd spread it all out, and now I'll go fetch her.'

Bessy ran off into the house-place.

'It's well enough in a country kind o' way,' said Molly, with the faint approbation of condescension. 'But if I'd thought on, I'd ha' brought 'em down a beast or two done i' sponge-cake, wi' currants for his eyes to give t' table an air.'

The door was opened, and Bessy came in smiling and blushing with proud pleasure. Her mother followed her on tip-toe, smoothing down her apron, and with her voice subdued to a whisper: –

'Ay, my lass, it *is* fine! But dunnot mak' an ado about it, let 'em think it's just our common way. If any one says aught about how good t' vittle is, tak' it calm, and say we'r better i' t' house, – it'll mak' 'em eat wi' a better appetite, and think the more on us. Sylvie, I'm much beholden t' ye for comin' so early, and helpin' t' lasses, but yo' mun come in t' house-place now, t' folks is gatherin', an' yo'r cousin's been asking after yo' a'ready.'

Molly gave her a nudge, which made Sylvia's face go all aflame with angry embarrassment. She was conscious that the watching which Molly had threatened her with began directly; for Molly went up to her husband, and whispered something to him which set him off in a chuckling laugh, and Sylvia was aware that his eyes followed her about with knowing looks all the evening. She would hardly speak to Philip, and pretended not to see his outstretched hand, but passed on to the chimney-corner, and tried to shelter herself behind the broad back of farmer Corney, who had no notion of relinquishing his customary place for all the young people who ever came to the house, – or for any old people either, for that matter. It was his household throne, and there he sat with no more idea of abdicating in favour of any comer than King George at St. James's.* But he was glad to see his friends; and had paid them the unwonted compliment of shaving on a week-day, and putting on his Sunday coat. The united efforts of wife and children had failed to persuade him to make any farther change in his attire; to all their arguments on this head he had replied, –

'Them as doesn't like t' see me i' my work-a-day wescut* and breeches may bide away.'

It was the longest sentence he said that day, but he repeated it several times over. He was glad enough to see all the young people, but they were not 'of his kidney',* as he expressed it to himself, and he did not feel any call upon himself to entertain them. He left that to his bustling wife, all smartness and smiles, and to his daughters and son-in-law. His efforts at hospitality consisted in sitting still, smoking his pipe; when any one came, he took it out of his mouth for an instant, and nodded his head in a cheerful friendly way, without a word of speech; and then returned to his smoking with the greater relish for the moment's intermission. He thought to himself: –

'They're a set o' young chaps as thinks more on t' lasses than on baccy; – they'll find out their mistake in time; give 'em time, give 'em time.'

And before eight o'clock, he went as quietly as a man of twelve stone can upstairs to bed, having made a previous arrangement with his wife that she should bring him up about two pounds of spiced beef, and a hot tumbler of stiff grog. But at the beginning of the evening he formed a good screen for Sylvia, who was rather a favourite with the old man, for twice he spoke to her.

'Feyther smokes?'

'Yes,' said Sylvia.

'Reach me t' baccy-box, my lass.'

And that was all the conversation that passed between her and her nearest neighbour for the first quarter of an hour after she came into company.

But, for all her screen, she felt a pair of eyes were fixed upon her with a glow of admiration deepening their honest brightness. Somehow, look in what direction she would, she caught the glance of those eyes before she could see anything else. So she played with her apron-strings, and tried not to feel so conscious. There were another pair of eyes, – not such beautiful, sparkling eyes, – deep-set, earnest, sad, nay, even gloomy, watching her every movement; but of this she was not aware. Philip had not recovered from the rebuff she had given him by refusing his offered hand, and was standing still, in angry silence, when Mrs Corney thrust a young woman just arrived upon his attention.

'Come, Measter Hepburn, here's Nancy Pratt wi'out ev'n a soul to speak t' her, an' yo' mopin' theere. She says she knows yo' by sight fra' having dealt at Foster's these six year. See if yo' can't find summut t' say t' each other, for I mun go pour out tea. Dixons, an' Walkers, an' Elliotts, an' Smiths is come,' said she, marking off the families on her fingers, as she looked round and called over their names; 'an' there's only Will Latham an' his two sisters, and Roger Harbottle, an' Taylor t' come; an' they'll turn up afore tea's ended.'

So she went off to her duty at the one table, which, placed alongside of the dresser, was the only article of furniture left in the middle of the room: all the seats being arranged as close to the four walls as could be managed. The candles of those days gave but a faint light compared to the light of the immense fire, which it was a point of hospitality to keep at the highest roaring, blazing pitch; the young women occupied the seats, with the exception of two or three of the elder ones, who, in an eager desire to show their capability, insisted on helping Mrs Corney in her duties, very much to her annoyance, as there were certain little contrivances for eking out cream, and adjusting the strength of the cups of tea to the worldly position of the intended drinkers, which she did not like every one to see. The young men, – whom tea did not embolden, and who had as yet had no chance of stronger liquor, – clustered in rustic shyness round the door, not speaking even to themselves, except now and then, when one, apparently the wag of the party, made some whispered remark, which set them all off laughing; but in a minute they checked themselves, and passed the back of their hands across their mouths to compose that unlucky feature, and then some would try to fix their eyes on the rafters of the ceiling, in a manner which was decorous if rather abstracted from the business in hand. Most of these were young farmers, with whom Philip had nothing in common, and from whom, in shy reserve, he had withdrawn himself when he first came in. But now he wished himself among them sooner than set to talk to Nancy Pratt, when he had nothing to say. And yet he might have had a companion less to his mind, for she was a decent young woman of a sober age, less inclined to giggle than many of the younger ones. But all the time that he was making commonplace remarks to her he was wondering if he had offended Sylvia, and why she would not shake hands with him, and this pre-occupation of his thoughts did not make him an agreeable companion. Nancy Pratt, who had been engaged for some years to a mate of a whaling-ship, perceived something of his state of mind, and took no offence at it; on the contrary, she tried to give him pleasure by admiring Sylvia.

'I've often heerd tell on her,' said she, 'but I niver thought she'd be so pretty, and so staid and quiet-like too. T' most part o' girls as has looks like hers are always gape-gazing* to catch other folks's eyes, and see what is thought on 'em; but she looks just like a child, a bit flustered wi' comin' into company, and gettin' into as dark a corner and bidin' as still as she can.'

Just then Sylvia lifted up her long, dark lashes, and catching the same glance which she had so often met before – Charley Kinraid was standing talking to Brunton on the opposite side of the fire-place – she started back into the shadow as if she had not expected it, and in so doing spilt her tea all over her gown. She could almost have cried, she felt herself so awkward, and as if everything was going wrong with her; she thought that every one would think she had never been in company before, and did not know how to behave; and while she was thus fluttered and crimson, she saw through her tearful eyes Kinraid on his knees before her, wiping her gown with his silk pocket handkerchief, and heard him speaking through all the buzz of commiserating voices.

'Your cupboard handle is so much i' th' way, – I hurt my elbow against it only this very afternoon.'

So perhaps it was no clumsiness of hers, – as they would all know, now, since he had so skilfully laid the blame somewhere else; and after all it turned out that her accident had been the means of bringing him across to her side, which was much more pleasant than having him opposite, staring at her; for now he began to talk to her, and this was very pleasant, although she was rather embarrassed at their *tête-à-tête* at first.

'I did not know you again when I first saw you,' said he, in a tone which implied a good deal more than was uttered in words.

'I knowed yo' at once,' she replied, softly, and then she blushed and played with her apron string, and wondered if she ought to have confessed to the clearness of her recollection.

'You're grown up into – well, perhaps it's not manners to say what you're grown into – anyhow, I shan't forget yo' again.'

More playing with her apron string, and head hung still lower down, though the corners of her mouth would go up in a shy smile of pleasure. Philip watched it all as greedily as if it gave him delight.

'Yo'r father, he'll be well and hearty, I hope?' asked Charley.

'Yes,' replied Sylvia, and then she wished she could originate some remark; he would think her so stupid if she just kept on saying such little short bits of speeches, and if he thought her stupid he might perhaps go away again to his former place.

But he was quite far enough gone in love of her beauty, and pretty modest ways, not to care much whether she talked or no, so long as she showed herself so pleasingly conscious of his close neighbourhood.

'I must come and see the old gentleman; and your mother, too,' he added more slowly, for he remembered that his visits last year had not been quite so much welcomed by Bell Robson as by her husband; perhaps it was because of the amount of drink which he and Daniel managed to get through of an evening. He resolved this year to be more careful to please the mother of Sylvia.

When tea was ended there was a great bustle and shifting of places, while Mrs Corney and her daughters carried out trays full of used cups, and great platters of uneaten bread and butter into the back-kitchen, to be washed up after the guests were gone. Just because she was so conscious that she did not want to move, and break up the little conversation between herself and Kinraid, Sylvia forced herself to be as active in the service going on as became a friend of the house; and she was too much her mother's own daughter to feel comfortable at leaving all the things in the disorder which to the Corney girls was second nature.

'This milk mun go back to t' dairy, I reckon,' said she, loading herself with milk and cream.

'Niver fash thysel'* about it,' said Nelly Corney, 'Christmas comes but onest a year, if it does go sour; and mother said she'd have a game at forfeits* first thing after tea to loosen folks's tongues, and mix up t' lads and lasses, so come along.'

But Sylvia steered her careful way to the cold chill of the dairy, and would not be satisfied till she had carried away all the unused provision into some fresher air than that heated by the fires and ovens used for the long day's cooking of pies and cakes and much roast meat.

When they came back a round of red-faced 'lads,' as young men up to five-and-thirty are called in Lancashire and Yorkshire if they are not married before, and lasses, whose age was not to be defined, were playing at some country game, in which the women were apparently more interested than the men, who looked shamefaced, and afraid of each other's ridicule. Mrs Corney, however, knew how to remedy this, and at a sign from her a great jug of beer was brought in. This jug was the pride of her heart, and was in the shape of a fat man in white knee-breeches, and a three-cornered hat; with one arm he supported the pipe in his broad, smiling mouth, and the other was placed akimbo and formed the handle. There was also a great china punch-bowl filled with grog made after an old ship-receipt current in these parts, but not too strong, because if their visitors had too much to drink at that early part of the evening 'it would spoil t' fun', as Nelly Corney had observed. Her father, however, after the notions of hospitality prevalent at that time in higher circles had stipulated that each man should have 'enough' before he left the house; enough meaning in Monkshaven parlance the liberty of getting drunk, if they thought fit to do it.

Before long one of the lads was seized with a fit of admiration for Toby* – the name of the old gentleman who contained liquor – and went up to the tray for a closer inspection. He was speedily followed by other amateurs of curious earthenware; and by-and-by Mr Brunton (who had been charged by his mother-in-law with the due supplying of liquor – by his father-in-law that every man should have his fill, and by his wife and her sisters that no one should have too much, at any rate at the beginning of the evening,) thought fit to carry out Toby to be replenished; and a faster spirit of enjoyment and mirth began to reign in the room.

Kinraid was too well seasoned to care what amount of liquor he drank; Philip had what was called a weak head, and disliked muddling himself with drink because of the immediate conse-quence of intense feelings of irritability, and the more distant one of a racking headache next day; so both these two preserved very much the same demeanour they had held at the beginning of the evening.

Sylvia was by all acknowledged and treated as the belle. When they played at blind-man's-buff, go where she would, she was always caught; she was called out repeatedly to do what was required in any game, as if all had a pleasure in seeing her light figure and deft ways. She was sufficiently pleased with this to have got over her shyness with all except Charley. When others paid her their rustic compliments she tossed her head, and made her little saucy repartees; but when he said something low and flattering, it was too honey-sweet to her heart to be thrown off thus. And, somehow, the more she yielded to this fascination the more she avoided Philip. He did not speak flatteringly – he did not pay compliments – he watched her with discontented, longing eyes, and grew more inclined every moment, as he remembered his anticipation, of a happy evening, to cry out in his heart *vanitas vanitatum.**

And now came crying the forfeits. Molly Brunton knelt down, her face buried in her mother's lap; the latter took out the forfeits one by one, and as she held them up, said the accustomed formula, –

'A fine thing and very fine thing, what must he (or she) do who owns this thing.'

One or two had been told to kneel to the prettiest, bow to the wittiest, and kiss those they loved best; others had had to bite an inch off the poker, or such plays upon words. And now came Sylvia's pretty new ribbon* that Philip had given her (he almost longed to snatch it out of Mrs Corney's hands and burn it before all their faces, so annoyed was he with the whole affair).

'A fine thing and a very fine thing – a most particular fine thing – choose how she came by it. What must she do as owns this thing?'

'She must blow out t' candle and kiss t' candlestick.'

In one instant Kinraid had hold of the only candle within reach, all the others had been put up high on inaccessible shelves and other places. Sylvia went up and blew out the candle, and before the sudden partial darkness was over he had taken the candle into his fingers, and, according to the traditional meaning of the words, was in the place of the candlestick, and as such was to be kissed. Every one laughed at innocent Sylvia's face as the meaning of her penance came into it, every one but Philip, who almost choked.

'I'm candlestick,' said Kinraid, with less of triumph in his voice than he would have had with any other girl in the room.

'Yo' mun kiss t' candlestick,' cried the Corneys, 'or yo'll niver get yo'r ribbon back.'

'And she sets a deal o' store by that ribbon,' said Molly Brunton, maliciously.

'I'll none kiss t' candlestick, nor him either,' said Sylvia, in a low voice of determination, turning away, full of confusion.

'Yo'll not get yo'r ribbon if yo' dunnot,' cried one and all.

'I don't care for t' ribbon,' said she, flashing up with a look at her tormentors, now her back was turned to Kinraid. 'An' I wunnot play any more at such like games,' she added, with fresh indignation rising in her heart as she took her old place in the corner of the room a little away from the rest.

Philip's spirits rose, and he yearned to go to her and tell her how he approved of her conduct. Alas, Philip! Sylvia, though as modest a girl as ever lived, was no prude, and had been brought up in simple, straightforward country ways; and with any other young man, excepting, perhaps, Philip's self, she would have thought no more of making a rapid pretence of kissing the hand or cheek of the temporary 'candlestick', than our ancestresses did in a much higher rank on similar occasions. Kinraid, though mortified by his public rejection, was more conscious of this than the inexperienced Philip; he resolved not to be baulked, and watched his opportunity. For the time he went on playing as if Sylvia's conduct had not affected him in the least, and as if he was hardly aware of her defection from the game. As she saw others submitting, quite as a matter of course, to similar penances, she began to be angry with herself for having thought twice about it, and almost to dislike herself for the strange consciousness which had made it at the time seem impossible to do what she was told. Her eyes kept filling with tears at her isolated position in the gay party, the thought of what a fool she had made of herself kept recurring to her mind; but no one saw her, she thought, thus crying; and, ashamed to be discovered when the party should pause in their game, she stole round behind them into the great chamber in which she had helped to lay out the supper, with the intention of bathing her eyes, and taking a drink of water. One instant Charley Kinraid was missing from the circle of which he was the life and soul; and then back he came with an air of satisfaction on his face, intelligible enough to those who had seen his game; but unnoticed by Philip, who, amidst the perpetual noise and movements around him, had not perceived Sylvia's leaving the room, until she came back at the end of about a quarter of an hour, looking lovelier than ever, her complexion brilliant, her eyes drooping, her hair neatly and freshly arranged, tied with a brown ribbon instead of that she was supposed to have forfeited. She looked as if she did not wish her return to be noticed, stealing softly behind the romping lads and lasses with noiseless motions, and altogether such a contrast to them in her cool freshness and modest neatness, that both Kinraid and Philip found it difficult to keep their eyes off her. But the former had a secret triumph in his heart which enabled him to go on with his merry-making as if it absorbed him; while Philip dropped out of the crowd and came up to where she was standing silently by Mrs Corney, who, arms akimbo, was laughing at the frolic and fun around her. Sylvia started a little when Philip spoke, and kept her soft eyes averted from him after the first glance; she answered him shortly, but with unaccustomed gentleness. He had only asked her when she would like him to take her home; and she, a little surprised at the idea of going home when to her the evening seemed only beginning, had answered –

'Go home? I don't know! It's New Year's eve!'

'Ay! but yo'r mother'll lie awake till yo' come home, Sylvie!'

But Mrs Corney, having heard his question, broke in with all sorts of upbraidings. 'Go home! Not see t' New Year in! Why, what should take 'em home these six hours? Wasn't there a moon as clear as day? and did such a time as this come often? And were they to break up the party before the New Year came in? And was there not supper, with a spiced round of beef that had been in pickle pretty nigh sin' Martinmas, and hams, and mince-pies, and what not? And if they thought any evil of her master's going to bed, or that by that early retirement he meant to imply that he did not bid his friends welcome, why he would not stay up beyond eight o'clock for King George upon his throne, as he'd tell them soon enough, if they'd only step upstairs and ask him. Well; she knowed what it was to want a daughter when she was ailing, so she'd say nought more, but hasten supper.'

And this idea now took possession of Mrs Corney's mind, for she would not willingly allow one of her guests to leave before they had done justice to her preparations; and, cutting her speech short, she hastily left Sylvia and Philip together.

His heart beat fast; his feeling towards her had never been so strong or so distinct as since her refusal to kiss the 'candlestick'. He was on the point of speaking, of saying something explicitly tender, when the wooden trencher which the party were using at their play, came bowling between him and Sylvia, and spun out its little period right betwixt them. Every one was moving from chair to chair, and when the bustle was over Sylvia was seated at some distance from him, and he left standing outside the circle, as if he were not playing. In fact, Sylvia had unconsciously taken his place as actor in the game while he remained spectator, and, as it turned out, an auditor of a conversation not intended for his ears. He was wedged against the wall, close to the great eight-day clock, with its round moon-like smiling face forming a ludicrous contrast to his long, sallow, grave countenance, which was pretty much at the same level above the sanded floor. Before him sat Molly Brunton and one of her sisters, their heads close together in too deep talk to attend to the progress of the game. Philip's attention was caught by the words –

'I'll lay any wager he kissed her when he ran off into t' parlour.'

'She's so coy she'd niver let him,' replied Bessy Corney.

'She couldn't help hersel'; and for all she looks so demure and prim now' (and then both heads were turned in the direction of Sylvia), 'I'm as sure as I'm born that Charley is not t' chap to lose his forfeit; and yet yo' see he says nought more about it, and she's left off being 'feared of him.'

There was something in Sylvia's look, ay, and in Charley Kinraid's, too, that shot conviction into Philip's mind. He watched them incessantly during the interval before supper; they were intimate, and yet shy with each other, in a manner that enraged while it bewildered Philip. What was Charley saying to her in that whispered voice, as they passed each other? Why did they linger near each other? Why did Sylvia look so dreamily happy, so startled at every call of the game, as if recalled from some pleasant idea? Why did Kinraid's eyes always seek her while hers were averted, or downcast, and her cheeks all a-flame? Philip's dark brow grew darker as he gazed. He, too, started when Mrs Corney, close at his elbow, bade him go in to

supper along with some of the elder ones, who were not playing;
for the parlour was not large enough to hold all at once, even
with the squeezing and cramming, and sitting together on chairs,
which was not at all out of etiquette at Monkshaven. Philip was
too reserved to express his disappointment and annoyance at
being thus arrested in his painful watch over Sylvia; but he had
no appetite for the good things set before him, and found it hard
work to smile a sickly smile when called upon by Josiah Pratt
for applause at some country joke. When supper was ended,
there was some little discussion between Mrs Corney and her
son-in-law as to whether the different individuals of the company should be called upon for songs or stories, as was the wont
at such convivial meetings. Brunton had been helping his
mother-in-law in urging people to eat, heaping their plates over
their shoulders with unexpected good things, filling the glasses
at the upper end of the table, and the mugs which supplied the
deficiency of glasses at the lower. And now, every one being
satisfied, not to say stuffed to repletion, the two who had been
attending to their wants stood still, hot and exhausted.

'They're a'most stawed,'* said Mrs Corney, with a pleased
smile. 'It'll be manners' t' ask some one as knows how to sing.'

'It may be manners for full men, but not for fasting,' replied
Brunton. 'Folks in t' next room will be wanting the victual, and
singing is allays out o' tune to empty bellies.'

'But there's them here as'll take it ill if they're not asked. I
heerd Josiah Pratt a-clearing his throat not a minute ago, an' he
thinks as much on his singin' as a cock does on his crowin'.'

'If one sings I'm afeard all on 'em will like to hear their own
pipes.'*

But their dilemma was solved by Bessy Corney, who opened
the door to see if the hungry ones outside might not come in for
their share of the entertainment; and in they rushed, bright and
riotous, scarcely giving the first party time to rise from their
seats ere they took their places. One or two young men, released
from all their previous shyness, helped Mrs Corney and her
daughters to carry off such dishes as were actually empty. There
was no time for changing or washing of plates; but then, as Mrs
Corney laughingly observed, –

'We're a' on us friends, and some on us mayhap sweethearts;
so no need to be particular about plates. Them as gets clean

ones is lucky; and them as doesn't, and cannot put up w' plates that has been used, mun go without.'

It seemed to be Philip's luck this night to be pent up in places; for again the space between the benches and the wall was filled up by the in-rush before he had time to make his way out; and all he could do was to sit quiet where he was.

But between the busy heads and over-reaching arms he could see Charley and Sylvia, sitting close together, talking and listening more than eating. She was in a new strange state of happiness not to be reasoned about, or accounted for, but in a state of more exquisite feeling than she had ever experienced before; when, suddenly lifting her eyes, she caught Philip's face of extreme displeasure.

'Oh,' said she, 'I must go. There's Philip looking at me so.'

'Philip!' said Kinraid, with a sudden frown upon his face. 'My cousin,' she replied, instinctively comprehending what had flashed into his mind, and anxious to disclaim the suspicion of having a lover. 'Mother told him to see me home, and he's noan one for staying up late.'

'But you needn't go. I'll see yo' home.'

'Mother's but ailing,' said Sylvia, a little conscience-smitten at having so entirely forgotten everything in the delight of the present, 'and I said I wouldn't be late.'

'And do you allays keep to your word?' asked he, with a tender meaning in his tone.

'Allays; leastways I think so,' replied she, blushing.

'Then if I ask you not to forget me, and you give me your word, I may be sure you'll keep it.'

'It wasn't I as forgot you,' said Sylvia, so softly as not to be heard by him.

He tried to make her repeat what she had said, but she would not, and he could only conjecture that it was something more tell-tale than she liked to say again, and that alone was very charming to him.

'I shall walk home with you,' said he, as Sylvia at last rose to depart, warned by a further glimpse of Philip's angry face.

'No!' said she, hastily, 'I can't do with yo';' for somehow she felt the need of pacifying Philip, and knew in her heart that a third person joining their *tête-à-tête* walk would only increase his displeasure.

'Why not?' said Charley, sharply.

'Oh! I don't know, only please don't!'

By this time her cloak and hood were on, and she was slowly making her way down her side of the room followed by Charley, and often interrupted by indignant remonstrances against her departure, and the early breaking-up of the party. Philip stood, hat in hand, in the doorway between the kitchen and parlour, watching her so intently that he forgot to be civil, and drew many a jest and gibe upon him for his absorption in his pretty cousin.

When Sylvia reached him, he said, –

'Yo're ready at last, are yo'?'

'Yes,' she replied, in her little beseeching tone. 'Yo've not been wanting to go long, han yo'? I ha' but just eaten my supper.'

'Yo've been so full of talk, that's been the reason your supper lasted so long. That fellow's none going wi' us?' said he sharply, as he saw Kinraid rummaging for his cap in a heap of men's clothes, thrown into the back-kitchen.

'No,' said Sylvia, in affright at Philip's fierce look and passionate tone. 'I telled him not.'

But at that moment the heavy outer door was opened by Daniel Robson himself – bright, broad, and rosy, a jolly impersonation of Winter. His large drover's coat was covered with snow-flakes, and through the black frame of the doorway might be seen a white waste world of sweeping fell and field, with the dark air filled with the pure down-fall. Robson stamped his snow-laden feet and shook himself well, still standing on the mat, and letting a cold frosty current of fresh air into the great warm kitchen. He laughed at them all before he spoke.

'It's a coud new year as I'm lettin' in though it's noan t' new year yet. Yo'll a' be snowed up, as sure as my name's Dannel, if yo' stop for twel' o'clock. Yo'd better mak' haste and go whoam. Why, Charley, my lad! how beest ta? who'd ha' thought o' seeing thee i' these parts again! Nay, missus, nay, t' new year mun find its way int' t' house by itsel' for me; for a ha' promised my oud woman to bring Sylvie whoam as quick as maybe; she's lyin' awake and frettin' about t' snow and what not. Thank yo' kindly, missus, but a'll tak' nought to eat; just a drop o' somethin' hot to keep out coud, and wish yo' a' the compliments o' the season. Philip, my man, yo'll not be sorry to be spared t' walk round by Haytersbank such a neet. My missus were i' such

a way about Sylvie that a thought a'd just step off mysel', and
have a peep at yo' a', and bring her some wraps. Yo'r sheep will
be a' folded,* a reckon, Measter Pratt, for there'll niver be a
nibble o' grass o' be seen this two month, accordin' to my
readin'; and a've been at sea long enough, and on land long
enough, t' know signs and wonders.* It's good stuff that, any
way, and worth comin' for,' after he had gulped down a
tumblerful of half-and-half grog. 'Kinraid, if ta doesn't come
and see me afore thou'rt many days ouder, thee and me'll have
words. Come, Sylvie, what art ta about, keepin' me here? Here's
Mistress Corney mixin' me another jorum.* Well, this time a'll
give "T' married happy, and t' single wed!"'

Sylvia was all this while standing by her father quite ready for
departure, and not a little relieved by his appearance as her
convoy home.

'I'm ready to see Haytersbank to-night, master!' said Kinraid,
with easy freedom – a freedom which Philip envied, but could
not have imitated, although he was deeply disappointed at the
loss of his walk with Sylvia, when he had intended to exercise
the power his aunt had delegated to him of remonstrance if her
behaviour had been light or thoughtless, and of warning if he
saw cause to disapprove of any of her associates.

After the Robsons had left, a blank fell upon both Charley
and Philip. In a few minutes, however, the former, accustomed
to prompt decision, resolved that she and no other should be
his wife. Accustomed to popularity among women, and well
versed in the incipient signs of their liking for him, he anticipated
no difficulty in winning her. Satisfied with the past, and pleasantly hopeful about the future, he found it easy to turn his
attention to the next prettiest girl in the room, and to make the
whole gathering bright with his ready good temper and buoyant
spirit.

Mrs Corney had felt it her duty to press Philip to stay, now
that, as she said, he had no one but himself to see home, and the
new year so near coming in. To any one else in the room she
would have added the clinching argument, 'A shall take it very
unkind if yo' go now'; but somehow she could not say this, for
in truth Philip's look showed that he would be but a wet blanket
on the merriment of the party. So, with as much civility as could
be mustered up between them, he took leave. Shutting the door
behind him, he went out into the dreary night, and began his

lonesome walk back to Monkshaven. The cold sleet almost
blinded him as the sea-wind drove it straight in his face; it cut
against him as it was blown with drifting force. The roar of the
wintry sea came borne on the breeze; there was more light from
the whitened ground than from that dark laden sky above. The
field-paths would have been a matter of perplexity, had it not
been for the well-known gaps in the dyke-side, which showed
the whitened land beyond, between the two dark stone walls.
Yet he went clear and straight along his way, having unconsciously left all guidance to the animal instinct which co-exists
with the human soul, and sometimes takes strange charge of the
human body, when all the nobler powers of the individual are
absorbed in acute suffering. At length he was in the lane, toiling
up the hill, from which, by day, Monkshaven might be seen.
Now all features of the landscape before him were lost in the
darkness of night, against which the white flakes came closer
and nearer, thicker and faster. On a sudden, the bells of
Monkshaven church rang out a welcome to the new year,
1796.* From the direction of the wind, it seemed as if the sound
was flung with strength and power right into Philip's face. He
walked down the hill to its merry sound – its merry sound, his
heavy heart. As he entered the long High Street of Monkshaven
he could see the watching lights put out in parlour, chamber, or
kitchen. The new year had come, and expectation was ended.
Reality had begun.

He turned to the right, into the court where he lodged with
Alice Rose. There was a light still burning there, and cheerful
voices were heard. He opened the door; Alice, her daughter, and
Coulson stood as if awaiting him. Hester's wet cloak hung on a
chair before the fire; she had her hood on, for she and Coulson
had been to the watch-night.

The solemn excitement of the services had left its traces upon
her countenance and in her mind. There was a spiritual light in
her usually shadowed eyes, and a slight flush on her pale cheek.
Merely personal and self-conscious feelings were merged in a
loving good-will to all her fellow-creatures. Under the influence
of this large charity, she forgot her habitual reserve, and came
forward as Philip entered to meet him with her New Year's
wishes – wishes that she had previously interchanged with the
other two.

'A happy New Year to you, Philip, and may God have you in his keeping all the days thereof!'

He took her hand, and shook it warmly in reply. The flush on her cheek deepened as she withdrew it. Alice Rose said something curtly about the lateness of the hour and her being much tired; and then she and her daughter went upstairs to the front chamber, and Philip and Coulson to that which they shared at the back of the house.

CHAPTER 13

Perplexities

Coulson and Philip were friendly, but not intimate. They never had had a dispute, they never were confidential with each other; in truth, they were both reserved and silent men, and, probably, respected each other the more for being so self-contained. There was a private feeling in Coulson's heart which would have made a less amiable fellow dislike Philip. But of this the latter was unconscious: they were not apt to exchange many words in the room which they occupied jointly.

Coulson asked Philip if he had enjoyed himself at the Corneys', and Philip replied, –

'Not much; such parties are noane to my liking.'

'And yet thou broke off from t' watch-night to go there.'

No answer; so Coulson went on, with a sense of the duty laid upon him, to improve the occasion – the first that had presented itself since the good old Methodist minister had given his congregation the solemn warning to watch over the opportunities of various kinds which the coming year would present.

'Jonas Barclay told us as the pleasures o' this world were like apples o' Sodom,* pleasant to look at, but ashes to taste.'

Coulson wisely left Philip to make the application for himself. If he did he made no sign, but threw himself on his bed with a heavy sigh.

'Are yo' not going to undress?' said Coulson, as he covered him up in bed.

There had been a long pause of silence. Philip did not answer

him, and he thought he had fallen asleep. But he was roused
from his first slumber by Hepburn's soft movements about the
room. Philip had thought better of it, and, with some penitence
in his heart for his gruffness to the unoffending Coulson, was
trying not to make any noise while he undressed.

But he could not sleep. He kept seeing the Corneys' kitchen
and the scenes that had taken place in it, passing like a pageant
before his closed eyes. Then he opened them in angry weariness
at the recurring vision, and tried to make out the outlines of the
room and the furniture in the darkness. The white ceiling sloped
into the whitewashed walls, and against them he could see the
four rush-bottomed chairs, the looking-glass hung on one side,
the old carved oak-chest (his own property, with the initials of
forgotten ancestors cut upon it), which held his clothes; the
boxes that belonged to Coulson, sleeping soundly in the bed in
the opposite corner of the room; the casement window in the
roof, through which the snowy ground on the steep hill-side
could be plainly seen; and when he got so far as this in the
catalogue of the room, he fell into a troubled feverish sleep,
which lasted two or three hours; and then he awoke with a start,
and a consciousness of uneasiness, though what about he could
not remember at first.

When he recollected all that had happened the night before, it
impressed him much more favourably than it had done at the
time. If not joy, hope had come in the morning;* and, at any
rate, he could be up and be doing, for the late wintry light was
stealing down the hill-side, and he knew that, although Coulson
lay motionless in his sleep, it was past their usual time of rising.
Still, as it was New Year's Day, a time of some licence, Philip
had mercy on his fellow-shopman, and did not waken him till
just as he was leaving the room.

Carrying his shoes in his hand, he went softly downstairs, for
he could see from the top of the flight that neither Alice nor her
daughter was down yet, as the kitchen shutters were not
unclosed. It was Mrs Rose's habit to rise early, and have all
bright and clean against her lodgers came down; but then, in
general, she went to rest before nine o'clock, whereas the last
night she had not gone till past twelve. Philip went about
undoing the shutters, and trying to break up the raking coal,*
with as little noise as might be, for he had compassion on the
tired sleepers. The kettle had not been filled, probably because

Mrs Rose had been unable to face the storm of the night before, in taking it to the pump just at the entrance of the court. When Philip came back from filling it, he found Alice and Hester both in the kitchen, and trying to make up for lost time by hastening over their work. Hester looked busy and notable* with her gown pinned up behind her, and her hair all tucked away under a clean linen cap; but Alice was angry with herself for her late sleeping, and that and other causes made her speak crossly to Philip, as he came in with his snowy feet and well-filled kettle.

'Look the' there! droppin' and drippin' along t' flags as was cleaned last night, and meddlin' wi' woman's work as man has no business wi'.'

Philip was surprised and annoyed. He had found relief from his own thoughts in doing what he believed would help others. He gave up the kettle to her snatching hands, and sat down behind the door in momentary ill-temper. But the kettle was better filled, and consequently heavier than the old woman expected, and she could not manage to lift it to the crook from which it generally hung suspended. She looked round for Hester, but she was gone into the back-kitchen. In a minute Philip was at her side, and had heaved it to its place for her. She looked in his face for a moment wistfully, but hardly condescended to thank him: at least the sound of the words did not pass the lips that formed them. Rebuffed by her manner, he went back to his old seat, and mechanically watched the preparations for breakfast; but his thoughts went back to the night before, and the comparative ease of his heart was gone. The first stir of a new day had made him feel as if he had had no sufficient cause for his annoyance and despondency the previous evening; but now, condemned to sit quiet, he reviewed looks and words, and saw just reason for his anxiety. After some consideration he resolved to go that very night to Haytersbank, and have some talk with either Sylvia or her mother; what the exact nature of this purposed conversation should be, he did not determine; much would depend on Sylvia's manner and mood, and on her mother's state of health; but at any rate something would be learnt.

During breakfast something was learnt nearer home; though not all that a man less unconscious and more vain than Philip might have discovered. He only found out that Mrs Rose was displeased with him for not having gone to the watchnight with

Hester, according to the plan made some weeks before. But he soothed his conscience by remembering that he had made no promise; he had merely spoken of his wish to be present at the service, about which Hester was speaking; and although at the time and for a good while afterwards, he had fully intended going, yet as there had been William Coulson to accompany her, his absence could not have been seriously noticed. Still he was made uncomfortable by Mrs Rose's change of manner; once or twice he said to himself that she little knew how miserable he had been during his 'gay evening', as she would persist in calling it, or she would not talk at him with such persevering bitterness this morning. Before he left for the shop, he spoke of his intention of going to see how his aunt was, and of paying her a New Year's Day visit.

Hepburn and Coulson took it in turns week and week about to go first home to dinner; the one who went first sat down with Mrs Rose and her daughter, instead of having his portion put in the oven to keep warm for him. To-day it was Hepburn's turn to be last. All morning the shop was full with customers, come rather to offer good wishes than to buy, and with an unspoken remembrance of the cake and wine which the two hospitable brothers Foster made a point of offering to all comers on New Year's Day. It was busy work for all – for Hester on her side, where caps, ribbons, and women's gear were exclusively sold – for the shopmen and boys in the grocery and drapery department. Philip was trying to do his business with his mind far away; and the consequence was that his manner was not such as to recommend him to the customers, some of whom recollected it as very different, courteous and attentive, if grave and sedate. One buxom farmer's wife noticed the change to him. She had a little girl with her, of about five years old, that she had lifted up on the counter, and who was watching Philip with anxious eyes, occasionally whispering in her mother's ear, and then hiding her face against her cloak.

'She's thought a deal o' coming to see yo', and a dunnot think as yo' mind her at all. My pretty, he's clean forgotten as how he said last New Year's Day, he'd gi' thee a barleysugar stick, if thou'd hem him a handkercher by this.'

The child's face was buried in the comfortable breadth of duffle at these words, while the little outstretched hand held a small square of coarse linen.

'Ay, she's noane forgotten it, and has done her five stitches a day, bless her; and a dunnot believe as yo' know her again. She's Phœbe Moorsom, and a'm Hannah, and a've dealt at t' shop reg'lar this fifteen year.'

'I'm very sorry,' said Philip 'I was up late last night, and I'm a bit dazed to-day. Well! this is nice work, Phœbe, and I'm sure I'm very much beholden to yo'. And here's five sticks o' barley-sugar, one for every stitch, and thank you kindly, Mrs Moorsom, too.'

Philip took the handkerchief, and hoped he had made honourable amends for his want of recognition. But the wee lassie refused to be lifted down, and whispered something afresh into her mother's ear, who smiled and bade her be quiet. Philip saw, however, that there was some wish ungratified on the part of the little maiden which he was expected to inquire into, and, accordingly, he did his duty.

'She's a little fool; she says yo' promised to gi'e her a kiss, and t' make her yo'r wife.'

The child burrowed her face closer into her mother's neck, and refused to allow the kiss which Philip willingly offered. All he could do was to touch the back of the little white fat neck with his lips. The mother carried her off only half satisfied, and Philip felt that he must try and collect his scattered wits, and be more alive to the occasion.

Towards the dinner-hour the crowd slackened; Hester began to replenish decanters and bottles, and to bring out a fresh cake before she went home to dinner; and Coulson and Philip looked over the joint present they always made to her on this day. It was a silk handkerchief of the prettiest colours they could pick out of the shop, intended for her to wear round her neck. Each tried to persuade the other to give it to her, for each was shy of the act of presentation. Coulson was, however, the most resolute; and when she returned from the parlour the little parcel was in Philip's hands.

'Here, Hester,' said he, going round the counter to her, just as she was leaving the shop. 'It's from Coulson and me; a handkerchief for yo' to wear; and we wish yo' a happy New Year, and plenty on 'em; and there's many a one wishes the same.'

He took her hand as he said this. She went a little paler, and her eyes brightened as though they would fill with tears as they met his; she could not have helped it, do what she would. But she only said, 'Thank yo' kindly', and going up to Coulson she repeated the words and action to him; and then they went off together to dinner.

There was a lull of business for the next hour. Jolm and Jeremiah were dining like the rest of the world. Even the elder errand-boy had vanished. Philip re-arranged disorderly goods; and then sat down on the counter by the window; it was the habitual place for the one who stayed behind; for excepting on market-day there was little or no custom during the noon-hour. Formerly he used to move the drapery with which the window was ornamented, and watch the passers-by with careless eye. But now, though he seemed to gaze abroad, he saw nothing but vacancy. All the morning since he got up he had been trying to fight through his duties – leaning against a hope – a hope that first had bowed, and then had broke as soon as he really tried its weight. There was not a sign of Sylvia's liking for him to be gathered from the most careful recollection of the past evening. It was of no use thinking that there was. It was better to give it up altogether and at once. But what if he could not? What if the thought of her was bound up with his life; and that once torn out by his own free will, the very roots of his heart must come also?

No; he was resolved he would go on; as long as there was life there was hope; as long as Sylvia remained unpledged to any one else, there was a chance for him. He would remodel his behaviour to her. He could not be merry and light-hearted like other young men; his nature was not cast in that mould; and the early sorrows that had left him a lonely orphan might have matured, but had not enlivened, his character. He thought with some bitterness on the power of easy talking about trifles which some of those he had met with at the Corneys' had exhibited. But then he felt stirring within him a force of enduring love which he believed to be unusual, and which seemed as if it must compel all things to his wish in the end. A year or so ago he had thought much of his own cleverness and his painfully acquired learning, and he had imagined that these were the qualities which were to gain Sylvia. But now, whether he had tried them and had failed to win even her admiration, or whether some true instinct had told him that a woman's love may be gained in many ways sooner than by mere learning, he was only angry with himself for his past folly in making himself her school –

nay, her taskmaster. To-night, though, he would start off on a new tack. He would not even upbraid her for her conduct the night before; he had shown her his displeasure at the time; but she should see how tender and forgiving he could be. He would lure her to him rather than find fault with her. There had perhaps been too much of that already.

When Coulson came back Philip went to his solitary dinner. In general he was quite alone while eating it; but to-day Alice Rose chose to bear him company. She watched him with a cold severe eye for some time, until he had appeased his languid appetite. Then she began with the rebuke she had in store for him; a rebuke the motives to which were not entirely revealed even to herself.

'Thou 're none so keen after thy food as common,' she began. 'Plain victuals goes ill down after feastin'.'

Philip felt the colour mount to his face; he was not in the mood for patiently standing the brunt of the attack which he saw was coming, and yet he had a reverent feeling for woman and for age. He wished she would leave him alone; but he only said – 'I had nought but a slice o' cold beef for supper, if you'll call that feasting.'

'Neither do godly ways savour delicately after the pleasures of the world,' continued she, unheeding his speech. 'Thou wert wont to seek the house of the Lord, and I thought well on thee; but of late thou'st changed, and fallen away, and I mun speak what is in my heart towards thee.'

'Mother,' said Philip, impatiently, (both he and Coulson called Alice 'mother' at times), 'I don't think I am fallen away, and any way I cannot stay now to be—it's New Year's Day, and t' shop is throng.'

But Alice held up her hand. Her speech was ready, and she must deliver it.

'Shop here, shop there. The flesh and the devil are gettin' hold on yo', and yo' need more nor iver to seek t' ways o' grace. New Year's Day comes and says, "Watch and pray", and yo' say, "Nay, I'll seek feasts and market-places, and let times and seasons come and go without heedin' into whose presence they're hastening me." Time was, Philip, when thou'd niver ha' letten a merry-making keep thee fra' t'watchnight, and t' company o' the godly.'

'I tell yo' it was no merry-making to me,' said Philip, with sharpness, as he left the house.

Alice sat down on the nearest seat, and leant her head on her wrinkled hand.

'He's tangled and snared,' said she; 'my heart has yearned after him, and I esteemed him as one o' the elect.* And more nor me yearns after him. O Lord, I have but one child! O Lord, spare her! But o'er and above a' I would like to pray for his soul, that Satan might not have it, for he came to me but a little lad.'

At that moment Philip, smitten by his conscience for his hard manner of speech, came back; but Alice did not hear or see him till he was close by her, and then he had to touch her to recall her attention.

'Mother,' said he, 'I was wrong. I'm fretted by many things. I shouldn't ha' spoken so. It was ill-done of me.'

'Oh, my lad!' said she, looking up and putting her thin arm on his shoulder as he stooped, 'Satan is desiring after yo' that he may sift yo' as wheat.* Bide at whoam, bide at whoam, and go not after them as care nought for holy things. Why need yo' go to Haytersbank this night?'

Philip reddened. He could not and would not give it up, and yet it was difficult to resist the pleading of the usually stern old woman.

'Nay,' said he, withdrawing himself ever so little from her hold; 'my aunt is but ailing, they're my own flesh and blood, and as good folks as needs be, though they mayn't be o' our – o' your way o' thinking in a' things.'

'Our ways – your ways o' thinking, says he, as if they were no longer his'n. And as good folks as need be,' repeated she, with returning severity. 'Them's Satan's words, tho' yo' spoke 'em, Philip. I can do nought again Satan, but I can speak to them as can; an' we'll see which pulls hardest, for it'll be better for thee to be riven and rent i' twain than to go body and soul to hell.'

'But don't think, mother,' said Philip, his last words of conciliation, for the clock had given warning for two, 'as I'm boun' for hell, just because I go t' see my own folks, all I ha' left o' kin.' And once more, after laying his hand with as much of a caress as was in his nature on hers, he left the house.

Probably Alice would have considered the first words that greeted Philip on his entrance into the shop as an answer to her prayer, for they were such as put a stop to his plan of going to see Sylvia that evening; and if Alice had formed her inchoate thoughts into words, Sylvia would have appeared as the nearest earthly representative of the spirit of temptation whom she dreaded for Philip.

As he took his place behind the counter, Coulson said to him in a low voice, –

'Jeremiah Foster has been round to bid us to sup wi' him to-night. He says that he and John have a little matter o' business to talk over with us.'

A glance from his eyes to Philip told the latter that Coulson believed the business spoken of had something to do with the partnership, respecting which there had been a silent intelligence for some time between the shopmen.

'And what did thou say?' asked Philip, doggedly unwilling, even yet, to give up his purposed visit.

'Say! why, what could a say, but that we'd come? There was summat up, for sure; and summat as he thought we should be glad on. I could tell it fra' t' look on his face.'

'I don't think as I can go,' said Philip, feeling just then as if the long-hoped-for partnership was as nothing compared to his plan. It was always distasteful to him to have to give up a project, or to disarrange an intended order of things, such was his nature; but to-day it was absolute pain to yield his own purpose.

'Why, man alive?' said Coulson, in amaze at his reluctance.

'I didn't say I mightn't go,' said Philip, weighing consequences, until called off to attend to customers.

In the course of the afternoon, however, he felt himself more easy in deferring his visit to Haytersbank till the next evening. Charley Kinraid entered the shop, accompanied by Molly Brunton and her sisters; and though they all went towards Hester's side of the shop, and Philip and Coulson had many people to attend to, yet Hepburn's sharpened ears caught much of what the young women were saying. From that he gathered that Kinraid had promised them New Year's gifts, for the purchase of which they were come; and after a little more listening he learnt that Kinraid was returning to Shields the next day, having only come over to spend a holiday with his relations, and being tied with ship's work at the other end. They all talked together lightly and merrily, as if his going or staying was almost a matter of indifference to himself and his cousins. The principal thought of the young women was to secure the articles they most fancied; Charley Kinraid was (so Philip thought) especially anxious that the youngest and prettiest should be pleased. Hepburn watched him perpetually with a kind of envy of his bright, courteous manner, the natural gallantry of the sailor. If it were but clear that Sylvia took as little thought of him as he did of her, to all appearance, Philip could even have given him praise for manly good looks, and a certain kind of geniality of disposition which made him ready to smile pleasantly at all strangers, from babies upwards.

As the party turned to leave the shop they saw Philip, the guest of the night before; and they came over to shake hands with him across the counter; Kinraid's hand was proffered among the number. Last night Philip could not have believed it possible that such a demonstration of fellowship should have passed between them; and perhaps there was a slight hesitation of manner on his part, for some idea or remembrance crossed Kinraid's mind which brought a keen searching glance into the eyes which for a moment were fastened on Philip's face. In spite of himself, and during the very action of handshaking, Philip felt a cloud come over his face, not altering or moving his features, but taking light and peace out of his countenance.

Molly Brunton began to say something, and he gladly turned to look at her. She was asking him why he went away so early, for they had kept it up for four hours after he left, and last of all, she added (turning to Kinraid), her cousin Charley had danced a hornpipe among the platters on the ground.

Philip hardly knew what he said in reply, the mention of that *pas seul** lifted such a weight off his heart. He could smile now, after his grave fashion, and would have shaken hands again with Kinraid had it been required; for it seemed to him that no one, caring ever so little in the way that he did for Sylvia, could have borne four mortal hours of a company where she had been, and was not; least of all could have danced a hornpipe, either from gaiety of heart, or even out of complaisance. He felt as if the yearning after the absent one would have been a weight to his legs, as well as to his spirit; and he imagined that all men were like himself.

CHAPTER 14

Partnership

As darkness closed in, and the New Year's throng became scarce, Philip's hesitation about accompanying Coulson faded away. He was more comfortable respecting Sylvia, and his going to see her might be deferred; and, after all, he felt that the wishes of his masters ought to be attended to, and the honour of an invitation to the private house of Jeremiah not to be slighted for anything short of a positive engagement. Besides, the ambitious man of business existed strongly in Philip. It would never do to slight advances towards the second great earthly object in his life; one also on which the first depended.

So when the shop was closed, the two set out down Bridge Street to cross the river to the house of Jeremiah Foster. They stood a moment on the bridge to breathe the keen fresh sea air after their busy day. The waters came down, swollen full and dark, with rapid rushing speed from the snow-fed springs high up on the moorland above. The close-packed houses in the old town seemed a cluster of white roofs irregularly piled against the more unbroken white of the hill-side. Lights twinkled here and there in the town, and were slung from stern and bow of the ships in the harbour. The air was very still, settling in for a frost; so still that all distant sounds seemed near: the rumble of a returning cart in the High Street, the voices on board ship, the closing of shutters and barring of doors in the new town to which they were bound. But the sharp air was filled, as it were, with saline particles in a freezing state; little pungent crystals of sea salt burning lips and cheeks with their cold keenness. It would not do to linger here in the very centre of the valley up which passed the current of atmosphere coming straight with the rushing tide from the icy northern seas. Besides, there was the unusual honour of a supper with Jeremiah Foster awaiting them. He had asked each of them separately to a meal before now; but they had never gone together, and they felt that there was something serious in the conjuncture.

They began to climb the steep heights leading to the freshly-built rows of the new town of Monkshaven, feeling as if they were rising into aristocratic regions where no shop profaned the streets. Jeremiah Foster's house was one of six, undistinguished in size, or shape, or colour; but noticed in the daytime by all passers-by for its spotless cleanliness of lintel and doorstep, window and window frame. The very bricks seemed as though they came in for the daily scrubbing which brightened handle, knocker, all down to the very scraper.

The two young men felt as shy of the interview with their master under such unusual relations of guest and host, as a girl does of her first party. Each rather drew back from the decided step of knocking at the door; but with a rebuffing shake at his own folly, Philip was the one to give a loud single rap. As if they had been waited for, the door flew open, and a middle-aged servant stood behind, as spotless and neat as the house itself, and smiled a welcome to the familiar faces.

'Let me dust yo' a bit, William,' said she, suiting the action to the word. 'Yo've been leanin' again some whitewash, a'll be bound. Ay, Philip,' continued she, turning him round with motherly freedom, 'yo'll do if yo'll but gi' your shoon a polishin' wipe on yon other mat. This'n for takin' t' roughest mud off. Measter allays polishes on that.'

In the square parlour the same precise order was observed. Every article of furniture was free from speck of dirt or particle of dust; and everything was placed either in a parallel line, or at exact right-angles with every other. Even John and Jeremiah sat in symmetry on opposite sides of the fire-place; the very smiles on their honest faces seemed drawn to a line of exactitude.

Such formality, however admirable, was not calculated to promote ease: it was not until after supper – until a good quantity of Yorkshire pie had been swallowed, and washed down, too, with the best and most generous wine in Jeremiah's cellar – that there was the least geniality among them, in spite of the friendly kindness of the host and his brother. The long silence, during which mute thanks for the meal were given, having come to an end, Jeremiah called for pipes, and three of the party began to smoke.

Politics in those days were tickle subjects to meddle with, even in the most private company. The nation was in a state of terror against France, and against any at home who might be supposed to sympathise with the enormities she had just been commit-ting.* The oppressive act against seditious meetings* had been passed the year before; and people were doubtful to what extremity of severity it might be construed. Even the law authorities forgot to be impartial, but either their alarms or their interests made too many of them vehement partisans instead of calm arbiters, and thus destroyed the popular confidence in what should have been considered the supreme tribunal of justice. Yet for all this, there were some who dared to speak of reform of Parliament, as a preliminary step to fair representation of the people, and to a reduction of the heavy war-taxation that was imminent, if not already imposed. But these pioneers of 1830* were generally obnoxious. The great body of the people gloried in being Tories and haters of the French, with whom they were on tenter-hooks to fight, almost unaware of the rising reputation of the young Corsican warrior,* whose name would be used ere a dozen years had passed to hush English babies with a terror such as that of Marlborough* once had for the French.

At such a place as Monkshaven all these opinions were held in excess. One or two might, for the mere sake of argument, dispute on certain points of history or government; but they took care to be very sure of their listeners before such arguments touched on anything of the present day; for it had been not unfrequently found that the public duty of prosecuting opinions not your own overrode the private duty of respecting confidence. Most of the Monkshaven politicians confined themselves, therefore, to such general questions as these: 'Could an Englishman lick more than four Frenchmen at a time?' 'What was the proper punishment for members of the Corresponding Society* (correspondence with the French directory), hanging and quartering, or burning?' 'Would the forthcoming child of the Princess of Wales be a boy or a girl? If a girl, would it be more loyal to call it Charlotte or Elizabeth?'*

The Fosters were quite secure enough of their guests this evening to have spoken freely on politics had they been so inclined. And they did begin on the outrages which had been lately offered to the king in crossing St James's Park* to go and open the House of Lords; but soon, so accustomed were their minds to caution and restraint, the talk dropped down to the high price of provisions. Bread at 1s. 3d. the quartern loaf, according to the London test. Wheat at 120s. per quarter, as the home-baking northerners viewed the matter; and then the conversation died away to an ominous silence. John looked at

Jeremiah, as if asking him to begin. Jeremiah was the host, and had been a married man. Jeremiah returned the look with the same meaning in it. John, though a bachelor, was the elder brother. The great church bell, brought from the Monkshaven monastery centuries ago, high up on the opposite hill-side, began to ring nine o'clock; it was getting late. Jeremiah began:

'It seems a bad time for starting any one on business, wi' prices and taxes and bread so dear; but John and I are getting into years, and we've no children to follow us: yet we would fain draw out of some of our worldly affairs. We would like to give up the shop, and stick to banking, to which there seemeth a plain path. But first there is the stock and goodwill of the shop to be disposed on.'

A dead pause. This opening was not favourable to the hopes of the two moneyless young men who had been hoping to succeed their masters by the more gradual process of partnership. But it was only the kind of speech that had been agreed upon by the two brothers with a view of impressing on Hepburn and Coulson the great and unusual responsibility of the situation into which the Fosters wished them to enter. In some ways the talk of many was much less simple and straightforward in those days than it is now. The study of effect shown in the London diners-out of the last generation, who prepared their conversation beforehand, was not without its parallel in humbler spheres, and for different objects than self-display. The brothers Foster had all but rehearsed the speeches they were about to make this evening. They were aware of the youth of the parties to whom they were going to make a most favourable proposal; and they dreaded that if that proposal was too lightly made, it would be too lightly considered, and the duties involved in it too carelessly entered upon. So the role of one brother was to suggest, that of the other to repress. The young men, too, had their reserves. They foresaw, and had long foreseen, what was coming that evening. They were impatient to hear it in distinct words; and yet they had to wait, as if unconscious, during all the long preamble. Do age and youth never play the same parts now? To return. John Foster replied to his brother:

'The stock and goodwill! That would take much wealth. And there will be fixtures to be considered. Philip, canst thee tell me the exact amount of stock in the shop at present?'

It had only just been taken; Philip had it at his fingers' ends.

'One thousand nine hundred and forty-one pounds, thirteen shillings and twopence.'

Coulson looked at him in a little dismay, and could not repress a sigh. The figures put into words and spoken aloud seemed to indicate so much larger an amount of money than when quickly written down in numerals. But Philip read the countenances, nay, by some process of which he was not himself aware, he read the minds of the brothers, and felt no dismay at what he saw there.

'And the fixtures?' asked John Foster.

'The appraiser valued them at two hundred and thirty-five pounds three and sixpence when father died. We have added to them since, but we will reckon them at that. How much does that make with the value of the stock? '

'Two thousand one hundred and seventy-six pounds, sixteen shillings and eightpence,' said Philip.

Coulson had done the sum quicker, but was too much disheartened by the amount to speak.

'And the goodwill?' asked the pitiless John. 'What dost thee set that at?'

'I think, brother, that that would depend on who came forward with the purchase-money of the stock and fixtures. To some folks we might make it sit easy, if they were known to us, and those as we wished well to. If Philip and William here, for instance, said they'd like to purchase the business, I reckon thee and me would not ask 'em so much as we should ask Millers' (Millers was an upstart petty rival shop at the end of the bridge in the New Town.)

'I wish Philip and William was to come after us,' said John. 'But that's out of the question,' he continued, knowing all the while that, far from being out of the question, it was the very question, and that it was as good as settled at this very time.

No one spoke. Then Jeremiah went on:

'It's out of the question, I reckon?'

He looked at the two young men. Coulson shook his head. Philip more bravely said, –

'I have fifty-three pounds seven and fourpence in yo'r hands, Master John, and it's all I have i' the world.'

'It's a pity,' said John, and again they were silent. Half-past nine struck. It was time to be beginning to make an end. 'Perhaps, brother, they have friends who could advance 'em the money. We might make it sit light to them, for the sake of their good service?'

Philip replied, –

'There's no one who can put forwards a penny for me: I have but few kin, and they have little to spare beyond what they need.'

Coulson said –

'My father and mother have nine on us.'

'Let alone, let alone!' said John, relenting fast; for he was weary of his part of cold, stern prudence. 'Brother, I think we have enough of this world's goods to do what we like wi' our own.'

Jeremiah was a little scandalized at the rapid melting away of assumed character, and took a good pull at his pipe before he replied –

'Upwards of two thousand pounds is a large sum to set on the well-being and well-doing of two lads, the elder of whom is not three-and-twenty. I fear we must look farther a-field.'

'Why, John,' replied Jeremiah, 'it was but yesterday thee saidst thee would rather have Philip and William than any men o' fifty that thee knowed. And now to bring up their youth again them.'

'Well, well! t' half on it is thine, and thou shalt do even as thou wilt. But I think as I must have security for my moiety, for it's a risk – a great risk. Have ye any security to offer? any expectations? any legacies, as other folk have a life interest in at present?'

No; neither of them had. So Jeremiah rejoined –

'Then, I suppose, I mun do as thee dost, John, and take the security of character. And it's a great security too, lads, and t' best o' all, and one that I couldn't ha' done without; no, not if yo'd pay me down five thousand for goodwill, and stock, and fixtures. For John Foster and Son has been a shop i' Monkshaven this eighty years and more; and I dunnot think there's a man living – or dead, for that matter – as can say Fosters wronged him of a penny, or gave short measure to a child or a Cousin Betty.'*

They all four shook hands round with the same heartiness as if it had been a legal ceremony necessary to the completion of the partnership. The old men's faces were bright with smiles; the eyes of the young ones sparkled with hope.

'But, after all,' said Jeremiah, 'we've not told you particulars. Yo're thanking us for a pig in a poke;* but we had more forethought, and we put all down on a piece o' paper.'

He took down a folded piece of paper from the mantel-shelf, put on his horn spectacles, and began to read aloud, occasionally peering over his glasses to note the effect on the countenances of the young men. The only thing he was in the habit of reading aloud was a chapter in the Bible daily to his housekeeper servant; and, like many, he reserved a peculiar tone for that solemn occupation – a tone which he unconsciously employed for the present enumeration of pounds, shillings, and pence.

'Average returns of the last three years, one hundred and twenty-seven pounds, three shillings, and seven penny and one-sixth a week. Profits thereupon thirty-four per cent – as near as may be. Clear profits of the concern, after deducting all expenses except rent – for t' house is our own – one thousand two hundred and two pound a year.'

This was far more than either Hepburn or Coulson had imagined it to be; and a look of surprise, almost amounting to dismay, crept over their faces, in spite of their endeavour to keep simply motionless and attentive.

'It's a deal of money, lads, and the Lord give you grace to guide it,' said Jeremiah, putting down his paper for a minute.

'Amen,' said John, shaking his head to give effect to his word.

'Now what we propose is this,' continued Jeremiah, beginning afresh to refer to his paper: 'We will call t' value of stock and fixtures two thousand one hundred and fifty. You may have John Holden, appraiser and auctioneer, in to set a price on them if yo' will; or yo' may look over books and bills; or, better still, do both, and so check one again 't other; but for t' sake o' making the ground o' the bargain,* state the sum as above; and I reckon it so much capital left in yo'r hands for the use o' which yo're bound to pay us five per cent quarterly – that's one hundred and seven pound ten per annum at least for t' first year; and after it will be reduced by the gradual payment on our money, which must be at the rate of twenty per cent, thus paying us our principal back in five years. And the rent, including all back yards, right of wharfage, warehouse, and premises, is reckoned by us to be sixty-five pound per annum. So yo' will have to pay us, John and Jeremiah Foster, brothers, six hundred and twelve pound ten out of the profits of the first year, leaving, at the present rate of profits, about five hundred and eighty-nine pound ten, for the share to be divided between yo'.'

The plan had, in all its details, been carefully arranged by the two brothers. They were afraid lest Hepburn and Coulson should be dazzled by the amount of profits, and had so arranged the sliding-scale of payment as to reduce the first year's income to what the elder men thought a very moderate sum, but what to the younger ones appeared an amount of wealth such as they, who had neither of them ever owned much more than fifty pounds, considered almost inexhaustible. It was certainly a remarkable instance of prosperity and desert meeting together so early in life.

For a moment or two the brothers were disappointed at not hearing any reply from either of them. Then Philip stood up, for he felt as if anything he could say sitting down would not be sufficiently expressive of gratitude, and William instantly followed his example. Hepburn began in a formal manner, something the way in which he had read in the York newspapers that honourable members* returned thanks when their health was given.

'I can hardly express my feelings' (Coulson nudged him) 'his feelings, too – of gratitude. Oh, Master John! Master Jeremiah, I thought it might come i' time; nay, I've thought it might come afore long; but I niver thought as it would be so much, or made so easy. We've got good kind friends – we have, have we not, William? – and we'll do our best, and I hope as we shall come up to their wishes.'

Philip's voice quivered a little, as some remembrance passed across his mind; at this unusual moment of expansion out it came. 'I wish mother could ha' seen this day.'

'She shall see a better day, my lad, when thy name and William's is painted over t' shop-door, and J. and J. Foster blacked out.'

'Nay, master,' said William, 'that mun never be. I'd a'most sooner not come in for the business. Anyhow, it must be "late J. and J. Foster", and I'm not sure as I can stomach that.'

'Well, well, William,' said John Foster, highly gratified, 'there be time enough to talk over that. There was one thing more to be said, was there not, brother Jeremiah? We do not wish to have this talked over in Monkshaven until shortly before the

time when yo' must enter on the business. We have our own
arrangements to make wi' regard to the banking concern, and
there'll be lawyer's work to do, after yo've examined books and
looked over stock again together; maybe we've overstated it, or
t' fixtures aren't worth so much as we said. Anyhow yo' must
each on yo' give us yo'r word for to keep fra' naming this night's
conversation to any one. Meantime, Jeremiah and I will have to
pay accounts, and take a kind of farewell of the merchants and
manufacturers with whom Fosters have had dealings this seventy
or eighty year; and when and where it seems fitting to us we will
take one of yo' to introduce as our successors and friends. But
all that's to come. But yo' must each give us yo'r word not to
name what has passed here to any one till further speech on the
subject has passed between us.'

Coulson immediately gave the promise. Philip's assent came
lagging. He had thought of Sylvia living, almost as much as of
the dead mother, whose last words had been a committal of her
child to the Father of the friendless;* and now that a short delay
was placed between the sight of the cup and his enjoyment of
it,* there was an impatient chafing in the mind of the composed
and self-restrained Philip; and then repentance quick as lightning
effaced the feeling, and he pledged himself to the secrecy which
was enjoined. Some few more details as to their mode of
procedure – of verifying the Fosters' statements, which to the
younger men seemed a perfectly unnecessary piece of business –
of probable journeys and introductions, and then farewell was
bidden, and Hepburn and Coulson were in the passage donning
their wraps, and rather to their indignation being assisted therein
by Martha, who was accustomed to the office with her own
master. Suddenly they were recalled into the parlour.

John Foster was fumbling with the papers a little nervously:
Jeremiah spoke –

'We have not thought it necessary to commend Hester Rose
to you; if she had been a lad she would have had a third o' the
business along wi' yo'. Being a woman, it's ill troubling her with
a partnership; better give her a fixed salary till such time as she
marries.'

He looked a little knowingly and curiously at the faces of the
young men he addressed. William Coulson seemed sheepish and
uncomfortable, but said nothing, leaving it as usual to Philip to
be spokesman.

'If we hadn't cared for Hester for hersel', master, we should ha' cared for her as being forespoken by yo'.* Yo' and Master John shall fix what we ought t' pay her; and I think I may make bold to say that, as our income rises, hers shall too – eh, Coulson?' (a sound of assent quite distinct enough), 'for we both look on her as a sister, and on Alice like a mother, as I told her only this very day.'

CHAPTER 15

A Difficult Question

Philip went to bed with that kind of humble penitent gratitude in his heart, which we sometimes feel after a sudden revulsion of feeling from despondency to hope. The night before it seemed as if all events were so arranged as to thwart him in his dearest wishes; he felt now as if his discontent and repining, not twenty-four hours before, had been almost impious, so great was the change in his circumstances for the better. Now all seemed promising for the fulfilment of what he most desired. He was almost convinced that he was mistaken in thinking that Kinraid had had anything more than a sailor's admiration for a pretty girl with regard to Sylvia; at any rate, he was going away to-morrow, in all probability not to return for another year (for Greenland ships left for the northern seas as soon as there was a chance of the ice being broken up), and ere then he himself might speak out openly, laying before her parents all his fortunate prospects, and before her all his deep passionate love.

So this night his prayers were more than the mere form that they had been the night before; they were a vehement expression of gratitude to God for having, as it were, interfered on his behalf, to grant him the desire of his eyes and the lust of his heart. He was like too many of us, he did not place his future life in the hands of God, and only ask for grace to do His will in whatever circumstances might arise; but he yearned in that terrible way after a blessing which, when granted under such circumstances, too often turns out to be equivalent to a curse. And that spirit brings with it the material and earthly idea that all events that favour our wishes are answers to our prayer; and so they are in one sense, but they need prayer in a deeper and higher spirit to keep us from the temptation to evil which such events invariably bring with them.

Philip little knew how Sylvia's time had been passed that day. If he had, he would have lain down this night with even a heavier heart than he had done on the last.

Charley Kinraid accompanied his cousins as far as the spot where the path to Haytersbank Farm diverged. Then he stopped his merry talk, and announced his intention of going to see farmer Robson. Bessy Corney looked disappointed and a little sulky; but her sister Molly Brunton laughed, and said, –

'Tell truth, lad! Dannel Robson'd niver have a call fra' thee if he hadn't a pretty daughter.'

'Indeed, but he would,' replied Charley, rather annoyed; 'when I've said a thing, I do it. I promised last night to go see him; besides, I like the old man.'

'Well! when shall we tell mother yo're comin' whoam?'

'Toward eight o'clock – maybe sooner.'

'Why it's bare five now! bless t' lad, does he think o' staying theere a'neet, and they up so late last night, and Mrs Robson ailing beside? Mother'll not think it kind on yo' either, will she, Bess?'

'I dunno. Charley mun do as he likes; I daresay no one'll miss him if he does bide away till eight.'

'Well, well! I can't tell what I shall do; but yo'd best not stop lingering here, for it's getting on, and there'll be a keen frost by t' look o' the stars.'

Haytersbank was closed for the night as far as it ever was closed; there were no shutters to the windows, nor did they care to draw the inside curtains, so few were the passers-by. The house door was fastened; but the shippen door* a little on in the same long low block of building stood open, and a dim light made an oblong upon the snowy ground outside. As Kinraid drew near he heard talking there, and a woman's voice; he threw a passing glance through the window into the fire-lit house-place, and seeing Mrs Robson asleep by the fireside in her easy-chair, he went on.

There was the intermittent sound of the sharp whistling of milk into the pail, and Kester, sitting on a three-legged stool, cajoling a capricious cow into letting her fragrant burden flow.

Sylvia stood near the farther window-ledge, on which a horn
lantern* was placed, pretending to knit at a grey worsted
stocking, but in reality laughing at Kester's futile endeavours,
and finding quite enough to do with her eyes, in keeping herself
untouched by the whisking tail, or the occasional kick. The
frosty air was mellowed by the warm and odorous breath of the
cattle – breath that hung about the place in faint misty clouds.
There was only a dim light; such as it was, it was not clearly
defined against the dark heavy shadow in which the old black
rafters and manger and partitions were enveloped.

As Charley came to the door, Kester was saying, 'Quiet wi'
thee, wench! Theere now, she's a beauty, if she'll stand still.
There's niver sich a cow i' t' Riding, if she'll only behave hersel'.
She's a bonny lass, she is; let down her milk, theere's a pretty! '

'Why, Kester,' laughed Sylvia, 'thou'rt asking her for her milk
wi' as many pretty speeches as if thou wert wooing a wife!'

'Hey, lass!' said Kester, turning a bit towards her, and shutting
one eye to cock the other the better upon her; an operation
which puckered up his already wrinkled face into a thousand
new lines and folds. 'An' how does thee know how a man woos
a wife, that thee talks so knowin' about it? That's tellin'. Some
un's been tryin' it on thee.'

'There's niver a one been so impudent,' said Sylvia, reddening
and tossing her head a little; 'I'd like to see 'em try me!'

'Well, well!' said Kester, wilfully misunderstanding her meaning, 'thou mun be patient, wench; and if thou's a good lass,
maybe thy turn 'll come and they 'll try it.'

'I wish thou'd talk of what thou's some knowledge on, Kester,
i'stead of i' that silly way,' replied Sylvia.

'Then a mun talk no more 'bout women, for they're past
knowin', an' druv e'en King Solomon* silly.'

At this moment Charley stepped in. Sylvia gave a little start
and dropped her ball of worsted. Kester made as though
absorbed in his task of cajoling Black Nell; but his eyes and ears
were both vigilant.

'I was going into the house, but I saw yo'r mother asleep, and
I didn't like to waken her, so I just came on here. Is yo'r father
to the fore?'*

'No,' said Sylvia, hanging down her head a little, wondering
if he could have heard the way in which she and Kester had
been talking, and thinking over her little foolish jokes with

anger against herself. 'Father is gone to Winthrop about some pigs as he's heerd on. He'll not be back till seven o'clock or so.'

It was but half-past five, and Sylvia in the irritation of the moment believed that she wished Kinraid would go. But she would have been extremely disappointed if he had. Kinraid himself seemed to have no thought of the kind. He saw with his quick eyes, not unaccustomed to women, that his coming so unexpectedly had fluttered Sylvia, and anxious to make her quite at her ease with him, and not unwilling to conciliate Kester, he addressed his next speech to him, with the same kind of air of interest in the old man's pursuit that a young man of a different class sometimes puts on when talking to the chaperone of a pretty girl in a ball-room.

'That's a handsome beast yo've just been milking, master.'

'Ay; but handsome is as handsome does. It were only yesterday as she aimed her leg right at t' pail wi' t' afterings* in. She knowed it were afterings as well as any Christian, and t' more t' mischief t' better she likes it; an' if a hadn't been too quick for her, it would have a' gone swash down i' t' litter.* This'n 's a far better cow i' t' long run, she's just a steady goer,' as the milky down-pour came musical and even from the stall next to Black Nell's.

Sylvia was knitting away vigorously, thinking all the while that it was a great pity she had not put on a better gown, or even a cap with brighter ribbon, and quite unconscious how very pretty she looked standing against the faint light, her head a little bent down; her hair catching bright golden touches, as it fell from under her little linen cap; her pink bedgown, confined by her apron-string, giving a sort of easy grace to her figure; her dark full linsey petticoat short above her trim ankles, looking far more suitable to the place where she was standing than her long gown of the night before would have done. Kinraid was wanting to talk to her, and to make her talk, but was uncertain how to begin. In the meantime Kester went on with the subject last spoken about.

'Black Nell's at her fourth calf now, so she ought to ha' left off her tricks and turned sober-like. But bless yo', there's some cows as 'll be skittish till they're fat for t' butcher. Not but what a like milking her better nor a steady goer; a man has allays summat to be watchin' for; and a'm kind o' set up when a've mastered her at last. T' young missus theere, she's mighty fond

o' comin' t' see Black Nell at her tantrums. She'd niver come
near me if a' cows were like this'n.'

'Do you often come and see the cows milked?' asked Kinraid.

'Many a time,' said Sylvia, smiling a little. 'Why, when we're
throng, I help Kester; but now we've only Black Nell and Daisy
giving milk. Kester knows as I can milk Black Nell quite easy,'
she continued, half vexed that Kester had not named this
accomplishment.

'Ay! when she's in a good frame o' mind, as she is some times.
But t' difficulty is to milk her at all times.'

'I wish I'd come a bit sooner. I should like t' have seen you
milk Black Nell,' addressing Sylvia.

'Yo'd better come to-morrow e'en, and see what a hand she'll
mak' on her,' said Kester.

'To-morrow night I shall be far on my road back to Shields.'

'To-morrow!' said Sylvia, suddenly looking up at him, and
then dropping her eyes, as she found he had been watching for
the effect of his intelligence on her.

'I mun be back at t' whaler, where I'm engaged,' continued
he. 'She's fitting up after a fresh fashion,* and as I've been one
as wanted new ways, I mun be on the spot for t' look after her.
Maybe I shall take a run down here afore sailing in March. I'm
sure I shall try.'

There was a good deal meant and understood by these last
few words. The tone in which they were spoken gave them a
tender intensity not lost upon either of the hearers. Kester
cocked his eye once more, but with as little obtrusiveness as he
could, and pondered the sailor's looks and ways. He remembered his coming about the place the winter before, and how
the old master had then appeared to have taken to him; but at
that time Sylvia had seemed to Kester too little removed from a
child to have either art or part in Kinraid's visits; now, however,
the case was different. Kester in his sphere – among his circle of
acquaintance, narrow though it was – had heard with much
pride of Sylvia's bearing away the bell* at church and at market,
wherever girls of her age were congregated. He was a north
countryman, so he gave out no further sign of his feelings than
his mistress and Sylvia's mother had done on a like occasion.

'T' lass is weel enough,' said he; but he grinned to himself,
and looked about, and listened to the hearsay of every lad,
wondering who was handsome, and brave, and good enough to

be Sylvia's mate. Now, of late, it had seemed to the canny farm-servant pretty clear that Philip Hepburn was 'after her'; and to Philip, Kester had an instinctive objection, a kind of natural antipathy such as has existed in all ages between the dwellers in a town and those in the country, between agriculture and trade. So, while Kinraid and Sylvia kept up their half-tender, half-jesting conversation, Kester was making up his slow persistent mind as to the desirability of the young man then present as a husband for his darling, as much from his being other than Philip in every respect, as from the individual good qualities he possessed. Kester's first opportunity of favouring Kinraid's suit consisted in being as long as possible over his milking; so never were cows that required such 'stripping',* or were expected to yield such 'afterings', as Black Nell and Daisy that night. But all things must come to an end; and at length Kester got up from his three-legged stool, on seeing what the others did not – that the dip-candle in the lantern was coming to an end – and that in two or three minutes more the shippen would be in darkness, and so his pails of milk be endangered. In an instant Sylvia had started out of her delicious dreamland, her drooping eyes were raised, and recovered their power of observation; her ruddy arms were freed from the apron in which she had enfolded them, as a protection from the gathering cold, and she had seized and adjusted the wooden yoke across her shoulders, ready to bear the brimming milk-pails to the dairy.

'Look yo' at her!' exclaimed Kester to Charley, as he adjusted the fragrant pails on the yoke. 'She thinks she's missus a'ready, and she's allays for carrying in t' milk since t' rhumatiz cotched my shouther i' t' back end;* and when she says "Yea," it's as much as my heed's worth to say "Nay."'

And along the wall, round the corner, down the round slippery stones of the rambling farmyard, behind the buildings, did Sylvia trip, safe and well-poised, though the ground wore all one coating of white snow, and in many places was so slippery as to oblige Kinraid to linger near Kester, the lantern-bearer. Kester did not lose his opportunity, though the cold misty night air provoked his asthmatic cough whenever he breathed, and often interrupted his words.

'She's a good wench – a good wench as iver was – an' come on a good stock, an' that's summat, whether in a cow or a woman. A've known her from a babby; she's a reet down good un.'

By this time they had reached the back kitchen door, just as Sylvia had unladen herself, and was striking a light with flint and tinder. The house seemed warm and inviting after the piercing outer air, although the kitchen into which they entered contained only a raked and slumbering fire at one end, over which, on a crook, hung the immense pan of potatoes cooking for the evening meal of the pigs. To this pan Kester immediately addressed himself, swinging it round with ease, owing to the admirable simplicity of the old-fashioned machinery. Kinraid stood between Kester and the door into the dairy, through which Sylvia had vanished with the milk. He half wished to conciliate Kester by helping him, but he seemed also attracted, by a force which annihilated his will, to follow her wherever she went. Kester read his mind.

'Let alone, let alone,' said he; 'pigs' vittle takes noan such dainty carryin' as milk. A may set it down an' niver spill a drop; she's noan fit for t' serve swine, nor yo' other, mester; better help her t' teem* t' milk.'

So Kinraid followed the light – his light – into the icy chill of the dairy, where the bright polished tin cans were quickly dimmed with the warm, sweet-smelling milk, that Sylvia was emptying out into the brown pans. In his haste to help her, Charley took up one of the pails.

'Eh? that'n 's to be strained. Yo' have a' the cow's hair in. Mother's very particular, and cannot abide a hair.'

So she went over to her awkward dairymaid, and before she – but not before he – was aware of the sweet proximity, she was adjusting his happy awkward arms to the new office of holding a milk-strainer over the bowl, and pouring the white liquid through it.

'There!' said she, looking up for a moment, and half blushing; 'now yo'll know how to do it next time.'

'I wish next time was to come now,' said Kinraid; but she had returned to her own pail, and seemed not to hear him. He followed her to her side of the dairy. 'I've but a short memory, can yo' not show me again how t' hold t' strainer?'

'No,' said she, half laughing, but holding her strainer fast in spite of his insinuating efforts to unlock her fingers. 'But there's no need to tell me yo've getten a short memory.'

'Why? what have I done? how dun you know it?'

'Last night,' she began, and then she stopped, and turned away her head, pretending to be busy in her daily duties of rinsing and such like.

'Well!' said he, half conjecturing her meaning, and flattered by it, if his conjecture were right. 'Last night – what?'

'Oh, yo' know!' said she, as if impatient at being both literally and metaphorically followed about, and driven into a corner.

'No; tell me,' persisted he.

'Well,' said she, 'if yo' will have it, I think yo' showed yo'd but a short memory when yo' didn't know me again, and yo' were five times at this house last winter, and that's not so long sin'. But I suppose yo' see a vast o' things on yo'r voyages by land or by sea, and then it's but natural yo' should forget.' She wished she could go on talking, but could not think of anything more to say just then; for, in the middle of her sentence, the flattering interpretation he might put upon her words, on her knowing so exactly the number of times he had been to Haytersbank, flashed upon her, and she wanted to lead the conversation a little farther afield – to make it a little less personal. This was not his wish, however. In a tone which thrilled through her, even in her own despite, he said, –

'Do yo' think that can ever happen again, Sylvia?'

She was quite silent; almost trembling. He repeated the question as if to force her to answer. Driven to bay, she equivocated.

'What happen again? Let me go, I dunno what yo're talking about, and I'm a'most numbed wi' cold.'

For the frosty air came sharp in through the open lattice window, and the ice was already forming on the milk. Kinraid would have found a ready way of keeping his cousins, or indeed most young women, warm; but he paused before he dared put his arm round Sylvia; she had something so shy and wild in her look and manner; and her very innocence of what her words, spoken by another girl, might lead to, inspired him with respect, and kept him in check. So he contented himself with saying, –

'I'll let yo' go into t' warm kitchen if yo'll tell me if yo' think I can ever forget yo' again.'

She looked up at him defiantly, and set her red lips firm. He enjoyed her determination not to reply to this question; it showed she felt its significance. Her pure eyes looked steadily into his; nor was the expression in his such as to daunt her or make her afraid. They were like two children defying each other; each determined to conquer. At last she unclosed her lips, and nodding her head as if in triumph, said, as she folded her arms once more in her check apron, –

'Yo'll have to go home some time.'

'Not for a couple of hours yet,' said he; 'and yo'll be frozen first; so yo'd better say if I can ever forget yo' again, without more ado.'

Perhaps the fresh voices breaking on the silence, – perhaps the tones were less modulated than they had been before, but anyhow Bell Robson's voice was heard calling Sylvia through the second door, which opened from the dairy to the house-place, in which her mother had been till this moment asleep. Sylvia darted off in obedience to the call; glad to leave him, as at the moment Kinraid resentfully imagined. Through the open door he heard the conversation between mother and daughter, almost unconscious of its meaning, so difficult did he find it to wrench his thoughts from the ideas he had just been forming with Sylvia's bright lovely face right under his eyes.

'Sylvia!' said her mother, 'who's yonder?' Bell was sitting up in the attitude of one startled out of slumber into intensity of listening; her hands on each of the chair-arms, as if just going to rise. 'There's a fremd* man i' t' house. I heerd his voice!'

'It's only – it's just Charley Kinraid; he was a-talking to me i' t' dairy.'

'I' t' dairy, lass! and how com'd he i' t' dairy?'

'He com'd to see feyther. Feyther asked him last night,' said Sylvia, conscious that he could overhear every word that was said, and a little suspecting that he was no great favourite with her mother.

'Thy feyther's out; how com'd he i' t' dairy?' persevered Bell.

'He com'd past this window, and saw yo' asleep, and didn't like for t' waken yo'; so he com'd on to t' shippen, and when I carried t' milk in—'

But now Kinraid came in, feeling the awkwardness of his situation a little, yet with an expression so pleasant and manly in his open face, and in his exculpatory manner, that Sylvia lost his first words in a strange kind of pride of possession in him, about which she did not reason nor care to define the grounds. But her mother rose from her chair somewhat formally, as if she did not intend to sit down again while he stayed, yet was too weak to be kept in that standing attitude long.

'I'm afeared, sir, Sylvie hasn't told yo' that my master's out, and not like to be in till late. He'll be main and sorry to have missed yo'.'

There was nothing for it after this but to go. His only comfort was that on Sylvia's rosy face he could read unmistakable signs of regret and dismay. His sailor's life, in bringing him suddenly face to face with unexpected events, had given him something of that self-possession which we consider the attribute of a gentleman; and with an apparent calmness which almost disappointed Sylvia, who construed it into a symptom of indifference as to whether he went or stayed, he bade her mother good-night, and only said, in holding her hand a minute longer than was absolutely necessary, –

'I'm coming back ere I sail; and then, maybe, you'll answer yon question.'

He spoke low, and her mother was rearranging herself in her chair, else Sylvia would have had to repeat the previous words. As it was, with soft thrilling ideas ringing through her, she could get her wheel, and sit down to her spinning by the fire; waiting for her mother to speak first, Sylvia dreamt her dreams.

Bell Robson was partly aware of the state of things, as far as it lay on the surface. She was not aware how deep down certain feelings had penetrated into the girl's heart who sat on the other side of the fire, with a little sad air diffused over her face and figure. Bell looked upon Sylvia as still a child, to be warned off forbidden things by threats of danger. But the forbidden thing was already tasted, and possible danger in it full acquisition only served to make it more precious-sweet.

Bell sat upright in her chair, gazing into the fire. Her milk-white linen mob-cap fringed round and softened her face, from which the usual apple-red was banished by illness, and the features, from the same cause, rendered more prominent and stern. She had a clean buff kerchief round her neck, and stuffed into the bosom of her Sunday woollen gown of dark blue, – if she had been in working-trim she would have worn a bedgown like Sylvia's. Her sleeves were pinned back at the elbows, and her brown arms and hard-working hands lay crossed in unwonted idleness on her check apron. Her knitting was by her side; and if she had been going through any accustomed calculation or consideration she would have had it busily clinking in her fingers. But she had something quite beyond common to think about, and, perhaps, to speak about; and for the minute she was not equal to knitting.

'Sylvie,' she began at length, 'did I e'er tell thee on Nancy Hartley as I knew when I were a child? I'm thinking a deal on her to-night; maybe it's because I've been dreaming on yon old times. She was a bonny lass as ever were seen, I've heerd folk say; but that were afore I knew her. When I knew her she were crazy, poor wench; wi' her black hair a-streaming down her back, and her eyes, as were a'most as black, allays crying out for pity, though never a word she spoke but "He once was here."* Just that o'er and o'er again, whether she were cold or hot, full or hungry, "He once was here," were all her speech. She had been farm-servant to my mother's brother – James Hepburn, thy great-uncle as was; she were a poor, friendless wench, a parish 'prentice, but honest and gaum-like,* till a lad, as nobody knowed, come o'er the hills one sheep-shearing fra' Whitehaven; he had summat to do wi' th' sea, though not rightly to be called a sailor: and he made a deal on Nancy Hartley, just to beguile the time like; and he went away and ne'er sent a thought after her more. It's the way as lads have; and there's no holding 'em when they're fellows as nobody knows – neither where they come fro', nor what they've been doing a' their lives, till they come athwart some poor wench like Nancy Hartley. She were but a softy* after all: for she left off doing her work in a proper manner. I've heerd my aunt say as she found out as summat was wrong wi' Nancy as soon as th' milk turned bingy,* for there ne'er had been such a clean lass about her milk-cans afore that; and from bad it grew to worse, and she would sit and do nothing but play wi' her fingers fro' morn till night, and if they asked her what ailed her, she just said, "He once was here"; and if they bid her go about her work, it were a' the same. And when they scolded her, and pretty sharp too, she would stand up and put her hair from her eyes, and look about her like a crazy thing searching for her wits, and ne'er finding them, for all she could think on was just, "He once was here." It were a caution to me again thinking a man t' mean what he says when he's a-talking to a young woman.'

'But what became on poor Nancy?' asked Sylvia.

'What should become on her or on any lass as gives hersel' up to thinking on a man who cares nought for her?' replied her mother, a little severely. 'She were crazed, and my aunt couldn't keep her on, could she? She did keep her a long weary time, thinking as she would, maybe, come to hersel', and, anyhow, she were a motherless wench. But at length she had for t' go where she came fro' – back to Keswick workhouse: and when last I heerd on her she were chained to th' great kitchen dresser i' t' workhouse; they'd beaten her till she were taught to be silent and quiet i' th' daytime; but at night, when she were left alone, she would take up th' oud cry; till it wrung their heart, so they'd many a time to come down and beat her again to get any peace. It were a caution to me, as I said afore, to keep fro' thinking on men as thought nought on me.'

'Poor crazy Nancy!' sighed Sylvia. The mother wondered if she had taken the 'caution' to herself, or was only full of pity for the mad girl, dead long before.

CHAPTER 16

The Engagement

'As the day lengthens so the cold strengthens.'* It was so that year; the hard frost which began on New Year's Eve lasted on and on into late February, black and bitter, but welcome enough to the farmers, as it kept back the too early growth of autumn-sown wheat, and gave them the opportunity of leading* manure. But it did not suit invalids as well, and Bell Robson, though not getting worse, did not make any progress towards amendment. Sylvia was kept very busy, notwithstanding that she had the assistance of a poor widow-woman in the neighbourhood on cleaning, or washing, or churning days. Her life was quiet and monotonous, although hard-working; and while her hands mechanically found and did their accustomed labour, the thoughts that rose in her head always centred on Charley Kinraid, his ways, his words, his looks, whether they all meant what she would fain believe they did, and whether, meaning love at the time, such a feeling was likely to endure. Her mother's story of crazy Nancy had taken hold of her; but not as a 'caution', rather as a parallel case to her own. Like Nancy, and borrowing the poor girl's own words, she would say softly to herself, 'He once was here';* but all along she believed in her heart he would come back again to her, though it touched her strangely to imagine the agonies of forsaken love.

Philip knew little of all this. He was very busy with facts and figures, doggedly fighting through the necessary business, and only now and then allowing himself the delicious relaxation of going to Haytersbank in an evening, to inquire after his aunt's health, and to see Sylvia; for the two Fosters were punctiliously anxious to make their shopmen test all their statements; insisting on an examination of the stock, as if Hepburn and Coulson were strangers to the shop; having the Monkshaven auctioneer in to appraise the fixtures and necessary furniture; going over the shop books for the last twenty years with their successors, an employment which took up evening after evening; and not unfrequently taking one of the young men on the long commercial journeys which were tediously made in a gig. By degrees both Hepburn and Coulson were introduced to distant manufacturers and wholesale dealers. They would have been willing to take the Fosters' word for every statement the brothers had made on New Year's Day; but this, it was evident, would not have satisfied their masters, who were scrupulous in insisting that whatever advantage there was should always fall on the side of the younger men.

When Philip saw Sylvia she was always quiet and gentle; perhaps more silent than she had been a year ago, and she did not attend so briskly to what was passing around her. She was rather thinner and paler; but whatever change there was in her was always an improvement in Philip's eyes, so long as she spoke graciously to him. He thought she was suffering from long-continued anxiety about her mother, or that she had too much to do; and either cause was enough to make him treat her with a grave regard and deference which had a repressed tenderness in it, of which she, otherwise occupied, was quite unaware. She liked him better, too, than she had done a year or two before, because he did not show her any of the eager attention which teased her then, although its meaning was not fully understood.

Things were much in this state when the frost broke, and milder weather succeeded. This was the time so long looked forward to by the invalid and her friends, as favouring the doctor's recommendation of change of air. Her husband was to take her to spend a fortnight with a kindly neighbour, who lived near the farm they had occupied, forty miles or so inland, before they came to Haytersbank. The widow-woman was to come and stay in the house, to keep Sylvia company, during her mother's absence. Daniel, indeed, was to return home after conveying his wife to her destination; but there was so much to be done on the land at this time of the year, that Sylvia would have been alone all day had it not been for the arrangement just mentioned.

There was active stirring in Monkshaven harbour as well as on shore. The whalers were finishing their fittings-out for the Greenland seas. It was a 'close' season, that is to say, there would be difficulty in passing the barrier of ice which lay between the ships and the whaling-grounds; and yet these must be reached before June, or the year's expedition would be of little avail. Every blacksmith's shop rung with the rhythmical clang of busy hammers, beating out iron, such as horseshoes, nails or stubs, into the great harpoons; the quays were thronged with busy and important sailors, rushing hither and thither, conscious of the demand in which they were held at this season of the year. It was war time, too. Many captains unable to procure men in Monkshaven would have to complete their crews in the Shetlands. The shops in the town were equally busy; stores had to be purchased by the whaling-masters, warm clothing of all sorts to be provided. These were the larger wholesale orders; but many a man, and woman, too, brought out their small hoards to purchase extra comforts, or precious keepsakes for some beloved one. It was the time of the great half-yearly traffic of the place; another impetus was given to business when the whalers returned in the autumn, and the men were flush of money,* and full of delight at once more seeing their homes and their friends.

There was much to be done in Fosters' shop, and later hours were kept than usual. Some perplexity or other was occupying John and Jeremiah Foster; their minds were not so much on the alert as usual, being engaged on some weighty matter of which they had as yet spoken to no one. But it thus happened that they did not give the prompt assistance they were accustomed to render at such times; and Coulson had been away on some of the new expeditions devolving on him and Philip as future partners. One evening after the shop was closed, while they were examining the goods, and comparing the sales with the entries in the day-book, Coulson suddenly inquired –

'By the way, Hester, does thee know where the parcel of best bandanas is gone? There was four left, as I'm pretty sure, when I set off to Sandsend; and to-day Mark Alderson came in, and would fain have had one, and I could find none nowhere.'

'I sold t' last to-day, to yon sailor, the specksioneer, who fought the press-gang same time as poor Darley were killed. He took it, and three yards of yon pink ribbon wi' t' black and yellow crosses on it, as Philip could never abide. Philip has got 'em i' t' book, if he'll only look.'

'Is he here again?' said Philip; 'I didn't see him. What brings him here, where he's noan wanted?'

'T' shop were throng wi' folk,' said Hester, 'and he knew his own mind about the handkercher, and didn't tarry long. Just as he was leaving, his eye caught on t' ribbon, and he came back for it. It were when yo' were serving Mary Darby and there was a vast o' folk about yo'.'

'I wish I'd seen him,' said Coulson. 'I'd ha' gi'en him a word and a look he'd not ha' forgotten in a hurry.'

'Why, what's up?' said Philip, surprised at William's unusual manner, and, at the same time, rather gratified to find a reflection of his own feelings about Kinraid. Coulson's face was pale with anger, but for a moment or two he seemed uncertain whether he would reply or not.

'Up!' said he at length. 'It's just this: he came after my sister for better nor two year; and a better lass – no, nor a prettier i' my eyes – niver broke bread. And then my master saw another girl, that he liked better' – William almost choked in his endeavour to keep down all appearance of violent anger, and then went on, 'and that he played t' same game wi', as I've heerd tell.'

'And how did thy sister take it?' asked Philip, eagerly.

'She died in a six-month,' said William; '*she* forgave him, but it's beyond me. I thought it were him when I heerd of t' work about Darley; Kinraid – and coming fra' Newcassel, where Annie lived 'prentice – and I made inquiry, and it were t' same man. But I'll say no more about him, for it stirs t' old Adam more nor I like, or is fitting.'

Out of respect to him, Philip asked no more questions, although there were many things that he fain would have known. Both Coulson and he went silently and grimly through the remainder of their day's work. Independent of any personal interest which either or both of them had or might have in Kinraid's being a light o' love, this fault of his was one with which the two grave, sedate young men had no sympathy. Their hearts were true and constant, whatever else might be their failings; and it is no new thing to 'damn the faults we have no mind to'.* Philip wished that it was not so late, or that very evening he would have gone to keep guard over Sylvia in her mother's absence – nay, perhaps he might have seen reason to give her a warning of some kind. But, if he had done so, it would have been locking the stable-door after the steed was stolen.* Kinraid had turned his steps towards Haytersbank Farm as soon as ever he had completed his purchases. He had only come that afternoon to Monkshaven, and for the sole purpose of seeing Sylvia once more before he went to fulfil his engagement as specksioneer in the *Urania*, a whaling-vessel that was to sail from North Shields on Thursday morning, and this was Monday.

Sylvia sat in the house-place, her back to the long low window, in order to have all the light the afternoon hour afforded for her work. A basket of her father's unmended stockings was on the little round table beside her, and one was on her left hand, which she supposed herself to be mending; but from time to time she made long pauses, and looked in the fire; and yet there was but little motion of flame or light in it out of which to conjure visions. It was 'redd up' for the afternoon; covered with a black mass of coal, over which the equally black kettle hung on the crook. In the back-kitchen Dolly Reid, Sylvia's assistant during her mother's absence, chanted a lugubrious ditty, befitting her condition as a widow, while she cleaned tins, and cans, and milking-pails. Perhaps these bustling sounds prevented Sylvia from hearing approaching footsteps coming down the brow with swift advance; at any rate, she started and suddenly stood up as some one entered the open door. It was strange she should be so much startled, for the person who entered had been in her thoughts all during those long pauses. Charley Kinraid and the story of crazy Nancy had been the subjects for her dreams for many a day, and many a night. Now he stood there, bright and handsome as ever, with just that much timidity in his face, that anxiety as to his welcome, which gave his accost an added charm, could she but have perceived it. But she was so afraid of herself, so unwilling to show what she felt, and how much she had been thinking of him in his absence, that her reception seemed cold and still. She did not come forward to meet him; she went crimson to the very roots of her hair; but that, in the waning light, he could not see; and she shook so that she felt as if she could hardly stand, but the tremor was not visible to him. She wondered if he remembered the kiss that had passed between them on New Year's Eve – the words that had been spoken in the dairy on New Year's Day; the tones, the looks, that had accompanied those words. But all she said was –

'I didn't think to see yo'. I thought yo'd ha' sailed.'

'I told yo' I should come back, didn't I?' said he, still standing, with his hat in his hand, waiting to be asked to sit down; and she, in her bashfulness, forgetting to give the invitation, but, instead, pretending to be attentively mending the stocking she held. Neither could keep quiet and silent long. She felt his eyes were upon her, watching every motion, and grew more and more confused in her expression and behaviour. He was a little taken aback by the nature of his reception, and was not sure at first whether to take the great change in her manner, from what it had been when last he saw her, as a favourable symptom or otherwise. By-and-by, luckily for him, in some turn of her arm to reach the scissors on the table, she caught the edge of her work-basket, and down it fell. She stooped to pick up the scattered stockings and ball of worsted, and so did he; and when they rose up, he had fast hold of her hand, and her face was turned away, half ready to cry.

'What ails yo' at me?' said he, beseechingly. 'Yo might ha' forgotten me; and yet I thought we made a bargain against forgetting each other.' No answer. He went on: 'Yo've never been out o' my thoughts, Sylvia Robson; and I'm come back to Monkshaven for nought but to see you once and again afore I go away to the northern seas. It's not two hour sin' I landed at Monkshaven, and I've been near neither kith nor kin as yet; and now I'm here you won't speak to me.'

'I don't know what to say,' said she, in a low, almost inaudible tone. Then hardening herself, and resolving to speak as if she did not understand his only half-expressed meaning, she lifted up her head, and all but looking at him – while she wrenched her hand out of his – she said: 'Mother's gone to Middleham for a visit, and feyther's out i' t' plough-field wi' Kester; but he'll be in afore long.'

Charley did not speak for a minute or so. Then he said –

'Yo're not so dull as to think I'm come all this way for t' see either your father or your mother. I've a great respect for 'em both; but I'd hardly ha' come all this way for to see 'em, and me bound to be back i' Shields, if I walk every step of the way, by Wednesday night. It's that yo' won't understand my meaning, Sylvia; it's not that yo' don't, or that yo' can't.' He made no effort to repossess himself of her hand. She was quite silent, but in spite of herself she drew long hard breaths. 'I may go back to where I came from,' he went on. 'I thought to go to sea wi' a blessed hope to cheer me up, and a knowledge o' some one as loved me as I'd left behind; some one as loved me half as much as I did her; for th' measure o' my love toward her is so great and mighty, I'd be content wi' half as much from her, till I'd taught her to love me more. But if she's a cold heart and cannot care for a honest sailor, why, then, I'd best go back at once.'

He made for the door. He must have been pretty sure from some sign or other, or he would never have left it to her womanly pride to give way, and for her to make the next advance. He had not taken two steps when she turned quickly towards him, and said something – the echo of which, rather than the words themselves, reached him.

'I didn't know yo' cared for me; yo' niver said so.' In an instant he was back at her side, his arm round her in spite of her short struggle, and his eager passionate voice saying, 'Yo' never knowed I loved you, Sylvia? say it again, and look i' my face while yo' say it, if yo' can. Why, last winter I thought yo'd be such a woman when yo'd come to be one as my een had never looked upon, and this year, ever sin' I saw yo' i' the kitchen corner sitting crouching behind my uncle, I as good as swore I'd have yo' for wife, or never wed at all. And it was not long ere yo' knowed it, for all yo' were so coy, and now yo' have the face – no, yo' have not the face – come, my darling, what is it?' for she was crying; and on his turning her wet blushing face towards him the better to look at it, she suddenly hid it in his breast. He lulled and soothed her in his arms, as if she had been

a weeping child and he her mother; and then they sat down on
the settle together, and when she was more composed they
began to talk. He asked her about her mother; not sorry in his
heart at Bell Robson's absence. He had intended if necessary to
acknowledge his wishes and desires with regard to Sylvia to her
parents; but for various reasons he was not sorry that circumstances had given him the chance of seeing her alone, and
obtaining her promise to marry him without being obliged to
tell either her father or her mother at present. 'I ha' spent my
money pretty free,' he said, 'and I've ne'er a penny to the fore,
and yo'r parents may look for something better for yo', my
pretty: but when I come back fro' this voyage I shall stand a
chance of having a share i' th' *Urania*, and maybe I shall be
mate as well as specksioneer; and I can get a matter of from
seventy to ninety pound a voyage, let alone th' half-guineas for
every whale I strike, and six shilling a gallon on th' oil; and if I
keep steady wi' Forbes and Company, they'll make me master i'
time, for I've had good schooling, and can work a ship as well
as any man; an' I leave yo' wi' yo'r parents, or take a cottage
for yo' nigh at hand; but I would like to have something to the
fore, and that I shall have, please God, when we come back i'
th' autumn. I shall go to sea happy, now, thinking I've yo'r
word. Yo're not one to go back from it, I'm sure, else it's a long
time to leave such a pretty girl as yo', and ne'er a chance of a
letter reaching yo' just to tell yo' once again how I love yo', and
to bid yo' not forget yo'r true love.'

'There'll be no need o' that,' murmured Sylvia.

She was too dizzy with happiness to have attended much to
his details of his worldly prospects, but at the sound of his
tender words of love her eager heart was ready to listen.

'I don't know,' said he, wanting to draw her out into more
confession of her feelings. 'There's many a one ready to come
after yo'; and yo'r mother is not o'er captivated wi' me; and
there's yon tall fellow of a cousin as looks black at me, for if I'm
not mista'en he's a notion of being sweet on yo'hisself.'

'Not he,' said Sylvia, with some contempt in her tone. 'He's
so full o' business and t' shop, and o' makin' money' and gettin'
wealth.'

'Ay, ay; but perhaps when he gets a rich man he'll come and
ask my Sylvia to be his wife, and what will she say then?'

'He'll niver come asking such a foolish question,' said she, a little impatiently; 'he knows what answer he'd get if he did.'

Kinraid said, almost as if to himself, 'Yo'r mother favours him though.' But she, weary of a subject she cared nothing about, and eager to identify herself with all his interests, asked him about his plans almost at the same time that he said these last words; and they went on as lovers do, intermixing a great many tender expressions with a very little conversation relating to facts.

Dolly Reid came in, and went out softly, unheeded by them. But Sylvia's listening ears caught her father's voice, as he and Kester returned homewards from their day's work in the plough-field; and she started away, and fled upstairs in shy affright, leaving Charley to explain his presence in the solitary kitchen to her father.

He came in, not seeing that any one was there at first; for they had never thought of lighting a candle. Kinraid stepped forward into the firelight; his purpose of concealing what he had said to Sylvia quite melted away by the cordial welcome her father gave him the instant that he recognized him.

'Bless thee, lad! who'd ha' thought o' seein' thee? Why, if iver a thought on thee at all, it were half way to Davis' Straits.* To be sure, t' winter's been a dree season, and thou'rt, maybe, i' t' reet on't to mak' a late start. Latest start as iver I made was ninth o' March, an' we struck thirteen whales that year.'

'I have something to say to you,' said Charley, in a hesitating voice, so different to his usual hearty way, that Daniel gave him a keen look of attention before he began to speak. And, perhaps, the elder man was not unprepared for the communication that followed. At any rate, it was not unwelcome. He liked Kinraid, and had strong sympathy not merely with what he knew of the young sailor's character, but with the life he led, and the business he followed. Robson listened to all he said with approving nods and winks, till Charley had told him everything he had to say; and then he turned and struck his broad horny palm into Kinraid's as if concluding a bargain, while he expressed in words his hearty consent to their engagement. He wound up with a chuckle, as the thought struck him that this great piece of business, of disposing of their only child, had been concluded while his wife was away.

'A'm noane so sure as t' missus 'll like it,' said he; 'tho' whativer she'll ha' to say again it, mischief only knows.* But she's noane keen on matterimony; though a have made her as good a man as there is in a' t' Ridings. Anyhow, a'm master, and that she knows. But maybe, for t' sake o' peace an' quietness – tho' she's niver a scolding tongue, that a will say for her – we'n best keep this matter to ourselves till thou comes int' port again. T' lass upstairs 'll like nought better than t' curl hersel' round a secret and purr o'er it, just as t' oud cat does o'er her blind kitten.* But thou'll be wanting to see t' lass, a'll be bound. An oud man like me isn't as good company as a pretty lass.' Laughing a low rich laugh over his own wit, Daniel went to the bottom of the stairs, and called, 'Sylvie, Sylvie! come down, lass! a's reet; come down!'

For a time there was no answer. Then a door was unbolted, and Sylvia said, 'I can't come down again. I'm noane comin' down again to-night.'

Daniel laughed the more at this, especially when he caught Charley's look of disappointment.

'Hearken how she's bolted her door. She'll noane come near us this neet. Eh! but she's a stiff* little 'un; she's been our only one, and we'n mostly let her have her own way. But we'll have a pipe and a glass; and that, to my thinking, is as good company as iver a woman i' Yorkshire.'

CHAPTER 17

Rejected Warnings

The post arrived at Monkshaven three times in the week; sometimes, indeed, there were not a dozen letters in the bag, which was brought thither by a man in a light mail-cart, who took the better part of a day to drive from York; dropping private bags here and there on the moors, at some squire's lodge or roadside inn. Of the number of letters that arrived in Monkshaven, the Fosters, shopkeepers and bankers, had the largest share.

The morning succeeding the day on which Sylvia had engaged herself to Kinraid, the Fosters seemed unusually anxious to obtain their letters. Several times Jeremiah came out of the parlour in which his brother John was sitting in expectant silence, and, passing through the shop, looked up and down the market-place in search of the old lame woman, who was charitably employed to deliver letters, and who must have been lamer than ever this morning, to judge from the lateness of her coming. Although none but the Fosters knew the cause of their impatience for their letters, yet there was such tacit sympathy between them and those whom they employed, that Hepburn, Coulson, and Hester were all much relieved when the old woman at length appeared with her basket of letters.

One of these seemed of especial consequence to the good brothers. They each separately looked at the direction, and then at one another; and without a word they returned with it unread into the parlour, shutting the door, and drawing the green silk curtain close, the better to read it in privacy.

Both Coulson and Philip felt that something unusual was going on, and were, perhaps, as full of consideration as to the possible contents of this London letter, as of attention to their more immediate business. But fortunately there was little doing in the shop. Philip, indeed, was quite idle when John Foster opened the parlour-door, and, half doubtfully, called him into the room. As the door of communication shut the three in, Coulson felt himself a little aggrieved. A minute ago Philip and he were on a level of ignorance, from which the former was evidently going to be raised. But he soon returned to his usual state of acquiescence in things as they were, which was partly constitutional, and partly the result of his Quaker training.

It was apparently by John Foster's wish that Philip had been summoned. Jeremiah, the less energetic and decided brother, was still discussing the propriety of the step when Philip entered.

'No need for haste, John; better not call the young man till we have further considered the matter.'

But the young man was there in presence; and John's will carried the day.

It seemed from his account to Philip (explanatory of what he, in advance of his brother's slower judgment, thought to be a necessary step), that the Fosters had for some time received anonymous letters, warning them, with distinct meaning, though in ambiguous terms, against a certain silk-manufacturer in Spitalfields, with whom they had had straightforward business dealings for many years; but to whom they had latterly advanced money. The letters hinted at the utter insolvency of this manufacturer. They had urged their correspondent to give them his name in confidence, and this morning's letter had brought it; but the name was totally unknown to them, though there seemed no reason to doubt the reality of either it or the address, the latter of which was given in full. Certain circumstances were mentioned regarding the transactions between the Fosters and this manufacturer, which could be known only to those who were in the confidence of one or the other; and to the Fosters the man was, as has been said, a perfect stranger. Probably, they would have been unwilling to incur the risk they had done on this manufacturer Dickinson's account, if it had not been that he belonged to the same denomination as themselves, and was publicly distinguished for his excellent and philanthropic character; but these letters were provocative of anxiety, especially since this morning's post had brought out the writer's full name, and various particulars showing his intimate knowledge of Dickinson's affairs.

After much perplexed consultation, John had hit upon the plan of sending Hepburn to London to make secret inquiries respecting the true character and commercial position of the man whose creditors, not a month ago, they had esteemed it an honour to be.

Even now Jeremiah was ashamed of their want of confidence in one so good; he believed that the information they had received would all prove a mistake, founded on erroneous grounds, if not a pure invention of an enemy, and he had only been brought partially to consent to the sending of Hepburn, by his brother's pledging himself that the real nature of Philip's errand should be unknown to any human creature, save them three.

As all this was being revealed to Philip, he sat apparently unmoved and simply attentive. In fact, he was giving all his mind to understanding the probabilities of the case, leaving his own feelings in the background till his intellect should have done its work. He said little; but what he did say was to the point, and satisfied both brothers. John perceived that his messenger would exercise penetration and act with energy; while Jeremiah was soothed by Philip's caution in not hastily admitting the probability of any charge against Dickinson, and in giving full weight to his previous good conduct and good character.

Philip had the satisfaction of feeling himself employed on a mission which would call out his powers, and yet not exceed them. In his own mind he forestalled the instructions of his masters, and was silently in advance of John Foster's plans and arrangements, while he appeared to listen to all that was said with quiet business-like attention.

It was settled that the next morning he was to make his way northwards to Hartlepool, whence he could easily proceed either by land or sea to Newcastle, from which place smacks were constantly sailing to London. As to his personal conduct and behaviour there, the brothers overwhelmed him with directions and advice; nor did they fail to draw out of the strong box in the thick wall of their counting-house a more than sufficient sum of money for all possible expenses. Philip had never had so much in his hands before, and hesitated to take it, saying it was more than he should require; but they repeated, with fresh urgency, their warnings about the terrible high prices of London, till he could only resolve to keep a strict account, and bring back all that he did not expend, since nothing but his taking the whole sum would satisfy his employers.

When he was once more behind the counter, he had leisure enough for consideration as far as Coulson could give it him. The latter was silent, brooding over the confidence which Philip had apparently received, but which was withheld from him. He did not yet know of the culminating point – of Philip's proposed journey to London; that great city of London, which, from its very inaccessibility fifty years ago, loomed so magnificent through the mist of men's imaginations. It is not to be denied that Philip felt exultant at the mere fact of 'going to London'. But then again, the thought of leaving Sylvia; of going out of possible daily reach of her; of not seeing her for a week – a fortnight; nay, he might be away for a month, – for no rash hurry was to mar his delicate negotiation, – gnawed at his heart, and spoilt any enjoyment he might have anticipated from gratified curiosity, or even from the consciousness of being trusted by those whose trust and regard he valued. The sense of what he was leaving grew upon him the longer he thought on the subject; he almost wished that he had told his masters earlier in the conversation of his unwillingness to leave Monkshaven for so long a time; and then again he felt that the gratitude he owed them quite prohibited his declining any task they might impose, especially as they had more than once said that it would not do for them to appear in the affair, and yet that to no one else could they entrust so difficult and delicate a matter. Several times that day, as he perceived Coulson's jealous sullenness, he thought in his heart that the consequence of the excessive confidence for which Coulson envied him was a burden from which he would be thankful to be relieved.

As they all sat at tea in Alice Rose's house-place, Philip announced his intended journey; a piece of intelligence he had not communicated earlier to Coulson because he had rather dreaded the increase of dissatisfaction it was sure to produce, and of which he knew the expression would be restrained by the presence of Alice Rose and her daughter.

'To Lunnon!' exclaimed Alice.

Hester said nothing.

'Well! some folks has the luck!' said Coulson.

'Luck!' said Alice, turning sharp round on him. 'Niver let me hear such a vain word out o' thy mouth, laddie, again. It's the Lord's doing, and luck's the devil's way o' putting it. Maybe it's to try Philip he's sent there; happen it may be a fiery furnace to him; for I've heerd tell it's full o' temptations, and he may fall into sin – and then where'd be the "luck" on it? But why art ta going? and the morning, say'st thou? Why, thy best shirt is in t' suds,* and no time for t' starch and iron it. Whatten the great haste as should take thee to Lunnon wi'out thy ruffled* shirt?'

'It's none o' my doing,' said Philip; 'there's business to be done, and John Foster says I'm to do it; and I'm to start to-morrow.'

'I'll not turn thee out wi'out thy ruffled shirt, if I sit up a' neet,' said Alice, resolutely.

'Niver fret thyself, mother, about t' shirt,' said Philip. 'If I need a shirt, London's not what I take it for if I can't buy mysel' one ready-made.'

'Hearken to him!' said Alice. 'He speaks as if buying o' ready-made shirts were nought to him, and he wi' a good half-dozen as I made mysel'. Eh, lad? but if that's the frame o' mind thou'rt in, Lunnon is like for to be a sore place o' temptation. There's pitfalls for men, and traps for money at ivery turn, as I've heerd say. It would ha' been better if John Foster had sent an older man on his business, whativer it be.'

'They seem to make a deal o' Philip all on a sudden,' said Coulson. 'He's sent for, and talked to i' privacy, while Hester and me is left i' t shop for t' bear t' brunt o' t' serving.'

'Philip knows,' said Hester, and then, somehow, her voice failed her and she stopped.

Philip paid no attention to this half-uttered sentence; he was eager to tell Coulson, as far as he could do so without betraying his masters' secret, how many drawbacks there were to his proposed journey, in the responsibility which it involved, and his unwillingness to leave Monkshaven: he said –

'Coulson, I'd give a deal it were thou that were going, and not me. At least, there is many a time I'd give a deal. I'll not deny but at other times I'm pleased at the thought on't. But, if I could I'd change places wi' thee at this moment.'

'It's fine talking,' said Coulson, half mollified, and yet not caring to show it. 'I make no doubt it were an even chance betwixt us two at first, which on us was to go; but somehow thou got the start* and thou'st stuck to it till it'n too late for aught but to say thou's sorry.'

'Nay, William,' said Philip, rising, 'it's an ill look-out for the future, if thee and me is to quarrel, like two silly wenches, o'er each bit of pleasure, or what thou fancies to be pleasure, as falls in t' way of either on us. I've said truth to thee, and played thee fair, and I've got to go to Haytersbank for to wish 'em good-by, so I'll not stay longer here to be misdoubted by thee.'

He took his cap and was gone, not heeding Alice's shrill inquiry as to his clothes and his ruffled shirt. Coulson sat still, penitent and ashamed; at length he stole a look at Hester. She was playing with her teaspoon, but he could see that she was choking down her tears; he could not choose but force her to speak with an ill-timed question.

'What's to do, Hester?' said he.

She lifted up those eyes, usually so soft and serene; now they were full of the light of indignation shining through tears.

'To do!' she said; 'Coulson, I'd thought better of thee, going and doubting and envying Philip, as niver did thee an ill turn, or said an ill word, or thought an ill thought by thee; and sending him away out o' t' house this last night of all, maybe, wi' thy envyings and jealousy.'

She hastily got up and left the room. Alice was away, looking up Philip's things for his journey. Coulson remained alone, feeling like a guilty child, but dismayed by Hester's words, even more than by his own regret at what he had said.

Philip walked rapidly up the hill-road towards Haytersbank. He was chafed and excited by Coulson's words, and the events of the day. He had meant to shape his life, and now it was, as it were, being shaped for him, and yet he was reproached for the course it was taking, as much as though he were an active agent; accused of taking advantage over Coulson, his intimate companion for years; he who esteemed himself above taking an unfair advantage over any man! His feeling on the subject was akin to that of Hazael, 'Is thy servant a dog that he should do this thing?'*

His feelings, disturbed on this one point, shook his judgment off its balance on another. The resolution he had deliberately formed of not speaking to Sylvia on the subject of his love till he could announce to her parents the fact of his succession to Fosters' business, and till he had patiently, with long-continuing and deep affection, worked his way into her regard, was set aside during the present walk. He would speak to her of his passionate attachment, before he left, for an uncertain length of time, and the certain distance of London. And all the modification on this point which his judgment could obtain from his impetuous and excited heart was, that he would watch her words and manner well when he announced his approaching absence, and if in them he read the slightest token of tender regretful feeling, he would pour out his love at her feet, not even urging the young girl to make any return, or to express the feelings of which he hoped the germ was already budding in her. He would be patient with her; he could not be patient himself. His heart beating, his busy mind rehearsing the probable coming scene, he turned into the field-path that led to Haytersbank. Coming along it, and so meeting him, advanced Daniel Robson, in earnest talk with Charley Kinraid. Kinraid, then, had been at the farm: Kinraid had been seeing Sylvia, her mother away. The thought of poor dead Annie Coulson flashed into Philip's mind. Could he be playing the same game with Sylvia? Philip set his teeth and tightened his lips at the thought of it. They had stopped talking; they had seen him already, or his impulse would have been to dodge behind the wall and avoid them; even though one of his purposes in going to Haytersbank had been to bid his uncle farewell.

Kinraid took him by surprise from the hearty greeting he gave him, and which Philip would fain have avoided. But the specksioneer was full of kindliness towards all the world, especially towards all Sylvia's friends, and, convinced of her great love towards himself, had forgotten any previous jealousy of Philip. Secure and exultant, his broad, handsome, weather-bronzed face was as great a contrast to Philip's long, thoughtful, sallow countenance, as his frank manner was to the other's cold reserve. It was some minutes before Hepburn could bring himself to tell the great event that was about to befall him before this third person whom he considered as an intrusive stranger. But as Kinraid seemed to have no idea of going on, and as there really was no reason why he and all the world should not know of Philip's intentions, he told his uncle that he was bound for London the next day on business connected with the Fosters.

Daniel was deeply struck with the fact that he was talking to a man setting off for London at a day's notice.

'Thou'll niver tell me this hasn't been brewin' longer nor twelve hours; thou's a sly close chap, and we hannot seen thee this se'nnight; thou'll ha' been thinkin' on this, and cogitating it, maybe, a' that time.'

'Nay,' said Philip, 'I knew nought about it last night; it's none o' my doing, going, for I'd liefer ha' stayed where I am.'

'Yo'll like it when once yo're there,' said Kinraid, with a travelled air of superiority, as Philip fancied.

'No, I shan't,' he replied, shortly. 'Liking has nought do do with it.'

'An' yo' knew nought about it last neet,' continued Daniel, musingly. 'Well, life's soon o'er; else when I were a young fellow, folks made their wills afore goin' to Lunnon.'

'Yet I'll be bound to say yo' niver made a will before going to sea,' said Philip, half smiling.

'Na, na; but that's quite another mak' o' thing; goin' to sea comes natteral to a man, but goin' to Lunnon, – I were once there, and were near deafened wi' t' throng and t' sound. I were but two hours i' t' place, though our ship lay a fortneet off Gravesend.'

Kinraid now seemed in a hurry; but Philip was stung with

curiosity to ascertain his movements, and suddenly addressed him:

'I heard yo' were i' these parts. Are you for staying here long?'

There was a certain abruptness in Philip's tone, if not in his words, which made Kinraid look in his face with surprise, and answer with equal curtness.

'I'm off i' th' mornin, and sail for the north seas day after.'

He turned away, and began to whistle, as if he did not wish for any further conversation with his interrogator. Philip, indeed, had nothing more to say to him: he had learned all he wanted to know.

'I'd like to bid good-by to Sylvie. Is she at home?' he asked of her father.

'A'm thinking thou'll not find her. She'll be off to Yesterbarrow t' see if she'd get a settin'* o' their eggs; her grey speckled hen is cluckin', and nought'll serve our Sylvia but their eggs to set her upon. But, for a' that, she mayn't be gone yet. Best go on and see for thysel'.'

So they parted; but Philip had not gone many steps before his uncle called him back, Kinraid slowly loitering on meanwhile. Robson was fumbling among some dirty papers he had in an old leather case, which he had produced out of his pocket.

'Fact is, Philip, t' pleugh's in a bad way, gearin'* and a', an' folk is talkin' on a new kind o' mak'; and if thou's bound for York—'

'I'm not going by York; I'm going by a Newcastle smack.'

'Newcassel – Newcassel – it's pretty much t' same. Here, lad, thou can read print easy; it's a bit as was cut out on a papper; there's Newcassel, and York, and Durham, and a vast more towns named, wheere folk can learn a' about t' new mak' o' pleugh.'

'I see,' said Philip: '"Robinson, Side, Newcastle, can give all requisite information."'

'Ay, ay,' said Robson; 'thou's hit t' marrow on t' matter.* Now, if thou'rt i' Newcassel, thou can learn all about it; thou'rt little better nor a woman, for sure, bein' mainly acquaint wi' ribbons,* but they'll tell thee – they'll tell thee, lad; and write down what they sayn, and what's to be t' price, and look sharp as to what kind o' folk they are as sells 'em, an' write and let me know. Thou'll be i' Newcassel to-morrow, maybe? Well, then, I'll reckon to hear fro' thee in a week, or, mayhap, less, – for t' land is backward, and I'd like to know about t' pleughs. I'd a month's mind* to write to Brunton, as married Molly Corney, but writin' is more i' thy way an' t' parson's nor mine; and if thou sells ribbons, Brunton sells cheese, and that's no better.'

Philip promised to do his best, and to write word to Robson, who, satisfied with his willingness to undertake the commission, bade him go on and see if he could not find the lass. Her father was right in saying that she might not have set out for Yesterbarrow. She had talked about it to Kinraid and her father in order to cover her regret at her lover's accompanying her father to see some new kind of harpoon about which the latter had spoken. But as soon as they had left the house, and she had covertly watched them up the brow in the field, she sate down to meditate and dream about her great happiness in being beloved by her hero, Charley Kinraid. No gloomy dread of his long summer's absence; no fear of the cold, glittering icebergs bearing mercilessly down on the *Urania*, nor shuddering anticipation of the dark waves of evil import, crossed her mind. He loved her, and that was enough. Her eyes looked, trance-like, into a dim, glorious future of life; her lips, still warm and reddened by his kiss, were just parted in a happy smile, when she was startled by the sound of an approaching footstep – a footstep quite familiar enough for her to recognize it, and which was unwelcome now, as disturbing her in the one blessed subject of thought in which alone she cared to indulge.

'Well, Philip! an' what brings *yo*' here?' was her rather ungracious greeting.

'Why, Sylvia, are yo' sorry to see me?' asked Philip, reproachfully. But she turned it off with assumed lightness.

'Oh, yes,' said she. 'I've been wanting yo' this week past wi' t' match to my blue ribbon yo' said yo'd get and bring me next time yo' came.'

'I've forgotten it, Sylvie. It's clean gone out of my mind,' said Philip, with true regret. 'But I've had a deal to think on,' he continued, penitently, as if anxious to be forgiven. Sylvia did not want his penitence, did not care for her ribbon, was troubled by his earnestness of manner – but he knew nothing of all that; he only knew that she whom he loved had asked him to do something for her, and he had neglected it; so, anxious to be excused and forgiven, he went on with the apology she cared not to hear.

If she had been less occupied with her own affairs, less engrossed with deep feeling, she would have reproached him, if only in jest, for his carelessness. As it was, she scarcely took in the sense of his words.

'You see, Sylvie, I've had a deal to think on; before long I intend telling yo' all about it; just now I'm not free to do it. And when a man's mind is full o' business, most particular when it's other folk's as is trusted to him, he seems to lose count on the very things he'd most care for at another time.' He paused a little.

Sylvia's galloping thoughts were pulled suddenly up by his silence; she felt that he wanted her to say something, but she could think of nothing besides an ambiguous –

'Well? '

'And I'm off to London i' t' morning,' added he, a little wistfully, almost as if beseeching her to show or express some sorrow at a journey, the very destination of which showed that he would be absent for some time.

'To Lunnon!' said she, with some surprise. 'Yo're niver thinking o' going to live theere, for sure!'

Surprise, and curiosity, and wonder; nothing more, as Philip's instinct told him. But he reasoned that first correct impression away with ingenious sophistry.

'Not to live there: only to stay for some time. I shall be back, I reckon, in a month or so.'

'Oh! that's nought of a going away,' said she, rather petulantly. 'Them as goes to t' Greenland seas has to bide away for six months and more,' and she sighed.

Suddenly a light shone down into Philip's mind. His voice was changed as he spoke next.

'I met that good-for-nothing chap, Kinraid, wi' yo'r father just now. He'll ha' been here, Sylvie?'

She stooped for something she had dropped, and came up red as a rose.

'To be sure; what then?' And she eyed him defiantly, though in her heart she trembled, she knew not why.

'What then? and yo'r mother away. He's no company for such as thee, at no time, Sylvie.'

'Feyther and me chooses our own company, without iver asking leave o' yo',' said Sylvia, hastily arranging the things in the little wooden work-box that was on the table, preparatory to putting it away. At the time, in his agitation, he saw, but did not affix any meaning to it, that the half of some silver coin was among the contents thus turned over before the box was locked.

'But thy mother wouldn't like it, Sylvie; he's played false wi' other lasses, he'll be playing thee false some o' these days, if thou lets him come about thee. He went on wi' Annie Coulson, William's sister, till he broke her heart; and sin then he's been on wi' others.'

'I dunnot believe a word on 't,' said Sylvia, standing up, all aflame.

'I niver telled a lie i' my life,' said Philip, almost choking with grief at her manner to him, and the regard for his rival which she betrayed. 'It were Willie Coulson as telled me, as solemn and serious as one man can speak to another; and he said it weren't the first nor the last time as he had made his own game with young women.'

'And how dare yo' come here to me wi' yo'r backbiting tales?' said Sylvia, shivering all over with passion.

Philip tried to keep calm, and to explain.

'It were yo'r own mother, Sylvia, as knowed yo' had no brother, or any one to see after yo'; and yo' so pretty, so pretty, Sylvia,' he continued, shaking his head, sadly, 'that men run after yo' against their will, as one may say; and yo'r mother made me watch o'er ye and see what company yo' kept, and who was following after yo', and to warn yo', if need were.'

'My mother niver bade yo' to come spying after me, and blaming me for seeing a lad as my feyther thinks well on. An' I don't believe a word about Annie Coulson; an' I'm not going to suffer yo' to come wi' yo'r tales to me; say 'em out to his face, and hear what he'll say to yo'.'

'Sylvie, Sylvie,' cried poor Philip, as his offended cousin rushed past him, and upstairs to her little bedroom, where he heard the sound of the wooden bolt flying into its place. He could hear her feet pacing quickly about through the unceiled rafters. He sat still in despair, his head buried in his two hands. He sate till it grew dusk, dark; the wood fire, not gathered together by careful hands, died out into grey ashes. Dolly Reid had done her work and gone home. There were but Philip and Sylvia in the house. He knew he ought to be going home, for he had much to do, and many arrangements to make. Yet it seemed as though he could not stir. At length he raised his stiffened body, and stood up, dizzy. Up the little wooden stairs he went, where he had never been before, to the small square landing, almost filled up with the great chest for oat-cake. He breathed hard for a minute, and then knocked at the door of Sylvia's room.

'Sylvie! I'm going away; say good-by.' No answer. Not a sound heard. 'Sylvie!' (a little louder, and less hoarsely spoken). There was no reply. 'Sylvie! I shall be a long time away; perhaps I may niver come back at all'; here he bitterly thought of an unregarded death. 'Say good-by.' No answer. He waited patiently. Can she be wearied out, and gone to sleep, he wondered. Yet once again – 'Good-by, Sylvie, and God bless yo'! I'm sorry I vexed yo'.'

No reply.

With a heavy, heavy heart he creaked down the stairs, felt for his cap, and left the house.

'She's warned, any way,' thought he. Just at that moment the little casement window of Sylvia's room was opened, and she said –

'Good-by, Philip!'

The window was shut again as soon as the words were spoken. Philip knew the uselessness of remaining; the need for his departure; and yet he stood still for a little time like one entranced, as if his will had lost all power to compel him to leave the place. Those two words of hers, which two hours before would have been so far beneath his aspirations, had now power to re-light hope, to quench reproach or blame.

'She's but a young lassie,' said he to himself; 'an' Kinraid has been playing wi' her, as such as he can't help doing, once they get among t' women. An' I came down sudden on her about Annie Coulson, and touched her pride. Maybe, too, it were ill advised to tell her how her mother was feared for her. I couldn't ha' left the place to-morrow if he'd been biding here; but he's off for half a year or so, and I'll be home again as soon as iver I can. In half a year such as he forgets, if iver he's thought serious about her; but in a' my lifetime, if I live to fourscore, I can niver forget. God bless her for saying, 'Good-by, Philip.' He repeated the words aloud in fond mimicry of her tones: 'Good-by, Philip.'

CHAPTER 18

Eddy in Love's Current

The next morning shone bright and clear, if ever a March morning did. The beguiling month was coming in like a lamb, with whatever storms it might go raging out. It was long since Philip had tasted the freshness of the early air on the shore, or in the country, as his employment at the shop detained him in Monkshaven till the evening. And as he turned down the quays (or staithes) on the north side of the river, towards the shore, and met the fresh sea-breeze blowing right in his face, it was impossible not to feel bright and elastic. With his knapsack slung over his shoulder, he was prepared for a good stretch towards Hartlepool, whence a coach would take him to Newcastle before night. For seven or eight miles the level sands were as short and far more agreeable a road than the up and down land-ways. Philip walked on pretty briskly, unconsciously enjoying the sunny landscape before him; the crisp curling waves rushing almost up to his feet, on his right hand, and then swishing back over the fine small pebbles into the great swelling sea. To his left were the cliffs rising one behind another, having deep gullies here and there between, with long green slopes upward from the land, and then sudden falls of brown and red soil or rock deepening to a yet greater richness of colour at their base towards the blue ocean before him. The loud, monotonous murmur of the advancing and receding waters lulled him into dreaminess; the sunny look of everything tinged his daydreams with hope. So he trudged merrily over the first mile or so; not an obstacle to his measured pace on the hard, level pavement; not a creature to be seen since he had left the little gathering of bare-legged urchins dabbling in the seapools near Monkshaven. The cares of land were shut out by the glorious barrier of rocks before him. There were some great masses that had been detached by the action of the weather, and lay half embedded in the sand, draperied over by the heavy pendent olive-green sea-weed. The waves were nearer at this point; the advancing sea came up with a mighty distant length of roar; here and there the smooth swell was lashed by the fret against unseen rocks into white breakers; but otherwise the waves came up from the

German Ocean upon that English shore with a long steady roll that might have taken its first impetus far away, in the haunt of the sea-serpent on the coast of 'Norroway over the foam'.* The air was soft as May; right overhead the sky was blue, but it deadened into gray near the sea lines. Flocks of seagulls hovered about the edge of the waves, slowly rising and turning their white underplumage to glimmer in the sunlight as Philip approached. The whole scene was so peaceful, so soothing, that it dispelled the cares and fears (too well founded in fact) which had weighed down on his heart during the dark hours of the past night.

There was Haytersbank gully opening down its green entrance among the warm brown bases of the cliffs. Below, in the sheltered brushwood, among the last year's withered leaves, some primroses might be found. He half thought of gathering Sylvia a posy of them, and rushing up to the farm to make a little farewell peace-offering. But on looking at his watch, he put all thoughts of such an action out of his head; it was above an hour later than he had supposed, and he must make all haste on to Hartlepool. Just as he was approaching this gully, a man came dashing down, and ran out some way upon the sand with the very force of his descent; then he turned to the left and took the direction of Hartlepool a hundred yards or so in advance of Philip. He never stayed to look round him, but went swiftly and steadily on his way. By the peculiar lurch in his walk – by everything – Philip knew it was the specksioneer, Kinraid.

Now the road up Haytersbank gully led to the farm, and nowhere else. Still any one wishing to descend to the shore might do so by first going up to the Robsons' house, and skirting the walls till they came to the little slender path down to the shore. But by the farm, by the very house-door they must of necessity pass. Philip slackened his pace, keeping under the shadow of the rock. By-and-by Kinraid, walking on the sunlit open sands, turned round and looked long and earnestly towards Haytersbank gully. Hepburn paused when he paused, but as intently as he looked at some object above, so intently did Hepburn look at him. No need to ascertain by sight towards whom his looks, his thoughts were directed. He took off his hat and waved it, touching one part of it as if with particular meaning. When he turned away at last, Hepburn heaved a heavy sigh, and crept yet more into the cold dank shadow of the cliffs.

Each step was now a heavy task, his sad heart tired and weary. After a while he climbed up a few feet, so as to mingle his form yet more completely with the stones and rocks around. Stumbling over the uneven and often jagged points, slipping on the seaweed, plunging into little pools of water left by the ebbing tide in some natural basins, he yet kept his eyes fixed as if in fascination on Kinraid, and made his way almost alongside of him. But the last hour had pinched Hepburn's features into something of the wan haggardness they would wear when he should first be lying still for ever.

And now the two men were drawing near a creek, about eight miles from Monkshaven. The creek was formed by a beck (or small stream) that came flowing down from the moors, and took its way to the sea between the widening rocks. The melting of the snows and running of the flooded water-springs above made this beck in the early spring-time both deep and wide. Hepburn knew that here they both must take a path leading inland to a narrow foot-bridge about a quarter of a mile up the stream; indeed from this point, owing to the jutting out of the rocks, the land path was the shortest; and this way lay by the water-side at an angle right below the cliff to which Hepburn's steps were leading him. He knew that on this long level field path he might easily be seen by any one following; nay, if he followed any one at a short distance, for it was full of turnings; and he resolved, late as he was, to sit down for a while till Kinraid was far enough in advance for him to escape being seen. He came up to the last rock behind which he could be concealed; seven or eight feet above the stream he stood, and looked cautiously for the specksioneer. Up by the rushing stream he looked, then right below.

'It is God's providence,' he murmured. 'It is God's providence.'

He crouched down where he had been standing and covered his face with his hands. He tried to deafen as well as to blind himself, that he might neither hear nor see anything of the coming event of which he, an inhabitant of Monkshaven at that day, well understood the betokening signs.

Kinraid had taken the larger angle of the sands before turning up towards the bridge. He came along now nearing the rocks. By this time he was sufficiently buoyant to whistle to himself. It steeled Philip's heart to what was coming to hear his rival

whistling, 'Weel may the keel row,' so soon after parting with
Sylvia.

The instant Kinraid turned the corner of the cliff, the ambush
was upon him. Four man-of-war's men sprang on him and
strove to pinion him.

'In the King's name!' cried they, with rough, triumphant jeers.

Their boat was moored not a dozen yards above; they were
sent by the tender of a frigate lying off Hartlepool for fresh
water. The tender was at anchor just beyond the jutting rocks in
face.

They knew that fishermen were in the habit of going to and
from their nets by the side of the creek; but such a prize as this
active, strong, and evidently superior sailor, was what they had
not hoped for, and their endeavours to secure him were in
proportion to the value of the prize.

Although taken by surprise, and attacked by so many, Kinraid
did not lose his wits. He wrenched himself free, crying out loud:

'Avast, I'm a protected whaler. I claim my protection. I've my
papers to show, I'm bonded specksioneer to the *Urania* whaler,
Donkin captain, North Shields port.'

As a protected whaler, the press-gang had, by the 17th section
of Act 26 Geo. III. no legal right to seize him, unless he had
failed to return to his ship by the 10th March following the date
of his bond. But of what use were the papers he hastily dragged
out of his breast; of what use were laws in those days of slow
intercourse with such as were powerful enough to protect, and
in the time of popular panic against a French invasion?

'D – n your protection,' cried the leader of the press-gang;
'come and serve his Majesty, that's better than catching whales.'

'Is it though?' said the specksioneer, with a motion of his
hand, which the swift-eyed sailor opposed to him saw and
interpreted rightly.

'Thou wilt, wilt thou? Close with him, Jack; and ware the
cutlass.'

In a minute his cutlass was forced from him, and it became a
hand-to-hand struggle, of which, from the difference in numbers, it was not difficult to foretell the result. Yet Kinraid made
desperate efforts to free himself; he wasted no breath in words,
but fought, as the men said, 'like a very devil'.

Hepburn heard loud pants of breath, great thuds, the dull
struggle of limbs on the sand, the growling curses of those who

thought to have managed their affair more easily; the sudden cry of some one wounded, not Kinraid he knew, Kinraid would have borne any pain in silence at such a moment; another wrestling, swearing, infuriated strife, and then a strange silence. Hepburn sickened at the heart; was then his rival dead? had he left this bright world? Lost his life – his love? For an instant Hepburn felt guilty of his death;* he said to himself he had never wished him dead, and yet in the struggle he had kept aloof, and now it might be too late for ever. Philip could not bear the suspense; he looked stealthily round the corner of the rock behind which he had been hidden, and saw that they had overpowered Kinraid, and, too exhausted to speak, were binding him hand and foot to carry him to their boat.

Kinraid lay as still as any hedgehog: he rolled when they pushed him; he suffered himself to be dragged without any resistance, any motion; the strong colour brought into his face while fighting was gone now, his countenance was livid pale; his lips were tightly held together, as if it cost him more effort to be passive, wooden, and stiff in their hands than it had done to fight and struggle with all his might. His eyes seemed the only part about him that showed cognizance of what was going on. They were watchful, vivid, fierce as those of a wild cat brought to bay, seeking in its desperate quickened brain for some mode of escape not yet visible, and in all probability never to become visible to the hopeless creature in its supreme agony.

Without a motion of his head, he was perceiving and taking in everything while he lay bound at the bottom of the boat. A sailor sat by his side, who had been hurt by a blow from him. The man held his head in his hand, moaning; but every now and then he revenged himself by a kick at the prostrate specksioneer, till even his comrades stopped their cursing and swearing at their prisoner for the trouble he had given them, to cry shame on their comrade. But Kinraid never spoke, nor shrank from the outstretched foot.

One of his captors, with the successful insolence of victory, ventured to jeer him on the supposed reason for his vehement and hopeless resistance.

He might have said yet more insolent things; the kicks might have hit harder; Kinraid did not hear or heed. His soul was beating itself against the bars of inflexible circumstance; review-ing in one terrible instant of time what had been, what might have been, what was. Yet while these thoughts thus stabbed him, he was still mechanically looking out for chances. He moved his head a little, so as to turn towards Haytersbank, where Sylvia must be quickly, if sadly, going about her simple daily work; and then his quick eye caught Hepburn's face, blanched with excitement rather than fear, watching eagerly from behind the rock, where he had sat breathless during the affray and the impressment of his rival.

'Come here, lad!' shouted the specksioneer as soon as he saw Philip, heaving and writhing his body the while with so much vigour that the sailors started away from the work they were engaged in about the boat, and held him down once more, as if afraid be should break the strong rope that held him like withes of green flax. But the bound man had no such notion in his head. His mighty wish was to call Hepburn near, that he might send some message by him to Sylvia. 'Come here, Hepburn,' he cried again, falling back this time so weak and exhausted that the man-of-war's men became sympathetic.

'Come down, peeping Tom, and don't be afeared.' they called out.

'I'm not afeared,' said Philip; 'I'm no sailor for yo t' impress me: nor have yo' any right to take that fellow; he is a Greenland specksioneer, under protection, as I know and can testify.'

'Yo' and yo'r testify go hang. Make haste, man, and hear what this gem'man, as was in a dirty blubbery whale-ship, and is now in his Majesty's service, has got to say. I dare say, Jack,' went on the speaker, 'it's some message to his sweetheart, asking her to come for to serve on board ship along with he, like Billy Taylor's young woman.'

Philip was coming towards them slowly, not from want of activity, but because he was undecided what he should be called upon to do or to say by the man whom he hated and dreaded, yet whom just now he could not help admiring.

Kinraid groaned with impatience at seeing one, free to move with quick decision, so slow and dilatory.

'Come on then,' cried the sailors, 'or we'll take you too on board, and run you up and down the main-mast a few times. Nothing like life aboard ship for quickening a land-lubber.'

'Yo'd better take him and leave me,' said Kinraid, grimly. 'I've been taught my lesson; and seemingly he has his yet to learn.'

'His Majesty isn't a schoolmaster to need scholars; but a jolly good captain to need men,' replied the leader of the gang, eyeing Philip nevertheless, and questioning within himself how far, with only two other available men, they durst venture on his capture as well as the specksioneer's. It might be done, he thought, even though there was this powerful captive aboard, and the boat to manage too; but, running his eye over Philip's figure, he decided that the tall stooping fellow was never cut out for a sailor, and that he should get small thanks if he captured him, to pay him for the possible risk of losing the other. Or else the mere fact of being a landsman was of as little consequence to the press-gang, as the protecting papers which Kinraid had vainly showed.

'Yon fellow wouldn't have been worth his grog this many a day, and be d – d to you,' said he, catching Hepburn by the shoulder, and giving him a push. Philip stumbled over something in this, his forced run. He looked down; his foot had caught in Kinraid's hat, which had dropped off in the previous struggle. In the band that went round the low crown, a ribbon was knotted; a piece of that same ribbon which Philip had chosen out, with such tender hope, to give to Sylvia for the Corneys' party on New Year's Eve. He knew every delicate thread that made up the briar-rose pattern; and a spasm of hatred towards Kinraid contracted his heart. He had been almost relenting into pity for the man captured before his eyes; now he abhorred him.

Kinraid did not speak for a minute or two. The sailors, who had begun to take him into favour, were all agog with curiosity to hear the message to his sweetheart, which they believed he was going to send. Hepburn's perceptions, quickened with his vehement agitation of soul, were aware of this feeling of theirs; and it increased his rage against Kinraid, who had exposed the idea of Sylvia to be the subject of ribald whispers. But the specksioneer cared little what others said or thought about the maiden, whom he yet saw before his closed eyelids as she stood watching him, from the Haytersbank gully, waving her hands, her handkerchief, all in one passionate farewell.

'What do yo' want wi' me?' asked Hepburn at last, in a gloomy tone. If he could have helped it, he would have kept silence till Kinraid spoke first; but he could no longer endure the sailors' nudges, and winks, and jests among themselves.

'Tell Sylvia,' said Kinraid —

'There's a smart name for a sweetheart,' exclaimed one of the men; but Kinraid went straight on, –

'What yo've seen; how I've been pressed by this cursed gang.'

'Civil words, messmate, if you please. Sylvia can't abide cursing and swearing, I'm sure. We're gentlemen serving his Majesty on board the *Alcestis*,* and this proper young fellow shall be helped on to more honour and glory than he'd ever get bobbing for whales. Tell Sylvia this, with my love; Jack Carter's love, if she's anxious about my name.'

One of the sailors laughed at this rude humour; another bade Carter hold his stupid tongue. Philip hated him in his heart. Kinraid hardly heard him. He was growing faint with the heavy blows he had received, the stunning fall he had met with, and the reaction from his dogged self-control at first.

Philip did not speak nor move.

'Tell her,' continued Kinraid, rousing himself for another effort, 'what yo've seen. Tell her I'll come back to her. Bid her not forget the great oath we took together this morning; she's as much my wife as if we'd gone to church; – I'll come back and marry her afore long.'

Philip said something inarticulately.

'Hurra!' cried Carter, 'and I'll be best man. Tell her, too, that I'll have an eye on her sweetheart, and keep him from running after other girls.'

'Yo'll have yo'r hands full, then,' muttered Philip, his passion boiling over at the thought of having been chosen out from among all men to convey such a message as Kinraid's to Sylvia.

'Make an end of yo'r d – d yarns, and be off,' said the man who had been hurt by Kinraid, and who had sate apart and silent till now.

Philip turned away; Kinraid raised himself and cried after him, –

'Hepburn, Hepburn! tell her—' what he added Philip could not hear, for the words were lost before they reached him in the outward noise of the regular splash of the oars and the rush of the wind down the gully, with which mingled the closer sound that filled his ears of his own hurrying blood surging up into his brain. He was conscious that he had said something in reply to Kinraid's adjuration that he would deliver his message to Sylvia, at the very time when Carter had stung him into fresh anger by the allusion to the possibility of the specksioneer's 'running after other girls', for, for an instant, Hepburn had been touched by the contrast of circumstances. Kinraid an hour or two ago, – Kinraid a banished man; for in those days, an impressed sailor might linger out years on some foreign station, far from those he loved, who all this time remained ignorant of his cruel fate.

But Hepburn began to wonder what he himself had said – how much of a promise he had made to deliver those last passionate words of Kinraid's. He could not recollect how much, how little he had said; he knew he had spoken hoarsely and low almost at the same time as Carter had uttered his loud joke. But he doubted if Kinraid had caught his words.

And then the dread Inner Creature,* who lurks in each of our hearts, arose and said, 'It is as well: a promise given is a fetter to the giver. But a promise is not given when it has not been received.'

At a sudden impulse, he turned again towards the shore when he had crossed the bridge, and almost ran towards the verge of the land. Then he threw himself down on the soft fine turf that grew on the margin of the cliffs overhanging the sea, and commanding an extent of view towards the north. His face supported by his hands, he looked down upon the blue rippling ocean, flashing here and there, into the sunlight in long, glittering lines. The boat was still in the distance, making her swift silent way with long regular bounds to the tender that lay in the offing.

Hepburn felt insecure, as in a nightmare dream, so long as the boat did not reach her immediate destination. His contracted eyes could see four minute figures rowing with ceaseless motion, and a fifth sat at the helm. But he knew there was a sixth, unseen, lying, bound and helpless, at the bottom of the boat; and his fancy kept expecting this man to start up and break his bonds, and overcome all the others, and return to the shore – free and triumphant.

It was by no fault of Hepburn's that the boat sped well away; that she was now alongside the tender, dancing on the waves; now emptied of her crew; now hoisted up to her place. No fault of his! and yet it took him some time before he could reason himself into the belief that his mad, feverish wishes not an hour before – his wild prayer to be rid of his rival, as he himself had scrambled onward over the rocks alongside of Kinraid's path on the sands – had not compelled the event.

'Anyhow,' thought he, as he rose up, 'my prayer is granted. God be thanked!'

Once more he looked out towards the ship. She had spread her beautiful great sails, and was standing out to sea in the glittering path of the descending sun.

He saw that he had been delayed on his road, and had lingered long. He shook his stiffened limbs, shouldered his knapsack, and prepared to walk on to Hartlepool as swiftly as he could.

CHAPTER 19

An Important Mission

Philip was too late for the coach he had hoped to go by, but there was another that left at night, and which reached Newcastle in the forenoon, so that, by the loss of a night's sleep, he might overtake his lost time. But, restless and miserable, he could not stop in Hartlepool longer than to get some hasty food at the inn from which the coach started. He acquainted himself with the names of the towns through which it would pass, and the inns at which it would stop, and left word that the coachman was to be on the look-out for him and pick him up at some one of these places.

He was thoroughly worn out before this happened – too much tired to gain any sleep in the coach. When he reached Newcastle, he went to engage his passage in the next London bound smack, and then directed his steps to Robinson's, in the Side, to make all the inquiries he could think of respecting the plough his uncle wanted to know about.

So it was pretty late in the afternoon, indeed almost evening, before he arrived at the small inn on the quay-side, where he intended to sleep. It was but a rough kind of place, frequented principally by sailors; he had been recommended to it by Daniel Robson, who had known it well in former days. The accommodation in it was, however, clean and homely, and the people keeping it were respectable enough in their way.

Still Hepburn was rather repelled by the appearance of the

sailors who sat drinking in the bar, and he asked, in a low voice, if there was not another room. The woman stared in surprise, and only shook her head. Hepburn went to a separate table, away from the roaring fire, which on this cold March evening was the great attraction, and called for food and drink. Then seeing that the other men were eyeing him with the sociable idea of speaking to him, he asked for pen and ink and paper, with the intention of defeating their purpose by pre-occupation on his part. But when the paper came, the new pen, the unused thickened ink, he hesitated long before he began to write; and at last he slowly put down the words, –

'DEAR AND HONOURED UNCLE,' —

There was a pause; his meal was brought and hastily swallowed. Even while he was eating it, he kept occasionally touching up the letters of these words. When he had drunk a glass of ale he began again to write: fluently this time, for he was giving an account of the plough. Then came another long stop; he was weighing in his own mind what he should say about Kinraid. Once he thought for a second of writing to Sylvia herself, and telling her—how much? She might treasure up her lover's words like grains of gold, while they were lighter than dust in their meaning to Philip's mind; words which such as the specksioneer used as counters* to beguile and lead astray silly women. It was for him to prove his constancy by action; and the chances of his giving such proof were infinitesimal in Philip's estimation. But should the latter mention the bare fact of Kinraid's impressment to Robson? That would have been the natural course of things, remembering that the last time Philip had seen either, they were in each other's company. Twenty times he put his pen to the paper with the intention of relating briefly the event that had befallen Kinraid; and as often he stopped, as though the first word would be irrevocable. While he thus sat pen in hand, thinking himself wiser than conscience, and looking on beyond the next step which she bade him take into an indefinite future, he caught some fragments of the sailors' talk at the other end of the room, which made him listen to their words. They were speaking of that very Kinraid, the thought of whom filled his own mind like an actual presence. In a rough, careless way they spoke of the specksioneer, with admiration enough for his powers as a sailor and harpooner; and from that they passed on to jesting mention of his power amongst women, and one or two girls' names were spoken of in connection with him. Hepburn silently added Annie Coulson and Sylvia Robson to this list, and his cheeks turned paler as he did so. Long after they had done speaking about Kinraid, after they had paid their shot,* and gone away, he sat in the same attitude, thinking bitter thoughts.

The people of the house prepared for bed. Their silent guest took no heed of their mute signs. At length the landlord spoke to him, and he started, gathered his wits together with an effort, and prepared to retire with the rest. But before he did so, he signed and directed the letter to his uncle, leaving it still open, however, in case some sudden feeling should prompt him to add a postscript. The landlord volunteered the information that the letter his guest had been writing must be posted early the next morning if it was going south; as the mails in that direction only left Newcastle every other day.

All night long Hepburn wearied himself with passionate tossings, prompted by stinging recollection. Towards morning he fell into a dead sound sleep. He was roused by a hasty knocking at the door. It was broad full daylight; he had overslept himself, and the smack was leaving by the early tide. He was even now summoned on board. He dressed, wafered his letter,* and rushed with it to the neighbouring post-office; and, without caring to touch the breakfast for which he paid, he embarked. Once on board, he experienced the relief which it always is to an undecided man, and generally is at first to any one who has been paltering* with duty, when circumstances decide for him. In the first case, it is pleasant to be relieved from the burden of decision; in the second, the responsibility seems to be shifted on to impersonal events.

And so Philip sailed out of the mouth of the Tyne on to the great open sea. It would be a week before the smack reached London, even if she pursued a tolerably straight course, but she had to keep a sharp look-out after possible impressment of her crew; and it was not until after many dodges and some adventures that, at the end of a fortnight from the time of his leaving Monkshaven, Philip found himself safely housed in London, and ready to begin the delicate piece of work which was given him to do.

He felt himself fully capable of unravelling each clue to information, and deciding on the value of the knowledge so gained. But during the leisure of the voyage he had wisely determined to communicate everything he learnt about Dickinson, in short, every step he took in the matter, by letter to his employers. And thus his mind both in and out of his lodgings might have appeared to have been fully occupied with the concerns of others.

But there were times when the miserable luxury of dwelling upon his own affairs was his – when he lay down in his bed till he fell into restless sleep – when the point to which his steps tended in his walks was ascertained. Then he gave himself up to memory, and regret which often deepened into despair, and but seldom was cheered by hope.

He grew so impatient of the ignorance in which he was kept – for in those days of heavy postage* any correspondence he might have had on mere Monkshaven intelligence* was very limited – as to the affairs at Haytersbank, that he cut out an advertisement respecting some new kind of plough, from a newspaper that lay in the chop-house* where he usually dined, and rising early the next morning he employed the time thus gained in going round to the shop where these new ploughs were sold.

That night he wrote another letter to Daniel Robson, with a long account of the merits of the implements he had that day seen. With a sick heart and a hesitating hand, he wound up with a message of regard to his aunt and to Sylvia; an expression of regard which he dared not make as warm as he wished, and which, consequently, fell below the usual mark attained by such messages, and would have appeared to any one who cared to think about it as cold and formal.

When this letter was despatched, Hepburn began to wonder what he had hoped for in writing it. He knew that Daniel could write – or rather that he could make strange hieroglyphics, the meaning of which puzzled others and often himself; but these pen-and-ink signs were seldom employed by Robson, and never, so far as Philip knew, for the purpose of letter-writing. But still he craved so for news of Sylvia – even for a sight of paper which she had seen, and perhaps touched – that he thought all his trouble about the plough (to say nothing of the one-and-twopence postage which he had prepaid in order to make sure of his letter's reception in the frugal household at Haytersbank) well lost for the mere chance of his uncle's caring enough for the intelligence to write in reply, or even to get some friend to write an answer; for in such case, perhaps, Philip might see her name mentioned in some way, even though it was only that she sent her duty to him.

But the post-office was dumb; no letter came from Daniel Robson. Philip heard, it is true, from his employers pretty frequently on business; and he felt sure they would have named it, if any ill had befallen his uncle's family, for they knew of the relationship and of his intimacy there. They generally ended their formal letters with as formal a summary of Monkshaven news; but there was never a mention of the Robsons, and that of itself was well, but it did not soothe Philip's impatient curiosity. He had never confided his attachment to his cousin to any one, it was not his way; but he sometimes thought that if Coulson had not taken his present appointment to a confidential piece of employment so ill, he would have written to him and asked him to go up to Haytersbank Farm, and let him know how they all were.

All this time he was transacting the affair on which he had been sent, with great skill; and, indeed, in several ways, he was quietly laying the foundation for enlarging the business in Monkshaven. Naturally grave and quiet, and slow to speak, he impressed those who saw him with the idea of greater age and experience than he really possessed. Indeed, those who encountered him in London, thought he was absorbed in the business of money-making. Yet before the time came when he could wind up affairs and return to Monkshaven, he would have given all he possessed for a letter from his uncle, telling him something about Sylvia. For he still hoped to hear from Robson, although he knew that he hoped against reason. But we often convince ourselves by good argument that what we wish for need never have been expected; and then, at the end of our reasoning, find that we might have saved ourselves the trouble, for that our wishes are untouched, and are as strong enemies to our peace of mind as ever. Hepburn's baulked hope was the Mordecai sitting in Haman's gate;* all his success in his errand to London, his well-doing in worldly affairs, was tasteless, and gave him no pleasure, because of this blank and void of all intelligence concerning Sylvia.

And yet he came back with a letter from the Fosters in his pocket, curt, yet expressive of deep gratitude for his discreet services in London; and at another time – in fact, if Philip's life had been ordered differently to what it was – it might have given this man a not unworthy pleasure to remember that without a penny of his own, simply by diligence, honesty, and faithful quick-sightedness as to the interests of his masters, he had risen to hold the promise of being their successor, and to be ranked by them as a trusted friend.

As the Newcastle smack neared the shore on her voyage home, Hepburn looked wistfully out for the faint grey outline of Monkshaven Priory against the sky, and the well-known cliffs; as if the masses of inanimate stone could tell him any news of Sylvia.

In the streets of Shields, just after landing, he encountered a neighbour of the Robsons, and an acquaintance of his own. By this honest man, he was welcomed as a great traveller is welcomed on his return from a long voyage, with many hearty good shakes of the hand, much repetition of kind wishes, and offers to treat him to drink. Yet, from some insurmountable feeling, Philip avoided all mention of the family who were the principal bond between the honest farmer and himself. He did not know why, but he could not bear the shock of first hearing her name in the open street, or in the rough public-house. And thus he shrank from the intelligence he craved to hear.

Thus he knew no more about the Robsons when he returned to Monkshaven, than he had done on the day when he had last seen them; and, of course, his first task there was to give a long *vivá voce* account of all his London proceedings to the two brothers Foster, who, considering that they had heard the result of everything by letter, seemed to take an insatiable interest in details.

He could hardly tell why, but even when released from the Fosters' parlour, he was unwilling to go to Haytersbank Farm. It was late, it is true, but on a May evening even country people keep up till eight or nine o'clock. Perhaps it was because Hepburn was still in his travel-stained dress; having gone straight to the shop on his arrival in Monkshaven. Perhaps it was because, if he went this night for the short half hour intervening before bed-time, he would have no excuse for paying a longer visit on the following evening. At any rate, he proceeded straight to Alice Rose's, as soon as he had finished his interview with his employers.

Both Hester and Coulson had given him their welcome home in the shop, which they had, however, left an hour or two before him.

Yet they gave him a fresh greeting, almost one in which surprise was blended, when he came to his lodgings. Even Alice seemed gratified by his spending this first evening with them, as if she had thought it might have been otherwise. Weary though he was, he exerted himself to talk and to relate what he had done and seen in London, as far as he could without breaking confidence with his employers. It was something to see the pleasure he gave to his auditors, although there were several mixed feelings in their minds to produce the expression of it which gratified him. Coulson was sorry for his former ungenerous reception of the news that Philip was going to London; Hester and her mother each secretly began to feel as if this evening was like more happy evenings of old, before the Robsons came to Haytersbank Farm; and who knows what faint delicious hopes this resemblance may not have suggested?

While Philip, restless and excited, feeling that he could not sleep, was glad to pass away the waking hours that must intervene before to-morrow night, at times, he tried to make them talk of what had happened in Monkshaven during his absence, but all had gone on in an eventless manner, as far as he could gather; if they knew of anything affecting the Robsons, they avoided speaking of it to him; and, indeed, how little likely were they ever to have heard their names while he was away?

CHAPTER 20

Loved and Lost*

Philip walked towards the Robsons' farm like a man in a dream, who has everything around him according to his wish, and yet is conscious of a secret mysterious inevitable drawback to his enjoyment. Hepburn did not care to think – would not realize what this drawback, which need not have been mysterious in his case, was.

The May evening was glorious in light and shadow. The

crimson sun warmed up the chilly northern air to a semblance
of pleasant heat. The spring sights and sounds were all about;
the lambs were bleating out their gentle weariness before they
sank to rest by the side of their mothers; the linnets were
chirping in every bush of golden gorse that grew out of the stone
walls; the lark was singing her good-night in the cloudless sky,
before she dropped down to her nest in the tender green wheat;
all spoke of brooding peace – but Philip's heart was not at
peace.

Yet he was going to proclaim his good fortune. His masters
had that day publicly announced that Coulson and he were to
be their successors, and he had now arrived at that longed-for
point in his business, when he had resolved to openly speak of
his love to Sylvia, and might openly strive to gain her love. But,
alas! the fulfilment of that wish of his had lagged sadly behind.
He was placed as far as he could, even in his most sanguine
moments, have hoped to be as regarded business, but Sylvia was
as far from his attainment as ever – nay, farther. Still the great
obstacle was removed in Kinraid's impressment. Philip took
upon himself to decide that, with such a man as the specksioneer, absence was equivalent to faithless forgetfulness. He
thought that he had just grounds for this decision in the account
he had heard of Kinraid's behaviour to Annie Coulson; to the
other nameless young girl, her successor in his fickle heart; in
the ribald talk of the sailors in the Newcastle public-house. It
would be well for Sylvia if she could forget as quickly; and, to
promote this oblivion, the name of her lover should never be
brought up, either in praise or blame. And Philip would be
patient and enduring; all the time watching over her, and
labouring to win her reluctant love.

There she was! He saw her as he stood at the top of the little
hill-path leading down to the Robsons' door. She was out of
doors, in the garden, which, at some distance from the house,
sloped up the bank on the opposite side of the gully; much too
far off to be spoken to – not too far off to be gazed at by eyes
that caressed her every movement. How well Philip knew that
garden; placed long ago by some tenant of the farm on a
southern slope; walled in with rough moorland stones; planted
with berry-bushes for use, and southernwood and sweetbriar
for sweetness of smell. When the Robsons had first come to
Haytersbank, and Sylvia was scarcely more than a pretty child,

how well he remembered helping her with the arrangement of this garden; laying out his few spare pence in hen-and-chicken daisies at one time, in flower-seeds at another; again in a rose-tree in a pot. He knew how his unaccustomed hands had laboured with the spade at forming a little primitive bridge over the beck in the hollow before winter streams should make it too deep for fording, how he had cut down branches of the mountain-ash and covered them over, yet decked with their scarlet berries, with sods of green turf, beyond which the brilliancy crept out; but now it was months and years since he had been in that garden, which had lost its charm for Sylvia, as she found the bleak sea-winds came up and blighted all endeavours at cultivating more than the most useful things – pot-herbs, marigolds,* potatoes, onions, and such-like. Why did she tarry there now, standing quite motionless up by the highest bit of wall, looking over the sea, with her hand shading her eyes? Quite motionless; as if she were a stone statue. He began to wish she would move – would look at him – but any way that she would move, and not stand gazing thus over that great dreary sea.

He went down the path with an impatient step, and entered the house-place. There sat his aunt spinning, and apparently as well as ever. He could hear his uncle talking to Kester in the neighbouring shippen; all was well in the household. Why was Sylvia standing in the garden in that strange quiet way?

'Why, lad! thou'rt a sight for sair een!'* said his aunt, as she stood up to welcome him back. 'An when didst ta come, eh? – but thy uncle will be glad to see thee, and to hear thee talk about yon pleughs; he's thought a deal o' thy letters. I'll go call him in.'

'Not yet,' said Philip, stopping her in her progress towards the door. 'He's busy talking to Kester. I'm in no haste to be gone. I can stay a couple of hours. Sit down, and tell me how you are yoursel' – and how iverything is. And I've a deal to tell you.'

'To be sure – to be sure. To think thou's been in Lunnon sin' I saw thee! – well to be sure! There's a vast o' coming and going i' this world. Thou'll mind yon specksioneer lad, him as was cousin to t' Corneys – Charley Kinraid?'

Mind him! As if he could forget him.

'Well! he's dead and gone.'

'Dead! Who told you? I don't understand,' said Philip, in strange bewilderment. Could Kinraid have tried to escape after all, and been wounded, killed in the attempt? If not, how should they know he was dead? Missing he might be, though how this should be known was strange, as he was supposed to be sailing to the Greenland seas. But dead! What did they mean? At Philip's worst moment of hatred he had hardly dared to wish him dead.

'Dunnot yo' mention it afore our Sylvia, we niver speak on him to her, for she takes it a deal to heart, though I'm thinkin' it were a good thing for her; for he'd got a hold of her – he had on Bessy Corney, too, as her mother told me, – not that I iver let on to them as Sylvia frets after him, so keep a calm sough, my lad. It's a girl's fancy – just a kind o' calf love; let it go by; and it's well for her he's dead, though it's hard to say so on a drowned man.'

'Drowned!' said Philip. 'How do yo' know?' half hoping that the poor drenched swollen body might have been found, and thus all questions and dilemmas solved. Kinraid might have struggled overboard with ropes or handcuffs on, and so have been drowned.

'Eh, lad! there's no misdoubtin' it. He were thought a deal on by t' captain o' t' *Urania*; and when he niver come back on t' day when she ought for to have sailed, he sent to Kinraid's people at Cullercoats, and they sent to Brunton's i' Newcassel, and they knew he'd been here. T' captain put off sailing for two or three days, that he might ha' that much law;* but when he heard as Kinraid were not at Corneys', but had left 'em a'most on to a week, he went off to them Northern seas wi' next best specksioneer he could find. For there's no use speaking ill on t' dead; an' though I couldn't abear his coming for iver about t' house, he were a rare good specksioneer, as I've been told.'

'But how do you know he was drowned?' said Philip, feeling guiltily disappointed at his aunt's story.

'Why, lad! I'm a'most ashamed to tell thee, I were sore put out mysel'; but Sylvia were so broken-hearted like I couldn't cast it up to her as I should ha' liked: th' silly lass had gone and gi'en him a bit o' ribbon, as many a one knowed, for it had been a vast noticed and admired that evenin' at th' Corneys' – New Year's Eve I think it were – and t' poor vain peacock had tied it on his hat, so that when t' tide – hist! there's Sylvie coming in at t' back door; never let on,' and in a forced made-up voice she inquired aloud, for hitherto she had been speaking almost in a whisper, –

'And didst ta see King George an' Queen Charlotte?'*

Philip could not answer – did not hear. His soul had gone out to meet Sylvia, who entered with quiet slowness quite unlike her former self. Her face was wan and white; her grey eyes seemed larger, and full of dumb tearless sorrow; she came up to Philip, as if his being there touched her with no surprise, and gave him a gentle greeting as if he were a familiar indifferent person whom she had seen but yesterday.

Philip, who had recollected the quarrel they had had, and about Kinraid too, the very last time they had met, had expected some trace of this remembrance to linger in her looks and speech to him. But there was no such sign; her great sorrow had wiped away all anger, almost all memory. Her mother looked at her anxiously, and then said in the same manner of forced cheerfulness which she had used before, –

'Here's Philip, lass, a' full o' Lunnon; call thy father in, an' we'll hear a' about t' new-fangled pleughs. It'll be rare an' nice a' sitting together again.'

Sylvia, silent and docile, went out to the shippen to obey her mother's wish. Bell Robson leant forward towards Philip, misinterpreting the expression on his face, which was guilt as much as sympathy, and checked the possible repentance which might have urged him on at that moment to tell all he knew, by saying, 'Lad! it's a' for t' best. He were noane good enough for her; and I misdoubt me he were only playin' wi' her as he'd done by others. Let her a-be, let her a-be; she'll come round to be thankful.'

Robson bustled in with loud welcome; all the louder and more talkative because he, like his wife, assumed a cheerful manner before Sylvia. Yet he, unlike his wife, had many a secret regret over Kinraid's fate. At first, while merely the fact of his disappearance was known, Daniel Robson had hit on the truth, and had stuck to his opinion that the cursed press-gang were at the bottom of it. He had backed his words by many an oath, and all the more because he had not a single reason to give that applied to the present occasion. No one on the lonely coast had remarked any sign of the presence of the men-of-war, or the tenders that accompanied them, for the purpose of impressment on the king's ships. At Shields, and at the mouth of the Tyne, where they lay in greedy wait, the owners of the *Urania* had caused strict search to be made for their skilled and protected specksioneer, but with no success. All this positive evidence in contradiction to Daniel Robson's opinion only made him cling to it the more; until the day when the hat was found on the shore with Kinraid's name written out large and fair in the inside, and the tell-tale bit of ribbon knotted in the band. Then Daniel, by a sudden revulsion, gave up every hope; it never entered his mind that it could have fallen off by any accident. No! now Kinraid was dead and drowned, and it was a bad job, and the sooner it could be forgotten the better for all parties; and it was well no one knew how far it had gone with Sylvia, especially now since Bessy Corney was crying her eyes out as if he had been engaged to her. So Daniel said nothing to his wife about the mischief that had gone on in her absence, and never spoke to Sylvia about the affair; only he was more than usually tender to her in his rough way, and thought, morning, noon, and night, on what he could do to give her pleasure, and drive away all recollection of her ill-starred love.

To-night be would have her sit by him while Philip told his stories, or heavily answered questions put to him. Sylvia sat on a stool by her father's knee, holding one of his hands in both of hers; and presently she laid down her head upon them, and Philip saw her sad eyes looking into the flickering fire-light with long unwinking stare, showing that her thoughts were far distant. He could hardly go on with his tales of what he had seen, and what done, he was so full of pity for her. Yet, for all his pity, he had now resolved never to soothe her with the knowledge of what he knew, nor to deliver the message sent by her false lover. He felt like a mother withholding something injurious from the foolish wish of her plaining* child.

But he went away without breathing a word of his good fortune in business. The telling of such kind of good fortune seemed out of place this night, when the thought of death and the loss of friends seemed to brood over the household, and cast its shadow there, obscuring for the time all worldly things.

And so the great piece of news came out in the ordinary course of gossip, told by some Monkshaven friend to Robson the next market day. For months Philip had been looking forward to the sensation which the intelligence would produce in the farm household, as a preliminary to laying his good fortune at Sylvia's feet. And they heard of it, and he away, and all chance of his making use of it in the manner he had intended vanished for the present.

Daniel was always curious after other people's affairs, and now was more than ever bent on collecting scraps of news which might possibly interest Sylvia, and rouse her out of the state of indifference as to everything into which she had fallen. Perhaps he thought that he had not acted altogether wisely in allowing her to engage herself to Kinraid, for he was a man apt to judge by results; and moreover he had had so much reason to repent of the encouragement which he had given to the lover whose untimely end had so deeply affected his only child, that he was more unwilling than ever that his wife should know of the length to which the affair had gone during her absence. He even urged secrecy upon Sylvia as a personal favour; unwilling to encounter the silent blame which he openly affected to despise.

'We'll noane fret thy mother by lettin' on how oft he came and went. She'll, maybe, be thinkin' he were for speakin' to thee, my poor lass; an' it would put her out a deal, for she's a woman of a stern mind towards matteremony. And she'll be noane so strong till summer-weather comes, and I'd be loth to give her aught to worrit hersel' about. So thee and me'll keep our own counsel.'

'I wish mother had been here, then she'd ha' known all, without my telling her.'

'Cheer up, lass; it's better as it is. Thou'll get o'er it sooner for havin' no one to let on to. A myself am noane going to speak on't again.'

No more he did; but there was a strange tenderness in his tones when he spoke to her; a half-pathetic way of seeking after her, if by any chance she was absent for a minute from the places where he expected to find her; a consideration for her, about this time, in his way of bringing back trifling presents, or small pieces of news that he thought might interest her, which sank deep into her heart.

'And what dun yo' think a' t' folks is talkin' on i' Monk-shaven?' asked he, almost before he had taken off his coat, on the day when he had heard of Philip's promotion in the world. 'Why, missus, thy nephew, Philip Hepburn, has got his name up

i' gold letters four inch long o'er Fosters' door! Him and
Coulson has set up shop together, and Fosters is gone out!'*

'That's t' secret of his journey t' Lunnon,' said Bell, more
gratified than she chose to show.

'Four inch long if they're there at all! I heerd on it at t' Bay
Horse first; but I thought yo'd niver be satisfied 'bout I seed it
wi' my own eyes. They do say as Gregory Jones, t' plumber, got
it done i' York, for that nought else would satisfy old Jeremiah.
It'll be a matter o' some hundreds a year i' Philip's pocket.'

'There'll be Fosters i' the' background, as one may say, to
take t' biggest share on t' profits,' said Bell.

'Ay, ay, that's but as it should be, for I reckon they'll ha' to
find t' brass* the first, my lass!' said he, turning to Sylvia. 'A'm
fain to tak' thee in to t' town next market day, just for thee t'
see 't. A'll buy thee a bonny ribbon for thy hair out o' t' cousin's
own shop.'

Some thought of another ribbon which had once tied up her
hair, and afterwards been cut in twain, must have crossed
Sylvia's mind, for she answered, as if she shrunk from her
father's words, –

'I cannot go, I'm noane wantin' a ribbon; I'm much obliged,
father, a' t' same.'

Her mother read her heart clearly, and suffered with her but
never spoke a word of sympathy. But she went on rather more
quickly than she would otherwise have done to question her
husband as to all he knew about this great rise of Philip's. Once
or twice Sylvia joined in with languid curiosity; but presently
she became tired and went to bed. For a few moments after she
left, her parents sat silent. Then Daniel, in a tone as if he were
justifying his daughter, and comforting himself as well as his
wife, observed that it was almost on for nine; the evenings were
light so long now. Bell said nothing in reply, but gathered up
her wool, and began to arrange the things for night.

By-and-by Daniel broke the silence by saying, –

'A thowt at one time as Philip had a fancy for our Sylvie.'

For a minute or two Bell did not speak. Then, with deeper
insight into her daughter's heart than her husband, in spite of
his greater knowledge of the events that had happened to affect
it, she said, –

'If thou's thinking on a match between 'em, it'll be a long

time afore th' poor sad wench is fit t' think on another man as sweetheart.'

'A said nought about sweethearts,' replied he, as if his wife had reproached him in some way. 'Woman's allays so full o' sweethearts and matteremony. A only said as a'd thowt once as Philip had a fancy for our lass, and a think so still; and he'll be worth his two hunder a year afore long. But a niver said nought about sweethearts.'

CHAPTER 21

A Rejected Suitor

There were many domestic arrangements to be made in connection with the new commercial ones which affected Hepburn and Coulson.

The Fosters, with something of the busybodiness which is apt to mingle itself with kindly patronage, had planned in their own minds that the Rose household should be removed altogether to the house belonging to the shop; and that Alice, with the assistance of the capable servant, who, at present, managed all John's domestic affairs, should continue as mistress of the house, with Philip and Coulson for her lodgers.

But arrangements without her consent did not suit Alice at any time, and she had very good reasons for declining to accede to this. She was not going to be uprooted at her time of life, she said, nor would she consent to enter upon a future which might be so uncertain. Why, Hepburn and Coulson were both young men, she said, and they were as likely to marry as not; and then the bride would be sure to wish to live in the good old-fashioned house at the back of the shop.

It was in vain she was told by every one concerned, that, in case of such an event, the first married partner should take a house of his own, leaving her in undisputed possession. She replied, with apparent truth, that both might wish to marry, and surely the wife of one ought to take possession of the house belonging to the business; that she was not going to trust herself to the fancies of young men, who were always, the best of them, going and doing the very thing that was most foolish in the way of marriage; of which state, in fact, she spoke with something of acrimonious contempt and dislike, as if young people always got mismatched, yet had not the sense to let older and wiser people choose for them.

'Thou'll not have been understanding why Alice Rose spoke as she did this morning,' said Jeremiah Foster to Philip, on the afternoon succeeding the final discussion of this plan. 'She was a-thinking of her youth, I reckon, when she was a well-favoured young woman, and our John was full of the thought of marrying her. As he could not have her, he has lived a bachelor all his days. But if I am not a vast mistaken, all that he has will go to her and to Hester, for all that Hester is the child of another man. Thee and Coulson should have a try for Hester, Philip. I have told Coulson this day of Hester's chances. I told him first because he is my wife's nephew; but I tell thee now, Philip. It would be a good thing for the shop if one of ye was married.'

Philip reddened. Often as the idea of marriage had come into his mind, this was the first time it had been gravely suggested to him by another. But he replied quietly enough.

'I don't think Hester Rose has any thought of matrimony.'

'To be sure not; it is for thee, or for William Coulson, to make her think. She, maybe, remembers enough of her mother's life with her father to make her slow to think on such things. But it's in her to think on matrimony; it's in all of us.'

'Alice's husband was dead before I knew her,' said Philip, rather evading the main subject.

'It was a mercy when he were taken. A mercy to them who were left, I mean. Alice was a bonny young woman, with a smile for everybody, when he wed her – a smile for every one except our John, who never could do enough to try and win one from her. But, no! she would have none of him, but set her heart on Jack Rose, a sailor in a whale-ship. And so they were married at last, though all her own folks were against it. And he was a profligate sinner, and went after other women, and drank, and beat her. She turned as stiff and as grey as thou seest her now within a year of Hester's birth. I believe they'd have perished for want and cold many a time if it had not been for John. If she ever guessed where the money came from, it must have hurt her pride above a bit, for she was always a proud woman. But mother's love is stronger than pride.'

Philip fell to thinking, a generation ago something of the same kind had been going on as that which he was now living through, quick with hopes and fears. A girl beloved by two – nay, those two so identical in occupation as he and Kinraid were – Rose identical even in character with what he knew of the specksioneer; a girl choosing the wrong lover, and suffering and soured all her life in consequence of her youth's mistake; was that to be Sylvia's lot? – or, rather, was she not saved from it by the event of the impressment, and by the course of silence he himself had resolved upon? Then he went on to wonder if the lives of one generation were but a repetition of the lives of those who had gone before, with no variation but from the internal cause that some had greater capacity for suffering than others. Would those very circumstances which made the interest of his life now, return, in due cycle, when he was dead and Sylvia was forgotten?

Perplexed thoughts of this and a similar kind kept returning into Philip's mind whenever he had leisure to give himself up to consideration of anything but the immediate throng* of business. And every time he dwelt on this complication and succession of similar events, he emerged from his reverie more and more satisfied with the course he had taken in withholding from Sylvia all knowledge of her lover's fate.

It was settled at length that Philip was to remove to the house belonging to the shop, Coulson remaining with Alice and her daughter. But in the course of the summer the latter told his partner that he had offered marriage to Hester on the previous day, and been refused. It was an awkward affair altogether, as he lived in their house, and was in daily companionship with Hester, who, however, seemed to preserve her gentle calmness, with only a tinge more of reserve in her manner to Coulson.

'I wish yo' could find out what she has again' me, Philip,' said Coulson, about a fortnight after he had made the proposal. The poor young man thought that Hester's composure of manner towards him since the event argued that he was not distasteful to her; and as he was now on very happy terms with Philip, he came constantly to him, as if the latter could interpret the meaning of all the little occurrences between him and his beloved. 'I'm o' right age, not two months betwixt us; and there's few in Monkshaven as would think on her wi' better prospects than me; and she knows my folks; we're kind o' cousins, in fact; and I'd be like a son to her mother; and there's noane i' Monkshaven as can speak again' my character. There's nought between yo' and her, is there, Philip?'

'I ha' told thee many a time that she and me is like brother and sister. She's no more thought on me nor I have for her. So be content wi't, for I'se not tell thee again.'

'Don't be vexed, Philip; if thou knew what it was to be in love, thou'd be always fancying things, just as I am.'

'I might be,' said Philip; 'but I dunnot think I should be always talking about my fancies.'

'I wunnot talk any more after this once, if thou'll just find out fra' thysel', as it were, what it is she has again' me. I'd go to chapel for iver with her, if that's what she wants. Just ask her, Philip.'

'It's an awkward thing for me to be melling wi','* said Hepburn, reluctantly.

'But thou said thee and she were like brother and sister; and a brother would ask a sister, and niver think twice about it.'

'Well, well,' replied Philip, 'I'll see what I can do; but, lad, I dunnot think she'll have thee. She doesn't fancy thee, and fancy is three parts o' love, if reason is t' other fourth.'

But somehow Philip could not begin on the subject with Hester. He did not know why, except that, as he said, 'it was so awkward.' But he really liked Coulson so much as to be anxious to do what the latter wished, although he was almost convinced that it would be of no use. So he watched his opportunity, and found Alice alone and at leisure one Sunday evening.

She was sitting by the window, reading her Bible, when he went in. She gave him a curt welcome, hearty enough for her, for she was always chary in her expressions of pleasure or satisfaction. But she took off her horn spectacles and placed them in the book to keep her place; and then turning more fully round on her chair, so as to face him, she said, –

'Well, lad! and how does it go on? Though it's not a day for t' ask about worldly things. But I niver see thee now but on Sabbath day, and rarely then. Still we munnot speak o' such things on t' Lord's day. So thee mun just say how t' shop is doing, and then we'll leave such vain talk.'

'T' shop is doing main an' well, thank ye, mother. But Coulson could tell yo' o' that any day.'

'I'd a deal rayther hear fra' thee, Philip. Coulson doesn't

know how t' manage his own business, let alone half the business as it took John and Jeremiah's heads – ay, and tasked 'em, too – to manage. I've no patience with Coulson.'

'Why? he's a decent young fellow as ever there is in Monkshaven.'

'He may be. He's noane cut his wisdom-teeth yet. But, for that matter, there's other folks as far fra' sense as he is.'

'Ay, and farther. Coulson mayn't be so bright at all times as he might be, but he's a steady-goer, and I'd back him again' any chap o' his age i' Monkshaven.'

'I know who I'd sooner back in many a thing, Philip!' She said it with so much meaning that he could not fail to understand that he himself was meant, and he replied, ingenuously enough, –

'If yo' mean me, mother, I'll noane deny that in a thing or two I may be more knowledgeable than Coulson. I've had a deal o' time on my hands i' my youth, and I'd good schooling as long as father lived.'

'Lad! it's not schooling, nor knowledge, nor book-learning as carries a man through t' world. It's mother-wit. And it's noane schooling, nor knowledge, nor book-learning as takes a young woman. It's summat as cannot be put into words.'

'That's just what I told Coulson!' said Philip, quickly. 'He were sore put about because Hester had gi'en him the bucket,*and came to me about it.'

'And what did thou say?' asked Alice, her deep eyes gleaming at him as if to read his face as well as his words. Philip, thinking he could now do what Coulson had begged of him in the neatest manner, went on, –

'I told him I'd help him all as I could—'

'Thou did, did thou? Well, well, there's nought sa queer as folks, that a will say,' muttered Alice, between her teeth.

' – but that fancy had three parts to do wi' love,' continued Philip, 'and it would be hard, maybe, to get a reason for her not fancying him. Yet I wish she'd think twice about it; he so set upon having her, I think he'll do himself a mischief wi' fretting, if it goes on as it is.'

'It'll noane go on as it is,' said Alice, with gloomy oracularness.

'How not?' asked Philip. Then, receiving no answer, he went on, 'He loves her true, and he's within a month or two on her age, and his character will bear handling on a' sides;* and his share on t' shop will be worth hundreds a year afore long.'

Another pause. Alice was trying to bring down her pride to say something, which she could not with all her efforts.

'Maybe yo'll speak a word for him, mother,' said Philip, annoyed at her silence.

'I'll do no such thing. Marriages are best made wi'out melling. How do I know but what she likes some one better?'

'Our Hester's not th' lass to think on a young man unless he's been a-wooing on her. And yo' know, mother, as well as I do – and Coulson does too – she's niver given any one a chance to woo her; living half her time here, and t'other half in t' shop, and niver speaking to no one by t' way.'

'I wish thou wouldn't come here troubling me on a Sabbath day wi' thy vanity and thy worldly talk. I'd liefer by far be i' that world wheere there's neither marrying nor giving in marriage,* for it's all a moithering mess here.' She turned to the closed Bible lying on the dresser, and opened it with a bang. While she was adjusting her spectacles on her nose, with hands trembling with passion, she heard Philip say, –

'I ask yo'r pardon, I'm sure. I couldn't well come any other day.'

'It's a' t' same – I care not. But thou might as well tell truth. I'll be bound thou's been at Haytersbank Farm some day this week?'

Philip reddened; in fact, he had forgotten how he had got to consider his frequent visits to the farm as a regular piece of occupation. He kept silence.

Alice looked at him with a sharp intelligence that read his silence through.

'I thought so. Next time thou thinks to thyself, "I'm more knowledgeable than Coulson", just remember Alice Rose's words, and they are these: – If Coulson's too thick-sighted to see through a board, thou'rt too blind to see through a window. As for comin' and speakin' up for Coulson, why, he'll be married to some one else afore t' year's out, for all he thinks he's so set upon Hester now. Go thy ways, and leave me to my Scripture, and come no more on Sabbath days wi' thy vain babbling.'

So Philip returned from his mission rather crestfallen, but quite as far as ever from 'seeing through a glass window'.

Before the year was out, Alice's prophecy was fulfilled. Coulson, who found the position of a rejected lover in the same house with the girl who had refused him, too uncomfortable to be endured, as soon as he was convinced that his object was decidedly out of his reach, turned his attention to some one else. He did not love his new sweetheart as he had done Hester: there was more of reason and less of fancy in his attachment. But it ended successfully; and before the first snow fell, Philip was best man at his partner's wedding.

CHAPTER 22

Deepening Shadows

But before Coulson was married, many small events happened – small events to all but Philip. To him they were as the sun and moon. The days when he went up to Haytersbank and Sylvia spoke to him, the days when he went up and she had apparently no heart to speak to any one, but left the room as soon as he came, or never entered it at all, although she must have known that he was there – these were his alternations from happiness to sorrow.

From her parents he always had a welcome. Oppressed by their daughter's depression of spirits, they hailed the coming of any visitor as a change for her as well as for themselves. The former intimacy with the Corneys was in abeyance for all parties, owing to Bessy Corney's out-spoken grief for the loss of her cousin, as if she had had reason to look upon him as her lover, whereas Sylvia's parents felt this as a slur upon their daughter's cause of grief. But although at this time the members of the two families ceased to seek after each other's society, nothing was said. The thread of friendship might be joined afresh at any time, only just now it was broken; and Philip was glad of it. Before going to Haytersbank he sought each time for some little present with which to make his coming welcome. And now he wished even more than ever that Sylvia had cared for learning; if she had he could have taken her many a pretty ballad, or story-book, such as were then in vogue. He did try her with the translation of the *Sorrows of Werther*, so popular at the time that it had a place in all pedlars' baskets, with *Law's Serious Call*, the *Pilgrim's Progress*, Klopstock's *Messiah*, and *Paradise Lost*.* But she could not read it for herself; and after turning the leaves languidly over, and smiling a little at the picture of Charlotte* cutting bread and butter in a left-handed manner, she put it aside on the shelf by the *Complete Farrier*,* and there Philip saw it, upside down and untouched, the next time he came to the farm.

Many a time during that summer did he turn to the few verses in Genesis in which Jacob's twice seven years' service* for Rachel is related, and try and take fresh heart from the reward which came to the patriarch's constancy at last. After trying books, nosegays, small presents of pretty articles of dress, such as suited the notions of those days, and finding them all received with the same languid gratitude, he set himself to endeavour to please her in some other way. It was time that he should change his tactics; for the girl was becoming weary of the necessity for thanking him, every time he came, for some little favour or other. She wished he would let her alone and not watch her continually with such sad eyes. Her father and mother hailed her first signs of impatient petulance towards him as a return to the old state of things before Kinraid had come to disturb the tenour of their lives; for even Daniel had turned against the specksioneer, irritated by the Corneys' loud moans over the loss of the man to whom their daughter said that she was attached. If Daniel wished for him to be alive again, it was mainly that the Corneys might be convinced that his last visit to the neighbourhood of Monkshaven was for the sake of the pale and silent Sylvia, and not for that of Bessy, who complained of Kinraid's untimely death rather as if by it she had been cheated of a husband than for any overwhelming personal love towards the deceased.

'If he were after her he were a big black scoundrel, that's what he were; and a wish he were alive again to be hung. But a dunnot believe it; them Corney lasses were allays a-talkin' an' a-thinkin' on sweethearts, and niver a man crossed t' threshold but they tried him on* as a husband. An' their mother were no better: Kinraid has spoken civil to Bessy as became a lad to a lass, and she makes an ado over him as if they'd been to church together not a week sin'.'

'I dunnot uphold t' Corneys; but Molly Corney – as is Molly Brunton now – used to speak on this dead man to our Sylvie as if he were her sweetheart in old days. Now there's no smoke without fire, and I'm thinking it's likely enough he were one of them fellows as is always after some lass or another, and, as often as not, two or three at a time. Now look at Philip, what a different one he is! He's niver thought on a woman but our Sylvie, I'll be bound. I wish he wern't so old-fashioned and faint-hearted.'

'Ay! and t' shop's doin' a vast o' business, I've heard say. He's a deal better company, too, nor he used to be. He'd a way o' preaching wi' him as a couldn't abide; but now he tak's his glass, an' holds his tongue, leavin' room for wiser men to say their say.'

Such was a conjugal colloquy about this time. Philip was gaining ground with Daniel, and that was something towards winning Sylvia's heart; for she was unaware of her father's change of feeling towards Kinraid, and took all his tenderness towards herself as if they were marks of his regard for her lost lover and his sympathy in her loss, instead of which he was rather feeling as if it might be a good thing after all that the fickle-hearted sailor was dead and drowned. In fact, Daniel was very like a child in all the parts of his character. He was strongly affected by whatever was present, and apt to forget the absent. He acted on impulse, and too often had reason to be sorry for it; but he hated his sorrow too much to let it teach him wisdom for the future. With all his many faults, however, he had something in him which made him be dearly loved, both by the daughter whom he indulged, and the wife who was in fact superior to him, but whom he imagined that he ruled with a wise and absolute sway.

Love to Sylvia gave Philip tact. He seemed to find out that to please the women of the household he must pay all possible attention to the man; and though he cared little in comparison for Daniel, yet this autumn he was continually thinking of how he could please him. When he had said or done anything to gratify or amuse her father, Sylvia smiled and was kind. What-ever he did was right with his aunt; but even she was unusually glad when her husband was pleased. Still his progress was slow towards his object; and often he sighed himself to sleep with the words, 'seven years; and maybe seven years more'. Then in his dreams he saw Kinraid again, sometimes struggling, sometimes sailing towards land, the only one on board a swift advancing ship, alone on deck, stern and avenging; till Philip awoke in remorseful terror.

Such and similar dreams returned with the greater frequency when, in the November of that year, the coast between Hartlepool and Monkshaven was overshadowed by the presence of guard-ships, driven south from their station at North Shields by the resolution which the sailors of that port had entered into to resist the press-gang, and the energy with which they had begun to carry out their determination. For on a certain Tuesday evening yet remembered by old inhabitants of North Shields, the sailors in the merchant service met together and overpowered the press-gang, dismissing them from the town with the highest contempt, and with their jackets reversed. A numerous mob went with them to Chirton Bar; gave them three cheers at parting, but vowed to tear them limb from limb should they seek to re-enter North Shields. But a few days afterwards some fresh cause of irritation arose, and five hundred sailors, armed with such swords and pistols as they could collect, paraded through the town in the most riotous manner, and at last attempted to seize the tender *Eleanor*, on some pretext of the ill-treatment of the impressed men aboard. This endeavour failed, however, owing to the energetic conduct of the officers in command. Next day this body of sailors set off for Newcastle; but learning, before they reached the town, that there was a strong military and civil force prepared to receive them there, they dispersed for the time; but not before the good citizens had received a great fright, the drums of the North Yorkshire militia beating to arms, and the terrified people rushing out into the streets to learn the reason of the alarm, and some of them seeing the militia, under the command of the Earl of Fauconberg, marching from the guard-house adjoining New Gate to the house of rendezvous for impressed seamen in the Broad Chase.

But a few weeks after, the impressment service took their revenge for the insults they had been subjected to in North Shields. In the dead of night a cordon was formed round that town by a regiment stationed at Tynemouth barracks; the press-gangs belonging to armed vessels lying off Shields harbour were let loose; no one within the circle could escape, and upwards of two hundred and fifty men, sailors, mechanics, labourers of every description, were forced on board the armed ships. With that prize they set sail, and wisely left the place, where deep passionate vengeance was sworn against them. Not all the dread of an invasion by the French could reconcile the people of these coasts to the necessity of impressment. Fear and confusion prevailed after this to within many miles of the sea-shore. A Yorkshire gentleman of rank said that his labourers dispersed like a covey of birds, because a press-gang was reported to have established itself so far inland as Tadcaster; and they only returned to work on the assurance from the steward of his master's protection, but even then begged leave to sleep on straw in the stables or outhouses belonging to their landlord, not daring to sleep at their own homes. No fish was caught, for the fishermen dared not venture out to sea; the markets were deserted, as the press-gangs might come down on any gathering of men; prices were raised, and many were impoverished; many others ruined. For in the great struggle in which England was then involved, the navy was esteemed her safeguard; and men must be had at any price of money, or suffering, or of injustice, Landsmen were kidnapped and taken to London; there, in too many instances, to be discharged without redress and penniless, because they were discovered to be useless for the purpose for which they had been taken.

Autumn brought back the whaling-ships. But the period of their return was full of gloomy anxiety, instead of its being the annual time of rejoicing and feasting; of gladdened households, where brave steady husbands or sons returned; of unlimited and reckless expenditure, and boisterous joviality among those who thought that they had earned unbounded licence on shore by their six months of compelled abstinence. In other years this had been the time for new and handsome winter clothing; for cheerful if humble hospitality; for the shopkeepers to display their gayest and best; for the public-houses to be crowded; for the streets to be full of blue jackets,* rolling along with merry words and open hearts. In other years the boiling-houses had been full of active workers, the staithes crowded with barrels, the ship-carpenters' yards thronged with seamen and captains; now a few men, tempted by high wages, went stealthily by back lanes to their work, clustering together, with sinister looks, glancing round corners, and fearful of every approaching foot-step, as if they were going on some unlawful business, instead of true honest work. Most of them kept their whalingknives about them ready for bloody defence if they were attacked. The shops were almost deserted; there was no unnecessary expenditure by the men; they dared not venture out to buy lavish presents for the wife or sweetheart or little children. The public-houses kept scouts on the look-out; while fierce men drank and swore deep oaths of vengeance in the bar – men who did not maunder in their cups, nor grow foolishly merry, but in whom liquor called forth all the desperate, bad passions of human nature.

Indeed, all along the coast of Yorkshire, it seemed as if a blight hung over the land and the people. Men dodged about their daily business with hatred and suspicion in their eyes, and many a curse went over the sea to the three fatal ships lying motionless at anchor three miles off Monkshaven. When first Philip had heard in his shop that these three men-of-war might be seen lying fell and still on the grey horizon, his heart sank, and he scarcely dared to ask their names. For if one should be the *Alcestis*; if Kinraid should send word to Sylvia; if he should say he was living, and loving, and faithful; if it should come to pass that the fact of the undelivered message sent by her lover through Philip should reach Sylvia's ears: what would be the position of the latter, not merely in her love – that, of course, would be hopeless – but in her esteem? All sophistry vanished; the fear of detection awakened Philip to a sense of guilt; and, besides, he found out, that, in spite of all idle talk and careless slander, he could not help believing that Kinraid was in terrible earnest when he uttered those passionate words, and entreated that they might be borne to Sylvia. Some instinct told Philip that if the specksioneer had only flirted with too many, yet that for Sylvia Robson his love was true and vehement. Then Philip tried to convince himself that, from all that was said of his previous character, Kinraid was not capable of an enduring constant attachment; and with such poor opiate to his conscience as he could obtain from this notion Philip was obliged to remain content, until, a day or two after the first intelligence of the presence of those three ships, he learned, with some trouble and pains, that their names were the *Megaera*, the *Bellerophon*, and the *Hanover*.*

Then he began to perceive how unlikely it was that the *Alcestis* should have been lingering on this shore all these many months. She was, doubtless, gone far away by this time; she had, probably, joined the fleet on the war station.* Who could tell what had become of her and her crew? she might have been in battle before now, and if so—

So his previous fancies shrank to nothing, rebuked for their improbability, and with them vanished his self-reproach. Yet there were times when the popular attention seemed totally absorbed by the dread of the press-gang; when no other subject was talked about – hardly, in fact, thought about. At such flows of panic, Philip had his own private fears lest a dash of light should come upon Sylvia, and she should suddenly see that Kinraid's absence might be accounted for in another way besides death. But when he reasoned, this seemed unlikely. No man-of-war had been seen off the coast, or, if seen, had never been spoken about, at the time of Kinraid's disappearance. If he had vanished this winter time, every one would have been convinced that the press-gang had seized upon him. Philip had never heard any one breathe the dreaded name of the *Alcestis*. Besides, he went on to think, at the farm they are out of hearing of this one great weary subject of talk. But it was not so, as he became convinced one evening. His aunt caught him a little aside while Sylvia was in the dairy, and her husband talking in the shippen with Kester.

'For good's sake, Philip, dunnot thee bring us talk about t' press-gang. It's a thing as has got hold on my measter, till thou'd think him possessed. He's speaking perpetual on it i' such a way, that thou'd think he were itching to kill 'em a' a'fore he tasted bread again. He really trembles wi' rage and passion; an' a' night it's just as bad. He starts up i' his sleep, swearing and cursing at 'em, till I'm sometimes afeard he'll mak' an end o' me by mistake. And what mun he do last night but open out on Charley Kinraid, and tell Sylvie he thought m'appen t' gang had got hold on him. It might make her cry a' her saut tears o'er again.'

Philip spoke, by no wish of his own, but as if compelled to speak.

'An' who knows but what it's true?'

The instant these words had come out of his lips he could have bitten his tongue off. And yet afterwards it was a sort of balm to his conscience that he had so spoken.

'What nonsense, Philip!' said his aunt; 'why, these fearsome

ships were far out o' sight when he went away,
and Sylvie just getting o'er her trouble so nice
master went on for to say if they'd getten hold
not a chap to stay wi' 'em; he'd gi'en proofs
'em, time on. He either ha' made off – an' then
should ha' heerd on him somehow – them Co
him still and they've a deal to do wi' his folk beyond Newcassel
– or, as my master says, he were just t' chap to hang or drown
hissel, sooner nor do aught against his will.'

'What did Sylvie say?' asked Philip, in a hoarse low voice.

'Say? why, a' she could say was to burst out crying, and after
a bit she just repeated her feyther's words, and said anyhow he
was dead, for he'd niver live to go to sea wi' a press-gang. She
knowed him too well for that. Thou sees she thinks a deal on
him for a spirited chap, as can do what he will. I belie' me she
first began to think on him time o' t' fight aboard th' *Good
Fortune*, when Darley were killed, and he would seem tame-like
to her if he couldn't conquer press-gangs and men-o'-war. She's
sooner think on him drowned, as she's ne'er to see him again.'

'It's best so,' said Philip, and then, to calm his unusually
excited aunt, he promised to avoid the subject of the press-gang
as much as possible.

But it was a promise very difficult of performance, for Daniel
Robson was, as his wife said, like one possessed. He could
hardly think of anything else, though he himself was occasionally weary of the same constantly recurring idea, and would fain
have banished it from his mind. He was too old a man to be
likely to be taken by them; he had no son to become their victim;
but the terror of them, which he had braved and defied in his
youth, seemed to come back and take possession of him in his
age; and with the terror came impatient hatred. Since his wife's
illness the previous winter he had been a more sober man until
now. He was never exactly drunk, for he had a strong, well-
seasoned head; but the craving to hear the last news of the
actions of the press-gang drew him into Monkshaven nearly
every day at this dead agricultural season of the year; and a
public-house is generally the focus from which gossip radiates;
and probably the amount of drink thus consumed weakened
Robson's power over his mind, and caused the concentration of
thought on one subject. This may be a physiological explanation

...what afterwards was spoken of as a supernatural kind of possession, leading him to his doom.

CHAPTER 23

Retaliation

The public-house that had been chosen by the leaders of the press-gang in Monkshaven at this time, for their rendezvous (or 'Randyvowse', as it was generally pronounced), was an inn of poor repute, with a yard at the back which opened on to the staithe or quay nearest to the open sea. A strong high stone wall bounded this grass-grown mouldy yard on two sides; the house, and some unused out-buildings, formed the other two. The choice of the place was good enough, both as to situation, which was sufficiently isolated, and yet near to the widening river; and as to the character of the landlord, John Hobbs was a failing man, one who seemed as if doomed to be unfortunate in all his undertakings, and the consequence of all this was that he was envious of the more prosperous, and willing to do anything that might bring him in a little present success in life. His household consisted of his wife, her niece, who acted as servant, and an out-of-doors man, a brother of Ned Simpson, the well-doing butcher, who at one time had had a fancy for Sylvia. But the one brother was prosperous, the other had gone on sinking in life, like him who was now his master. Neither Hobbs nor his man Simpson were absolutely bad men; if things had gone well with them they might each have been as scrupulous and conscientious as their neighbours, and even now, supposing the gain in money to be equal, they would sooner have done good than evil; but a very small sum was enough to turn the balance. And in a greater degree than in most cases was the famous maxim of Rochefoucault true with them; for in the misfortunes of their friends they seemed to see some justification of their own.* It was blind fate dealing out events, not that the events themselves were the inevitable consequences of folly or misconduct. To such men as these the large sum offered by the lieutenant of the press-gang for the accommodation of the Mariner's Arms was simply and immediately irresistible. The best room in the dilapidated house was put at the service of the commanding officer of the impress service, and all other arrangements made at his desire, irrespective of all the former unprofitable sources of custom and of business. If the relatives both of Hobbs and of Simpson had not been so well known and so prosperous in the town, they themselves would have received more marks of popular ill opinion than they did during the winter the events of which are now being recorded. As it was, people spoke to them when they appeared at kirk or at market, but held no conversation with them; no, not although they each appeared better dressed than they had either of them done for years past, and although their whole manner showed a change, inasmuch as they had been formerly snarling and misanthropic, and were now civil almost to deprecation.

Every one who was capable of understanding the state of feeling in Monkshaven at this time must have been aware that at any moment an explosion might take place; and probably there were those who had judgment enough to be surprised that it did not take place sooner than it did. For until February there were only occasional cries and growls of rage, as the press-gang made their captures first here, then there; often, apparently, tranquil for days, then heard of at some distance along the coast, then carrying off a seaman from the very heart of the town. They seemed afraid of provoking any general hostility, such as that which had driven them from Shields, and would have conciliated the inhabitants if they could; the officers on the service and on board the three men-of-war coming often into the town, spending largely, talking to all with cheery friendliness, and making themselves very popular in such society as they could obtain access to at the houses of the neighbouring magistrates or at the rectory. But this, however agreeable, did not forward the object the impress service had in view; and, accordingly, a more decided step was taken at a time when, although there was no apparent evidence as to the fact, the town was full of the Greenland mariners coming quietly in to renew their yearly engagements, which, when done, would legally entitle them to protection from impressment. One night – it was on a Saturday, February 23rd, when there was a bitter black frost, with a north-east wind sweeping through the streets, and men and women were close shut in their houses – all were

startled in their household content and warmth by the sound of
the firebell busily swinging, and pealing out for help. The fire-
bell was kept in the market-house where High Street and Bridge
Street met: every one knew what it meant. Some dwelling or
maybe a boiling-house was on fire, and neighbourly assistance
was summoned with all speed, in a town where no water was
laid on, nor fire-engines kept in readiness. Men snatched up
their hats, and rushed out, wives following, some with the
readiest wraps they could lay hands on, with which to clothe
the over-hasty husbands, others from that mixture of dread and
curiosity which draws people to the scene of any disaster. Those
of the market people who were making the best of their way
homewards, having waited in the town till the early darkness
concealed their path, turned back at the sound of the ever-
clanging fire-bell, ringing out faster and faster as if the danger
became every instant more pressing.

As men ran against or alongside of each other, their breathless
question was ever, 'Where is it?' and no one could tell; so they
pressed onwards into the market-place, sure of obtaining the
information desired there, where the fire-bell kept calling out
with its furious metal tongue.

The dull oil-lamps in the adjoining streets only made darkness
visible* in the thronged market-place, where the buzz of many
men's unanswered questions was rising louder and louder. A
strange feeling of dread crept over those nearest to the closed
market-house. Above them in the air the bell was still clanging;
but before them was a door fast shut and locked; no one to
speak and tell them why they were summoned – where they
ought to be. They were at the heart of the mystery, and it was a
silent blank! Their unformed dread took shape at the cry from
the outside of the crowd, from where men were still coming
down the eastern side of Bridge Street. 'The gang! the gang!'
shrieked out some one. 'The gang are upon us! Help! help!'
Then the fire-bell had been a decoy; a sort of seething the kid in
its mother's milk,* leading men into a snare through their
kindliest feelings. Some dull sense of this added to utter dismay,
and made them struggle and strain to get to all the outlets save
that in which a fight was now going on; the swish of heavy
whips, the thud of bludgeons, the groans, the growls of wounded
or infuriated men, coming with terrible distinctness through the
darkness to the quickened ear of fear.

A breathless group rushed up the blackness of a narrow entry to stand still awhile, and recover strength for fresh running. For a time nothing but heavy pants and gasps were heard amongst them. No one knew his neighbour, and their good feeling, so lately abused and preyed upon, made them full of suspicion. The first who spoke was recognized by his voice.

'Is it thee, Daniel Robson?' asked his neighbour, in a low tone.

'Ay! Who else should it be?'

'A dunno.'

'If a am to be any one else, I'd like to be a chap of nobbut eight stun.* A'm welly done for!'

'It were as bloody a shame as iver I heerd on. Who's to go t' t' next fire, a'd like to know?'

'A tell yo' what, lads,' said Daniel, recovering his breath, but speaking in gasps. 'We were a pack o' cowards to let 'em carry off yon chaps as easy as they did, a'm reckoning!'

'A think so, indeed,' said another voice.

Daniel went on –

'We was two hunder, if we was a man; an' t' gang has niver numbered above twelve.'

'But they was armed. A seen t' glitter on their cutlasses,' spoke out a fresh voice.

'What then!' replied he who had latest come, and who stood at the mouth of the entry. 'A had my whalin' knife wi' me i' my pea-jacket as my missus threw at me, and a'd ha' ripped 'em up as soon as winkin', if a could ha' thought what was best to do wi' that d – d bell makin' such a din reet above us. A man can but die onest, and we was ready to go int' t' fire for t' save folks' lives, and yet we'd none on us t' wit to see as we might ha' saved yon poor chaps as screeched out for help.'

'They'll ha' getten 'em to t' Randyvowse by now,' said some one.

'They cannot tak' 'em aboard till morning; t' tide won't serve,' said the last speaker but one.

Daniel Robson spoke out the thought that was surging up into the brain of every one there.

'There's a chance for us a'. How many be we?' By dint of touching each other the numbers were counted. Seven. 'Seven. But if us seven turns out and rouses t' town, there'll be many a score ready to gang* to t' Mariners' Arms, and it'll be easy work reskyin' them chaps as is pressed. Us seven, each man jack on us, go and seek up his friends, and get him as well as he can to t' church steps; then, mebbe, there'll be some theere as'll not be so soft as we was, lettin' them poor chaps be carried off from under our noses, just becase our ears was busy listenin' to yon confounded bell, whose clip-clappin' tongue a'll tear out afore this week is out.'

Before Daniel had finished speaking, those nearest to the entrance muttered their assent to his project, and had stolen off, keeping to the darkest side of the streets and lanes, which they threaded in different directions; most of them going straight as sleuth-hounds to the haunts of the wildest and most desperate portion of the seafaring population of Monkshaven. For, in the breasts of many, revenge for the misery and alarm of the past winter took a deeper and more ferocious form than Daniel had thought of when he made his proposal of a rescue. To him it was an adventure like many he had been engaged in in his younger days; indeed, the liquor he had drunk had given him a fictitious youth for the time; and it was more in the light of a rough frolic of which he was to be the leader, that he limped along (always lame from old attacks of rheumatism), chuckling to himself at the apparent stillness of the town, which gave no warning to the press-gang at the Rendezvous of anything in the wind. Daniel, too, had his friends to summon; old hands like himself, but 'deep uns', also, like himself, as he imagined.

It was nine o'clock when all who were summoned met at the church steps; and by nine o'clock, Monkshaven, in those days, was more quiet and asleep than many a town at present is at midnight. The church and churchyard above them were flooded with silver light, for the moon was high in the heavens: the irregular steps were here and there in pure white clearness, here and there in blackest shadow. But more than half way up to the top, men clustered like bees all pressing so as to be near enough to question those who stood nearest to the planning of the attack. Here and there, a woman, with wild gestures and shrill voice, that no entreaty would hush down to the whispered pitch of the men, pushed her way through the crowd – this one imploring immediate action, that adjuring those around her to smite and spare not those who had carried off her 'man', – the father, the breadwinner. Low down in the darkened silent town were many whose hearts went with the angry and excited crowd, and who would bless them and caress them for that night's deeds. Daniel soon found himself a laggard in planning, compared to some of those around him. But when, with the rushing sound of many steps and but few words, they had arrived at the blank, dark, shut-up Mariners' Arms, they paused in surprise at the uninhabited look of the whole house: it was Daniel once more who took the lead.

'Speak 'em fair,' said he; 'try good words first. Hobbs'll mebbe let 'em out quiet, if we can catch a word wi' him. A say, Hobbs,' said he, raising his voice, 'is a' shut up for t' neet; for a'd be glad of a glass. A'm Dannel Robson, thou knows.'

Not one word in reply, any more than from the tomb; but his speech had been heard nevertheless. The crowd behind him began to jeer and to threaten: there was no longer any keeping down their voices, their rage, their terrible oaths. If doors and windows had not of late been strengthened with bars of iron in anticipation of some such occasion, they would have been broken in with the onset of the fierce and now yelling crowd, who rushed against them with the force of a battering-ram, to recoil in baffled rage from the vain assault. No sign, no sound from within, in that breathless pause.

'Come away round here! a've found a way to t' back o' behint, where belike it's not so well fenced,' said Daniel, who had made way for younger and more powerful men to conduct the assault, and had employed his time meanwhile in examining the back premises. The men rushed after him, almost knocking him down, as he made his way into the lane into which the doors of the outbuildings belonging to the inn opened. Daniel had already broken the fastening of that which opened into a damp, mouldy-smelling shippen, in one corner of which a poor lean cow shifted herself on her legs, in an uneasy, restless manner, as her sleeping-place was invaded by as many men as could cram themselves into the dark hold. Daniel, at the end farthest from the door, was almost smothered before he could break down the rotten wooden shutter, that, when opened, displayed the weedy yard of the old inn, the full clear light defining the outline of each blade of grass by the delicate black shadow behind.

This hole, used to give air and light to what had once been a stable, in the days when horse travellers were in the habit of coming to the Mariners' Arms, was large enough to admit the passage of a man; and Daniel, in virtue of its discovery, was the first to get through. But he was larger and heavier than he had been; his lameness made him less agile, and the impatient crowd behind him gave him a helping push that sent him down on the round stones with which the yard was paved, and for the time disabled him so much that he could only just crawl out of the way of leaping feet and heavy nailed boots, which came through the opening till the yard was filled with men, who now set up a fierce, derisive shout, which, to their delight, was answered from within. No more silence, no more dead opposition: a living struggle, a glowing, raging fight; and Daniel thought he should be obliged to sit there still, leaning against the wall, inactive, while the strife and the action were going on in which he had once been foremost.

He saw the stones torn up; he saw them used with good effect on the unguarded back-door; he cried out in useless warning as he saw the upper windows open, and aim taken among the crowd; but just then the door gave way, and there was an involuntary forward motion in the throng, so that no one was so disabled by the shots as to prevent his forcing his way in with the rest. And now the sounds came veiled by the walls as of some raging ravening beast growling over his prey; the noise came and went – once utterly ceased; and Daniel raised himself with difficulty to ascertain the cause, when again the roar came clear and fresh, and men poured into the yard again, shouting and rejoicing over the rescued victims of the press-gang. Daniel hobbled up, and shouted, and rejoiced, and shook hands with the rest, hardly caring to understand that the lieutenant and his gang had quitted the house by a front window, and that all had poured out in search of them; the greater part, however, returning to liberate the prisoners, and then glut their vengeance on the house and its contents.

From all the windows, upper and lower, furniture was now being thrown into the yard. The smash of glass, the heavier crash of wood, the cries, the laughter, the oaths, all excited Daniel to the utmost; and, forgetting his bruises, he pressed forwards to lend a helping hand. The wild, rough success of his scheme almost turned his head. He hurraed at every flagrant piece of destruction; he shook hands with every one around him, and, at last, when the destroyers inside paused to take breath, he cried out, –

'If a was as young as onest a was, a'd have t' Randyvowse down, and mak' a bonfire on it. We'd ring t' fire-bell then t' some purpose.'

No sooner said than done. Their excitement was ready to take the slightest hint of mischief; old chairs, broken tables, odd drawers, smashed chests, were rapidly and skilfully heaped into a pyramid, and one, who at the first broaching of the idea had gone for live coals the speedier to light up the fire, came now through the crowd with a large shovelful of red-hot cinders. The rioters stopped to take breath and look on like children at the uncertain flickering blaze, which sprang high one moment, and dropped down the next only to creep along the base of the heap of wreck, and make secure of its future work. Then the lurid blaze darted up wild, high, and irrepressible; and the men around gave a cry of fierce exultation, and in rough mirth began to try and push each other in. In one of the pauses of the rushing, roaring noise of the flames, the moaning low and groan of the poor alarmed cow fastened up in the shippen caught Daniel's ear, and he understood her groans as well as if they had been words. He limped out of the yard through the now deserted house, where men were busy at the mad work of destruction, and found his way back to the lane into which the shippen opened. The cow was dancing about at the roar, and dazzle, and heat of the fire; but Daniel knew how to soothe her, and in a few minutes he had a rope round her neck, and led her gently out from the scene of her alarm. He was still in the lane when Simpson, the man-of-all-work at the Mariners' Arms, crept out of some hiding-place in the deserted out-building, and stood suddenly face to face with Robson.

The man was white with fear and rage.

'Here, tak' thy beast, and lead her wheere she'll noane hear yon cries and shouts. She's fairly moithered* wi' heat an' noise.'

'They're brennin'* ivery rag I have i' t'world,' gasped out Simpson: 'I niver had much, and now I'm a beggar.'

'Well! thou shouldn't ha' turned again' thine own townfolks, and harboured t' gang. Sarves thee reet. A'd noane be here leadin' beasts if a were as young as a were; a'd be in t' thick on it.'

'It was thee set 'm on – a heerd thee – a see'd thee a helping on 'em t' break in; they'd niver ha' thought on attackin' t' house, and settin' fire to yon things, if thou hadn't spoken on it.'

Simpson was now fairly crying. But Daniel did not realize what the loss of all the small property he had in the world was to the poor fellow (rapscallion though he was, broken down, unprosperous ne'er-do-weel!) in his pride at the good work he believed he had set on foot.

'Ay,' said he; 'it's a great thing for folk to have a chap for t' lead 'em wi' a head on his shoulders. A misdoubt me if there were a felly theere as would ha' thought o' routling out* yon wasps' nest; it tak's a deal o' mother-wit to be up to things. But t' gang'll niver harbour theere again, one while. A only wish we'd cotched 'em. An' a should like t' ha' gi'en Hobbs a bit o' my mind.'

'He's had his sauce,' said Simpson, dolefully. 'Him and me is ruined.'

'Tut, tut, thou's got thy brother, he's rich enough. And Hobbs'll do a deal better; he's had his lesson now, and he'll stick to his own side time to come. Here, tak' thy beast an' look after her, for my bones is achin'. An' mak' thysel' scarce, for some o' them fellys has getten their blood up, an' wunnot be for treating thee o'er well if they fall in wi' thee.'

'Hobbs ought to be served out;* it were him as made t' bargain wi' lieutenant; and he's off safe wi' his wife and his money bag, and a'm left a beggar this neet i' Monkshaven street. My brother and me has had words, and he'll do nought for me but curse me. A had three crown-pieces, and a good pair o' breeches, and a shirt, and a dare say better nor two pair o' stockings. A wish t' gang, and thee, and Hobbs and them mad folk up yonder, were a' down i' hell, a do.'

'Coom, lad,' said Daniel, noways offended at his companion's wish on his behalf. 'A'm noane flush* mysel', but here's half-a-crown and tuppence; it's a' a've getten wi' me, but it'll keep thee and t' beast i' food and shelter to-neet, and get thee a glass o' comfort, too. A had thought o' takin' one mysel', but a shannot ha' a penny left, so a'll just toddle whoam to my missus.'

Daniel was not in the habit of feeling any emotion at actions not directly affecting himself; or else he might have despised the poor wretch who immediately clutched at the money, and overwhelmed that man with slobbery thanks whom he had not a minute before been cursing. But all Simpson's stronger passions had been long ago used up; now he only faintly liked and disliked, where once he loved and hated; his only vehement feeling was for himself; that cared for, other men might wither or flourish as best suited them.

Many of the doors which had been close shut when the crowd went down the High Street, were partially open as Daniel slowly returned; and light streamed from them on the otherwise dark road. The news of the successful attempt at rescue had reached those who had sat in mourning and in desolation an hour or two ago, and several of these pressed forwards as from their watching corner they recognized Daniel's approach; they pressed forward into the street to shake him by the hand, to thank him (for his name had been bruited abroad as one of those who had planned the affair), and at several places he was urged to have a dram – urgency that he was loath for many reasons to refuse, but his increasing uneasiness and pain made him for once abstinent, and only anxious to get home and rest. But he could not help being both touched and flattered at the way in which those who formed his 'world' looked upon him as a hero; and was not insensible to the words of blessing which a wife, whose husband had been impressed and rescued this night, poured down upon him as he passed.

'Theere, theere, – dunnot crack thy throat wi' blessin'. Thy man would ha' done as much for me, though mebbe he mightn't ha' shown so much gumption and capability; but them's gifts, and not to be proud on.'

When Daniel reached the top of the hill on the road home, he turned to look round; but he was lame and bruised, he had gone along slowly, the fire had pretty nearly died out, only a red hue in the air about the houses at the end of the long High Street, and a hot lurid mist against the hill-side beyond where the Mariners' Arms had stood, were still left as signs and token of the deed of violence.

Daniel looked and chuckled. 'That comes o' ringin' t' fire-bell,' said he to himself; 'it were shame for it to be tellin' a lie, poor oud story-teller.'

CHAPTER 24

Brief Rejoicing

Daniel's unusually late absence from home disturbed Bell and Sylvia not a little. He was generally at home between eight and nine on market days. They expected to see him the worse for liquor at such times; but this did not shock them; he was no worse than most of his neighbours, indeed better than several, who went off once or twice a year, or even oftener, on drinking bouts of two or three days' duration, returning pale, sodden, and somewhat shame-faced, when all their money was gone; and, after the conjugal reception was well over, settling down into hard-working and decently sober men until the temptation again got power over them. But, on market days, every man drank more than usual; every bargain or agreement was ratified by drink; they came from greater or less distances, either afoot or on horseback, and the 'good accommodation for man and beast' (as the old inn-signs expressed it) always included a considerable amount of liquor to be drunk by the man.

Daniel's way of announcing his intention of drinking more than ordinary was always the same. He would say at the last moment, 'Missus, I've a mind to get fuddled to-neet', and be off, disregarding her look of remonstrance, and little heeding the injunctions she would call after him to beware of such and such companions, or to attend to his footsteps on his road home.

But this night he had given no such warning. Bell and Sylvia put the candle on the low window-seat at the usual hour to guide him through the fields – it was a habit kept up even on moonlight nights like this – and sat on each side of the fire, at first scarcely caring to listen, so secure were they of his return. Bell dozed, and Sylvia sat gazing at the fire with abstracted eyes, thinking of the past year and of the anniversary which was approaching of the day when she had last seen the lover whom she believed to be dead, lying somewhere fathoms deep beneath the surface of that sunny sea on which she looked day by day without ever seeing his up-turned face through the depths, with whatsoever heart-sick longing for just one more sight she yearned and inwardly cried. If she could set her eyes on his bright, handsome face, that face which was fading from her memory, overtasked in the too frequent efforts to recall it; if she could but see him once again, coming over the waters beneath which he lay with supernatural motion, awaiting her at the stile, with the evening sun shining ruddy into his bonny eyes, even though, after that one instant of vivid and visible life, he faded into mist; if she could but see him now, sitting in the faintly flickering fire-light in the old, happy, careless way, on a corner of the dresser, his legs dangling, his busy fingers playing with some of her woman's work; – she wrung her hands tight together as she implored some, any Power, to let her see him just once again – just once – for one minute of passionate delight. Never again would she forget that dear face, if but once more she might set her eyes upon it.

Her mother's head fell with a sudden jerk, and she roused herself up; and Sylvia put by her thought of the dead, and her craving after his presence, into that receptacle of her heart where all such are kept closed and sacred from the light of common day.

'Feyther's late,' said Bell.

'It's gone eight,' replied Sylvia.

'But our clock is better nor an hour forrard,' answered Bell.

'Ay, but t' wind brings Monkshaven bells clear to-night. I heard t' eight o'clock bell ringing not five minutes ago.'

It was the fire-bell, but she had not distinguished the sound.

There was another long silence; both wide awake this time.

'He'll have his rheumatics again,' said Bell.

'It's cold for sartin,' said Sylvia. 'March weather come afore its time. But I'll make him a treacle-posset; it's a famous thing for keeping off hoasts.'*

The treacle-posset was entertainment enough for both while it was being made. But once placed in a little basin in the oven, there was again time for wonder and anxiety.

'He said nought about having a bout,* did he, mother?' asked Sylvia at length.

'No,' said Bell, her face a little contracting. After a while she added, 'There's many a one as has husbands that goes off drinking without iver saying a word to their wives. My master is none o' that mak'.'

'Mother,' broke in Sylvia again, 'I'll just go and get t' lantern out of t' shippen, and go up t' brow, and mebbe to t' ash-field end.'

'Do, lass,' said her mother. 'I'll get my wraps and go with thee.'

'Thou shall do niver such a thing,' said Sylvia. 'Thou's too frail to go out i' t' night air such a night as this.'

'Then call Kester up.'

'Not I. I'm noane afraid o' t' dark.'

'But of what thou mayst meet i' t' dark, lass?'

Sylvia shivered all over at the sudden thought, suggested by this speech of her mother's, that the idea that had flashed into her own mind of going to look for her father might be an answer to the invocation to the Powers which she had made not long ago, that she might indeed meet her dead lover at the ash-field stile;* but though she shivered as this superstitious fancy came into her head, her heart beat firm and regular; not from darkness nor from the spirits of the dead was she going to shrink; her great sorrow had taken away all her girlish nervous fear.

She went; and she came back. Neither man nor spirit had she seen; the wind was blowing on the height enough to sweep all creatures before it; but no one was coming.

So they sat down again to keep watch. At length his step was heard close to the door; and it startled them even in their state of expectation.

'Why, feyther!' cried Sylvia as he entered; while his wife stood up trembling, but not saying a word.

'A'm a'most done up,' said he, sitting heavily down on the chair nearest the door.

'Poor old feyther!' said Sylvia, stooping to take off his heavy clogged shoes; while Bell took the posset out of the oven.

'What's this? posset? what creatures women is for slops,' said he; but he drank it all the same, while Sylvia fastened the door, and brought the flaring candle from the window-seat. The fresh arrangement of light displayed his face blackened with smoke, and his clothes disarranged and torn.

'Who's been melling wi' thee?' asked Bell.

'No one has melled wi' me; but a've been mellin' wi' t' gang at last.'

'Thee: they niver were for pressing thee!' exclaimed both the women at once.

'No! they knowed better. They'n getten their belly-full as it is. Next time they try it on, a reckon they'll ax if Daniel Robson is wi'in hearin'. A've led a resky this neet, and saved nine or ten

honest chaps as was pressed, and carried off to t' Randyvowse.
Me and some others did it. And Hobbs' things and t' lieutenant's
is a' burnt; and by this time a reckon t' Randyvowse is pretty
nigh four walls, ready for a parish-pound.'*

'Thou'rt niver for saying thou burnt it down wi' t' gang in it,
for sure?' asked Bell.

'Na, na, not this time. T' gang fled up t' hill like coneys; and
Hobbs and his folks carried off a bag o' money; but t' oud
tumbledown place is just a heap o' brick and mortar; an' t'
furniture is smoulderin' int' ashes; and, best of a', t' men is free,
and will niver be cotched wi'a fire-bell again.'

And so he went on to tell of the ruse by which they had been
enticed into the market-place; interrupted from time to time by
their eager questions, and interrupting himself every now and
then with exclamations of weariness and pain, which made him
at last say, –

'Now a'm willing to tell yo' a' about it to-morrow, for it's not
ivery day a man can do such great things; but to-neet a mun go
to bed, even if King George were wantin' for to know how a
managed it a'.'

He went wearily upstairs, and wife and daughter both strove
their best to ease his aching limbs, and make him comfortable.
The warming-pan, only used on state occasions,* was taken
down and unpapered for his service; and as he got between the
warm sheets, he thanked Sylvia and her mother in a sleepy voice,
adding, –

'It's a vast o' comfort to think on yon poor lads as is sleepin'
i' their own homes this neet,' and then slumber fell upon him,
and he was hardly roused by Bell's softly kissing his weatherbeaten cheek, and saying low, –

'God bless thee, my man! Thou was allays for them that was
down and put upon.'

He murmured some monosyllabic reply, unheard by his wife,
who stole away to undress herself noiselessly, and laid herself
down on her side of the bed as gently as her stiffened limbs
would permit.

They were late in rising the next morning. Kester was long
since up and at his work among the cattle before he saw the
house-door open to admit the fresh chill morning air; and even
then Sylvia brushed softly, and went about almost on tiptoe.
When the porridge was ready, Kester was called in to his

breakfast, which he took sitting at the dresser with the family. A large wooden platter stood in the middle; and each had a bowl of the same material filled with milk. The way was for every one to dip his pewter spoon into the central dish, and convey as much or as little as he liked at a time of the hot porridge into his pure fresh milk. But to-day Bell told Kester to help himself all at once, and to take his bowl up to the master's room and keep him company. For Daniel was in bed, resting from his weariness, and bemoaning his painful bruises whenever he thought of them. But his mind was still so much occupied with the affair of the previous night, that Bell judged rightly that a new listener would give ease to his body as well as to his mind, and her proposal of Kester's carrying up his breakfast had been received by Daniel with satisfaction.

So Kester went up slowly, carrying his over-full basin tenderly, and seated himself on the step leading down into the bed-room (for levels had not been calculated when the old house was built) facing his master, who, half sitting up in the blue check bed, not unwillingly began his relation again; to which Kester listened so attentively, that his spoon was often arrested in its progress from the basin to his mouth, open ready to receive it, while he gazed with unwinking eyes at Daniel narrating his exploits.

But after Daniel had fought his battles o'er again to every auditor within his reach, he found the seclusion of his chamber rather oppressive, without even the usual week-days' noises below; so after dinner, though far from well, he came down and wandered about the stable and the fields nearest to the house, consulting with Kester as to crops and manure for the most part; but every now and then breaking out into an episodical chuckle over some part of last night's proceedings. Kester enjoyed the day even more than his master, for he had no bruises to remind him that, although a hero, he was also flesh and blood.

When they returned to the house they found Philip there, for it was already dusk. It was Kester's usual Sunday plan to withdraw to bed at as early an hour as he could manage to sleep, often in winter before six; but now he was too full of interest in what Philip might have to tell of Monkshaven news to forego his Sabbath privilege of spending the evening sitting on the chair at the end of the dresser behind the door.

Philip was as close to Sylvia as he could possibly get without giving her offence, when they came in. Her manner was listless and civil; she had lost all that active feeling towards him which made him positively distasteful, and had called out her girlish irritation and impertinence. She now was rather glad to see him than otherwise. He brought some change into the heavy monotony of her life, – monotony so peaceful until she had been stirred by passion out of that content with the small daily events which had now become burdensome recurrences. Insensibly to herself she was becoming dependent on his timid devotion, his constant attention; and he, lover-like, once so attracted, in spite of his judgment, by her liveliness and piquancy, now doted on her languor, and thought her silence more sweet than words.

He had only just arrived when master and man came in. He had been to afternoon chapel; none of them had thought of going to the distant church; worship with them was only an occasional duty, and this day their minds had been too full of the events of the night before. Daniel sat himself heavily down in his accustomed chair, the three-cornered arm-chair in the fireside corner, which no one thought of anybody else ever occupying on any occasion whatever. In a minute or two he interrupted Philip's words of greeting and inquiry by breaking out into the story of the rescue of last night. But to the mute surprise of Sylvia, the only one who noticed it, Philip's face, instead of expressing admiration and pleasant wonder, lengthened into dismay; once or twice he began to interrupt, but stopped himself as if he would consider his words again. Kester was never tired of hearing his master talk; by long living together they understood every fold of each other's minds, and small expressions had much significance to them. Bell, too, sat thankful that her husband should have done such deeds. Only Sylvia was made uneasy by Philip's face and manner. When Daniel had ended there was a great silence, instead of the questions and compliments he looked to receive. He became testy, and turning to Bell, said, –

'My nephew looks as though he was a-thinking more on t' little profit he has made on his pins an' bobs, than as if he was heeding how honest men were saved from being haled out to yon tender, an' carried out o' sight o' wives and little 'uns for iver. Wives an' little 'uns may go to t' workhouse or clem* for aught he cares.'

Philip went very red, and then more sallow then usual. He had not been thinking of Charley Kinraid, but of quite another thing, while Daniel had told his story; but this last speech of the old man's brought up the remembrance that was always quick, do what he would to smother or strangle it. He did not speak for a moment or two, then he said, –

'To-day has not been like Sabbath in Monkshaven. T' rioters, as folks call 'em, have been about all night. They wanted to give battle to t' men-o'-war's men; and it were taken up by th' better end, and they've sent to my Lord Malton for t' militia; and they're come into t' town, and they're hunting for a justice for t' read th' act;* folk do say there'll be niver a shop opened to-morrow.'

This was rather a more serious account of the progress of the affair than any one had calculated upon. They looked grave upon it awhile, then Daniel took heart and said, –

'A think we'd done a'most enough last neet; but men's not to be stopped wi' a straw when their blood is up; still it's hard lines to call out t' sojers, even if they be but militia. So what we seven hatched in a dark entry has ta'en a lord to put a stop to 't!' continued he, chuckling a little, but more faintly this time.

Philip went on, still graver than before, boldly continuing to say what he knew would be discordant to the family he loved so well.

'I should ha' telled yo' all about it; I thought on it just as a bit o' news; I'd niver thought on such a thing as uncle there having been in it, and I'm main sorry to hear on it, I am.'

'Why?' said Sylvia, breathlessly.

'It's niver a thing to be sorry on. I'm proud and glad,' said Bell.

'Let-a-be, let-a-be,' said Daniel, in much dudgeon. 'A were a fool to tell him o' such-like doings, they're noane i' his line; we'll talk on yard measures now.'

Philip took no notice of this poor attempt at sarcasm: he seemed as if lost in thought, then he said, –

'I'm vexed to plague yo', but I'd best say all I've got i' my mind. There was a vast o' folk at our chapel speaking about it – last night's doings and this morning's work – and how them as set it afoot was assured o' being clapt int' prison and tried for it; and when I heered uncle say as he was one, it like ran through me; for they say as t' justices will be all on t' Government side, and mad for vengeance.'

For an instant there was dead silence. The women looked at

each other with blank eyes, as if they were as yet unable to take in the new idea that the conduct which had seemed to them a subject for such just pride could be regarded by any one as deserving of punishment or retribution. Daniel spoke before they had recovered from their amazement.

'A'm noane sorry for what a did, an' a'd do it again to-neet, if need were. So theere's for thee. Thou may tell t' justices fra' me that a reckon a did righter nor them, as letten poor fellys be carried off i' t' very midst o' t' town they're called justices for.'

Perhaps Philip had better have held his tongue; but he believed in the danger, which he was anxious to impress upon his uncle, in order that, knowing what was to be apprehended, the latter might take some pains to avert it.

He went on.

'But they're making a coil* about th' Randyvowse being all destroyed!'

Daniel had taken down his pipe from the shelf in the chimney corner, and was stuffing tobacco into the bowl. He went on pretending to do this a little while after it was filled; for, to tell the truth, he was beginning to feel uncomfortable at the new view of his conduct presented to him. Still he was not going to let this appear, so lifting up his head with an indifferent air he lighted the pipe, blew into it, took it out and examined it as if something were wrong about it, and until that was put to rights he was unable to attend to anything else; all the while the faithful three who hung upon his well-being, gazing, breathless, at his proceedings, and anxious for his reply.

'Randyvowse!' said he at length; 'it were a good job it were brenned down, for such a harbour for vermin a never seed: t' rats ran across t' yard by hunders an' thousands; an it were no man's property as a've heerd tell, but belonged to Chancery, up i' Lunnon; so wheere's t' harm done, my fine felly?'

Philip was silent. He did not care to brave any further his uncle's angry frown and contracted eye. If he had only known of Daniel Robson's part in the riot before he had left the town, he would have taken care to have had better authority for the reality of the danger which he had heard spoken about, and in which he could not help believing. As it was, he could only keep quiet until he had ascertained what was the legal peril overhanging the rioters, and how far his uncle had been recognized.

Daniel went on puffing angrily. Kester sighed audibly, and

then was sorry he had done so, and began to whistle. Bell, full
of her new fear, yet desirous to bring all present into some kind
of harmony, said, –

'It'll ha' been a loss to John Hobbs – all his things burnt, or
trampled on. Mebbe he deserved it all, but one's a kind o' tender
feeling to one's tables and chairs, special if one's had t' bees-
waxing on 'em.'

'A wish he'd been burnt on t' top on 'em, a do,' growled out
Daniel, shaking the ash out of his pipe.

'Don't speak so ill o' thysel',' said his wife. 'Thou'd ha' been
t' first t' pluck him down if he'd screeched out.'

'An' a'll warrant if they come about wi' a paper asking for
feyther's name to make up for what Hobbs has lost by t' fire,
feyther 'll be for giving him summut,' said Sylvia.

'Thou knows nought about it,' said Daniel. 'Hold thy tongue
next time till thou's axed to speak, my wench.'

His sharp irritated way of speaking was so new to Sylvia, that
the tears sprang to her eyes, and her lip quivered. Philip saw it
all, and yearned over her. He plunged headlong into some other
subject to try and divert attention from her; but Daniel was too
ill at ease to talk much, and Bell was obliged to try and keep up
the semblance of conversation, with an occasional word or two
from Kester, who seemed instinctively to fall into her way of
thinking, and to endeavour to keep the dark thought in the
background.

Sylvia stole off to bed; more concerned at her father's angry
way of speaking than at the idea of his being amenable to law
for what he had done; the one was a sharp present evil, the
other something distant and unlikely. Yet a dim terror of this
latter evil hung over her, and once upstairs she threw herself on
her bed and sobbed. Philip heard her where he sat near the
bottom of the short steep staircase, and at every sob the cords
of love round his heart seemed tightened, and he felt as if he
must there and then do something to console her.

But, instead, he sat on talking of nothings, a conversation in
which Daniel joined with somewhat of surliness, while Bell,
grave and anxious, kept wistfully looking from one to the other,
desirous of gleaning some further information on the subject
which had begun to trouble her mind. She hoped some chance
would give her the opportunity of privately questioning Philip,
but it seemed to be equally her husband's wish to thwart any

such intention of hers. He remained in the house-place till after Philip had left, although he was evidently so much fatigued as to give some very distinct, though unintentional, hints to his visitor to be gone.

At length the house-door was locked on Philip, and then Daniel prepared to go to bed. Kester had left for his loft above the shippen more than an hour before. Bell had still to rake the fire, and then she would follow her husband upstairs.

As she was scraping up the ashes, she heard, intermixed with the noise she was making, the sound of some one rapping gently at the window. In her then frame of mind she started a little; but on looking round, she saw Kester's face pressed against the glass, and, reassured, she softly opened the door. There he stood in the dusk outer air, distinct against the grey darkness beyond, and in his hand something which she presently perceived was a pitchfork.

'Missus!' whispered he, 'a've watched t' maister t' bed; an' now a'd be greatly beholden to yo' if yo'd let me just lay me down i' t' house-place. A'd warrant niver a constable i' a' Monkshaven should get sight o' t' maister, an' me below t' keep ward.'

Bell shivered a little.

'Nay, Kester,' said she, putting her hand kindly on his shoulder; 'there's nought for t' fear. Thy master is not one for t' hurt nobody; and I dunnot think they can harm him for setting yon poor chaps free, as t' gang catched i' their wicked trap.'

Kester stood still; then he shook his head slowly.

'It's t' work at t' Randyvowse as a'm afeared on. Some folks thinks such a deal o' a bonfire. Then a may lay me down afore t' fire, missus?' said he, beseechingly.

'Nay, Kester – 'she began; but suddenly changing, she said, 'God bless thee, my man; come in and lay thee down on t' settle, and I'll cover thee up wi' my cloak as hangs behind t' door. We're not many on us that love him, an' we'll be all on us under one roof, an' niver a stone wall or a lock betwixt us.'

So Kester took up his rest in the house-place that night, and none knew of it besides Bell.

CHAPTER 25

Coming Troubles

The morning brought more peace if it did not entirely dissipate fear. Daniel seemed to have got over his irritability, and was unusually kind and tender to wife and daughter, especially striving by silent little deeds to make up for the sharp words he had said the night before to the latter.

As if by common consent, all allusion to the Saturday night's proceedings was avoided. They spoke of the day's work before them; of the crops to be sown; of the cattle; of the markets; but each one was conscious of a wish to know more distinctly what were the chances of the danger that, to judge from Philip's words, hung over them, falling upon them and cutting them off from all these places for the coming days.

Bell longed to send Kester down into Monkshaven as a sort of spy to see how the land lay; but she dared not manifest her anxiety to her husband, and could not see Kester alone. She wished that she had told him to go to the town, when she had had him to herself in the house-place the night before; now it seemed as though Daniel were resolved not to part from him, and as though both had forgotten that any peril had been anticipated. Sylvia and her mother, in like manner, clung together, not speaking of their fears, yet each knowing that it was ever present in the other's mind.

So things went on till twelve o'clock – dinner-time. If at any time that morning they had had the courage to speak together on the thought which was engrossing all their minds, it is possible that some means might have been found to avert the calamity that was coming towards them with swift feet. But among the uneducated – the partially educated – nay, even the weakly educated – the feeling exists which prompted the futile experiment of the well-known ostrich.* They imagine that, by closing their own eyes to apprehended evil, they avert it. The expression of fear is supposed to accelerate the coming of its cause. Yet, on the other hand, they shrink from acknowledging the long continuance of any blessing, in the idea that when unusual happiness is spoken about, it disappears. So, although perpetual complaints of past or present grievances and sorrows are most common among this class, they shrink from embodying apprehensions for the future in words, as if it then took shape and drew near.

They all four sat down to dinner, but not one of them was inclined to eat. The food was scarcely touched on their plates, yet they were trying to make talk among themselves as usual; they seemed as though they dared not let themselves be silent, when Sylvia, sitting opposite to the window, saw Philip at the top of the brow, running rapidly towards the farm. She had been so full of the anticipation of some kind of misfortune all the morning that she felt now as if this was the very percussive circumstance she had been expecting; she stood up, turning quite white, and, pointing with her finger, said, –

'There he is!'

Every one at table stood up too. An instant afterwards, Philip, breathless, was in the room.

He gasped out, 'They're coming! the warrant is out. You must go. I hoped you were gone.'

'God help us!' said Bell, and sat suddenly down, as if she had received a blow that made her collapse into helplessness; but she got up again directly.

Sylvia flew for her father's hat. He really seemed the most unmoved of the party.

'A'm noane afeared,' said he. 'A'd do it o'er again, a would; an' a'll tell 'em so. It's a fine time o' day when men's to be trapped and carried off, an' them as lays traps to set 'em free is to be put i' t' lock-ups for it.'

'But there was rioting, beside the rescue; t' house was burnt,' continued eager, breathless Philip.

'An' a'm noane goin' t' say a'm sorry for that, neyther; tho', mebbe, a wouldn't do it again.'

Sylvia had his hat on his head by this time; and Bell, wan and stiff, trembling all over, had his over-coat, and his leather purse with the few coins she could muster, ready for him to put on.

He looked at these preparations, at his wife and daughter, and his colour changed from its ruddy brown.

'A'd face lock-ups, an' a fair spell o' jail, but for these,' said he, hesitating.

'Oh!' said Philip, 'for God's sake, lose no time, but be off.'

'Where mun he go?' asked Bell, as if Philip must decide all.

'Anywhere, anywhere, out of this house – say Haverstone.

This evening, I'll go and meet him there and plan further; only be off now.' Philip was so keenly eager, he hardly took note at the time of Sylvia's one vivid look of unspoken thanks, yet he remembered it afterwards.

'A'll dang 'em dead,' said Kester, rushing to the door, for he saw what the others did not – that all chance of escape was over; the constables were already at the top of the little fieldpath not twenty yards off.

'Hide him, hide him,' cried Bell, wringing her hands in terror; for she, indeed they all, knew that flight would now be impossible. Daniel was heavy, rheumatic, and, moreover, had been pretty severely bruised on that unlucky night.

Philip, without another word, pushed Daniel before him upstairs, feeling that his own presence at Haytersbank Farm at that hour of the day would be a betrayal. They had just time to shut themselves up in the larger bed-room, before they heard a scuffle and the constables' entry downstairs.

'They're in,' said Philip, as Daniel squeezed himself under the bed; and then they held quite still, Philip as much concealed by the scanty, blue-check curtain as he could manage to be. They heard a confusion of voices below, a hasty moving of chairs, a banging of doors, a further parley, and then a woman's scream, shrill and pitiful; then steps on the stairs.

'That screech spoiled all,' sighed Philip.

In one instant the door was opened, and each of the hiders was conscious of the presence of the constables, although at first the latter stood motionless, surveying the apparently empty room with disappointment. Then in another moment they had rushed at Philip's legs, exposed as these were. They drew him out with violence, and then let him go.

'Measter Hepburn!' said one in amaze. But immediately they put two and two together; for in so small a place as Monkshaven every one's relationships and connections, and even likings, were known; and the motive of Philip's coming out to Haytersbank was perfectly clear to these men.

'T' other 'll not be far off,' said the other constable. 'His plate were downstair, full o' victual; a seed Measter Hepburn a-walking briskly before me as a left Monkshaven.'

'Here he be, here he be,' called out the other man, dragging Daniel out by his legs, 'we've getten him.'

Daniel kicked violently, and came out from his hiding-place in a less ignominious way than by being pulled out by his heels.

He shook himself, and then turned, facing his captors.

'A wish a'd niver hidden mysel'; it were his doing,' jerking his thumb towards Philip: 'a'm ready to stand by what a've done. Yo've getten a warrant, a'll be bound, for them justices is grand at writin' when t' fight's over.'

He was trying to carry it off with bravado, but Philip saw that he had received a shock, from his sudden look of withered colour and shrunken feature.

'Don't handcuff him,' said Philip, putting money into the constable's hand 'You'll be able to guard him well enough without them things.'

Daniel turned round sharp at this whisper.

'Let-a-be, let-a-be, my lad,' he said. 'It'll be summut to think on i' t' lock-up how two able-bodied fellys were so afeared on t' chap as reskyed them honest sailors o' Saturday neet, as they mun put him i' gyves, and he sixty-two come Martinmas, and sore laid up wi' t' rheumatics.' .

But it was difficult to keep up this tone of bravado when he was led a prisoner through his own house-place, and saw his poor wife quivering and shaking all over with her efforts to keep back all signs of emotion until he was gone; and Sylvia standing by her mother, her arm round Bell's waist and stroking the poor shrunken fingers which worked so perpetually and nervously in futile unconscious restlessness. Kester was in a corner of the room, sullenly standing.

Bell quaked from head to foot as her husband came down-stairs a prisoner. She opened her lips several times with an uneasy motion,* as if she would fain say something, but knew not what. Sylvia's passionate swollen lips and her beautiful defiant eyes gave her face quite a new aspect; she looked a helpless fury.

'A may kiss my missus, a reckon,' said Daniel, coming to a standstill as he passed near her.

'Oh, Dannel, Dannel!' cried she, opening her arms wide to receive him. 'Dannel, Dannel, my man!' and she shook with her crying, laying her head on his shoulder, as if he was all her stay and comfort.

'Come, missus! come, missus!' said he, 'there couldn't be more ado if a'd been guilty of murder, an' yet a say again, as a said

afore, a'm noane ashamed o' my doings. Here, Sylvie, lass, tak'
thy mother off me, for a cannot do it mysel', it like sets me off.'*
His voice was quavering as he said this. But he cheered up a
little and said, 'Now, good-by, oud wench' (kissing her), 'and
keep a good heart, and let me see thee lookin' lusty and strong
when a come back. Good-by, my lass; look well after mother,
and ask Philip for guidance if it's needed.'

He was taken out of his home, and then arose the shrill cries
of the women; but in a minute or two they were checked by the
return of one of the constables, who, cap in hand at the sight of
so much grief, said, –

'He wants a word wi' his daughter.'

The party had come to a halt about ten yards from the house.
Sylvia, hastily wiping her tears on her apron, ran out and threw
her arms round her father, as if to burst out afresh on his neck.

'Nay, nay, my wench, it's thee as mun be a comfort to mother:
nay, nay, or thou'll niver hear what a've got to say. Sylvie, my
lass, a'm main and sorry a were so short wi' thee last neet; a ax
thy pardon, lass, a were cross to thee, and sent thee to thy bed
wi' a sore heart. Thou munnot think on it again, but forgie me,
now a'm leavin' thee.'

'Oh, feyther! feyther!' was all Sylvia could say; and at last
they had to make as though they would have used force to
separate her from their prisoner. Philip took her hand, and
softly led her back to her weeping mother.

For some time nothing was to be heard in the little farmhouse
kitchen but the sobbing and wailing of the women. Philip stood
by silent, thinking, as well as he could, for his keen sympathy
with their grief, what had best be done next. Kester, after some
growls at Sylvia for having held back the uplifted arm which he
thought might have saved Daniel by a well-considered blow on
his captors as they entered the house, went back into his shippen
– his cell for meditation and consolation, where he might hope
to soothe himself before going out to his afternoon's work;
labour which his master had planned for him that very morning,
with a strange foresight, as Kester thought, for the job was one
which would take him two or three days without needing any
further directions than those he had received, and by the end of
that time he thought that his master would be at liberty again.
So he – so they all thought in their ignorance and inexperience.

Although Daniel himself was unreasoning, hasty, impulsive –

in a word, often thinking and acting very foolishly – yet, somehow, either from some quality in his character, or from the loyalty of nature in those with whom he had to deal in his every-day life, he had made his place and position clear as the arbiter and law-giver of his household. On his decision, as that of husband, father, master, perhaps superior natures waited. So now that he was gone and had left them in such strange new circumstances so suddenly, it seemed as though neither Bell nor Sylvia knew exactly what to do when their grief was spent, so much had every household action and plan been regulated by the thought of him. Meanwhile Philip had slowly been arriving at the conclusion that he was more wanted at Monkshaven to look after Daniel's interests, to learn what were the legal probabilities in consequence of the old man's arrest, and to arrange for his family accordingly, than standing still and silent in the Haytersbank kitchen, too full of fellow-feeling and heavy foreboding to comfort, awkwardly unsympathetic in appearance from the very aching of his heart.

So when his aunt, with instinctive sense of regularity and propriety, began to put away the scarcely tasted dinner, and Sylvia, blinded with crying, and convulsively sobbing, was yet trying to help her mother, Philip took his hat, and brushing it round and round with the sleeve of his coat, said, –

'I think I'll just go back, and see how matters stand.' He had a more distinct plan in his head than these words implied, but it depended on so many contingencies of which he was ignorant that he said only these few words; and with a silent resolution to see them again that day, but a dread of being compelled to express his fears, so far beyond theirs, he went off without saying anything more. Then Sylvia lifted up her voice with a great cry. Somehow she had expected him to do something – what, she did not know; but he was gone, and they were left without stay or help.

'Hush thee, hush thee,' said her mother, trembling all over herself; 'it's for the best. The Lord knows.'

'But I niver thought he'd leave us,' moaned Sylvia, half in her mother's arms, and thinking of Philip. Her mother took the words as applied to Daniel.

'And he'd niver ha' left us, my wench, if he could ha' stayed.'

'Oh, mother, mother, it's Philip as has left us, and he could ha' stayed.'

'He'll come back, or mebbe send, I'll be bound. Leastways he'll be gone to see feyther, and he'll need comfort most on all in a fremd place – in Bridewell* – and niver a morsel of victual or a piece o' money.' And now she sat down, and wept the dry hot tears that come with such difficulty to the eyes of the aged. And so – first one grieving, and then the other, and each draining her own heart of every possible hope by way of comfort, alternately trying to cheer and console – the February afternoon passed away; the continuous rain closing in the daylight even earlier than usual, and adding to the dreariness, with the natural accompaniments of wailing winds, coming with long sweeps over the moors, and making the sobbings at the windows that always sound like the gasps of some one in great agony. Meanwhile Philip had hastened back to Monkshaven. He had no umbrella, he had to face the driving rain for the greater part of the way, but he was thankful to the weather, for it kept men indoors, and he wanted to meet no one, but to have time to think and mature his plans. The town itself was, so to speak, in mourning. The rescue of the sailors was a distinctly popular movement; the subsequent violence (which had, indeed, gone much further than has been described, after Daniel left it) was, in general considered as only a kind of due punishment inflicted in wild justice* on the press-gang and their abettors. The feeling of the Monkshaven people was, therefore, in decided opposition to the vigorous steps taken by the county magistrates, who, in consequence of an appeal from the naval officers in charge of the impressment service, had called out the militia (from a distant and inland county) stationed within a few miles, and had thus summarily quenched the riots that were continuing on the Sunday morning after a somewhat languid fashion; the greater part of the destruction of property having been accomplished during the previous night. Still there was little doubt but that the violence would have been renewed as evening drew on, and the more desperate part of the population and the enraged sailors had had the Sabbath leisure to brood over their wrongs, and to encourage each other in a passionate attempt at redress, or revenge. So the authorities were quite justified in the decided steps they had taken, both in their own estimation then, and now, in ours, looking back on the affair in cold blood. But at the time feeling ran strongly against them; and all means of expressing itself in action being prevented, men brooded sullenly in their own houses. Philip, as the representative of the family, the head of which was now suffering for his deeds in the popular cause, would have met with more sympathy, ay, and more respect than he imagined, as he went along the streets, glancing from side to side, fearful of meeting some who would shy him as the relation of one who had been ignominiously taken to Bridewell a few hours before. But in spite of this wincing of Philip's from observation and remark, he never dreamed of acting otherwise than as became a brave true friend. And this he did, and would have done, from a natural faithfulness and constancy of disposition, without any special regard for Sylvia.

He knew his services were needed in the shop; business which he had left at a moment's warning awaited him, unfinished; but at this time he could not bear the torture of giving explanations, and alleging reasons to the languid intelligence and slow sympathies of Coulson.

He went to the offices of Mr Donkin, the oldest established and most respected attorney in Monkshaven – he who had been employed to draw up the law papers and deeds of partnership consequent on Hepburn and Coulson succeeding to the shop of John and Jeremiah Foster, Brothers.

Mr Donkin knew Philip from this circumstance. But, indeed, nearly every one in Monkshaven knew each other; if not enough to speak to, at least enough to be acquainted with the personal appearance and reputation of most of those whom they met in the streets. It so happened that Mr Donkin had a favourable opinion of Philip; and perhaps for this reason the latter had a shorter time to wait before he obtained an interview with the head of the house, than many of the clients who came for that purpose from town or country for many miles round.

Philip was ushered in. Mr Donkin sat with his spectacles pushed up on his forehead, ready to watch his countenance and listen to his words.

'Good afternoon, Mr Hepburn!'

'Good afternoon, sir.' Philip hesitated how to begin. Mr Donkin became impatient, and tapped with the fingers of his left hand on his desk. Philip's sensitive nerves felt and rightly interpreted the action.

'Please, sir, I'm come to speak to you about Daniel Robson, of Haytersbank Farm.'

'Daniel Robson?' said Mr Donkin, after a short pause, to try and compel Philip into speed in his story.

'Yes, sir. He's been taken up on account of this affair, sir, about the press-gang on Saturday night.'

'To be sure! I thought I knew the name.' And Mr Donkin's face became graver, and the expression more concentrated. Looking up suddenly at Philip, he said, 'You are aware that I am the clerk to the magistrates?'

'No, sir,' in a tone that indicated the unexpressed 'What then?'

'Well, but I am. And so of course, if you want my services or advice in favour of a prisoner whom they have committed, or are going to commit, you can't have them, that's all.'

'I am very sorry – very!' said Philip; and then he was again silent for a period; long enough to make the busy attorney impatient.

'Well, Mr Hepburn, have you anything else to say to me?'

'Yes, sir. I've a deal to ask of you; for you see I don't rightly understand what to do; and yet I'm all as Daniel's wife and daughter has to look to; and I've their grief heavy on my heart. You could not tell me what is to be done with Daniel, could you, sir?'

'He'll be brought up before the magistrates to-morrow morning for final examination, along with the others, you know, before he's sent to York Castle to take his trial at the spring assizes.'

'To York Castle, sir?'

Mr Donkin nodded, as if words were too precious to waste.

'And when will he go?' asked poor Philip, in dismay.

'To-morrow: most probably as soon as the examination is over. The evidence is clear as to his being present, aiding and abetting, – indicted on the 4th section of 1 George I,* statute 1, chapter 5. I'm afraid it's a bad look-out. Is he a friend of yours, Mr Hepburn?'

'Only an uncle, sir,' said Philip, his heart getting full; more from Mr Donkin's manner than from his words. 'But what can they do to him, sir?'

'Do?' Mr Donkin half smiled at the ignorance displayed. 'Why, hang him, to be sure; if the judge is in a hanging mood. He's been either a principal in the offence, or a principal in the second degree, and, as such, liable to the full punishment. I drew up the warrant myself this morning, though I left the exact name to be filled up by my clerk.'

'Oh, sir! can you do nothing for me?' asked Philip, with sharp beseeching in his voice. He had never imagined that it was a capital offence; and the thought of his aunt's and Sylvia's ignorance of the possible fate awaiting him whom they so much loved, was like a stab to his heart.

'No, my good fellow. I'm sorry; but, you see, it's my duty to do all I can to bring criminals to justice.'

'My uncle thought he was doing such a fine deed.'

'Demolishing and pulling down, destroying and burning dwelling-houses and outhouses,' said Mr Donkin. 'He must have some peculiar notions.'

'The people is so mad with the press-gang, and Daniel has been at sea hisself; and took it so to heart when he heard of mariners and seafaring folk being carried off, and just cheated into doing what was kind and helpful – leastways, what would have been kind and helpful, if there had been a fire. I'm against violence and riots myself, sir, I'm sure; but I cannot help thinking as Daniel had a deal to justify him on Saturday night, sir.'

'Well; you must try and get a good lawyer to bring out all that side of the question. There's a good deal to be said on it; but it's my duty to get up all the evidence to prove that he and others were present on the night in question; so, as you'll perceive, I can give you no help in defending him.'

'But who can, sir? I came to you as a friend who, I thought, would see me through it. And I don't know any other lawyer; leastways, to speak to.'

Mr Donkin was really more concerned for the misguided rioters than he was aware; and he was aware of more interest than he cared to express. So he softened his tone a little, and tried to give the best advice in his power.

'You'd better go to Edward Dawson on the other side of the river; he that was articled clerk with me two years ago, you know. He's a clever fellow, and has not too much practice; he'll do the best he can for you. He'll have to be at the court-house, tell him, to-morrow morning at ten, when the justice meet. He'll watch the case for you; and then he'll give you his opinion, and tell you what to do. You can't do better than follow his advice. I must do all I can to collect evidence for a conviction, you know.'

Philip stood up, looked at his hat, and then came forward and laid down six and eightpence* on the desk in a blushing, awkward way.

'Pooh! pooh!' said Mr Donkin, pushing the money away. 'Don't be a fool; you'll need it all before the trial's over. I've done nothing, man. It would be a pretty thing for me to be feed by both parties.'

Philip took up the money, and left the room. In an instant he came back again, glanced furtively at Mr Donkin's face, and then, once more having recourse to brushing his hat, he said, in a low voice –

'You'll not be hard upon him, sir, I hope?'

'I must do my duty,' replied Mr Donkin, a little sternly, 'without any question of hardness.'

Philip, discomfited, left the room; an instant of thought and Mr Donkin had jumped up, and hastening to the door he opened it and called after Philip.

'Hepburn – Hepburn – I say, he'll be taken to York as soon as may be to-morrow morning; if any one wants to see him before then, they'd better look sharp about it.'

Philip went quickly along the streets towards Mr Dawson's, pondering upon the meaning of all that he had heard, and what he had better do. He had made his plans pretty clearly out by the time he arrived at Mr Dawson's smart door in one of the new streets on the other side of the river. A clerk as smart as the door answered Philip's hesitating knock, and replied to his inquiry as to whether Mr Dawson was at home, in the negative, adding, after a moment's pause –

'He'll be at home in less than an hour; he's only gone to make Mrs Dawson's will – Mrs Dawson, of Collyton – she's not expected to get better.'

Probably the clerk of an older-established attorney would not have given so many particulars as to the nature of his master's employment; but, as it happened it was of no consequence, the unnecessary information made no impression on Philip's mind; he thought the matter over, and then said –

'I'll be back in an hour, then. It's gone a quarter to four; I'll be back before five, tell Mr Dawson.'

He turned on his heel and went back to the High Street as fast as he could, with a far more prompt and decided step than before. He hastened through the streets, emptied by the bad weather, to the principal inn of the town, the George – the sign of which was fastened to a piece of wood stretched across the narrow street; and going up to the bar with some timidity (for the inn was frequented by the gentry of Monkshaven and the neighbourhood, and was considered as a touch above such customers as Philip), he asked if he could have a tax-cart* made ready in a quarter of an hour, and sent up to the door of his shop.

'To be sure he could; how far was it to go?'

Philip hesitated before he replied –

'Up the Knotting Lane, to the stile leading down to Hayters-bank Farm; they'll have to wait there for some as are coming.'

'They must not wait long such an evening as this; standing in such rain and wind as there'll be up there, is enough to kill a horse.'

'They shan't wait long,' said Philip, decisively: 'in a quarter of an hour, mind.'

He now went back to the shop, beating against the storm, which was increasing as the tide came in and the night hours approached.

Coulson had no word for him, but he looked reproachfully at his partner for his long, unexplained absence. Hester was putting away the ribbons and handkerchiefs, and bright-coloured things which had been used to deck the window; for no more customers were likely to come this night through the blustering weather to a shop dimly lighted by two tallow candles and an inefficient oil-lamp. Philip came up to her, and stood looking at her with unseeing eyes; but the strange consciousness of his fixed stare made her uncomfortable, and called the faint flush to her pale cheeks, and at length compelled her, as it were, to speak, and break the spell of the silence. So, curiously enough, all three spoke at once. Hester asked (without looking at Philip) –

'Yo're sadly wet, I'm feared?'

Coulson said –

'Thou might have a bit o' news to tell one after being on the gad all afternoon.'

Philip whispered to Hester –

'Wilt come into t' parlour? I want a word wi' thee by oursel's.'

Hester quietly finished rolling up the ribbon she had in her hands when he spoke, and then followed him into the room behind the shop before spoken of.

Philip set down on the table the candle which he had brought out of the shop, and turning round to Hester, took her trembling hand into both of his, and gripping it nervously, said –

'Oh! Hester, thou must help me – thou will, will not thou?'

Hester gulped down something that seemed to rise in her throat and choke her, before she answered.

'Anything, thou knows, Philip.'

'Yes, yes, I know. Thou sees the matter is this: Daniel Robson – he who married my aunt – is taken up for yon riot on Saturday night at t' Mariners' Arms—'

'They spoke on it this afternoon; they said the warrant was out,' said Hester, filling up the sentence as Philip hesitated, lost for an instant in his own thoughts.

'Ay! the warrant is out, and he's in t' lock-up, and will be carried to York Castle to-morrow morn; and I'm afeared it will go bad with him; and they at Haytersbank is not prepared, and they must see him again before he goes. Now, Hester, will thou go in a tax-cart as will be here in less than ten minutes from t' George, and bring them back here, and they must stay all night for to be ready to see him to-morrow before he goes? It's dree weather for them, but they'll not mind that.'

He had used words as if he was making a request to Hester; but he did not seem to await her answer, so sure was he that she would go. She noticed this, and noticed also that the rain was spoken of in reference to them, not to her. A cold shadow passed over her heart, though it was nothing more than she already knew – that Sylvia was the one centre of his thoughts and his love.

'I'll go put on my things at once,' said she, gently.

Philip pressed her hand tenderly, a glow of gratitude over-spread him.

'Thou's a real good one, God bless thee!' said he. 'Thou must take care of thyself, too,' continued he; 'there's wraps and plenty i' th' house, and if there are not, there's those i' the shop as 'll be none the worse for once wearing at such a time as this; and wrap thee well up, and take shawls and cloaks for them, and mind as they put 'em on. Thou'll have to get out at a stile, I'll tell t' driver where; and thou must get over t' stile and follow t' path down two fields, and th' house is right before ye, and bid 'em make haste and lock up th' house, for they mun stay all night here. Kester 'll look after things.'

All this time Hester was hastily putting on her hat and cloak, which she had fetched from the closet where they usually hung through the day; now she stood listening, as it were, for final directions.

'But suppose they will not come,' said she; 'they dunnot know me, and mayn't believe my words.'

'They must,' said he, impatiently. 'They don't know what awaits 'em,' he continued. 'I'll tell thee, because thou 'll not let out, and it seems as if I mun tell some one – it were such a shock – he's to be tried for 's life. They know not it's so serious; and, Hester,' said he, going on in his search after sympathy, 'she's like as if she was bound up in her father.'

His lips quivered as he looked wistfully into Hester's face at these words. No need to tell her who was *she*. No need to put into words the fact, told plainer than words could have spoken it, that his heart was bound up in Sylvia.

Hester's face, instead of responding to his look, contracted a little, and, for the life of her, she could not have helped saying, –

'Why don't yo' go yourself, Philip?'

'I can't, I can't,' said he, impatiently. 'I'd give the world to go, for I might be able to comfort her; but there's lawyers to see, and iver so much to do, and they've niver a man friend but me to do it all. Yo'll tell her,' said Philip, insinuatingly, as if a fresh thought had struck him, 'as how I would ha' come. I would fain ha' come for 'em, myself, but I couldn't, because of th' lawyer, – mind yo' say because of th' lawyer. I'd be loath for her to think I was minding any business of my own at this time; and, whatever yo' do, speak hopeful, and, for t' life of yo', don't speak of th' hanging, it's likely it's a mistake o' Donkin's; and anyhow – there's t' cart – anyhow I should perhaps not ha' telled thee, but it's a comfort to make a clean breast to a friend at times. God bless thee, Hester. I don't know what I should ha' done without thee,' said he, as he wrapped her well up in the cart, and placed the bundles of cloaks and things by her side.

Along the street, in the jolting cart, as long as Hester could see the misty light streaming out of the shop door, so long was Philip standing bareheaded in the rain looking after her. But she knew that it was not her own poor self that attracted his lingering gaze. It was the thought of the person she was bound to.

CHAPTER 26

A Dreary Vigil

Through the dark rain, against the cold wind, shaken over the rough stones, went Hester in the little tax-cart. Her heart kept rising against her fate; the hot tears came unbidden to her eyes. But rebellious heart was soothed, and hot tears were sent back to their source before the time came for her alighting.

The driver turned his horse in the narrow lane, and shouted after her an injunction to make haste, as, with her head bent low, she struggled down to the path to Haytersbank Farm. She saw the light in the window from the top of the brow, and involuntarily she slackened her pace. She had never seen Bell Robson, and would Sylvia recollect her? If she did not, how awkward it would be to give the explanation of who she was, and what her errand was, and why she was sent. Nevertheless, it must be done; so on she went, and standing within the little porch, she knocked faintly at the door; but in the bluster of the elements the sound was lost. Again she knocked, and now the murmur of women's voices inside was hushed, and some one came quickly to the door, and opened it sharply.

It was Sylvia. Although her face was completely in shadow, of course Hester knew her well; but she, if indeed she would have recognized Hester less disguised, did not know in the least who the woman, muffled up in a great cloak, with her hat tied down with a silk handkerchief, standing in the porch at this time of night, could be. Nor, indeed, was she in a mood to care or to inquire. She said hastily, in a voice rendered hoarse and arid with grief:

'Go away. This is no house for strangers to come to. We've enough on our own to think on;' and she hastily shut the door in Hester's face, before the latter could put together the right words in which to explain her errand. Hester stood outside in the dark, wet porch discomfited, and wondering how next to obtain a hearing through the shut and bolted door. Not long did she stand, however; some one was again at the door, talking in a voice of distress and remonstrance, and slowly unbarring the bolts. A tall, thin figure of an elderly woman was seen against the warm fire-light inside as soon as the door was opened; a hand was put out, like that which took the dove into the ark,* and Hester was drawn into the warmth and the light, while Bell's voice went on speaking to Sylvia before addressing the dripping stranger –

'It's not a night to turn a dog fra' t' door; it's ill letting our grief harden our hearts. But oh! missus (to Hester), yo' mun forgive us, for a great sorrow has fallen upon us this day, an' we're like beside ourselves wi' crying an' plaining.'

Bell sat down, and threw her apron over her poor worn face, as if decently to shield the signs of her misery from a stranger's gaze. Sylvia, all tear-swollen, and looking askance and almost fiercely at the stranger who had made good her intrusion, was drawn, as it were, to her mother's side, and, kneeling down by her, put her arms round her waist, and almost lay across her lap, still gazing at Hester with cold, distrustful eyes, the expression of which repelled and daunted that poor, unwilling messenger, and made her silent for a minute or so after her entrance. Bell suddenly put down her apron.

'Yo're cold and drenched,' said she. 'Come near to t' fire and warm yo'rsel'; yo' mun pardon us if we dunnot think on everything at onest.'

"Yo're very kind, very kind indeed,' said Hester, touched by the poor woman's evident effort to forget her own grief in the duties of hospitality, and loving Bell from that moment.

'I'm Hester Rose,' she continued, half addressing Sylvia, who she thought might remember the name, 'and Philip Hepburn has sent me in a tax-cart to t' stile yonder, to fetch both on yo' back to Monkshaven.' Sylvia raised her head and looked intently at Hester. Bell clasped her hands tight together and leant forwards.

'It's my master as wants us?' said she, in an eager, questioning tone.

'It's for to see yo'r master,' said Hester. 'Philip says he'll be sent to York to-morrow, and yo'll be fain to see him before he goes; and if yo'll come down to Monkshaven tonight, yo'll be on t' spot again' the time comes when t' justices will let ye.'

Bell was up and about, making for the place where she kept her out-going things, almost before Hester had begun to speak. She hardly understood about her husband's being sent to York, in the possession of the idea that she might go and see him. She did not understand or care how, in this wild night, she was to get to Monkshaven; all she thought of was, that she might go and see her husband. But Sylvia took in more points than her mother, and, almost suspiciously, began to question Hester.

'Why are they sending him to York? What made Philip leave us? Why didn't he come hissel'?'

'He couldn't come hissel', he bade me say; because he was bound to be at the lawyer's at five, about yo'r father's business. I think yo' might ha' known he would ha' come for any business of his own; and, about York, it's Philip as telled me, and I never asked why. I never thought on yo'r asking me so many questions. I thought yo'd be ready to fly on any chance o' seeing your father.' Hester spoke out the sad reproach that ran from her heart to her lips. To distrust Philip! to linger when she might hasten!

'Oh!' said Sylvia, breaking out into a wild cry, that carried with it more conviction of agony than much weeping could have done. 'I may be rude and hard, and I may ask strange questions, as if I cared for t' answers yo' may gi' me; an', in my heart o' hearts, I care for nought but to have father back wi' us, as love him so dear. I can hardly tell what I say, much less why I say it. Mother is so patient, it puts me past mysel',* for I could fight wi' t' very walls, I'm so mad wi' grieving. Sure, they'll let him come back wi' us to-morrow, when they hear from his own sel' why he did it?'

She looked eagerly at Hester for an answer to this last question, which she had put in a soft, entreating tone, as if with Hester herself the decision rested. Hester shook her head. Sylvia came up to her and took her hands, almost fondling them.

'Yo' dunnot think they'll be hard wi' him when they hear all about it, done yo'? Why, York Castle's t' place they send a' t' thieves and robbers to, not honest men like feyther.'

Hester put her hand on Sylvia's shoulder with a soft, caressing gesture.

'Philip will know,' she said, using Philip's name as a kind of spell – it would have been so to her. 'Come away to Philip,' said she again, urging Sylvia, by her looks and manner, to prepare for the little journey. Sylvia moved away for this purpose, saying to herself, –

'It's going to see feyther: he will tell me all.'

Poor Mrs Robson was collecting a few clothes for her husband with an eager, trembling hand, so trembling that article after article fell to the floor, and it was Hester who picked them up;

and at last, after many vain attempts by the grief-shaken woman, it was Hester who tied the bundle, and arranged the cloak, and fastened down the hood; Sylvia standing by, not unobservant, though apparently absorbed in her own thoughts.

At length, all was arranged, and the key given over to Kester.

As they passed out into the storm, Sylvia said to Hester, –

"Thou's a real good wench. Thou's fitter to be about mother than me. I'm but a cross-patch at best, an' now it's like as if I was no good to nobody.'

Sylvia began to cry, but Hester had no time to attend to her, even had she the inclination: all her care was needed to help the hasty, tottering steps of the wife, who was feebly speeding up the wet and slippery brow to her husband. All Bell thought of was that 'he' was at the end of her toil. She hardly understood when she was to see him; her weary heart and brain had only received one idea – that each step she was now taking was leading her to him. Tired and exhausted with her quick walk up hill, battling all the way with wind and rain, she could hardly have held up another minute when they reached the tax-cart in the lane, and Hester had almost to lift her on to the front seat by the driver. She covered and wrapped up the poor old woman, and afterwards placed herself in the straw at the back of the cart, packed up close by the shivering, weeping Sylvia.

Neither of them spoke a word at first; but Hester's tender conscience smote her for her silence before they had reached Monkshaven. She wanted to say some kind word to Sylvia, and yet knew not how to begin. Somehow, without knowing why, or reasoning upon it, she hit upon Philip's message as the best comfort in her power to give. She had delivered it before, but it had been apparently little heeded.

'Philip bade me say it was business as kept him from fetching' yo' hissel' – business wi' the lawyer, about – about yo'r father.'

'What do they say?' said Sylvia, suddenly, lifting her bowed head, as though she would read her companion's face in the dim light.

'I dunnot know,' said Hester, sadly. They were now jolting over the paved streets, and not a word could be spoken. They were now at Philip's door, which was opened to receive them even before they arrived, as if some one had been watching and listening. The old servant, Phœbe, the fixture in the house, who had belonged to it and to the shop for the last twenty years, came out, holding a candle and sheltering it in her hand from the weather, while Philip helped the tottering steps of Mrs Robson as she descended behind. As Hester had got in last, so she had now to be the first to move. Just as she was moving, Sylvia's cold little hand was laid on her arm.

'I am main and thankful to yo'. I ask yo'r pardon for speaking cross, but, indeed, my heart's a'most broken wi' fear about feyther.'

The voice was so plaintive, so full of tears, that Hester could not but yearn towards the speaker. She bent over and kissed her cheek, and then clambered unaided down by the wheel on the dark side of the cart. Wistfully she longed for one word of thanks or recognition from Philip, in whose service she had performed this hard task; but he was otherwise occupied, and on casting a further glance back as she turned the corner of the street, she saw Philip lifting Sylvia carefully down in his arms from her footing on the top of the wheel, and then they all went into the light and the warmth, the door was shut, the lightened cart drove briskly away, and Hester, in rain, and cold, and darkness, went homewards with her tired sad heart.

Philip had done all he could, since his return from lawyer Dawson's, to make his house bright and warm for the reception of his beloved. He had a strong apprehension of the probable fate of poor Daniel Robson; he had a warm sympathy with the miserable distress of the wife and daughter; but still at the back of his mind his spirits danced as if this was to them a festal occasion. He had even taken unconscious pleasure in Phœbe's suspicious looks and tones, as he had hurried and superintended her in her operations. A fire blazed cheerily in the parlour, almost dazzling to the travellers brought in from the darkness and the rain; candles burned – two candles, much to Phœbe's discontent. Poor Bell Robson had to sit down almost as soon as she entered the room, so worn out was she with fatigue and excitement; yet she grudged every moment which separated her, as she thought, from her husband.

'I'm ready now,' said she, standing up, and rather repulsing Sylvia's caress; 'I'm ready now,' said she, looking eagerly at Philip, as if for him to lead the way.

'It's not to-night,' replied he, almost apologetically. 'You can't see him to-night; it's to-morrow morning before he goes to

York; it was better for yo' to be down here in town ready; and beside I didn't know when I sent for ye that he was locked up for the night.'

'Well-a day, well-a-day,' said Bell, rocking herself backwards and forwards, and trying to soothe herself with these words. Suddenly she said, –

'But I've brought his comforter wi' me – his red woollen comforter* as he's allays slept in this twelvemonth past; he'll get his rheumatiz again; oh, Philip, cannot I get it to him?'

'I'll send it by Phœbe,' said Philip, who was busy making tea, hospitable and awkward.

'Cannot I take it mysel'?' repeated Bell. 'I could make surer nor anybody else; they'd maybe not mind yon woman – Phœbe d'ye call her?'

'Nay, mother,' said Sylvia, 'thou's not fit to go.'

'Shall I go?' asked Philip, hoping she would say 'no,' and be content with Phœbe, and leave him where he was.

'Oh, Philip, would yo'?' said Sylvia, turning round.

'Ay,' said Bell, 'if thou would take it they'd be minding yo'.'

So there was nothing for it but for him to go, in the first hush of his delightful rites of hospitality.

'It's not far,' said he, consoling himself rather than them. 'I'll be back in ten minutes, the tea is maskit,* and Phœbe will take yo'r wet things and dry 'em by t' kitchen fire; and here's the stairs,' opening a door in the corner of the room, from which the stairs immediately ascended. 'There's two rooms at the top; that to t' left is all made ready, t' other is mine,' said he, reddening a little as he spoke. Bell was busy undoing her bundle with trembling fingers.

'Here,' said she; 'and oh, lad, here's a bit o' peppermint cake; he's main and fond on it, and I catched sight on it by good luck just t' last minute.'

Philip was gone, and the excitement of Bell and Sylvia flagged once more, and sank into wondering despondency. Sylvia, however, roused herself enough to take off her mother's wet clothes, and she took them timidly into the kitchen and arranged them before Phœbe's fire.

Phœbe opened her lips once or twice to speak in remonstrance, and then, with an effort, gulped her words down; for her sympathy, like that of all the rest of the Monkshaven world, was in favour of Daniel Robson; and his daughter might place her dripping cloak this night wherever she would, for Phœbe.

Sylvia found her mother still sitting on the chair next the door, where she had first placed herself on entering the room.

'I'll gi'e yo' some tea, mother,' said she, struck with the shrunken look of Bell's face.

'No, no,' said her mother. 'It's not manners for t' help oursel's.'

'I'm sure Philip would ha' wished yo' for to take it,' said Sylvia, pouring out a cup.

Just then he returned, and something in his look, some dumb expression of delight at her occupation, made her blush and hesitate for an instant; but then she went on, and made a cup of tea ready, saying something a little incoherent all the time about her mother's need of it. After tea Bell Robson's weariness became so extreme, that Philip and Sylvia urged her to go to bed. She resisted a little, partly out of 'manners', and partly because she kept fancying, poor woman, that somehow or other her husband might send for her. But about seven o'clock Sylvia persuaded her to come upstairs. Sylvia, too, bade Philip good-night, and his look followed the last wave of her dress as she disappeared up the stairs; then leaning his chin on his hand, he gazed at vacancy and thought deeply – for how long he knew not, so intent was his mind on the chances of futurity.

He was aroused by Sylvia's coming downstairs into the sitting-room again. He started up.

'Mother is so shivery,' said she. 'May I go in there,' indicating the kitchen, 'and make her a drop of gruel?'

'Phœbe shall make it, not you,' said Philip, eagerly preventing her, by going to the kitchen door and giving his orders.

When he turned round again, Sylvia was standing over the fire, leaning her head against the stone mantel-piece for the comparative coolness. She did not speak at first, or take any notice of him. He watched her furtively, and saw that she was crying, the tears running down her cheeks, and she too much absorbed in her thoughts to wipe them away with her apron.

While he was turning over in his mind what he could best say to comfort her (his heart, like hers, being almost too full for words), she suddenly looked him full in the face, saying, –

'Philip! won't they soon let him go? what can they do to him?' Her open lips trembled while awaiting his answer, the tears came up and filled her eyes. It was just the question he had most dreaded; it led to the terror that possessed his own mind, but which he had hoped to keep out of hers. He hesitated. 'Speak, lad!' said she, impatiently, with a little passionate gesture. 'I can see thou knows!'

He had only made it worse by consideration; he rushed blindfold at a reply.

'He's ta'en up for felony.'

'Felony,' said she. 'There thou're out,* he's in for letting yon men out; thou may call it rioting if thou's a mind to set folks again' him, but it's too bad to cast such hard words at him as yon – felony,' she repeated, in a half-offended tone.

'It's what the lawyers call it,' said Philip, sadly; 'it's no word o' mine.'

'Lawyers is allays for making the worst o' things,' said she, a little pacified, 'but folks shouldn't allays believe them.'

'It's lawyers as has to judge i' t' long run.'

'Cannot the justices, Mr Harter and them as is no lawyers, give him a sentence to-morrow, wi'out sending him to York?'

'No!' said Philip, shaking his head. He went to the kitchen door and asked if the gruel was not ready, so anxious was he to stop the conversation at this point; but Phœbe, who held her young master in but little respect, scolded him for a stupid man, who thought, like all his sex, that gruel was to be made in a minute, whatever the fire was, and bade him come and make it for himself if he was in such a hurry.

He had to return discomfited to Sylvia, who meanwhile had arranged her thoughts ready to return to the charge.

'And say he's sent to York, and say he's tried theere, what's t' worst they can do again' him?' asked she, keeping down her agitation to look at Philip the more sharply. Her eyes never slackened their penetrating gaze at his countenance, until he replied, with the utmost unwillingness, and most apparent confusion, –

'They may send him to Botany Bay.'*

He knew that he held back a worse contingency, and he was mortally afraid that she would perceive this reserve. But what he did say was so much beyond her utmost apprehension, which had only reached to various terms of imprisonment, that she did not imagine the dark shadow lurking behind. What he had said was too much for her. Her eyes dilated, her lips blanched, her pale cheeks grew yet paler. After a minute's look into his face, as if fascinated by some horror, she stumbled backwards into the chair in the chimney corner, and covered her face with her hands, moaning out some inarticulate words.

Philip was on his knees by her, dumb from excess of sympathy, kissing her dress, all unfelt by her; he murmured half-words, he began passionate sentences that died away upon his lips; and she – she thought of nothing but her father, and was possessed and rapt out of herself by the dread of losing him to that fearful country which was almost like the grave to her, so all but impassable was the gulf. But Philip knew that it was possible that the separation impending might be that of the dark, mysterious grave – that the gulf between the father and child might indeed be that which no living, breathing, warm human creature can ever cross.

'Sylvie, Sylvie!' said he, – and all their conversation had to be carried on in low tones and whispers, for fear of the listening ears above, – 'don't – don't, thou'rt rending my heart. Oh, Sylvie, hearken. There's not a thing I'll not do; there's not a penny I've got, – th' last drop of blood that's in me, – I'll give up my life for his.'

'Life,' said she, putting down her hands, and looking at him as if her looks could pierce his soul; 'who talks o' touching his life? Thou're going crazy, Philip, I think;' but she did not think so, although she would fain have believed it. In her keen agony she read his thoughts as though they were an open page;* she sat there, upright and stony, the conviction creeping over her face like the grey shadow of death. No more tears, no more trembling, almost no more breathing. He could not bear to see her, and yet she held his eyes, and he feared to make the effort necessary to move or to turn away, lest the shunning motion should carry conviction to her heart. Alas! conviction of the probable danger to her father's life was already there: it was that that was calming her down, tightening her muscles, bracing her nerves. In that hour she lost all her early youth.

'Then he may be hung,' said she, low and solemnly, after a long pause. Philip turned away his face, and did not utter a word. Again deep silence, broken only by some homely sound in the kitchen. 'Mother must not know on it,' said Sylvia, in the same tone in which she had spoken before.

'It's t' worst as can happen to him,' said Philip. 'More likely he'll be transported: maybe he'll be brought in innocent after all.'

'No,' said Sylvia, heavily, as one without hope – as if she were reading some dreadful doom in the tablets of the awful future. 'They'll hang him. Oh, feyther! feyther!' she choked out, almost stuffing her apron into her mouth to deaden the sound, and catching at Philip's hand, and wringing it with convulsive force, till the pain that he loved was nearly more than he could bear. No words of his could touch such agony; but irrepressibly, and as he would have done it to a wounded child, he bent over her, and kissed her with a tender, trembling kiss. She did not repulse it, probably she did not even perceive it.

At that moment Phœbe came in with the gruel. Philip saw her, and knew, in an instant, what the old woman's conclusion must needs be; but Sylvia had to be shaken by the now standing Philip, before she could he brought back to the least consciousness of the present time. She lifted up her white face to understand his words, then she rose up like one who slowly comes to the use of her limbs.

'I suppose I mun go,' she said; 'but I'd sooner face the dead. If she asks me, Philip, what mun I say?'

'She'll not ask yo',' said he, 'if yo' go about as common. She's never asked yo' all this time, an' if she does, put her on to me. I'll keep it from her as long as I can; I'll manage better nor I've done wi' thee, Sylvie,' said he, with a sad, faint smile, looking with fond penitence at her altered countenance.

'Thou mustn't blame thysel',' said Sylvia, seeing his regret. 'I brought it on me mysel'; I thought I would ha' t' truth, whativer came on it, and now I'm not strong enough to stand it, God help me!' she continued, piteously.

'Oh, Sylvie, let me help yo'! I cannot do what God can, – I'm not meaning that, but I can do next to Him of any man. I have loved yo' for years an' years, in a way it's terrible to think on, if my love can do nought now to comfort yo' in your sore distress.'

'Cousin Philip,' she replied, in the same measured tone in which she had always spoken since she had learnt the extent of her father's danger, and the slow stillness of her words was in harmony with the stony look of her face, 'thou's a comfort to me, I couldn't bide my life without thee; but I cannot take in the thought o' love, it seems beside me quite; I can think on nought but them that is quick and them that is dead.'

CHAPTER 27

Gloomy Days

Philip had money in the Fosters' bank, not so much as it might have been if he had not had to pay for the furniture in his house. Much of this furniture was old, and had belonged to the brothers Foster, and they had let Philip have it at a very reasonable rate; but still the purchase of it had diminished the amount of his savings. But on the sum which he possessed he drew largely – he drew all – nay, he overdrew his account somewhat, to his former masters' dismay, although the kindness of their hearts overruled the harder arguments of their heads.

All was wanted to defend Daniel Robson at the approaching York assizes. His wife had handed over to Philip all the money or money's worth she could lay her hands upon. Daniel himself was not one to be much beforehand with the world;* but to Bell's thrifty imagination the round golden guineas, tied up in the old stocking foot against rent-day, seemed a mint of money on which Philip might draw infinitely. As yet she did not comprehend the extent of her husband's danger. Sylvia went about like one in a dream, keeping back the hot tears that might interfere with the course of life she had prescribed for herself in that terrible hour when she first learnt all. Every penny of money either she or her mother could save went to Philip. Kester's hoard, too, was placed in Hepburn's hands at Sylvia's earnest entreaty; for Kester had no great opinion of Philip's judgment, and would rather have taken his money straight himself to Mr Dawson, and begged him to use it for his master's behoof.

Indeed, if anything, the noiseless breach between Kester and Philip had widened of late. It was seed-time, and Philip, in his great anxiety for every possible interest that might affect Sylvia, and also as some distraction from his extreme anxiety about her father, had taken to study agriculture of an evening in some old books which he had borrowed – *The Farmer's Complete Guide*,* and such like; and from time to time he came down upon the practical dogged Kester with directions gathered from the theories in his books. Of course the two fell out, but without many words. Kester persevered in his old ways, making light of Philip and his books in manner and action, till at length Philip withdrew from the contest. 'Many a man may lead a horse to water, but there's few can make him drink,' and Philip certainly was not one of those few. Kester, indeed, looked upon him with jealous eyes on many accounts. He had favoured Charley Kinraid as a lover of Sylvia's; and though he had no idea of the truth – though he believed in the drowning of the specksioneer as much as any one – yet the year which had elapsed since Kinraid's supposed death was but a very short while to the middle-aged man, who forgot how slowly time passes with the young; and he could often have scolded Sylvia, if the poor girl had been a whit less heavy at heart than she was, for letting Philip come so much about her – come, though it was on her father's business. For the darkness of their common dread drew them together, occasionally to the comparative exclusion of Bell and Kester, which the latter perceived and resented. Kester even allowed himself to go so far as to wonder what Philip could want with all the money, which to him seemed unaccountable; and once or twice the ugly thought crossed his mind, that shops conducted by young men were often not so profitable as when guided by older heads, and that some of the coin poured into Philip's keeping might have another destination than the defence of his master. Poor Philip! and he was spending all his own, and more than all his own money, and no one ever knew it, as he had bound down his friendly bankers to secrecy.

Once only Kester ventured to speak to Sylvia on the subject of Philip. She had followed her cousin to the field just in front of their house, just outside the porch, to ask him some question she dared not put in her mother's presence – (Bell, indeed, in her anxiety, usually absorbed all the questions when Philip came) – and stood, after Philip had bid her good-by, hardly thinking about him at all, but looking unconscious after him as he ascended the brow; and at the top he had turned to take a last glance at the place his love inhabited, and, seeing her, he had waved his hat in gratified farewell. She, meanwhile, was roused from far other thoughts than of him, and of his now acknowledged love, by the motion against the sky, and was turning back into the house when she heard Kester's low hoarse call, and saw him standing at the shippen door.

'Come hither, wench,' said he, indignantly; 'is this a time for courtin'?'

'Courting?' said she, drawing up her head, and looking back at him with proud defiance.

'Ay, courtin'! what other mak' o' thing is't when thou's gazin' after yon meddlesome chap, as if thou'd send thy eyes after him, and he making marlocks* back at thee? It's what we ca'ed courtin' i' my young days anyhow. And it's noane a time for a wench to go courtin' when her feyther's i' prison,' said he, with a consciousness as he uttered these last words that he was cruel and unjust and going too far, yet carried on to say them by his hot jealousy against Philip.

Sylvia continued looking at him without speaking: she was too much offended for expression.

'Thou may glower an' thou may look, lass,' said he, 'but a'd thought better on thee. It's like last week thy last sweetheart were drowned; but thou'st not one to waste time i' rememberin' them as is gone – if, indeed, thou iver cared a button for yon Kinraid – if it wasn't a make-believe.'

Her lips were contracted and drawn up, showing her small glittering teeth, which were scarcely apart as she breathed out –

'Thou thinks so, does thou, that I've forgotten *him*? Thou'd better have a care o' thy tongue.'

Then, as if fearful that her self-command might give way, she turned into the house; and going through the kitchen like a blind person, she went up to her now unused chamber, and threw herself, face downwards, flat on her bed, almost smothering herself.

Ever since Daniel's committal, the decay that had imperceptibly begun in his wife's bodily and mental strength during her illness of the previous winter, had been making quicker progress. She lost her reticence of speech, and often talked to herself. She had not so much forethought as of old; slight differences, it is true, but which, with some others of the same description, gave foundation for the homely expression which some now applied to Bell, 'She'll never be t' same woman again.'

This afternoon she had cried herself to sleep in her chair after Philip's departure. She had not heard Sylvia's sweeping passage through the kitchen; but half an hour afterwards she was startled up by Kester's abrupt entry.

'Where's Sylvie?' asked he.

'I don't know,' said Bell, looking scared, and as if she was ready to cry. 'It's no news about him?' said she, standing up, and supporting herself on the stick she was now accustomed to use.

'Bless yo', no, dunnot be afeared, missus; it's only as a spoke hasty to t' wench, an' a want t' tell her as a'm sorry,' said Kester, advancing into the kitchen, and looking round for Sylvia.

'Sylvie, Sylvie!' shouted he; 'she mun be i' t' house.'

Sylvia came slowly down the stairs, and stood before him. Her face was pale, her mouth set and determined; the light of her eyes veiled in gloom. Kester shrank from her look, and even more from her silence.

'A'm come to ax pardon,' said he, after a little pause.

She was still silent.

'A'm noane above axing pardon, though a'm fifty and more, and thee's but a silly wench, as a've nursed i' my arms. A'll say before thy mother as a ought niver to ha' used them words, and as how a'm sorry for 't.'

'I don't understand it all,' said Bell, in a hurried and perplexed tone. 'What has Kester been saying, my lass?' she added, turning to Sylvia.

Sylvia went a step or two nearer to her mother, and took hold of her hand as if to quieten her; then facing once more round, she said deliberately to Kester, –

'If thou wasn't Kester, I'd niver forgive thee. Niver,' she added, with bitterness, as the words he had used recurred to her mind. 'It's in me to hate thee now, for saying what thou did; but thou're dear old Kester after all, and I can't help mysel', I mun needs forgive thee,' and she went towards him. He took her little head between his horny hands and kissed it. She looked up with tears in her eyes, saying softly, –

'Niver say things like them again. Niver speak on—'

'A'll bite my tongue off first,' he interrupted.

He kept his word.

In all Philip's comings and goings to and from Haytersbank Farm at this time, he never spoke again of his love. In look, words, manner, he was like a thoughtful, tender brother; nothing more. He could be nothing more in the presence of the great dread which loomed larger upon him after every conversation with the lawyer.

For Mr Donkin had been right in his prognostication. Government took up the attack on the Rendezvous with a high and heavy hand. It was necessary to assert authority which had been of late too often braved. An example must be made, to strike dismay into those who opposed and defied the press-gang; and all the minor authorities who held their powers from Government were in a similar manner severe and relentless in the execution of their duty. So the attorney, who went over to see the prisoner in York Castle, told Philip. He added that Daniel still retained his pride in his achievement, and could not be brought to understand the dangerous position in which he was placed; that when pressed and questioned as to circumstances that might possibly be used in his defence, he always wandered off to accounts of previous outrages committed by the press-gang, or to passionate abuse of the trick by which men had been lured from their homes on the night in question to assist in putting out an imaginary fire, and then seized and carried off. Some of this very natural indignation might possibly have some effect on the jury; and this seemed the only ground of hope, and was indeed a slight one, as the judge was likely to warn the jury against allowing their natural sympathy in such a case to divert their minds from the real question.

Such was the substance of what Philip heard, and heard repeatedly, during his many visits to Mr Dawson. And now the time of trial drew near; for the York assizes opened on March the twelfth;* not much above three weeks since the offence was committed which took Daniel from his home and placed him in peril of death.

Philip was glad that, the extremity of his danger never having been hinted to Bell, and travelling some forty miles being a most unusual exertion at that time to persons of her class, the idea of going to see her husband at York had never suggested itself to Bell's mind. Her increasing feebleness made this seem a step only to be taken in case of the fatal extreme necessity; such was the conclusion that both Sylvia and he had come to; and it was the knowledge of this that made Sylvia strangle her own daily longing to see her father. Not but that her hopes were stronger than her fears. Philip never told her the causes for despondency; she was young, and she, like her father, could not understand how fearful sometimes is the necessity for prompt and severe punishment of rebellion against authority.

Philip was to be in York during the time of the assizes; and it was understood, almost without words, that if the terrible worst occurred, the wife and daughter were to come to York as soon as might be. For this end Philip silently made all the necessary arrangements before leaving Monkshaven. The sympathy of all men was with him; it was too large an occasion for Coulson to be anything but magnanimous. He urged Philip to take all the time requisite; to leave all business cares to him. And as Philip went about pale and sad, there was another cheek that grew paler still, another eye that filled with quiet tears as his heaviness of heart became more and more apparent. The day for opening the assizes came on. Philip was in York Minster, watching the solemn antique procession in which the highest authority in the county accompanies the judges to the house of the Lord, to be there admonished as to the nature of their duties. As Philip listened to the sermon with a strained and beating heart, his hopes rose higher than his fears for the first time, and that evening he wrote his first letter to Sylvia.

'DEAR SYLVIA,

'It will be longer first than I thought for. Mr Dawson says Tuesday in next week. But keep up your heart. I have been hearing the sermon to-day which is preached to the judges; and the clergyman said so much in it about mercy and forgiveness, I think they cannot fail to be lenient this assize. I have seen uncle, who looks but thin, but is in good heart: only he will keep saying he would do it over again if he had the chance, which neither Mr Dawson nor I think is wise in him, in especial as the gaoler is by and hears every word as is said. He was very fain of hearing all about home; and wants you to rear Daisy's calf, as he thinks she will prove a good one. He bade me give his best love to you and my aunt, and his kind duty to Kester.

'Sylvia, will you try and forget how I used to scold you about your writing and spelling, and just write me two or three lines. I think I would rather have them badly spelt than not, because then I shall be sure they are yours. And never mind about capitals; I was a fool to say such a deal about them, for a man does just as well without them. A letter from you would do a vast to keep me patient all these days till Tuesday. Direct –

'Mr. Philip Hepburn,

'Care of Mr Fraser, Draper,

'Micklegate, York.

'My affectionate duty to my aunt.

'Your respectful cousin and servant,

'PHILIP HEPBURN.

'P.S. The sermon was grand. The text was Zachariah vii. 9,
'Execute true judgment and show mercy.'* God grant it may have
put mercy into the judge's heart as is to try my uncle.'

Heavily the days passed over. On Sunday Bell and Sylvia went
to church, with a strange, half-superstitious feeling, as if they
could propitiate the Most High to order the events in their
favour by paying Him the compliment of attending to duties in
their time of sorrow which they had too often neglected in their
prosperous days.

But He 'who knoweth our frame, and remembereth that we
are dust;',* took pity upon His children, and sent some of His
blessed peace into their hearts, else they could scarce have
endured the agony of suspense of those next hours. For as they
came slowly and wearily home from church, Sylvia could no
longer bear her secret, but told her mother of the peril in which
Daniel stood. Cold as the March wind blew, they had not felt it,
and had sate down on a hedge bank for Bell to rest. And then
Sylvia spoke, trembling and sick for fear, yet utterly unable to
keep silence any longer. Bell heaved up her hands, and let them
fall down on her knees before she replied.

'The Lord is above us,' said she, solemnly. 'He has sent a fear
o' this into my heart afore now. I niver breathed it to thee, my
lass—'

'And I niver spoke on it to thee, mother, because—'

Sylvia choked with crying, and laid her head on her mother's
lap, feeling that she was no longer the strong one and the
protector, but the protected. Bell went on, stroking her head,

'The Lord is like a tender nurse as weans a child to look on
and to like what it lothed once. He has sent me dreams as has
prepared me for this, if so be it comes to pass.'

'Philip is hopeful,' said Sylvia, raising her head and looking
through her tears at her mother.

''Ay, he is. And I cannot tell, but I think it's not for nought as
the Lord has ta'en away all fear o' death out o' my heart. I think
He means as Daniel and me is to go hand-in-hand through the
valley – like as we walked up to our wedding in Crosthwaite
Church. I could never guide th' house without Daniel, and I
should be feared he'd take a deal more nor is good for him
without me.'

'But me, mother, thou's forgetting me,' moaned out Sylvia. 'Oh, mother, mother, think on me!'

'Nay, my lass, I'm noane forgetting yo'. I'd a sore heart a' last winter a-thinking on thee, when that chap Kinraid were hanging about thee. I'll noane speak ill on the dead, but I were uneasy-like. But sin' Philip and thee seem to ha' made it up—' Sylvia shivered, and opened her mouth to speak, but did not say a word, 'and sin' the Lord has been comforting me, and talking to me many a time when thou's thought I were asleep, things has seemed to redd theirselves up, and if Daniel goes, I'm ready to follow. I could niver stand living to hear folks say he'd been hung; it seems so unnatural and shameful.'

'But, mother, he won't! – he shan't be hung!' said Sylvia, springing to her feet. 'Philip says he won't.'

Bell shook her head. They walked on, Sylvia both disheartened and almost irritated at her mother's despondency. But before they went to bed at night Bell said things which seemed as though the morning's feelings had been but temporary, and as if she was referring every decision to the period of her husband's return. 'When father comes home',* seemed a sort of burden at the beginning or end of every sentence, and this reliance on his certain coming back to them was almost as great a trial to Sylvia as the absence of all hope had been in the morning. But that instinct told her that her mother was becoming incapable of argument, she would have asked her why her views were so essentially changed in so few hours. This inability of reason in poor Bell made Sylvia feel very desolate.

Monday passed over – how, neither of them knew, for neither spoke of what was filling the thoughts of both. Before it was light on Tuesday morning, Bell was astir.

'It's very early, mother,' said weary, sleepy Sylvia, dreading returning consciousness.

'Ay, lass!' said Bell, in a brisk, cheerful tone; 'but he'll, maybe, be home to-night, and I'se bound to have all things ready for him.'

'Anyhow,' said Sylvia, sitting up in bed, 'he couldn't come home to-night.'

'Tut, lass! thou doesn't know how quick a man comes home to wife and child. I'll be a' ready at any rate.'

She hurried about in a way which Sylvia wondered to see; till at length she fancied that perhaps her mother did so to drive away thought. Every place was cleaned; there was scarce time allowed for breakfast; till at last, long before midday, all the work was done, and the two sat down to their spinning-wheels. Sylvia's spirits sank lower and lower at each speech of her mother's, from whose mind all fear seemed to have disappeared, leaving only a strange restless kind of excitement.

'It's time for t' potatoes,' said Bell, after her wool had snapped many a time from her uneven tread.

'Mother,' said Sylvia, 'it's but just gone ten!'

'Put 'em on,' said Bell, without attending to the full meaning of her daughter's words. 'It'll, maybe, hasten t' day on if we get dinner done betimes.'

'But Kester is in t' Far Acre field, and he'll not be home till noon.'

This seemed to settle matters for a while; but then Bell pushed her wheel away, and began searching for her hood and cloak. Sylvia found them for her, and then asked sadly –

'What does ta want 'em for, mother?'

'I'll go up t' brow and through t' field, and just have a look down t' lane.'

'I'll go wi' thee,' said Sylvia, feeling all the time the uselessness of any looking for intelligence from York so early in the day. Very patiently did she wait by her mother's side during the long half-hour which Bell spent in gazing down the road for those who never came.

When they got home Sylvia put the potatoes on to boil; but when dinner was ready and the three were seated at the dresser, Bell pushed her plate away from her, saying it was so long after dinner time that she was past eating. Kester would have said something about its being only half-past twelve, but Sylvia gave him a look beseeching silence, and he went on with his dinner without a word, only brushing away the tears from his eyes with the back of his hand from time to time.

'A'll noane go far fra' home t' rest o' t' day,' said he, in whisper to Sylvia, as he went out.

'Will this day niver come to an end?' cried Bell, plaintively.

'Oh, mother! it'll come to an end some time, niver fear. I've heerd say –

> Be the day weary or be the day long
> At length it ringeth to even-song.'*

'To even-song – to even-song,' repeated Bell. 'D'ye think now that even-song means death, Sylvie?'

'I cannot tell – I cannot bear it. Mother,' said Sylvia, in despair, 'I'll make some clap-bread: that's a heavy job, and will while away t' afternoon.'

'Ay, do!' replied the mother. 'He'll like it fresh – he'll like it fresh.'

Murmuring and talking to herself, she fell into a doze, from which Sylvia was careful not to disturb her.

The days were now getting long, although as cold as ever; and at Haytersbank Farm the light lingered, as there was no near horizon to bring on early darkness. Sylvia had all ready for her mother's tea against she wakened; but she slept on and on, the peaceful sleep of a child, and Sylvia did not care to waken her. Just after the sun had set, she saw Kester outside the window making signs to her to come out. She stole out on tip-toe by the back-kitchen, the door of which was standing open. She almost ran against Philip, who did not perceive her, as he was awaiting her coming the other way round the corner of the house, and who turned upon her a face whose import she read in an instant. 'Philip!' was all she said, and then she fainted at his feet, coming down with a heavy bang on the round paving-stones of the yard.

'Kester! Kester!' he cried, for she looked like one dead, and with all his strength the wearied man could not lift her and carry her into the house.

With Kester's help she was borne into the back-kitchen, and Kester rushed to the pump for some cold water to throw over her.

While Philip, kneeling at her head, was partly supporting her in his arms, and heedless of any sight or sound, the shadow of some one fell upon him. He looked up and saw his aunt; the old dignified, sensible expression on her face, exactly like her former self, composed, strong, and calm.

'My lass,' said she, sitting down by Philip, and gently taking her out of his arms into her own. 'Lass, bear up! we mun bear up, and be agait* on our way to him, he'll be needing us now. Bear up, my lass! the Lord will give us strength. We mun go to him; ay, time's precious; thou mun cry the cry at after!'

Sylvia opened her dim eyes, and heard her mother's voice; the ideas came slowly into her mind, and slowly she rose up, standing still, like one who has been stunned, to regain her strength; and then, taking hold of her mother's arm, she said, in a soft, strange voice –

'Let's go. I'm ready.'

CHAPTER 28

The Ordeal

It was the afternoon of an April day in that same year, and the sky was blue above, with little sailing white clouds catching the pleasant sunlight. The earth in that northern country had scarcely yet put on her robe of green. The few trees grew near brooks running down from the moors and the higher ground. The air was full of pleasant sounds prophesying of the coming summer. The rush, and murmur, and tinkle of the hidden watercourses; the song of the lark poised high up in the sunny air; the bleat of the lambs calling to their mothers – everything inanimate was full of hope and gladness.

For the first time for a mournful month the front door of Haytersbank Farm was open; the warm spring air might enter, and displace the sad dark gloom, if it could. There was a newly-lighted fire in the unused grate; and Kester was in the kitchen, with his clogs off his feet, so as not to dirty the spotless floor, stirring here and there, and trying in his awkward way to make things look home-like and cheerful. He had brought in some wild daffodils which he had been to seek in the dawn, and he placed them in a jug on the dresser. Dolly Reid, the woman who had come to help Sylvia during her mother's illness a year ago, was attending to something in the back-kitchen, making a noise among the milk-cans, and singing a ballad to herself as she worked; yet every now and then she checked herself in her singing, as if a sudden recollection came upon her that this was neither the time nor the place for songs. Once or twice she took up the funeral psalm which is sung by the bearers of the body in that country –

Our God, our help in ages past.*

But it was of no use: the pleasant April weather out of doors, and perhaps the natural spring in the body, disposed her nature to cheerfulness, and insensibly she returned to her old ditty.

Kester was turning over many things in his rude honest mind as he stood there, giving his finishing touches every now and then to the aspect of the house-place, in preparation for the return of the widow and daughter of his old master.

It was a month and more since they had left home; more than a fortnight since Kester, with three halfpence in his pocket, had set out after his day's work to go to York – to walk all night long, and to wish Daniel Robson his last farewell.

Daniel had tried to keep up and had brought out one or two familiar, thread-bare, well-worn jokes, such as he had made Kester chuckle over many a time and oft, when the two had been together afield or in the shippen at the home which he should never more see. But no 'Old Grouse in the gun-room'* could make Kester smile, or do anything except groan in but a heart-broken sort of fashion, and presently the talk had become more suitable to the occasion, Daniel being up to the last the more composed of the two; for Kester, when turned out of the condemned cell, fairly broke down into the heavy sobbing he had never thought to sob again on earth. He had left Bell and Sylvia in their lodging at York, under Philip's care; he dared not go to see them; he could not trust himself; he had sent them his duty, and bade Philip tell Sylvia that the game-hen had brought out fifteen chickens at a hatch.

Yet although Kester sent this message through Philip – although he saw and recognized all that Philip was doing in their behalf, in the behalf of Daniel Robson, the condemned felon, his honoured master – he liked Hepburn not a whit better than he had done before all this sorrow had come upon them.

Philip had, perhaps, shown a want of tact in his conduct to Kester. Acute with passionate keenness in one direction, he had a sort of dull straightforwardness in all others. For instance, he had returned Kester the money which the latter had so gladly advanced towards the expenses incurred in defending Daniel. Now the money which Philip gave him back was part of an advance which Foster Brothers had made on Philip's own account. Philip had thought that it was hard on Kester to lose his savings in a hopeless cause, and had made a point of repaying the old man; but Kester would far rather have felt that the earnings of the sweat of his brow had gone in the attempt to save his master's life than have had twice ten times as many golden guineas.

Moreover, it seemed to take his action in lending his hoard out of the sphere of love, and make it but a leaden common loan, when it was Philip who brought him the sum, not Sylvia into whose hands he had given it.

With these feelings Kester felt his heart shut up as he saw the long-watched-for two coming down the little path with a third person; with Philip holding up the failing steps of poor Bell Robson, as, loaded with her heavy mourning, and feeble from the illness which had detained her in York ever since the day of her husband's execution, she came faltering back to her desolate home. Sylvia was also occupied in attending to her mother; once or twice, when they paused a little, she and Philip spoke, in the familiar way in which there is no coyness nor reserve. Kester caught up his clogs, and went quickly out through the back-kitchen into the farm-yard, not staying to greet them, as he had meant to do; and yet it was dull-sighted of him not to have perceived that whatever might be the relations between Philip and Sylvia, he was sure to have accompanied them home; for, alas! he was the only male protector of their blood remaining in the world. Poor Kester, who would fain have taken that office upon himself, chose to esteem himself cast off, and went heavily about the farm-yard, knowing that he ought to go in and bid such poor welcome as he had to offer, yet feeling too much to like to show himself before Philip.

It was long, too, before any one had leisure to come and seek him. Bell's mind had flashed up for a time, till the fatal day, only to be reduced by her subsequent illness into complete and hopeless childishness. It was all Philip and Sylvia could do to manage her in the first excitement of returning home; her restless inquiry for him who would never more be present in the familiar scene, her feverish weariness and uneasiness, all required tender soothing and most patient endurance of her refusals to be satisfied with what they said or did.

At length she took some food, and, refreshed by it, and warmed by the fire, she sank asleep in her chair. Then Philip would fain have spoken with Sylvia before the hour came at which he must return to Monkshaven, but she eluded him, and went in search of Kester, whose presence she had missed.

She had guessed some of the causes which kept him from greeting them on their first return. But it was not as if she had shaped these causes into the definite form of words. It is astonishing to look back and find how differently constituted were the minds of most people fifty or sixty years ago; they felt, they understood, without going through reasoning or analytic processes, and if this was the case among the more educated people, of course it was still more so in the class to which Sylvia belonged. She knew by some sort of intuition that if Philip accompanied them home (as, indeed, under the circumstances, was so natural as to be almost unavoidable), the old servant and friend of the family would absent himself; and so she slipped away at the first possible moment to go in search of him. There he was in the farm-yard, leaning over the gate that opened into the home-field, apparently watching the poultry that scratched and pecked at the new-springing grass with the utmost relish. A little farther off were the ewes with their new-dropped lambs, beyond that the great old thorn-tree with its round fresh clusters of buds, again beyond that there was a glimpse of the vast sunny rippling sea; but Sylvia knew well that Kester was looking at none of these things. She went up to him and touched his arm. He started from his reverie, and turned round upon her with his dim eyes full of unshed tears. When he saw her black dress, her deep mourning, he had hard work to keep from breaking out, but by dint of a good brush of his eyes with the back of his hand, and a moment's pause, he could look at her again with tolerable calmness.

'Why, Kester: why didst niver come to speak to us?' said Sylvia, finding it necessary to be cheerful if she could.

'A dun know; niver ax me. A say, they'n gi'en* Dick Simpson' (whose evidence had been all material against poor Daniel Robson at the trial) 'a' t' rotten eggs and fou' things they could o' Saturday, they did,' continued he, in a tone of satisfaction; 'ay, and they niver stopped t' see whether t' eggs were rotten or fresh when their blood was up – nor whether stones was hard or soft,' he added, in a lower tone, and chuckling a little.

Sylvia was silent. He looked at her now, chuckling still. Her face was white, her lips tightened, her eyes a-flame. She drew a long breath.

'I wish I'd been theere! I wish I could do him an ill turn,' sighed she, with some kind of expression on her face that made Kester quail a little.

'Nay, lass! he'll get it fra' others. Niver fret thysel' about sich rubbish. A'n done ill to speak on him.'

'No! thou hasn't. Them as was friends o' father's I'll love for iver and iver; them as helped for t' hang him' (she shuddered from head to foot – a sharp irrepressible shudder!) 'I'll niver forgive – niver!'

'Niver's a long word,' said Kester, musingly. 'A could horse-whip him, or cast stones at him, or duck him mysel'; but, lass! niver's a long word!'

'Well! niver heed if it is – it's me as said it, and I'm turned savage late days. Come in, Kester, and see poor mother.'

'A cannot,' said he, turning his wrinkled puckered face away, that she might not see the twitchings of emotion on it. 'There's kine to be fetched up, and what not, and he's theere, isn't he, Sylvie?' facing round upon her with inquisitiveness. Under his peering eyes she reddened a little.

'Yes, if it's Philip thou means; he's been all we've had to look to sin'.' Again the shudder.

'Well, now he'll be seein' after his shop, a reckon?'

Sylvia was calling to the old mare nibbling tufts of early-springing grass here and there, and half unconsciously coaxing the creature to come up to the gate to be stroked. But she heard Kester's words well enough, and so he saw, although she made this excuse not to reply. But Kester was not to be put off.

'Folks is talkin' about thee and him; thou'll ha' to mind lest thee and him gets yo'r names coupled together.'

'It's right down cruel on folks, then,' said she, crimsoning from some emotion. 'As if any man as was a man wouldn't do all he could for two lone women at such a time – and he a cousin, too! Tell me who said so,' continued she, firing round at Kester, 'and I'll niver forgive 'em – that's all.'

'Hoots!'* said Kester, a little conscious that he himself was the principal representative of that name of multitude folk. 'Here's a pretty lass; she's got "a'll niver forgi' e" at her tongue's end wi' a vengeance.'

Sylvia was a little confused.

'Oh, Kester, man,' said she, 'my heart is sore again' every one, for feyther's sake.'

And at length the natural relief of plentiful tears came; and

Kester, with instinctive wisdom, let her weep undisturbed: indeed, he cried not a little himsel. They were interrupted by Philip's voice from the back-door.

'Sylvie; your mother's awake, and wants you!'

'Come, Kester, come,' and taking hold of him she drew him with her into the house.

Bell rose as they came in, holding by the arms of the chair. At first she received Kester as though he had been a stranger.

'I'm glad to see yo', sir; t' master's out, but he'll be in afore long. It'll be about t' lambs yo're come, mebbe?'

'Mother!' said Sylvia, 'dunnot yo' see? it's Kester, – Kester, wi' his Sunday clothes on.'

'Kester! ay, sure it is; my eyes have getten so sore and dim of late; just as if I'd been greeting.* I'm sure, lad, I'm glad to see thee! It's a long time I've been away, but it were not pleasure-seeking as took me, it were business o' some mak' – tell him, Sylvie, what it were, for my head's clean gone.* I only know I wouldn't ha' left home if I could ha' helped it; for I think I should ha' kept my health better if I'd bided at home wi' my master. I wonder as he's not comed in for t' bid me welcome? Is he far afield, think ye, Kester?'

Kester looked at Sylvia, mutely imploring her to help him out in the dilemma of answering, but she was doing all she could to help crying. Philip came to the rescue.

'Aunt,' said he, 'the clock has stopped; can you tell me where t' find t' key, and I'll wind it up.'

'T' key,' said she, hurriedly, 't' key, it's behind th' big Bible on yon shelf. But I'd rayther thou wouldn't touch it, lad; it's t' master's work, and he distrusts folk meddling wi' it.'

Day after day there was this constant reference to her dead husband. In one sense it was a blessing; all the circumstances attendant on his sad and untimely end were swept out of her mind along with the recollection of the fact itself. She referred to him as absent, and had always some plausible way of accounting for it, which satisfied her own mind; and, accordingly they fell into the habit of humouring her, and speaking of him as gone to Monkshaven, or afield, or wearied out, and taking a nap upstairs, as her fancy led her to believe for the moment. But this forgetfulness, though happy for herself, was terrible for her child. It was a constant renewing of Sylvia's grief, while her mother could give her no sympathy, no help, or strength in any circumstances that arose out of this grief. She was driven more and more upon Philip; his advice and his affection became daily more necessary to her.

Kester saw what would be the end of all this more clearly than Sylvia did herself; and, impotent to hinder what he feared and disliked, he grew more and more surly every day. Yet he tried to labour hard and well for the interests of the family, as if they were bound up in his good management of the cattle and land. He was out and about by the earliest dawn, working all day long with might and main. He bought himself a pair of new spectacles, which might, he fancied, enable him to read the *Farmer's Complete Guide*, his dead master's *vade-mecum**. But he had never learnt more than his capital letters, and had forgotten many of them; so the spectacles did him but little good. Then he would take the book to Sylvia, and ask her to read to him the instructions he needed; instructions, be it noted, that he would formerly have despised as mere book-learning: but his present sense of responsibility had made him humble.

Sylvia would find the place with all deliberation: and putting her finger under the line to keep the exact place of the word she was reading, she would strive in good earnest to read out the directions given; but when every fourth word had to be spelt, it was rather hopeless work, especially as all these words were unintelligible to the open-mouthed listener, however intent he might be. He had generally to fall back on his own experience; and, guided by that, things were not doing badly in his estimation, when, one day, Sylvia said to him, as they were in the hay-field, heaping up the hay into cocks with Dolly Reid's assistance –

'Kester – I didn't tell thee – there were a letter from Measter Hall, Lord Malton's steward, that came last night and that Philip read me.'

She stopped for a moment.

'Ay, lass! Philip read it thee, and whatten might it say?'

'Only that he had an offer for Haytersbank Farm, and would set mother free to go as soon as t' crops was off t' ground.'

She sighed a little as she said this.

'"Only" sayst ta? Whatten business has he for to go an' offer to let t' farm afore iver he were told as yo' wished to leave it?' observed Kester, in high dudgeon.

'Oh!' replied Sylvia, throwing down her rake, as if weary of life. 'What could we do wi' t' farm and land? If it were all dairy I might ha' done, but wi' so much on it arable.'

'And if 'tis arable is not I allays to t' fore?'

'Oh, man, dunnot find fault wi' me! I'm just fain to lie down and die, if it were not for mother.'

'Ay! thy mother will be sore unsettled if thou's for quitting Haytersbank,' said merciless Kester.

'I cannot help it; I cannot help it! What can I do? It would take two pair o' men's hands to keep t' land up as Measter Hall likes it; and beside—'

'Beside what?' said Kester, looking up at her with his sudden odd look, one eye shut, the other open: there she stood, her two hands clasped tight together, her eyes filling with tears, her face pale and sad. 'Beside what?' he asked again, sharply.

'T' answer's sent to Measter Hall – Philip wrote it last night; so there's no use planning and fretting, it were done for t' best, and mun be done.' She stooped and picked up her rake, and began tossing the hay with energy, the tears streaming down her cheeks unheeded. It was Kester's turn to throw down his rake. She took no notice, he did not feel sure that she had observed his action. He began to walk towards the field gate; this movement did catch her eye, for in a minute her hand was on his arm, and she was stooping forward to look into his face. It was working and twitching with emotion. 'Kester! oh, man! speak out, but dunnot leave me a this-ns.* What could I ha' done? Mother is gone dateless* wi' sorrow, and I am but a young lass, i' years I mean; for I'm old enough wi' weeping.'

'I'd ha' put up for t' farm mysel', sooner than had thee turned out,' said Kester, in a low voice; then working himself up into a passion, as a new suspicion crossed his mind, he added, 'An' what for didn't yo' tell me on t' letter? Yo' were in a mighty hurry to settle it a', and get rid on t' oud place.'

'Measter Hall had sent a notice to quit on Midsummer day; but Philip had answered it hisself. Thou knows I'm not good at reading writing, 'special when a letter's full o' long words, and Philip had ta'en it in hand to answer.'

'Wi'out asking thee?'

Sylvia went on without minding the interruption.

'And Measter Hall makes a good offer, for t' man as is going to come in will take t' stock and a' t' implements; and if mother – if we – if I – like, th' furniture and a'—'

'Furniture!' said Kester, in grim surprise. 'What's to come o' t'missus and thee, that yo'll not need a bed to lie on, or a pot to boil yo'r vittel in?'

Sylvia reddened, but kept silence.

'Cannot yo' speak?'

'Oh, Kester, I didn't think thou'd turn again' me, and me so friendless. It's as if I'd been doin' something wrong, and I have so striven to act as is best; there's mother as well as me to be thought on.'

'Cannot yo' answer a question?' said Kester, once more. 'Whatten's up that t'missus and yo'll not need bed and table, pots and pans?'

'I think I'm going to marry Philip,' said Sylvia, in so low a tone, that if Kester had not suspected what her answer was to be, he could not have understood it.

After a moment's pause he recommenced his walk towards the field gate. But she went after him and held him tight by the arm, speaking rapidly.

'Kester, what could I do? What can I do? He's my cousin, and mother knows him, and likes him; and he's been so good to us in a' this time o' trouble and heavy grief, and he'll keep mother in comfort all t' rest of her days.'

'Ay, and thee in comfort. There's a deal in a well-filled purse in a wench's eyes, or one would ha' thought it weren't so easy forgettin' yon lad as loved thee as t' apple on his eye.*'

'Kester, Kester,' she cried, 'I've niver forgotten Charley; I think on him, I see him ivery night lying drowned at t' bottom o' t' sea. Forgotten him! Man! it's easy talking!' She was like a wild creature that sees its young, but is unable to reach it without a deadly spring, and yet is preparing to take that fatal leap. Kester himself was almost startled, and yet it was as if he must go on torturing her.

'An' who told thee so sure and certain as he were drowned? He might ha' been carried off by t' press-gang as well as other men.'

'Oh! if I were but dead that I might know all!' cried she, flinging herself down on the hay.

Kester kept silence. Then she sprang up again, and looking with eager wistfulness into his face, she said, –

'Tell me t' chances. Tell me quick! Philip's very good and kind, and he says he shall die if I will not marry him, and there's no home for mother and me, – no home for her, for as for me I dunnot care what becomes on me; but if Charley's alive I cannot marry Philip – no, not if he dies for want o'me – and as for mother, poor mother, Kester, it's an awful strait; only first tell me if there's a chance, just one in a thousand, only one in a hundred thousand, as Charley were ta'en by t' gang?' She was breathless by this time, what with her hurried words, and what with the beating of her heart. Kester took time to answer. He had spoken before too hastily, this time he weighed his words.

'Kinraid went away from this here place t' join his ship. An' he niver joined it no more; an' t' captain an' all his friends at Newcassel as iver were, made search for him, on board t' king's ships. That's more nor fifteen month ago, an' nought has iver been heerd on him by any man. That's what's to be said on one side o' t' matter. Then on t' other there's this as is known. His hat were cast up by t' sea wi' a ribbon in it, as there's reason t' think as he'd not ha' parted wi' so quick if he'd had his own will.'

'But yo' said as he might ha' been carried off by t' gang – yo' did, Kester, tho' now yo're a' for t'other side.'

'My lass, a'd fain have him alive, an' a dunnot fancy Philip for thy husband; but it's a serious judgment as thou's put me on, an' a'm trying it fair. There's allays one chance i' a thousand as he's alive, for no man iver saw him dead. But t' gang were noane about Monkshaven then: there were niver a tender on t' coast nearer than Shields, an' those theere were searched.'

He did not say any more, but turned back into the field, and took up his hay-making again.

Sylvia stood quite still, thinking, and wistfully longing for some kind of certainty.

Kester came up to her.

'Sylvie, thou knows Philip paid me back my money, and it were eight pound fifteen and three-pence; and t' hay and stock 'll sell for summat above t' rent, and a've a sister as is a decent widow-woman, tho' but badly off, livin' at Dale End; and if thee and thy mother 'll go live wi' her, a'll give thee well on to all a can earn, and it'll be a matter o' five shilling a week. But dunnot go and marry a man as thou's noane taken wi', and another as is most like for t' be dead, but who, mebbe, is alive, havin' a pull on thy heart.'

Sylvia began to cry as if her heart was broken. She had

promised herself more fully to Philip the night before than she had told Kester; and, with some pains and much patience, her cousin, her lover, alas! her future husband, had made the fact clear to the bewildered mind of her poor mother, who had all day long shown that her mind and heart were full of the subject, and that the contemplation of it was giving her as much peace as she could ever know. And now Kester's words came to call up echoes in the poor girl's heart. Just as she was in this miserable state, wishing that the grave lay open before her, and that she could lie down, and be covered up by the soft green turf from all the bitter sorrows and carking cares and weary bewilderments of this life; wishing that her father was alive, that Charley was once more here; that she had not repeated the solemn words by which she had promised herself to Philip only the very evening before, she heard a soft, low whistle, and, looking round unconsciously, there was her lover and affianced husband, leaning on the gate, and gazing into the field with passionate eyes, devouring the fair face and figure of her, his future wife.

'Oh, Kester,' said she once more, 'what mun I do? I'm pledged to him as strong as words can make it, and mother blessed us both wi' more sense than she's had for weeks. Kester, man, speak! Shall I go and break it all off? – say.'

'Nay, it's noane for me t' say; m'appen thou's gone too far. Them above only knows what is best.'

Again that long, cooing whistle. 'Sylvie!'

'He's been very kind to us all,' said Sylvia, laying her rake down with slow care, 'and I'll try t' make him happy.'

CHAPTER 29

Wedding Raiment

Philip and Sylvia were engaged. It was not so happy a state of things as Philip had imagined. He had already found that out, although it was not twenty-four hours since Sylvia had promised to be his. He could not have defined why he was dissatisfied; if he had been compelled to account for his feeling, he would

probably have alleged as a reason that Sylvia's manner was so
unchanged by her new position towards him. She was quiet and
gentle; but no shyer, no brighter, no coyer, no happier, than she
had been for months before. When she joined him at the field-
gate, his heart was beating fast, his eyes were beaming out love
at her approach. She neither blushed nor smiled, but seemed
absorbed in thought of some kind. But she resisted his silent
effort to draw her away from the path leading to the house, and
turned her face steadily homewards. He murmured soft words,
which she scarcely heard. Right in their way was the stone
trough for the fresh-bubbling water, that, issuing from a roadside spring, served for all the household purposes of Haytersbank Farm. By it were the milkcans, glittering and clean. Sylvia
knew she should have to stop for these, and carry them back
home in readiness for the evening's milking; and at this time,
during this action, she resolved to say what was on her mind.

They were there. Sylvia spoke.

'Philip, Kester has been saying as how it might ha' been—'

'Well!' said Philip.

Sylvia sat down on the edge of the trough, and dipped her
hot little hand in the water. Then she went on quickly, and
lifting her beautiful eyes to Philip's face, with a look of inquiry
– 'He thinks as Charley Kinraid may ha' been took by t' press-
gang.'

It was the first time she had named the name of her former
lover to her present one since the day, long ago now, when they
had quarrelled about him; and the rosy colour flushed her all
over; but her sweet, trustful eyes never flinched from their
steady, unconscious gaze.

Philip's heart stopped beating; literally, as if he had come to a
sudden precipice, while he had thought himself securely walking
on sunny greensward. He went purple all over from dismay; he
dared not take his eyes away from that sad, earnest look of hers,
but he was thankful that a mist came before them and drew a
veil before his brain. He heard his own voice saying words he
did not seem to have framed in his own mind.

'Kester's a d——d fool,' he growled.

'He says there's mebbe but one chance i' a hundred,' said
Sylvia, pleading, as it were, for Kester; 'but oh! Philip, think yo'
there's just that one chance?'

'Ay, there's a chance, sure enough,' said Philip, in a kind of

fierce despair that made him reckless what he said or did.
'There's a chance, I suppose, for iverything i' life as we have not
seen with our own eyes as it may not ha' happened. Kester may
say next as there's a chance as your father is not dead, because
we none on us saw him—'

'Hung,' he was going to have said, but a touch of humanity
came back into his stony heart. Sylvia sent up a little sharp cry
at his words. He longed at the sound to take her in his arms and
hush her up, as a mother hushes her weeping child. But the very
longing, having to be repressed, only made him more beside
himself with guilt, anxiety, and rage. They were quite still now.
Sylvia looking sadly down into the bubbling, merry, flowing
water: Philip glaring at her, wishing that the next word were
spoken, though it might stab him to the heart. But she did not
speak.

At length, unable to bear it any longer, he said, 'Thou sets a
deal o' store on that man, Sylvie.'

If 'that man' had been there at the moment, Philip would have
grappled with him, and not let go his hold till one or the other
were dead. Sylvia caught some of the passionate meaning of the
gloomy, miserable tone of Philip's voice as he said these words.
She looked up at him.

'I thought yo' knowed that I cared a deal for him.'

There was something so pleading and innocent in her pale,
troubled face, so pathetic in her tone, that Philip's anger, which
had been excited against her, as well as against all the rest of the
world, melted away into love; and once more he felt that have
her for his own he must, at any cost. He sat down by her, and
spoke to her in quite a different manner to that which he had
used before, with a ready tact and art which some strange
instinct or tempter 'close at his ear'* supplied.

'Yes, darling, I knew yo' cared for him. I'll not say ill of him
that is – dead – ay, dead and drowned – whatever Kester may
say – before now; but if I chose I could tell tales.'

'No! tell no tales; I'll not hear them,' said she, wrenching
herself out of Philip's clasping arm. 'They may misca'* him for
iver, and I'll not believe 'em.'

'I'll niver miscall one who is dead,' said Philip; each new
unconscious sign of the strength of Sylvia's love for her former
lover only making him the more anxious to convince her that he
was dead, only rendering him more keen at deceiving his own

conscience by repeating to it the lie that long ere this Kinraid was in all probability dead – killed by either the chances of war or tempestuous sea; that, even if not, he was as good as dead to her; so that the word 'dead' might be used in all honest certainty, as in one of its meanings Kinraid was dead for sure.

'Think yo' that if he were not dead he wouldn't ha' written ere this to some one of his kin, if not to thee? Yet none of his folk Newcassel-way but believe him dead.'

'So Kester says,' sighed Sylvia.

Philip took heart. He put his arm softly round her again, and murmured –

'My lassie, try not to think on them as is gone, as is deed, but t' think a bit more on him as loves yo' wi' heart, and soul, and might, and has done iver sin' he first set eyes on yo'. Oh, Sylvie, my love for thee is just terrible.'

At this moment Dolly Reid was seen at the back-door of the farmhouse, and catching sight of Sylvia, she called out –

'Sylvia, thy mother is axing for thee, and I cannot make her mind easy.'

In a moment Sylvia had sprung up from her seat, and was running in to soothe and comfort her mother's troubled fancies.

Philip sat on by the well-side, his face buried in his two hands. Presently he lifted himself up, drank some water eagerly out of his hollowed palm, sighed, and shook himself, and followed his cousin into the house. Sometimes he came unexpectedly to the limits of his influence over her. In general she obeyed his expressed wishes with gentle indifference, as if she had no preferences of her own; once or twice he found that she was doing what he desired out of the spirit of obedience, which, as her mother's daughter, she believed to be her duty towards her affianced husband. And this last motive for action depressed her lover more than anything. He wanted the old Sylvia back again; captious, capricious, wilful, haughty, merry, charming. Alas! that Sylvia was gone for ever.

But once especially his power, arising from whatever cause, was stopped entirely short – was utterly of no avail.

It was on the occasion of Dick Simpson's mortal illness. Sylvia and her mother kept aloof from every one. They had never been intimate with any family but the Corneys, and even this friend-ship had considerably cooled since Molly's marriage, and most especially since Kinraid's supposed death, when Bessy Corney and Sylvia had been, as it were, rival mourners. But many people, both in Monkshaven and the country round about, held the Robson family in great respect, although Mrs Robson herself was accounted 'high' and 'distant'; and poor little Sylvia, in her heyday of beautiful youth and high spirits, had been spoken of as 'a bit flighty', and 'a set-up lassie'. Still, when their great sorrow fell upon them, there were plenty of friends to sympathize deeply with them; and, as Daniel had suffered in a popular cause, there were even more who, scarcely knowing them personally, were ready to give them all the marks of respect and friendly feeling in their power. But neither Bell nor Sylvia were aware of this. The former had lost all perception of what was not immediately before her; the latter shrank from all encounters of any kind with a sore heart, and sensitive avoidance of everything that could make her a subject of remark. So the poor afflicted people at Haytersbank knew little of Monkshaven news. What little did come to their ears came through Dolly Reid, when she returned from selling the farm produce of the week; and often, indeed, even then she found Sylvia too much absorbed in other cares or thoughts to listen to her gossip. So no one had ever named that Simpson was supposed to be dying till Philip began on the subject one evening. Sylvia's face suddenly flashed into glow and life.

'He's dying, is he? t' earth is well rid on such a fellow!'

'Eh, Sylvie, that's a hard speech o' thine!' said Philip; 'it gives me but poor heart to ask a favour of thee!'

'If it's aught about Simpson,' replied she, and then she interrupted herself – 'But say on; it were ill-mannered in me for t' interrupt yo'.'

'Thou would be sorry to see him, I think, Sylvie. He cannot get over the way, t' folk met him, and pelted him when he came back fra' York, – and he's weak and faint, and beside himself at times; and he'll lie a-dreaming, and a-fancying they're all at him again, hooting, and yelling, and pelting him.'

'I'm glad on 't,' said Sylvia; 'it's t' best news I've heered for many a day, – he, to turn again' feyther, who gave him money for t' get a lodging that night, when he'd no place to go to. It were his evidence as hung feyther; and he's rightly punished for it now.'

'For a' that, – and he's done a vast o' wrong beside, he's dying now, Sylvie!'

'Well! let him die – it's t' best thing he could do!'

'But he's lying i' such dree poverty, and niver a friend to go near him, – niver a person to speak a kind word t' him.'

'It seems as yo've been speaking wi' him, at any rate,' said Sylvia, turning round on Philip.

'Ay. He sent for me by Nell Manning, th' old beggar woman, who sometimes goes in and makes his bed for him, poor wretch, – he's lying in t' ruins of th' cowhouse of th' Mariner's Arms, Sylvie.'

'Well!' said she, in the same hard, dry tone.

'And I went and fetched th' parish doctor, for I thought he'd ha' died before my face, – he was so wan, and ashen-grey, so thin, too, his eyes seem pushed out of his bony face.'

'That last time – feyther's eyes were starting, wild-like, and as if he couldn't meet ours, or bear the sight on our weeping.'

It was a bad look-out for Philip's purpose; but after a pause he went bravely on.

'He's a poor dying creature, anyhow. T' doctor said so, and told him he hadn't many hours, let alone days, to live.'

'And he'd shrink fra' dying wi' a' his sins on his head?' said Sylvia, almost exultingly.

Philip shook his head. 'He said this world had been too strong for him, and men too hard upon him; he could niver do any good here, and he thought he should, maybe, find folks i' t' next place more merciful.'

'He'll meet feyther theere,' said Sylvia, still hard and bitter.

'He's a poor ignorant creature, and doesn't seem to know rightly who he's like to meet; only he seems glad to get away fra' Monkshaven folks; he were really hurt, I am afeared, that night, Sylvie, – and he speaks as if he'd had hard times of it ever since he were a child, – and he talks as if he were really grieved for t' part t' lawyers made him take at th' trial, – they made him speak, against his will, he says.'

'Couldn't he ha' bitten his tongue out?' asked Sylvia. 'It's fine talking o' sorrow when the thing is done!'

'Well, anyhow he's sorry now; and he's not long for to live. And, Sylvie, he bid me ask thee, if, for the sake of all that is dear to thee both here, and i' th' world to come, thou'd go wi' me, and just say to him that thou forgives him his part that day.'

'He sent thee on that errand, did he? And thou could come and ask me? I've a mind to break it off for iver wi' thee, Philip.'

She kept gasping, as if she could not say any more. Philip watched and waited till her breath came, his own half choked.

'Thee and me was niver meant to go together. It's not in me to forgive, – I sometimes think it's not in me to forget. I wonder, Philip, if thy feyther had done a kind deed – and a right deed – and a merciful deed – and some one as he'd been good to, even i' t' midst of his just anger, had gone and let on about him to th' judge, as was trying to hang him, – and had getten him hanged, – hanged dead, so that his wife were a widow, and his child fatherless for ivermore, – I wonder if thy veins would run milk and water, so that thou could go and make friends, and speak soft wi' him as had caused thy feyther's death?'

'It's said in t' Bible, Sylvie, that we're to forgive.'

'Ay, there's some things as I know I niver forgive; and there's others as I can't – and I won't, either.'

'But, Sylvie, yo' pray to be forgiven your trespasses, as you forgive them as trespass against you.'

'Well, if I'm to be taken at my word, I'll noane pray at all, that's all. It's well enough for them as has but little to forgive to use them words; and I don't reckon it's kind, or pretty behaved in yo', Philip, to bring up Scripture again' me. Thou may go about thy business.'

'Thou'rt vexed with me, Sylvie; and I'm not meaning but that it would go hard with thee to forgive him; but I think it would be right and Christian-like i' thee, and that thou'd find thy comfort in thinking on it after. If thou'd only go, and see his wistful eyes – I think they'd plead wi' thee more than his words, or mine either.'

'I tell thee my flesh and blood wasn't made for forgiving and forgetting. Once for all, thou must take my word. When I love I love, and when I hate I hate, and him as has done harm to me, or to mine, I may keep fra' striking or murdering, but I'll niver forgive. I should be just a monster, fit to be shown at a fair, if I could forgive him as got feyther hanged.'

Philip was silent, thinking what more he could urge.

'Yo'd better be off,' said Sylvia, in a minute or two. 'Yo' and me has got wrong, and it'll take a night's sleep to set us right. Yo've said all yo' can for him; and perhaps it's not yo' as is to blame, but yo'r nature. But I'm put out wi' thee, and want thee out o' my sight for awhile.'

One or two more speeches of this kind convinced him that it

would be wise in him to take her at her word. He went back to
Simpson, and found him, though still alive, past the understanding of any words of human forgiveness. Philip had almost
wished he had not troubled or irritated Sylvia by urging the
dying man's request: the performance of this duty seemed now
to have been such a useless office.

After all, the performance of a duty is never a useless office,
though we may not see the consequences, or they may be quite
different to what we expected or calculated on. In the pause of
active work, when daylight was done, and the evening shades
came on, Sylvia had time to think; and her heart grew sad and
soft, in comparison to what it had been when Philip's urgency
had called out all her angry opposition. She, thought of her
father – his sharp passions, his frequent forgiveness, or rather
his forgetfulness that he had even been injured. All Sylvia's
persistent or enduring qualities were derived from her mother,
her impulses from her father. It was her dead father whose
example filled her mind this evening in the soft and tender
twilight. She did not say to herself that she would go and tell
Simpson that she forgave him; but she thought that if Philip
asked her again that she should do so.

But when she saw Philip again he told her that Simpson was
dead; and passed on from what he had reason to think would
be an unpleasant subject to her. Thus he never learnt how her
conduct might have been more gentle and relenting than her
words – words which came up into his memory at a future time,
with full measure of miserable significance.

In general, Sylvia was gentle and good enough; but Philip
wanted her to be shy and tender with him, and this she was not.
She spoke to him, her pretty eyes looking straight and com-
posedly at him. She consulted him like the family friend that he
was: she met him quietly in all the arrangements for the time of
their marriage, which she looked upon more as a change of
home, as the leaving of Haytersbank, as it would affect her
mother, than in any more directly personal way. Philip was
beginning to feel, though not as yet to acknowledge, that the
fruit he had so inordinately longed for was but of the nature of
an apple of Sodom.

Long ago, lodging in widow Rose's garret, he had been in the
habit of watching some pigeons that were kept by a neighbour;
the flock disported themselves on the steep tiled roofs just

opposite to the attic window, and insensibly Philip grew to know their ways, and one pretty, soft little dove was somehow perpetually associated in his mind with his idea of his cousin Sylvia. The pigeon would sit in one particular place, sunning herself, and puffing out her feathered breast, with all the blue and rose-coloured lights gleaming in the morning rays, cooing softly to herself as she dressed her plumage. Philip fancied that he saw the same colours in a certain piece of shot silk – now in the shop; and none other seemed to him so suitable for his darling's wedding-dress. He carried enough to make a gown, and gave it to her one evening, as she sat on the grass just outside the house, half attending to her mother, half engaged in knitting stockings for her scanty marriage outfit. He was glad that the sun was not gone down, thus allowing him to display the changing colours in fuller light. Sylvia admired it duly; even Mrs Robson was pleased and attracted by the soft yet brilliant hues. Philip whispered to Sylvia – (he took delight in whispers, – she, on the contrary, always spoke to him in her usual tone of voice) –

'Thou'lt look so pretty in it, sweetheart, – o' Thursday fortnight!'

'Thursday fortnight. On the fourth yo're thinking on. But I cannot wear it then, – I shall be i' black.'

'Not on that day, sure!' said Philip.

'Why not? There's nought t' happen on that day for t' make me forget feyther. I couldn't put off my black, Philip, – no, not to save my life! Yon silk is just lovely, far too good for the likes of me, – and I'm sure I'm much beholden to yo'; and I'll have it made up first of any gown after last April come two years, – but, oh, Philip, I cannot put off my mourning!'

'Not for our wedding-day!' said Philip, sadly.

'No, lad, I really cannot. I'm just sorry about it, for I see thou'rt set upon it; and thou'rt so kind and good, I sometimes think I can niver be thankful enough to thee. When I think on what would ha' become of mother and me if we hadn't had thee for a friend i' need, I'm noane ungrateful, Philip; tho' I sometimes fancy thou'rt thinking I am.'

'I don't want yo' to be grateful, Sylvie,' said poor Philip, dissatisfied, yet unable to explain what he did want; only knowing that there was something he lacked, yet fain would have had.

As the marriage-day drew near, all Sylvia's care seemed to be for her mother; all her anxiety was regarding the appurtenances of the home she was leaving. In vain Philip tried to interest her in details of his improvements or contrivances in the new home to which he was going to take her. She did not tell him; but the idea of the house behind the shop was associated in her mind with two times of discomfort and misery. The first time she had gone into the parlour about which Philip spoke so much was at the time of the press-gang riot, when she had fainted from terror and excitement; the second was on that night of misery when she and her mother had gone in to Monkshaven, to bid her father farewell before he was taken to York; in that room, on that night, she had first learnt something of the fatal peril in which he stood. She could not show the bright shy curiosity about her future dwelling that is common enough with girls who are going to be married. All she could do was to restrain herself from sighing, and listen patiently, when he talked on the subject. In time he saw that she shrank from it; so he held his peace, and planned and worked for her in silence, – smiling to himself as he looked on each completed arrangement for her pleasure or comfort; and knowing well that her happiness was involved in what fragments of peace and material comfort might remain to her mother.

The wedding-day drew near apace. It was Philip's plan that after they had been married in Kirk Moorside Church, he and his Sylvia, his cousin, his love, his wife, should go for the day to Robin Hood's Bay, returning in the evening to the house behind the shop in the market-place. There they were to find Bell Robson installed in her future home; for Haytersbank Farm was to be given up to the new tenant on the very day of the wedding. Sylvia would not be married any sooner; she said that she must stay there till the very last; and had said it with such determination that Philip had desisted from all urgency at once.

He had told her that all should be settled for her mother's comfort during their few hours' absence; otherwise Sylvia would not have gone at all. He told her he should ask Hester, who was always so good and kind – who never yet had said him nay, to go to church with them as bridesmaid – for Sylvia would give no thought or care to anything but her mother – and that they would leave her at Haytersbank as they returned from church; she would manage Mrs Robson's removal – she would do this –

do that – do everything. Such friendly confidence had Philip in Hester's willingness and tender skill. Sylvia acquiesced at length, and Philip took upon himself to speak to Hester on the subject.

'Hester,' said he, one day when he was preparing to go home after the shop was closed; 'would yo' mind stopping a bit? I should like to show yo' the place now it's done up; and I've a favour to ask on yo' besides.' He was so happy he did not see her shiver all over. She hesitated just a moment before she answered, –

'I'll stay, if thou wishes it, Philip. But I'm no judge o' fashions and such like.'

'Thou'rt a judge o' comfort, and that's what I've been aiming at. I were niver so comfortable in a' my life as when I were a lodger at thy house,' said he, with brotherly tenderness in his tone. 'If my mind had been at ease I could ha' said I niver were happier in all my days than under thy roof; and I know it were thy doing for the most part. So come along, Hester, and tell me if there's aught more I can put in for Sylvie.'

It might not have been a very appropriate text, but such as it was the words, 'From him that would ask of thee turn not thou away',* seemed the only source of strength that could have enabled her to go patiently through the next half-hour. As it was, she unselfishly brought all her mind to bear upon the subject; admired this, thought and decided upon that, as one by one Philip showed her all his alterations and improvements. Never was such a quiet little bit of unconscious and unrecognized heroism. She really ended by such a conquest of self that she could absolutely sympathize with the proud expectant lover, and had quenched all envy of the beloved, in sympathy with the delight she imagined Sylvia must experience when she discovered all these proofs of Philip's fond consideration and care. But it was a great strain on the heart, that source of life; and when Hester returned into the parlour, after her deliberate survey of the house, she felt as weary and depressed in bodily strength as if she had gone through an illness of many days. She sat down on the nearest chair, and felt as though she never could rise again. Philip, joyous and content, stood near her talking.

'And, Hester,' said he, 'Sylvie has given me a message for thee – she says thou must be her bridesmaid – she'll have none other.'

'I cannot,' said Hester, with sudden sharpness.

'Oh, yes, but yo' must. It wouldn't be like my wedding if thou wasn't there: why I've looked upon thee as a sister iver since I came to lodge with thy mother.'

Hester shook her head. Did her duty require her not to turn away from this asking, too? Philip saw her reluctance, and, by intuition rather than reason, he knew that what she would not do for gaiety or pleasure she would consent to, if by so doing she could render any service to another. So he went on.

'Besides, Sylvie and me has planned to go for our wedding jaunt to Robin Hood's Bay. I ha' been to engage a shandry* this very morn, before t' shop was opened; and there's no one to leave wi' my aunt. Th' poor old body is sore crushed with sorrow; and is, as one may say, childish at times; she's to come down here, that we may find her when we come back at night; and there's niver a one she'll come with so willing and so happy as with thee, Hester. Sylvie and me has both said so.' – Hester looked up in his face with her grave honest eyes.

'I cannot go to church wi' thee, Philip; and thou must not ask me any further. But I'll go betimes to Haytersbank Farm, and I'll do my best to make the old lady happy, and to follow out thy directions in bringing her here before nightfall.'

Philip was on the point of urging her afresh to go with them to church; but something in her eyes brought a thought across his mind, as transitory as a breath passes over a looking-glass, and he desisted from his entreaty, and put away his thought as a piece of vain coxcombry, insulting to Hester. He passed rapidly on to all the careful directions rendered necessary by her compliance with the latter part of his request, coupling Sylvia's name with his perpetually; so that Hester looked upon her as a happy girl, as eager in planning all the details of her marriage as though no heavy shameful sorrow had passed over her head not many months ago.

Hester did not see Sylvia's white, dreamy, resolute face, that answered the solemn questions of the marriage service in a voice that did not seem her own. Hester was not with them to notice the heavy abstraction that made the bride as if unconscious of her husband's loving words, and then start and smile, and reply with a sad gentleness of tone. No! Hester's duty lay in conveying the poor widow and mother down from Haytersbank to the new home in Monkshaven; and for all Hester's assistance and thoughtfulness, it was a dreary, painful piece of work – the poor old woman crying like a child, with bewilderment at the

confused bustle which, in spite of all Sylvia's careful forethought, could not be avoided on this final day, when her
mother had to be carried away from the homestead over which
she had so long presided. But all this was as nothing to the
distress which overwhelmed poor Bell Robson when she entered
Philip's house; the parlour – the whole place so associated with
the keen agony she had undergone there, that the stab of
memory penetrated through her deadened senses, and brought
her back to misery. In vain Hester tried to console her by telling
her the fact of Sylvia's marriage with Philip in every form of
words that occurred to her. Bell only remembered her husband's
fate, which filled up her poor wandering mind, and coloured
everything; insomuch that Sylvia not being at hand to reply to
her mother's cry for her, the latter imagined that her child, as
well as her husband, was in danger of trial and death, and
refused to be comforted by any endeavour of the patient
sympathizing Hester. In a pause of Mrs Robson's sobs, Hester
heard the welcome sound of the wheels of the returning shandry,
bearing the bride and bridegroom home. It stopped at the door
– an instant, and Sylvia, white as a sheet at the sound of her
mother's wailings, which she had caught while yet at a distance,
with the quick ears of love, came running in; her mother feebly
rose and tottered towards her, and fell into her arms, saying,
'Oh! Sylvie, Sylvie, take me home, and away from this cruel
place!'

Hester could not but be touched with the young girl's manner
to her mother – as tender, as protecting as if their relation to
each other had been reversed, and she was lulling and tenderly
soothing a wayward, frightened child. She had neither eyes nor
ears for any one till her mother was sitting in trembling peace,
holding her daughter's hand tight in both of hers, as if afraid of
losing sight of her: then Sylvia turned to Hester, and, with the
sweet grace which is a natural gift to some happy people,
thanked her; in common words enough she thanked her, but in
that nameless manner, and with that strange, rare charm which
made Hester feel as if she had never been thanked in all her life
before; and from that time forth she understood, if she did not
always yield to, the unconscious fascination which Sylvia could
exercise over others at times.

Did it enter into Philip's heart to perceive that he had wedded
his long-sought bride in mourning raiment, and that the first

sounds which greeted them as they approached their home were those of weeping and wailing?

CHAPTER 30

Happy Days

And now Philip seemed as prosperous as his heart could desire. The business flourished, and money beyond his moderate wants came in. As for himself he required very little; but he had always looked forward to placing his idol in a befitting shrine;* and means for this were now furnished to him. The dress, the comforts, the position he had desired for Sylvia, were all hers. She did not need to do a stroke of household work if she preferred to 'sit in her parlour and sew up a seam'.* Indeed Phœbe resented any interference in the domestic labour, which she had performed so long, that she looked upon the kitchen as a private empire of her own. 'Mrs Hepburn' (as Sylvia was now termed) had a good dark silk gown-piece in her drawers, as well as the poor dove-coloured, against the day when she chose to leave off mourning; and stuff for either grey or scarlet cloaks was hers at her bidding.

What she cared for far more were the comforts with which it was in her power to surround her mother. In this Philip vied with her; for besides his old love, and new pity for his aunt Bell, he never forgot how she had welcomed him to Haytersbank, and favoured his love to Sylvia, in the yearning days when he little hoped he should ever win his cousin to be his wife. But even if he had not had these grateful and affectionate feelings towards the poor woman, he would have done much for her if only to gain the sweet, rare smiles which his wife never bestowed upon him so freely as when she saw him attending to 'mother', for so both of them now called Bell. For her creature comforts, her silk gowns, and her humble luxury, Sylvia did not care; Philip was almost annoyed at the indifference she often manifested to all his efforts to surround her with such things. It was even a hardship to her to leave off her country dress, her uncovered hair, her linsey petticoat, and loose bed-gown, and to don a stiff and stately gown for her morning dress. Sitting in the dark parlour at the back of the shop, and doing 'white work',* was much more wearying to her than running out into the fields to bring up the cows, or spinning wool, or making up butter. She sometimes thought to herself that it was a strange kind of life where there were no out-door animals to look after; the 'ox and the ass' had hitherto come into all her ideas of humanity; and her care and gentleness had made the dumb creatures round her father's home into mute friends with loving eyes, looking at her as if wistful to speak in words the grateful regard that she could read without the poor expression of language.

She missed the free open air, the great dome of sky above the fields; she rebelled against the necessity of 'dressing' (as she called it) to go out, although she acknowledged that it was a necessity where the first step beyond the threshold must be into a populous street.

It is possible that Philip was right at one time when he had thought to win her by material advantages; but the old vanities had been burnt out of her by the hot iron of acute suffering. A great deal of passionate feeling still existed, concealed and latent; but at this period it appeared as though she were indifferent to most things, and had lost the power of either hoping or fearing much. She was stunned into a sort of temporary numbness on most points; those on which she was sensitive being such as referred to the injustice and oppression of her father's death, or anything that concerned her mother.

She was quiet even to passiveness in all her dealings with Philip; he would have given not a little for some of the old bursts of impatience, the old pettishness, which, naughty as they were, had gone to form his idea of the former Sylvia. Once or twice he was almost vexed with her for her docility; he wanted her so much to have a will of her own, if only that he might know how to rouse her to pleasure by gratifying it. Indeed he seldom fell asleep at nights without his last thoughts being devoted to some little plan for the morrow, that he fancied she would like; and when he wakened in the early dawn he looked to see if she were indeed sleeping by his side, or whether it was not all a dream that he called Sylvia 'wife'.

He was aware that her affection for him was not to be spoken of in the same way as his for her, but he found much happiness in only being allowed to love and cherish her; and with the patient perseverance that was one remarkable feature in his character, he went on striving to deepen and increase her love when most other men would have given up the endeavour, made themselves content with half a heart, and turned to some other object of attainment. All this time Philip was troubled by a dream that recurred whenever he was over-fatigued, or otherwise not in perfect health. Over and over again in this first year of married life he dreamt this dream; perhaps as many as eight or nine times, and it never varied. It was always of Kinraid's return; Kinraid was full of life in Philip's dream, though in his waking hours he could and did convince himself by all the laws of probability that his rival was dead. He never remembered the exact sequence of events in that terrible dream after he had roused himself, with a fight and a struggle, from his feverish slumbers. He was generally sitting up in bed when he found himself conscious, his heart beating wildly, with a conviction of Kinraid's living presence somewhere near him in the darkness. Occasionally Sylvia was disturbed by his agitation, and would question him about his dreams, having, like most of her class at that time, great faith in their prophetic interpretation; but Philip never gave her any truth in his reply.

After all, and though he did not acknowledge it even to himself, the long-desired happiness was not so delicious and perfect as he had anticipated. Many have felt the same in their first year of married life; but the faithful, patient nature that still works on, striving to gain love, and capable itself of steady love all the while, is a gift not given to all.

For many weeks after their wedding, Kester never came near them: a chance word or two from Sylvia showed Philip that she had noticed this and regretted it; and, accordingly, he made it his business at the next leisure opportunity to go to Haytersbank (never saying a word to his wife of his purpose), and seek out Kester.

All the whole place was altered! It was new white-washed, new thatched: the patches of colour in the surrounding ground were changed with altered tillage; the great geraniums were gone from the window, and instead, was a smart knitted blind. Children played before the house door; a dog lying on the step flew at Philip; all was so strange, that it was even the strangest thing of all for Kester to appear where everything else was so altered!

Philip had to put up with a good deal of crabbed* behaviour on the part of the latter before he could induce Kester to promise to come down into the town and see Sylvia in her new home.

Somehow, the visit when paid was but a failure; at least, it seemed so at the time, though probably it broke the ice of restraint which was forming over the familiar intercourse between Kester and Sylvia. The old servant was daunted by seeing Sylvia in a strange place, and stood, sleeking his hair down, and furtively looking about him, instead of seating himself on the chair Sylvia had so eagerly brought forward for him.

Then his sense of the estrangement caused by their new positions infected her, and she began to cry pitifully, saying, –

'Oh, Kester! Kester! tell me about Haytersbank! Is it just as it used to be in feyther's days?'

'Well, a cannot say as it is,' said Kester, thankful to have a subject started. 'They'n pleughed up t' oud pasture-field, and are settin' it for 'taters. They're not for much cattle, isn't Higginses. They'll be for corn in t' next year, a reckon, and they'll just ha' their pains for their payment.* But they're allays so pig-headed, is folk fra' a distance.'

So they went on discoursing on Haytersbank and the old days, till Bell Robson, having finished her afternoon nap, came slowly down-stairs to join them; and after that the conversation became so broken up, from the desire of the other two to attend and reply as best they could to her fragmentary and disjointed talk, that Kester took his leave before long; falling, as he did so, into the formal and unnaturally respectful manner which he had adopted on first coming in.

But Sylvia ran after him, and brought him back from the door.

'To think of thy going away, Kester, without either bit or drink; nay, come back wi' thee, and taste wine and cake.'

Kester stood at the door, half shy, half pleased, while Sylvia, in all the glow and hurry of a young housekeeper's hospitality, sought for the decanter of wine, and a wine-glass in the corner cupboard, and hastily cut an immense wedge of cake, which she crammed into his hand in spite of his remonstrances; and then she poured him out an overflowing glass of wine, which Kester would far rather have gone without, as he knew manners too well to suppose that he might taste it without having gone through the preliminary ceremony of wishing the donor health and happiness. He stood red and half smiling, with his cake in one hand, his wine in the other, and then began, –

'Long may ye live,
Happy ma' ye be,
And blest with a num'rous
Pro-ge-ny.'*

'Theere, that's po'try for yo' as I larnt i' my youth. But there's a deal to be said as cannot be put int' po'try, an' yet a cannot say it, somehow. It 'd tax a parson t' say a' as a've getten i' my mind. It's like a heap o' woo' just after shearin' time; it's worth a deal, but it tak's a vast o' combin', an' cardin', an' spinnin' afore it can be made use on. If a were up to t' use o' words, a could say a mighty deal; but somehow a'm tongue-teed when a come to want my words most, so a'll only just mak' bold t' say as a think yo've done pretty well for yo'rsel', getten a house-full o' furniture (looking around him as he said this), an' vittle an' clothin' for t' axing, belike, an' a home for t' missus in her time o' need; an' mebbe not such a bad husband as a once thought yon man 'ud mak'; a'm not above sayin' as he's, mebbe, better nor a took him for; – so here's to ye both, and wishin' ye health and happiness, ay, and money to buy yo' another, as country folk say.'

Having ended his oration, much to his own satisfaction, Kester tossed off his glass of wine, smacked his lips, wiped his mouth with the back of his hand, pocketed his cake, and made off.

That night Sylvia spoke of his visit to her husband. Philip never said how he himself had brought it to pass, nor did he name the fact that he had heard the old man come in just as he himself had intended going into the parlour for tea, but had kept away, as he thought Sylvia and Kester would most enjoy their interview undisturbed. And Sylvia felt as if her husband's silence was unsympathizing, and shut up the feelings that were just beginning to expand towards him. She sank again into the listless state of indifference from which nothing but some reference to former days, or present consideration for her mother, could rouse her.

Hester was almost surprised at Sylvia's evident liking for her. By slow degrees Hester was learning to love the woman, whose position as Philip's wife she would have envied so keenly had she not been so truly good and pious. But Sylvia seemed as though she had given Hester her whole affection all at once. Hester could not understand this, while she was touched and melted by the trust it implied. For one thing Sylvia remembered and regretted – her harsh treatment of Hester the rainy, stormy night on which the latter had come to Haytersbank to seek her and her mother, and bring them into Monkshaven to see the imprisoned father and husband. Sylvia had been struck with Hester's patient endurance of her rudeness, a rudeness which she was conscious that she herself should have immediately and vehemently resented. Sylvia did not understand how a totally different character from hers might immediately forgive the anger she could not forget; and because Hester had been so meek at the time, Sylvia, who knew how passing and transitory was her own anger, thought that all was forgotten; while Hester believed that the words, which she herself could not have uttered except under deep provocation, meant much more than they did, and admired and wondered at Sylvia for having so entirely conquered her anger against her.

Again, the two different women were divergently affected by the extreme fondness which Bell had shown towards Hester ever since Sylvia's wedding-day. Sylvia, who had always received more love from others than she knew what to do with, had the most entire faith in her own supremacy in her mother's heart, though at times Hester would do certain things more to the poor old woman's satisfaction. Hester, who had craved for the affection which had been withheld from her, and had from that one circumstance become distrustful of her own power of inspiring regard, while she exaggerated the delight of being beloved, feared lest Sylvia should become jealous of her mother's open display of great attachment and occasional preference for Hester. But such a thought never entered Sylvia's mind. She was more thankful than she knew how to express towards any one who made her mother happy; as has been already said, the contributing to Bell Robson's pleasures earned Philip more of his wife's smiles than anything else. And Sylvia threw her whole heart into the words and caresses she lavished on Hester whenever poor Mrs Robson spoke of the goodness and kindness of the latter. Hester attributed more virtue to these sweet words and deeds of gratitude than they deserved; they did not imply in

Sylvia any victory over evil temptation, as they would have done in Hester.

It seemed to be Sylvia's fate to captivate more people than she cared to like back again. She turned the heads of John and Jeremiah Foster, who could hardly congratulate Philip enough on his choice of a wife.

They had been prepared to be critical on one who had interfered with their favourite project of a marriage between Philip and Hester; and, though full of compassion for the cruelty of Daniel Robson's fate, they were too completely men of business not to have some apprehension that the connection of Philip Hepburn with the daughter of a man who was hanged, might injure the shop over which both his and their name appeared. But all the possible proprieties demanded that they should pay attention to the bride of their former shopman and present successor; and the very first visitors whom Sylvia had received after her marriage had been John and Jeremiah Foster, in their sabbath-day clothes. They found her in the parlour (so familiar to both of them!) clear-starching her mother's caps, which had to be got up in some particular fashion that Sylvia was afraid of dictating to Phœbe.

She was a little disturbed at her visitors discovering her at this employment; but she was on her own ground, and that gave her self-possession; and she welcomed the two old men so sweetly and modestly, and looked so pretty and feminine, and, besides, so notable in her handiwork, that she conquered all their prejudices at one blow; and their first thought on leaving the shop was how to do her honour, by inviting her to a supper party at Jeremiah Foster's house.

Sylvia was dismayed when she was bidden to this wedding feast, and Philip had to use all his authority, though tenderly, to make her consent to go at all. She had been to merry country parties like the Corneys', and to bright haymaking romps in the open air; but never to a set stately party at a friend's house.

She would fain have made attendance on her mother an excuse; but Philip knew he must not listen to any such plea, and applied to Hester in the dilemma, asking her to remain with Mrs Robson while he and Sylvia went out visiting; and Hester had willingly, nay, eagerly consented – it was much more to her taste than going out.

So Philip and Sylvia set out, arm-in-arm, down Bridge Street, across the bridge, and then clambered up the hill. On the way he gave her the directions she asked for about her behaviour as bride and most honoured guest; and altogether succeeded, against his intention and will, in frightening her so completely as to the grandeur and importance of the occasion, and the necessity of remembering certain set rules, and making certain set speeches and attending to them when the right time came, that, if any one so naturally graceful could have been awkward, Sylvia would have been so that night.

As it was, she sat, pale and weary-looking, on the very edge of her chair; she uttered the formal words which Philip had told her were appropriate to the occasion, and she heartily wished herself safe at home and in bed. Yet she left but one unanimous impression on the company when she went away, namely, that she was the prettiest and best-behaved woman they had ever seen, and that Philip Hepburn had done well in choosing her, felon's daughter though she might be.

Both the hosts had followed her into the lobby to help Philip in cloaking her, and putting on her pattens.* They were full of old-fashioned compliments and good-wishes; one speech of theirs came up to her memory in future years: –

'Now, Sylvia Hepburn,' said Jeremiah, 'I've known thy husband long, and I don't say but what thou hast done well in choosing him; but if he ever neglects or ill-uses thee, come to me, and I'll give him a sound lecture on his conduct. Mind, I'm thy friend from this day forrards, and ready to take thy part against him!'

Philip smiled as if the day would never come when he should neglect or ill-use his darling; Sylvia smiled a little, without much attending to, or caring for, the words that were detaining her, tired as she was; John and Jeremiah chuckled over the joke; but the words came up again in after days, as words idly spoken sometimes do.

Before the end of that first year, Philip had learnt to be jealous of his wife's new love for Hester. To the latter, Sylvia gave the free confidence on many things which Philip fancied she withheld from him. A suspicion crossed his mind, from time to time, that Sylvia might speak of her former lover to Hester. It would be not unnatural, he thought, if she did so, believing him to be dead; but the idea irritated him.

He was entirely mistaken, however; Sylvia, with all her

apparent frankness, kept her deep sorrows to herself. She never mentioned her father's name, though he was continually present to her mind. Nor did she speak of Kinraid to human being, though, for his sake, her voice softened when, by chance, she spoke to a passing sailor; and for his sake her eyes lingered on such men longer than on others, trying to discover in them something of the old familiar gait; and partly for his dead sake, and partly because of the freedom of the outlook and the freshness of the air, she was glad occasionally to escape from the comfortable imprisonment* of her 'parlour', and the close streets around the market-place, and to mount the cliffs and sit on the turf, gazing abroad over the wide still expanse of the open sea; for, at that height, even breaking waves only looked like broken lines of white foam on the blue watery plain.

She did not want any companion on these rambles, which had somewhat of the delight of stolen pleasures; for all the other respectable matrons and town-dwellers whom she knew were content to have always a business object for their walk, or else to stop at home in their own households; and Sylvia was rather ashamed of her own yearnings for solitude and open air, and the sight and sound of the mother-like sea. She used to take off her hat, and sit there, her hands clasping her knees, the salt air lifting her bright curls, gazing at the distant horizon over the sea, in a sad dreaminess of thought; if she had been asked on what she meditated, she could not have told you.

But, by-and-by, the time came when she was a prisoner in the house; a prisoner in her room, lying in bed with a little baby by her side – her child, Philip's child. His pride, his delight knew no bounds; this was a new fast tie between them; this would reconcile her to the kind of life that, with all its respectability and comfort, was so different from what she had lived before, and which Philip had often perceived that she felt to be dull and restraining. He already began to trace in the little girl, only a few days old, the lovely curves that he knew so well by heart in the mother's face. Sylvia, too, pale, still, and weak, was very happy; yes, really happy for the first time since her irrevocable marriage. For its irrevocableness had weighed much upon her with a sense of dull hopelessness; she felt all Philip's kindness, she was grateful to him for his tender regard towards her mother, she was learning to love him as well as to like and respect him. She did not know what else she could have done but marry so true a friend, and she and her mother so friendless; but, at the same time, it was like lead on her morning spirits when she awoke and remembered that the decision was made, the deed was done, the choice taken which comes to most people but once in their lives. Now the little baby came in upon this state of mind like a ray of sunlight into a gloomy room.

Even her mother was rejoiced and proud; even with her crazed brain and broken heart, the sight of sweet, peaceful infancy brought light to her. All the old ways of holding a baby, of hushing it to sleep, of tenderly guarding its little limbs from injury, came back, like the habits of her youth, to Bell; and she was never so happy or so easy in her mind, or so sensible and connected in her ideas, as when she had Sylvia's baby in her arms.

It was a pretty sight to see, however familiar to all of us such things may be – the pale, worn old woman, in her quaint, old-fashioned country dress, holding the little infant on her knees, looking at its open, unspeculative eyes, and talking the little language to it as though it could understand; the father on his knees, kept prisoner by a small, small finger curled round his strong and sinewy one, and gazing at the tiny creature with wondering idolatry; the young mother, fair, pale, and smiling, propped up on pillows in order that she, too, might see the wonderful babe; it was astonishing how the doctor could come and go without being drawn into the admiring vortex, and look at this baby just as if babies came into the world every day.

'Philip,' said Sylvia, one night, as he sat as still as a mouse in her room, imagining her to be asleep. He was by her bed-side in a moment.

'I've been thinking what she's to be called. Isabella, after mother; and what were yo'r mother's name?'

'Margaret,' said he.

'Margaret Isabella; Isabella Margaret. Mother's called Bell. She might be called Bella.'

'I could ha' wished her to be called after thee.'

She made a little impatient movement.

'Nay; Sylvia's not a lucky name. Best be called after thy mother and mine. And I want for to ask Hester to be godmother.'

'Anything thou likes, sweetheart. Shall we call her Rose, after Hester Rose?'

'No, no!' said Sylvia; 'she mun be called after my mother, or thine, or both. I should like her to be called Bella, after mother, because she's so fond of baby.'

'Anything to please thee, darling.'

'Don't say that as if it didn't signify; there's a deal in having a pretty name,' said Sylvia, a little annoyed. 'I ha' allays hated being called Sylvia. It were after father's mother, Sylvia Steele.'

'I niver thought any name in a' the world so sweet and pretty as Sylvia,' said Philip, fondly; but she was too much absorbed in her own thoughts to notice either his manner or his words.

'There, yo'll not mind if it is Bella, because yo' see my mother is alive to be pleased by its being named after her, and Hester may be godmother, and I'll ha' t' dove-coloured silk as yo' gave me afore we were married made up into a cloak for it to go to church in.'

'I got it for thee,' said Philip, a little disappointed. 'It'll be too good for the baby.'

'Eh! but I'm so careless, I should be spilling something on it? But if thou got it for me I cannot find i' my heart for t' wear it on baby, and I'll have it made into a christening gown for mysel'. But I'll niver feel at my ease in it, for fear of spoiling it.'

'Well! an' if thou does spoil it, love, I'll get thee another. I make account of riches only for thee; that I may be able to get thee whativer thou's a fancy for, for either thysel', or thy mother.'

She lifted her pale face from her pillow, and put up her lips to kiss him for these words.

Perhaps on that day Philip reached the zenith of his life's happiness.

CHAPTER 31

Evil Omens

The first step in Philip's declension happened in this way. Sylvia had made rapid progress in her recovery; but now she seemed at a stationary point of weakness; wakeful nights succeeding to languid days. Occasionally she caught a little sleep in the afternoons, but she usually awoke startled and feverish.

One afternoon Philip had stolen upstairs to look at her and his child; but the efforts he made at careful noiselessness made the door creak on its hinges as he opened it. The woman employed to nurse her had taken the baby into another room that no sound might rouse her from her slumber; and Philip would probably have been warned against entering the chamber where his wife lay sleeping had he been perceived by the nurse. As it was, he opened the door, made a noise, and Sylvia started up, her face all one flush, her eyes wild and uncertain; she looked about her as if she did not know where she was; pushed the hair off her hot forehead; all which actions Philip saw, dismayed and regretful. But he kept still, hoping that she would lie down and compose herself. Instead she stretched out her arms imploringly, and said, in a voice full of yearning and tears, –

'Oh! Charley! come to me – come to me!' and then as she more fully became aware of the place where she was, her actual situation, she sank back and feebly began to cry. Philip's heart boiled within him; any man's would under the circumstances, but he had the sense of guilty concealment to aggravate the intensity of his feelings. Her weak cry after another man, too, irritated him, partly through his anxious love, which made him wise to know how much physical harm she was doing herself. At this moment he stirred, or unintentionally made some sound: she started up afresh, and called out, –

'Oh, who's theere? Do, for God's sake, tell me who yo' are!'

'It's me,' said Philip, coming forwards, striving to keep down the miserable complication of love and jealousy, and remorse and anger, that made his heart beat so wildly, and almost took him out of himself. Indeed, he must have been quite beside himself for the time, or he could never have gone on to utter the unwise, cruel words he did. But she spoke first, in a distressed and plaintive tone of voice.

'Oh, Philip, I've been asleep, and yet I think I was awake! And I saw Charley Kinraid as plain as iver I see thee now, and he wasn't drowned at all. I'm sure he's alive somewheere; he were so clear and life-like. Oh! what shall I do? what shall I do?'

She wrung her hands in feverish distress. Urged by passionate feelings of various kinds, and also by his desire to quench the agitation which was doing her harm, Philip spoke, hardly knowing what he said.

'Kinraid's dead, I tell yo', Sylvie! And what kind of a woman are yo' to go dreaming of another man i' this way, and taking on so about him, when yo're a wedded wife, with a child as yo've borne to another man?'

In a moment he could have bitten out his tongue. She looked at him with the mute reproach which some of us see (God help us!) in the eyes of the dead, as they come before our sad memories in the night-season; looked at him with such a solemn, searching look, never saying a word of reply or defence. Then she lay down, motionless and silent. He had been instantly stung with remorse for his speech; the words were not beyond his lips when an agony had entered his heart; but her steady, dilated eyes had kept him dumb and motionless as if by a spell.

Now he rushed to the bed on which she lay, and half knelt, half threw himself upon it, imploring her to forgive him; regardless for the time of any evil consequences to her, it seemed as if he must have her pardon – her relenting – at any price, even if they both died in the act of reconciliation. But she lay speechless, and, as far as she could be, motionless, the bed trembling under her with the quivering she could not still.

Philip's wild tones caught the nurse's ears, and she entered full of the dignified indignation of wisdom.

'Are yo' for killing yo'r wife, measter?' she asked. 'She's noane so strong as she can bear flytin'* and scoldin', nor will she be for many a week to come. Go down wi' ye, and leave her i' peace if yo're a man as can be called a man!'

Her anger was rising as she caught sight of Sylvia's averted face. It was flushed crimson, her eyes full of intense emotion of some kind, her lips compressed; but an involuntary twitching overmastering her resolute stillness from time to time. Philip, who did not see the averted face, nor understand the real danger in which he was placing his wife, felt as though he must have one word, one responsive touch of the hand which lay passive in his, which was not even drawn away from the kisses with which he covered it, any more than if it had been an impassive stone. The nurse had fairly to take him by the shoulders, and turn him out of the room.

In half an hour the doctor had to be summoned. Of course, the nurse gave him her version of the events of the afternoon,

with much *animus* against Philip; and the doctor thought it his
duty to have some very serious conversation with him.

'I do assure you, Mr Hepburn, that, in the state your wife has
been in for some days, it was little less than madness on your
part to speak to her about anything that could give rise to strong
emotion.'

'It was madness, sir!' replied Philip, in a low, miserable tone
of voice. The doctor's heart was touched, in spite of the nurse's
accusations against the scolding husband. Yet the danger was
now too serious for him to mince matters.

'I must tell you that I cannot answer for her life, unless the
greatest precautions are taken on your part, and unless the
measures I shall use have the effect I wish for in the next twenty-
four hours. She is on the verge of a brain fever. Any allusion to
the subject which has been the final cause of the state in which
she now is must be most cautiously avoided, even to a chance
word which may bring it to her memory.'

And so on; but Philip seemed to hear only this: then he might
not express contrition, or sue for pardon, he must go on
unforgiven through all this stress of anxiety; and even if she
recovered the doctor warned him of the undesirableness of
recurring to what had passed!

Heavy miserable times of endurance and waiting have to be
passed through by all during the course of their lives; and Philip
had had his share of such seasons, when the heart, and the will,
and the speech, and the limbs, must be bound down with strong
resolution to patience.

For many days, nay, for weeks, he was forbidden to see Sylvia,
as the very sound of his footstep brought on a recurrence of the
fever and convulsive movement. Yet she seemed, from questions
she feebly asked the nurse, to have forgotten all that had
happened on the day of her attack from the time when she
dropped off to sleep. But how much she remembered of after
occurrences no one could ascertain. She was quiet enough when,
at length, Philip was allowed to see her. But he was half jealous
of his child, when he watched how she could smile at it, while
she never changed a muscle of her face at all he could do or say.

And of a piece with this extreme quietude and reserve was her
behaviour to him when at length she had fully recovered, and
was able to go about the house again. Philip thought many a

time of the words she had used long before – before their marriage. Ominous words they were.

'It's not in me to forgive; I sometimes think it's not in me to forget.'

Philip was tender even to humility in his conduct towards her. But nothing stirred her from her fortress of reserve. And he knew she was so different; he knew how loving, nay, passionate, was her nature – vehement, demonstrative – oh! how could he stir her once more into expression, even if the first show or speech she made was of anger? Then he tried being angry with her himself; he was sometimes unjust to her consciously and of a purpose, in order to provoke her into defending herself, and appealing against his unkindness. He only seemed to drive her love away still more.

If any one had known all that was passing in that household, while yet the story of it was not ended, nor, indeed, come to its crisis, their hearts would have been sorry for the man who lingered long at the door of the room in which his wife sat cooing and talking to her baby, and sometimes laughing back to it, or who was soothing the querulousness of failing age with every possible patience of love; sorry for the poor listener who was hungering for the profusion of tenderness thus scattered on the senseless air, yet only by stealth caught the echoes of what ought to have been his.

It was so difficult to complain, too, impossible, in fact. Everything that a wife could do from duty she did; but the love seemed to have fled, and, in such cases, no reproaches or complaints can avail to bring it back. So reason outsiders, and are convinced of the result before the experiment is made. But Philip could not reason, or could not yield to reason – and so he complained and reproached. She did not much answer him; but he thought that her eyes expressed the old words, –

'It's not in me to forgive; I sometimes think it's not in me to forget.'

However, it is an old story, an ascertained fact, that, even in the most tender and stable masculine natures, at the supremest seasons of their lives, there is room for other thoughts and passions than such as are connected with love. Even with the most domestic and affectionate men, their emotions seem to be kept in a cell distinct and away from their actual lives. Philip had other thoughts and other occupations than those connected with his wife during all this time.

An uncle of his mother's, a Cumberland 'statesman',* of whose existence he was barely conscious, died about this time, leaving to his unknown great-nephew four or five hundred pounds, which put him at once in a different position with regard to his business. Henceforward his ambition was roused, – such humble ambition as befitted a shop-keeper in a country town sixty or seventy years ago. To be respected by the men around him had always been an object with him, and was, perhaps, becoming more so than ever now, as a sort of refuge from his deep, sorrowful mortification in other directions. He was greatly pleased at being made a sidesman;* and, in preparation for the further honour of being churchwarden, he went regularly twice a day to church on Sundays. There was enough religious feeling in him to make him disguise the worldly reason for such conduct from himself. He believed that he went because he thought it right to attend public worship in the parish church whenever it was offered up; but it may be questioned of him, as of many others, how far he would have been as regular in attendance in a place where he was not known. With this, however, we have nothing to do. The fact was that he went regularly to church, and he wished his wife to accompany him to the pew, newly painted, with his name on the door, where he sat in full sight of the clergyman and congregation.

Sylvia had never been in the habit of such regular church-going, and she felt it as a hardship, and slipped out of the duty as often as ever she could. In her unmarried days, she and her parents had gone annually to the mother-church of the parish in which Haytersbank was situated: on the Monday succeeding the Sunday next after the Romish Saint's Day, to whom the church was dedicated,* there was a great feast or wake held, and, on the Sunday, all the parishioners came to church from far and near. Frequently, too, in the course of the year, Sylvia would accompany one or other of her parents to Scarby Moorside* afternoon service, – when the hay was got in, and the corn not ready for cutting, or the cows were dry and there was no afternoon milking. Many clergymen were languid in those days, and did not too curiously inquire into the reasons which gave them such small congregations in country parishes.

Now she was married, this weekly church-going which Philip

seemed to expect from her, became a tie and a small hardship, which connected itself with her life of respectability and prosperity. 'A crust of bread and liberty'* was much more accordant to Sylvia's nature than plenty of creature comforts and many restraints. Another wish of Philip's, against which she said no word, but constantly rebelled in thought and deed, was his desire that the servant he had engaged during the time of her illness to take charge of the baby, should always carry it whenever it was taken out for a walk. Sylvia often felt, now she was strong, as if she would far rather have been without the responsibility of having this nursemaid, of whom she was, in reality, rather afraid. The good side of it was that it set her at liberty to attend to her mother at times when she would have been otherwise occupied with her baby; but Bell required very little from any one: she was easily pleased, unexacting, and methodical even in her dotage; preserving the quiet, undemonstrative habits of her earlier life now that the faculty of reason, which had been at the basis of the formation of such habits, was gone. She took great delight in watching the baby, and was pleased to have it in her care for a short time, but she dozed so much that it prevented her having any strong wish on the subject.

So Sylvia contrived to get her baby as much as possible to herself, in spite of the nursemaid; and, above all, she would carry it out, softly cradled in her arms, warm pillowed on her breast, and bear it to the freedom and solitude of the seashore on the west side of the town, where the cliffs were not so high, and there was a good space of sand and shingle at all low tides.

Once here, she was as happy as she ever expected to be in this world. The fresh sea-breeze restored something of the colour of former days to her cheeks, the old buoyancy to her spirits; here she might talk her heart-full of loving nonsense to her baby; here it was all her own; no father to share in it, no nursemaid to dispute the wisdom of anything she did with it. She sang to it, she tossed it; it crowed and it laughed back again, till both were weary; and then she would sit down on a broken piece of rock, and fall to gazing on the advancing waves catching the sunlight on their crests, advancing, receding, for ever and for ever, as they had done all her life long – as they did when she had walked with them that once by the side of Kinraid; those cruel waves that, forgetful of the happy lovers' talk by the side of their waters, had carried one away, and drowned him deep till he was dead. Every time she sat down to look at the sea, this process of thought was gone through up to this point; the next step would, she knew, bring her to the question she dared not, must not ask. He was dead; he must be dead; for was she not Philip's wife? Then came up the recollection of Philip's speech, never forgotten, only buried out of sight: 'What kind of a woman are yo' to go on dreaming of another man, and yo' a wedded wife?' She used to shudder as if cold steel had been plunged into her warm, living body as she remembered these words; cruel words, harmlessly provoked. They were too much associated with physical pains to be dwelt upon; only their memory was always there. She paid for these happy rambles with her baby by the depression which awaited her on her re-entrance into the dark, confined house that was her home; its very fulness of comfort was an oppression. Then, when her husband saw her pale and fatigued, he was annoyed, and sometimes upbraided her for doing what was so unnecessary as to load herself with her child. She knew full well it was not that that caused her weariness. By-and-by, when he inquired and discovered that all these walks were taken in one direction, out towards the sea, he grew jealous of her love for the inanimate ocean. Was it connected in her mind with the thought of Kinraid? Why did she so perseveringly, in wind or cold, go out to the sea-shore; the western side, too, where, if she went but far enough, she would come upon the mouth of the Haytersbank gully, the point at which she had last seen Kinraid? Such fancies haunted Philip's mind for hours after she had acknowledged the direction of her walks. But he never said a word that could distinctly tell her he disliked her going to the sea, otherwise she would have obeyed him in this, as in everything else; for absolute obedience to her husband seemed to be her rule of life at this period – obedience to him who would so gladly have obeyed her smallest wish had she but expressed it! She never knew that Philip had any painful association with the particular point on the sea-shore that she instinctively avoided, both from a con-sciousness of wifely duty, and also because the sight of it brought up so much sharp pain.

Philip used to wonder if the dream that preceded her illness was the suggestive cause that drew her so often to the shore. Her illness consequent upon that dream had filled his mind, so that for many months he himself had had no haunting vision of Kinraid to disturb his slumbers. But now the old dream of Kinraid's actual presence by Philip's bedside began to return with fearful vividness. Night after night it recurred; each time with some new touch of reality, and close approach; till it was as if the fate that overtakes all men were then, even then, knocking at his door.

In his business Philip prospered. Men praised him because he did well to himself. He had the perseverance, the capability for head-work and calculation, the steadiness and general fore-thought which might have made him a great merchant if he had lived in a large city. Without any effort of his own, almost, too, without Coulson's being aware of it, Philip was now in the position of superior partner; the one to suggest and arrange, while Coulson only carried out the plans that emanated from Philip. The whole work of life was suited to the man: he did not aspire to any different position, only to the full development of the capabilities of that which he already held. He had originated several fresh schemes with regard to the traffic of the shop; and his old masters, with all their love of tried ways, and distrust of everything new, had been candid enough to confess that their successors' plans had resulted in success. 'Their successors.' Philip was content with having the power when the exercise of it was required, and never named his own important share in the new improvements. Possibly, if he had, Coulson's vanity might have taken the alarm, and he might not have been so acquiescent for the future. As it was, he forgot his own subordinate share, and always used the imperial 'we', 'we thought', 'it struck us', etc.

CHAPTER 32

Rescued from the Waves

Meanwhile Hester came and went as usual; in so quiet and methodical a way, with so even and undisturbed a temper, that she was almost forgotten when everything went well in the shop or household. She was a star, the brightness of which was only recognized in times of darkness. She herself was almost surprised at her own increasing regard for Sylvia. She had not thought she should ever be able to love the woman who had been such a laggard in acknowledging Philip's merits; and from all she had ever heard of Sylvia before she came to know her, from the angry words with which Sylvia had received her when she had first gone to Haytersbank Farm, Hester had intended to remain on friendly terms, but to avoid intimacy. But her kindness to Bell Robson had won both the mother's and daughter's hearts; and in spite of herself, certainly against her own mother's advice, she had become the familiar friend and welcome guest of the household.

Now the very change in Sylvia's whole manner and ways, which grieved and vexed Philip, made his wife the more attractive to Hester. Brought up among Quakers, although not one herself, she admired and respected the staidness and outward peacefulness common amongst the young women of that sect. Sylvia, whom she had expected to find volatile, talkative, vain, and wilful, was quiet and still, as if she had been born a Friend: she seemed to have no will of her own; she served her mother and child for love; she obeyed her husband in all things, and never appeared to pine after gaiety or pleasure. And yet at times Hester thought, or rather a flash came across her mind, as if all things were not as right as they seemed. Philip looked older, more care-worn; nay, even Hester was obliged to allow to herself that she had heard him speak to his wife in sharp, aggrieved tones. Innocent Hester! she could not understand how the very qualities she so admired in Sylvia were just what were so foreign to her nature that the husband, who had known her from a child, felt what an unnatural restraint she was putting upon herself, and would have hailed petulant words or wilful actions with an unspeakable thankfulness for relief.

One day – it was in the spring of 1798 – Hester was engaged to stay to tea with the Hepburns, in order that after that early meal she might set to again in helping Philip and Coulson to pack away the winter cloths and flannels, for which there was no longer any use. The tea-time was half-past four; about four o'clock a heavy April shower came on, the hail pattering against the window-panes so as to awaken Mrs Robson from her afternoon's nap. She came down the corkscrew stairs, and found Phœbe in the parlour arranging the tea-things.

Phoebe and Mrs Robson were better friends than Phœbe and her young mistress; and so they began to talk a little together in a comfortable, familiar way. Once or twice Philip looked in, as if he would be glad to see the tea-table in readiness; and then Phœbe would put on a spurt of busy bustle, which ceased almost as soon as his back was turned, so eager was she to obtain Mrs Robson's sympathy in some little dispute that had occurred between her and the nursemaid. The latter had misappropriated some hot water, prepared and required by Phœbe, to the washing of the baby's clothes; it was a long story, and would have tired the patience of any one in full possession of their senses; but the details were just within poor Bell's comprehension, and she was listening with the greatest sympathy. Both the women were unaware of the lapse of time; but it was of consequence to Philip, as the extra labour was not to be begun until after tea, and the daylight hours were precious.

At a quarter to five Hester and he came in, and then Phœbe began to hurry. Hester went up to sit by Bell and talk to her. Philip spoke to Phœbe in the familiar words of countryfolk. Indeed, until his marriage, Phœbe had always called him by his Christian name, and had found it very difficult to change it into 'master'.

'Where's Sylvie?' said he.

'Gone out wi' t' babby,' replied Phœbe.

'Why can't Nancy carry it out?' asked Philip.

It was touching on the old grievance: he was tired, and he spoke with sharp annoyance. Phœbe might easily have told him the real state of the case; Nancy was busy at her washing, which would have been reason enough. But the nursemaid had vexed her, and she did not like Philip's sharpness, so she only said, –

'It's noane o' my business; it's yo' t' look after yo'r own wife and child; but yo'r but a lad after a'.'

This was not a conciliatory speech, and just put the last stroke to Philip's fit of ill-temper.

'I'm not for my tea to-night,' said he, to Hester, when all was ready. 'Sylvie's not here, and nothing is nice, or as it should be. I'll go and set to on t' stock-taking. Don't yo' hurry, Hester; stop and chat a bit with th' old lady.'

'Nay, Philip,' said Hester, 'thou's sadly tired; just take this cup o' tea; Sylvia 'll be grieved if yo' haven't something.'

'Sylvia doesn't care whether I'm full or fasting,' replied he,

impatiently putting aside the cup. 'If she did she'd ha' taken care
to be in, and ha' seen to things being as I like them.'

Now in general Philip was the least particular of men about
meals; and to do Sylvia justice, she was scrupulously attentive
to every household duty in which old Phœbe would allow her to
meddle, and always careful to see after her husband's comforts.
But Philip was too vexed at her absence to perceive the injustice
of what he was saying, nor was he aware how Bell Robson had
been attending to what he said. But she was sadly discomfited
by it, understanding just enough of the grievance in hand to
think that her daughter was neglectful of those duties which she
herself had always regarded as paramount to all others; nor
could Hester convince her that Philip had not meant what he
said; neither could she turn the poor old woman's thoughts from
the words which had caused her distress.

Presently Sylvia came in, bright and cheerful, although breathless with hurry.

'Oh,' said she, taking off her wet shawl, 'we've had to shelter
from such a storm of rain, baby and me – but see! she's none
the worse for it, as bonny as iver, bless her.'

Hester began some speech of admiration for the child in order
to prevent Bell from delivering the lecture she felt sure was
coming down on the unsuspecting Sylvia; but all in vain.

'Philip's been complaining on thee, Sylvie,' said Bell, in the
way in which she had spoken to her daughter when she was a
little child; grave and severe in tone and look, more than in
words. 'I forget justly what about, but he spoke on thy neglect-
ing him continual. It's not right, my lass, it's not right; a woman
should – but my head's very tired, and all I can think on to say
is, it's not right.'

'Philip been complaining of me, and to mother!' said Sylvia,
ready to burst into tears, so grieved and angry was she.

'No!' said Hester, 'thy mother has taken it a little too strong;
he were vexed like at his tea not being ready.'

Sylvia said no more, but the bright colour faded from her
cheek, and the contraction of care returned to her brow. She
occupied herself with taking off her baby's walking things.
Hester lingered, anxious to soothe and make peace; she was
looking sorrowfully at Sylvia, when she saw tears dropping on
the baby's cloak, and then it seemed as if she must speak a word
of comfort before going to the shop-work, where she knew she

was expected by both Philip and Coulson. She poured out a cup
of tea, and coming close up to Sylvia, and kneeling down by
her, she whispered, –

'Just take him this into t' ware-room; it'll put all to rights if
thou'll take it to him wi' thy own hands.'

Sylvia looked up, and Hester then more fully saw how she
had been crying. She whispered in reply, for fear of disturbing
her mother, –

'I don't mind anything but his speaking ill on me to mother. I
know I'm for iver trying and trying to be a good wife to him,
an' it's very dull work; harder than yo' think on, Hester, – an' I
would ha' been home for tea to-night only I was afeard of baby
getting wet wi' t' storm o' hail as we had down on t' shore; and
we sheltered under a rock. It's a weary coming home to this
dark place, and to find my own mother set against me.'

'Take him his tea, like a good lassie. I'll answer for it he'll be
all right. A man takes it hardly when he comes in tired, a-
thinking his wife 'll be there to cheer him up a bit, to find her
off, and niver know nought of t' reason why.'

'I'm glad enough I've getten a baby,' said Sylvia, 'but for
aught else I wish I'd niver been married, I do!'

'Hush thee, lass!' said Hester, rising up indignant; 'now that
is a sin. Eh! if thou only knew the lot o' some folk. But let's talk
no more on that, that cannot be helped; go, take him his tea, for
it's a sad thing to think on him fasting all this time.'

Hester's voice was raised by the simple fact of her change of
position; and the word fasting caught Mrs Robson's ear, as she
sat at her knitting by the chimney-corner.

'Fasting? he said thou didn't care if he were full or fasting.
Lassie! it's not right in thee, I say; go, take him his tea at once.'

Sylvia rose, and gave up the baby, which she had been
suckling, to Nancy, who having done her washing, had come
for her charge, to put it to bed. Sylvia kissed it fondly, making a
little moan of sad, passionate tenderness as she did so. Then she
took the cup of tea; but she said, rather defiantly, to Hester, –

'I'll go to him with it, because mother bids me, and it'll ease
her mind.'

Then louder to her mother, she added, –

'Mother, I'll take him his tea, though I couldn't help the being
out.'

If the act itself was conciliatory, the spirit in which she was

going to do it was the reverse. Hester followed her slowly into
the ware-room, with intentional delay, thinking that her presence might be an obstacle to their mutually understanding one
another. Sylvia held the cup and plate of bread and butter out
to Philip, but avoided meeting his eye, and said not a word of
explanation, or regret, or self-justification. If she had spoken,
though ever so crossly, Philip would have been relieved, and
would have preferred it to her silence. He wanted to provoke
her to speech, but did not know how to begin.

'Thou's been out again wandering on that sea-shore!' said he.
She did not answer him. 'I cannot think what's always taking
thee there, when one would ha' thought a walk up to Esdale
would be far more sheltered, both for thee and baby in such
weather as this. Thou'll be having that baby ill some of these
days.'

At this, she looked up at him, and her lips moved as though
she were going to say something. Oh, how he wished she would,
that they might come to a wholesome quarrel, and a making
friends again, and a tender kissing, in which he might whisper
penitence for all his hasty words, or unreasonable vexation. But
she had come resolved not to speak, for fear of showing too
much passion, too much emotion. Only as she was going away
she turned and said, –

'Philip, mother hasn't many more years to live; dunnot grieve
her, and set her again' me by finding fault wi' me afore her. Our
being wed were a great mistake; but before t' poor old widow
woman let us make as if we were happy.'

'Sylvie! Sylvie!' he called after her. She must have heard, but
she did not turn. He went after her, and seized her by the arm
rather roughly; she had stung him to the heart with her calm
words, which seemed to reveal a long-formed conviction.

'Sylvie!' said he, almost fiercely, 'what do yo' mean by what
yo've said? Speak! I will have an answer.'

He almost shook her: she was half frightened by his vehemence of behaviour, which she took for pure anger, while it was
the outburst of agonized and unrequited love.

'Let me go! Oh, Philip, yo' hurt me!'

Just at this moment Hester came up; Philip was ashamed of
his passionate ways in her serene presence, and loosened his
grasp of his wife, and she ran away; ran into her mother's empty
room, as to a solitary place, and there burst into that sobbing,

miserable crying which we instinctively know is too surely lessening the length of our days on earth to be indulged in often.

When she had exhausted that first burst and lay weak and quiet for a time, she listened in dreading expectation of the sound of his footstep coming in search of her to make friends. But he was detained below on business, and never came. Instead, her mother came clambering up the stairs; she was now in the habit of going to bed between seven and eight, and to-night she was retiring at even an earlier hour.

Sylvia sprang up and drew down the window-blind, and made her face and manner as composed as possible, in order to soothe and comfort her mother's last waking hours. She helped her to bed with gentle patience; the restraint imposed upon her by her tender filial love was good for her, though all the time she was longing to be alone to have another wild outburst. When her mother was going off to sleep, Sylvia went to look at her baby, also in a soft sleep. Then she gazed out at the evening sky, high above the tiled roofs of the opposite houses, and the longing to be out under the peaceful heavens took possession of her once more.

'It's my only comfort,' said she to herself; 'and there's no earthly harm in it. I would ha' been at home to his tea, if I could; but when he doesn't want me, and mother doesn't want me, and baby is either in my arms or asleep; why, I'll go and cry my fill out under yon great quiet sky. I cannot stay in t' house to be choked up wi' my tears, nor yet to have him coming about me either for scolding or peace-making.'

So she put on her things and went out again; this time along the High Street, and up the long flights of steps towards the parish church, and there she stood and thought that here she had first met Kinraid, at Darley's burying, and she tried to recall the very look of all the sad, earnest faces round the open grave – the whole scene, in fact; and let herself give way to the miserable regrets she had so often tried to control. Then she walked on, crying bitterly, almost unawares to herself; on through the high, bleak fields at the summit of the cliffs; fields bounded by loose stone fences, and far from all sight of the habitation of man. But, below, the sea rose and raged; it was high water at the highest tide, and the wind blew gustily from the land, vainly combating the great waves that came invincibly up with a roar and an impotent furious dash against the base of the cliffs below.

Sylvia heard the sound of the passionate rush and rebound of many waters, like the shock of mighty guns, whenever the other sound of the blustering gusty wind was lulled for an instant. She was more quieted by this tempest of the elements than she would have been had all nature seemed as still as she had imagined it to be while she was yet in-doors and only saw a part of the serene sky.

She fixed on a certain point, in her own mind, which she would reach, and then turn back again. It was where the outline of the land curved inwards, dipping into a little bay. Here the field-path she had hitherto followed descended somewhat abruptly to a cluster of fishermen's cottages, hardly large enough to be called a village; and then the narrow roadway wound up the rising ground till it again reached the summit of the cliffs that stretched along the coast for many and many a mile.

Sylvia said to herself that she would turn homewards when she came within sight of this cove, Headlington Cove, they called it. All the way along she had met no one since she had left the town, but just as she had got over the last stile, or ladder of stepping-stones, into the field from which the path descended, she came upon a number of people – quite a crowd, in fact; men moving forward in a steady line, hauling at a rope, a chain, or something of that kind; boys, children, and women holding babies in their arms, as if all were fain to come out and partake in some general interest.

They kept within a certain distance from the edge of the cliff, and Sylvia, advancing a little, now saw the reason why. The great cable the men held was attached to some part of a smack, which could now be seen by her in the waters below, half dismantled, and all but a wreck, yet with her deck covered with living men, as far as the waning light would allow her to see. The vessel strained to get free of the strong guiding cable; the tide was turning, the wind was blowing off shore, and Sylvia knew without being told, that almost parallel to this was a line of sunken rocks that had been fatal to many a ship before now, if she had tried to take the inner channel instead of keeping out to sea for miles, and then steering in straight for Monkshaven port. And the ships that had been thus lost had been in good plight and order compared to this vessel, which seemed nothing but a hull without mast or sail.

By this time, the crowd – the fishermen from the hamlet down below, with their wives and children – all had come but the bedridden – had reached the place where Sylvia stood. The women, in a state of wild excitement, rushed on, encouraging their husbands and sons by words, even while they hindered them by actions; and, from time to time, one of them would run to the edge of the cliff and shout out some brave words of hope in her shrill voice to the crew on the deck below. Whether these latter heard it or not, no one could tell; but it seemed as if all human voice must be lost in the tempestuous stun and tumult of wind and wave. It was generally a woman with a child in her arms who so employed herself. As the strain upon the cable became greater, and the ground on which they strove more uneven, every hand was needed to hold and push, and all those women who were unencumbered held by the dear rope on which so many lives were depending. On they came, a long line of human beings, black against the ruddy sunset sky. As they came near Sylvia, a woman cried out, –

'Dunnot stand idle, lass, but houd on* wi' us; there's many a bonny life at stake, and many a mother's heart a-hangin' on this bit o' hemp. Tak' houd, lass, and give a firm grip, and God remember thee i' thy need.'

Sylvia needed no second word; a place was made for her, and in an instant more the rope was pulling against her hands till it seemed as though she was holding fire in her bare palms. Never a one of them thought of letting go for an instant, though when all was over many of their hands were raw and bleeding. Some strong, experienced fishermen passed a word along the line from time to time, giving directions as to how it should be held according to varying occasions, but few among the rest had breath or strength enough to speak. The women and children that accompanied them ran on before breaking down the loose stone fences, so as to obviate delay or hindrance; they talked continually, exhorting, encouraging, explaining. From their many words and fragmentary sentences, Sylvia learnt that the vessel was supposed to be a Newcastle smack sailing from London, that had taken the dangerous inner channel to save time, and had been caught in the storm, which she was too crazy* to withstand; and that if by some daring contrivance of the fishermen who had first seen her the cable had not been got ashore, she would have been cast upon the rocks before this, and 'all on board perished'.

'It were dayleet then,' quoth one woman; 'a could see their faces, they were so near. They were as pale as dead men, an' one was prayin' down on his knees. There was a king's officer aboard, for I saw t' gowd about him.'

'He'd maybe come from these hom'ard parts, and be comin' to see his own folk; else it's no common for king's officers to sail in aught but king's ships.'

'Eh! but it's gettin' dark! See there's t' leeghts in t' houses in t' New Town! T' grass is crispin' wi' t' white frost under our feet. It'll be a hard tug round t' point, and then she'll be gettin' into still waters.'

One more great pull and mighty strain, and the danger was past; the vessel – or what remained of her – was in the harbour, among the lights and cheerful sounds of safety. The fishermen sprang down the cliff to the quay side, anxious to see the men whose lives they had saved; the women, weary and over-excited, began to cry. Not Sylvia, however; her fount of tears had been exhausted earlier in the day: her principal feeling was of gladness and high rejoicing that they were saved who had been so near to death not half an hour before.

She would have liked to have seen the men, and shaken hands with them all round. But instead she must go home, and well would it be with her if she was in time for her husband's supper, and escaped any notice of her absence. So she separated herself from the groups of women who sat on the grass in the churchyard, awaiting the return of such of their husbands as could resist the fascinations of the Monkshaven public-houses. As Sylvia went down the church steps, she came upon one of the fishermen who had helped to tow the vessel into port.

'There was seventeen men and boys aboard her, and a navy-lieutenant as had comed as passenger. It were a good job as we could manage her. Good-neet to thee, thou'll sleep all t' sounder for havin' lent a hand.'

The street air felt hot and close after the sharp keen atmosphere of the heights above; the decent shops and houses had all their shutters put up, and were preparing for their early bed-time. Already lights shone here and there in the upper chambers, and Sylvia scarcely met any one.

She went round up the passage from the quay side, and in by the private door. All was still, the basins of bread and milk that she and her husband were in the habit of having for supper stood in the fender before the fire, each with a plate upon them. Nancy had gone to bed, Phœbe dozed in the kitchen; Philip was still in the ware-room, arranging goods and taking stock along with Coulson, for Hester had gone home to her mother.

Sylvia was not willing to go and seek out Philip, after the manner in which they had parted. All the despondency of her life became present to her again as she sat down within her home. She had forgotten it in her interest and excitement, but now it came back again.

Still she was hungry, and youthful, and tired. She took her basin up, and was eating her supper when she heard a cry of her baby upstairs, and ran away to attend to it. When it had been fed and hushed away to sleep, she went in to see her mother, attracted by some unusual noise in her room.

She found Mrs Robson awake, and restless, and ailing; dwelling much on what Philip had said in his anger against Sylvia. It was really necessary for her daughter to remain with her; so Sylvia stole out, and went quickly down-stairs to Philip – now sitting tired and worn out, and eating his supper with little or no appetite – and told him she meant to pass the night with her mother.

His answer of acquiescence was so short and careless, or so it seemed to her, that she did not tell him any more of what she had done or seen that evening, or even dwell upon any details of her mother's indisposition.

As soon as she had left the room, Philip set down his half-finished basin of bread and milk, and sat long, his face hidden in his folded arms. The wick of the candle grew long and black, and fell, and sputtered, and guttered; he sat on, unheeding either it or the pale grey fire that was dying out – dead at last.

CHAPTER 33

An Apparition

Mrs Robson was very poorly all night long. Uneasy thoughts seemed to haunt and perplex her brain, and she neither slept nor woke, but was restless and uneasy in her talk and movements.

Sylvia lay down by her, but got so little sleep, that at length she preferred sitting in the easy-chair by the bedside. Here she dropped off to slumber in spite of herself; the scene of the evening before seemed to be repeated; the cries of the many people, the heavy roar and dash of the threatening waves, were repeated in her ears; and something was said to her through all the conflicting noises – what it was she could not catch, though she strained to hear the hoarse murmur that, in her dream, she believed to convey a meaning of the utmost importance to her.

This dream, that mysterious, only half-intelligible sound, recurred whenever she dozed, and her inability to hear the words uttered distressed her so much, that at length she sat bolt upright, resolved to sleep no more. Her mother was talking in a half-conscious way; Philip's speech of the evening before was evidently running in her mind.

'Sylvie, if thou're not a good wife to him, it'll just break my heart outright. A woman should obey her husband, and not go her own gait. I never leave the house wi'out telling father, and getting his leave.'

And then she began to cry pitifully, and to say unconnected things, till Sylvia, to soothe her, took her hand, and promised never to leave the house without asking her husband's permission, though in making this promise, she felt as if she were sacrificing her last pleasure to her mother's wish; for she knew well enough that Philip would always raise objections to the rambles which reminded her of her old free open-air life.

But to comfort and cherish her mother she would have done anything; yet this very morning that was dawning, she must go and ask his permission for a simple errand, or break her word.

She knew from experience that nothing quieted her mother so well as balm-tea;* it might be that the herb really possessed some sedative power; it might be only early faith, and often repeated experience, but it had always had a tranquillizing effect; and more than once, during the restless hours of the night, Mrs Robson had asked for it; but Sylvia's stock of last year's dead leaves was exhausted. Still she knew where a plant of balm grew in the sheltered corner of Haytersbank Farm garden; she knew that the tenants who had succeeded them in the occupation of the farm had had to leave it in consequence of a death, and that the place was unoccupied; and in the darkness she had planned that if she could leave her mother after the dawn came, and she had attended to her baby, she would walk quickly to the old garden, and gather the tender sprigs which she was sure to find there.

Now she must go and ask Philip; and till she held her baby to her breast, she bitterly wished that she were free from the duties and chains of matrimony. But the touch of its waxen fingers, the hold of its little mouth, made her relax into docility and gentleness. She gave it back to Nancy to be dressed, and softly opened the door of Philip's bed-room.

'Philip!' said she, gently. 'Philip!'

He started up from dreams of her; of her, angry. He saw her there, rather pale with her night's watch and anxiety, but looking meek, and a little beseeching.

'Mother has had such a bad night! she fancied once as some balm-tea would do her good – it allays used to: but my dried balm is all gone, and I thought there'd be sure to be some in t' old garden at Haytersbank. Feyther planted a bush just for mother, wheere it allays came up early, nigh t' old elder-tree; and if yo'd not mind, I could run theere while she sleeps, and be back again in an hour, and it's not seven now.'

'Thou's not wear thyself out with running, Sylvie,' said Philip, eagerly; 'I'll get up and go myself, or, perhaps,' continued he, catching the shadow that was coming over her face, 'thou'd rather go thyself: it's only that I'm so afraid of thy tiring thyself.'

'It'll not tire me,' said Sylvia. 'Afore I was married, I was out often far farther than that, afield to fetch up t' kine, before my breakfast.'

'Well, go if thou will,' said Philip. 'But get somewhat to eat first, and don't hurry; there's no need for that.'

She had got her hat and shawl, and was off before he had finished his last words.

The long High Street was almost empty of people at that early hour; one side was entirely covered by the cool morning shadow which lay on the pavement, and crept up the opposite houses till only the topmost story caught the rosy sunlight. Up the hill-road, through the gap in the stone wall, across the dewy fields, Sylvia went by the very shortest path she knew.

She had only once been at Haytersbank since her wedding-day. On that occasion the place had seemed strangely and dissonantly changed by the numerous children who were diverting themselves before the open door, and whose playthings and clothes strewed the house-place, and made it one busy scene of confusion and untidiness, more like the Corneys' kitchen in former times, than her mother's orderly and quiet abode. Those little children were fatherless now; and the house was shut up, awaiting the entry of some new tenant. There were no shutters to shut; the long low window was blinking in the rays of the morning sun; the house and cow-house doors were closed, and no poultry wandered about the field in search of stray grains of corn, or early worms. It was a strange and unfamiliar silence, and struck solemnly on Sylvia's mind. Only a thrush in the old orchard down in the hollow, out of sight, whistled and gurgled with continual shrill melody.

Sylvia went slowly past the house and down the path leading to the wild, deserted bit of garden. She saw that the last tenants had had a pump sunk for them, and resented the innovation, as though the well she was passing could feel the insult. Over it grew two hawthorn trees; on the bent trunk of one of them she used to sit, long ago: the charm of the position being enhanced by the possible danger of falling into the well and being drowned. The rusty unused chain was wound round the wind-lass; the bucket was falling to pieces from dryness. A lean cat came from some outhouse, and mewed pitifully with hunger; accompanying Sylvia to the garden, as if glad of some human companionship, yet refusing to allow itself to be touched. Primroses grew in the sheltered places, just as they formerly did; and made the uncultivated ground seem less deserted than the garden, where the last year's weeds were rotting away, and cumbering the ground.

Sylvia forced her way through the berry bushes to the herb-plot, and plucked the tender leaves she had come to seek; sighing a little all the time. Then she retraced her steps; paused softly before the house-door, and entered the porch and kissed the senseless wood.*

She tried to tempt the poor gaunt cat into her arms, meaning to carry it home and befriend it; but it was scared by her endeavour and ran back to its home in the outhouse, making a green path across the white dew of the meadow. Then Sylvia began to hasten home, thinking, and remembering – at the stile that led into the road she was brought short up.

Some one stood in the lane just on the other side of the gap; his back was to the morning sun; all she saw at first was the uniform of a naval officer, so well known in Monkshaven in those days.

Sylvia went hurrying past him, not looking again, although her clothes almost brushed his, as he stood there still. She had not gone a yard – no, not half a yard – when her heart leaped up and fell again dead within her,* as if she had been shot.

'Sylvia!' he said, in a voice tremulous with joy and passionate love. 'Sylvia!'

She looked round; he had turned a little, so that the light fell straight on his face. It was bronzed, and the lines were strengthened; but it was the same face she had last seen in Haytersbank Gully three long years ago, and had never thought to see in life again.

He was close to her and held out his fond arms, she went fluttering towards their embrace, as if drawn by the old fascination; but when she felt them close round her, she started away, and cried out with a great pitiful shriek, and put her hands up to her forehead as if trying to clear away some bewildering mist.

Then she looked at him once more, a terrible story in her eyes, if he could but have read it.

Twice she opened her stiff lips to speak, and twice the words were overwhelmed by the surges of her misery, which bore them back into the depths of her heart.

He thought that he had come upon her too suddenly, and he attempted to soothe her with soft murmurs of love, and to woo her to his outstretched hungry arms once more. But when she saw this motion of his, she made a gesture as though pushing him away; and with an inarticulate moan of agony she put her hands to her head once more, and turning away began to run blindly towards the town for protection.

For a minute or so he was stunned with surprise at her behaviour; and then he thought it accounted for by the shock of his accost,* and that she needed time to understand the unexpected joy. So he followed her swiftly, ever keeping her in view, but not trying to overtake her too speedily.

'I have frightened my poor love,' he kept thinking. And by this thought he tried to repress his impatience and check the speed he longed to use; yet he was always so near behind that her quickened sense heard his well-known footsteps following, and a mad notion flashed across her brain that she would go to the wide full river, and end the hopeless misery she felt enshrouding her. There was a sure hiding-place from all human reproach and heavy mortal woe beneath the rushing waters borne landwards by the morning tide.

No one can tell what changed her course; perhaps the thought of her sucking child; perhaps her mother; perhaps an angel of God; no one on earth knows, but as she ran along the quay-side she all at once turned up an entry, and through an open door.

He, following all the time, came into a quiet dark parlour, with a cloth and tea-things on the table ready for breakfast; the change from the bright sunny air out of doors to the deep shadow of this room made him think for the first moment that she had passed on, and that no one was there, and he stood for an instant baffled, and hearing no sound but the beating of his own heart; but an irrepressible sobbing gasp made him look round, and there he saw her cowered behind the door, her face covered tight up, and sharp shudders going through her whole frame.

'My love, my darling!' said he, going up to her, and trying to raise her, and to loosen her hands away from her face. 'I've been too sudden for thee: it was thoughtless in me; but I have so looked forward to this time, and seeing thee come along the field, and go past me, but I should ha' been more tender and careful of thee. Nay! let me have another look of thy sweet face.'

All this he whispered in the old tones of manoeuvring love, in that voice she had yearned and hungered to hear in life, and had not heard, for all her longing, save in her dreams.

She tried to crouch more and more into the corner, into the hidden shadow – to sink into the ground out of sight.

Once more he spoke, beseeching her to lift up her face, to let him hear her speak.

But she only moaned.

'Sylvia!' said he, thinking he could change his tactics, and pique her into speaking, that he would make pretence of suspicion and offence.

'Sylvia! one would think you weren't glad to see me back again at length. I only came in late last night, and my first thought on wakening was of you; it has been ever since I left you.'

Sylvia took her hands away from her face; it was grey as the face of death; her awful eyes were passionless in her despair.

'Where have yo' been?' she asked, in slow, hoarse tones, as if her voice were half strangled within her.

'Been!' said he, a red light coming into his eyes, as he bent his looks upon her; now, indeed, a true and not an assumed suspicion entering his mind.

'Been!' he repeated; then, coming a step nearer to her, and taking her hand, not tenderly this time, but with a resolution to be satisfied.

'Did not your cousin – Hepburn, I mean – did not he tell you? – he saw the press-gang seize me – I gave him a message to you – I bade you keep true to me as I would be to you.'

Between every clause of this speech he paused and gasped for her answer; but none came. Her eyes dilated and held his steady gaze prisoner as with a magical charm – neither could look away from the other's wild, searching gaze. When he had ended, she was silent for a moment, then she cried out, shrill and fierce –

'Philip!' No answer.

Wilder and shriller still, 'Philip!' she cried.

He was in the distant ware-room completing the last night's work before the regular shop hours began; before breakfast, also, that his wife might not find him waiting and impatient.

He heard her cry; it cut through doors, and still air, and great bales of woollen stuff; he thought that she had hurt herself, that her mother was worse, that her baby was ill, and he hastened to the spot whence the cry proceeded.

On opening the door that separated the shop from the sitting-room, he saw the back of a naval officer, and his wife on the ground, huddled up in a heap; when she perceived him come in, she dragged herself up by means of a chair, groping like a blind person, and came and stood facing him.

The officer turned fiercely round, and would have come towards Philip, who was so bewildered by the scene that even yet he did not understand who the stranger was – did not perceive for an instant that he saw the realization of his greatest dread.

But Sylvia laid her hand on Kinraid's arm, and assumed to herself the right of speech. Philip did not know her voice, it was so changed.

'Philip,' she said, 'this is Kinraid come back again to wed me. He is alive; he has niver been dead, only taken by t' press-gang. And he says yo' saw it, and knew it all t' time. Speak, was it so?'

Philip knew not what to say, whither to turn, under what refuge of words or acts to shelter.

Sylvia's influence was keeping Kinraid silent, but he was rapidly passing beyond it.

'Speak!' he cried, loosening himself from Sylvia's light grasp, and coming towards Philip, with a threatening gesture. 'Did I not bid you tell her how it was? Did I not bid you say how I would be faithful to her, and she was to be faithful to me? Oh! you damned scoundrel! have you kept it from her all that time, and let her think me dead, or false? Take that!'

His closed fist was up to strike the man, who hung his head with bitterest shame and miserable self-reproach; but Sylvia came swift between the blow and its victim.

'Charley, thou shan't strike him,' she said. 'He is a damned scoundrel' (this was said in the hardest, quietest tone), 'but he is my husband.'

'Oh! thou false heart!' exclaimed Kinraid, turning sharp on her. 'If ever I trusted woman, I trusted you, Sylvia Robson.'

He made as though throwing her from him, with a gesture of contempt that stung her to life.

'Oh, Charley!' she cried, springing to him, 'dunnot cut me to the quick; have pity on me, though he had none. I did so love thee; it was my very heart-strings as gave way when they told me thou was drowned – feyther, and th' Corneys, and all, iverybody. Thy hat and t' bit o' ribbon I gave thee were found drenched and dripping wi' sea-water; and I went mourning for thee all the day long – dunnot turn away from me; only hearken this once, and then kill me dead, and I'll bless yo' – and have niver been mysel' since; niver ceased to feel t' sun grow dark and th' air chill and dreary when I thought on t' time when thou was alive. I did, my Charley, my own love! And I thought thou was dead for iver, and I wished I were lying bes'ide thee. Oh,

Charley! Philip, theere, where he stands, could tell yo' this was true. Philip, wasn't it so?'

'Would God I were dead!' moaned forth the unhappy, guilty man. But she had turned to Kinraid, and was speaking again to him, and neither of them heard or heeded him – they were drawing closer and closer together – she, with her cheeks and eyes aflame, talking eagerly.

'And feyther was taken up, and all for setting some free as t' press-gang had gotten by a foul trick; and he were put i' York prison, and tried, and hung! – hung! Charley! – good kind feyther was hung on a gallows; and mother lost her sense and grew silly in grief, and we were like to be turned out on t' wide world, and poor mother dateless – and I thought yo' were dead – oh! I thought yo' were dead, I did – oh, Charley, Charley!'

By this time they were in each other's arms, she with her head on his shoulder, crying as if her heart would break.

Philip came forwards and took hold of her to pull her away; but Charley held her tight, mutely defying Philip. Unconsciously she was Philip's protection, in that hour of danger, from a blow which might have been his death if strong will could have aided it to kill.

'Sylvie!' said he grasping her tight. 'Listen to me. He didn't love yo' as I did. He had loved other women. I, yo' – yo' alone. He loved other girls before yo', and had left off loving 'em. I – I wish God would free my heart from the pang; but it will go on till I die, whether yo' love me or not. And then – where was I? Oh! that very night that he was taken, I was a-thinking on yo' and on him; and I might ha' given yo' his message, but I heard them speaking of him as knew him well; talking of his false fickle ways. How was I to know he would keep true to thee? It might be a sin in me, I cannot say; my heart and my sense are gone dead within me. I know this, I've loved yo' as no man but me ever loved before. Have some pity and forgiveness on me, if it's only because I've been so tormented with my love.'

He looked at her with feverish eager wistfulness, it faded away into despair as she made no sign of having even heard his words. He let go his hold of her, and his arm fell loosely by his side.

'I may die,' he said, 'for my life is ended!'

'Sylvia!' spoke out Kinraid, bold and fervent, 'your marriage is no marriage. You were tricked into it. You are my wife, not his. I am your husband; we plighted each other our troth. See! here is my half of the sixpence.'*

He pulled it out from his bosom, tied by a black ribbon round his neck.

'When they stripped me and searched me in th' French prison, I managed to keep this. No lies can break the oath we swore to each other. I can get your pretence of a marriage set aside. I'm in favour with my admiral, and he'll do a deal for me, and back me out.* Come with me; your marriage shall be set aside, and we'll be married again, all square and above board. Come away. Leave that damned fellow to repent of the trick he played an honest sailor; we'll be true, whatever has come and gone. Come, Sylvia.'

His arm was round her waist, and he was drawing her towards the door, his face all crimson with eagerness and hope. Just then the baby cried.

'Hark!' said she, starting away from Kinraid, 'baby's crying for me. His child – yes, it is his child – I'd forgotten that – forgotten all. I'll make my vow now, lest I lose mysel' again. I'll never forgive yon man, nor live with him as his wife again. All that's done and ended. He's spoilt my life – he's spoilt it for as long as iver I live on this earth; but neither yo' nor him shall spoil my soul. It goes hard wi' me, Charley, it does indeed. I'll just give yo' one kiss – one little kiss – and then, so help me God, I'll niver see nor hear till – no, not that, not that is needed – I'll niver see – sure that's enough – I'll niver see yo' again on this side heaven, so help me God! I'm bound and tied, but I've sworn my oath to him as well as yo': there's things I will do, and there's things I won't. Kiss me once more. God help me, he's gone!'

CHAPTER 34

A Reckless Recruit

She lay across a chair, her arms helplessly stretched out, her face unseen. Every now and then a thrill ran through her body: she was talking to herself all the time with incessant low incontinence* of words.

Philip stood near her, motionless: he did not know whether she was conscious of his presence; in fact, he knew nothing but that he and she were sundered for ever; he could only take in that one idea, and it numbed all other thought.

Once more her baby cried for the comfort she alone could give. She rose to her feet, but staggered when she tried to walk; her glazed eyes fell upon Philip as he instinctively made a step to hold her steady. No light came into her eyes any more than if she had looked upon a perfect stranger; not even was there the contraction of dislike. Some other figure filled her mind, and she saw him no more than she saw the inanimate table. That way of looking at him withered him up more than any sign of aversion would have done.

He watched her laboriously climb the stairs, and vanish out of sight; and sat down with a sudden feeling of extreme bodily weakness.

The door of communication between the parlour and the shop was opened. That was the first event of which Philip took note; but Phœbe had come in unawares to him, with the intention of removing the breakfast things on her return from market, and seeing them unused, and knowing that Sylvia had sat up all night with her mother, she had gone back to the kitchen. Philip had neither seen nor heard her.

Now Coulson came in, amazed at Hepburn's non-appearance in the shop.

'Why! Philip, what's ado? How ill yo' look, man!' exclaimed he, thoroughly alarmed by Philip's ghastly appearance. 'What's the matter?'

'I!' said Philip, slowly gathering his thoughts. 'Why should there be anything the matter?'

His instinct, quicker to act than his reason, made him shrink from his misery being noticed, much more made any subject for explanation or sympathy.

'There may be nothing the matter wi' thee,' said Coulson, 'but thou's the look of a corpse on thy face. I was afeard something was wrong, for it's half-past nine, and thee so punctual!'

He almost guarded Philip into the shop, and kept furtively watching him, and perplexing himself, with Philip's odd strange ways.

Hester, too, observed the heavy broken-down expression on

Philip's ashen face, and her heart ached for him; but after that first glance, which told her so much, she avoided all appearance of noticing or watching. Only a shadow brooded over her sweet, calm face, and once or twice she sighed to herself.

It was market-day, and people came in and out, bringing their store of gossip from the country, or the town – from the farm or the quay-side.

Among the pieces of news, the rescue of the smack the night before furnished a large topic; and by-and-by Philip heard a name that startled him into attention.

The landlady of a small public-house much frequented by sailors was talking to Coulson.

'There was a sailor aboard of her as knowed Kinraid by sight, in Shields, years ago; and he called him by his name afore they were well out o' t' river. And Kinraid was no ways set up, for all his lieutenant's uniform (and eh! but they say he looks handsome in it!); but he tells 'm all about it – how he was pressed aboard a man-o'-war, an' for his good conduct were made a warrant officer, boatswain, or something!'

All the people in the shop were listening now; Philip alone seemed engrossed in folding up a piece of cloth, so as to leave no possible chance of creases in it; yet he lost not a syllable of the good woman's narration.

She, pleased with the enlarged audience her tale had attracted, went on with fresh vigour.

'An' there's a gallant captain, one Sir Sidney Smith,* and he'd a notion o' goin' smack into a French port, an' carryin' off a vessel from right under their very noses; an' says he, "Which of yo' British sailors 'll go along with me to death or glory?" So Kinraid stands up like a man, an' "I'll go with yo', captain," he says. So they, an' some others as brave, went off, an' did their work, an' choose whativer it was, they did it famously; but they got caught by them French, an' were clapped into prison i' France for iver so long; but at last one Philip – Philip somethin' (he were a Frenchman, I know)* – helped 'em to escape, in a fishin'-boat. But they were welcomed by th' whole British squadron as was i' t' Channel for t' piece of daring they'd done i' cuttin' out t' strip from a French port; an' Captain Sir Sidney Smith was made an admiral, an' him as we used t' call Charley Kinraid, the specksioneer, is made a lieutenant, an' a commissioned officer i' t' King's service; and is come to great glory, and slep in my house this very blessed night as is just past!'

A murmur of applause and interest and rejoicing buzzed all around Philip. All this was publicly known about Kinraid, – and how much more? All Monkshaven might hear to-morrow – nay, to-day – of Philip's treachery to the hero of the hour; how he had concealed his fate, and supplanted him in his love.

Philip shrank from the burst of popular indignation which he knew must follow. Any wrong done to one who stands on the pinnacle of the people's favour is resented by each individual as a personal injury; and among a primitive set of country-folk, who recognize the wild passion in love, as it exists untamed by the trammels of reason and self-restraint, any story of baulked affections, or treachery in such matters, spreads like wildfire.

Philip knew this quite well; his doom of disgrace lay plain before him, if only Kinraid spoke the word. His head was bent down while he thus listened and reflected. He half resolved on doing something; he lifted up his head, caught the reflection of his face in the little strip of glass on the opposite side, in which the women might look at themselves in their contemplated purchases, and quite resolved.

The sight he saw in the mirror was his own long, sad, pale face, made plainer and greyer by the heavy pressure of the morning's events. He saw his stooping figure, his rounded shoulders, with something like a feeling of disgust at his personal appearance as he remembered the square, upright build of Kinraid; his fine uniform, with epaulette and sword-belt; his handsome brown face; his dark eyes, splendid with the fire of passion and indignation; his white teeth, gleaming out with the terrible smile of scorn.

The comparison drove Philip from passive hopelessness to active despair.

He went abruptly from the crowded shop into the empty parlour, and on into the kitchen, where he took up a piece of bread, and heedless of Phœbe's look and words, began to eat it before he even left the place; for he needed the strength that food would give; he needed it to carry him out of the sight and the knowledge of all who might hear what he had done, and point their fingers at him.

He paused a moment in the parlour, and then, setting his teeth tight together, he went upstairs.

First of all he went into the bit of a room opening out of theirs, in which his baby slept. He dearly loved the child, and many a time would run in and play a while with it; and in such gambols he and Sylvia had passed their happiest moments of wedded life.

The little Bella was having her morning slumber; Nancy used to tell long afterwards how he knelt down by the side of her cot, and was so strange she thought he must have prayed, for all it was nigh upon eleven o'clock, and folk in their senses only said their prayers when they got up, and when they went to bed.

Then he rose, and stooped over, and gave the child a long, lingering, soft, fond kiss.

And on tip-toe he passed away into the room where his aunt lay; his aunt who had been so true a friend to him! He was thankful to know that in her present state she was safe from the knowledge of what was past, safe from the sound of the shame to come.

He had not meant to see Sylvia again; he dreaded the look of her hatred, her scorn, but there, outside her mother's bed, she lay, apparently asleep. Mrs Robson, too, was sleeping, her face towards the wall. Philip could not help it; he went to have one last look at his wife. She was turned towards her mother, her face averted from him; he could see the tear-stains, the swollen eyelids, the lips yet quivering: he stooped down, and bent to kiss the little hand that lay listless by her side. As his hot breath neared that hand it was twitched away, and a shiver ran through the whole prostrate body. And then he knew that she was not asleep, only worn out by her misery, – misery that he had caused.

He sighed heavily; but he went away, downstairs, and away for ever. Only as he entered the parlour his eyes caught on two silhouettes, one of himself, one of Sylvia, done in the first month of their marriage, by some wandering artist, if so he could be called. They were hanging against the wall in little oval wooden frames; black profiles, with the lights done in gold; about as poor semblances of humanity as could be conceived; but Philip went up, and after looking for a minute or so at Sylvia's, he took it down, and buttoned his waistcoat over it.

It was the only thing he took away from his home.

He went down the entry on to the quay. The river was there, and waters, they say, have a luring power, and a weird promise of rest in their perpetual monotony of sound. But many people were there, if such a temptation presented itself to Philip's mind; the sight his fellow-townsmen, perhaps of his acquaintances, drove him up another entry – the town is burrowed with such – back into the High Street, which he straightway crossed into a well-known court, out of which rough steps led to the summit of the hill, and on to the fells and moors beyond.

He plunged and panted up this rough ascent. From the top he could look down on the whole town lying below, severed by the bright shining river into two parts. To the right lay the sea, shimmering and heaving; there were the cluster of masts rising out of the little port; the irregular roofs of the houses; which of them, thought he, as he carried his eye along the quay-side to the market-place, which of them was his? and he singled it out in its unfamiliar aspect, and saw the thin blue smoke rising from the kitchen chimney, where even now Phœbe was cooking the household meal that he never more must share.

Up at that thought and away, he knew not nor cared not whither. He went through the ploughed fields where the corn was newly springing; he came down upon the vast sunny sea, and turned his back upon it with loathing; he made his way inland to the high green pastures; the short upland turf above which the larks hung poised 'at heaven's gate'.* He strode along, so straight and heedless of briar and bush, that the wild black cattle ceased from grazing, and looked after him with their great blank puzzled eyes.

He had passed all enclosures and stone fences now, and was fairly on the desolate brown moors; through the withered last year's ling and fern, through the prickly gorse, he tramped, crushing down the tender shoots of this year's growth, and heedless of the startled plover's cry, goaded by the furies.* His only relief from thought, from the remembrance of Sylvia's looks and words, was in violent bodily action.

So he went on till evening shadows and ruddy evening lights came out upon the wild fells.

He had crossed roads and lanes, with a bitter avoidance of men's tracks; but now the strong instinct of self-preservation came out, and his aching limbs, his weary heart, giving great pants and beats for a time, and then ceasing altogether till a mist swam and quivered before his aching eyes, warned him that he must find some shelter and food, or lie down to die. He fell down now, often; stumbling over the slightest obstacle. He had passed the cattle pastures; he was among the blackfaced sheep; and they, too, ceased nibbling, and looked after him, and somehow, in his poor wandering imagination, their silly faces turned to likenesses of Monkshaven people – people who ought to be far, far away.

'Thou'll be belated* on these fells, if thou doesn't tak' heed,' shouted some one.

Philip looked abroad to see whence the voice proceeded.

An old stiff-legged shepherd, in a smock-frock, was within a couple of hundred yards. Philip did not answer, but staggered and stumbled towards him.

'Good lork!' said the man, 'wheere hast ta been? Thou's seen Oud Harry,* I think, thou looks so scared.'

Philip rallied himself, and tried to speak up to the old standard of respectability; but the effort was pitiful to see, had any one been by, who could have understood the pain it caused to restrain cries of bodily and mental agony.

'I've lost my way, that's all.'

'Twould ha' been enough, too, I'm thinkin', if I hadn't come out after t' ewes. There's t' Three Griffins near at hand: a sup o' Hollands 'll set thee to reeghts.'

Philip followed faintly. He could not see before him, and was guided by the sound of footsteps rather than by the sight of the figure moving onwards. He kept stumbling; and he knew that the old shepherd swore at him; but he also knew such curses proceeded from no ill-will, only from annoyance at the delay in going and 'seein' after t' ewes'. But had the man's words conveyed the utmost expression of hatred, Philip would neither have wondered at them, nor resented them.

They came into a wild mountain road, unfenced from the fells. A hundred yards off, and there was a small public-house, with a broad ruddy oblong of firelight shining across the tract.

'Theere!' said the old man. 'Thee cannot well miss that. A dunno tho', thee bees sich a gawby.'*

So he went on, and delivered Philip safely up to the landlord.

'Here's a felly as a fund on t' fell side, just as one as if he were drunk; but he's sober enough, a reckon, only summat's wrong i' his head, a'm thinkin'.'

'No!' said Philip, sitting down on the first chair he came to.

'I'm right enough; just fairly wearied out: lost my way,' and he fainted.

There was a recruiting sergeant of marines sitting in the house-place, drinking. He, too, like Philip, had lost his way; but was turning his blunder to account by telling all manner of wonderful stories to two or three rustics who had come in ready to drink on any pretence; especially if they could get good liquor without paying for it.

The sergeant rose as Philip fell back, and brought up his own mug of beer, into which a noggin of gin had been put (called in Yorkshire 'dog's-nose'). He partly poured and partly spilt some of this beverage on Philip's face; some drops went through the pale and parted lips, and with a start the worn-out man revived.

'Bring him some victual, landlord,' called out the recruiting sergeant. 'I'll stand shot.'*

They brought some cold bacon and coarse oat-cake. The sergeant asked for pepper and salt; minced the food fine and made it savoury, and kept administering it by teaspoonfuls; urging Philip to drink from time to time from his own cup of dog's-nose.

A burning thirst, which needed no stimulant from either pepper or salt, took possession of Philip, and he drank freely, scarcely recognizing what he drank. It took effect on one so habitually sober, and he was soon in that state when the imagination works wildly and freely.

He saw the sergeant before him, handsome, and bright, and active, in his gay red uniform, without a care, as it seemed to Philip, taking life lightly; admired and respected everywhere because of his cloth.

If Philip were gay, and brisk, well-dressed like him, returning with martial glory to Monkshaven, would not Sylvia love him once more? Could not he win her heart? He was brave by nature, and the prospect of danger did not daunt him, if ever it presented itself to his imagination.

He thought he was cautious in entering on the subject of enlistment with his new friend, the sergeant; but the latter was twenty times as cunning as he, and knew by experience how to bait his hook.

Philip was older by some years than the regulation age; but, at that time of great demand for men, the question of age was lightly entertained. The sergeant was profuse in statements of the advantages presented to a man of education in his branch of the service; how such a one was sure to rise; in fact, it would have seemed from the sergeant's account, as though the difficulty consisted in remaining in the ranks.

Philip's dizzy head thought the subject over and over again, each time with failing power of reason.

At length, almost, as it would seem, by some sleight of hand, he found the fatal shilling* in his palm, and had promised to go before the nearest magistrate to be sworn in as one of his Majesty's marines the next morning. And after that he remembered nothing more.

He wakened up in a little truckle-bed* in the same room as the sergeant, who lay sleeping the sleep of full contentment; while gradually, drop by drop, the bitter recollections of the day before came, filling up Philip's cup of agony.

He knew that he had received the bounty-money;* and though he was aware that he had been partly tricked into it, and had no hope, no care, indeed, for any of the advantages so liberally promised him the night before, yet he was resigned, with utterly despondent passiveness, to the fate to which he had pledged himself. Anything was welcome that severed him from his former life, that could make him forget it, if that were possible; and also welcome anything which increased the chances of death without the sinfulness of his own participation in the act. He found in the dark recess of his mind the dead body of his fancy of the previous night; that he might come home, handsome and glorious, to win the love that had never been his.

But he only sighed over it, and put it aside out of his sight – so full of despair was he. He could eat no breakfast, though the sergeant ordered of the best. The latter kept watching his new recruit out of the corner of his eye, expecting a remonstrance, or dreading a sudden bolt.

But Philip walked with him the two or three miles in the most submissive silence, never uttering a syllable of regret or repentance; and before Justice Cholmeley, of Holm Fell Hall,* he was sworn into his Majesty's service, under the name of Stephen Freeman.* With a new name, he began a new life. Alas! the old life lives for ever!

CHAPTER 35

Things Unutterable*

After Philip had passed out of the room, Sylvia lay perfectly still, from very exhaustion. Her mother slept on, happily unconscious of all the turmoil that had taken place; yes, happily, though the heavy sleep was to end in death. But of this her daughter knew nothing, imagining that it was refreshing slumber, instead of an ebbing of life. Both mother and daughter lay motionless till Phœbe entered the room to tell Sylvia that dinner was on the table.

Then Sylvia sat up, and put back her hair, bewildered and uncertain as to what was to be done next; how she should meet the husband to whom she had discarded all allegiance, repudiated the solemn promise of love and obedience which she had vowed.

Phœbe came into the room, with natural interest in the invalid, scarcely older than herself.

'How is t' old lady?' asked she, in a low voice.

Sylvia turned her head round to look; her mother had never moved, but was breathing in a loud uncomfortable manner, that made her stoop over her to see the averted face more nearly.

'Phœbe!' she cried, 'come here! She looks strange and odd; her eyes are open, but don't see me. Phœbe! Phœbe!'

'Sure enough, she's in a bad way!' said Phœbe, climbing stiffly on to the bed to have a nearer view. 'Hold her head a little up t' ease her breathin' while I go for master; he'll be for sendin' for t' doctor, I'll be bound.'

Sylvia took her mother's head and laid it fondly on her breast, speaking to her and trying to rouse her; but it was of no avail: the hard, stertorous breathing grew worse and worse.

Sylvia cried out for help; Nancy came, the baby in her arms. They had been in several times before that morning; and the child came smiling and crowing at its mother, who was supporting her own dying parent.

'Oh, Nancy!' said Sylvia; 'what is the matter with mother? yo' can see her face; tell me quick!'

Nancy set the baby on the bed for all reply, and ran out of the room, crying out,

'Master! master! Come quick! T' old missus is a-dying!'

This appeared to be no news to Sylvia, and yet the words came on her with a great shock, but for all that she could not cry; she was surprised herself at her own deadness of feeling.

Her baby crawled to her, and she had to hold and guard both her mother and her child. It seemed a long, long time before any one came, and then she heard muffled voices, and a heavy tramp: it was Phœbe leading the doctor upstairs, and Nancy creeping in behind to hear his opinion.

He did not ask many questions, and Phœbe replied more frequently to his inquiries than did Sylvia, who looked into his face with a blank, tearless, speechless despair, that gave him more pain than the sight of her dying mother.

The long decay of Mrs Robson's faculties and health, of which he was well aware, had in a certain manner prepared him for some such sudden termination of the life whose duration was hardly desirable, although he gave several directions as to her treatment; but the white, pinched face, the great dilated eye, the slow comprehension of the younger woman, struck him with alarm; and he went on asking for various particulars, more with a view of rousing Sylvia, if even it were to tears, than for any other purpose that the information thus obtained could answer.

'You had best have pillows propped up behind her — it will not be for long; she does not know that you are holding her, and it is only tiring you to no purpose!'

Sylvia's terrible stare continued; he put his advice into action, and gently tried to loosen her clasp, and tender hold. This she resisted; laying her cheek against her poor mother's unconscious face.

'Where is Hepburn?' said he. 'He ought to be here!'

Phœbe looked at Nancy, Nancy at Phœbe. It was the latter who replied,

'He's neither i' t' house nor i' t' shop. A seed him go past t' kitchen window better nor an hour ago; but neither William Coulson nor Hester Rose knows where he's gone to.'

Dr Morgan's lips were puckered up into a whistle, but he made no sound.

'Give me baby!' he said, suddenly. Nancy had taken her up off the bed where she had been sitting, encircled by her mother's arm. The nursemaid gave her to the doctor. He watched the mother's eye, it followed her child, and he was rejoiced. He gave a little pinch to the baby's soft flesh, and she cried out piteously; again the same action, the same result. Sylvia laid her mother down, and stretched out her arms for her child, hushing it, and moaning over it.

'So far so good!' said Dr Morgan to himself. 'But where is the husband? He ought to be here.' He went downstairs to make inquiry for Philip; that poor young creature, about whose health he had never felt thoroughly satisfied since the fever after her confinement, was in an anxious condition, and with an inevitable shock awaiting her. Her husband ought to be with her, and supporting her to bear it.

Dr Morgan went into the shop. Hester alone was there. Coulson had gone to his comfortable dinner at his well-ordered house, with his common-place wife. If he had felt anxious about Philip's looks and strange disappearance, he had also managed to account for them in some indifferent way.

Hester was alone with the shop-boy; few people came in during the universal Monkshaven dinner-hour. She was resting her head on her hand, and puzzled and distressed about many things – all that was implied by the proceedings of the evening before between Philip and Sylvia; and that was confirmed by Philip's miserable looks and strange abstracted ways to-day. Oh! how easy Hester would have found it to make him happy! not merely how easy, but what happiness it would have been to her to merge her every wish into the one great object of fulfilling his will. To her, an on-looker, the course of married life, which should lead to perfect happiness, seemed so plain! Alas! it is often so! and the resisting forces which make all such harmony and delight impossible are not recognized by the bystanders, hardly by the actors. But if these resisting forces are only superficial, or constitutional, they are but the necessary discipline here, and do not radically affect the love which will make all things right in heaven.

Some glimmering of this latter comforting truth shed its light on Hester's troubled thoughts from time to time. But again, how easy would it have been to her to tread the maze that led to Philip's happiness; and how difficult it seemed to the wife he had chosen!

She was aroused by Dr Morgan's voice.

'So both Coulson and Hepburn have left the shop to your

care, Hester. I want Hepburn, though; his wife is in a very
anxious state. Where is he? can you tell me?'

'Sylvia in an anxious state! I've not seen her to-day, but last
night she looked as well as could be.'

'Ay, ay; but many a thing happens in four-and-twenty hours.
Her mother is dying, may be dead by this time; and her husband
should be there with her. Can't you send for him?'

'I don't know where he is,' said Hester. 'He went off from
here all on a sudden, when there was all the market-folks in t'
shop; I thought he'd maybe gone to John Foster's about th'
money, for they was paying a deal in. I'll send there and inquire.'

No! the messenger brought back word that he had not been
seen at their bank all morning. Further inquiries were made by
the anxious Hester, by the doctor, by Coulson; all they could
learn was that Phœbe had seen him pass the kitchen window
about eleven o'clock, when she was peeling the potatoes for
dinner; and two lads playing on the quay-side thought they had
seen him among a group of sailors; but these latter, as far as
they could be identified, had no knowlededge of his appearance
among them.

Before night the whole town was excited about his disappearance. Before night Bell Robson had gone to her long home.*
And Sylvia still lay quiet and tearless, apparently more unmoved
than any other creature by the events of the day, and the strange
vanishing of her husband.

The only thing she seemed to care for was her baby; she held
it tight in her arms, and Dr Morgan bade them leave it there, its
touch might draw the desired tears into her weary, sleepless
eyes, and charm the aching pain out of them.

They were afraid lest she should inquire for her husband,
whose non-appearance at such a time of sorrow to his wife must
(they thought) seem strange to her. And night drew on while
they were all in this state. She had gone back to her own room
without a word when they had desired her to do so; caressing
her child in her arms, and sitting down on the first chair she
came to, with a heavy sigh, as if even this slight bodily exertion
had been too much for her. They saw her eyes turn towards the
door every time it was opened, and they thought it was with
anxious expectation of one who could not be found, though
many were seeking for him in all probable places.

When night came some one had to tell her of her husband's

disappearance; and Dr Morgan was the person who undertook this.

He came into her room about nine o'clock; her baby was sleeping in her arms; she herself pale as death, still silent and tearless, though strangely watchful of gestures and sounds, and probably cognizant of more than they imagined.

'Well, Mrs Hepburn,' said he, as cheerfully as he could, 'I should advise your going to bed early; for I fancy your husband won't come home to-night. Some journey or other, that perhaps Coulson can explain better than I can, will most likely keep him away till to-morrow. It's very unfortunate that he should be away at such a sad time as this, as I'm sure he'll feel when he returns; but we must make the best of it.'

He watched her to see the effect of his words.

She sighed, that was all. He still remained a little while. She lifted her head up a little and asked,

'How long do yo' think she was unconscious, doctor? Could she hear things, think yo', afore she fell into that strange kind o' slumber?'

'I cannot tell,' said he, shaking his head. 'Was she breathing in that hard snoring kind of way when you left her this morning?'

'Yes, I think so; I cannot tell, so much has happened.'

'When you came back to her, after your breakfast, I think you said she was in much the same position?'

'Yes, and yet I may be telling yo' lies; if I could but think: but it's my head as is aching so; doctor, I wish yo'd go, for I need being alone, I'm so mazed.'

'Good-night, then, for you're a wise woman, I see, and mean to go to bed, and have a good night with baby there.'

But he went down to Phœbe, and told her to go in from time to time, and see how her mistress was.

He found Hester Rose and the old servant together; both had been crying, both were evidently in great trouble about the death and the mystery of the day.

Hester asked if she might go up and see Sylvia, and the doctor gave his leave, talking meanwhile with Phœbe over the kitchen fire. Hester came down again without seeing Sylvia. The door of the room was bolted, and everything quiet inside.

'Does she know where her husband is, think you?' asked the doctor at this account of Hester's. 'She's not anxious about him at any rate: or else the shock of her mother's death has been too much for her. We must hope for some change in the morning; a good fit of crying, or a fidget about her husband, would be more natural. Good-night to you both,' and off he went.

Phœbe and Hester avoided looking at each other at these words. Both were conscious of the probability of something having gone seriously wrong between the husband and wife. Hester had the recollection of the previous night, Phœbe the untasted breakfast of to-day to go upon.

She spoke first.

'A just wish he'd come home to still folks' tongues. It need niver ha' been known if t' old lady hadn't died this day of all others. It's such a thing for t' shop t' have one o' t' partners missin', an' no one for t' know what's comed on him. It niver happened i' Fosters' days, that's a' I know.'

'He'll maybe come back yet,' said Hester. 'It's not so very late.'

'It were market day, and a',' continued Phoebe, 'just as if everything mun go wrong together; an' a' t' country customers'll go back wi' fine tale i' their mouths, as Measter Hepburn was strayed an' missin' just like a beast o' some kind.'

'Hark! isn't that a step?' said Hester suddenly, as a footfall sounded in the now quiet street; but it passed the door, and the hope that had arisen on its approach fell as the sound died away.

'He'll noane come to-night,' said Phœbe, who had been as eager a listener as Hester, however. 'Thou'd best go thy ways home; a shall stay up, for it's not seemly for us a' t' go to our beds, an' a corpse in t' house; an' Nancy, as might ha' watched, is gone to her bed this hour past, like a lazy boots as she is. A can hear, too, if t' measter does come home; tho' a'll be bound he wunnot; choose wheere he is, he'll be i' bed by now, for it's well on to eleven. I'll let thee out by t' shop door, and stand by it till thou's close at home, for it's ill for a young woman to be i' t' street so late.'

So she held the door open, and shaded the candle from the flickering outer air, while Hester went to her home with a heavy heart.

Heavily and hopelessly did they all meet in the morning. No news of Philip, no change in Sylvia; an unceasing flow of angling and conjecture and gossip radiating from the shop into the town.

Hester could have entreated Coulson on her knees to cease from repeating the details of a story of which every word touched on a raw place in her sensitive heart; moreover, when they talked together so eagerly, she could not hear the coming footsteps on the pavement without.

Once some one hit very near the truth in a chance remark.

'It seems strange,' she said, 'how as one man turns up, another just disappears. Why, it were but upo' Tuesday as Kinraid come back, as all his own folk had thought to be dead; and next day here's Measter Hepburn as is gone no one knows wheere!'

'That's t' way i' this world,' replied Coulson, a little sententiously. 'This life is full o' changes o' one kind or another; them that's dead is alive; and as for poor Philip, though he was alive, he looked fitter to be dead when he came into t' shop o' Wednesday morning.'

'And how does she take it?' nodding to where Sylvia was supposed to be.

'Oh! she's not herself, so to say. She were just stunned by finding her mother was dying in her very arms when she thought as she were only sleeping; yet she's never been able to cry a drop; so that t' sorrow's gone inwards on her brain, and from all I can hear, she doesn't rightly understand as her husband is missing. T' doctor says if she could but cry, she'd come to a juster comprehension of things.'

'And what do John and Jeremiah Foster say to it all?'

'They're down here many a time in t' day to ask if he's come back, or how she is; for they made a deal on 'em both. They're going t' attend t' funeral to-morrow, and have given orders as t' shop is to be shut up in t' morning.'

To the surprise of every one, Sylvia, who had never left her room since the night of her mother's death, and was supposed to be almost unconscious of all that was going on in the house, declared her intention of following her mother to the grave. No one could do more than remonstrate: no one had sufficient authority to interfere with her. Dr Morgan even thought that she might possibly be roused to tears by the occasion; only he begged Hester to go with her, that she might have the solace of some woman's company.

She went through the greater part of the ceremony in the same hard, unmoved manner in which she had received everything for days past.

But on looking up once, as they formed round the open grave, she saw Kester, in his Sunday clothes, with a bit of new crape round his hat, crying as if his heart would break over the coffin of his good, kind mistress.

His evident distress, the unexpected sight, suddenly loosed the fountain of Sylvia's tears, and her sobs grew so terrible that Hester feared she would not be able to remain until the end of the funeral. But she struggled hard to stay till the last, and then she made an effort to go round by the place where Kester stood.

'Come and see me,' was all she could say for crying: and Kester only nodded his head – he could not speak a word.

CHAPTER 36

Mysterious Tidings

That very evening Kester came, humbly knocking at the kitchen-door. Phœbe opened it. He asked to see Sylvia.

'A know not if she'll see thee,' said Phœbe. 'There's no makin' her out; sometimes she's for one thing, sometimes she's for another.'

'She bid me come and see her,' said Kester. 'Only this mornin', at missus' buryin', she told me to come.'

So Phœbe went off to inform Sylvia that Kester was there; and returned with the desire that he would walk into the parlour. An instant after he was gone, Phœbe heard him return, and carefully shut the two doors of communication between the kitchen and sitting-room.

Sylvia was in the latter when Kester came in, holding her baby close to her; indeed, she seldom let it go now-a-days to any one else, making Nancy's place quite a sinecure, much to Phœbe's indignation.

Sylvia's face was shrunk, and white, and thin; her lovely eyes alone retained the youthful, almost childlike, expression. She went up to Kester, and shook his horny hand, she herself trembling all over.

'Don't talk to me of her,' she said hastily. 'I cannot stand it. It's a blessing for her to be gone, but, oh —'

She began to cry, and then cheered herself up, and swallowed down her sobs.

'Kester,' she went on, hastily, 'Charley Kinraid isn't dead; dost ta know? He's alive, and he were here o' Tuesday – no, Monday, was it? I cannot tell – but he were here!'

'A knowed as he weren't dead. Every one is a-speaking on it. But a didn't know as thee'd ha' see'n him. A took comfort i' thinkin as thou'd ha' been wi' thy mother a' t' time as he were i' t' place.'

'Then he's gone?' said Sylvia.

'Gone; ay, days past. As far as a know, he but stopped a' neet. A thought to mysel' (but yo' may be sure a said nought to nobody), he's heerd as our Sylvia were married, and has put it in his pipe, and ta'en hisser' off to smoke it.'

'Kester!' said Sylvia, leaning forwards, and whispering. 'I saw him. He was here. Philip saw him. Philip had known as he wasn't dead a' this time!'

Kester stood up suddenly.

'By goom,* that chap has a deal t' answer for.'

A bright red spot was on each of Sylvia's white cheeks; and for a minute or so neither of them spoke.

Then she went on, still whispering out her words.

'Kester, I'm more afeared than I dare tell any one: can they ha' met, think yo'? T' very thought turns me sick. I told Philip my mind, and took a vow again' him – but it would be awful to think on harm happening to him through Kinraid. Yet he went out that morning, and has niver been seen or heard on sin'; and Kinraid were just fell* again' him, and as for that matter, so was I; but —'

The red spot vanished as she faced her own imagination.

Kester spoke.

'It's a thing as can be easy looked into. What day an' time were it when Philip left this house?'

'Tuesday – the day she died. I saw him in her room that morning between breakfast and dinner; I could a'most swear to its being close after eleven. I mind counting t' clock.* It was that very morn as Kinraid were here.'

'A'll go an' have a pint o' beer at t' King's Arms, down on t' quay-side; it were theere he put up at. An' a'm pretty sure as he only stopped one night, and left i' t' morning betimes. But a'll go see.'

'Do,' said Sylvia, 'and go out through t' shop; they're all watching and watching me to see how I take things; and daren't let on about t' fire as is burning up my heart. Coulson is i' t' shop, but he'll not notice thee like Phœbe.'

By-and-by Kester came back. It seemed as though Sylvia had never stirred; she looked eagerly at him, but did not speak.

'He went away i' Rob Mason's mail-cart, him as tak's t' letters to Hartlepool. T' lieutenant (as they ca' him down at t' King's Arms; they're as proud on his uniform as if it had been a new-painted sign to swing o'er their doors), t' lieutenant had reckoned upo' stayin' longer wi' 'em; but he went out betimes o' Tuesday morn', an' came back a' ruffled up,* an' paid his bill – paid for his breakfast, though he touched noane on it – an' went off i' Rob postman's mail-cart, as starts reg'lar at ten o'clock. Corneys has been theere askin' for him, an' makin' a piece o' work,* as he niver went near 'em; and they bees cousins. Niver a one among 'em knows as he were here as far as a could mak' out.'

'Thank yo', Kester,' said Sylvia, falling back in her chair, as if all the energy that had kept her stiff and upright was gone now that her anxiety was relieved.

She was silent for a long time; her eyes shut, her cheek laid on her child's head. Kester spoke next.

'A think it's pretty clear as they'n niver met. But it's a' t' more wonder where thy husband's gone to. Thee and him had words about it, and thou telled him thy mind, thou said?'

'Yes,' said Sylvia, not moving. 'I'm afeared lest mother knows what I said to him, there, where she's gone to – I am – ' the tears filled her shut eyes, and came softly overflowing down her cheeks; 'and yet it were true, what I said, I cannot forgive him; he's just spoilt my life, and I'm not one-and-twenty yet, and he knowed how wretched, how very wretched, I were. A word fra' him would ha' mended it a'; and Charley had bid him speak the word, and give me his faithful love, and Philip saw my heart ache day after day, and niver let on as him I was mourning for was alive, and had sent me word as he'd keep true to me, as I were to do to him.'

'A wish a'd been theere; a'd ha' felled him to t' ground,' said Kester, clenching his stiff, hard hand with indignation.

Sylvia was silent again: pale and weary she sat, her eyes still shut.

Then she said,

'Yet he were so good to mother; and mother loved him so. Oh, Kester!' lifting herself up, opening her great wistful eyes, 'it's well for folks as can die; they're spared a deal o' misery.'

'Ay!' said he. 'But there's folk as one 'ud like to keep fra' shirkin' their misery. Think yo' now as Philip is livin'?'

Sylvia shivered all over, and hesitated before she replied.

'I dunnot know. I said such things; he deserved 'em all—'

'Well, well, lass!' said Kester, sorry that he had asked the question which was producing so much emotion of one kind or another. 'Neither thee nor me can tell; we can neither help nor hinder, seein' as he's ta'en hissel' off out on our sight, we'd best not think on him. A'll try an' tell thee some news, if a can think on it wi' my mind full. Thou knows Haytersbank folk ha' flitted, and t' oud place is empty?'

'Yes!' said Sylvia, with the indifference of one wearied out with feeling.

'A only telled yo' t' account like for me bein' at a loose end i' Monkshaven. My sister, her as lived at Dale End an' is a widow, has comed int' town to live; an' a'm lodgin' wi' her, an' jobbin' about.* A'm gettin' pretty well to do, an' a'm noane far t' seek, an' a'm going now: only first a just wanted for t' say as a'm thy oldest friend, a reckon, and if a can do a turn for thee, or go an errand, like as a've done to-day, or if it's any comfort to talk a bit to one who's known thy life from a babby, why yo've only t' send for me, an' a'd come if it were twenty mile. A'm lodgin' at Peggy Dawson's, t' lath and plaster cottage at t' right hand o' t' bridge, a' among t' new houses, as they're thinkin' o' buildin' near t' sea: no one can miss it.'

He stood up and shook hands with her. As he did so, he looked at her sleeping baby.

'She's liker yo' than him. A think a'll say, God bless her.'

With the heavy sound of his out-going footsteps, baby awoke. She ought before this time to have been asleep in her bed, and the disturbance made her cry fretfully.

'Hush thee, darling, hush thee!' murmured her mother; 'there's no one left to love me but thee, and I cannot stand thy weeping, my pretty one. Hush thee, my babe, hush thee!'

She whispered soft in the little one's ear as she took her upstairs to bed.

About three weeks after the miserable date of Bell Robson's death and Philip's disappearance, Hester Rose received a letter from him. She knew the writing on the address well; and it made her tremble so much that it was many minutes before she dared to open it, and make herself acquainted with the facts it might disclose.

But she need not have feared; there were no facts told, unless the vague date of 'London' might be something to learn. Even that much might have been found out by the post-mark, only she had been too much taken by surprise to examine it.

It ran as follows:

'DEAR HESTER, –

'Tell those whom it may concern, that I have left Monkshaven for ever. No one need trouble themselves about me; I am provided for. Please to make my humble apologies to my kind friends, the Messrs Foster, and to my partner, William Coulson. Please to accept of my love, and to join the same to your mother. Please to give my particular and respectful duty and kind love to my aunt Isabella Robson. Her daughter Sylvia knows what I have always felt, and shall always feel, for her better than I can ever put into language, so I send her no message; God bless and keep my child. You must all look on me as one dead;* as I am to you, and maybe shall soon be in reality.

'Your affectionate and obedient friend to command,

'PHILIP HEPBURN.

'P.S. – Oh, Hester for God's sake and mine, look after ("my wife," scratched out) Sylvia and my child. I think Jeremiah Foster will help you to be a friend to them. This is the last solemn request of P. H. She is but very young.'

Hester read this letter again and again, till her heart caught the echo of its hopelessness, and sank within her. She put it in her pocket, and reflected upon it all the day long as she served in the shop.

The customers found her as gentle, but far more inattentive than usual. She thought that in the evening she would go across the bridge, and consult with the two good old brothers Foster. But something occurred to put off the fulfilment of this plan.

That same morning Sylvia had preceded her, with no one to consult, because consultation would have required previous confidence, and confidence would have necessitated such a confession about Kinraid as it was most difficult for Sylvia to make. The poor young wife yet felt that some step must be taken by her; and what it was to be she could not imagine.

She had no home to go to; for as Philip was gone away, she remained where she was only on sufferance; she did not know what means of livelihood she had; she was willing to work, nay, would be thankful to take up her old life of country labour; but with her baby, what could she do?

In this dilemma, the recollection of the old man's kindly speech and offer of assistance, made, it is true, half in joke, at the end of her wedding visit, came into her mind; and she resolved to go and ask for some of the friendly counsel and assistance then offered.

It would be the first time of her going out since her mother's funeral, and she dreaded the effort on that account. More even than on that account did she shrink from going into the streets again. She could not get over the impression that Kinraid must be lingering near; and she distrusted herself so much that it was a positive terror to think of meeting him again. She felt as though, if she but caught a sight of him, the glitter of his uniform, or heard his well-known voice in only a distant syllable of talk, her heart would stop, and she should die from very fright of what would come next. Or rather so she felt, and so she thought before she took her baby in her arms, as Nancy gave it to her after putting on its out-of-door attire.

With it in her arms she was protected, and the whole current of her thoughts was changed. The infant was wailing, and suffering with its teething, and the mother's heart was so occupied in soothing and consoling her moaning child, that the dangerous quay-side and the bridge were passed almost before she was aware; nor did she notice the eager curiosity and respectful attention of those she met who recognized her even through the heavy veil* which formed part of the draping mourning provided for her by Hester and Coulson, in the first unconscious days after her mother's death.

Though public opinion as yet reserved its verdict upon Philip's disappearance – warned possibly by Kinraid's story against hasty decisions and judgments in such times as those of war and general disturbance – yet every one agreed that no more pitiful fate could have befallen Philip's wife.

Marked out by her striking beauty as an object of admiring interest even in those days when she sat in girlhood's smiling peace by her mother at the Market Cross – her father had lost his life in a popular cause, and ignominious as the manner of his death might be, he was looked upon as a martyr to his zeal in avenging the wrongs of his townsmen; Sylvia had married amongst them too, and her quiet daily life was well known to them; and now her husband had been carried off from her side just on the very day when she needed his comfort most.

For the general opinion was that Philip had been 'carried off' – in seaport towns such occurrences were not uncommon in those days – either by land-crimps or water-crimps.*

So Sylvia was treated with silent reverence, as one sorely afflicted, by all the unheeded people she met in her faltering walk to Jeremiah Foster's.

She had calculated her time so as to fall in with him at his dinner hour, even though it obliged her to go to his own house rather than to the bank where he and his brother spent all the business hours of the day.

Sylvia was so nearly exhausted by the length of her walk and the weight of her baby, that all she could do when the door was opened was to totter into the nearest seat, sit down, and begin to cry.

In an instant kind hands were about her, loosening her heavy cloak, offering to relieve her of her child, who clung to her all the more firmly, and some one was pressing a glass of wine against her lips.

'No, sir, I cannot take it! wine allays gives me th' headache; if I might have just a drink o' water. Thank you, ma'am' (to the respectable-looking old servant), 'I'm well enough now; and perhaps, sir, I might speak a word with yo', for it's that I've come for.'

'It's a pity, Sylvia Hepburn, as thee didst not come to me at the bank, for it's been a long toil for thee all this way in the heat, with thy child. But if there's aught I can do or say for thee, thou hast but to name it, I am sure. Martha! wilt thou relieve her of her child while she comes with me into the parlour?'

But the wilful little Bella stoutly refused to go to any one, and Sylvia was not willing to part with her, tired though she was.

So the baby was carried into the parlour, and much of her after-life depended on this trivial fact.

Once installed in the easy-chair, and face to face with Jeremiah, Sylvia did not know how to begin.

Jeremiah saw this, and kindly gave her time to recover herself, by pulling out his great gold watch, and letting the seal dangle before the child's eyes, almost within reach of the child's eager little fingers.

'She favours you a deal,' said he, at last. 'More than her father,' he went on, purposely introducing Philip's name, so as to break the ice; for he rightly conjectured she had come to speak to him about something connected with her husband.

Still Sylvia said nothing; she was choking down tears and shyness, and unwillingness to take as confidant a man of whom she knew so little, on such slight ground (as she now felt it to be) as the little kindly speech with which she had been dismissed from that house the last time that she entered it.

'It's no use keeping yo', sir,' she broke out at last. It's about Philip as I comed to speak. Do yo' know any thing whatsoever about him? He niver had a chance o' saying anything, I know; but maybe he's written?'

'Not a line, my poor young woman!' said Jeremiah, hastily putting an end to that vain idea.

'Then he's either dead or gone away for iver,' she whispered. 'I mun be both feyther and mother to my child.'

'Oh! thee must not give it up,' replied he. 'Many a one is carried off to the wars, or to the tenders o' men-o'-war, and then they turn out to be unfit for service, and are sent home. Philip 'll come back before the year's out; thee'll see that.'

'No; he'll niver come back. And I'm not sure as I should iver wish him t' come back, if I could but know what was gone wi' him.* Yo' see, sir, though I were sore set again' him, I shouldn't like harm to happen him.'

'There is something behind all this that I do not understand. Can thee tell me what it is?'

'I must, sir, if yo're to help me wi' your counsel; and I came up here to ask for it.'

Another long pause, during which Jeremiah made a feint of playing with the child, who danced and shouted with tantalized impatience at not being able to obtain possession of the seal, and at length stretched out her soft round little arms to go to the owner of the coveted possession. Surprise at this action roused Sylvia, and she made some comment upon it.

'I niver knew her t' go to any one afore. I hope she'll not be troublesome to yo', sir?'

The old man, who had often longed for a child of his own in days gone by, was highly pleased by this mark of baby's confidence, and almost forgot, in trying to strengthen her regard by all the winning wiles in his power, how her poor mother was still lingering over some painful story which she could not bring herself to tell.

'I'm afeared of speaking wrong again' any one, sir. And mother were so fond o' Philip; but he kept something from me as would ha' made me a different woman, and some one else, happen, a different man. I were troth-plighted wi' Kinraid the specksioneer, him as was cousin to th' Corneys o' Moss Brow, and comed back lieutenant i' t' navy last Tuesday three weeks, after ivery one had thought him dead and gone these three years.'

She paused.

'Well?' said Jeremiah, with interest; although his attention appeared to be divided between the mother's story and the eager playfulness of the baby on his knee.

'Philip knew he were alive; he'd seen him taken by t' press-gang, and Charley had sent a message to me by Philip.'

Her white face was reddening, her eyes flashing at this point of her story.

'And he niver told me a word on it, not when he saw me like to break my heart in thinking as Kinraid were dead; he kept it a' to hissel'; and watched me cry, and niver said a word to comfort me wi' t' truth. It would ha' been a great comfort, sir, only t' have had his message if I'd niver ha' been to see him again. But Philip niver let on to any one, as I iver heared on, that he'd seen Charley that morning as t' press-gang took him. Yo' know about feyther's death, and how friendless mother and me was left? and so I married him; for he were a good friend to us then, and I were dazed like wi' sorrow, and could see naught else to do for mother. He were allays very tender and good to her, for sure.'

Again a long pause of silent recollection, broken by one or two deep sighs.

'If I go on, sir, now, I mun ask yo' to promise as yo'll niver tell. I do so need some one to tell me what I ought to do, and I were led here, like,* else I would ha' died wi' it all within my teeth. Yo'll promise, sir?'

Jeremiah Foster looked in her face, and seeing the wistful, eager look, he was touched almost against his judgment into giving the promise required; she went on.

'Upon a Tuesday morning, three weeks ago, I think, tho' for t' matter o' time it might ha' been three years, Kinraid come home; come back for t' claim me as his wife, and I were wed to Philip! met him i' t' road at first; and I couldn't tell him theere. He followed me into t' house – Philip's house, sir, behind t' shop – and somehow I told him all, how I were a wedded wife to another. Then he up and said I'd a false heart – me false, sir, as had eaten my daily bread in bitterness, and had wept t' nights through, all for sorrow and mourning for his death! Then he said as Philip knowed all t' time he were alive and coming back for me; and I couldn't believe it. and I called Philip, and he come, and a' that Charley had said were true; and yet I were Philip's wife! So I took a mighty oath, and I said as I'd niver hold Philip to be my lawful husband again, nor iver forgive him for t' evil he'd wrought us, but hold him as a stranger and one as had done me a heavy wrong.'

She stopped speaking; her story seemed to her to end there. But her listener said, after a pause,

'It were a cruel wrong, I grant thee that; but thy oath were a sin, and thy words were evil, my poor lass. What happened next?'

'I don't justly remember,' she said, wearily. 'Kinraid went away, and mother cried out; and I went to her. She were asleep, I thought, so I lay down by her, to wish I were dead, and to think on what would come on my child if I died; and Philip came in softly, and I made as if I were asleep; and that's t' very last as I've iver seen or heared of him.'

Jeremiah Foster groaned as she ended her story. Then he pulled himself up, and said, in a cheerful tone of voice,

'He'll come back, Sylvia Hepburn. He'll think better of it: never fear!'

'I fear his coming back!' said she. 'That's what I'm feared on;

I would wish as I knew on his well-doing i' some other place; but him and me can niver live together again.'

'Nay,' pleaded Jeremiah. 'Thee art sorry for what thee said; thee were sore put about,* or thee wouldn't have said it.'

He was trying to be a peace-maker, and to heal over conjugal differences; but he did not go deep enough.

'I'm not sorry,' said she, slowly. 'I were too deeply wronged to be "put about"; that would go off wi' a night's sleep. It's only the thought of mother (she's dead and happy, and knows nought of all this, I trust) that comes between me and hating Philip. I'm not sorry for what I said.'

Jeremiah had never met with any one so frank and undisguised in expressions of wrong feeling, and he scarcely knew what to say.

He looked extremely grieved, and not a little shocked. So pretty and delicate a young creature to use such strong relentless language!

She seemed to read his thoughts, for she made answer to them.

'I dare say you think I'm very wicked, sir, not to be sorry. Perhaps I am. I can't think o' that for remembering how I've suffered; and he knew how miserable I was, and might ha' cleared my misery away wi' a word; and he held his peace, and now it's too late! I'm sick o' men and their cruel, deceitful ways. I wish I were dead.'

She was crying before she had ended this speech, and seeing her tears, the child began to cry too, stretching out its little arms to go back to its mother. The hard stony look on her face melted away into the softest, tenderest love as she clasped the little one to her, and tried to soothe its frightened sobs.

A bright thought came into the old man's mind.

He had been taking a complete dislike to her till her pretty way with her baby showed him that she had a heart of flesh within her.

'Poor little one!' said he, 'thy mother had need love thee, for she's deprived thee of thy father's love. Thou'rt half-way to being an orphan; yet I cannot call thee one of the fatherless to whom God will be a father.* Thou'rt a desolate babe, thou may'st well cry; thine earthly parents have forsaken thee, and I know not if the Lord will take thee up.'

Sylvia looked up at him affrighted; holding her baby tighter to her, she exclaimed,

'Don't speak so, sir! it's cursing, sir! I haven't forsaken her! Oh, sir! those are awful sayings.'

'Thee hast sworn never to forgive thy husband, nor to live with him again. Dost thee know that by the law of the land, he may claim his child; and then thou wilt have to forsake it, or to be forsworn? Poor little maiden!' continued he, once more luring the baby to him with the temptation of the watch and chain.

Sylvia thought for a while before speaking. Then she said,

'I cannot tell what ways to take.* Whiles I think my head is crazed. It were a cruel turn he did me!'

'It was. I couldn't have thought him guilty of such baseness.'

This acquiescence, which was perfectly honest on Jeremiah's part, almost took Sylvia by surprise. Why might she not hate one who had been both cruel and base in his treatment of her? And yet she recoiled from the application of such hard terms by another to Philip, by a cool-judging and indifferent person, as she esteemed Jeremiah to be. From some inscrutable turn in her thoughts, she began to defend him, or at least to palliate the harsh judgment which she herself had been the first to pronounce.

'He were so tender to mother; she were dearly fond on him; he niver spared aught he could do for her, else I would niver ha' married him.'

'He was a good and kind-hearted lad from the time he was fifteen. And I never found him out in any falsehood, no more did my brother.'

'But it were all the same as a lie,' said Sylvia, swiftly changing her ground, 'to leave me to think as Charley were dead, when he knowed all t' time he were alive.'

'It was. It was a self-seeking lie; putting thee to pain to get his own ends. And the end of it has been that he is driven forth like Cain.'

'I niver told him to go, sir.'

'But thy words sent him forth, Sylvia.'

'I cannot unsay them, sir; and I believe as I should say them again.'

But she said this as one who rather hopes for a contradiction.

All Jeremiah replied, however, was, 'Poor wee child!' in a pitiful tone, addressed to the baby.

Sylvia's eyes filled with tears.

'Oh, sir, I'll do anything as iver yo' can tell me for her. That's what I came for t' ask yo'. I know I mun not stay theere, and Philip gone away; and I dunnot know what to do: and I'll do aught, only I must keep her wi' me. Whativer can I do, sir?'

Jeremiah thought it over for a minute or two. Then he replied,

'I must have time to think. I must talk it over with brother John.'

'But yo've given me yo'r word, sir!' exclaimed she.

'I have given thee my word never to tell any one of what has passed between thee and thy husband, but I must take counsel with my brother as to what is to be done with thee and thy child, now that thy husband has left the shop.'

This was said so gravely as almost to be a reproach, and he got up, as a sign that the interview was ended.

He gave the baby back to its mother; but not without a solemn blessing, so solemn that, to Sylvia's superstitious and excited mind, it undid the terrors of what she had esteemed to be a curse.

'The Lord bless thee and keep thee! The Lord make His face to shine upon thee!*

All the way down the hill-side, Sylvia kept kissing the child, and whispering to its unconscious ears, –

'I'll love thee for both, my treasure, I will. I'll lap thee round wi' my love, so as thou shall niver need a feyther's.'

CHAPTER 37

Bereavement

Hester had been prevented by her mother's indisposition from taking Philip's letter to the Fosters, to hold a consultation with them over its contents.

Alice Rose was slowly failing, and the long days which she had to spend alone told much upon her spirits, and consequently upon her health.

All this came out in the conversation which ensued after reading Hepburn's letter in the little parlour at the bank on the day after Sylvia had had her confidential interview with Jeremiah Foster.

He was a true man of honour, and never so much as alluded to her visit to him; but what she had then told him influenced him very much in the formation of the project which he proposed to his brother and Hester.

He recommended her remaining where she was, living still in the house behind the shop; for he thought within himself that she might have exaggerated the effect of her words upon Philip; that, after all, it might have been some cause totally disconnected with them, which had blotted out her husband's place among the men of Monkshaven; and that it would be so much easier for both to resume their natural relations, both towards each other and towards the world, if Sylvia remained where her husband had left her – in an expectant attitude, so to speak.

Jeremiah Foster questioned Hester straitly about her letter: whether she had made known its contents to any one. No, not to any one. Neither to her mother nor to William Coulson? No, to neither.

She looked at him as she replied to his inquiries, and he looked at her, each wondering if the other could be in the least aware that a conjugal quarrel might be at the root of the dilemma in which they were placed by Hepburn's disappearance.

But neither Hester, who had witnessed the misunderstanding between the husband and wife on the evening, before the morning on which Philip went away, nor Jeremiah Foster, who had learnt from Sylvia the true reason of her husband's disappearance, gave the slightest reason to the other to think that they each supposed they had a clue to the reason of Hepburn's sudden departure.

What Jeremiah Foster, after a night's consideration, had to propose was this; that Hester and her mother should come and occupy the house in the market-place, conjointly with Sylvia and her child. Hester's interest in the shop was by this time acknowledged. Jeremiah had made over to her so much of his share in the business, that she had a right to be considered as a kind of partner; and she had long been the superintendent of that department of goods which were exclusively devoted to women. So her daily presence was requisite for more reasons than one.

Yet her mother's health and spirits were such as to render it unadvisable that the old woman should be too much left alone; and Sylvia's devotion to her own mother seemed to point her out as the very person who could be a gentle and tender companion to Alice Rose during those hours when her own daughter would necessarily be engaged in the shop.

Many desirable objects seemed to be gained by this removal of Alice: an occupation was provided for Sylvia, which would detain her in the place where her husband had left her, and where (Jeremiah Foster fairly expected in spite of his letter) he was likely to come back to find her; and Alice Rose, the early love of one of the brothers, the old friend of the other, would be well cared for, and under her daughter's immediate supervision during the whole of the time that she was occupied in the shop.

Philip's share of the business, augmented by the money which he had put in from the legacy of his old Cumberland uncle, would bring in profits enough to support Sylvia and her child in ease and comfort until that time, which they all anticipated, when he should return from his mysterious wandering – mysterious, whether his going forth had been voluntary or involuntary.

Thus far was settled; and Jeremiah Foster went to tell Sylvia of the plan.

She was too much a child, too entirely unaccustomed to any independence of action, to do anything but leave herself in his hands. Her very confession, made to him the day before, when she sought his counsel, seemed to place her at his disposal. Otherwise, she had had notions of the possibility of a free country life once more – how provided for and arranged she hardly knew; but Haytersbank was to let, and Kester disengaged, and it had just seemed possible that she might have to return to her early home, and to her old life. She knew that it would take much money to stock the farm again, and that her hands were tied from much useful activity by the love and care she owed to her baby. But still, somehow, she hoped and she fancied, till Jeremiah Foster's measured words and carefully-arranged plan made her silently relinquish her green, breezy vision.

Hester, too, had her own private rebellion – hushed into submission by her gentle piety. If Sylvia had been able to make

Philip happy, Hester could have felt lovingly and almost grate-
fully towards her; but Sylvia had failed in this.

Philip had been made unhappy, and was driven forth a
wanderer into the wide world – never to come back! And his
last words to Hester, the postscript of his letter, containing the
very pith of it, was to ask her to take charge and care of the wife
whose want of love towards him had uprooted him from the
place where he was valued and honoured.

It cost Hester many a struggle and many a self-reproach
before she could make herself feel what she saw all along – that
in everything Philip treated her like a sister. But even a sister
might well be indignant if she saw her brother's love disregarded
and slighted, and his life embittered by the thoughtless conduct
of a wife! Still Hester fought against herself, and for Philip's
sake she sought to see the good in Sylvia, and she strove to love
her as well as to take care of her.

With the baby, of course, the case was different. Without
thought or struggle, or reason, every one loved the little girl.
Coulson and his buxom wife, who were childless, were never
weary of making much of her. Hester's happiest hours were
spent with that little child. Jeremiah Foster almost looked upon
her as his own from the day when she honoured him by yielding
to the temptation of the chain and seal, and coming to his knee;
not a customer to the shop but knew the smiling child's sad
history, and many a country-woman would save a rosy-cheeked
apple from out her store that autumn to bring it on next market-
day for 'Philip Hepburn's baby, as had lost its father, bless it.'

Even stern Alice Rose was graciously inclined towards the
little Bella; and though her idea of the number of the elect was
growing narrower and narrower every day, she would have been
loth to exclude the innocent little child, that stroked her
wrinkled cheeks so softly every night in return for her blessing,
from the few that should be saved. Nay, for the child's sake, she
relented towards the mother; and strove to have Sylvia rescued
from the many castaways with fervent prayer, or, as she phrased
it, 'wrestling with the Lord'.

Alice had a sort of instinct that the little child, so tenderly
loved by, so fondly loving, the mother whose ewe-lamb she was,
could not be even in heaven without yearning for the creature
she had loved best on earth; and the old woman believed that
this was the principal reason for her prayers for Sylvia; but

unconsciously to herself, Alice Rose was touched by the filial attentions she constantly received from the young mother, whom she believed to be foredoomed to condemnation.

Sylvia rarely went to church or chapel, nor did she read her Bible; for though she spoke little of her ignorance, and would fain, for her child's sake, have remedied it now it was too late, she had lost what little fluency of reading she had ever had, and could only make out her words with much spelling and difficulty. So the taking her Bible in hand would have been a mere form; though of this Alice Rose knew nothing.

No one knew much of what was passing in Sylvia; she did not know herself. Sometimes in the nights she would waken, crying, with a terrible sense of desolation; every one who loved her, or whom she had loved, had vanished out of her life; every one but her child, who lay in her arms, warm and soft.

But then Jeremiah Foster's words came upon her; words that she had taken for cursing at the time; and she would so gladly have had some clue by which to penetrate the darkness of the unknown region from whence both blessing and cursing came, and to know if she had indeed done something which should cause her sin to be visited on that soft, sweet, innocent darling.

If any one would teach her to read! If any one would explain to her the hard words she heard in church or chapel, so that she might find out the meaning of sin and godliness! – words that had only passed over the surface of her mind till now! For her child's sake she should like to do the will of God, if she only knew what that was, and how to be worked out in her daily life.

But there was no one she dared confess her ignorance to and ask information from. Jeremiah Foster had spoken as if her child, sweet little merry Bella, with a loving word and a kiss for every one, was to suffer heavily for the just and true words her wronged and indignant mother had spoken. Alice always spoke as if there were no hope for her; and blamed her, nevertheless, for not using the means of grace that it was not in her power to avail herself of.

And Hester, that Sylvia would fain have loved for her uniform gentleness and patience with all around her, seemed so cold in her unruffled and undemonstrative behaviour; and moreover, Sylvia felt that Hester blamed her perpetual silence regarding Philip's absence without knowing how bitter a cause Sylvia had for casting him off.

The only person who seemed to have pity upon her was Kester; and his pity was shown in looks rather than words; for when he came to see her, which he did from time to time, by a kind of mutual tacit consent, they spoke but little of former days.

He was still lodging with his sister, widow Moore, working at odd jobs, some of which took him into the country for weeks at a time. But on his returns to Monkshaven he was sure to come and see her and the little Bella; indeed, when his employment was in the immediate neighbourhood of the town, he never allowed a week to pass away without a visit.

There was not much conversation between him and Sylvia at such times. They skimmed over the surface of the small events in which both took an interest; only now and then a sudden glance, a checked speech, told each that there were deeps not forgotten, although they were never mentioned.

Twice Sylvia – below her breath – had asked Kester, just as she was holding the door open for his departure, if anything had ever been heard of Kinraid since his one night's visit to Monkshaven: each time (and there was an interval of some months between the inquiries) the answer had been simply, no.

To no one else would Sylvia ever have named his name. But indeed she had not the chance, had she wished it ever so much, of asking any questions about him from any one likely to know. The Corneys had left Moss Brow at Martinmas, and gone many miles away towards Horncastle. Bessy Corney, it is true, was married and left behind in the neighbourhood; but with her Sylvia had never been intimate; and what girlish friendship there might have been between them had cooled very much at the time of Kinraid's supposed death three years before.*

One day before Christmas in this year, 1798,* Sylvia was called into the shop by Coulson, who, with his assistant, was busy undoing the bales of winter goods supplied to them from the West Riding, and other places. He was looking at a fine Irish poplin dress-piece when Sylvia answered to his call.

'Here! do you know this again?' asked he, in the cheerful tone of one sure of giving pleasure.

'No! have I iver seen it afore?'

'Not this, but one for all t' world like it.'

She did not rouse up too much interest, but looked at it as if trying to recollect where she could have seen its like.

'My missus had one on at th' party at John Foster's last March, and yo' admired it a deal. And Philip, he thought o' nothing but how he could get yo' just such another, and he set a vast o' folk agait for to meet wi' its marrow; and what he did just the very day afore he went away so mysterious was to write through Dawson Brothers, o' Wakefield, to Dublin, and order that one should be woven for yo'. Jemima had to cut a bit off hers for to give him t' exact colour.'

Sylvia did not say anything but that it was very pretty, in a low voice, and then she quickly left the shop, much to Coulson's displeasure.

All the afternoon she was unusually quiet and depressed.

Alice Rose, sitting helpless in her chair, watched her with keen eyes.

At length, after one of Sylvia's deep, unconscious sighs, the old woman spoke:

'It's religion as must comfort thee, child, as it's done many a one afore thee.'

'How?' said Sylvia, looking up, startled to find herself an object of notice.

'How?' (The answer was not quite so ready as the precept had been.) 'Read thy Bible, and thou wilt learn.'

'But I cannot read,' said Sylvia, too desperate any longer to conceal her ignorance.

'Not read! and thee Philip's wife as was such great scholar! Of a surety the ways o' this life are crooked!* There was our Hester, as can read as well as any minister, and Philip passes over her to go and choose a young lass as cannot read her Bible.'

'Was Philip and Hester—'

Sylvia paused, for though a new curiosity had dawned upon her, she did not know how to word her question.

'Many a time and oft have I seen Hester take comfort in her Bible when Philip was following after thee. She knew where to go for consolation.'

'I'd fain read,' said Sylvia, humbly, 'if anybody would learn me; for perhaps it might do me good; I'm noane so happy.'

Her eyes, as she looked up at Alice's stern countenance, were full of tears.

The old woman saw it, and was touched, although she did not immediately show her sympathy. But she took her own time, and made no reply.

The next day, however, she bade Sylvia come to her, and then and there, as if her pupil had been a little child, she began to teach Sylvia to read the first chapter of Genesis; for all other reading but the Scriptures was as vanity to her, and she would not condescend to the weakness of other books. Sylvia was now, as ever, slow at book-learning; but she was meek and desirous to be taught, and her willingness in this respect pleased Alice, and drew her singularly towards one who, from being a pupil, might become a convert.

All this time Sylvia never lost the curiosity that had been excited by the few words Alice had let drop about Hester and Philip, and by degrees she approached the subject again, and had the idea then started confirmed by Alice, who had no scruple in using the past experience of her own, of her daughter's, or of any one's life, as an instrument to prove the vanity of setting the heart on anything earthly.

This knowledge, unsuspected before, sank deep into Sylvia's thoughts, and gave her a strange interest in Hester – poor Hester, whose life she had so crossed and blighted, even by the very blighting of her own. She gave Hester her own former passionate feelings for Kinraid, and wondered how she herself should have felt towards any one who had come between her and him, and wiled his love away. When she remembered Hester's unfailing sweetness and kindness towards herself from the very first, she could better bear the comparative coldness of her present behaviour.

She tried, indeed, hard to win back the favour she had lost; but the very means she took were blunders, and only made it seem to her as if she could never again do right in Hester's eyes.

For instance, she begged her to accept and wear the pretty poplin gown which had been Philip's especial choice; feeling within herself as if she should never wish to put it on, and as if the best thing she could do with it was to offer it to Hester. But Hester rejected the proffered gift with as much hardness of manner as she was capable of assuming; and Sylvia had to carry it upstairs and lay it by for the little daughter, who, Hester said, might perhaps learn to value things that her father had given especial thought to.

Yet Sylvia went on trying to win Hester to like her once more; it was one of her great labours, and learning to read from Hester's mother was another.

Alice, indeed, in her solemn way, was becoming quite fond of Sylvia; if she could not read or write, she had a deftness and gentleness of motion, a capacity for the household matters which fell into her department, that had a great effect on the old woman, and for her dear mother's sake Sylvia had a stock of patient love ready in her heart for all the aged and infirm that fell in her way. She never thought of seeking them out, as she knew that Hester did; but then she looked up to Hester as some one very remarkable for her goodness. If only she could have liked her!

Hester tried to do all she could for Sylvia. Philip had told her to take care of his wife and child; but she had the conviction that Sylvia had so materially failed in her duties as to have made her husband an exile from his home – a penniless wanderer, wifeless and childless, in some strange country whose very aspect was friendless, while the cause of all lived on in the comfortable home where he had placed her, wanting for nothing – an object of interest and regard to many friends – with a lovely little child to give her joy for the present, and hope for the future; while he, the poor outcast, might even lie dead by the wayside. How could Hester love Sylvia?

Yet they were frequent companions that ensuing spring. Hester was not well; and the doctors said that the constant occupation in the shop was too much for her, and that she must, for a time at least, take daily walks into the country.

Sylvia used to beg to accompany her; she and the little girl often went with Hester up the valley of the river to some of the nestling farms that were hidden in the more sheltered nooks – for Hester was bidden to drink milk warm from the cow; and to go into the familiar haunts about a farm was one of the few things in which Sylvia seemed to take much pleasure. She would let little Bella toddle about while Hester sat and rested: and she herself would beg to milk the cow destined to give the invalid her draught.

One May evening the three had been out on some such expedition; the country side still looked grey and bare, though the leaves were showing on the willow and blackthorn and sloe, and by the tinkling runnels, making hidden music along the copse side, the pale delicate primrose buds were showing amid their fresh, green, crinkled leaves. The larks had been singing all the afternoon, but were now dropping down into their nests in the pasture fields; the air had just the sharpness in it which goes along with a cloudless evening sky at that time of the year.

But Hester walked homewards slowly and languidly, speaking no word. Sylvia noticed this at first without venturing to speak, for Hester was one who disliked having her ailments noticed. But after a while Hester stood still in a sort of weary dreamy abstraction; and Sylvia said to her,

'I'm afeared yo're sadly tired. Maybe we've been too far.'

Hester almost started.

'No!' said she, 'it's only my headache which is worse to-night. It has been bad all day; but since I came out it has felt just as if there were great guns booming, till I could almost pray 'em to be quiet. I am so weary o' th' sound.'

She stepped out quickly towards home after she had said this, as if she wished for neither pity nor comment on what she had said.

CHAPTER 38

The Recognition

Far away, over sea and land, over sunny sea again, great guns were booming on that 7th of May, 1799.*

The Mediterranean came up with a long roar on a beach glittering white with snowy sand, and the fragments of innumerable sea-shells, delicate and shining as porcelain. Looking at that shore from the sea, a long ridge of upland ground, beginning from an inland depth, stretched far away into the ocean on the right, till it ended in a great mountainous bluff, crowned with the white buildings of a convent sloping rapidly down into the blue water at its base.

In the clear eastern air, the different characters of the foliage that clothed the sides of that sea-washed mountain might be discerned from a long distance by the naked eye; the silver grey of the olive-trees near its summit; the heavy green and bossy forms of the sycamores lower down; broken here and there by a solitary terebinth or ilex tree, of a deeper green and a wider spread; till the eye fell below on the maritime plain, edged with the white seaboard and the sandy hillocks; with here and there feathery palm-trees, either isolated or in groups – motionless and distinct against the hot purple air.

Look again; a little to the left on the sea-shore there are the white walls of a fortified town, glittering in sunlight, or black in shadow.

The fortifications themselves run out into the sea, forming a port and a haven against the wild Levantine storms; and a lighthouse rises out of the waves to guide mariners into safety.

Beyond this walled city, and far away to the left still, there is the same wide plain shut in by the distant rising ground, till the upland circuit comes closing in to the north, and the great white rocks meet the deep tideless ocean with its intensity of blue colour.

Above, the sky is literally purple with heat; and the pitiless light smites the gazer's weary eye as it comes back from the white shore. Nor does the plain country in that land offer the refuge and rest of our own soft green. The limestone rock underlies the vegetation, and gives a glittering, ashen hue to all the bare patches, and even to the cultivated parts which are burnt up early in the year. In spring-time alone does the country look rich and fruitful; then the cow-fields of the plain show their capability of bearing, 'some fifty, some an hundred fold';* down by the brook Kishon, flowing not far from the base of the mountainous promontory to the south, there grow the broad green fig-trees, cool and fresh to look upon; the orchards are full of glossy-leaved cherry-trees; the tall amaryllis puts forth crimson and yellow glories in the fields, rivalling the pomp of King Solomon;* the daisies and the hyacinths spread their myriad flowers; the anemones, scarlet as blood, run hither and thither over the ground like dazzling flames of fire.

A spicy odour lingers in the heated air; it comes from the multitude of aromatic flowers that blossom in the early spring. Later on they will have withered and faded, and the corn will have been gathered, and the deep green of the eastern foliage will have assumed a kind of gray-bleached tint.

Even now in May, the hot sparkle of the everlasting sea, the terribly clear outline of all objects, whether near or distant, the fierce sun right overhead, the dazzling air around, were inexpressibly wearying to the English eyes that kept their skilled watch, day and night, on the strongly-fortified coast-town that lay out a little to the northward of where the British ships were anchored.

They had kept up a flanking fire for many days in aid of those besieged in St Jean d'Acre;* and at intervals had listened, impatient, to the sound of the heavy siege guns, or the sharper rattle of the French musketry.

In the morning, on the 7th of May, a man at the masthead of the *Tigre* sang out that he saw ships in the offing; and in reply to the signal that was hastily run up, he saw the distant vessels hoist friendly flags. That May morning was a busy time. The besieged Turks took heart of grace; the French outside, under the command of their great general, made hasty preparations for a more vigorous assault than all the many, both vigorous and bloody, that had gone before (for the siege was now at its fifty-first day), in hopes of carrying the town by storm before the reinforcement coming by sea could arrive; and Sir Sidney Smith, aware of Buonaparte's desperate intention, ordered all the men, both sailors and marines, that could be spared from the necessity of keeping up a continual flanking fire from the ships upon the French, to land, and assist the Turks and the British forces already there in the defence of the old historic city.

Lieutenant Kinraid, who had shared his captain's daring adventure off the coast of France three years before, who had been a prisoner with him and Westley Wright, in the Temple at Paris,*and had escaped with them, and, through Sir Sidney's earnest recommendation, been promoted from being a warrant officer to the rank of lieutenant, received on this day the honour from his admiral of being appointed to an especial post of danger. His heart was like a war-horse, and said, Ha, ha!* as the boat bounded over the waves that were to land him, under the ancient machicolated walls where the Crusaders made their last stand in the Holy Land. Not that Kinraid knew or cared one jot about those gallant knights of old: all he knew was, that the French, under Boney, were trying to take the town from the Turks, and that his admiral said they must not, and so they should not.

He and his men landed on that sandy shore, and entered the town by the water-port gate; he was singing to himself his own country song, –

Weel may the keel row, the keel row, etc.,

and his men, with sailors' aptitude for music, caught up the air, and joined in the burden with inarticulate sounds.

So, with merry hearts, they threaded the narrow streets of Acre, hemmed in on either side by the white walls of Turkish houses, with small grated openings high up, above all chance of peeping intrusion.

Here and there they met an ample-robed and turbaned Turk going along with as much haste as his stately self-possession would allow. But the majority of the male inhabitants were gathered together to defend the breach, where the French guns thundered out far above the heads of the sailors.

They went along none the less merrily for the sound to Djezzar Pacha's garden,* where the old Turk sat on his carpet, beneath the shade of a great terebinth tree, listening to the interpreter, who made known to him the meaning of the eager speeches of Sir Sidney Smith and the colonel of the marines.

As soon as the admiral saw the gallant sailors of HMS *Tigre*, he interrupted the council of war without much ceremony, and going to Kinraid, he despatched them, as before arranged, to the North Ravelin,* showing them the way with rapid, clear directions.

Out of respect to him, they had kept silent while in the strange, desolate garden; but once more in the streets, the old Newcastle song rose up again till the men were, perforce, silenced by the haste with which they went to the post of danger.

It was three o'clock in the afternoon. For many a day these very men had been swearing at the terrific heat at this hour – even when at sea, fanned by the soft breeze; but now, in the midst of hot smoke, with former carnage tainting the air, and with the rush and whizz of death perpetually whistling in their ears, they were uncomplaining and light-hearted. Many an old joke, and some new ones, came brave and hearty, on their cheerful voices, even though the speaker was veiled from sight in great clouds of smoke, cloven only by the bright flames of death.

A sudden message came; as many of the crew of the *Tigre* as were under Lieutenant Kinraid's command were to go down to the Mole, to assist the new reinforcements (seen by the sailor from the masthead at day-dawn), under command of Hassan Bey, to land at the Mole, where Sir Sidney then was.

Off they went, almost as bright and thoughtless as before,

though two of their number lay silent for ever at the North Ravelin – silenced in that one little half-hour. And one went along with the rest, swearing lustily at his ill-luck in having his right arm broken, but ready to do good business with his left.

They helped the Turkish troops to land more with goodwill than tenderness; and then, led by Sir Sidney, they went under the shelter of English guns to the fatal breach, so often assailed, so gallantly defended, but never so fiercely contested as on this burning afternoon. The ruins of the massive wall that here had been broken down by the French, were used by them as stepping stones to get on a level with the besieged, and so to escape the heavy stones which the latter hurled down; nay, even the dead bodies of the morning's comrades were made into ghastly stairs.

When Djezzar Pacha heard that the British sailors were defending the breach, headed by Sir Sidney Smith, he left his station in the palace garden, gathered up his robes in haste, and hurried to the breach; where, with his own hands, and with right hearty good-will, he pulled the sailors down from the post of danger, saying that if he lost his English friends he lost all!

But little recked the crew of the *Tigre* of the one old man – Pacha or otherwise – who tried to hold them back from the fight; they were up and at the French assailants clambering over the breach in an instant; and so they went on, as if it were some game at play instead of a deadly combat, until Kinraid and his men were called off by Sir Sidney, as the reinforcement of Turkish troops under Hassan Bey were now sufficient for the defence of that old breach in the walls, which was no longer the principal object of the French attack; for the besiegers had made a new and more formidable breach by their incessant fire, knocking down whole streets of the city walls.

'Fight your best, Kinraid!' said Sir Sidney, 'for there's Boney on yonder hill looking at you.'

And sure enough, on a rising ground, called Richard Cœur de Lion's Mount, there was a half-circle of French generals, on horseback, all deferentially attending to the motions, and apparently to the words, of a little man in their centre; at whose bidding the aide-de-camp galloped swift with messages to the more distant French camp.

The two ravelins which Kinraid and his men had to occupy, for the purpose of sending a flanking fire upon the enemy, were not ten yards from that enemy's van.

But at length there was a sudden rush of the French to that part of the wall where they imagined they could enter unopposed.

Surprised at this movement, Kinraid ventured out of the shelter of the ravelin to ascertain the cause; he, safe and untouched during that long afternoon of carnage, fell now, under a stray musket-shot, and lay helpless and exposed upon the ground undiscerned by his men, who were recalled to help in the hot reception which had been planned for the French; who, descending the city walls into the Pacha's garden, were attacked with sabre and dagger, and lay headless corpses under the flowering rose-bushes, and by the fountain side.

Kinraid lay beyond the ravelins, many yards outside the city walls.

He was utterly helpless, for the shot had broken his leg. Dead bodies of Frenchmen lay strewn around him; no Englishman had ventured out so far.

All the wounded men that he could see were French; and many of these, furious with pain, gnashed their teeth at him and cursed him aloud, till he thought that his best course was to assume the semblance of death; for some among these men were still capable of dragging themselves up to him, and by concentrating all their failing energies into one blow, put him to a speedy end.

The outlying pickets of the French army were within easy rifle shot; and his uniform, although less conspicuous in colour than that of the marines, by whose sides he had been fighting, would make him a sure mark if he so much as moved his arm. Yet how he longed to turn, if ever so slightly, so that the cruel slanting sun might not beat full into his aching eyes. Fever, too, was coming upon him; the pain in his leg was every moment growing more severe; the terrible thirst of the wounded, added to the heat and fatigue of the day, made his lips and tongue feel baked and dry, and his whole throat seemed parched and wooden. Thoughts of other days, of cool Greenland seas, where ice abounded, of grassy English homes, began to make the past more real than the present.

With a great effort he brought his wandering senses back; he knew where he was now, and could weigh the chances of his life, which were but small; the unwonted tears came to his eyes as he thought of the newly-made wife in her English home, who might never know how he died thinking of her.

Suddenly he saw a party of English marines advance, under shelter of the ravelin, to pick up the wounded, and bear them within the walls for surgical help. They were so near he could see their faces, could hear them speak; yet he durst not make any sign to them when he lay within range of the French picket's fire.

For one moment he could not resist raising his head, to give himself a chance for life; before the unclean creatures that infest a camp came round in the darkness of the night to strip and insult the dead bodies, and to put to death such as had yet the breath of life within them. But the setting sun came full into his face, and he saw nothing of what he longed to see.

He fell back in despair; he lay there to die.

That strong clear sunbeam had wrought his salvation.

He had been recognized as men are recognized when they stand in the red glare of a house on fire;* the same despair of help, of hopeless farewell to life, stamped on their faces in blood-red light.

One man left his fellows, and came running forwards, forwards in among the enemy's wounded, within range of their guns; he bent down over Kinraid; he seemed to understand without a word; he lifted him up, carrying him like a child;* and with the vehement energy that is more from the force of will than the strength of body, he bore him back to within the shelter of the ravelin – not without many shots being aimed at them, one of which hit Kinraid in the fleshy part of his arm.

Kinraid was racked with agony from his dangling broken leg, and his very life seemed leaving him; yet he remembered afterwards how the marine recalled his fellows, and how, in the pause before they returned, his face became like one formerly known to the sick senses of Kinraid; yet it was too like a dream, too utterly improbable to be real.

Yet the few words this man said, as he stood breathless and alone by the fainting Kinraid, fitted in well with the belief conjured up by his personal appearance. He panted out, –

'I niver thought you'd ha' kept true to her!'

And then the others came up; and while they were making a sling of their belts, Kinraid fainted utterly away, and the next time that he was fully conscious, he was lying in his berth in the

Tigre, with the ship surgeon setting his leg. After that he was too feverish for several days to collect his senses. When he could first remember, and form a judgment upon his recollections, he called the man especially charged to attend upon him, and bade him go and make inquiry in every possible manner for a marine named Philip Hepburn, and, when he was found, to entreat him to come and see Kinraid.

The sailor was away the greater part of the day, and returned unsuccessful in his search; he had been from ship to ship, hither and thither; he had questioned all the marines he had met with, no one knew anything of any Philip Hepburn.

Kinraid passed a miserably feverish night, and when the doctor exclaimed the next morning at his retrogression, he told him, with some irritation, of the ill-success of his servant; he accused the man of stupidity, and wished fervently that he were able to go himself.

Partly to soothe him, the doctor promised that he would undertake the search for Hepburn, and he engaged faithfully to follow all Kinraid's eager directions; not to be satisfied with men's careless words, but to look over muster-rolls and ships' books.

He, too, brought the same answer, however unwillingly given.

He had set out upon the search so confident of success, that he felt doubly discomfited by failure. However, he had persuaded himself that the lieutenant had been partially delirious from the effects of his wound, and the power of the sun shining down just where he lay. There had, indeed, been slight symptoms of Kinraid's having received a sun-stroke; and the doctor dwelt largely on these in his endeavour to persuade his patient that it was his imagination which had endued a stranger with the lineaments of some former friend.

Kinraid threw his arms out of bed with impatience at all this plausible talk, which was even more irritating than the fact that Hepburn was still undiscovered.

'The man was no friend of mine; I was like to have killed him when last I saw him. He was a shopkeeper in a country town in England. I had seen little enough of him; but enough to make me able to swear to him anywhere, even in a marine's uniform, and in this sweltering country.'

'Faces once seen, especially in excitement, are apt to return upon the memory in cases of fever,' quoth the doctor, sententiously.

The attendant sailor, reinstalled to some complacency by the failure of another in the search in which he himself had been unsuccessful, now put in his explanation.

'Maybe it was a spirit. It's not th' first time as I've heered of a spirit coming upon earth to save a man's life i' time o' need. My father had an uncle, a west country grazier. He was a-coming over Dartmoor in Devonshire one moonlight night with a power o'* money as he'd got for his sheep at t' fair. It were stowed i' leather bags under th' seat o' th' gig. It were a rough kind o' road, both as a road and in character, for there'd been many robberies there of late, and th' great rocks stood convenient for hiding-places. All at once father's uncle feels as if some one were sitting beside him on th' empty seat; and he turns his head and looks, and there he sees his brother sitting – his brother as had been dead twelve year and more. So he turns his head back again, eyes right, and never says a word, but wonders what it all means. All of a sudden two fellows come out upo' th' white road from some black shadow, and they looked, and they let th' gig go past, father's uncle driving hard, I'll warrant him. But for all that he heard one say to t' other, "By—, there's *two* on 'em!" Straight on he drove faster than ever, till he saw th' far lights of some town or other. I forget its name, though I've heered it many a time; and then he drew a long breath, and turned his head to look at his brother, and ask him how he'd managed to come out of his grave i' Barum churchyard, and th' seat was as empty as it had been when he set out; and then he knew that it were a spirit come to help him against th' men who thought to rob him, and would likely enough ha' murdered him.'

Kinraid had kept quiet through this story. But when the sailor began to draw the moral, and to say, 'And I think I may make bold to say, sir, as th' marine who carried you out o' th' Frenchy's gun-shot was just a spirit come to help you,' he exclaimed impatiently, swearing a great oath as he did so, 'It was no spirit, I tell you; and I was in my full senses. It was a man named Philip Hepburn. He said words to me, or over me, as none but himself would have said. Yet we hated each other like poison; and I can't make out why he should be there and putting himself in danger to save me. But so it was; and as you can't find him, let me hear no more of your nonsense. It was him, and not my fancy, doctor. It was flesh and blood, and not a spirit, Jack. So get along with you, and leave me quiet.' All this time Stephen Freeman lay friendless, sick, and shattered, on board the *Theseus*.*

He had been about his duty close to some shells that were placed on her deck; a gay young midshipman was thoughtlessly striving to get the fusee out of one of these by a mallet and spike-nail that lay close at hand; and a fearful explosion ensued, in which the poor marine, cleaning his bayonet near, was shockingly burnt and disfigured, the very skin of all the lower part of his face being utterly destroyed by gunpowder. They said it was a mercy that his eyes were spared; but he could hardly feel anything to be a mercy, as he lay tossing in agony, burnt by the explosion, wounded by splinters, and feeling that he was disabled for life, if life itself were preserved. Of all that suffered by that fearful accident (and they were many) none was so forsaken, so hopeless, so desolate, as the Philip Hepburn about whom such anxious inquiries were being made at that very time.

CHAPTER 39

Confidences

It was a little later on in that same summer that Mrs Brunton came to visit her sister Bessy.

Bessy was married to a tolerably well-to-do farmer who lived at an almost equal distance between Monkshaven and Hartswell; but from old habit and convenience the latter was regarded as the Dawsons' market-town; so Bessy seldom or never saw her old friends in Monkshaven.

But Mrs Brunton was far too flourishing a person not to speak out her wishes, and have her own way. She had no notion, she said, of coming such a long journey only to see Bessy and her husband, and not to have a sight of her former acquaintances at Monkshaven. She might have added, that her new bonnet and cloak would be as good as lost if it was not displayed among those who, knowing her as Molly Corney, and being less fortunate in matrimony than she was, would look upon it with wondering admiration, if not with envy.

So one day farmer Dawson's market cart deposited Mrs Brunton in all her bravery* at the shop in the market-place, over which Hepburn and Coulson's names still flourished in joint partnership.

After a few words of brisk recognition to Coulson and Hester, Mrs Brunton passed on into the parlour and greeted Sylvia with boisterous heartiness.

It was now four years and more since the friends had met; and each secretly wondered how they had ever come to be friends. Sylvia had a country, raw, spiritless look to Mrs Brunton's eye; Molly was loud and talkative, and altogether distasteful to Sylvia, trained in daily companionship with Hester to appreciate soft slow speech, and grave thoughtful ways.

However, they kept up the forms of their old friendship, though their hearts had drifted far apart. They sat hand in hand while each looked at the other with eyes inquisitive as to the changes which time had made. Molly was the first to speak.

'Well, to be sure! how thin and pale yo've grown, Sylvia! Matrimony hasn't agreed wi' yo' as well as it's done wi' me. Brunton is allays saying (yo' know what a man he is for his joke) that if he'd ha' known how many yards o' silk I should ha' ta'en for a gown, he'd ha' thought twice afore he'd ha' married me. Why, I've gained a matter o' thirty pound o' flesh sin' I were married!'

'Yo' do look brave and hearty!' said Sylvia, putting her sense of her companion's capacious size and high colour into the prettiest words she could.

'Eh! Sylvia! but I know what it is,' said Molly, shaking her head. 'It's just because o' that husband o' thine as has gone and left thee; thou's pining after him, and he's not worth it. Brunton said, when he heared on it – I mind he was smoking at t' time, and he took his pipe out of his mouth, and shook out t' ashes as grave as any judge – "The man," says he, "as can desert a wife like Sylvia Robson as was, deserves hanging!" That's what he says! Eh! Sylvia, but speakin' o' hanging I was so grieved for yo' when I heared of yo'r poor feyther! Such an end for a decent man to come to! Many a one come an' called on me o' purpose to hear all I could tell 'em about him!'

'Please don't speak on it!' said Sylvia, trembling all over.

'Well, poor creature, I wunnot. It is hard on thee, I grant. But to give t' devil his due, it were good i' Hepburn to marry thee, and so soon after there was a' that talk about thy feyther. Many a man would ha' drawn back, choose howiver far they'd gone. I'm noane so sure about Charley Kinraid. Eh, Sylvia! only think on his being alive after all. I doubt if our Bessy would ha' wed Frank Dawson if she'd known as he wasn't drowned. But it's as well she did, for Dawson's a man o' property, and has getten twelve cows in his cow-house, beside three right down good horses; and Kinraid were allays a fellow wi' two strings to his bow. I've allays said and do maintain, that he went on pretty strong* wi' yo', Sylvie; and I will say I think he cared more for yo' than for our Bessy, though it were only yesterday at e'en she were standing out that he liked her better than yo'. Yo'll ha' heared on his grand marriage?'

'No!' said Sylvia, with eager painful curiosity.

'No! It was in all t' papers! I wonder as yo' didn't see it. Wait a minute! I cut it out o' t' *Gentleman's Magazine,** as Brunton bought o' purpose, and put it i' my pocket-book when I were a-coming here: I know I've got it somewheere.'

She took out her smart crimson pocket-book, and rummaged in the pocket until she produced a little crumpled bit of printed paper, from which she read aloud,

'On January the third, at St Mary Redcliffe, Bristol, Charles Kinraid, Esq., lieutenant Royal Navy, to Miss Clarinda Jackson, with a fortune of 10,000*l.*'

'Theere!' said she, triumphantly, 'it's something, as Brunton says, to be cousin to that.'

'Would yo' let me see it?' said Sylvia, timidly.

Mrs Brunton graciously consented; and Sylvia brought her newly acquired reading-knowledge, hitherto principally exercised on the Old Testament, to bear on these words.

There was nothing wonderful in them, nothing that she might not have expected; and yet the surprise turned her giddy for a moment or two. She never thought of seeing him again, never. But to think of his caring for another woman as much as he had done for her, nay, perhaps more!

The idea was irresistibly forced upon her that Philip would not have acted so; it would have taken long years before he could have been induced to put another on the throne she had once occupied. For the first time in her life she seemed to recognize the real nature of Philip's love.

But she said nothing but 'Thank yo'', when she gave the scrap of paper back to Molly Brunton. And the latter continued giving her information about Kinraid's marriage.

'He were down in t' west, Plymouth or somewheere, when he met wi' her. She's no feyther; he'd been in t' sugar-baking business; but from what Kinraid wrote to old Turner, th' uncle as brought him up at Cullercoats, she's had t' best of edications: can play on t' instrument and dance t' shawl dance; and Kinraid had all her money settled on her, though she said she'd rayther give it all to him, which I must say, being his cousin, was very pretty on her. He's left her now, having to go off in t' *Tigre*, as is his ship, to t' Mediterranean seas; and she's written to offer to come and see old Turner, and make friends with his relations, and Brunton is going to gi'e me a crimson satin as soon as we know for certain when she's coming, for we're sure to be asked out to Cullercoats.'

'I wonder if she's very pretty?' asked Sylvia, faintly, in the first pause in this torrent of talk.

'Oh! she's a perfect beauty, as I understand. There was a traveller as come to our shop as had been at York, and knew some of her cousins theere, that were in t' grocery line – her mother was a York lady – and they said she was just a picture of a woman, and iver so many gentlemen had been wantin' to marry her, but she just waited for Charley Kinraid, yo' see!'

'Well, I hope they'll be happy; I'm sure I do!' said Sylvia.

'That's just luck. Some folks is happy i' marriage, and some isn't. It's just luck, and there's no forecasting it. Men is such unaccountable animals, there's no prophesyin' upon 'em. Who'd ha' thought of yo'r husband, him as was so slow and sure – steady Philip, as we lasses used to ca' him – makin' a moonlight flittin',* and leavin' yo' to be a widow bewitched?'

'He didn't go at night,' said Sylvia, taking the words 'moonlight flitting' in their literal sense.

'No! Well, I only said "moonlight flittin'" just because it come uppermost and I knowed no better. Tell me all about it, Sylvie, for I can't mak' it out from what Bessy says. Had he and yo' had words? – but in course yo' had.'

At this moment Hester came into the room; and Sylvia joyfully availed herself of the pretext for breaking off the conversation that had reached this painful and awkward point. She detained Hester in the room for fear lest Mrs Brunton should repeat her inquiry as to how it all happened that Philip had gone away; but the presence of a third person seemed as though it would be but little restraint upon the inquisitive Molly, who repeatedly bore down upon the same questions till she nearly drove Sylvia distracted, between her astonishment at the news of Kinraid's marriage; her wish to be alone and quiet, so as to realize the full meaning of that piece of intelligence; her desire to retain Hester in the conversation; her efforts to prevent Molly's recurrence to the circumstances of Philip's disappearance, and the longing – more vehement every minute – for her visitor to go away and leave her in peace. She became so disturbed with all these thoughts and feelings that she hardly knew what she was saying, and assented or dissented to speeches without there being either any reason or truth in her words.

Mrs Brunton had arranged to remain with Sylvia while the horse rested, and had no compunction about the length of her visit. She expected to be asked to tea, as Sylvia found out at last, and this she felt would be the worst of all, as Alice Rose was not one to tolerate the coarse, careless talk of such a woman as Mrs Brunton without uplifting her voice in many a testimony against it. Sylvia sat holding Hester's gown tight in order to prevent her leaving the room, and trying to arrange her little plans so that too much discordance should not arise to the surface. Just then the door opened, and little Bella came in from the kitchen in all the pretty, sturdy dignity of two years old, Alice following her with careful steps, and protecting, outstretched arms, a slow smile softening the sternness of her grave face; for the child was the unconscious darling of the household, and all eyes softened into love as they looked on her. She made straight for her mother with something grasped in her little dimpled fist; but half-way across the room she seemed to have become suddenly aware of the presence of a stranger, and she stopped short, fixing her serious eyes full on Mrs Brunton, as if to take in her appearance, nay, as if to penetrate down into her very real self, and then, stretching out her disengaged hand, the baby spoke out the words that had been hovering about her mother's lips for an hour past.

'Do away!' said Bella, decisively.

'What a perfect love!' said Mrs Brunton, half in real admiration, half in patronage. As she spoke, she got up and went towards the child, as if to take her up.

'Do away! do away!' cried Bella, in shrill affright at this movement.

'Dunnot,' said Sylvia; 'she's shy; she doesn't know strangers.'

But Mrs Brunton had grasped the struggling, kicking child by this time, and her reward for this was a vehement little slap in the face.

'Yo' naughty little spoilt thing!' said she, setting Bella down in a hurry. 'Yo' deserve a good whipping, yo' do, and if yo' were mine yo' should have it.'

Sylvia had no need to stand up for the baby who had run to her arms, and was soothing herself with sobbing on her mother's breast; for Alice took up the defence.

'The child said, as plain as words could say, "go away", and if thou wouldst follow thine own will instead of heeding her wish, thou mun put up with the wilfulness of the old Adam, of which it seems to me thee hast gotten thy share at thirty as well as little Bella at two.'

'Thirty!' said Mrs Brunton, now fairly affronted. 'Thirty! why, Sylvia, yo' know I'm but two years older than yo'; speak to that woman an' tell her as I'm only four and twenty. Thirty, indeed!'

'Molly's but four and twenty,' said Sylvia, in a pacificatory tone.

'Whether she be twenty, or thirty, or forty, is alike to me,' said Alice. 'I meant no harm. I meant but for t' say as her angry words to the child bespoke her to be one of the foolish. I know not who she is, nor what her age may be.'

'She's an old friend of mine,' said Sylvia. 'She's Mrs Brunton now, but when I knowed her she was Molly Corney.'

'Ay! and yo' were Sylvia Robson, and as bonny and light-hearted a lass as any in a' t' Riding, though now yo're a poor widow bewitched, left wi' a child as I mustn't speak a word about, an' living wi' folk as talk about t' old Adam as if he wasn't dead and done wi' long ago! It's a change, Sylvia, as makes my heart ache for yo', to think on them old days when yo' were so thought on yo' might have had any man, as Brunton often says; it were a great mistake as yo' iver took up wi' yon man as has run away. But seven year'll soon be past fro' t' time he went off, and yo'll only be six-and-twenty then, and there'll be a chance of a better husband for yo' after all, so keep up yo'r heart, Sylvia.'

Molly Brunton had put as much venom as she knew how into this speech, meaning it as a vengeful payment for the supposition of her being thirty, even more than for the reproof for her angry words about the child. She thought that Alice Rose must be either mother or aunt to Philip, from the serious cast of countenance that was remarkable in both; and she rather exulted in the allusion to a happier second marriage for Sylvia with which she had concluded her speech. It roused Alice, however, as effectually as if she had been really a blood relation to Philip; but for a different reason. She was not slow to detect the intentional offensiveness to herself in what had been said; she was indignant at Sylvia for suffering the words spoken to pass unanswered; but in truth they were too much in keeping with Molly Brunton's character to make as much impression on Sylvia as they did on a stranger; and besides, she felt as if the less reply Molly received, the less likely would it be that she would go on in the same strain. So she coaxed and chattered to her child, and behaved like a little coward in trying to draw out of the conversation, while at the same time listening attentively.

'As for Sylvia Hepburn as was Sylvia Robson, she knows my mind,' said Alice, in grim indignation. 'She's humbling herself now, I trust and pray, but she was light-minded and full of vanity when Philip married her, and it might ha' been a lift towards her salvation in one way; but it pleased the Lord to work in a different way, and she mun wear her sackcloth and ashes in patience.* So I'll say naught more about her. But for him as is absent, as thee hast spoken on so lightly and reproachfully, I'd have thee to know he were one of a different kind to any thee ever knew, I reckon. If he were led away by a pretty face to slight one as was fitter for him, and who had loved him as the apple of her eye, it's him as is suffering for it, inasmuch as he's a wanderer from his home, and an outcast from wife and child.'

To the surprise of all, Molly's words of reply were cut short even when they were on her lips, by Sylvia. Pale, fire-eyed, and excited, with Philip's child on one arm, and the other stretched out, she said, –

'Noane can tell – noane know. No one shall speak a judgment 'twixt Philip and me. He acted cruel and wrong by me. But I've said my words to him hissel', and I'm noane going to make any plaint to others; only them as knows should judge. And it's not fitting, it's not' (almost sobbing), 'to go on wi' talk like this afore me.'

The two – for Hester, who was aware that her presence had only been desired by Sylvia as a check to an unpleasant *tête-à-tête* conversation, had slipped back to her business as soon as her mother came in – the two looked with surprise at Sylvia; her words, her whole manner, belonged to a phase of her character which seldom came uppermost, and which had not been perceived by either of them before.

Alice Rose, though astonished, rather approved of Sylvia's speech; it showed that she had more serious thought and feeling on the subject than the old woman had given her credit for; her general silence respecting her husband's disappearance had led Alice to think that she was too childish to have received any deep impression from the event. Molly Brunton gave vent to her opinion on Sylvia's speech in the following words: –

'Hoighty-toighty! That tells tales, lass. If yo' treated steady Philip to many such looks an' speeches as yo'n given us now, it's easy t' see why he took hisself off. Why, Sylvia, I niver saw it in yo' when yo' was a girl; yo're grown into a regular little vixen, theere wheere yo' stand!'

Indeed she did look defiant, with the swift colour flushing her cheeks to crimson on its return, and the fire in her eyes not yet died away. But at Molly's jesting words she sank back into her usual look and manner, only saying quietly, –

'It's for noane to say whether I'm vixen or not, as doesn't know th' past things as is buried in my heart. But I cannot hold them as my friends as go on talking on either my husband or me before my very face. What he was, I know; and what I am, I reckon he knows. And now I'll go hurry tea, for yo'll be needing it, Molly!'

The last clause of this speech was meant to make peace; but Molly was in twenty minds as to whether she should accept the olive-branch or not. Her temper, however, was of that obtuse kind which is not easily ruffled; her mind, stagnant in itself, enjoyed excitement from without; and her appetite was invariably good, so she stayed, in spite of the inevitable *tête-à-tête* with Alice. The latter, however, refused to be drawn into conversation again; replying to Mrs Brunton's speeches with a curt yes or no, when, indeed, she replied at all.

When all were gathered at tea, Sylvia was quite calm again; rather paler than usual, and very attentive and subdued in her behaviour to Alice; she would evidently fain have been silent, but as Molly was her own especial guest, that could not be, so all her endeavours went towards steering the conversation away from any awkward points. But each of the four, let alone little Bella, was thankful when the market-cart drew up at the shop door, that was to take Mrs Brunton back to her sister's house.

When she was fairly off, Alice Rose opened her mouth in strong condemnation; winding up with –

'And if aught in my words gave thee cause for offence, Sylvia, it was because my heart rose within me at the kind of talk thee and she had been having about Philip, and her evil and light-minded counsel to thee about waiting seven years, and then wedding another.'

Hard as these words may seem when repeated, there was something of a nearer approach to an apology in Mrs Rose's manner than Sylvia had ever seen in it before. She was silent for a few moments, then she said, –

'I ha' often thought of telling yo' and Hester, special-like, when yo've been so kind to my little Bella, that Philip an' me could niver come together again; no, not if he came home this very night—'

She would have gone on speaking, but Hester interrupted her with a low cry of dismay.

Alice said, –

'Hush thee, Hester. It's no business o' thine. Sylvia Hepburn, thou'rt speaking like a silly child.'

'No. I'm speaking like a woman; like a woman as finds out she's been cheated by men as she trusted, and as has no help for it. I'm noane going to say any more about it. It's me as has been wronged, and as has to bear it: only I thought I'd tell yo' both this much, that yo' might know somewhat why he went away, and how I said my last word about it.'

So indeed it seemed. To all questions and remonstrances from Alice, Sylvia turned a deaf ear. She averted her face from Hester's sad, wistful looks; only when they were parting for the night, at the top of the little staircase, she turned, and putting her arms round Hester's neck she laid her head on her neck, and whispered, –

'Poor Hester – poor, poor Hester if yo' an' he had but been married together, what a deal o' sorrow would ha' been spared to us all!'

Hester pushed her away as she finished these words; looked searchingly into her face, her eyes, and then followed Sylvia into her room, where Bella lay sleeping, shut the door, and almost knelt down at Sylvia's feet, clasping her, and hiding her face in the folds of the other's gown.

'Sylvia, Sylvia,' she murmured, 'some one has told you – I thought no one knew – it's no sin – it's done away with now – indeed it is – it was long ago – before yo' were married; but I cannot forget. It was a shame, perhaps, to have thought on it iver, when he niver thought o' me; but I niver believed as any one could ha' found it out. I'm just fit to sink into t' ground, what wi' my sorrow and my shame.'

Hester was stopped by her own rising sobs, immediately she was in Sylvia's arms. Sylvia was sitting on the ground holding her, and soothing her with caresses and broken words.

'I'm allays saying t' wrong things,' said she. 'It seems as if I were all upset to-day; and indeed I am;' she added, alluding to the news of Kinraid's marriage she had yet to think upon.

'But it wasn't yo', Hester: it were nothing yo' iver said, or did, or looked, for that matter. It were yo'r mother as let it out.'

'Oh, mother! mother!' wailed out Hester; 'I niver thought as any one but God would ha' known that I had iver for a day thought on his being more to me than a brother.'

Sylvia made no reply, only went on stroking Hester's smooth brown hair, off which her cap had fallen. Sylvia was thinking how strange life was, and how love seemed to go all at cross purposes; and was losing herself in bewilderment at the mystery of the world; she was almost startled when Hester rose up, and taking Sylvia's hands in both of hers, and looking solemnly at her, said, –

'Sylvia, yo' know what has been my trouble and my shame, and I'm sure yo're sorry for me – for I will humble myself to yo', and own that for many months before yo' were married, I felt my disappointment like a heavy burden laid on me by day and by night; but now I ask yo', if yo've any pity for me for what I went through, or if yo've any love for me because of yo'r dead mother's love for me, or because of any fellowship, or daily breadliness between us two, – put the hard thoughts of Philip away from out yo'r heart; he may ha' done yo' wrong, anyway yo' think that he has; I niver knew him aught but kind and good; but if he comes back from wheriver in th' wide world he's gone to (and there's not a night but I pray God to keep him, and send him safe back), yo' put away the memory of past injury, and forgive it all, and be, what yo' can be, Sylvia, if yo've a mind to, just the kind, good wife he ought to have.'

'I cannot; yo' know nothing about it, Hester.'

'Tell me, then,' pleaded Hester.

'No!' said Sylvia, after a moment's hesitation; 'I'd do a deal for yo', I would, but I daren't forgive Philip, even if I could; I took a great oath again' him. Ay, yo' may look shocked at me, but it's him as yo' ought for to be shocked at if yo' knew all. I said I'd niver forgive him; I shall keep to my word.'

'I think I'd better pray for his death, then,' said Hester, hopelessly, and almost bitterly, loosing her hold of Sylvia's hands.

'If it weren't for baby theere, I could think as it were my death as 'ud be best. Them as one thinks t' most on, forgets one soonest.'

It was Kinraid to whom she was alluding; but Hester did not understand her; and after standing for a moment in silence, she kissed her, and left her for the night.

CHAPTER 40

An Unexpected Messenger

After this agitation, and these partial confidences, no more was said on the subject of Philip for many weeks. They avoided even the slightest allusion to him; and none of them knew how seldom or how often he might be present in the minds of the others.

One day the little Bella was unusually fractious with some slight childish indisposition, and Sylvia was obliged to have recourse to a never-failing piece of amusement; namely, to take the child into the shop, when the number of new, bright-coloured articles was sure to beguile the little girl out of her fretfulness. She was walking along the high terrace of the counter, kept steady by her mother's hand, when Mr Dawson's market-cart once more stopped before the door. But it was not Mrs Brunton who alighted now; it was a very smartly-dressed, very pretty young lady, who put one dainty foot before the other with care, as if descending from such a primitive vehicle were a new occurrence in her life. Then she looked up at the names above the shop door, and after ascertaining that this was indeed the place she desired to find, she came in blushing.

'Is Mrs Hepburn at home?' she asked of Hester, whose position in the shop brought her forwards to receive the customers, while Sylvia drew Bella out of sight behind some great bales of red flannel.

'Can I see her?' the sweet, south-country voice went on, still addressing Hester. Sylvia heard the inquiry, and came forwards, with a little rustic awkwardness, feeling both shy and curious.

'Will yo' please walk this way, ma'am?' said she, leading her visitor back into her own dominion of the parlour, and leaving Bella to Hester's willing care.

'You don't know me!' said the pretty young lady, joyously. 'But I think you knew my husband. I am Mrs Kinraid!'

A sob of surprise rose to Sylvia's lips – she choked it down, however, and tried to conceal any emotion she might feel, in placing a chair for her visitor, and trying to make her feel welcome, although, if the truth must be told, Sylvia was wondering all the time why her visitor came, and how soon she would go.

'You knew Captain Kinraid, did you not?' said the young lady, with innocent inquiry; to which Sylvia's lips formed the answer, 'Yes,' but no clear sound issued therefrom.

'But I know your husband knew the captain; is he at home yet? Can I speak to him? I do so want to see him.'

Sylvia was utterly bewildered; Mrs Kinraid, this pretty, joyous, prosperous little bird of a woman, Philip, Charley's wife, what could they have in common? what could they know of each other? All she could say in answer to Mrs Kinraid's eager questions, and still more eager looks, was, that her husband was from home, had been long from home: she did not know where he was, she did not know when he would come back.

Mrs Kinraid's face fell a little, partly from her own real disappointment, partly out of sympathy with the hopeless, indifferent tone of Sylvia's replies.

'Mrs Dawson told me he had gone away rather suddenly a year ago, but I thought he might be come home by now. I am expecting the captain early next month. Oh! how I should have liked to see Mr Hepburn, and to thank him for saving the captain's life!'

'What do yo' mean?' asked Sylvia, stirred out of all assumed indifference. 'The captain! is that' (not 'Charley,' she could not use that familiar name to the pretty young wife before her) 'yo'r husband?'

'Yes, you knew him, didn't you? when he used to be staying with Mr Corney, his uncle?'

'Yes, I knew him; but I don't understand. Will yo' please to tell me all about it, ma'am?' said Sylvia, faintly.

'I thought your husband would have told you all about it; I hardly know where to begin. You know my husband is a sailor?'

Sylvia nodded assent, listening greedily, her heart beating thick all the time.

'And he's now a Commander in the Royal Navy, all earned by his own bravery! Oh! I am so proud of him!'

So could Sylvia have been if she had been his wife; as it was, she thought how often she had felt sure that he would be a great man some day.

'And he has been at the siege of Acre.'

Sylvia looked perplexed at these strange words, and Mrs Kinraid caught the look.

'St Jean d'Acre, you know – though it's fine saying "you know," when I didn't know a bit about it myself till the captain's ship was ordered there, though I was the head girl at Miss Dobbin's* in the geography class – Acre is a seaport town, not far from Jaffa, which is the modern name for Joppa, where St Paul went to long ago; you've read of that, I'm sure, and Mount Carmel, where the prophet Elijah* was once, all in Palestine, you know, only the Turks have got it now?'

'But I don't understand yet,' said Sylvia, plaintively; 'I daresay it's all very true about St Paul, but please, ma'am, will yo' tell me about yo'r husband and mine – have they met again?'

'Yes, at Acre, I tell you,' said Mrs Kinraid, with pretty petulance. 'The Turks held the town, and the French wanted to take it; and we, that is the British Fleet, wouldn't let them. So Sir Sidney Smith, a commodore and a great friend of the captain's, landed in order to fight the French; and the captain and many of the sailors landed with him; and it was burning hot; and the poor captain was wounded, and lay a-dying of pain and thirst within the enemy's – that is the French – fire; so that they were ready to shoot any one of his own side who came near him. They thought he was dead himself, you see, as he was very near; and would have been too, if your husband had not come out of shelter, and taken him up in his arms or on his back (I couldn't make out which), and carried him safe within the walls.'

'It couldn't have been Philip,' said Sylvia, dubiously.

'But it was. The captain says so; and he's not a man to be mistaken. I thought I'd got his letter with me; and I would have read you a part of it, but I left it at Mrs Dawson's in my desk; and I can't send it to you,' blushing as she remembered certain passages in which 'the captain' wrote very much like a lover, 'or else I would. But you may be quite sure it was your husband that ventured into all that danger to save his old friend's life, or the captain would not have said so.'

'But they weren't – they weren't – not to call great friends.'

'I wish I'd got the letter here; I can't think how I could be so stupid; I think I can almost remember the very words, though – I've read them over so often. He says, "Just as I gave up all hope, I saw one Philip Hepburn, a man whom I had known at Monkshaven, and whom I had some reason to remember well" – (I'm sure he says so – "remember well"), "he saw me too, and came at the risk of his life to where I lay. I fully expected he would be shot down; and I shut my eyes not to see the end of my last chance. The shot rained about him, and I think he was hit; but he took me up and carried me under cover." I'm sure he says that, I've read it over so often; and he goes on and says how he hunted for Mr Hepburn all through the ships, as soon as ever he could; but he could hear nothing of him, either alive or dead. Don't go so white, for pity's sake!' said she, suddenly startled by Sylvia's blanching colour. 'You see, because he couldn't find him alive is no reason for giving him up as dead; because his name wasn't to be found on any of the ships' books;

so the captain thinks he must have been known by a different name to his real one. Only he says he should like to have seen him to have thanked him; and he says he would give a deal to know what has become of him; and as I was staying two days at Mrs Dawson's, I told them I must come over to Monkshaven, if only for five minutes, just to hear if your good husband was come home, and to shake his hands, that helped to save my own dear captain.'

'I don't think it could have been Philip,' reiterated Sylvia.

'Why not?' asked her visitor; 'you say you don't know where he is; why mightn't he have been there where the captain says he was?'

'But he wasn't a sailor, nor yet a soldier.'

'Oh! but he was. I think somewhere the captain calls him a marine; that's neither one nor the other, but a little of both. He'll be coming home some day soon; and then you'll see!'

Alice Rose came in at this minute, and Mrs Kinraid jumped to the conclusion that she was Sylvia's mother, and in her overflowing gratitude and friendliness to all the family of him who had 'saved the captain', she went forward, and shook the old woman's hand in that pleasant confiding way that wins all hearts.

'Here's your daughter, ma'am!' said she to the half-astonished, half-pleased Alice. 'I'm Mrs Kinraid, the wife of the captain that used to be in these parts, and I'm come to bring her news of her husband, and she don't half believe me, though it's all to his credit, I'm sure.'

Alice looked so perplexed that Sylvia felt herself bound to explain.

'She says he's either a soldier or a sailor, and a long way off at some place named in t' Bible.'

'Philip Hepburn led away to be a soldier!' said she, 'who had once been a Quaker?'*

'Yes, and a very brave one too, and one that it would do my heart good to look upon,' exclaimed Mrs Kinraid. 'He's been saving my husband's life in the Holy Land, where Jerusalem is, you know.'

'Nay!' said Alice, a little scornfully. 'I can forgive Sylvia for not being over keen to credit thy news. Her man of peace becoming a man of war; and suffered to enter Jerusalem, which is a heavenly and a typical city* at this time; while me, as is one of the elect, is obliged to go on dwelling in Monkshaven, just like any other body.'

'Nay, but,' said Mrs Kinraid, gently, seeing she was touching on delicate ground, 'I did not say he had gone to Jerusalem, but my husband saw him in those parts, and he was doing his duty like a brave, good man; ay, and more than his duty; and, you may take my word for it, he'll be at home some day soon, and all I beg is that you'll let the captain and me know, for I'm sure if we can, we'll both come and pay our respects to him. And I'm very glad I've seen you,' said she, rising to go, and putting out her hand to shake that of Sylvia; 'for, besides being Hepburn's wife, I'm pretty sure I've heard the captain speak of you; and if ever you come to Bristol I hope you'll come and see us on Clifton Downs.'

She went away, leaving Sylvia almost stunned by the new ideas presented to her. Philip, soldier! Philip in a battle risking his life. Most strange of all, Charley and Philip once more meeting together, not as rivals or as foes, but as saviour and saved! Add to all this the conviction, strengthened by every word that happy, loving wife had uttered, that Kinraid's old, passionate love for herself had faded away and vanished utterly: its very existence apparently blotted out of his memory. She had torn up her love for him by the roots, but she felt as if she could never forget that it had been.

Hester brought back Bella to her mother. She had not liked to interrupt the conversation with the strange lady before; and now she found her mother in an obvious state of excitement; Sylvia quieter than usual.

'That was Kinraid's wife, Hester! Him that was th' specksioneer as made such a noise about t' place at the time of Darley's death. He's now a captain – a navy captain, according to what she says. And she'd fain have us believe that Philip is abiding in all manner of Scripture places; places as has been long done away with, but the similitude whereof is in the heavens, where the elect shall one day see them. And she says Philip is there, and a soldier, and that he saved her husband's life, and is coming home soon. I wonder what John and Jeremiah 'll say to his soldiering then? It 'll noane be to their taste, I'm thinking.'

This was all very unintelligible to Hester, and she would dearly have liked to question Sylvia; but Sylvia sat a little apart, with Bella on her knee, her cheek resting on her child's golden curls, and her eyes fixed and almost trance-like, as if she were seeing things not present.

So Hester had to be content with asking her mother as many elucidatory questions as she could; and after all did not gain a very clear idea of what had really been said by Mrs Kinraid, as her mother was more full of the apparent injustice of Philip's being allowed the privilege of treading on holy ground – if, indeed, that holy ground existed on this side heaven, which she was inclined to dispute – than to confine herself to the repetition of words, or narration of facts.

Suddenly Sylvia roused herself to a sense of Hester's deep interest and balked inquiries, and she went over the ground rapidly.

'Yo'r mother says right – she is his wife. And he's away fighting; and got too near t' French as was shooting and firing all round him; and just then, according to her story, Philip saw him, and went straight into t' midst o' t' shots, and fetched him out o' danger. That's what she says, and upholds.'

'And why should it not be?' asked Hester, her cheek flushing.

But Sylvia only shook her head, and said,

'I cannot tell. It may be so. But they'd little cause to be friends, and it seems all so strange – Philip a soldier, and them meeting theere after all!'

Hester laid the story of Philip's bravery to her heart – she fully believed in it. Sylvia pondered it more deeply still; the causes for her disbelief, or, at any rate, for her wonder, were unknown to Hester! Many a time she sank to sleep with the picture of the event narrated by Mrs Kinraid as present to her mind as her imagination or experience could make it: first one figure prominent, then another. Many a morning she wakened up, her heart beating wildly, why, she knew not, till she shuddered at the remembrance of the scenes that had passed in her dreams: scenes that might be acted in reality that very day; for Philip might come back, and then?

And where was Philip all this time, these many weeks, these heavily passing months?

CHAPTER 41

The Bedesman of St Sepulchre

Philip lay long ill on board the hospital ship. If his heart had been light, he might have rallied sooner; but he was so depressed he did not care to live. His shattered jawbone, his burnt and blackened face, his many injuries of body, were torture to both his physical frame, and his sick, weary heart. No more chance for him, if indeed there ever had been any, of returning gay and gallant, and thus regaining his wife's love. This had been his poor, foolish vision in the first hour of his enlistment; and the vain dream had recurred more than once in the feverish stage of excitement which the new scenes into which he had been hurried as a recruit had called forth. But that was all over now. He knew that it was the most unlikely thing in the world to have come to pass; and yet those were happy days when he could think of it as barely possible. Now all he could look forward to was disfigurement, feebleness, and the bare pittance that keeps pensioners from absolute want.

Those around him were kind enough to him in their fashion, and attended to his bodily requirements; but they had no notion of listening to any revelations of unhappiness, if Philip had been the man to make confidences of that kind. As it was, he lay very still in his berth, seldom asking for anything, and always saying he was better, when the ship-surgeon came round with his daily inquiries. But he did not care to rally, and was rather sorry to find that his case was considered so interesting in a surgical point of view, that he was likely to receive a good deal more than the average amount of attention. Perhaps it was owing to this that he recovered at all. This doctors said it was the heat that made him languid, for that his wounds and burns were all doing well at last; and by-and-by they told him they had ordered him 'home'. His pulse sank under the surgeon's finger at the mention of the word; but he did not say a word. He was too indifferent to life and the world to have a will; otherwise they might have kept their pet patient a little longer where he was.

Slowly passing from ship to ship as occasion served; resting here and there in garrison hospitals, Philip at length reached Portsmouth on the evening of a September day in 1799.* The transport-ship in which he was, was loaded with wounded and invalided soldiers and sailors; all who could manage it in any way struggled on deck to catch the first view of the white coasts of England. One man lifted his arm, took off his cap, and feebly waved it aloft, crying, 'Old England for ever!' in a faint shrill voice, and then burst into tears and sobbed aloud. Others tried to pipe up 'Rule Britannia',* while more sat, weak and motionless, looking towards the shores that once, not so long ago, they never thought to see again. Philip was one of these; his place a little apart from the other men. He was muffled up in a great military cloak that had been given him by one of his officers; he felt the September breeze chill after his sojourn in a warmer climate, and in his shattered state of health.

As the ship came in sight of Portsmouth harbour, the signal flags ran up the ropes; the beloved Union Jack floated triumphantly over all. Return signals were made from the harbour; on board all became bustle and preparation for landing; while on shore there was the evident movement of expectation, and men in uniform were soon pressing their way to the front, as if to them belonged the right of reception. They were the men from the barrack hospital, that had been signalled for, come down with ambulance litters and other marks of forethought for the sick and wounded, who were returning to the country for which they had fought and suffered.

With a dash and a great rocking swing the vessel came up to her appointed place, and was safely moored. Philip sat still, almost as if he had no part in the cries of welcome, the bustling care, the loud directions that cut the air around him, and pierced his nerves through and through. But one in authority gave the order; and Philip, disciplined to obedience, rose to find his knapsack and leave the ship. Passive as he seemed to be, he had his likings for particular comrades; there was one especially, a man as different from Philip as well could be, to whom the latter had always attached himself; a merry fellow from Somersetshire, who was almost always cheerful and bright, though Philip had overheard the doctors say he would never be the man he was before he had that shot through the side. This marine would often sit making his fellows laugh, and laughing himself at his own good-humoured jokes, till so terrible a fit of coughing came on that those around him feared he would die in the paroxysm. After one of these fits he had gasped out some words, which led

Philip to question him a little; and it turned out that in the quiet little village of Potterne, far inland, nestled beneath the high stretches of Salisbury Plain, he had a wife and a child, a little girl, just the same age even to a week as Philip's own little Bella. It was this that drew Philip towards the man; and this that made Philip wait and go ashore along with the poor consumptive marine.

The litters had moved off towards the hospital, the sergeant in charge had given his words of command to the remaining invalids, who tried to obey them to the best of their power, falling into something like military order for their march; but soon, very soon, the weakest broke step, and lagged behind; and felt as if the rough welcomes and rude expressions of sympathy from the crowd around were almost too much for them. Philip and his companion were about midway, when suddenly a young woman with a child in her arms forced herself through the people, between the soldiers who kept pressing on either side, and threw herself on the neck of Philip's friend.

'Oh Jem!' she sobbed. 'I've walked all the road from Potterne. I've never stopped but for food and rest for Nelly, and now I've got you once again, I've got you once again, bless God for it!'

She did not seem to see the deadly change that had come over her husband since she parted with him, a ruddy young labourer; she had got him once again, as she phrased it, and that was enough for her; she kissed his face, his hands, his very coat, nor would she be repulsed from walking beside him and holding his hand, while her little girl ran along scared by the voices and the strange faces, and clinging to her mammy's gown.

Jem coughed, poor fellow! he coughed his churchyard cough; and Philip bitterly envied him – envied his life, envied his approaching death; for was he not wrapped round with that woman's tender love, and is not such love stronger than death? Philip had felt as if his own heart was grown numb, and as though it had changed to a cold heavy stone. But at the contrast of this man's lot to his own, he felt that he had yet the power of suffering left to him.

The road they had to go was full of people, kept off in some measure by the guard of soldiers. All sorts of kindly speeches, and many a curious question, were addressed to the poor invalids as they walked along. Philip's jaw, and the lower part of his face, were bandaged up; his cap was slouched down; he held his cloak about him, and shivered within its folds.

They came to a standstill from some slight obstacle at the corner of a street. Down the causeway of this street a naval officer with a lady on his arm was walking briskly, with a step that told of health and a light heart. He stayed his progress though, when he saw the convoy of maimed and wounded men; he said something, of which Philip only caught the words, 'same uniform', 'for his sake', to the young lady, whose cheek blanched a little, but whose eyes kindled. Then leaving her for an instant, he pressed forward; he was close to Philip, – poor sad Philip absorbed in his own thoughts, – so absorbed that he noticed nothing till he heard a voice at his ear, having the Northumbrian burr, the Newcastle inflections which he knew of old, and that were to him like the sick memory of a deadly illness; and then he turned his muffled face to the speaker, though he knew well enough who it was, and averted his eyes after one sight of the handsome, happy man, – the man whose life he had saved once, and would save again, at the risk of his own, but whom, for all that, he prayed that he might never meet more on earth.

'Here, my fine fellow, take this,' forcing a crown piece into Philip's hand. 'I wish it were more; I'd give you a pound if I had it with me.'

Philip muttered something, and held out the coin to Captain Kinraid, of course in vain; nor was there time to urge it back upon the giver, for the obstacle to their progress was suddenly removed, the crowd pressed upon the captain and his wife, the procession moved on, and Philip along with it, holding the piece in his hand, and longing to throw it far away. Indeed he was on the point of dropping it, hoping to do so unperceived, when he bethought him of giving it to Jem's wife, the footsore woman, limping happily along by her husband's side. They thanked him, and spoke in his praise more than he could well bear. It was no credit to him to give that away which burned his fingers as long as he kept it.

Philip knew that the injuries he had received in the explosion on board the *Theseus* would oblige him to leave the service. He also believed that they would entitle him to a pension. But he had little interest in his future life; he was without hope, and in a depressed state of health. He remained for some little time stationary, and then went through all the forms of dismissal on account of wounds received in service, and was turned out loose upon the world, uncertain where to go, indifferent as to what became of him.

It was fine, warm October weather as he turned his back upon the coast, and set off on his walk northwards. Green leaves were yet upon the trees; the hedges were one flush of foliage and the wild rough-flavoured fruits of different kinds; the fields were tawny with the uncleared-off stubble, or emerald green with the growth of the aftermath. The roadside cottage gardens were gay with hollyhocks and Michaelmas daisies and marigolds, and the bright panes of the windows glittered through a veil of China roses.

The war was a popular one, and, as a natural consequence, soldiers and sailors were heroes everywhere. Philip's long drooping form, his arm hung in a sling, his face scarred and blackened, his jaw bound up with a black silk handkerchief; these marks of active service were reverenced by the rustic cottagers as though they had been crowns and sceptres. Many a hard-handed labourer left his seat by the chimney corner, and came to his door to have a look at one who had been fighting the French, and pushed forward to have a grasp of the stranger's hand as he gave back the empty cup into the good wife's keeping, for the kind homely women were ever ready with milk or homebrewed to slake the feverish traveller's thirst when he stopped at their doors and asked for a drink of water.

At the village public-house he had had a welcome of a more interested character, for the landlord knew full well that his circle of customers would be large that night, if it was only known that he had within his doors a soldier or a sailor who had seen service. The rustic politicians would gather round Philip, and smoke and drink, and then question and discuss till they were drouthy* again; and in their sturdy obtuse minds they set down the extra glass and the supernumerary pipe to the score of patriotism.

Altogether human nature turned its sunny side out to Philip just now; and not before he needed the warmth of brotherly kindness to cheer his shivering soul. Day after day he drifted northwards, making but the slow progress of a feeble man, and yet this short daily walk tired him so much that he longed for rest – for the morning to come when he needed not to feel that in the course of an hour or two he must be up and away.

He was toiling on with this longing at his heart when he saw that he was drawing near a stately city, with a great old cathedral in the centre keeping solemn guard. This place might be yet two or three miles distant; he was on a rising ground looking down upon it. A labouring man passing by, observed his pallid looks and his languid attitude, and told him for his comfort, that if he turned down a lane to the left a few steps farther on, he would find himself at the Hospital of St Sepulchre,* where bread and beer were given to all comers, and where he might sit him down and rest awhile on the old stone benches within the shadow of the gateway. Obeying these directions, Philip came upon a building which dated from the time of Henry the Fifth.* Some knight who had fought in the French wars of that time, and had survived his battles and come home to his old halls, had been stirred up by his conscience, or by what was equivalent in those days, his confessor, to build and endow a hospital for twelve decayed soldiers,* and a chapel wherein they were to attend the daily masses he ordained to be said till the end of all time (which eternity lasted rather more than a century, pretty well for an eternity bespoken by a man), for his soul and the souls of those whom he had slain. There was a large division of the quadrangular building set apart for the priest who was to say these masses; and to watch over the well-being of the bedesmen. In process of years the origin and primary purpose of the hospital had been forgotten by all excepting the local antiquaries; and the place itself came to be regarded as a very pleasant quaint set of almshouses; and the warden's office (he who should have said or sung his daily masses was now called the warden, and read daily prayers and preached a sermon on Sundays) an agreeable sinecure.

Another legacy of old Sir Simon Bray was that of a small croft of land, the rent or profits of which were to go towards giving to all who asked for it a manchet* of bread and a cup of good beer. This beer was, so Sir Simon ordained, to be made after a certain receipt which he left, in which ground ivy took the place of hops. But the receipt, as well as the masses, was modernized according to the progress of time.

Philip stood under a great broad stone archway; the backdoor into the warden's house was on the right side; a kind of buttery-hatch was placed by the porter's door on the opposite side. After some consideration, Philip knocked at the closed shutter, and the signal seemed to be well understood. He heard a movement within; the hatch was drawn aside, and his bread and beer were handed to him by a pleasant-looking old man, who proved himself not at all disinclined for conversation.

'You may sit down on yonder bench,' said he. 'Nay, man! sit i' the sun, for it's a chilly place this, and then you can look through the grate and watch th' old fellows toddling about in th' quad.'

Philip sat down where the warm October sun slanted upon him, and looked through the iron railing at the peaceful sight.

A great square of velvet lawn, intersected diagonally with broad flag-paved walks, the same kind of walk going all round the quadrangle; low two-storied brick houses, tinted grey and yellow by age, and in many places almost covered with vines, Virginian creepers, and monthly roses; before each house a little plot of garden ground, bright with flowers, and evidently tended with the utmost care; on the farther side the massive chapel; here and there an old or infirm man sunning himself, or leisurely doing a bit of gardening, or talking to one of his comrades – the place looked as if care and want, and even sorrow, were locked out and excluded by the ponderous gate through which Philip was gazing.

'It's a nice enough place, bean't it?' said the porter interpreting Philip's looks pretty accurately. 'Leastways, for them as likes it. I've got a bit weary on it myself; it's so far from th' world, as a man may say; not a decent public within a mile and a half, where one can hear a bit o' news of an evening.'

'I think I could make myself very content here,' replied Philip. 'That's to say, if one were easy in one's mind.'

'Ay, ay, my man. That's it everywhere. Why, I don't think that I could enjoy myself – not even at th' White Hart, where they give you as good a glass of ale for twopence as anywhere i' th' four kingdoms – I couldn't, to say, flavour my ale even there, if my old woman lay a-dying; which is a sign as it's the heart, and not the ale, as makes the drink.'

Just then the warden's back-door opened, and out came the warden himself, dressed in full clerical costume.

He was going into the neighbouring city, but he stopped to speak to Philip, the wounded soldier; and all the more readily because his old faded uniform told the warden's experienced eye that he had belonged to the Marines.

'I hope you enjoy the victual provided for you by the founder of St Sepulchre,' said he, kindly. 'You look but poorly, my good fellow, and as if a slice of good cold meat would help your bread down.'

'Thank you, sir!' said Philip. 'I'm not hungry, only weary, and glad of a draught of beer.'

'You've been in the Marines, I see. Where have you been serving?'

'I was at the siege of Acre, last May, sir.'

'At Acre! Were you, indeed? Then perhaps you know my boy Harry? He was in the – th.'

'It was my company,' said Philip, warming up a little. Looking back upon his soldier's life, it seemed to him to have many charms, because it was so full of small daily interests.

'Then, did you know my son, Lieutenant Pennington?'

'It was he that gave me this cloak, sir, when they were sending me back to England. I had been his servant for a short time before I was wounded by the explosion on board the *Theseus*, and he said I should feel the cold of the voyage. He's very kind; and I've heard say he promises to be a first-rate officer.'

'You shall have a slice of roast beef, whether you want it or not,' said the warden, ringing the bell at his own back-door. 'I recognize the cloak now – the young scamp! How soon he has made it shabby, though,' he continued, taking up a corner where there was an immense tear not too well botched up. 'And so you were on board the *Theseus* at the time of the explosion? Bring some cold meat here for the good man – or stay! Come in with me, and then you can tell Mrs Pennington and the young ladies all you know about Harry, – and the siege, – and the explosion.'

So Philip was ushered into the warden's house and made to eat roast beef almost against his will; and he was questioned and cross-questioned by three eager ladies, all at the same time, as it seemed to him. He had given all possible details on the subjects about which they were curious; and was beginning to consider how he could best make his retreat, when the younger Miss Pennington went up to her father – who had all this time stood, with his hat on, holding his coat-tails over his arms, with his back to the fire. He bent his ear down a very little to hear some whispered suggestion of his daughter's, nodded his head, and then went on questioning Philip, with kindly inquisitiveness and patronage, as the rich do question the poor.

'And where are you going to now?'

Philip did not answer directly. He wondered in his own mind where he was going. At length he said,

'Northwards, I believe. But perhaps I shall never reach there.'

'Haven't you friends? Aren't you going to them?'

There was again a pause; a cloud came over Philip's countenance. He said,

'No! I'm not going to my friends. I don't know that I've got any left.'

They interpreted his looks and this speech to mean that he had either lost his friends by death, or offended them by enlisting.

The warden went on,

'I ask, because we've got a cottage vacant in the mead. Old Dobson, who was with General Wolfe at the taking of Quebec,* died a fortnight ago. With such injuries as yours, I fear you'll never be able to work again. But we require strict testimonials as to character,' he added, with as penetrating a look as he could summon up at Philip.

Philip looked unmoved, either by the offer of the cottage, or the allusion to the possibility of his character not being satisfactory. He was grateful enough in reality, but too heavy at heart to care very much what became of him.

The warden and his family, who were accustomed to consider settlement at St Sepulchre's as the sum of all good to a worn-out soldier, were a little annoyed at Philip's cool way of receiving the proposition. The warden went on to name the contingent advantages.

'Besides the cottage, you would have a load of wood for firing on All Saints', on Christmas, and on Candlemas days – a blue gown and suit of clothes to match every Michaelmas, and a shilling a day to keep yourself in all other things. Your dinner you would have with the other men, in hall.'

'The warden himself goes into hall every day, and sees that everything is comfortable, and says grace,' added the warden's lady.

'I know I seem stupid,' said Philip, almost humbly, 'not to be more grateful, for it's far beyond what I iver expected or thought for again, and it's a great temptation, for I'm just worn out with fatigue. Several times I've thought I must lie down under a hedge, and just die for very weariness. But once I had a wife and a child up in the north,' he stopped.

'And are they dead?' asked one of the young ladies in a soft sympathizing tone. Her eyes met Philip's, full of dumb woe. He tried to speak; he wanted to explain more fully, yet not to reveal the truth.

'Well!' said the warden, thinking he perceived the real state of things, 'what I propose is this. You shall go into old Dobson's house at once, as a kind of probationary bedesman. I'll write to Harry, and get your character from him. Stephen Freeman I think you said your name was? Before I can receive his reply you'll have been able to tell how you'd like the kind of life; and at any rate you'll have the rest you seem to require in the meantime. You see, I take Harry's having given you that cloak as a kind of character,' added he, smiling kindly. 'Of course you'll have to conform to rules just like all the rest, – chapel at eight, dinner at twelve, lights out at nine; but I'll tell you the remainder of our regulations as we walk across quad to your new quarters.'

And thus Philip, almost in spite of himself, became installed in a bedesman's house at St Sepulchre.

CHAPTER 42

A Fable at Fault

Philip took possession of the two rooms which had belonged to the dead Sergeant Dobson. They were furnished sufficiently for every comfort by the trustees of the hospital. Some little fragments of ornament, some small articles picked up in distant countries, a few tattered books, remained in the rooms as legacies from their former occupant.

At first the repose of the life and the place was inexpressibly grateful to Philip. He had always shrunk from encountering strangers, and displaying his blackened and scarred countenance to them, even where such disfigurement was most regarded as a mark of honour. In St Sepulchre's he met none but the same set day after day, and when he had once told the tale of how it happened and submitted to their gaze, it was over for ever, if he so minded. The slight employment his garden gave him – there was a kitchen-garden behind each house, as well as the flower-plot in front – and the daily arrangement of his parlour and chamber were, at the beginning of his time of occupation, as much bodily labour as he could manage. There was something stately and utterly removed from all Philip's previous existence in the forms observed at every day's dinner, when the twelve bedesmen met in the large quaint hall, and the warden came in in his college-cap and gown to say the long Latin grace which wound up with something very like a prayer for the soul of Sir Simon Bray. It took some time to get a reply to ship letters in those times when no one could exactly say where the fleet might be found.

And before Dr Pennington had received the excellent charac-ter of Stephen Freeman, which his son gladly sent in answer to his father's inquiries, Philip had become restless and uneasy in the midst of all this peace and comfort.

Sitting alone over his fire in the long winter evenings, the scenes of his past life rose before him; his childhood; his aunt Robson's care of him; his first going to Foster's shop in Monkshaven; Haytersbank Farm, and the spelling lessons in the bright warm kitchen there; Kinraid's appearance; the miserable night of the Corneys' party; the farewell he had witnessed on Monkshaven sands; the press-gang, and all the long conse-quences of that act of concealment; poor Daniel Robson's trial and execution; his own marriage; his child's birth; and then he came to that last day at Monkshaven: and he went over and over again the torturing details, the looks of contempt and anger, the words of loathing indignation, till he almost brought himself, out of his extreme sympathy with Sylvia, to believe that he was indeed the wretch she had considered him to be.

He forgot his own excuses for having acted as he had done; though these excuses had at one time seemed to him to wear the garb of reasons. After long thought and bitter memory came some wonder. What was Sylvia doing now? Where was she? What was his child like – his child as well as hers? And then he remembered the poor footsore wife and the little girl she carried in her arms, that was just the age of Bella; he wished he had noticed that child more, that a clear vision of it might rise up when he wanted to picture Bella.

One night he had gone round this mill-wheel circle of ideas till he was weary to the very marrow of his bones. To shake off the monotonous impression he rose to look for a book amongst the old tattered volumes, hoping that he might find something that would sufficiently lay hold of him to change the current of his thoughts. There was an odd volume of *Peregrine Pickle*;* a book of sermons; half an army list* of 1774, and the *Seven Champions of Christendom*.* Philip took up this last, which he had never seen before. In it he read how Sir Guy, Earl of Warwick,* went to fight the Paynim* in his own country, and was away for seven long years; and when he came back his own wife Phillis, the countess in her castle, did not know the poor travel-worn hermit, who came daily to seek his dole of bread at her hands along with many beggars and much poor. But at last, when he lay a-dying in his cave in the rock, he sent for her by a secret sign known but to them twain. And she came with great speed, for she knew it was her lord who had sent for her; and they had many sweet and holy words together before he gave up the ghost, his head lying on her bosom.

The old story known to most people from their childhood was all new and fresh to Philip. He did not quite believe in the truth of it, because the fictitious nature of the histories of some of the other Champions of Christendom was too patent. But he could not help thinking that this one might be true; and that Guy and Phillis might have been as real flesh and blood, long, long ago, as he and Sylvia had ever been. The old room, the quiet moonlit quadrangle into which the cross-barred casement looked, the quaint aspect of everything that he had seen for weeks and weeks; all this predisposed Philip to dwell upon the story he had just been reading as a faithful legend of two lovers whose bones were long since dust. He thought that if he could thus see Sylvia, himself unknown, unseen – could live at her gates, so to speak, and gaze upon her and his child – some day too, when he lay a-dying, he might send for her, and in soft words of mutual forgiveness breathe his life away in her arms. Or perhaps— and so he lost himself, and from thinking, passed on to dreaming. All night long Guy and Phillis, Sylvia and his child, passed in and out of his visions; it was impossible to make the fragments of his dreams cohere; but the impression made upon him by them was not the less strong for this. He felt as if he were called to Monkshaven, wanted at Monkshaven, and to

Monkshaven he resolved to go; although when his reason overtook his feeling, he knew perfectly how unwise it was to leave a home of peace and tranquillity and surrounding friendliness, to go to a place where nothing but want and wretchedness awaited him unless he made himself known; and if he did, a deeper want, a more woeful wretchedness, would in all probability be his portion.

In the small oblong of looking-glass hung against the wall, Philip caught the reflection of his own face, and laughed scornfully at the sight. The thin hair lay upon his temples in the flakes that betoken long ill-health, his eyes were the same as ever, and they had always been considered the best feature in his face; but they were sunk in their orbits, and looked hollow and gloomy. As for the lower part of his face, blackened, contracted, drawn away from his teeth, the outline entirely changed by the breakage of his jaw-bone, he was indeed a fool if he thought himself fit to go forth to win back that love which Sylvia had forsworn. As a hermit and a beggar, he must return to Monkshaven, and fall perforce into the same position which Guy of Warwick had only assumed. But still he should see his Phillis, and might feast his sad hopeless eyes from time to time with the sight of his child. His small pension of sixpence a day would keep him from absolute want of necessaries.

So that very day he went to the warden and told him he thought of giving up his share in the bequest of Sir Simon Bray. Such a relinquishment had never occurred before in all the warden's experience; and he was very much inclined to be offended.

'I must say that for a man not to be satisfied as a bedesman of St Sepulchre's argues a very wrong state of mind, and a very ungrateful heart.'

'I'm sure, sir, it's not from any ingratitude, for I can hardly feel thankful enough to you and to Sir Simon, and to madam, and the young ladies, and all my comrades in the hospital, and I niver expect to be either so comfortable or so peaceful again, but—'

'But? What can you have to say against the place, then? Not but what there are always plenty of applicants for every vacancy; only I thought I was doing a kindness to a man out of Harry's company. And you'll not see Harry either; he's got his leave in March!'

'I'm very sorry. I should like to have seen the lieutenant again. But I cannot rest any longer so far away from – people I once knew.'

'Ten to one they're dead, or removed, or something or other by this time; and it'll serve you right if they are. Mind! no one can be chosen twice to be a bedesman of St Sepulchre's.'

The warden turned away; and Philip, uneasy at staying, disheartened at leaving, went to make his few preparations for setting out once more on his journey northwards. He had to give notice of his change of residence to the local distributor of pensions; and one or two farewells had to be taken, with more than usual sadness at the necessity; for Philip, under his name of Stephen Freeman, had attached some of the older bedesmen a good deal to him, from his unselfishness, his willingness to read to them, and to render them many little services, and, perhaps, as much as anything, by his habitual silence, which made him a convenient recipient of all their garrulousness. So before the time for his departure came, he had the opportunity of one more interview with the warden, of a more friendly character than that in which he gave up his bedesmanship. And so far it was well; and Philip turned his back upon St Sepulchre's with his sore heart partly healed by his four months' residence there.

He was stronger, too, in body, more capable of the day-after-day walks that were required of him. He had saved some money from his allowance as bedesman and from his pension, and might occasionally have taken an outside place on a coach, had it not been that he shrank from the first look of every stranger upon his disfigured face. Yet the gentle, wistful eyes, and the white and faultless teeth always did away with the first impression as soon as people became a little acquainted with his appearance.

It was February when Philip left St Sepulchre's. It was the first week in April when he began to recognize the familiar objects between York and Monkshaven. And now he began to hang back, and to question the wisdom of what he had done – just as the warden had prophesied that he would. The last night of his two hundred mile walk he slept at the little inn at which he had been enlisted nearly two years before. It was by no intention of his that he rested at that identical place. Night was drawing on; and, in making, as he thought, a short cut, he had missed his way, and was fain to seek shelter where he might find it. But it brought him very straight face to face with his life at that time, and ever since. His mad, wild hopes – half the result of intoxication, as he now knew – all dead and gone; the career then freshly opening shut up against him now; his youthful strength and health changed into premature infirmity, and the home and the love that should have opened wide its doors to console him for all, why in two years Death might have been busy, and taken away from him his last feeble chance of the faint happiness of seeing his beloved without being seen or known of her. All that night and all the next day, the fear of Sylvia's possible death overclouded his heart. It was strange that he had hardly ever thought of this before; so strange, that now, when the terror came, it took possession of him, and he could almost have sworn that she must be lying dead in Monkshaven churchyard. Or was it little Bella, that blooming, lovely babe, whom he was never to see again? There was the tolling of mournful bells in the distant air to his disturbed fancy, and the cry of the happy birds, the plaintive bleating of the new-dropped lambs, were all omens of evil import to him.

As well as he could, he found his way back to Monkshaven, over the wild heights and moors he had crossed on that black day of misery; why he should have chosen that path he could not tell – it was as if he were led, and had no free will of his own.

The soft clear evening was drawing on, and his heart beat thick, and then stopped, only to start again with fresh violence. There he was, at the top of the long, steep lane that was in some parts a literal staircase leading down from the hill-top into the High Street, through the very entry up which he had passed when he shrank away from his former and his then present life. There he stood, looking down once more at the numerous irregular roofs, the many stacks of chimneys below him, seeking out that which had once been his own dwelling – who dwelt there now?

The yellower gleams grew narrower; the evening shadows broader, and Philip crept down the lane a weary, woeful man. At every gap in the close-packed buildings he heard the merry music of a band, the cheerful sound of excited voices. Still he descended slowly, scarcely wondering what it could be, for it was not associated in his mind with the one pervading thought of Sylvia.

When he came to the angle of junction between the lane and the High Street, he seemed plunged all at once into the very centre of the bustle, and he drew himself up into a corner of deep shadow, from whence he could look out upon the street.

A circus was making its grand entry into Monkshaven, with all the pomp of colour and of noise that it could muster. Trumpeters in parti-coloured clothes rode first, blaring out triumphant discord. Next came a gold-and-scarlet chariot drawn by six piebald horses, and the windings of this team through the tortuous narrow street were pretty enough to look upon. In the chariot sat kings and queens, heroes and heroines, or what were meant for such; all the little boys and girls running alongside of the chariot envied them; but they themselves were very much tired, and shivering with cold in their heroic pomp of classic clothing. All this Philip might have seen; did see, in fact; but heeded not one jot. Almost opposite to him, not ten yards apart, standing on the raised step at the well-known shop door, was Sylvia, holding a child, a merry dancing child, up in her arms to see the show. She too, Sylvia, was laughing for pleasure, and for sympathy with pleasure. She held the little Bella aloft that the child might see the gaudy procession the better and the longer, looking at it herself with red lips apart and white teeth glancing through; then she turned to speak to some one behind her – Coulson, as Philip saw the moment afterwards; his answer made her laugh once again. Philip saw it all; her bonny careless looks, her pretty matronly form, her evident ease of mind and prosperous outward circumstances. The years that he had spent in gloomy sorrow, amongst wild scenes, on land or by sea, his life in frequent peril of a bloody end, had gone by with her like sunny days; all the more sunny because he was not there. So bitterly thought the poor disabled marine, as weary and despairing, he stood in the cold shadow and looked upon the home that should have been his haven, the wife that should have welcomed him, the child that should have been his comfort. He had banished himself from his home; his wife had forsworn him; his child was blossoming into intelligence unwitting of any father. Wife, and child, and home, were all doing well without him; what madness had tempted him thither? an hour ago, like a fanciful fool, he had thought she might be dead – dead with sad penitence for her cruel words at her heart – with mournful wonder at the unaccounted-for absence of her child's father preying on her spirits, and in some measure causing the death he had apprehended. But to look at her there where she stood, it did not seem as if she had had an hour's painful thought in all her blooming life.

Ay! go in to the warm hearth, mother and child, now the gay cavalcade has gone out of sight, and the chill of night has succeeded to the sun's setting. Husband and father, steal out into the cold dark street, and seek some poor cheap lodging where you may rest your weary bones, and cheat your more weary heart into forgetfulness in sleep. The pretty story of the Countess Phillis, who mourned for her husband's absence so long, is a fable of old times; or rather say Earl Guy* never wedded his wife, knowing that one she loved better than him was alive all the time she had believed him to be dead.

CHAPTER 43

The Unknown

A few days before that on which Philip arrived at Monkshaven, Kester had come to pay Sylvia a visit. As the earliest friend she had, and also as one who knew the real secrets of her life, Sylvia always gave him the warm welcome, the cordial words, and the sweet looks in which the old man delighted. He had a sort of delicacy of his own which kept him from going to see her too often, even when he was stationary at Monkshaven; but he looked forward to the times when he allowed himself this pleasure as a child at school looks forward to its holidays. The time of his service at Haytersbank had, on the whole, been the happiest in all his long monotonous years of daily labour. Sylvia's father had always treated him with the rough kindness of fellowship; Sylvia's mother had never stinted him in his meat or grudged him his share of the best that was going; and once, when he was ill for a few days in the loft above the cow-house, she had made him possets, and nursed him with the same tenderness which he remembered his mother showing to him when he was a little child, but which he had never experienced since then. He had known Sylvia herself, as bud, and sweet

promise of blossom; and just as she was opening into the full-
blown rose, and, if she had been happy and prosperous, might
have passed out of the narrow circle of Kester's interests, one
sorrow after another came down upon her pretty innocent head,
and Kester's period of service to Daniel Robson, her father, was
tragically cut short. All this made Sylvia the great centre of the
faithful herdsman's affection; and Bella, who reminded him of
what Sylvia was when first Kester knew her, only occupied the
second place in his heart, although to the child he was much
more demonstrative of his regard than to the mother.

He had dressed himself in his Sunday best, and although it
was only Thursday, had forestalled his Saturday's shaving; he
had provided himself with a paper of humbugs for the child –
'humbugs' being the north-country term for certain lumps of
toffy, well flavoured with peppermint – and now he sat in the
accustomed chair, as near to the door as might be, in Sylvia's
presence, coaxing the little one, who was not quite sure of his
identity, to come to him, by opening the paper parcel, and
letting its sweet contents be seen.

'She's like thee – and yet she favours her feyther,' said he; and
the moment he had uttered the incautious words he looked up
to see how Sylvia had taken the unpremeditated, unusual
reference to her husband. His stealthy glance did not meet her
eye; but though he thought she had coloured a little, she did not
seem offended as he had feared. It was true that Bella had her
father's grave, thoughtful, dark eyes, instead of her mother's
grey ones, out of which the childlike expression of wonder
would never entirely pass away. And as Bella slowly and half
distrustfully made her way towards the temptation offered her,
she looked at Kester with just her father's look.

Sylvia said nothing in direct reply; Kester almost thought she
could not have heard him. But, by-and-by, she said, –

'Yo'll have heared how Kinraid – who's a captain now, and
grand officer – has gone and got married.'

'Nay!' said Kester, in genuine surprise. 'He niver has, for
sure!'

'Ay, but he has,' said Sylvia. 'And I'm sure I dunnot see why
he shouldn't.'

'Well, well!' said Kester, not looking up at her, for he caught
the inflections in the tones of her voice. 'He were a fine stirrin'
chap, yon; an' he were allays for doin' summut; an' when he

fund as he couldn't ha' one thing as he'd set his mind on, a reckon he thought he mun put up wi' another.'

'It 'ud be no "putting up",' said Sylvia. 'She were staying at Bessy Dawson's, and she come here to see me – she's as pretty a young lady as yo'd see on a summer's day; and a real lady, too, wi' a fortune. She didn't speak two words wi'out bringing in her husband's name, – "the captain", as she called him.'

'An' she come to see thee?' said Kester, cocking his eye at Sylvia with the old shrewd look. 'That were summut queer,* weren't it?'

Sylvia reddened a good deal.

'He's too fause to have spoken to her on me, in t' old way, – as he used for t' speak to me. I were nought to her but Philip's wife.'

'An' what t' dickins* had she to do wi' Philip?' asked Kester, in intense surprise; and so absorbed in curiosity that he let the humbugs all fall out of the paper upon the floor, and the little Bella sat down, plump, in the midst of treasures as great as those fabled to exist on Tom Tiddler's ground.*

Sylvia was again silent; but Kester, knowing her well, was sure that she was struggling to speak, and bided his time without repeating his question.

'She said – and I think her tale were true, though I cannot get to t' rights on it, think on it as I will – as Philip saved her husband's life somewheere nearabouts to Jerusalem. She would have it that t' captain – for I think I'll niver ca' him Kinraid again – was in a great battle, and were near upon being shot by t' French, when Philip – our Philip – come up and went right into t' fire o' t' guns, and saved her husband a life. And she spoke as if both she and t' captain were more beholden to Philip than words could tell. And she come to see me, to try and get news on him.'

'It's a queer kind o' story,' said Kester, meditatively. 'A should ha' thought as Philip were more likely to ha' gi'en him a shove into t' thick on it, than t' help him out o' t' scrape.'

'Nay!' said Sylvia, suddenly looking straight at Kester; 'yo're out theere. Philip had a deal o' good in him. And I dunnot think as he'd ha' gone and married another woman so soon, if he'd been i' Kinraid's place.'

'An' yo've niver heared on Philip sin' he left?' asked Kester, after a while.

'Niver; nought but what she told me. And she said that t' captain made inquiry for him right and left, as soon after that happened as might be, and could hear niver a word about him. No one had seen him, or knowed his name.'

'Yo' niver heared of his goin' for t' be a soldier?' persevered Kester.

'Niver. I've told yo' once. It were unlike Philip to think o' such a thing.'

'But thou mun ha' been thinkin' on him at times i' a' these years. Bad as he'd behaved hissel', he were t' feyther o' thy little un. What did ta think he had been agait on when he left here? '

'I didn't know. I were noane so keen a-thinking on him at first. I tried to put him out o' my thoughts a'together, for it made me like mad to think how he'd stood between me and – that other. But I'd begun to wonder and to wonder about him, and to think I should like to hear as he were doing well. I reckon I thought he were i' London, wheere he'd been that time afore, yo' know, and had allays spoke as if he'd enjoyed hissel' tolerable; and then Molly Brunton told me on t' other one's marriage; and, somehow, it gave me a shake in my heart, and I began for to wish I hadn't said all them words i' my passion; and then that fine young lady come wi' her story – and I've thought a deal on it since, – and my mind has come out clear. Philip's dead, and it were his spirit as come to t' other's help in his time o' need. I've heared feyther say as spirits cannot rest i' their graves for trying to undo t' wrongs they've done i' their bodies.'

'Them's my conclusions,' said Kester, solemnly. 'A was fain fo' t' hear what were yo'r judgments first; but them's the conclusions I comed to as soon as I heared t' tale.'

'Let alone that one thing,' said Sylvia, 'he were a kind, good man.'

'It were a big deal on a "one thing", though,' said Kester. 'It just spoilt yo'r life, my poor lass; an' might ha' gone near to spoilin' Charley Kinraid's too.'

'Men takes a deal more nor women to spoil their lives,' said Sylvia, bitterly.

'Not a' mak' o' men. I reckon, lass, Philip's life were pretty well on for bein' spoilt at after he left here; and it were, mebbe, a good thing he got rid on it so soon.'

'I wish I'd just had a few kind words wi' him, I do,' said Sylvia, almost on the point of crying.

'Come, lass, it's as ill moanin' after what's past as it 'ud be for me t' fill my eyes wi' weepin' after t' humbugs as this little wench o' thine has grubbed up* whilst we'n been talkin'. Why there's not one on 'em left!'

She's a sad spoilt little puss!' said Sylvia, holding out her arms to the child, who ran into them, and began patting her mother's cheeks, and pulling at the soft brown curls tucked away beneath the matronly cap. 'Mammy spoils her, and Hester spoils her—'

'Granny Rose doesn't spoil me,' said the child, with quick, intelligent discrimination, interrupting her mother's list.

'No; but Jeremiah Foster does above a bit. He'll come in fro' t' bank, Kester, and ask for her, a'most ivery day. And he'll bring her things in his pocket; and she's so fause, she allays goes straight to peep in, and then he shifts t' apple or t' toy into another. Eh! but she's a little fause one,' – half devouring the child with her kisses. 'And he comes and takes her a walk oftentimes, and he goes as slow as if he were quite an old man, to keep pace wi' Bella's steps. I often run upstairs and watch 'em out o' t' window; he doesn't care to have me with 'em, he's so fain t' have t' child all to hisself.'

'She's a bonny un, for sure,' said Kester; 'but not so pretty as thou was, Sylvie. A've niver tell'd thee what a come for tho', and it's about time for me t' be goin'. A'm off to t' Cheviots to-morrow morn t' fetch home some sheep as Jonas Blundell has purchased. It'll be a job o' better nor two months a reckon.'

'It'll be a nice time o' year,' said Sylvia, a little surprised at Kester's evident discouragement at the prospect of the journey or absence; he had often been away from Monkshaven for a longer time without seeming to care so much about it.

'Well, yo' see it's a bit hard upon me for t' leave my sister – she as is t' widow-woman, wheere a put up when a'm at home. Things is main an' dear; four-pound loaves is at sixteenpence;* an' there's a deal o' talk on a famine i' t' land; an' whaten a paid for my victual an' t' bed i' t' lean-to helped t' oud woman a bit, – an' she's sadly down i' t' mouth, for she cannot hear on a lodger for t' tak' my place, for she's moved o'er to t' other side o' t' bridge for t' be nearer t' new buildings, an' t' grand new walk they're makin' round t' cliffs, thinkin' she'd be likelier t' pick up a labourer as would be glad on a bed near his work. A'd ha' liked to ha' set her agait wi' a 'sponsible lodger afore a'd ha' left, for she's just so softhearted, any scamp may put upon her if he nobbut gets houd on her blind side.'*

'Can I help her?' said Sylvia, in her eager way. 'I should be so glad; and I've a deal of money by me—'

'Nay, my lass,' said Kester, 'thou munnot go off so fast;* it were just what I were feared on i' tellin' thee. I've left her a bit o' money, and I'll mak' shift to send her more; it's just a kind word, t' keep up her heart when I'm gone, as I want. If thou'd step in and see her fra' time to time, and cheer her up a bit wi' talkin' to her on me, I'd tak' it very kind, and I'd go off wi' a lighter heart.'

'Then I'm sure I'll do it for yo', Kester. I niver justly feel like mysel' when yo're away, for I'm lonesome enough at times. She and I will talk a' t' better about yo' for both on us grieving after yo'.'

So Kester took his leave, his mind set at ease by Sylvia's promise to go and see his sister pretty often during his absence in the North.

But Sylvia's habits were changed since she, as a girl at Haytersbank, liked to spend half her time in the open air, running out perpetually without anything on to scatter crumbs to the poultry, or to take a piece of bread to the old carthorse, to go up to the garden for a handful of herbs, or to clamber to the highest point around to blow the horn which summoned her father and Kester home to dinner. Living in a town where it was necessary to put on hat and cloak before going out into the street, and then to walk in a steady and decorous fashion, she had only cared to escape down to the freedom of the sea-shore until Philip went away; and after that time she had learnt so to fear observation as a deserted wife, that nothing but Bella's health would have been a sufficient motive to take her out of doors. And, as she had told Kester, the necessity of giving the little girl a daily walk was very much lightened by the great love and affection which Jeremiah Foster now bore to the child. Ever since the day when the baby had come to his knee, allured by the temptation of his watch, he had apparently considered her as in some sort belonging to him; and now he had almost come to think that he had a right to claim her as his companion in his walk back from the bank to his early dinner, where a high chair was always placed ready for the chance of her coming to share his meal. On these occasions he generally brought her back to the shop-door when he returned to his afternoon's work at the bank. Sometimes, however, he would leave word that she was to be sent for from his house in the New Town, as his business at the bank for that day was ended. Then Sylvia was compelled to put on her things, and fetch back her darling; and excepting for this errand she seldom went out at all on week-days.

About a fortnight after Kester's farewell call, this need for her visit to Jeremiah Foster's arose; and it seemed to Sylvia that there could not be a better opportunity of fulfilling her promise and going to see the widow Dobson, whose cottage was on the other side of the river, low down on the cliff side, just at the bend and rush of the full stream into the open sea. She set off pretty early in order to go there first. She found the widow with her house-place tidied up after the midday meal, and busy knitting at the open door – not looking at her rapid-clicking needles, but gazing at the rush and recession of the waves before her; yet not seeing them either, – rather seeing days long past.

She started into active civility as soon as she recognized Sylvia, who was to her as a great lady, never having known Sylvia Robson in her wild childish days. Widow Dobson was always a little scandalized at her brother Christopher's familiarity with Mrs Hepburn.

She dusted a chair which needed no dusting, and placed it for Sylvia, sitting down herself on a three-legged stool to mark her sense of the difference in their conditions, for there was another chair or two in the humble dwelling; and then the two fell into talk – first about Kester, whom his sister would persist in calling Christopher, as if his dignity as her elder brother was compromised by any familiar abbreviation; and by-and-by she opened her heart a little more.

'A could wish as a'd learned write-of-hand,' said she; 'for a've that for to tell Christopher as might set his mind at ease. But yo' see, if a wrote him a letter he couldn't read it; so a just comfort mysel' wi' thinkin' nobody need learn writin' unless they'n got friends as can read. But a reckon he'd ha' been glad to hear as a've getten a lodger.' Here she nodded her head in the direction of the door opening out of the houseplace into the 'lean-to,' which Sylvia had observed on drawing near the cottage, and the recollection of the mention of which by Kester had enabled her to identify widow Dobson's dwelling. 'He's a-bed yonder,' the latter continued, dropping her voice. 'He's a queer-lookin' tyke, but a don't think as he's a bad un.'

'When did he come?' said Sylvia, remembering Kester's account of his sister's character, and feeling as though it behoved her, as Kester's confidante on this head, to give cautious and prudent advice.

'Eh! a matter of a s'ennight ago. A'm noane good at mindin' time; he's paid me his rent twice, but then he were keen to pay aforehand. He'd comed in one night, an' sat him down afore he could speak, he were so done up; he'd been on tramp this many a day, a reckon. "Can yo' give me a bed?" says he, panting like, after a bit. "A chap as a met near here says as yo've a lodging for t' let." "Ay," says a, "a ha' that; but yo mun pay me a shilling a week for 't." Then my mind misgive me, for a thought he hadn't a shilling i' t' world, an' yet if he hadn't, a should just ha' gi'en him t' bed a' t' same: a'm not one as can turn a dog out if he comes t' me wearied of his life. So he outs wi' a shillin', an' lays it down on t' table, 'bout a word. "A'll not trouble yo' long," says he. "A'm one as is best out o' t' world," he says. Then a thought as a'd been a bit hard upon him. An' says I, "A'm a widow-woman, and one as has getten but few friends:" for yo' see a were low about our Christopher's goin' away north; "so a'm forced-like to speak hard to folk; but a've made mysel' some stirabout* for my supper; and if yo'd like t' share an' share about wi' me, it's but puttin' a sup more watter to 't, and God's blessing 'll be on 't, just as same as if 't were meal." So he ups wi' his hand afore his e'en, and says not a word. At last he says, "Missus," says he, "can God's blessing be shared by a sinner – one o' t' devil's children?" says he. For the Scriptur' says he's t' father o' lies."* So a were puzzled-like; an' at length a says, "Thou mun ask t' parson that; a'm but a poor faint-hearted widow-woman; but a've allays had God's blessing somehow, now a bethink me, an' a'll share it wi' thee as far as my will goes." So he raxes* his hand across t' table, an' mutters summat, as he grips mine. A thought it were Scriptur' as he said, but a'd needed a' my strength just then for t' lift t' pot off t' fire – it were t' first vittle a'd tasted sin' morn, for t' famine comes down like stones on t' head o' us poor folk: an' a' a said were just "Coom along, chap, an' fa' to; an' God's blessing be on him as eats most." An' sin that day him and me's been as thick as thieves, only he's niver telled me nought of who he is, or wheere he comes fra'. But a think he's one o' them poor colliers, as has getten brunt i' t' coal-pits; for, t' be sure, his face is a' black wi' fire-marks; an' o' late days he's ta'en t' his bed, an' just lies there sighing, – for one can hear him plain as dayleet thro' t' bit partition wa'.'

As a proof of this, a sigh – almost a groan – startled the two women at this very moment.

'Poor fellow!' said Sylvia, in a soft whisper. 'There's more sore hearts i' t' world than one reckons for!' But after a while, she bethought her again of Kester's account of his sister's 'softness'; and she thought that it behoved her to give some good advice. So she added, in a sterner, harder tone – 'Still, yo' say yo' know nought about him; and tramps is tramps a' t' world over; and yo're a widow, and it behoves yo' to be careful. I think I'd just send him off as soon as he's a bit rested. Yo' say he's plenty o' money?'

'Nay! A never said that. A know nought about it. He pays me aforehand; an' he pays me down for whativer a've getten for him; but that's but little; he's noane up t' his vittle, though a've made him some broth as good as a could make 'em.'

'I wouldn't send him away till he was well again, if I were yo'; but I think yo'd be better rid on him,' said Sylvia. 'It would be different if yo'r brother were in Monkshaven.' As she spoke she rose to go.

Widow Dobson held her hand in hers for a minute, then the humble woman said, –

'Yo'll noane be vexed wi' me, missus, if a cannot find i' my heart t' turn him out till he wants to go hissel'? For a wouldn't like to vex yo', for Christopher's sake; but a know what it is for t' feel for friendless folk, an' choose what may come on it, I cannot send him away.'

'No!' said Sylvia. 'Why should I be vexed? it's no business o' mine. Only I should send him away if I was yo'. He might go lodge wheere there was men-folk, who know t' ways o' tramps, and are up to them.'

Into the sunshine went Sylvia. In the cold shadow the miserable tramp lay sighing. She did not know that she had been so near to him towards whom her heart was softening, day by day.

CHAPTER 44

First Words

It was the spring of 1800.* Old people yet can tell of the hard famine of that year. The harvest of the autumn before had failed; the war and the corn laws had brought the price of corn up to a famine rate; and much of what came into the market was unsound, and consequently unfit for food, yet hungry creatures bought it eagerly, and tried to cheat disease by mixing the damp, sweet, clammy flour with rice or potato meal. Rich families denied themselves pastry and all unnecessary and luxurious uses of wheat in any shape; the duty on hair-powder was increased;* and all these palliatives were but as drops in the ocean of the great want of the people.

Philip, in spite of himself, recovered and grew stronger; and as he grew stronger hunger took the place of loathing dislike to food. But his money was all spent; and what was his poor pension of sixpence a day in that terrible year of famine? Many a summer's night he walked for hours and hours round the house which once was his, which might be his now, with all its homely, blessed comforts, could he but go and assert his right to it. But to go with authority, and in his poor, maimed guise assert that right, he had need be other than Philip Hepburn. So he stood in the old shelter of the steep, crooked lane opening on to the hill out of the marketplace, and watched the soft fading of the summer's eve into night; the closing of the once familiar shop; the exit of good, comfortable William Coulson, going to his own home, his own wife, his comfortable, plentiful supper. Then Philip – there were no police in those days, and scarcely an old watchman in that primitive little town – would go round on the shady sides of streets, and, quickly glancing about him, cross the bridge, looking on the quiet, rippling stream, the grey shimmer foretelling the coming dawn over the sea, the black masts and rigging of the still vessels against the sky; he could see with his wistful, eager eyes the shape of the windows – the window of the very room in which his wife and child slept, unheeding of him, the hungry, broken-hearted outcast. He would go back to his lodging, and softly lift the latch of the door; still more softly, but never without an unspoken, grateful prayer, pass by the poor sleeping woman who had given him a shelter and her share of God's blessing – she who, like him, knew not the feeling of satisfied hunger; and then he laid him down on the narrow pallet in the lean-to, and again gave Sylvia happy lessons in the kitchen at Haytersbank, and the dead were alive; and Charley Kinraid, the specksioneer, had never come to trouble the hopeful, gentle peace.

For widow Dobson had never taken Sylvia's advice. The tramp known to her by the name of Freeman – that in which he received his pension – lodged with her still, and paid his meagre shilling in advance, weekly. A shilling was meagre in those hard days of scarcity. A hungry man might easily eat the produce of a shilling in a day.

Widow Dobson pleaded this to Sylvia as an excuse for keeping her lodger on; to a more calculating head it might have seemed a reason for sending him away.

'Yo' see, missus,' said she, apologetically, to Sylvia, one evening, as the latter called upon the poor widow before going to fetch little Bella (it was now too hot for the child to cross the bridge in the full heat of the summer sun, and Jeremiah would take her up to her supper instead) – 'Yo' see, missus, there's not a many as 'ud take him in for a shillin' when it goes so little way; or if they did, they'd take it out on him some other way, an' he's not getten much else, a reckon. He ca's me granny, but a'm vast mista'en if he's ten year younger nor me; but he's getten a fine appetite of his own, choose how young he may be; an' a can see as he could eat a deal more nor he a getten money to buy, an' it's few as can mak' victual go farther nor me. Eh, missus, but yo' may trust me a'll send him off when times is better; but just now it would be sendin' him to his death; for a ha' plenty and to spare, thanks be to God an' yo'r bonny face.'

So Sylvia had to be content with the knowledge that the money she gladly gave to Kester's sister went partly to feed the lodger who was neither labourer nor neighbour, but only just a tramp, who, she feared, was preying on the good old woman. Still the cruel famine cut sharp enough to penetrate all hearts; and Sylvia, an hour after the conversation recorded above, was much touched, on her return from Jeremiah Foster's with the little merry, chattering Bella, at seeing the feeble steps of one, whom she knew by description must be widow Dobson's lodger, turn up from the newly-cut road which was to lead to the terrace walk round the North Cliff, a road which led to no dwelling but widow Dobson's. Tramp, and vagrant, he might be in the eyes of the law; but, whatever his character, Sylvia could see him before her in the soft dusk, creeping along, over the bridge, often stopping to rest and hold by some support, and then going on again towards the town, to which she and happy little Bella were wending.

A thought came over her: she had always fancied that this unknown man was some fierce vagabond, and had dreaded lest in the lonely bit of road between widow Dobson's cottage and the peopled highway, he should fall upon her and rob her if he learnt that she had money with her; and several times she had gone away without leaving the little gift she had intended, because she imagined that she had seen the door of the small chamber in the 'lean-to' open softly while she was there, as if the occupant (whom widow Dobson spoke of as never leaving the house before dusk, excepting once a week) were listening for the chink of the coin in her little leathern purse. Now that she saw him walking before her with heavy languid steps, this fear gave place to pity; she remembered her mother's gentle superstition which had prevented her from ever sending the hungry empty away, for fear lest she herself should come to need bread.

'Lassie,' said she to little Bella, who held a cake which Jeremiah's housekeeper had given her tight in her hand, 'yon poor man theere is hungry; will Bella give him her cake, and mother will make her another to-morrow twice as big?'

For this consideration, and with the feeling of satisfaction which a good supper not an hour ago gives even to the hungry stomach of a child of three years old, Bella, after some thought, graciously assented to the sacrifice.

Sylvia stopped, the cake in her hand, and turned her back to the town, and to the slow wayfarer in front. Under the cover of her shawl she slipped a half-crown deep into the crumb of the cake, and then restoring it to little Bella, she gave her her directions.

'Mammy will carry Bella; and when Bella goes past the poor man, she shall give him the cake over mammy's shoulder. Poor man is so hungry; and Bella and mammy have plenty to eat, and to spare.'

The child's heart was touched by the idea of hunger, and her little arm was outstretched ready for the moment her mother's hurried steps took her brushing past the startled, trembling Philip.

'Poor man, eat this; Bella not hungry.'

They were the first words he had ever heard his child utter. The echoes of them rang in his ears as he stood endeavouring to hide his disfigured face by looking over the parapet of the bridge down upon the stream running away towards the ocean, into which his hot tears slowly fell, unheeded by the weeper. Then he changed the intention with which he had set out upon his nightly walk, and turned back to his lodging.

Of course the case was different with Sylvia; she would have forgotten the whole affair very speedily, if it had not been for little Bella's frequent recurrence to the story of the hungry man, which had touched her small sympathies with the sense of an intelligible misfortune. She liked to act the dropping of the bun into the poor man's hand as she went past him, and would take up any article near her in order to illustrate the gesture she had used. One day she got hold of Hester's watch for this purpose, as being of the same round shape as the cake; and though Hester, for whose benefit the child was repeating the story in her broken language for the third or fourth time, tried to catch the watch as it was intended that she should (she being the representative of the 'hungry man' for the time being), it went to the ground with a smash that frightened the little girl, and she began to cry at the mischief she had done.

'Don't cry, Bella,' said Hester. 'Niver play with watches again. I didn't see thee at mine, or I'd ha' stopped thee in time. But I'll take it to old Darley's on th' quay-side, and maybe he'll soon set it to rights again. Only Bella must niver play with watches again.'

'Niver no more!' promised the little sobbing child. And that evening Hester took her watch down to old Darley's.

This William Darley was the brother of the gardener at the rectory; the uncle to the sailor who had been shot by the press-gang years before, and to his bed-ridden sister. He was a clever mechanician, and his skill as a repairer of watches and chronometers* was great among the sailors, with whom he did a very irregular sort of traffic, conducted often without much use of money, but rather on the principle of barter, they bringing him foreign coins and odd curiosities picked up on their travels in exchange for his services to their nautical instruments or their watches. If he had ever had capital to extend his business, he might have been a rich man; but it is to be doubted whether he would have been as happy as he was now in his queer little habitation of two rooms, the front one being both shop and workshop, the other serving the double purpose of bedroom and museum.

The skill of this odd-tempered, shabby old man was some-times sought by the jeweller who kept the more ostentatious shop in the High Street; but before Darley would undertake any 'tickle'* piece of delicate workmanship for the other, he sneered at his ignorance, and taunted and abused him well. Yet he had soft places in his heart, and Hester Rose had found her way to one by her patient, enduring kindness to his bedridden niece. He never snarled at her as he did at too many; and on the few occasions when she had asked him to do anything for her, he had seemed as if she were conferring the favour on him, not he on her, and only made the smallest possible charge.

She found him now sitting where he could catch the most light for his work, spectacles on nose, and microscope in hand.

He took her watch, and examined it carefully without a word in reply to her. Then he began to open it and take it to pieces, in order to ascertain the nature of the mischief.

Suddenly he heard her catch her breath with a checked sound of surprise. He looked at her from above his spectacles; she was holding a watch in her hand which she had just taken up off the counter.

'What's amiss wi' thee now?' said Darley. 'Hast ta niver seen a watch o' that mak' afore? or is it them letters on t' back, as is so wonderful?'

Yes, it was those letters – that interlaced, old-fashioned cipher. That Z. H. that she knew of old stood for Zachary Hepburn, Philip's father. She knew how Philip valued this watch. She remembered having seen it in his hands the very day before his disappearance, when he was looking at the time in his annoy-ance at Sylvia's detention in her walk with baby. Hester had no doubt that he had taken this watch as a matter of course away with him. She felt sure that he would not part with this relic of his dead father on any slight necessity. Where, then, was Philip? – by what chance of life or death had this, his valued property, found its way once more to Monkshaven?

'Where did yo' get this?' she asked, in as quiet a manner as she could assume, sick with eagerness as she was.

To no one else would Darley have answered such a question. He made a mystery of most of his dealings; not that he had anything to conceal, but simply because he delighted in concealment. He took it out of her hands, looked at the number marked inside, and the maker's name – 'Natteau Gent, York' – and then replied, –

'A man brought it me yesterday, at nightfall, for t' sell it. It's a matter o' forty years old. Natteau Gent has been dead and in his grave pretty nigh as long as that. But he did his work well when he were alive; and so I gave him as brought it for t' sell about as much as it were worth, i' good coin. A tried him first i' t' bartering line, but he wouldn't bite; like enough he wanted food, – many a one does now-a-days.'

'Who was he?' gasped Hester.

'Bless t' woman! how should I know?'

'What was he like? – how old? – tell me.'

'My lass, a've summut else to do wi' my eyes than go peering into men's faces i' t' dusk light.'

'But yo' must have had light for t' judge about the watch.'

'Eh! how sharp we are! A'd a candle close to my nose. But a didn't tak' it up for to gaze int' his face. That wouldn't be manners, to my thinking.'

Hester was silent. Then Darley's heart relented.

'If yo're so set upo' knowing who t' fellow was, a could, mebbe, put yo' on his tracks.'

'How?' said Hester, eagerly. 'I do want to know. I want to know very much, and for a good reason.'

'Well, then, a'll tell yo'. He's a queer tyke, that one is. A'll be bound he were sore pressed for t' brass; yet he out's wi' a good half-crown, all wrapped up i' paper, and he axes me t' make a hole in it. Says I, "It's marring good king's coin; at after a've made a hole in 't, it'll never pass current again." So he mumbles, and mumbles, but for a' that it must needs be done; and he's left it here, and is t' call for 't to-morrow at e'en.'

'Oh, William Darley!' said Hester, clasping her hands tight together. 'Find out who he is, where he is – anything – everything about him – and I will so bless yo'.'

Darley looked at her sharply, but with some signs of sympathy on his grave face. 'My woman,' he said, 'a could ha' wished as

yo'd niver seen t' watch. It's poor, thankless work thinking too
much on one o' God's creatures. But a'll do thy bidding,' he
continued, in a lighter and different tone. 'A'm a 'cute old
badger when need be. Come for thy watch in a couple o' days,
and a'll tell yo' all as a've learnt.'

So Hester went away, her heart beating with the promise of
knowing something about Philip, – how much, how little, in
these first moments, she dared not say even to herself. Some
sailor newly landed from distant seas might have become
possessed of Philip's watch in far-off latitudes; in which case,
Philip would be dead. That might be. She tried to think that this
was the most probable way of accounting for the watch. She
could be certain as to the positive identity of the watch – being
in William Darley's possession. Again, it might be that Philip
himself was near at hand – was here in this very place – starving,
as too many were, for insufficiency of means to buy the high-
priced food. And then her heart burnt within her as she thought
of the succulent, comfortable meals which Sylvia provided every
day – nay, three times a day – for the household in the market-
place, at the head of which Philip ought to have been; but his
place knew him not.* For Sylvia had inherited her mother's
talent for housekeeping, and on her, in Alice's decrepitude and
Hester's other occupations in the shop, devolved the cares of
due provision for the somewhat heterogeneous family.

And Sylvia! Hester groaned in heart over the remembrance of
Sylvia's words, 'I can niver forgive him the wrong he did to me,'
that night when Hester had come, and clung to her, making the
sad, shameful confession of her unreturned love.

What could ever bring these two together again? Could Hester
herself – ignorant of the strange mystery of Sylvia's heart, as
those who are guided solely by obedience to principle must ever
be of the clue to the actions of those who are led by the
passionate ebb and flow of impulse? Could Hester herself? Oh!
how should she speak, how should she act, if Philip were near –
if Philip were sad and in miserable estate? Her own misery at
this contemplation of the case was too great to bear; and she
sought her usual refuge in the thought of some text, some
promise of Scripture, which should strengthen her faith.

'With God all things are possible,' said she, repeating the
words as though to lull her anxiety to rest.

Yes; with God all things are possible. But ofttimes He does

his work with awful instruments. There is a peacemaker whose name is Death.

CHAPTER 45

Saved and Lost

Hester went out on the evening of the day after that on which the unknown owner of the half-crown had appointed to call for it again at William Darley's. She had schooled herself to believe that time and patience would serve her best. Her plan was to obtain all the knowledge about Philip that she could in the first instance; and then, if circumstances allowed it, as in all probability they would, to let drop by drop of healing, peacemaking words and thoughts fall on Sylvia's obdurate, unforgiving heart. So Hester put on her things, and went out down towards the old quay-side on that evening after the shop was closed.

Poor Sylvia! She was unforgiving, but not obdurate to the full extent of what Hester believed. Many a time since Philip went away had she unconsciously missed his protecting love; when folks spoke shortly to her, when Alice scolded her as one of the non-elect, when Hester's gentle gravity had something of severity in it; when her own heart failed her as to whether her mother would have judged that she had done well, could that mother have known all, as possibly she did by this time. Philip had never spoken otherwise than tenderly to her during the eighteen months of their married life, except on the two occasions before recorded: once when she referred to her dream of Kinraid's possible return, and once again on the evening of the day before her discovery of his concealment of the secret of Kinraid's involuntary disappearance.

After she had learnt that Kinraid was married, her heart had still more strongly turned to Philip; she thought that he had judged rightly in what he had given as the excuse for his double dealing; she was even more indignant at Kinraid's fickleness than she had any reason to be; and she began to learn the value of such enduring love as Philip's had been – lasting ever since the days when she first began to fancy what a man's love for a woman should be, when she had first shrunk from the tone of tenderness he put into his especial term for her, a girl of twelve – 'Little lassie', as he was wont to call her.

But across all this relenting came the shadow of her vow – like the chill of a great cloud passing over a sunny plain. How should she decide? what would be her duty, if he came again, and once more called her 'wife'? She shrank from such a possibility with all the weakness and superstition of her nature; and this it was which made her strengthen herself with the re-utterance of unforgiving words; and shun all recurrence to the subject on the rare occasion when Hester had tried to bring it back, with a hope of softening the heart which to her appeared altogether hardened on this one point.

Now, on this bright summer evening, while Hester had gone down to the quay-side, Sylvia stood with her out-of-door things on in the parlour, rather impatiently watching the sky, full of hurrying clouds, and flushing with the warm tints of the approaching sunset. She could not leave Alice: the old woman had grown so infirm that she was never left by her daughter and Sylvia at the same time; yet Sylvia had to fetch her little girl from the New Town, where she had been to her supper at Jeremiah Foster's. Hester had said that she should not be away more than a quarter of an hour; and Hester was generally so punctual that any failure of hers, in this respect, appeared almost in the light of an injury on those who had learnt to rely upon her. Sylvia wanted to go and see widow Dobson, and learn when Kester might be expected home. His two months were long past; and Sylvia had heard through the Fosters of some suitable and profitable employment for him, of which she thought he would be glad to know as soon as possible. It was now some time since she had been able to get so far as across the bridge; and, for aught she knew, Kester might already be come back from his expedition to the Cheviots. Kester was come back. Scarce five minutes had elapsed after these thoughts had passed through her mind before his hasty hand lifted the latch of the kitchen-door, his hurried steps brought him face to face with her. The smile of greeting was arrested on her lips by one look at him: his eyes staring wide, the expression on his face wild, and yet pitiful.

'That's reet,' said he, seeing that her things were already on. 'Thou're wanted sore. Come along.'

'Oh! dear God! my child!' cried Sylvia, clutching at the chair near her; but recovering her eddying senses with the strong fact before her that whatever the terror was, she was needed to combat it.

'Ay; thy child!' said Kester, taking her almost roughly by the arm, and drawing her away with him out through the open doors on to the quay-side.

'Tell me!' said Sylvia, faintly, 'is she dead?'

'She's safe now,' said Kester. 'It's not her – it's him as saved her as needs yo', if iver husband needed a wife.'

'He? – who? O Philip! Philip! is it yo' at last?'

Unheeding what spectators might see her movements, she threw up her arms and staggered against the parapet of the bridge they were then crossing.

'He! – Philip! – saved Bella? Bella, our little Bella, as got her dinner by my side, and went out wi' Jeremiah, as well as could be. I cannot take it in; tell me, Kester.' She kept trembling so much in voice and in body, that he saw she could not stir without danger of falling until she was calmed; as it was, her eyes became filmy from time to time, and she drew her breath in great heavy pants, leaning all the while against the wall of the bridge.

'It were no illness,' Kester began. 'T' little un had gone for a walk wi' Jeremiah Foster, an' he were drawn for to go round t' edge o' t' cliff, wheere they's makin' t' new walk reet o'er t' sea. But it's but a bit on a pathway now; an' t' one was too oud, an' t' other too young for t' see t' water comin' along wi' great leaps; it's allays for comin' high up again' t' cliff, an' this spring-tide it's comin' in i' terrible big waves. Some one said as they passed t' man a-sittin' on a bit on a rock up above – a dunnot know, a only know as a heared a great fearful screech i' t' air. A were just a-restin' me at after a'd comed in, not half an hour i' t' place. A've walked better nor a dozen mile to-day; an' a ran out, an' a looked, an' just on t' walk, at t' turn, was t' swish of a wave runnin' back as quick as t' mischief int' t' sea, an' oud Jeremiah standin' like one crazy, lookin' o'er int' t' watter; an' like a stroke o' leeghtnin' comes a man, an' int' t' very midst o' t' great waves like a shot; an' then a knowed summut were in t' watter as were nearer death than life; an' a seemed to misdoubt me that it were our Bella; an' a shouts an' a cries for help, an' a goes mysel' to t' very edge o' t' cliff, an' a bids oud Jeremiah, as

was like one beside hissel', houd tight on me, for he were good
for nought else; an' a bides my time, an' when a sees two arms
houdin' out a little drippin' streamin' child, a clutches her by
her waist-band, an' hauls her to land. She's noane t' worse for
her bath, a'll be bound.'

'I mun go – let me,' said Sylvia, struggling with his detaining
hand, which he had laid upon her in the fear that she would slip
down to the ground in a faint, so ashen-grey was her face. 'Let
me, – Bella, I mun go see her.'

He let go, and she stood still, suddenly feeling herself too
weak to stir.

'Now, if yo'll try a bit to be quiet, a'll lead yo' along; but yo'
mun be a steady and brave lass.'

'I'll be aught if yo' only let me see Bella,' said Sylvia, humbly.

'An' yo' niver ax at after him as saved her,' said Kester,
reproachfully.

'I know it's Philip,' she whispered, 'and yo' said he wanted
me; so I know he's safe; and, Kester, I think I'm 'feared on him,
and I'd like to gather courage afore seeing him, and a look at
Bella would give me courage. It were a terrible time when I saw
him last, and I did say—'

'Niver think on what thou did say; think on what thou will
say to him now, for he lies a-dyin'! He were dashed again t' cliff
an' bruised sore in his innards afore t' men as come wi' a boat
could pick him up.'

She did not speak; she did not even tremble now; she set her
teeth together, and, holding tight by Kester, she urged him on;
but when they came to the end of the bridge, she seemed
uncertain which way to turn.

'This way,' said Kester. 'He's been lodgin' wi' Sally this nine
week, an' niver a one about t' place as knowed him; he's been i'
t' wars an' getten his face brunt.'

'And he was short o' food,' moaned Sylvia, 'and we had
plenty, and I tried to make yo'r sister turn him out, and send
him away. Oh! will God iver forgive me?'

Muttering to herself, breaking her mutterings with sharp cries
of pain, Sylvia, with Kester's help, reached widow Dobson's
house. It was no longer a quiet, lonely dwelling. Several sailors
stood about the door, awaiting, in silent anxiety, for the verdict
of the doctor, who was even now examining Philip's injuries.

Two or three women stood talking eagerly, in low voices, in the doorway.

But when Sylvia drew near the men fell back; and the women moved aside as though to allow her to pass, all looking upon her with a certain amount of sympathy, but perhaps with rather more of antagonistic wonder as to how she was taking it – she who had been living in ease and comfort while her husband's shelter was little better than a hovel, her husband's daily life a struggle with starvation; for so much of the lodger at widow Dobson's was popularly known; and any distrust of him as a stranger and a tramp was quite forgotten now.

Sylvia felt the hardness of their looks, the hardness of their silence; but it was as nothing to her. If such things could have touched her at this moment, she would not have stood still right in the midst of their averted hearts, and murmured something to Kester. He could not hear the words uttered by that hoarse choked voice, until he had stooped down and brought his ear to the level of her mouth.

'We'd better wait for t' doctors to come out,' she said again. She stood by the door, shivering all over, almost facing the people in the road, but with her face turned a little to the right, so that they thought she was looking at the pathway on the cliff-side, a hundred yards or so distant, below which the hungry waves still lashed themselves into high ascending spray; while nearer to the cottage, where their force was broken by the bar at the entrance to the river, they came softly lapping up the shelving shore.

Sylvia saw nothing of all this, though it was straight before her eyes. She only saw a blurred mist; she heard no sound of waters, though it filled the ears of those around. Instead she heard low whispers pronouncing Philip's earthly doom.

For the doctors were both agreed; his internal injury was of a mortal kind, although, as the spine was severely injured above the seat of the fatal bruise, he had no pain in the lower half of his body.

They had spoken in so low a tone that John Foster, standing only a foot or so away, had not been able to hear their words. But Sylvia heard each syllable there where she stood outside, shivering all over in the sultry summer evening. She turned round to Kester.

'I mun go to him, Kester; thou'll see that noane come in to us, when t' doctors come out.'

She spoke in a soft, calm voice; and he, not knowing what she had heard, made some easy conditional promise. Then those opposite to the cottage door fell back, for they could see the grave doctors coming out, and John Foster, graver, sadder still, following them. Without a word to them, – without a word even of inquiry – which many outside thought and spoke of as strange – white-faced, dry-eyed Sylvia slipped into the house out of their sight.

And the waves kept lapping on the shelving shore.*

The room inside was dark, all except the little halo or circle of light made by a dip candle. Widow Dobson had her back to the bed – her bed – on to which Philip had been borne in the hurry of terror as to whether he was alive or whether he was dead. She was crying – crying quietly, but the tears down-falling fast, as, with her back to the lowly bed, she was gathering up the dripping clothes cut off from the poor maimed body by the doctors' orders. She only shook her head as she saw Sylvia, spirit-like, steal in – white, noiseless, and upborne from earth.

But noiseless as her step might be, he heard, he recognized, and with a sigh he turned his poor disfigured face to the wall, hiding it in the shadow.

He knew that she was by him; that she had knelt down by his bed; that she was kissing his hand, over which the languor of approaching death was stealing. But no one spoke.

At length he said, his face still averted, speaking with an effort,

'Little lassie, forgive me now! I cannot live to see the morn!'

There was no answer, only a long miserable sigh, and he felt her soft cheek laid upon his hand, and the quiver that ran through her whole body.

'I did thee a cruel wrong,' he said, at length. 'I see it now. But I'm a dying man. I think that God will forgive me – and I've sinned against Him; try, lassie – try, my Sylvie – will not thou forgive me?'

He listened intently for a moment. He heard through the open window the waves lapping on the shelving shore. But there came no word from her; only that same long shivering, miserable sigh broke from her lips at length.

'Child,' said he, once more. 'I ha' made thee my idol;* and if

I could live my life o'er again I would love my God more, and thee less;* and then I shouldn't ha' sinned this sin against thee. But speak one word of love to me – one little word, that I may know I have thy pardon.'

'Oh, Philip! Philip!' she moaned, thus adjured.

Then she lifted her head, and said,

'Them were wicked, wicked words, as I said; and a wicked vow as I vowed; and Lord God Almighty has ta'en me at my word. I'm sorely punished, Philip, I am indeed.'

He pressed her hand, he stroked her cheek. But he asked for yet another word.

'I did thee a wrong. In my lying heart I forgot to do to thee as I would have had thee to do to me. And I judged Kinraid in my heart.'

'Thou thought as he was faithless and fickle,' she answered quickly; 'and so he were. He were married to another woman not so many weeks at after thou went away. Oh, Philip, Philip! and now I have thee back, and—'

'Dying' was the word she would have said, but first the dread of telling him what she believed he did not know, and next her passionate sobs, choked her.

'I know,' said he, once more stroking her cheek, and soothing her with gentle, caressing hand. 'Little lassie!' he said, after a while when she was quiet from very exhaustion, 'I niver thought to be so happy again. God is very merciful.'

She lifted up her head, and asked wildly, 'Will He iver forgive me, think yo'? I drove yo' out fra' yo'r home, and sent yo' away to t' wars, wheere yo' might ha' getten yo'r death; and when yo' come back, poor and lone, and weary I told her for t' turn yo' out, for a' I knew yo' must be starving in these famine times. I think I shall go about among them as gnash their teeth for iver, while yo' are wheere all tears are wiped away.'*

'No!' said Philip, turning round his face, forgetful of himself in his desire to comfort her. 'God pities us as a father pities his poor wandering children; the nearer I come to death the clearer I see Him. But you and me have done wrong to each other; yet we can see now how we were led to it; we can pity and forgive one another. I'm getting low and faint, lassie; but thou must remember this: God knows more, and is more forgiving than either you to me, or me to you. I think and do believe as we shall meet together before His face; but then I shall ha' learnt to love thee second to Him; not first, as I have done here upon the earth.'

Then he was silent – very still. Sylvia knew – widow Dobson had brought it in – that there was some kind of medicine, sent by the hopeless doctors, lying upon the table hard by, and she softly rose and poured it out and dropped it into the half-open mouth. Then she knelt down again, holding the hand feebly stretched out to her, and watching the faint light in the wistful loving eyes. And in the stillness she heard the ceaseless waves lapping against the shelving shore.

Something like an hour before this time, which was the deepest midnight of the summer's night, Hester Rose had come hurrying up the road to where Kester and his sister sat outside the open door, keeping their watch under the star-lit sky, all others having gone away, one by one, even John and Jeremiah Foster having returned to their own house, where the little Bella lay, sleeping a sound and healthy slumber after her perilous adventure.

Hester had heard but little from William Darley as to the owner of the watch and the half-crown; but he was chagrined at the failure of all his skilful interrogations to elicit the truth, and promised her further information in a few days, with all the more vehemence because he was unaccustomed to be baffled. And Hester had again whispered to herself 'Patience! Patience!' and had slowly returned back to her home to find that Sylvia had left it, why she did not at once discover. But, growing uneasy as the advancing hours neither brought Sylvia nor little Bella to their home, she had set out for Jeremiah Foster's as soon as she had seen her mother comfortably asleep in her bed; and then she had learnt the whole story, bit by bit, as each person who spoke broke in upon the previous narration with some new particular. But from no one did she clearly learn whether Sylvia was with her husband, or not; and so she came speeding along the road, breathless, to where Kester sat in wakeful, mournful silence, his sister's sleeping head lying on his shoulder, the cottage door open, both for air and that there might be help within call if needed; and the dim slanting oblong of the interior light lying across the road.

Hester came panting up, too agitated and breathless to ask how much was truth of the fatal, hopeless tale which she had heard. Kester looked at her without a word. Through this solemn momentary silence the lapping of the ceaseless waves was heard, as they came up close on the shelving shore.

'He? Philip?' said she. Kester shook his head sadly.

'And his wife – Sylvia?' said Hester.

'In there with him, alone,' whispered Kester.

Hester turned away, and wrung her hands together.

'Oh, Lord God Almighty!' said she, 'was I not even worthy to bring them together at last?' And she went away slowly and heavily back to the side of her sleeping mother. But 'Thy will be done' was on her quivering lips before she lay down to her rest.

The soft grey dawn lightens the darkness of a midsummer night soon after two o'clock. Philip watched it come, knowing that it was his last sight of day, – as we reckon days on earth.

He had been often near death as a soldier; once or twice, as when he rushed into fire to save Kinraid, his chances of life had been as one to a hundred: but yet he had had a chance. But now there was the new feeling – the last new feeling which we shall any of us experience in this world – that death was not only close at hand, but inevitable.

He felt its numbness stealing up him – stealing up him. But the head was clear, the brain more than commonly active in producing vivid impressions.

It seemed but yesterday since he was a little boy at his mother's knee, wishing with all the earnestness of his childish heart to be like Abraham, who was called the friend of God, or David, who was said to be the man after God's own heart, or St John,* who was called 'the Beloved'. As very present seemed the day on which he made resolutions of trying to be like them; it was in the spring, and some one had brought in cowslips; and the scent of those flowers was in his nostrils now, as he lay a-dying – his life ended, his battles fought, his time for 'being good' over and gone – the opportunity, once given in all eternity, past.

All the temptations that had beset him rose clearly before him; the scenes themselves stood up in their solid materialism – he could have touched the places; the people, the thoughts, the arguments that Satan had urged in behalf of sin, were reproduced with the vividness of a present time. And he knew that the thoughts were illusions, the arguments false and hollow; for in that hour came the perfect vision of the perfect truth: he saw the 'way to escape' which had come along with the temptation;

now, the strong resolve of an ardent boyhood, with all a life before it to show the world 'what a Christian might be' and then the swift, terrible now, when his naked, guilty soul shrank into the shadow of God's mercy-seat, out of the blaze of His anger against all those who act a lie.

His mind was wandering, and he plucked it back. Was this death in very deed? He tried to grasp at the present, the earthly present, fading quick away. He lay there on the bed – on Sally Dobson's bed in the house-place, not on his accustomed pallet in the lean-to. He knew that much. And the door was open into the still, dusk night; and through the open casement he could hear the lapping of the waves on the shelving shore, could see the soft grey dawn over the sea – he knew it was over the sea – he saw what lay unseen behind the poor walls of the cottage. And it was Sylvia who held his hand tight in her warm, living grasp; it was his wife whose arm was thrown around him, whose sobbing sighs shook his numbed frame from time to time.

'God bless and comfort my darling,' he said to himself. 'She knows me now. All will be right in heaven – in the light of God's mercy.'

And then he tried to remember all that he had ever read about God, and all that the blessed Christ – that bringeth glad tidings of great joy* unto all people, had said of the Father, from whom He came. Those sayings dropped like balm down upon his troubled heart and brain. He remembered his mother, and how she had loved him; and he was going to a love wiser, tenderer, deeper than hers.

As he thought this, he moved his hands as if to pray; but Sylvia clenched her hold, and he lay still, praying all the same for her, for his child, and for himself. Then he saw the sky redden with the first flush of dawn; he heard Kester's long-drawn sigh of weariness outside the open door.

He had seen widow Dobson pass through long before to keep the remainder of her watch on the bed in the lean-to, which had been his for many and many a sleepless and tearful night. Those nights were over – he should never see that poor chamber again, though it was scarce two feet distant. He began to lose all sense of the comparative duration of time: it seemed as long since kind Sally Dobson had bent over him with soft, lingering look, before going into the humble sleeping-room – as long as it was since his boyhood, when he stood by his mother dreaming of the life that should be his, with the scent of the cowslips tempting him to be off to the woodlands where they grew. Then there came a rush and an eddying through his brain – his soul trying her wings for the long flight. Again he was in the present: he heard the waves lapping against the shelving shore once again.

And now his thoughts came back to Sylvia. Once more he spoke aloud, in a strange and terrible voice, which was not his. Every sound came with efforts that were new to him.

'My wife! Sylvie! Once more – forgive me all.'

She sprang up, she kissed his poor burnt lips; she held him in her arms, she moaned, and said,

'Oh, wicked me! forgive me – me – Philip!'

Then he spoke, and said, 'Lord, forgive us our trespasses as we forgive each other!' And after that the power of speech was conquered by the coming death. He lay very still, his consciousness fast fading away, yet coming back in throbs, so that he knew it was Sylvia who touched his lips with cordial, and that it was Sylvia who murmured words of love in his ear. He seemed to sleep at last, and so he did – a kind of sleep, but the light of the red morning sun fell on his eyes, and with one strong effort he rose up, and turned so as once more to see his wife's pale face of misery.

'In heaven,' he cried, and a bright smile came on his face, as he fell back on his pillow.

Not long after Hester came, the little Bella scarce awake in her arms, with the purpose of bringing his child to see him ere yet he passed away. Hester had watched and prayed through the livelong night. And now she found him dead, and Sylvia, tearless and almost unconscious, lying by him, her hand holding his, her other thrown around him.

Kester, poor old man, was sobbing bitterly; but she not at all.

Then Hester bore her child to her, and Sylvia opened wide her miserable eyes, and only stared, as if all sense was gone from her. But Bella suddenly rousing up at the sight of the poor, scarred, peaceful face, cried out, –

'Poor man who was so hungry. Is he not hungry now?'

'No,' said Hester, softly. 'The former things are passed away – and he is gone where there is no more sorrow, and no more pain.'*

But then she broke down into weeping and crying. Sylvia sat up and looked at her.

'Why do yo' cry, Hester?' she said. 'Yo' niver said that yo' wouldn't forgive him as long as yo' lived. Yo' niver broke the heart of him that loved yo', and let him almost starve at yo'r very door. Oh, Philip! my Philip, tender and true.'

Then Hester came round and closed the sad half-open eyes; kissing the calm brow with a long farewell kiss. As she did so, her eye fell on a black ribbon round his neck. She partly lifted it out; to it was hung a half-crown piece.'*

'This is the piece he left at William Darley's to be bored,' said she, 'not many days ago.'

Bella had crept to her mother's arms as a known haven in this strange place; and the touch of his child loosened the fountains of her tears. She stretched out her hand for the black ribbon, put it round her own neck; after a while she said,

'If I live very long, and try hard to be very good all that time, do yo' think, Hester, as God will let me to him where he is?'

Monkshaven is altered now into a rising bathing place. Yet, standing near the site of widow Dobson's house on a summer's night, at the ebb of a spring-tide, you may hear the waves come lapping up the shelving shore with the same ceaseless, ever recurrent sound as that which Philip listened to in the pauses between life and death.

And so it will be until 'there shall be no more sea'.*

But the memory of man fades away. A few old people can still tell you the tradition of the man who died in a cottage somewhere about this spot, – died of starvation while his wife lived in hard-hearted plenty not two good stone-throws away. This is the form into which popular feeling, and ignorance of the real facts, have moulded the story. Not long since a lady went to the 'Public Baths',* a handsome stone building erected on the very site of widow Dobson's cottage, and finding all the rooms engaged she sat down and had some talk with the bathing woman; and, as it chanced, the conversation fell on Philip Hepburn and the legend of his fate.

'I knew an old man when I was a girl,' said the bathing woman, 'as could niver abide to hear t' wife blamed. He would say nothing again' th' husband; he used to say as it were not fit for men to be judging; that she had had her sore trial, as well as Hepburn hisself.'

The lady asked, 'What became of the wife?'

'She was a pale, sad woman, allays dressed in black. I can just remember her when I was a little child, but she died before her daughter was well grown up; and Miss Rose took t' lassie, as had always been like her own.'

'Miss Rose?'

'Hester Rose! have yo' niver heared of Hester Rose, she as founded t' alms-houses for poor disabled sailors and soldiers on t' Horncastle road? There's a piece o' stone in front to say that "This building is erected in memory of P. H." – and some folk will have it P. H. stands for t' name o' th' man as was starved to death.'

'And the daughter?'

'One o' th' Fosters, them as founded t' Old Bank, left her a vast o' money; and she were married to a distant cousin of theirs, and went off to settle in America many and many a year ago.'

NOTES

Generally speaking, words or phrases found in a good dictionary are not listed below unless their usage is distinctive. Definitions of words in dialect are given where there is little indication of the meaning from the sound or spelling of the word, but since so much of the conversation in this novel is in dialect the reader must expect to engage with the characters and learn to appreciate their local idiom. We have consulted the World's Classics edition of *Sylvia's Lovers*, edited by Andrew Sanders, and wish to express my thanks to him for his help with these notes. We also wish to thank Dr Jennifer Fellows for her invaluable work on the text and the notes.

Epigraph
p. 1 Oh for thy voice to soothe and bless: the lines are taken from *In Memoriam A.H.H.*, LVI, 26–8. Published anonymously in 1850, this great poem by Alfred, Lord Tennyson (1809–92) is his tribute to his close friend Arthur Hallam, who had died suddenly in 1833. The three lines sound the theme of tragic loss in *Sylvia's Lovers*.

Chapter 1: Monkshaven
p. 3 Monkshaven: modelled on Whitby, 'a town of considerable importance even at the period of the Norman Conquest, occupies a beautiful position on both banks of the Esk at its junction with the sea' (from *The North Sea Pilot*, III, 1914).

p. 3 a throneless queen: in August 1561, the Catholic Mary Queen of Scots (1542–87) left France, where she had lived in exile for thirteen years, and sailed to reclaim her rightful throne in Scotland. During the voyage, Mary's fleet was spotted off Flamborough Head, 40 km. south of Whitby, an incident which probably gave rise to rumours of her landing at other points along this stretch of coast. Later, Mary's right to the Scottish as well as to the English throne would be contested, and she would again become a 'throneless queen'. She was executed by Queen Elizabeth I in 1587 (see Antonia Fraser, *Mary Queen of Scots*, 1969, p. 136).

p. 3   a great monastery: the monastery at Whitby, founded in the seventh century, was destroyed by Viking raiders in 867 AD. It was refounded after the Norman Conquest. According to George Young, 'The history of our Abbey naturally divides itself into two periods; – the Saxon, and the Norman or English period ... as the monastery of Whitby, erected after the Conquest, was founded on the site of Lady Hilda's monastery, it may be regarded as a revival of that ancient establishment' (George Young, *A History of Whitby*, 1817, vol. I, p. 238).

p. 3   the Dee: the river Esk.

p. 3   the German Ocean: the North Sea.

p. 4   blubber and whalebone: the fat of whales and the elastic horny substance found in their upper jaws. The first is used for train-oil (see below), the second for stiffening in dresses, corsets, whips, etc.

p. 4   'staithes': landing-stages, wharves.

p. 4   train-oil: oil from the blubber of a whale.

p. 5   scaur: cliff, ridge of hill.

p. 5   black-faced sheep: a hardier breed than others, their presence an indication of the wildness of the landscape and the consequent toughness of existence.

p. 6   'old man': the Southernwood, having hoary foliage.

p. 7   the termination of the American war: the War of Independence against British control began in 1775 and ended in 1783 at the Peace of Paris, with full recognition of the autonomy of the United States.

p. 7   in 1793 the proceedings of the French had set Europe on fire: among other things this meant the execution of the king, Louis XVI, in January, and the entry of Britain and other European states into the war against France, where the excesses of the Reign of Terror were to occur in 1794.

p. 7   We had our ships; but where were our men?: Gaskell is ironically echoing the patriotic 'Heart of oak are our ships!/Heart of oak are our men', from David Garrick's play *Harlequin's Invasion* (1759). The words were set to music by William Boyce. Garrick (1717–79) was a celebrated actor–manager–dramatist and a friend of Dr Johnson; 1759 was the *annus mirabilis*, with British colonial victories against the

French, including the capture of Quebec. Another line from the song, which she does not quote, carries an even deeper irony – 'To honour we call you, not press you like slaves'.

p. 7 '**press-warrants**': these gave authority granting permission to impress men into the army or the navy, their origin dating back at least to the end of the previous century.

p. 7 **in the hold of the tender**: the lower part of the supply vessel.

p. 7 **Lord Thurlow … Tower Hill … the attorney-general**: Lord Thurlow (1731–1806) was Solicitor-General in 1770, Attorney-General in the following year, and Lord Chancellor from 1778 until his dismissal in 1792. Ironically, during his time as Attorney-General he had to act for the Admiralty against one John Tubbs, who claimed that he had been wrongfully impressed, claiming exemption as a Thames waterman. Thurlow argued successfully that Tubbs was not exempt, and just after this successfully again resisted a bill introduced to abolish the press-gang, which was defeated 'by a two to one majority' (Robert Gore-Brown, *Chancellor Thurlow*, 1953, p. 95). Gore-Brown also notes a scurrilous pamphlet which refers to the impressment of 'Lord Churlow' as 'he was returning home from Council buttoned up as usual in his old rusty brown coat … and away they hurried his Lordship to the house of rendezvous on Tower Hill' (ibid., p. 138). Another reference is to be found in John Lord Campbell's *Lives of the Lord Chancellors*, 5th edition, 1868, vol. VII, p. 303, where he relates an anecdote from Baron Maseres, who told the story of how Thurlow when Attorney-General had, 'by way of frolic', dressed up as a sailor and been seized by a press-gang late at night in Long Acre. They carried him 'to their rendezvous at the Tower'; hence Gaskell's memory slip about the place of his impressment.

p. 7 '**mop**': a fair for hiring servants and farm-labourers, generally held before Michaelmas (29 September), with another held afterwards at which those who had not found jobs offered themselves again for employment.

p. 10 **overhaste in getting rich**: see Proverbs 28:22 ('He that hasteth to be rich *hath* an evil eye').

p. 10 **a Quaker**: the Christian sect known as the religious Society of Friends was founded by George Fox in the late 1640s. Quakers were sober in dress, espoused pacifism, rejected the Established Church and worshipped in meetings where they would be moved to pray. Andrew

White stresses their influence on eighteenth-century Whitby in his *A History of Whitby* (1993). Their reputation for honesty and directness ensured that they made their way in the community.

p. 10 Lieutenant Atkinson: the name may be deliberately chosen because of its local relevance. In *The Streets of Whitby and their Associations*, Hugh Kendall (revised Burnett, 1988) reports an attack on the press-gang in Whitby in 1793: 'An old man of seventy years of age, by name William Atkinson, was arrested on a charge of inciting, and afterwards hanged at York Castle; but there is little doubt that he was made a scapegoat for others' (p. 36).

p. 11 'varmint': vermin.

p. 11 the *Aurora*: note the choice of names (some drawn from actual ships), some admittedly commonplace, for the vessels. Aurora was the Roman goddess of dawn, perhaps an ironic choice since the 'living cargoes' are being taken into the darkness of war.

p. 11 Randyvow-house: from the French *rendezvous*, meeting-place, regular haunt. The local dialect conveniently assimilates this, since 'randy' has to do with wild drinking, but also means unmanageable and rash, words which would describe Daniel Robson and the mob which destroys the building. The treacherous ringing of the firebell brings him to a rendezvous with death. Note the reference to 'rendezvous' in the impressment of Thurlow above.

Chapter 2: Home from Greenland
p. 11 October of the year 1796: a rare error by Gaskell. As Sanders points out, once the rest of the chronology of the novel is established, this must be amended to 1793. But there is another less obvious but important slip. According to Young (writing in 1817), the *latest* arrival of a whaler from the Greenland seas was 'that of the Two Sisters, Agar, on Sept 8, 1790' (*A History of Whitby*, vol. II, p. 567).

p. 12 'rating': telling-off.

p. 12 the nine tails of a 'cat': the instrument of punishment used in the armed services (particularly the navy) of the time and also in slave labour: the handle was made of rope, and one end had nine branches or tails of log line with three or more knots in each one.

p. 12 sultana: the wife or concubine of a sultan, or other female member of his family, here sitting with legs crossed in eastern fashion.

p. 12 topped t' brow: came over the hill.

p. 13   a deal o' rubble: trivialities.

p. 14   every peg o' words: note the domestic image (of a clothes-line). Such usages convey the authenticity of the characters in their daily lives, part of Gaskell's unforced realism.

p. 15   the bar ... Dee: the sandbank at the mouth of the harbour or estuary of the Esk.

p. 15   Is ta ...?: Are you?

p. 16   betimes: (too) late.

p. 16   creepie-stools: stools which were very low to the ground.

p. 16   vast ... skeps: many ... receptacles, baskets.

p. 16   lamiter: cripple.

p. 16   beating her anchor: freeing it so that it can be lowered.

p. 17   *Resolution*: in fourteen voyages a whaler thus named brought home 298 whales (Young, *A History of Whitby*, vol. II, p. 566). It was also the name of one of Captain Cook's ships.

p. 17   happen: perhaps.

p. 17   manifest: the list of goods carried, for checking by the customs officers.

p. 17   Fishburn: a famous name in Whitby history. The yard built the three ships which took Captain Cook on his voyages of discovery, and Thomas Fishburn's residence lent its name to that part of the neighbourhood known as Fishburn Park.

p. 17   St Abb's Head: an actual place, on the Scottish North Sea coastline north of Berwick upon Tweed.

p. 17   specksioneer: the chief harpooner of a whaler, usually in charge of cutting up the blubber. This first mention of Kinraid is significant: he is always a leader among men (and women). Gaskell's focus on him is reflected in one of her proposed titles for the novel, which was simply *The Specksioneer*.

p. 18   mak o' mischief: not clear from the context here. It probably means 'getting herself into a state', or the equivalent.

p. 18   press: crowd.

p. 19   Weel may the keel row ...: this song is one of the most popular of all Northumbrian songs and is an important unifying moral index in the novel, heard here at the moment of crisis, hummed by Kinraid (to Philip's anger) just before his impressment, and welling up at crisis point again at the Siege of Acre.

p. 20   t' huxters: petty tradesmen or shopkeepers in a small way of business.

Chapter 3: Buying a New Cloak
p. 22   Foster's shop: based on the shop owned by Jonathan and Joseph Sanders, Quaker brothers who came to Whitby (Jonathan founded the business in 1779) from Guisborough. According to Kendall (*The Streets of Whitby and their Associations*, 1948), the bank and shop were at 93 Church Street.

p. 22   mercery: a shop devoted to textiles, clothes, silks, etc.

p. 23   William Coulson: a prominent Whitby name. William Coulson the shipbuilder came to Whitby from Scarborough in 1835, his yard, the Whitehall yard, being 'the longest lived of all Whitby yards, which built its last ship in 1902' (Young, *A History of Whitby*, Ch. 4).

p. 24   the ribbons in the shop window: the first mention of the symbolic sequence which shows Gaskell's attention to the detailed stitching of her plot fabric. Philip chooses for Sylvia a briar-rose ribbon ('sweetness and thorns'), which she later uses as a forfeit at a party; at the same party she wears a brown ribbon in her hair which marks her acceptance of Kinraid's attentions; and later Kinraid buys a bandanna and three yards of pink ribbon with black crosses. When Kinraid is impressed, Philip stumbles against his hat and sees this patterned ribbon, 'so that a spasm of hatred towards Kinraid contracted in his heart'. The sequence underpins character, situation, love, loss, possession.

p. 27   looking their eyes out: staring for all they were worth.

p. 27   King George: George III (1760–1820).

p. 27   dropt out o' t' lift: fallen from the sky, the heavens.

p. 28   as if they had been a Greek chorus: in a Greek classical tragedy. The phrase is appropriate to the contemporary tragedy being enacted here, since the Chorus does not influence the course of tragic events but merely comments on them. It is a demonstration of public – and more particularly female – impotence in the face of force.

p. 29   cobles: flat-bottomed fishing-boats commonly in use in north-east England. White points out that they 'were so made as to be able to beach stern-first on a sandy shore' (*A History of Whitby*, Ch. 5).

p. 30   **marred**: upsetting, spoiling (causing such distress).

p. 30   **a turn**: a fainting fit.

p. 30   **rage together ... like the very heathen**: an echo of Psalms 2:1 ('Why do the heathen rage . . .?').

p. 31   **"The old Adam"**: the first man is in his state of original sin, hence a phrase indicating the unregenerate nature of man.

Chapter 4: Philip Hepburn
p. 33   **chine**: narrow ravine.

p. 33   **sea-wrack**: seaweed thrown up by the sea or already growing on the shore.

p. 33   **osier baskets**: baskets made from the pliant branches of the willow.

p. 34   **clap-bread**: oatmeal cake, beaten up or rolled thin, and baked hard.

p. 34   **'turf cakes'**: cakes baked on a low-burning peat fire.

p. 34   **'singing hinnies'**: cakes baked on a circular iron plate which appear to give off a singing sound as they are cooked. The traditional song 'Billy Boy' in one of its many variants contains the lines, 'She can make an Irish stew/ Ay, an' singing hinnies too.'

p. 35   **bishopped**: burned.

p. 35   **a' reet**: all right.

p. 35   **Hollands**: Dutch gin.

p. 35   **in a peck o' troubles**: worrying, fretting.

p. 35   **browhead**: top of the hill.

p. 36   **agate**: about, active.

p. 36   **i' sperits . . .' potticary's**: preserved in spirits according to the practice of an apothecary.

p. 36   **get shut on us**: get rid of us.

p. 36   **pottering**: doing something feebly, idly, ineffectually.

p. 36   **keen set**: hungry, having an appetite.

p. 36   grog: spirits, originally rum and water.

p. 37   whittle: large knife.

p. 37   cotched up: taken, here 'captured'.

p. 37   at war wi' the French: this began in 1793. See second note to p. 7.

p. 37   where t' shoe pinches: where the trouble lies.

p. 37   junk: rubbish (in terms of food).

p. 37   carnal-mindedness and poesies: Daniel really means that he does not take any account of the love and domestic side of the lives of those impressed. He is turning his back on sentiment, another significant comment on his character.

p. 37   whittle: cut (their way out) with a sharp knife.

p. 38   isn't breeched: not grown up, not yet in trousers.

p. 38   Militiaman pays in person: i.e. by having to serve his country.

p. 38   When I gived my vote to Measter Cholmley: note Gaskell's use of a locally impressive family name. As White points out, Whitby lost representation in Parliament at the Restoration (1660), and it was not until 1832 that it was represented and 'even then the town was not at first listed among the new boroughs created by the Reform Act' (*A History of Whitby*, Ch. 1). The first MP was a Conservative, Aaron Chapman, who served until 1847.

p. 38   Parliament House: Daniel's singular is here emphatic of his simple-mindedness, which, in a way, is responsible for his having to pay with his life.

p. 38   div: if.

p. 38   that piece o'work: that deed.

p. 39   nation's nowheere: see Introduction pp. xxiv–xxv, for a discussion of the force and relevance of this.

p. 39   Measter Pitt: the younger William Pitt (1759–1806). He had become Prime Minister at the age of 24 (1783) but failed to make provision for the possibility of a long war with France.

p. 40   'traddle': the dialect form of 'treadle' – the lever worked by the foot. Sylvia is using a spinning-wheel.

p. 40   spot: stain.

p. 41 again: against.

p. 41 go whistle for my vote: ask me in vain to vote for him. Cholmley is one of the most prominent names in the history of Whitby: Henrietta Street, named after Nathaniel Cholmley's wife, who disappeared in a landslide in 1787, a few years before the main narrative action of *Sylvia's Lovers*.

p. 42 Let a' be: Leave me alone.

Chapter 5: Story of the Press-Gang
p. 43 the three Ridings: these were the administrative areas of York-shire – East, North and West.

p. 43 pin a dish-clout to his tail: attach a kitchen-cloth to his coat-tails, make him look ridiculous: 'a punishment often threatened by the female servants in a kitchen, to a man who pries too minutely into the secrets of that place' (*1811 Dictionary of the Vulgar Tongue*).

p. 43 dree work ... nursing th' fire: it is weary, miserable, having him just sitting around.

p. 43 Madame de Maintenon's difficulty: Madame de Maintenon (1635–1719) was the mistress of the 'Sun King', Louis XIV of France, before marrying him in 1684. She exerted a powerful influence over him until his death in 1715 but found it difficult to keep him amused because of his temperament, according to the duc de Saint-Simon in his *Mémoires* (Sanders).

p. 43 scouted: scornfully rejected.

p. 44 Martinmas: St Martin's Day, 11 November.

p. 45 fettle it, an' do it up: mend, repair and get it ready.

p. 45 mooney: staring, vacant, acting listlessly.

p. 45 deep and fause: clever and cunning, shrewd.

p. 45 Solomon ... Queen of Sheba: while the queen of Sheba could not trick the wise King Solomon, she nonetheless managed to obtain from him what she wanted. See I Kings 10:7ff., and particularly verse 13: 'And king Solomon gave unto the queen of Sheba all her desire, whatsoever she asked, beside that which Solomon gave her of his royal bounty.'

p. 45 cachinnation: loud laughing.

p. 45 shot: small stones or pebbles.

p. 45   ta'en . . . on t' reet side: got round him, persuaded him.

p. 45   permiskus: casually.

p. 45   felley: fellow.

p. 45   strike an' a half o' maut: generous measure (more than half again) of malt, thus making a strong beer.

p. 45   set up his back: become angry, annoyed.

p. 46   leagues o' hail: shouting distance.

p. 46   a natural: reduced to being an idiot.

p. 46   professional-wise: i.e. cross-legged.

p. 46   or that were required to mend each other: i.e. the materials required for mending (such as scraps of cloth for patches).

p. 47   t' ninth part's: even this small amount.

p. 47   after t' winders: window-tax was imposed in 1695 and not abolished until 1851.

p. 47   moither: worry, perplex.

p. 48   had a run for 't: it had to dodge the customs, it was smuggled.

p. 48   lustier by a deal: fuller-figured (because of what she was carrying).

p. 48   domestic Jupiter: a passing humorous glance. Jupiter was the chief Roman god.

p. 48   wark: pain, heartache.

p. 49   mought: might.

p. 50   mak' o' goin' on: way of proceeding.

p. 51   ware: warn.

p. 52   cried for quarter: indicated that they wished to surrender.

p. 52   waur: worse.

Chapter 6: The Sailor's Funeral
p. 53   'dab-wash': quick and superficial washing.

p. 54   nowt so weel: nothing so well.

p. 55   Rain is over and gone: Song of Solomon 2:11 – ('the rain is over *and* gone').

p. 56 set me: accompany me.

p. 56 wer: our.

p. 57 galraverging: gallivanting, enjoying oneself.

p. 58 answered: done him good.

p. 58 scrimpit: niggardly, scanty, mean.

p. 58 main: really, very.

p. 59 St Martin's summer: fine, mild weather for the season, about Martinmas (see first note to p. 44).

p. 59 'the heat o' th' sun . . .': see *Cymbeline*, IV.ii.259–60 ('Fear no more the heat o' th' sun/Nor the furious winter's rages').

p. 60 St Nicholas: patron saint of, among others, sailors, as well as being the original of 'Father Christmas'.

p. 60 rosemary . . . 'for remembrance': the echo is of Ophelia's plaintive lament for her father, Polonius, in *Hamlet*, IV.v.174.

p. 62 Wesley . . . an Oxford man: John Wesley (1703–91), the founder of Methodism, was educated at Charterhouse and at Lincoln College, Oxford. As Sanders notes, he had been a regular visitor to Whitby and recorded his appreciation of the Methodist community there.

p. 62 a rabid Independent: a keen member of the Congregational Church, which believed in the self-government of individual churches.

p. 62 'In the midst of life we are in death': from *The Book of Common Prayer*: the Burial of the Dead.

p. 63 the King could do no wrong . . . the glorious Revolution: Gaskell is here stressing the paradoxical views of the preacher, who apparently believed in the Divine Right of Kings, a doctrine held by the Stuart dynasty, who were deposed in the 'Glorious Revolution' of 1688 by which the succession passed to William of Orange, who became king of England with his wife Mary as queen.

p. 64 'It is the Lord's doing': Psalm 118:23 ('This is the Lord's doing; it is marvellous in our eyes').

p. 65 the last long, lingering look: an echo of Thomas Gray's 'Elegy Written in a Country Churchyard' (1751), line 88 ('Nor cast one longing, lingering look behind').

Chapter 7: Tête-à-tête – The Will

p. 67 he'll have to stand his trial . . .: Daniel is hanged for his part in the attack on the Randyvowse, but Kinraid, guilty and later impressed and promoted in the service, is not subjected to legal punishment, an oblique Gaskellian comment on the injustice of the times.

p. 68 look on wi' yo'r hands hanging by yo'r side: another superbly prophetic if casual hint – this is precisely what Philip does when he sees Kinraid taken by the gang.

p. 68 t' flag's down: for fear of reprisals, or perhaps to give the impression that the gang has left.

p. 68 strong: boldly, aggressively.

p. 69 Mason *On Self-Knowledge,* and Law's *Serious Call*: John Mason (1706–63) was a prominent Nonconformist. His treatise *On Self-Knowledge* was published in 1743. William Law (1686–1761) was an influential English churchman, whose *Devout Call to a Serious and Holy Life* (1728) is his most famous work. It exerted a profound effect upon Dr Johnson and the Wesleys among others.

p. 69 Pharisaism: being self-righteous, arrogant.

p. 69 Friend: synonymous with the word Quaker, as indicated in the text.

p. 70 one of those who went to mock, but remained to pray: an echo of the description of the village preacher's effect ('Truth from his lips prevailed with double sway/And fools, who came to scoff, remained to pray') in 'The Deserted Village' (1770), lines 179–80, by Oliver Goldsmith (1730–74).

p. 71 'dread the grave as little as her bed': from the evening hymn by Thomas Ken (1631–1711) ('Teach me to live, that I may dread/The grave as little as my bed').

p. 74 a spread-eagle: extravagant, spread like the wings of an eagle, flamboyant.

p. 74 fly-legs and cob-webs: a further comment (from Alice) on the thin and extended nature of the handwriting.

p. 74 'In the name of the Father . . .': an insight into Alice's devout nature. For her, the Lord's Prayer is the final legal stamp.

p. 74 t' episcopal persuasion: accepting government by bishops.

p. 74   third day, ninth month: precise dating – though if the novel, as suggested by Sanders, begins in October 1793, Alice is surely wrong (or Gaskell is), since this occurs shortly after Darley's funeral.

p. 75   paste: dough of flour.

p. 75   chancery: court of the Lord Chancellor, a division of the High Court. It was notorious for delays in settling claims to property and possessions, and is mercilessly satirized in Charles Dickens's *Bleak House* (1852).

p. 75   world's gear: material possessions.

p. 76   We'll take a turn at t' will next First Day: we'll resume preparing the will on the next Sunday (called the First Day by members of the Society of Friends).

p. 76   a call . . . had been called: he was certain to die.

p. 77   gnashing o' teeth: Luke 13:28 ('There shall be weeping and gnashing of teeth').

Chapter 8: Attraction and Repulsion
p. 78   pared up: trimmed, shaved, ready.

p. 79   crack on: boast of.

p. 80   chops and changes: variable moods.

p. 80   Little Red Riding Hood: a casually appropriate physical comparison, with the innuendo in the background from Philip that Kinraid is the wolf.

p. 81   fine and vexed: very upset.

p. 81   a crack o' no time: very soon.

p. 82   Michaelmas Day: the feast of St Michael, 29 September.

p. 82   he's ta'en a turn to betterin': his condition is improving.

p. 82   a deep set: a cunning lot.

p. 84   likely: likely to do well, promising, good-looking.

p. 84   the brilliant northern lights: electrical atmospherics, streamers of light in the sky above the North Pole, known as the Aurora Borealis.

p. 84   'for I loves the tossin' say': heaving sea (source not identified).

p. 85   to boot: in addition.

p. 85 'Abednego': the name of one of Daniel's three friends who were delivered from the fiery furnace (Daniel 3:12–30).

p. 86 has stuck by me sore: has rankled with me.

p. 86 'I sent my love a letter . . .': identified by Sanders as being from volume II of Robert Archibald Smith's *The Scottish Minstrel* (1821–4), slightly misquoted here. Its resonance in the plot heightens the pathos of Sylvia's 'unlettered' state and her late (one is inclined to say too late) wish to learn.

p. 87 dip-candle: one made by putting the wick in hot tallow quickly.

p. 87 John Bullish: John Bull is the humorous caricature of the English people collectively. It derives from Arbuthnot's satire 'The History of John Bull' (1712), where the Church of England is represented as being his mother.

p. 87 Nelson and the North: a strange reference. Horatio Nelson (1758–1805) would be in the Mediterranean in command of the *Agamemnon* if we are in 1793, while the 'North' does not properly fit any other battle location of the time. But it may be a casual echo of Thomas Campbell's (1777–1844) 'Battle of the Baltic', the opening lines of which are 'Of Nelson and the North/Sing the glorious day's renown'. The occasion is Nelson's famous victory at Copenhagen on 2 April 1801, an event outside the time-span of *Sylvia's Lovers*.

p. 88 a pair o' gloves: a present which signifies courtship.

p. 88 sa mim: prim, demure.

Chapter 9: The Specksioneer
p. 89 cranching: crunching.

p. 91 duty on salt: first introduced in 1702, and bitterly resented during this hard war period; the taxes were not abolished until 1825 (Sanders).

p. 91 It may seem curious to trace up . . .: Gaskell striking an omniscient note, suggesting that severe taxation breeds dishonesty rather than truthfulness.

p. 91 to see th' last man out: to outlive everybody.

p. 92 making play: creating difficulties, trying to stay free.

p. 92 reeved: put through (the fins, to secure them).

p. 92   **Noah's grandfather:** proverbial phrase, strictly a reference to Methuselah, who lived for 969 years (Genesis 5:27).

p. 92   **to sweep th' fish:** to clean it out thoroughly.

p. 92   **moulds:** earth (he is thinking of being suffocated as a miner), but it is also an ironic comment on land burial instead of a watery grave.

p. 93   **M or N?:** from the Catechism in the *Book of Common Prayer*.

p. 93   **turn-in:** period of rest.

p. 94   **th' mouth o' Hell:** possibly another Tennyson echo, of lines 25 and 47 in 'The Charge of the Light Brigade' (1854) ('Into the mouth of Hell' and 'Back from the mouth of Hell').

p. 94   **dwined:** pined, dwindled.

p. 95   **t' *Aimwell* of Whitby:** appropriate name for a whaler, but note that Gaskell has also used the factual Whitby here instead of Monkshaven. The *Aimwell* is mentioned as a particularly successful whaler by Young (*A History of Whitby*, vol. II, p. 566).

p. 95   **cotched:** caught.

p. 96   **wheniver t' maggot stirs i' her head:** whenever she wants to.

p. 96   **or iver:** before.

p. 96   **stopped an oud maid:** remained unmarried (since I would be dead).

p. 97   **Sylvia dreamed of burning volcanoes . . .:** Sylvia's dreams are an important index to her subconscious sexuality, as we see later when she is married to Philip but still longs for Kinraid.

Chapter 10: A Refractory Pupil
p. 98   **farred:** removed.

p. 98   **a set on 'em:** a complete list of words.

p. 99   **barm:** yeast, but also froth, nonsense.

p. 102   **calm sough:** quiet tongue, silence.

p. 105   **left on hand:** unmarried.

p. 105   **gets off quickest:** marries soonest.

p. 106   **'Charley Kinraid be hung!':** even Molly's exclamation here carries some weight in the unfolding narrative: Kinraid might have been hanged for his own actions against the press-gang earlier.

p. 106   **t' Side**: at this time the main street of Newcastle.

p. 106   **turns over**: makes a profit of.

p. 106   **out o' t' road**: out of the way.

p. 106   **cropping out of**: being introduced into.

Chapter 11: Visions of the Future
p. 108   **pet**: temper.

p. 112   **as peaked and pined as a Methody preacher after a love-feast**: as thin and pale as a Methodist after one of their religious services on brotherly love (note Bell's sharpness of tongue).

p. 113   **whatten ... next thing?**: and most important, what do they say of her?.

p. 113   **All Souls' Day**: 2 November.

p. 113   **marlock**: frolic about, be noisy.

p. 114   **venture**: investment.

p. 115   **Sarvant**: 'Your servant' (form of polite address).

p. 116   **set up**: conceited, vain.

p. 116   **a weaver**: a very poor specimen.

p. 116   **lile**: little.

p. 116   **kittle**: difficult, awkward to deal with.

p. 116   **chary of herself**: reserved.

p. 117   **shrined in the dearest sanctuary of his being**: imagery which again suggests the earlier title of *Philip's Idol*.

p. 117   **'Give me Sylvia, or else I die'**: a movingly prophetic inward exclamation within the context of the plot.

p. 118   **gig**: light carriage.

Chapter 12: New Year's Fête
p. 120   **hissen**: himself.

p. 120   **oat-cake folk ... pie-crust**: ordinary people ... superior.

p. 120   **many a wrinkle**: a hint or tip (on how to behave yourself).

p. 121 **cut t' best on 'em out:** show how superior you are.

p. 121 **watch-night:** religious service held on the last night of the year.

p. 121 **make shift:** put myself out.

p. 122 **Mavor's Spelling-book:** Sanders asserts that this was first published in 1801, in which case Gaskell is guilty of a minor anachronism.

p. 122 **mentor:** adviser, guide; from the Greek Mentor who guided the young Telemachus in Homer's *Odyssey*.

p. 123 **Yates and Peels:** Robert Peel set up in 1764, with his brother-in-law Mr Haworth and a neighbour Mr Yates, a calico-printing firm in Blackburn which effectively became the founding industry in Lancashire. He was the grandfather of the statesman and Tory Minister Sir Robert Peel (1788–1850).

p. 123 **palempours:** more commonly palampores, patterned chintz bedcovers, made in India.

p. 126 **St James's:** the royal residence, the palace.

p. 127 **wescut:** waistcoat.

p. 127 **'of his kidney':** of his way of thinking, his type.

p. 129 **gape-gazing:** seeking to attract by looking fixedly, 'gazing' at people in order to draw attention to themselves.

p. 130 **Niver fash thysel':** don't worry, don't disturb yourself.

p. 130 **forfeits:** game which consists of having to do something (a forfeit) if you answer wrongly.

p. 131 **Toby:** a large jug for holding liquor, shaped like a stout old man wearing a three-cornered hat.

p. 132 **'*vanitas vanitatum*':** vanity of vanities (cf. Ecclesiastes 1:2; *vanitas* means emptiness or fruitlessness).

p. 132 **Sylvia's pretty new ribbon:** again the associations are ironic – in giving up Philip's present to her she is 'forfeiting' him in favour of Kinraid, whom she is later to 'forfeit' because of his supposed death. The following conversation stresses that she must kiss the 'candlestick' or forgo her ribbon.

p. 136 **stawed:** full up, having eaten as much as they can take.

p. 136 **pipes:** voices.

p. 139   a' folded: all penned in.

p. 139   signs and wonders: the indications of what the weather will be like; an echo of Exodus 7:3 ('and multiply my signs and my wonders in the land of Egypt').

p. 139   jorum: large drinking-bowl.

p. 140   the new year, 1796: see note to p. 74. This should be 1795.

Chapter 13: Perplexities
p. 141   like apples o' Sodom: mythic fruit said to grow by the Dead Sea, externally tempting but, as Colson comments, filled with ashes.

p. 142   joy, hope had come in the morning: an echo of Psalms 30:5 ('weeping may endure for a night, but joy *cometh* in the morning'.)

p. 142   raking coal: large lumps used to keep the fire in during the night.

p. 143   notable: capable; clever and industrious in household management and occupations (*OED*).

p. 143   the elect: those chosen by God for salvation.

p. 148   sift yo' as wheat: do as he wants with you (and see Luke 22:31: 'Satan hath desired *to have* you, that he may sift *you* as wheat').

p. 150   *pas seul*: solo dance (a reference to Kinraid's hornpipe).

Chapter 14: Partnership
p. 152   the enormities she had just been committing: a reference to the Reign of Terror in France in 1793–4. By July of the latter year, 1250 people had been guillotined in Paris; there was equal severity in the provinces, with attacks on all suspected of royalist sympathies, while in May Christianity was abolished in favour of the cult of reason. But Robespierre (1758–94) was himself executed in July, and the Directory was established in 1795.

p. 152   The oppressive act against seditious meetings: the Seditious Meetings Act was passed in 1795 and forbade for three years any meetings of more than fifty people unless licensed by the local magistracy. Lectures outside universities were similarly censored.

p. 153   these pioneers of 1830: presumably a reference to the electoral reform agitation culminating in the passing of the First Reform Bill of 1832, which abolished certain corrupt or 'rotten' boroughs and slightly extended the franchise.

p. 153 the young Corsican warrior: Napoleon Buonaparte (1769–1821) was born in Ajaccio. He had taken part in the Siege of Toulon (1793), became a general at the age of 24, and conquered Lombardy in a brilliant campaign in Italy in 1796–7. He later became emperor of the French and was finally defeated by the Duke of Wellington and the Prussian Blucher at Waterloo in 1815. He is well in evidence at the Siege of Acre (Ch. 38).

p. 153 Marlborough: John Churchill, Duke of Marlborough (1650–1722). Commander-in-chief under Queen Anne, he won outstanding victories against the French at Blenheim (1704), Ramillies (1706), Oudenaard (1708) and Malplaquet (1709).

p. 153 the Corresponding Society: this had been formed in 1792 for the encouragement of discussion about the constitution, and was sympathetic to the French. But with the advent of the war it became gradually disillusioned (though still posing a threat), and in 1798 the London branch discussed the possibility of forming resistance to any projected French invasion.

p. 153 the Princess of Wales ... Charlotte or Elizabeth: her daughter was born on 7 January 1796, and was in fact called Charlotte Augusta. The dissolute Prince of Wales had married Caroline of Brunswick on 8 April 1795. They separated shortly afterwards. The princess Charlotte died in childbirth in 1817.

p. 153 outrages which had been lately offered to the King in crossing St James's Park: the incident is fully reported in the *Annual Register*, 38 (1796): 'In his way to the house of lords, which lay through the park, his coach was surrounded on every side, by persons of all descriptions, demanding peace and the dismission of Mr Pitt. Some voices were even heard exclaiming no king, and stones were thrown at the state-coach as it drew near to the Horse-guards. In passing through Palace-yard, one of the windows was broken, it was said, by a bullet discharged from an air-gun. These outrages were repeated on the king's return from the house, and he narrowly escaped the fury of the populace, in his way back from St James's Palace to Buckingham House' (p. 9). As a result, a bill to secure the safety of the king's person (as well as the Seditious Meetings Bill) was carried in November 1795.

p. 156 Cousin Betty: harmless madwoman or vagrant.

p. 157 a pig in a poke: something you don't know the worth or value of.

p. 157   the ground o' the bargain: the basis of the agreement.

p. 158   honourable members: of the House of Commons, MPs.

p. 159   Father of the friendless: see Psalms 68:5 ('A father of the fatherless . . .').

p. 159   a short delay was placed . . . the cup and his enjoyment of it: unobtrusive irony here, referring to the proverb 'there's many a slip 'twixt cup and lip'.

p. 160   we . . . forespoken by yo': we would have cared for Hester because you wished it.

Chapter 15: A Difficult Question
p. 161   shippen door: the door of the cowshed.

p. 162   a horn lantern: a lantern whose sides were made from transparent horn.

p. 162   King Solomon: see note to p. 45, and Ecclesiastes 7:26 ('And I find more bitter than death the woman, whose heart is snares and nets . . .').

p. 162   to the fore: about, here.

p. 163   t' afterings: the last milk that comes before the udder is empty.

p. 163   swash down i' t' litter: spill, splash down in the straw.

p. 164   fitting up after a fresh fashion: being overhauled and refurbished.

p. 164   bearing away the bell: taking first place because of her looks.

p. 165   'stripping': drawing off the last milk by pressure of thumb and finger.

p. 165   t' rhumatiz . . . back end: since I got (rheumatism) in my shoulder (blade).

p. 166   teem: pour from one receptacle into another.

p. 168   fremd: strange.

p. 170   Nancy Hartley . . . 'He once was here': this story is to echo the main story of Sylvia's lovers, each of whom 'once was here' later. The phrase comes back to Sylvia in her terrible loneliness and adversity, the pathos of the crazed girl having a searing equivalence to her own suffering.

p. 170   **gaum-like**: sensible.

p. 170   **softy**: simple-minded person.

p. 170   **bingy**: sour.

Chapter 16: The Engagement

p. 171   **"As the day lengthens, so the cold strengthens"**: proverbial, meaning that February and March are colder than December and January.

p. 171   **leading**: spreading over the land as fertilizer.

p. 172   **"He once was here"**: notice how Sylvia innocently appropriates the phrase to herself at this stage.

p. 173   **flush of money**: with plenty to spend.

p. 175   **"damn the faults we have no mind to"**: Sanders points out that this is reminiscent of a couplet from *Hudibras* (1663–78), a satire on Puritanism, by Samuel Butler (1612–80): 'Compound for sins they are inclin'd to/By damning those they have no mind to' (lines 213–4).

p. 175   **locking the stable-door . . . stolen**: being too late.

p. 179   **Davis' Straits**: named after their discoverer, John Davis (*c.* 1550–1605), English navigator who made three voyages to the Arctic (1585–7), the straits are between Greenland and Baffin Island.

p. 180   **mischief only knows**: i.e. the Devil only knows.

p. 180   **t' oud cat does 'er her blind kitten**: domestic image which stresses the pathos of Sylvia's coming situation.

p. 180   **stiff**: obstinate.

Chapter 17: Rejected Warnings

p. 184   **t' suds**: being washed.

p. 184   **ruffled**: ornamented with gathered frill of lace at cuff or neck. Obviously a best or fashionable shirt.

p. 185   **got the start**: had the advantage.

p. 186   **Hazael, "Is thy servant a dog that he should do this thing?"**: cf. II Kings 8:13. Hazael became king of Aram, as prophesied by Elisha.

p. 188   **settin'**: of a hen, sitting (in order to hatch out).

p. 188   **gearin'**: implements.

p. 188   **t'marrow on t' matter**: the truth or fact of the thing.

p. 188   acquaint wi' ribbons: unconsciously ironic comment on Philip's concerns.

p. 189   a month's mind: a strong inclination.

Chapter 18: Eddy in Love's Current

p. 194   "Norroway over the foam": from the fourth verse, added by Sir Walter Scott (1771–1832) in his *Minstrelsy of the Scottish Border* (1803), of the anonymous ballad of 'Sir Patrick Spens'.

p. 197   Hepburn felt guilty of his death: another fine example of the author's conciseness, for hereafter Kinraid is to all intents and purposes dead.

p. 200   the *Alcestis*: a deftly ironic choice of name, since Alcestis in Greek mythology is synonymous with self-sacrifice. Sylvia sacrifices herself in marriage to Philip, while the latter is unable at this point to sacrifice himself for his rival Kinraid, though in rescuing him later he does so.

p. 201   the dread Inner Creature: the Devil, temptation.

Chapter 19: An Important Mission

p. 203   counters: chips.

p. 204   shot: share of the bill.

p. 204   wafered his letter: sealed it, with a small disc of dried paste.

p. 204   paltering: being equivocal, indecisive.

p. 205   heavy postage: i.e. costly, since this is in the period before the introduction of the Penny Post by Rowland Hill in 1840.

p. 205   intelligence: news.

p. 205   chop-house: common eating-place.

p. 206   the Mordecai sitting in Haman's gate: see Esther 2–6 for the full story of Mordecai saving King Ahasuerus' life and of the persecution of the Jews by Haman, against which Mordecai protests. Haman is later hanged on the gallows he has prepared for Mordecai.

Chapter 20: Loved and Lost

p. 208   Loved and Lost: The chapter title is not only a comment on the immediate action and the main theme, but another echo of Tennyson's *In Memoriam* (section XXVII): ''Tis better to have loved and lost/Than never to have loved at all', a sentiment perhaps at variance with Sylvia's present, and even later, mood. Curiously, Tennyson's

Enoch Arden, published in 1864, after *Sylvia's Lovers*, has a similar plot. Enoch marries Annie, who is loved by his friend Philip. In order to earn money, Enoch goes to sea, but is shipwrecked for ten years. Annie has a dream which she interprets as his death, and marries Philip, who has protected her. Enoch returns, discovers Annie's marriage, but decides to do nothing. He dies, his identity revealed, as he wished, only after his death.

p. 210 **marigolds**: these have medicinal properties. The flowers were sometimes made into a conserve, or used as a soup flavouring or to provide a yellow colouring for cheese.

p. 210 **sair een**: sore eyes.

p. 211 **that much law**: so that he was within the law (in terms of the time for sailing).

p. 212 **King George an' Queen Charlotte**: George III died in 1820, his wife Charlotte Sophia in 1818. They had fifteen children, the eldest succeeding as George IV.

p. 213 **plaining**: fretful.

p. 215 **gone out**: given up the business.

p. 215 **t' brass**: money.

Chapter 21: A Rejected Suitor
p. 218 **throng**: here 'pressure'.

p. 219 **melling wi'**: meddling with, interfering.

p. 220 **gi'en him the bucket**: (presumably) rejected him.

p. 221 **his character will bear handling on a' sides**: his integrity will bear any amount of inspection.

p. 221 **neither marrying nor giving in marriage**: a straight echo of Matthew 24:38.

Chapter 22: Deepening Shadows
p. 223 **the *Sorrows of Werther* ... Law's *Serious Call*, the *Pilgrim's Progress*, Klopstock's *Messiah*, and *Paradise Lost***: the first is by Goethe (1749–1832), and was published in 1774; it is in strange company here, though this is a mark of its sensational success; in essence it is a tragic love-story. For Law's *Serious Call*, see first note to p. 69. The *Pilgrim's Progress* (1678) by John Bunyan (1628–88) is the classic popular allegory of Christianity which had a wide and continuing

appeal. Friedrich Gottfried Klopstock (1724–1803) was a German poet, who completed his *Messiah* in 1773. *Paradise Lost* is the epic poem in blank verse on the Fall of Man by John Milton (1608–74).

p. 223 the picture of Charlotte: Charlotte is the object of young Werther's hopeless love in Goethe's work mentioned above.

p. 223 the *Complete Farrier*: Sanders suggests that this may be *The Experienced Farrier*, which was originally published in 1678.

p. 223 Jacob's twice seven years' service: Genesis 29:20–1. Jacob serves seven years for Laban's daughter Rachel and claims her by agreement after that time, but she is the younger daughter and by law cannot take precedence over her elder sister, Leah. Having been tricked into sleeping with Leah, Jacob is required to serve another seven years before finally being rewarded with Rachel.

p. 223 tried him on: assessed his potential.

p. 226 blue jackets: sailors, seamen in the Royal Navy.

p. 227 *Megaera ... Bellerophon ... Hanover*: note the range of names, the classical references balancing the patriotic choice of *Hanover*, the ruling dynasty of England since the accession of George I in 1714.

p. 228 the war station: another clue as to the time and state of the war.

Chapter 23: Retaliation

p. 230 the famous maxim of Rochefoucault ... for in the misfortunes of their friends...: La Rochefoucauld (1613–80), French writer. His *Réflexions: ou, Sentences et maximes morales*, appeared in 1665. Gaskell's paraphrase is of *maxime 99*.

p. 232 made darkness visible: a conscious assimilation of 'No light, but rather darkness visible' from *Paradise Lost*, 1.63.

p. 232 seething the kid in its mother's milk: seething means boiling or soaking. At the literal level, this would violate the biblical prohibition handed down to Moses on Mount Sinai (see Exodus 23: 19); as a metaphor it suggests that the action of the press-gang is a violation of the most profane sort – an abomination against the sacred feelings bonding the members of a community.

p. 233 nobbut eight stun: weighing no more than 8 stones (112 lbs).

p. 233 **to gang:** to go.

p. 237 **moithered:** worried, confused, upset.

p. 237 **brennin':** burning.

p. 238 **routling out:** hunting out (cited in Wright's *The English Dialect Dictionary*, 1905, from *Sylvia's Lovers*).

p. 238 **served out:** to get what he deserves.

p. 238 **A'm noane flush:** I haven't got much.

Chapter 24: Brief Rejoicing
p. 241 **treacle-posset ... hoasts:** hot milk drink curdled with treacle, used as a remedy for colds and coughs.

p. 241 **a bout:** i.e. of getting drunk.

p. 242 **her dead lover at the ash-field stile:** these reiterations are a considered stress of the poignancy of Sylvia's situation both now and later.

p. 243 **a parish-pound:** an enclosure maintained by the local village for detaining stray or wandering cattle.

p. 243 **warming-pan ... state occasions:** Daniel is an old man who needs to be kept warm after his exertions; the tragic state occasion to come is his execution.

p. 245 **clem:** starve.

p. 246 **th' act:** the Riot Act. See note to p. 258.

p. 247 **coil:** row, trouble.

Chapter 25: Coming Troubles
p. 250 **the well-known ostrich:** which buried his head in the sand to avoid trouble.

p. 253 **with an uneasy motion:** this appears to be a subliminal Gaskellian echo of a phrase, appropriately enough, from *The Rime of the Ancient Mariner* ('with a short uneasy motion', lines 386 and 388) by Samuel Taylor Coleridge (1772–1832).

p. 254 **sets me off:** reduces me to tears.

p. 256 **fremd ... Bridewell:** strange ... prison, the latter named from the St Bride's Well in London.

p. 256 **inflicted in wild justice:** Patsy Stoneman (*Elizabeth Gaskell*,

1987, p. 142) locates 'wild justice' in the fourth essay of Francis Bacon (1561–1626), English statesman and philosopher, as defining revenge.

p. 258 **4th section of 1 George I**: the Riot Act. This was passed in 1715 virtually at the beginning of the Hanoverian accession. It laid down that a gathering of more than twelve people must disperse when ordered to do so by a magistrate. It was initially designed to protect the throne against the Jacobites; technically it remained in force until 1967.

p. 260 **six and eightpence**: one-third of a pound, the standard legal consultation fee.

p. 261 **tax-cart**: two-wheeled open cart drawn by a single horse, generally used for agricultural purposes. At this time a reduced duty or tax was required, though this was later removed.

Chapter 26: A Dreary Vigil
p. 265 **like that which took the dove into the ark**: see Genesis 8:9; the hand is Noah's, the dove being used three times to see if the Flood is subsiding.

p. 266 **past mysel'**: out of my mind.

p. 269 **comforter**: long woollen scarf.

p. 269 **maskit**: made, fully infused, ready to drink.

p. 271 **thou're out**: you're wrong.

p. 271 **Botany Bay**: an inlet in New South Wales, a few miles from Sydney. It was discovered by Captain Cook in 1770, its name becoming synonymous with the convict settlement, though this was abolished in 1840. Deportation to Australia would be common in the period: cf. the fate of Hetty Sorrel in George Eliot's *Adam Bede* (1859), where the fictional time is 1799–1807.

p. 272 **as though they were an open page**: a subtly ironic image, since Sylvia cannot read ordinary print.

Chapter 27: Gloomy Days
p. 274 **beforehand with the world**: i.e. making provision for the future (by saving).

p. 274 **the old stocking-foot**: for money to be stored in, on the premises so that you could keep your eye on it.

p. 274 *The Farmer's Complete Guide*: identified by Sanders as being first published in 1760.

p. 276   marlocks: flirtatious looks.

p. 278   **March the twelfth:** again Gaskell is keeping a tight hold on her chronology, but we might note the speed with which Daniel is brought to trial, the need being to make an example of him and thus deter others from interfering with the operations of the press-gang.

p. 280   **"Execute true judgment and show mercy":** even here the use of 'execute' carries its own ominous weight.

p. 280   **'knoweth our frame and remembereth that we are dust':** Psalms 103:14 ('For he knoweth our frame; he remembereth that we are dust').

p. 281   **'When father comes home':** Sylvia is perhaps unconsciously again associating with Nancy Hartley's 'He once was here'.

p. 282   **'Be the day weary, or be the day long . . .':** Sanders notes this as being an alternative version of the proverbial 'Be the day never so long, at length cometh evensong.'

p. 283   agait: going.

Chapter 28: The Ordeal
p. 284   **Our God, our help in ages past:** commonly, 'O God, our help in ages past', a hymn by Isaac Watts (1674–1748) derived from Psalm 30.

p. 285   **Old Grouse in the gun-room':** Gaskell is quoting from *She Stoops to Conquer*, II. i, by Oliver Goldsmith (1730–74).

p. 287   **gi'en:** here the meaning is 'thrown at'.

p. 288   **'Hoots':** an expression of dissatisfaction, disbelief, intended to discredit what has been said.

p. 289   greeting: weeping.

p. 289   **my head's clean gone:** poignantly, this indicates Bell's own recognition that she is confused, has lost her reason.

p. 290   *vade-mecum*: small manual or reference book.

p. 291   a this-ns: like this.

p. 291   dateless: out of her mind.

p. 292   **t' apple on his eye:** his specially chosen one: see Psalms 17:8 ('Keep me as the apple of the eye . . .').

Chapter 29: Wedding Raiment

p. 296 'close at his ear': the echo is of *Paradise Lost*, IV.800, where Satan is 'Squat like a toad, close at the ear of Eve'.

p. 296 misca': condemn, abuse.

p. 305 'From him that would ask of thee turn not thou away': Matthew 5:42 ('Give to him that asketh thee, and from him that would borrow of thee turn not thou away').

p. 307 shandry: light cart, one-horse carriage.

Chapter 30: Happy Days

p. 307 placing his idol ... shrine: another reminder that one of the early titles for the novel was *Philip's Idol*, with Gaskell here giving Philip's error a twist which looks back to the motto on the title-page of the novel.

p. 307 'sit in her parlour and sew up a seam': Sanders notes this as a variant on the nursery-rhyme line 'But sit on a cushion/And sew a fine seam'.

p. 308 'white work': delicate, fine embroidery in white on white cloth.

p. 310 crabbed: irritable.

p. 310 their pains for their payment: nothing but their trouble as their reward.

p. 311 'Long may ye live ...': as Sanders says, a traditional blessing at a wedding. He also points out that in a letter to Mary Howitt (*Letters*, no. 28, 18 August 1838) Gaskell describes how both verses of this song of 'rural composition' were used at her own wedding in 1832.

p. 314 pattens: overshoes, usually of wood, worn so that mud, water, etc. may be negotiated without getting shoes dirty or wet.

p. 315 the comfortable imprisonment: a significant image, repeated in related forms, to indicate the nature of Sylvia's emotional as well as physical confinement.

Chapter 31: Evil Omens

p. 319 flytin': nagging; criticizing errors.

p. 322 'statesman': here, a yeoman, a man who farms his own land.

p. 322 **sidesman:** assistant churchwarden who takes collections, shows worshippers to their seats, in church.

p. 322 **the Romish Saint's Day, to whom the church was dedicated:** St Nicholas.

p. 322 **Scarby Moorside:** as Sanders correctly notes, changed from 'Kirby Moorside', which occurs in the early editions of the novel, after it was pointed out to Gaskell that there was an actual Kirby Moorside twenty miles from Whitby.

p. 323 **'A crust of bread and liberty':** from Alexander Pope (1688–1744), 'An Imitation of the Sixth Satire of the Second Book of Horace' (1738), line 223.

Chapter 32: Rescued from the Waves
p. 333 **houd on:** take hold (of the rope).

p. 333 **crazy:** shaky, unsound.

Chapter 33: An Apparition
p. 336 **balm-tea:** infusion of herb leaves from balm-mint to soothe the taker into sleep.

p. 338 **and kissed the senseless wood:** one of the most moving and telling moments in the novel. Life has become inanimate, unfeeling to Sylvia, except for the beloved past (hence her gesture).

p. 339 **her heart leaped up and fell again dead within her:** note the associations of the graphic language – the first half of this a reminiscence of Wordsworth ('My heart leaps up . . .'), the second the deaths she has become accustomed to, those of her father and, until this shock, of Kinraid.

p. 339 **accost:** sudden approach to her.

p. 344 **my half of the sixpence:** again, there is perhaps a deliberate irony in this custom of pledging themselves through the two halves of a coin, which is in turn exactly half of the one shilling which betokens another pledge – the signing on for king and country shortly to be undertaken by Philip.

p. 344 **back me out:** support, corroborate me.

Chapter 34: A Reckless Recruit
p. 344 **incontinence:** here a fine way of expressing Sylvia's state of mind through her uncontrolled speech.

p. 346 Sir Sidney Smith: first name William (1764–1840), English naval commander who had helped to burn the French fleet and arsenal at Toulon (1793). On 18 April 1796 he had captured a French privateer at Havre-de-Grace, but the following day was captured himself with a number of his men (one of whom by chance was called Coulson). They were ultimately transferred to the Temple in Paris, and were later helped to escape by 'an engineer officer of rank, and a secret royalist, devoutly attached to the exiled family of France', one Colonel Phelypeaux. The latter accompanied him to London, which they reached on 8 May 1798, and was largely responsible (according to Smith) for organizing the defence of Acre, where he died almost a year later, a 'sacrifice to his zeal' and 'from exposure to the sun, which brought on a fever' (see John Barrow, *The Life and Correspondence of Sir William Sidney Smith*, 1848, vol. I, pp. 188–281).

p. 346 Philip somethin' (he were a Frenchman, I know) . . .: see note preceding on Phelypeaux.

p. 349 'at heaven's gate': Shakespeare, Sonnet 29 ('Like to the lark at break of day arising/From sullen earth, sings hymns at heaven's gate', (lines 11–12), and also *Cymbeline*, II.iii.19 ('Hark, hark! the lark at heaven's gate sings').

p. 349 the furies: in Greek mythology, the three goddesses sent to avenge wrongdoing, hence representing an avenging spirit.

p. 350 belated: overtaken by darkness.

p. 350 Oud Harry: synonymous with the Devil.

p. 350 gawby: blockhead, simpleton.

p. 351 stand shot: make oneself responsible for payment.

p. 352 the fatal shilling: the payment given to a recruit in return for which he binds himself to serve in the army.

p. 352 truckle-bed: low bed on wheels and thus easily stored.

p. 352 bounty-money: the sum paid to recruits on enlistment.

p. 352 Justice Cholmeley, of Holm-Fell Hall . . .: again Gaskell is using the weight of the celebrated local family as a kind of oblique authentication.

p. 352 Stephen Freeman: Philip is nominally freed from his past, but imprisoned in the service.

Chapter 35: Things Unutterable

p. 353 **Things Unutterable**: Cf. 'Sighed and looked unutterable things', from 'The Seasons' ('Summer', line 188) by James Thomson (1700–48).

p. 356 **her long home**: i.e. death – see Ecclesiastes 12:5 ('because man goeth to his long home, and the mourners go about the streets').

Chapter 36: Mysterious Tidings

p. 361 **By goom**: by God, 'gum' or 'goom' being a corruption of God and used in trivial oaths.

p. 361 **fell**: angry.

p. 361 **I mind counting t' clock**: I remember noticing the time.

p. 362 **ruffled up**: out of temper, upset.

p. 362 **makin' a piece o' work**: complaining.

p. 363 **jobbin' about**: doing odd jobs.

p. 364 **look on me as one dead**: Philip has now taken upon himself to be what he had contrived Kinraid should be.

p. 365 **the heavy veil**: note the subtle echo of the novel's epigraph.

p. 366 **land-crimps and water-crimps**: agents who capture and impress men for service in the army or navy.

p. 367 **what was gone wi' him**: what had happened to him.

p. 369 **I were led here, like**: you have brought me to this confidence.

p. 370 **put about**: upset, distressed.

p. 370 **fatherless . . . father**: cf. first note to p. 159.

p. 371 **what ways to take**: how to act.

p. 372 **"The Lord bless thee . . . shine upon thee!"**: an echo of Numbers 6:24–5.

Chapter 37: Bereavement

p. 377 **Kinraid's supposed death three years before**: another considered chronological stress.

p. 377 **One day before Christmas in this year, 1798**: as above, which it immediately follows.

p. 378 **the ways o' this life are crooked!**: an echo of Proverbs 2:15.

Chapter 38: The Recognition

p. 381   7th of May, 1799: the siege lasted for sixty days, beginning in March and being raised on 20 May. On 14 May Smith wrote to his brother that eleven separate assaults had been repulsed (Barrow, *Life and Correspondence of . . . Smith*, vol. I, p. 296).

p. 382   'some fifty, some an hundred fold' . . .: cf. Matthew 13:8 ('some an hundredfold, some sixtyfold, some thirtyfold').

p. 382   rivalling the pomp of King Solomon: a reference to Matthew 6:28–9.

p. 383   St Jean d'Acre: the seaport in Syria (now in Israel), at the foot of Mount Carmel, captured with terrible losses by Richard Coeur de Lion and Philip Augustus in 1191. It was essential to Napoleon's strategic plan against Egypt and the Ottoman Empire.

p. 383   shared his captain's daring adventure off the coast of France three years before . . . Westley Wright in the Temple at Paris: see note to p. 346, and note further Gaskell's ingenuity in having her fictional character integrated into the factual past action.

p. 383   His heart was like a war-horse, and said, Ha, ha!: an echo of Job 39:25.

p. 384   Djezzar Pacha's garden: Djezzar Pasha was governor or ruler of that part of Syria which contains Jaffa and El Arish; his seat of residence was St Jean d'Acre.

p. 384   Ravelin: trench.

p. 387   as men are recognized when they stand . . . house on fire: the association is with Daniel Robson at the burning of the Randyvowse.

p. 387   carrying him like a child: the reader has to suspend disbelief, since Philip is physically incapable of doing this even if the army has hardened him.

p. 389   a power o': a lot of.

p. 390   *Theseus*: on 15 May, Smith wrote to Earl St Vincent about 'a most melancholy accident which happened yesterday on board his majesty's ship Theseus, occasioned by the bursting of seventy shells at the fore-part of Captain Miller's cabin, by which he lost his life, as he did likewise twenty-five men' (Barrow, *Life and Correspondence of . . . Smith*, vol. I, p. 299). They were preparing unexploded enemy shells for use against their attackers.

Chapter 39: Confidences
p. 391   **bravery**: fine clothes.

p. 392   **pretty strong**: seriously.

p. 393   *Gentleman's Magazine*: founded in 1731, it ceased publication in 1914. Dr Johnson was an early contributor.

p. 396   **a moonlight flittin'**: leaving without warning, surreptitiously.

p. 402   **sackcloth and ashes**: see Daniel 9:3.

Chapter 40: An Unexpected Messenger
p. 402   **Miss Dobbin's**: Dobbin is the dull but loyal and long-suffering hero of the Novel Without a Hero, William Makepeace Thackeray's *Vanity Fair* (1847–8). Gaskell occasionally uses names which have resonances outside her own fiction.

p. 402   **Mount Carmel ... the prophet Elijah**: now in Haifa, Israel, Mount Carmel was the spot from which Elijah challenged the prophets of Baal (I Kings 18).

p. 404   **who had once been a Quaker**: Alice Rose's surprise derives from the fact that Quakers are committed pacifists. Her comment seems to be wishful thinking, since the text makes clear that Philip is not a Quaker.

p. 404   **a heavenly and a typical city**: the celestial or spiritual Jerusalem as distinct from the one on earth.

Chapter 41: The Bedesman of St Sepulchre
p. 407   **a September day in 1799**: another chronological notation.

p. 408   **'Rule Britannia'**: words by James Thomson (see note to p. 353), set to music by Thomas Arne (1710–78). The song occurs in the masque *Alfred* (1740).

p. 411   **drouthy**: thirsty, dry.

p. 412   **the Hospital of St Sepulchre**: based on that of St Cross near Winchester, already given contemporary notoriety by Anthony Trollope in his novel *The Warden* (1855). It was founded by Henry de Blois in 1157. The reverend Francis North, fifth earl of Guildford, is believed to have accumulated more than £300,000 since 1808 from the mastership of the hospital and from other livings which he was not legally entitled to hold at the same time.

p. 412   **Henry the Fifth**: King of England, 1413–22, he defeated the

French at Agincourt in 1415 in pursuit of his aim to bring France under British rule.

p. 412   to build and endow a hospital for twelve decayed soldiers: directly paralleled in Trollope's *The Warden*, where Hiram's Hospital is established under a similar bequest to house twelve elderly men.

p. 412   manchet: a roll of fine wheaten bread.

p. 415   General Wolfe at the taking of Quebec: in September 1759, when Wolfe was killed at the moment of victory over the French General Montcalm.

Chapter 42: A Fable at Fault
p. 418   Peregrine Pickle: the second novel, published in 1751, of Tobias Smollett (1721–71).

p. 418   an army list: an official register of all commissioned officers.

p. 418   the Seven Champions of Christendom: book by the writer of romances Richard Johnson (1573–1659); the first part appeared in 1596. The seven 'champions' are St George of England, St Denys of France, St Antony of Italy, St Andrew of Scotland, St James of Spain, St Patrick of Ireland and St David of Wales.

p. 418   Sir Guy, Earl of Warwick: as Sanders points out, Sir Guy could hardly be included in the above. The exploits of Sir Guy are recorded in prose and verse. Phillis (or Felice) insisted that he distinguish himself by knightly deeds before she would accept him; after his marriage he embarked on a further series of adventures in honour of God. His deeds encompassed Germany, Greece, the Holy Land and England, where he slew the Danish giant Colbrand at Winchester. After all his achievements he became a hermit in Warwick. He went to his own castle unrecognized and received bread from the hands of his wife; as he lay dying he sent her a ring so that she would recognize who he was. The parallels with the Philip–Sylvia story are obvious.

p. 418   Paynim: Muslim.

p. 423   Countess Phillis ... Earl Guy: notice how Gaskell uses the fable so that the perspective is from Philip's consciousness of what he thinks has happened – that Sylvia has been happy while he has been suffering, and that she should have married 'one she loved better'.

Chapter 43: The Unknown
p. 425   summut queer: a little surprising.

p. 425   t' dickens: the Devil.

p. 425   **fabled to exist on Tom Tiddler's ground**: any place where money or goods etc. are easily acquired (proverbial).

p. 427   **grubbed up**: eaten.

p. 427   **four-pound loaves is at sixteenpence**: the price of bread is an index to the economic conditions of the poor in the late eighteenth and early nineteenth centuries, the regulations on the importing and export-ing of grain protecting the home producer at the expense of the consumer. These 'Corn Laws' were abolished in 1846.

p. 428   **gets houd on her blind side**: the meaning is, wins her round, discovers her weakness and soft-heartedness.

p. 428   **munnot go off so fast**: must not react so impetuously.

p. 430   **stirabout**: a kind of porridge or improvised pudding.

p. 430   **t' father o' lies**: cf. John 8:44 ('for he is a liar, and the father of it').

p. 430   **raxes**: reaches, stretches.

Chapter 44: First Words
p. 432   **the spring of 1800**: from this we can calculate how long Philip has been in Monkshaven.

p. 432   **the duty on hair-powder was increased**: this tax had been introduced in 1795.

p. 435   **chronometers**: time-measuring instruments used in navigation.

p. 436   **'tickle'**: tricky, delicate.

p. 438   **but his place knew him not**: cf. Job 7:10 ('neither shall his place know him any more').

Chapter 45: Saved and Lost
p. 444   **And the waves kept lapping on the shelving shore**: this becomes a refrain as Philip dies, reminding one of the death of little Paul in Dickens's *Dombey and Son* (1848) and of the poem 'What are the wild waves saying?' by the nineteenth-century poet Joseph Edwards Carpenter.

p. 444   **I ha' made thee my idol**: another crucial reference to and reminder of the earlier title. The theme of reconciliation through Christian forgiveness, so characteristic of Gaskell, is here being invoked.

p. 445   **if I could live my life o'er again . . . and thee less**: I am indebted to Dr Jennifer Fellows for pointing out to me that in the Middle English *Guy of Warwick*, Guy says much the same thing to Felice.

p. 445 **wheere all tears are wiped away**: cf. Revelation 7:17, 21:4 ('God shall wipe away all tears from their eyes').

p. 447 **Abraham ... David ... St John**: 'Abraham my friend' (Isaiah 41:8), 'the Lord will seek a man after his own heart' (I Samuel 13:14), 'the disciple he loved' (John 13:23).

p. 448 **bringeth glad tidings of great joy ...**: cf. Luke 2:10 ('I bring you good tidings of great joy').

p. 449 **"The former things are passed away ... no more pain"**: cf. Revelation 21:4.

p. 450 **her eye fell on a black ribbon round his neck ... to it was hung a half-crown piece**: this is the final twist in the ribbon-and-coin series of associations, with Philip's love more complete than Kinraid's, being of greater and more enduring value.

p. 450 **'there shall be no more sea'**: an echo of Revelation 21:1 ('and there was no more sea').

p. 450 **the 'Public Baths'**: according to White (*A History of Whitby*, p. 41), the baths, museum and library in Whitby were built in 1827.

ELIZABETH GASKELL AND HER CRITICS

By the time *Sylvia's Lovers* was published in 1863, Elizabeth Gaskell had an assured reputation as a novelist. Although in the preceding years she had written a number of stories and novellas, as well as *The Life of Charlotte Brontë* (1857), she had not published a novel since *North and South* (1855). Contemporary reviewers recognized *Sylvia's Lovers* as a departure in terms of both location and period. The contemporary extracts given below are from Angus Easson's excellent *Elizabeth Gaskell: The Critical Heritage* (Routledge, 1992) and convey the contrasting reactions of the time.

The first is from an unsigned review of the novel which appeared in the *Saturday Review* of 4 April 1863 (*The Critical Heritage*, pp. 446–9):

It is often very difficult to express a feeling of dissatisfaction and avoid the appearance of cavilling and hypercriticism. Besides, if a fairly good book is given us, it seems ungracious to quarrel with the writer for not making it better. Mrs Gaskell's former works are to blame for having raised our expectations to such a height that nothing short of equal excellence will satisfy us, and we cannot but think that in *Sylvia's Lovers* she has fallen below her own standard. She is not one of those hasty and facile writers whose 'clever books', as the advertisements say, 'are in every one's hands', and, we may add, are quickly laid down after having produced their few hours' excitement, and left small trace upon the reader's mind. No one needs to be told in what style Mrs Gaskell writes, for her excellence in that respect is established; but people want to know what she has to say. Classification frequently misguides, and we can scarcely say in what class we should rank *Sylvia's Lovers*, or to what other novel we should liken it. A story, in some hands, becomes a well-managed puzzle, and there are ten people who relish an interesting plot to one who can judge of style, or appreciate sentiment; but a good plot is always acknowledged to be essential to the success and popularity of a novel, and in *Sylvia's Lovers* the plot lacks unity and sequence. There are some romantic incidents and attempts to elaborate character, but it is not always satisfactorily brought out. In the first volume there is a vast amount of description, and a good deal of writing which must have been laborious work, and which is certainly tedious reading. No doubt, the aim of the author's minute description of localities is to give an air of reality, a characteristic background to the figures, and this is often the effect; but novelists should be cautioned against a propensity to dwell on and linger over what is, after all, the easiest part of their craft.

Mary Barton was one of the first of a series of novels illustrative of artisan life; and it still remains a genuine and very interesting description of the Lancashire operative, whatever may be thought of the writer's views, and apart from the mere narrative. Mrs Gaskell has now turned to fresh pasture, and has shown her familiarity with the dialect and habits of the Yorkshire folk of the sea-coast. She describes a state of society which has passed away, and asks us to go back to the end of the last century. To many it would be easier to revive a more distant period, for it is too long ago to be remembered by many, and not long enough to have passed into the domain of history. The press-gang is an instance in point. All the iniquity of that obsolete institution, which is made to play an important part in the story, is here recalled and execrated; and we feel an irrepressible satisfaction, when thinking of present foreign grievances and oppressions, that such a system should have so completely passed away as to make its former existence almost incredible to this generation . . .

There are three careful studies in this novel – Daniel Robson, Sylvia's father, her mother, and the farm servant, Kester – the first being the most highly elaborated . . .

In Sylvia's character the interest ought to centre, as she is the sole heroine; yet we never can be brought to care much about her. When the book which narrates her history is closed, we remember nothing very distinctly except her beauty and her trials. The sketch of the shopwoman Hester leaves a stronger impression. Sylvia has two lovers – the first being Philip Hepburn, her cousin, who has loved her passionately from childhood. He is a specimen of a very properly behaved, commendable young draper, self-educated, and anxious to instruct his pretty cousin, who can neither read nor write, and who is perfectly contented with her ignorance and does not care to be coaxed out of it ... Most readers will prefer the second lover, Charley Kinraid, the manly dashing lad, whom Sylvia first sees, pale and haggard from wounds, standing by the grave of a whaler messmate who had been shot by the men-of-war's men for resisting the 'King's kidnapping'. At this funeral the whole of Monkshaven was gathered in dumb anger and sympathy for the dead ... and here, as in some other instances, Mrs Gaskell is highly successful in describing the wild contagious emotions and confusion of a surging crowd whose angry passions have been excited by oppression almost to frenzy. All a young girl's natural enthusiasm was called out by Kinraid's character, which displayed the sort of heroism most easy to comprehend – namely, resistance to oppression, and recklessness of life ... The pretty face makes no permanent impression on the sailor; but with Sylvia it was very different. Kinraid filled the narrow circle over which her fancy could wander and brood. To those who theorize on love as if it were entirely under the control of reason, it will be incomprehensible that such a feeling should arise unbidden, and grow scarcely acknowledged in her heart. Love stories were as nought to the ignorant country girl, and she had not listened to any second-hand experience of the passion; but she loved Kinraid instinctively, and during his absence was more than ever irritated against Philip, who, though rebuffed, still prostrated himself at her feet ...

It is often a matter of complaint that novels flag towards the end; but in this story the last of the three volumes is, in some respects, the best. The web of circumstances becomes more intricate, and, with the shifting and contending feelings to be delineated, Mrs Gaskell exhibits her power of insight and expression. There is a great deal about the mercer's shop, and two Quaker brothers who give up their business to Philip and his fellow-shopman; yet, with the exception of the shopwoman Hester, and quaint old Kester, there are no secondary characters who are not rather dull and commonplace. Several of the personages, indeed, are wholly unnecessary to the conduct of the tale, and are merely impediments in the narrative, which, with many affecting incidents and striking scenes, does not gain that hold on the imagination of the reader which Mrs Gaskell has before commanded. We need scarcely say that Kinraid returns, and his meeting with Sylvia is the most powerful scene in the book. The language is very forcible in its homely dialect, without the slightest exaggeration. Mrs Gaskell has finely marked the ebb and flow of passion, and made very tangible the overwhelming despair which Sylvia feels when her lover's presence makes known her husband's deceit. The story does not end at this point, and the current of events takes a totally unexpected, yet natural, direction.

Another unsigned notice, this time from the *Examiner*, picks out both the realism and the elements of poetic tragedy (*The Critical Heritage*, pp. 441–2).

This is a novel to read slowly, as one reads a poem. Its plot is of such a tale as Crabbe might have chosen for his verse, and although written in prose, it deals, among simple and unfashionable people, with the truest poetry of life, in thought, feeling, and action. Every incident is alive with subtle touches of humour or pathos, and in its harmony of colouring, the skilful grouping of its characters, and the quick sense of life and nature shown in its minutest detail, stands before the reader as a picture by a sterling artist. Mrs Gaskell has never written with more care than in this novel. The Yorkshire dialect of nearly all the dialogues is so skilfully managed, that without being a stumbling-block to any reader, it gives the charm of a Doric simplicity to the whole idyll. The shrewd character painting, the incessant blending of the sights and sounds of nature with the action of the story, the spirit of kindly human fellowship and the high sense of human duty belong to the unaffected English of the narrative itself, rich in fresh thought and true refinement of expression. Were the story of the book poor, it would be commended by the manner of the telling. In its whole texture *Sylvia's Lovers* is as lawn to sackcloth compared with the coarse 'sensation' tales of late forced into fashion, which produce a striking plot, as one might produce a striking pattern by daubs with a tar brush on the miller's sacking.

In story as in style the contrast is complete. In *Sylvia's Lovers*, though strong interest is excited, and none who have tears for an imagined grief will pass with dry eyes through the closing chapters either of the second or of the third volume, there is no bigamist, no murderer, no villain at all. There are the shortcomings of human weakness common to us all, the lesser conflicts of character wherein no small part of all human life consists; but there is not a person in the book of either sex who does not accredit the sound doctrine at which they who live healthily must needs arrive in their mature years, although its evidences are not clear to youth, that men and women are good fellows in the main. The true artist shrinks from nothing so much as the mere dull reproduction of deformity. Crime of course must be always a common element in tragic narrative, but then it must be introduced not for its own sake but as an active power, through which souls are tried and the great depths of man's nature may be stirred. A great crime establishes among a group of surrounding persons strong exceptional conditions of life; exceptional because it is below the common nature of men to be greatly criminal. The true poet, novelist, or dramatist, uses the crime not as a condition interesting in itself, but as productive of conditions under which the spirit of a man shows in its strong emotion forces that would, in repose, not be apparent. The objection against such books as 'Lady Audley's Secret', apart from the fact that they show only the coarsest sense of literature in their writing, is not that they are tales of crime, but that they are ill-written tales of sordid crime, of crime meanly committed for poor, sneaking ends, and dilated upon for their own sake as interesting matters of concealment and detection . . .

All the stir of emotion that can be produced by a great crime, Mrs Gaskell has obtained in *Sylvia's Lovers* without the production of a criminal. There is great iniquity, but it is the iniquity of an abstraction; relentless, powerful, impalpable as the Fate of a Greek Tragedy; iniquity of Law, mainly in the activity of the press-gang among the seafaring men of coast towns during the war with France at the close of the last century, and subordinately in the undue severity of penal law at the same date. We are reminded that there was no deliberate wickedness in the motives that maintained at that time in great vigour the system of impressment, and that backed it with the strong arm of the law. Those persons concerned in execution of the law who appear in the tale are represented only as men with the same kindly sympathies as their neighbours. But the evil Law is the dread shadowy Fate, against which hearts beat and souls chafe in vain.

An unsigned review, this time in the *Daily News*, is concerned largely with plot summary, the descriptive criticism of the time often taking this form (*The Critical Heritage*, pp. 445–6).

The subjects chosen by Mrs Gaskell in this work are of a nature to test to the utmost her literary skill and her power of interesting her readers. That she possesses great force of style and no common ability in drawing character is sufficiently proved by her former works. We also acknowledge her narrative faculty, and her vigour in description. It would, however, require almost superhuman powers to invest with anything like interest a series of dreary images and comfortless events like that which forms the staple of the work before us. Yorkshire wolds, bleak and barren, swept by cutting winds, drenched with continuous rains, or swathed in impenetrable fogs – a farm house, which is a picture of hard penury, inhabited by a family sunk in the most profound ignorance – are not objects upon which the eye can dwell with either pleasure or curiosity. Sylvia, the heroine of the tale, is presented to us as a beautiful human animal, without a thought beyond the shippen and its cows, or the farm and its produce, ignorant of the merest elements of education, and depending solely upon such sympathy as her unsophisticated nature can awaken for the interest we are expected to take in her fortunes. We do not mean to say that the grandest heroism and noblest virtues may not be exemplified in low life, but it is trying the patience of readers too far to compel them to wade through three volumes of unpronounceable *patois* and miserable incidents in order to follow the trail of persons who display a very ordinary amount of either heroism or virtue. It avails nothing that Sylvia's father gets hanged, for an attack upon a pressgang; that one of her lovers is impressed and carried off to the wars: we pity her mother, but we cannot get up a spark of interest in herself. The other lover, a quakerish young shopkeeper, might, indeed, though not favoured by Sylvia, have enlisted our sympathies did he not go about his wooing in such a hang-dog fashion. By suppressing the message entrusted to him for Sylvia by his kidnapped rival . . . the shopkeeper obtains her hand, without any congratulations on our part. Yet when he has succoured her mother in helpless distress, and surrounded her with every possible proof of his affection – when, after several years of happy domesticity and the birth of a child, the kidnapped man returns, and she agrees with him in the presence of her husband that the said husband is a 'damned soundrel', we must confess to a slight feeling of disgust. That the husband should be such a villanous milksop as to stand it, however, deprives him of all our sympathy. We read with slight attention how she pronounces 'a deep divorcing vow' against the husband – how he enlists for a soldier, leaving the self-willed vixen all his lands and livings – how the circumvented man comforts himself with a much more suitable wife, and how the wanderer returns wounded and weak to die miserably in the arms of his wife, exchanging mutual penitence and forgiveness.

The next review, though unsigned, is by the novelist and critic Geraldine Jewsbury (1812–80). It appeared in the *Athenaeum* on 28 February 1863 (*The Critical Heritage*, pp. 432–5). Again there is plot summary, but note the emotional responses to character. Despite the subjectivity there is some appreciation of Gaskell's art. It is genuinely sympathetic, apart from its condescension over 'the provincial dialect and the peculiar orthography'.

The story of 'Sylvia's Lovers' is laid in humble life, and is narrated chiefly in the broad vernacular Yorkshire dialect, which, although it gives the local colour, is a drawback to the comfort of the reader, and fatiguing to the eye. But for true artistic workmanship we think 'Sylvia's Lovers' superior to any of Mrs Gaskell's former works. The scene of the story is laid at a fishing-town on the Yorkshire coast, called here Monkhaven [*sic*]; the time, the close of the last century, when the war with France was rife, and pressgangs were in all their cruel authority. Monkhaven was the seat of the Greenland whaling-trade; and the best scene in the book is the description of the return of a whaling-vessel, the first of the season, waiting to get over the bar, all the inhabitants assembled in breathless excitement to hear news of sons, brothers, husbands and lovers who had sailed on the voyage. Just as she clears the bar and gets in, the pressgang is upon her, seizing half-a-dozen of the crew, and carrying them off to the rendezvous, without allowing them a word with their half-frantic relations waiting and watching for them. It is a highly-wrought scene, and yet there is not a trace of straining for effect or of exaggeration; it is true pathos, and relies only on the simple truth of the reality. Sylvia, the heroine, is the daughter of a retired whaling-sailor, who has become a farmer, but who still loves whaling and smuggling far better than ploughing or seeing after sheep and cattle. Old Daniel Robson is a capital portrait; Sylvia is as charming and pretty a damsel as ever tormented the heart of a lover; but she has a dash of fierce, persistent resentment in her character that effectually redeems her from perfection. The mother is an excellent and skilfully-drawn character – a respectable, sensible, religious woman, whose one inconsistent act had been the choice of her husband; but she behaves so wisely and well, that it would have been a pity to deprive her of such an opportunity to exercise her virtues. Sylvia's cousin, Philip, is desperately in love with her, against all his sense of prudence; for he is as wise and excellent and disagreeable a young man as can well be imagined. There is no fault to be found with him, except that he is detestable. Sylvia hates him, and the reader sympathizes with her heartily; and yet he never does anything but good, nor says anything but what is unexceptionable. He loves Sylvia with a remorseless pertinacity which affects the reader with a positive dread, it is so certain to tire down all opposition and wear out obstacles: of course he suffers a great deal, and the reader feels a malignant pleasure in every rebuff he receives. He is a man who can talk of the respect due to the law to the poor people who are driven wild by seeing the pressgang carry off their relatives as they touch the land. In one of the returning whalers which the pressgang boards, a young man distinguishes himself by his resistance, and gets nearly killed; in fact, there are several lives lost in the affray. This young man is the type of a fine, high-spirited sailor: Sylvia exalts him into a hero; he tells tales of adventure which would have won Desdemona herself. He falls in love with Sylvia; and though the mother favours Philip and does not like Charley, circumstances are, however, propitious, – the father gives his consent, and the two plight their troth; but they have to part immediately, for he has to join his ship, a whaler: he is the best harpooner in all the service. On his road he is seized by a pressgang in the sight of Philip, to whom he gives a message for Sylvia. Philip never delivers it; lets her believe he is dead; sees her breaking heart, and only thinks of the steadily-increasing chances for himself to win her. Mrs Gaskell tries very hard to furnish him with redeeming traits of character, and to make excuses, and to get up the reader's pity for him, but quite in vain. Poor old Daniel, the father, gets mixed up in a riot and a rescue from a pressgang, in which a house is broken into and destroyed. For this he is committed to York Castle, and takes his trial, is condemned to be hanged, and the law takes its course. This part is told vaguely and feebly. Mrs Gaskell does not let her sympathies go with the poor old man, and she shrinks from this part of her narrative; it is hastily huddled over. After this terrible catastrophe, Sylvia and her mother are left helpless and alone, with no one to assist them or protect them but Philip, who has certainly been a good friend in their trouble. Sylvia marries him for the sake of a home for her mother. The real genius of the story now begins. Nothing can be more true and delicately indicated than the cold, disappointed married life of Philip. The treachery he has practised begins for the first time to weigh heavily upon him: his punishment lies in his sin; even the reader feels sorry for him. Of course, Charley Kinraid comes home, and Sylvia learns the truth.

There is a very strong scene, excellently done: the fierce unforgiving side of Sylvia's character comes out towards her husband. She has by this time a child: this, and her sense of honour, enable her to refuse to leave him; but he cannot stand her wild, contemptuous, indignant misery, he leaves home, and in a fit of reckless despair enlists for a soldier, and never lets his wife know what has become of him. Years pass by, and the triumph of Mrs Gaskell's art is shown in her power to bring over the sympathy of the reader to Philip. Charley goes away and makes a fine marriage; he has risen to be an officer, and become so prosperous that the reader cares no more for him. Philip saves his life; but he meets with no success himself; he is in a terrific explosion, and scarred, maimed, and disfigured so as not to be recognized. He is sent to England and discharged. His deep, passionate love for his wife remains all unchanged; but he dares not return to her – the memory of her curse lies heavy on him. The reader not only forgives him, but the intensest sympathy is roused for him. We will not spoil the reader's interest, by narrating the end of the story; it is very finely worked up, and is as true as it is powerful. When the reader has got over the provincial dialect and the peculiar orthography, there will be nothing more to find fault with.

Comparisons with George Eliot were inevitable. The unsigned notice in the *Reader* of 28 February 1863 (*The Critical Heritage*, pp. 437–9) not only considers the subject painful but draws hardly tenable analogies with *Adam Bede*.

'Sylvia's Lovers', although we look upon it as a better novel than 'Mary Barton', will not, for several reasons, share the popularity of its predecessor. Some of these reasons might be reckoned by many among its merits. Those who remember the state of feeling with regard to the relations of labour and capital fifteen years ago, will not doubt that some part of the very lively interest excited by the 'novel of Manchester life' was due to its entanglement with a complex problem of the day. But critics who believe all adventitious interest of this kind to be as dangerous to the effect of art as a stripe of bright colour running across a beautiful pattern, – who doubt whether problems of this kind are a good field for the powers of women – nay, who feel quite certain that novels are not a good occasion for discussing such, will find with unmixed satisfaction that Mrs Gaskell's last novel opens no issues of this nature. Our attention to an interesting and pathetic story is not carried out of the picture, as it were, by any introduction of an element foreign to art. Mrs Gaskell's last novel is, moreover, very superior to her first, in the absolute exclusion of all 'gentility'. She keeps on her own peculiar ground from the beginning of the book to the end, and those feebler touches, which her vigorous style in dealing with favourable material brought out so forcibly in her earlier novels, are thereby avoided. The quality of the novel which will, we imagine, most detract from its general popularity is its exceeding painfulness. This, in itself, is neither good nor bad – a tragedy cannot be too tragic. But we do not find all that in a very painful story we unconsciously demand. Thackeray had a good right to give us a novel without a hero, but a novelist who takes us into the dark recesses which only a few human beings are called upon to tread, owes us the compensation of a central image of large and lofty proportions, excelling, not necessarily in virtue, but in energy, in revelation, in strength – owes us, in short, the relief of poetry, as it is defined in the noble words of Bacon, – 'The use of this feigned history hath been to give some shadow of satisfaction to the mind in those points wherein the nature of things both deny it.

A more ample greatness, a more exact goodness, and a more absolute variety, than is to be found – in the nature of things', he concludes, but we would alter it to 'the nature of *man*'.

Here our author fails. She does, indeed, leave a large space for her central figure, and spends much pains in the elaboration of his portrait, but the conception is feeble, and the execution indistinct. Philip Hepburn is Sylvia's lover and nothing more. Take from him the love which leads him into the basest perfidy, and which, therefore, eminently needs the background of a rich and glowing character, and he becomes a mere blank, while his wife is drawn with so much force and solidity, that the extreme flatness of his portrait tells like a false note. We cannot help comparing him with Adam Bede, and the difference of the two impressions of character, is the difference between a name written on loose sand, and one engraved on a gem. The dashing young sailor, whose gallantry wins him a captaincy, is a stock novel character, it is true, but the superior crispness and decision of execution so far compensates for the common-place ideal, that we find ourselves regretting at every turn that he, instead of his uncouth and yet insipid rival, does not occupy the place of honour in the story. This is the capital flaw in the book, and it is, to our thinking, something more than an artistic flaw. Hepburn is so evidently intended to interest us on the moral side of his character, that the absence of any remorse for his treachery, apart from the fear of and regret for its consequences, strikes us somewhat painfully. And though the occasion demands the exclusion of all bitter feeling, we yet are somewhat revolted when his wife, repenting of what seems to us her righteous indignation against him, laments him (Chapter 45) with the words, 'Oh, Philip, my Philip, tender and *true*!' Mrs Gaskell is too much inclined to confuse the sharp line which divides those temptations which are and are not possible to a character she intends to retain its hold on our respect.

Nevertheless, the story has a noble moral, put in the mouth of the dying Philip (Chapter 45). 'Child', he said, 'I ha' made thee my idol; and if I could live my life o'er again I would love my God more, and thee less; and then I shouldn't have sinned this sin against thee.' This is the key-note of the book, but to give it full effect the character of Philip should have been altogether different. Milton's division, 'He for God only, she for God in him', – might be owing to a low conception of the woman's ideal, but to sacrifice honour and duty for one beloved object is the woman's temptation, and the character which is to yield to it and yet retain our sympathy should retain the attraction of a somewhat feminine grace. This the uncouth shopman is entirely and designedly without, and loses thereby as much in an artistic as in a moral point of view.

We have dwelt too long on the one great want of a story whose excellence forces us to try it by a very high standard, to do more than indicate very slightly either its few remaining defects, or its many lesser merits. Our favourite passages are those fresh country scenes where we seem to breathe the pure dewy air of the Georgics, though there are not wanting passages of great vigour (as for instance, the description of the fire [Chapter 23]), which will excite more general admiration. We cannot reckon the scene at the storming of St Jean d'Acre (Chapter 38) among these, but it is the only too ambitious passage in the book. We regret this failure the more, as the author might easily have spared us this journey to Palestine and back by merely giving a letter actually quoted. When we have added that the first half of the first volume is very decidedly inferior to the rest, and that there is a superficial resemblance to George Eliot's Hetty in the heroine, which is quite lost sight of as we advance, we have noticed almost everything we regret in a book, the merits of which could not be exhausted in a much longer space.

Since 1952, when Annette Hopkins's Elizabeth Gaskell: Her Life and Work was published, there has been increasing interest both in the fiction and The Life of Charlotte Brontë. The centenary of Gaskell's death in 1965 saw more studies and the publication of her letters. A set of critical extracts is given below, ranging from treatments of the composition of Sylvia's Lovers to recent feminist readings. Evaluation of these extracts has not been included, but they are a representative choice, offering some idea of the density of Gaskell studies as her reputation has grown. This is from Winifred Gérin, Elizabeth Gaskell: A Biography (Oxford: Clarendon Press, 1976), pp. 212–15:

Without 'a word of it written yet' in late October, she had, however, been so busy planning and reading for it and had it so well advanced in her mind as to warrant her sudden visit to Whitby at the beginning of November. Julia, aged 13 and out-growing her strength, was made the excuse for this apparently uncalled for and unseasonal rush to the cold east coast in winter. Not even to George Smith did she give her true reason for the journey, she was keeping the plot and setting of her book a complete secret. Taking Meta (and Hearn) with her as well as Julia (not only as confidante but as illustrator of selected views) she left home on Monday, 31 October, stayed overnight at York (which the girls had not seen before) and reached Whitby the next day without having booked lodgings. They found rooms easily, however, at 1 Abbey Terrace, with a fine view of the sea and an admirable landlady, Mrs Rose, who supplied all their needs, including recommendations and introductions to townsfolk likely to provide Mrs Gaskell with local lore. They stayed for a fortnight. Though the weather, to judge from Mrs Gaskell's letters, was consistently bad, they did 'nothing but go out', as she reported to Marianne who was keeping house at home.

A fortnight, in the short days of November, was little enough time in which to gather the accurate and detailed descriptions of the town and surrounding countryside she was able to provide as the setting of her novel. All her work depended to a considerable degree on atmosphere, on the character of the places in which she set her dramas. There were the strongly etched streets and old houses of Ruth's native 'assize town' in the eastern counties (Ipswich); and the Welsh village and Lancashire shore in the same novel; the Greenhey Fields of *Mary Barton*; the smoke-laden sky of *North and South* – all of which had a vital symbolic part to play in their respective tales. It was to be even more so in *Sylvia's Lovers*. Whitby was the setting and its character had to be evoked first by observation and then by imposing her own vision on what she saw, by bringing out a certain grandeur in the place which was both literally and symbolically true of it. She had found an ideal setting in fact, and one that deeply moved her. Her descriptions of the high surrounding cliffs, holding up like a beacon to the ships at sea the noble ruined profile of the abbey, of the steep streets and cobbled lanes leading to the harbour, of the heathery grassy heights slashed by chines and dotted with sheep farms where the life of the rural community was centred, are fine spontaneous evocations. But not even the casual observer can overlook where the heart of Whitby beats, down at the little narrow harbour where the Esk frets its way out to sea, and the fishing fleets come and go. It was there in the days about which Mrs Gaskell wished to write that the twice yearly drama of the whalers' departure and return was played out. So impressive a spectacle, so momentous a yearly enterprise for the community that lived by the produce of the sea, could not be lost on a woman of her wide sympathies and passionate response to the sea and sea-faring folk. Here was everything to hand, danger, heroism, high drama, and tragedy, in the daily lives of these people. She was determined to see, hear, or read every traceable fact about the past of the place and its people. She worked indefatigably and missed little of the scene about her, noting the 'red and fluted tiles of the gabled houses of the town', the emplacement of the Butter

Cross, the 'mists and sea-fogs' prevalent on that coast, the country sounds within earshot of the sea – the 'cackle of the geese blending with the tones of the great church bell'. The book itself opens with a memorable passage on the whalers' return:

> The narrow harbour at the mouth of the river was crowded with small vessels of all descriptions, making an intricate forest of masts. Beyond lay the sea, like a flat pavement of sapphire, scarcely a ripple varying its sunny surface, that stretched out leagues away till it blended with the softened azure of the sky. On this blue, trackless water floated scores of white-sailed fishing boats, apparently motionless, unless you measured their progress by some land-mark; but, still, and silent, and distant as they seemed, the consciousness that there were men on board, each going forth into the great deep, added unspeakably to the interest felt in watching them.

Of the story which begins with an evocation of careless youth, self-assured manhood, high spirits, and healthy pursuits, she herself ultimately said it was the saddest she had ever written. The tragedy emerged from the varied material at her command, and the period she chose for her action – the anti-press gang riots that took place in the town in 1793 at the height of the French wars. Into that central and verifiable incident she wove the drama of Charlie Kinraid – the 'Specksioneer', as the chief harpooner on every whaler was called, who was loved by Sylvia and 'impressed' unknown to her. He is assumed lost at sea but returns to find her married most unwillingly to his rival Philip Hepburn. Here was the theme known to her from early womanhood when she was much influenced by Crabbe and the theme of his poem 'Ruth' which was published in 1819. At that time it was her ambition to write like him, as she confided to Mary Howitt. It fitted perfectly into the framework of the Whitby riots provoked by the press-gang, and the whole drama of the arctic fisheries about which she had read in Dr Scoresby's book. While at Whitby she took every opportunity for gathering first-hand accounts of those events from the old people who still remembered them. One old resident, George Corney, lent her a copy of Young's *History of Whitby* (published 1817), the standard work on the town, which she read in the evenings during her visit. She made use of Mr Corney's name in the book for the family of Sylvia's cousins. He was thanked for his pains, as Mrs Chadwick relates, by receiving an inscribed copy of *Sylvia's Lovers* on publication, which was treasured and handed down in the family.

From T. W. Craik, *Elizabeth Gaskell and the Provincial Novel* (London: Methuen, 1975), pp. 147–51:

The position of the narrator and the personality revealed become equally absorbed into the texture as a whole. Measured in terms of proportions, *Sylvia's Lovers* has more of itself covered by the author's narrative than by dialogue or action, but such a statement is misleading. Elizabeth Gaskell has always avoided as far as possible projecting her own personality as narrator, still less has she ever had a consciously adopted authorial tone. Here, even what she has is further reduced, and, when compelled to use it, she does so most sparingly, and intermingles it with other parts of the novel's technique.

General expectations in the English nineteenth-century novel are that the writer will find it necessary to render in his own voice information as to facts about situation and setting, will need at times to pass judgement on events or character, will have to provide description of character and of setting, make analyses of situations or thoughts and states of mind, and establish some sort of direct personal relationship with the reader. At all these points the ultimate consequence will be a distancing of the author from the experience he is transcribing, and a further distancing, through the author, of the reader. Such distancing is necessary and valuable to many writers, since it allows assessment and judgement, and proportioning. Elizabeth Gaskell's purposes, however, are otherwise: concerned though she is with assessment, judgement and proportion, she always prefers to allow these to emerge through the closest possible contact between the reader and the experience, uncoloured by the sense of a narrator as a medium.

She establishes her position of near-invisibility relative to both the narrative and the reader as early as possible. Her opening chapter is a masterpiece of unobtrusive art. It is necessarily wholly expository, because she cannot begin her story until she has established the sense of the time and the setting which will enclose it. She thus faces the problem of virtually all novelists, from Scott onwards, who choose to write of a time and place that are not the norm for the reader. Anything like Jane Austen's dramatic economical beginnings with the bare essentials leading instantly into

the situation or event are impossible. Most novelists faced with
this task follow Scott, by establishing a relationship between the
author and the reader which imposes an attitude to the material.
Scott frequently devotes a chapter or more to this purpose, giving
sources and establishing his own speaking voice, of which the
beginning of *Waverley* provides a fairly compact example:

> The title of this work has not been chosen without the grave
> and solid deliberation which matters of importance demand
> from the prudent. Even its first or general denomination was
> the result of no common research or selection, although,
> according to the example of my predecessors, I had only to seize
> upon the most sounding and euphonic surname that English
> history or topography affords, and elect it at once as the title of
> my work and the name of my hero. But, alas, what could my
> readers have expected from the chivalrous epithets of Howard,
> Mordaunt, Mortimer or Stanley, ... but pages of iniquity
> similar to those which have been so christened for half a century
> past? I must modestly admit I am too diffident of my own merit
> to place it in unnecessary opposition to preconceived associa-
> tions. I have therefore like a maiden knight with his white
> shield, assumed for my hero, WAVERLEY, an uncontaminated
> name, bearing with its sound little of good or evil, excepting
> what the reader shall hereafter be pleased to affix to it.

This (like most of Scott's rather unfairly maligned leisurely
openings) is vital to establish a mutual relationship, so that the
reader will trust the writer's perspective and judgement on the
story proper. The method is a good one, and serves different
writers, with different ends. George Eliot follows him, though
with greater brevity, in for example, *Adam Bede*:

> With a single drop of ink for a mirror, the Egyptian sorcerer
> undertakes to reveal to any chance comer far-reaching visions
> of the past. This is what I undertake to do for you, reader. With
> this drop of ink at the end of my pen, I will show you the roomy
> workshop of Mr Jonathan Burge, carpenter and builder, in the
> village of Hayslope, as it appeared on the eighteenth of June, in
> the year of our Lord 1799.

and Trollope, as here, in the opening of *Doctor Thorne*:

> Before the reader is introduced to the modest country medical

practitioner who is to be the chief personage of the following tale, it will be well that he should be made acquainted with some particulars as to the locality in which, and the neighbours among whom, our doctor followed his profession.

Such examples as these few out of many demonstrate that novelists in general feel that the need to get into touch with the reader takes precedence over the statement of facts of time or place, the more especially when establishing time and place has to be done before action can begin. Elizabeth Gaskell takes the greater risk, of the more direct method, depending upon establishing the reader's trust, not by charming him, by presenting personal credentials, but simply from the nature of her fact:

On the north-eastern shore of England there is a town called Monkshaven, containing at the present day about fifteen thousand inhabitants. There were, however, but half the number at the end of the last century, and it was at that period that the events narrated in the following pages occurred.

She does not hide behind the conscious claim to be inventing, but determines to convince as fact convinces. It is the most neutral of methods, in that, though it sets up few expectations, and in isolation seems even a little bleak, it sets up no false ones, wholly avoiding the dangers of daunting the reader with the rather ponderous considering of what it will avoid, like Scott's, or the possible unattractiveness of too close contact, like George Eliot's, and above all avoids what amounts to the semi-deceitful self-excusing of George Eliot and Trollope. There is undoubtedly a sense of duplicity and the inverted boast about all these three, who are implying with pseudo-modesty that they are only inventing what is in its nature inferior to fact, to reality, with the intention of disarming the reader and engaging his sympathy for what they intend to make, ultimately, in their various ways, more exciting, or significant, or attractive than 'reality'. Elizabeth Gaskell has always been as conscious as any of them that there must be a discernible likeness between the actual and invented fiction, and just as conscious that the purposes and value of fiction cannot be judged merely by how far it recreates the actual; but she has never chosen to point out this likeness by using her own personality.

When she moves on to setting her scene, she continues to remain virtually invisible, delineating it, not as she herself responds to it, but by every other method at her disposal, to persuade the reader that what she selects is what any observer would see, so that no sense of a narrative *persona* is perceived. She equally skilfully avoids the feeling that the third participant in this trio of author and material and reader is merely a watcher of print on a page:

> Somehow in this country sea-thoughts followed the thinker far inland; whereas in most other parts of the island, at five miles from the ocean, he has all but forgotten the existence of such an element as salt water.

In such a passage, where the 'thinker' may be a character, or the author, or the reader himself, the separation between them becomes as insignificant as possible. She employs 'you', as the most universal pronoun, equivalent to the impersonal 'one':

> in the moorland hollows, as in these valleys, trees and under-wood grew and flourished; so that, while on the bare swells of the high land you shivered at the waste desolation of the scenery, when you dropped into these wooded 'bottoms' you were charmed with the nestling shelter they gave.

She continues to give this feeling of the universal truth of her facts by introducing the responses of those who experience them, as well as of the observer:

> It was also not surprising that the whole town had an amphibi-ous appearance, to a degree unusual even in a sea-port. Every one depended on the whale-fishery, and almost every male inhabitant had been, or hoped to be, a sailor. Down by the river the smell was almost intolerable to any but Monkshaven people during certain seasons of the year; but on these unsavoury 'staithes' the old men and children lounged for hours, almost as if they revelled in the odours of train-oil.

Detachment as well as engagement are thus precisely established and regulated: detachment without any loss of sympathy with Monkshaven and its folk by the comparison with sea-ports in general, and by the delicately unobtrusive humour of the single epithet 'amphibious', and the verb 'revelled', which at the same time compel the reader to participate in the sensuous experience. Thus in regulating the distance between observer and subject, Elizabeth Gaskell obscures the difference between author and reader, who, almost falling together into a single identity at such points as this, can separate, where Elizabeth Gaskell uses the authorial 'I', into entities who, though separate, think alike. When, a few sentences later, she observes

> There was also a dread and an irritation in every one's mind, at the time of which I write, in connection with the neighbouring sea.

the 'I' is an entirely trustworthy medium, scarcely felt as a separate person.

From Angus Easson, *Elizabeth Gaskell* (London: Routledge and Kegan Paul, 1979), pp. 170-3:

The first volume of the novel ends with Sylvia committed to Charley Kinraid, and Philip at a height of his business career in the Fosters' offer of partnership; the second, after Charley's disappearance and Robson's death, ends with Philip engaged to Sylvia – indeed in Gaskell's original writing, probably ended with Sylvia's breaking to Kester (Chapter 28) her acceptance of Philip and determination to stand by that decision. Even transference of the next chapter, 'Wedding Raiment', to be the last of Volume 2 does not alter that emphasis on Philip having achieved what ought to be his personal ideal, as the partnership was his worldly one. And the third volume shows the destruction of both his public and emotional life. As with *Ruth*, her other three-volume novel, Gaskell seems to have borne the physical format of issue in mind as a factor in the shape of the story. But a comparison between the two novels (and the centrality of the female character and the nature of her personal crisis makes this easy) shows how Gaskell has progressed in her art. There is none of the smudging at vital points, either in terms of plot or character; things not shown to us (Daniel Robson's trial, for instance) are fully accounted for, lightly in terms of detail, but subtly, even painfully, in their effects upon the women who wait, so there are no vague gaps as there was earlier between Ruth departing for London and her arrival in Wales. Gaskell is now also certain how to handle the relationship between subject and mood. A jarring in *Ruth* may be felt between on the one hand the idyllic, apparently historical tone of much of the story – located in the old town at the opening, the natural description, the life of the Bensons – and on the other, the 'problem' nature of Ruth's situation, the exposure Gaskell sought to make of a contemporary outrage that would seem better suited to the world of Manchester.

In *Sylvia's Lovers* this harmony of subject and mood is above all in landscape. The natural scene plays its part in the relationship between sea and moorland, between fishing town and farm, between character and action, establishing a world where even the dweller inland is aware of the sea, and where war and the clash of nations make themselves known not only in expensive bread but in the more immediate terms of the press-gang and its preying on the very life-blood of the community, the men who are its sailors. When Gaskell describes Monkshaven and its hinterland, she is already setting the story in motion:

> There was a comparative fertility and luxuriance down below in the rare green dales. The narrow meadows stretching along the brookside seemed as though the cows could really satisfy their hunger in the deep rich grass; whereas on the higher lands the scanty herbage was hardly worth the fatigue of moving about in search of it. Even in these 'bottoms' the piping sea-winds, following the current of the stream, stunted and cut low any trees; but still there was rich, thick underwood, tangled and tied together with brambles, and briar-roses, and honey-suckle . . . But for twenty miles inland there was no forgetting the sea, nor the sea-trade; refuse, shell-fish, sea-weed, the offal of the melting-houses, were the staple manure of the district; great ghastly whale-jaws, bleached bare and white, were the arches over the gate-posts to many a field or moorland stretch. Out of every family of several sons, however agricultural their position might be, one had gone to sea, and the mother looked wistfully seaward at the changes of the keen piping moorland winds.

The very land runs down to the sea rather than inland, so that Kinraid, having taken his farewell of Sylvia, bursts before Philip's gaze onto the beach by a valley leading down from Haytersbank. To Philip, Sylvia might seem to look down to the town and the security of himself, a landsman, but the reader feels how through Charley's defiance of the press-gang and the yarns swapped between him and her father, it is beyond the town that she looks and out to sea and to romance. Importantly, part of her swing back to Philip and part of her understanding of the man, even though she did not love him, comes as she recognizes the truth of Clarinda Kinraid's account of Philip saving Charley. Philip may be rejected, but she does not doubt his bravery and admires it in action beyond the seas.

Sylvia is the undoubted centre of the novel. Although *Sylvia's Lovers* was the last of the novel's proposed titles – *The Specksioneer* stressed Kinraid, the later *Philip's Idol* emphasized Hepburn – it gives the right sense of her dealings with other people, a still centre (her physical situation at Monkshaven unmoved, at least) who by her very being draws men into this emotional identity. She begins as a free-natured girl, slightly wilful in her desire for a cloak of brilliant red rather than the useful grey duffle (not a question of warmth or durability: the quality is the same, whatever the colour), playful as she washes her feet before she and Molly put on their shoes for town, yet already open in her nature – an openness unconscious and possibly uncontrollable. When the whaler comes in she accepts naturally the joyful handclasp of the girl who calls out, 'She's o'er t'bar! She's o'er t'bar! I'm boun' to tell mother!' The contrast with Philip is clear enough. He takes on himself the position of moral guardian and Sylvia understandably resents his asking how she knows such a girl, as she did his insisting that it was the grey duffle she wanted, not the red. Her resentment is as understandable as his wish to show love by the affectionate care he hopes will one day be his right. Philip's tenderness is clear, however unwelcome. He is a lover able already to draw so much pleasure from her mere presence that when he is to accompany her home he anticipates 'so keenly the pleasure awaiting him in the walk that he was almost surprised by the gravity of his companion'. Charley Kinraid's role as yet is more covert. Molly Corney has already hinted (boasted, rather) that Charley is more than cousin to her and Sylvia, drawn by the death of the seaman and Kinraid's heroic stand against the press-gang, feels that the harpooner is Molly's by right. She accepts readily enough the proposal to go and see the fashionable cut of cloaks at church the day of the seaman's funeral, an occasion which she cannot anyway treat with the simple levity of Molly's excuse for going and where she and Kinraid are brought into physical proximity. Her emotional responsiveness has already been established by handclasp and faint when the whaler came in. Touched by the service and burial, her sensibility expands. Sylvia is not yet fully aware, indeed, is never fully aware on the rational level, though she is to feel more in years to come and feel more intensely, but she is open to impressions. Because more finely attuned she is aware of the implications of relationships and actions, suffers more than ordinary folk, and in suffering is set apart. What the ordinary character collapses under or does not notice, the tragic character bears.

From Jenny Uglow, *Elizabeth Gaskell: A Habit of Stories* (London: Faber & Faber, 1993), pp. 513–15:

In *Sylvia's Lovers*, even more than in *Mary Barton*, Gaskell kept faith with the expression of the people. Speech, as William had insisted in his 'Lectures on Lancashire Dialect', has its own history and evolution, displaying regional, class and individual variants: Gaskell carefully gave Bell Robson Cumbrian forms to fit her origins. The manuscript reveals numerous alterations of word endings and technical details such as variations of the definite article – the, th', t' – and in the second edition she meticulously corrected the dialect wherever Lancashire forms had corrupted Yorkshire ('ne'er' to 'niver'; 'dost na' to 'dostn' t'). So precise was she that her idioms entered Wright's *English Dialect Dictionary* (such as: 'main an' ' – very; 'a coil' – a fuss; 'maskit' – infused; 't'fettling' – repairing), while other terms were included in locally compiled glossaries.

Such details, imperceptible to most of her readers, were in tune with her determination to gather the 'unimportant' chaff and dust of past lives. Diction and syntax are carefully adapted to the speaker, reflecting relationships as well as origins: the intimate second person 'yo' as opposed to the formal plural 'ye', or the Quaker 'thee' and 'thou'. Gradations are tenderly charted. Bell comes from a higher class than her husband (before her marriage she was a Preston, of that familiar Lakeland 'Statesman' class) and it irritates Daniel when she uses a word beyond his comprehension, like 'pretext', which he then promptly misuses. The misconception of meaning is more than merely verbal, as Sylvia recognizes when she wishes her mother had not spoken in favour of the grey cloak:

'Ay! but mother's words are scarce, and weigh heavy. Feyther's liker me, and we talk a deal o' rubble; but mother's words are liker to hewn stone. She puts a deal o' meaning in 'em' (Chapter 2).

Daniel's 'deal o' rubble', gathered over a wandering life, has rough eloquence, like John Barton's Manchester speech, but his words spring from passion and his rash use of them is his downfall. Over a year before he spurs on the crowd in the riot, Bell blanches at his angry speeches about the press-gang:

> 'Ay, missus, yo' may look. I wunnot pick and choose my words, noather for yo' nor for nobody, when I speak o' that daumed gang. I'm noane ashamed o' my words. They're true, and I'm ready to prove 'em' (Chapter 4).

Through the words native to them the inarticulate become articulate, even while they feel outcast from language. When the Robsons' farmhand Kester, who has loved Sylvia since she was a baby, visits her after her marriage, he recites the old sanding rhyme Gaskell heard at her own wedding, looking to the continuation of life through 'fruitful progeny':

> 'Theere, that's po'try for yo' as I larnt i' my youth. But there's a deal to be said as cannot be put int' po'try, an' yet a cannot say it, somehow. It'd tax a parson t' say a' as a've getten i' my mind. It's like a heap o' woo' just after shearin'-time; it's worth a deal, but it tak's a vast o' combin', an' cardin', an' spinnin', afore it can be made use on. If a were up to t' use o' words, a could say a mighty deal; but somehow a'm tongue-teed when a come to want my words most.' (Chapter 30)

Kester's image of the sheared wool, drawn from life, is as vivid as any poetry. Sylvia's resistance to literacy may be foolish, but it is also understood as loyalty to the unregulated oral vigour of her class. As such it contrasts to the upward aspirations of Philip, who reads aloud in a high-pitched voice 'which deprived words of their reality', or to the Foster brothers in their spotless, right-angled room, the smiles on their honest faces 'drawn to a line of exactitude', preparing their conversation 'like London diners-out of the last generation', intoning articles of trade like articles of faith. Jeremiah reads his Bible daily to the housekeeper: 'like many, he reserved a peculiar tone for that solemn occupation – and one which he unconsciously employed for the present enumeration of pounds, shillings and pence'.

The voices of the new bourgeoisie sound forced compared with Sylvia's 'natural' expression, but Gaskell respects these people too and does not mock them. As Philip points out, Sylvia's objection to printed books with their 'new-fangled words' confines her to the past. She must use her head as well as her heart and adapt to the wider culture, just as she must look at the globe to find other places than Greenland and the Arctic seas. And, as he sketches his map, she does begin to look outward, although still from the vantage of the local: 'even she became a little interested in starting from a great black spot called Monkshaven, and in the shaping of land and sea around that one centre'. Words also map the world. Every life, explains Philip, has its own language; hers of woman's work, his of the shop, that of the 'folks in fields' and the 'high English that parsons and lawyers speak'. *Sylvia's Lovers* is full of such vocabularies, creating a complex, developing and competing universe through the words of land, sea, trade, church, state and war.

From Patsy Stoneman, *Elizabeth Gaskell* (Brighton: Harvester, 1987), pp. 149–53:

Sylvia's Lovers is the third of Elizabeth Gaskell's novels to hinge around a lie (see *Ruth*, *North and South*), and each lie derives from a denial of female sexuality. When Philip allows Sylvia to believe that Kinraid is dead he not only makes it more likely that she will marry him but he also defines her femininity in a way which is acceptable to him. Sylvia's passion for Kinraid confirms her as a sexual being, whereas Philip wants her to be a 'pretty, soft little dove'. When he assumes the rights of a brother to '"watch o'er ye and see what company yo' kept"' he is authorised by Sylvia's mother, who sees her as a child 'to be warned off forbidden things by threats of danger'. Thus, in persisting in his lie, 'he felt like a mother withholding something injurious from the foolish wish of her plaining child', perpetuating the 'protective' parental stance which deprives women of adult status.

The more Philip is convinced of the strength of Sylvia's love for Kinraid, the more anxious he becomes

to convince her that he was dead . . . repeating . . . the lie that long ere this Kinraid was in all probability dead . . . that, even if not, he was as good as dead to her; so that the word 'dead' might be used in all honest certainty, as in one of its meanings Kinraid was dead for sure.

For Philip, Kinraid symbolises Sylvia's sexual autonomy, and he exerts his authority over her to assert that her independent sexuality is and must be dead if she is to be his wife. Their marriage is appropriately like a funeral; Philip 'wedded his long-sought bride in mourning raiment, and ... the first sounds which greeted them as they approached their home were those of weeping and wailing'. He regrets what he has done, and wants 'the old Sylvia back', but 'Alas! that Sylvia was gone for ever'. The text again inverts an accepted maxim: 'Philip was beginning to feel ... that the fruit he had so inordinately longed for was but of the nature of an apple of Sodom'. In *Paradise Lost* (X, 560–70), Sodom apples represent indulged sensuality, and William Coulson uses the phrase in this sense (*SL:* 155), but Philip's ashes in the mouth are the result of sexuality denied. '"Mrs Hepburn"' leads the life of Curly Locks, a domestic 'idol in a befitting shrine', but at night Philip looks 'to see if she were indeed sleeping by his side, or whether it was not all a dream that he called Sylvia "wife"'.

Sylvia's sexuality, however, is not dead but repressed, and Philip's unconscious desire evokes the figure of Kinraid, who was its visible sign: 'all this time Philip was troubled by a dream ... a conviction of Kinraid's living presence somewhere near him in the darkness'. When Sylvia speaks of her own dream of Kinraid, however, he finds it intolerable; '"what kind of a woman are yo' to go dreaming of another man ... when yo're a wedded wife?"'. Before long Philip is jealous of anyone who receives her love – Hester, the baby and even 'the inanimate ocean'.

Sylvia, meanwhile, 'was glad occasionally to escape from the comfortable imprisonment of her "parlour" into 'solitude and open air, and the sight and sound of the mother-like sea'. Both 'sea' and 'mother' are ambiguous terms in *Sylvia's Lovers*; her mother's surveillance, perpetuated by Philip, denies to Sylvia both Kinraid and sexual maturity, but her mother's impulse to succour the needy, manifested in Sylvia's effort to save the sinking ship, brings back Kinraid and a crisis of adult autonomy. Like the mother, the sea is the site both of love and death, both of Kinraid's parting pledge and of his disappearance and Philip's denial, and provokes in Sylvia a complication of emotions involving physical and ideological 'death': Kinraid 'was dead; he must be dead; for was she not Philip's wife?' Recalling what Philip said about her dream, she shuddered 'as if cold steel had been plunged into her warm, living body' and when she sees Kinraid again, 'her heart leaped up and fell again dead within her, as if she had been shot'. Sylvia's 'death' takes the feminine form of silence. After Philip's 'cold steel' speech 'she lay down, motionless and silent', 'her lips compressed' as Hester's are from long usage. 'Nothing stirred her from her fortress of reserve, but though 'she said no word', she 'constantly rebelled in thought and deed'. Quiet as a Quaker, her stillness is the result of 'unnatural restraint'. Eventually, feeling that she ' "cannot stay in t'house to be choked up wi' [her] tears" ', she runs out into a storm and, like Ruth, is 'quieted by this tempest of the elements'. As in Chapter 3, her emotion is shaped by communal feeling, and as part of a crowd she unwittingly helps save the ship on which Kinraid is returning.

Kinraid's return is the Freudian 'return of the repressed', initially 'unutterable' (heading to Chapter 35) and, as in the conclusion to *Ruth*, madness threatens: she speaks 'with incessant low incontinence of words', and understands only that Philip ' "kept something from me as would ha' made me a different woman" ', and understands only that Philip ' "kept something from me as would ha' made me a different woman" '. Unlike Ruth, however, Sylvia never connived at the lie denying her sexuality. She was 'no prude, and had been brought up in simple, straightforward country ways'. The historical setting releases Elizabeth Gaskell from the disabling Victorian concept of innocence which entangles *Ruth* and *North and South*, and allows her to present Philip's Puritan ethic as an imposed ideology. Sylvia's response to Kinraid's return is not shame but indignation, expressed in the crude terms of her father's 'wild justice'. She 'assume[s] to herself the right of speech', and, 'with her cheeks and eyes aflame', makes a vow of implacable enmity to Philip.

From Jane Spencer, *Elizabeth Gaskell* (London: Macmillan, 1993), pp. 110–13:

Other characters in the novel construct histories by telling the story of their own lives or by interpreting other people's stories. Thus in William Coulson's version of history, his sister died mainly because of her disappointed love for Charley Kinraid, who 'kept company' with her for two years and then left her – an event that does not seem to be part of Kinraid's own complacent view of his past. Daniel Robson, like Philip, evidently trusts history to repeat itself. Kinraid's courtship of Sylvia reminds him of his courtship of Bell; and his approval of Kinraid as a suitor is based on what the two men have in common: both have been specksioneers in whaling-ships, both have defied the law, and both can win women's interest with their tall tales of adventurous life in the man's world of the seas. While these characters make up kinds of history, they formulate no ideas about it. Philip, on the other hand, is capable of generalising from his experience and trying out the notion of a cyclic view of history. As he does so the Yorkshire dialect of his direct speeches gives way to a modern, standard language use, suggesting a momentary collapsing of the distance between narrator and character. It is as if Philip is now sharing the role of the historian.

There remains a distinction, though, between the narrator's attitude to events and Philip Hepburn's. She does not share his cyclic view of history; rather, she reveals how the various characters, from their different points of view, perceive different parallels between past and present. Philip takes Alice Rose's disastrous marriage to a whaler who 'went after other women, and drank, and beat her' as a prediction of Sylvia's likely fate if she marries Kinraid; Daniel Robson, without consciously considering the matter, takes his own, in his view satisfactory, marriage as a good omen for his daughter's marriage to another sailor. Yet what the narrative has revealed of Kinraid's character does not warrant the assumption that he would behave like Jack Rose, while the indications of some of Bell Robson's difficulties with married life, and her evident wish that her daughter not marry a similar kind of man, belie her husband's optimistic view of Sylvia and Kinraid's relationship. The historical parallels Philip notices have no predictive force: no determinism, Gaskell places moral responsibility firmly on the individual's reaction to historical predicament. Philip notices the parallel between Jack Rose and Charley Kinraid, but does not understand the parallel between his own position, as rejected lover, and John Foster's. Foster has reacted to rejection by quietly offering Alice Rose financial help, and by planning to leave all his money to her daughter – a complete contrast to Philip's selfish pursuit of Sylvia. The novel's view of history is that it is a series of stories that it is up to the individual to interpret: viewed as simple reflections of the individual's own preoccupations they merely help compound existing errors, but viewed as moral example they might help him or her to act well.

Philip, with his oppressive pursuit of Sylvia, and the cruel deception that he so carefully rationalises, is the most culpable character in the novel, the one least the victim of external forces. Yet this is what makes him interesting to Gaskell, and makes her focus on him as tragic hero rather than on Daniel Robson, the rebellious but doomed victim of government injustice. In the end she is less interested in exploring the historical conflict between governors and governed than in the internal conflicts of characters seen as relatively free moral agents. Daniel Robson's fate illustrates the helplessness of an ordinary man caught up in historical events beyond his control; Philip's does not, though he becomes a soldier and returns from the wars a broken man. He chooses to enlist out of shame when Kinraid returns and Sylvia rejects her husband, and by saving Kinraid's life on the battlefield he atones for his earlier action. History, as exemplified in the siege of Acre, has become mere background for the working-out of an individual's moral salvation. Gaskell's treatment of the siege of Acre has been criticised as a melodramatic lapse in a realistic historical novel, but it is necessary to understand its function: the rehabilitation of a form of heroism even as conventional battle-heroics are mocked. The soldiers understand little of the causes of the war and Kinraid's courage goes along with a childish naïvety: real heroism is not in battle but in Philip's rescue of the man he had wronged and hated.

As J. M. Rignall has pointed out, Sylvia's two lovers swop roles during the novel: Kinraid from being the representative of an old heroic way of life changes to become a social success in the new century; Philip, the unheroic, new bourgeois man, becomes a heroic rescuer and a social outcast. The changes are entirely consistent with the two men's characters: Kinraid's opportunism, Philip's obsessive commitment. Thus the novel resists any schematic linking of characters' social position and occupation to the historical narrative of the decline of old ways of life and the development of nineteenth-century society. Character is strongly influenced but not completely determined by social, regional and historical position; individual temperament is given a great deal of weight too. At the end of the novel the historical narrative recedes and there is a brief picture of Monkshaven as it is in the narrator's own time, no longer a whaling community but a Victorian seaside resort. Kinraid, the former whaler, would be more at home there than Philip.

From Andrew Sanders, *The Victorian Historical Novel 1840–1880* (London: Macmillan, 1978), pp. 206–7:

The actions of the press-gang in and around Monkshaven fully justify Daniel Robson's passionately rooted hatred of its interference, and he is not alone in seeing it as a challenge both to his private independence and to the maintenance of order and dignity in society. Monkshaven mourns as a community when a sailor is killed resisting empressment, but Mrs Gaskell balances the indignation she clearly shares with her characters against a disinclination to condemn the State, the law, or the officers of the law. It is more than simply an attempt at fair-mindedness on her part, for, as in *Mary Barton* or *North and South*, she seems too ready to accept the basic structure of society to offer any challenge beyond a moral one. She demands a similar acceptance and a similar charity of her central characters, and acknowledges both the strength of a conservative spirit and the real difficulties which beset those who seek a fundamental change in the social order. With Dickens she looks first to a change in heart before she dares to consider the prospect of the coming of the millennium. In *Sylvia's Lovers* she embodies her own fears, and something of her own dilemma, in the divided response of the vicar of Monkshaven to popular dissent from authority. There is sufficient critical detachment for her not to comment on his compromise, and there is a wit and gentleness reminiscent of George Eliot's portraits of clergymen. She presents Dr Wilson as a 'kindly, peaceable old man, hating strife and troubled waters above everything', while offering us an equally telling account of the troubled waters. When Dr Wilson is called upon to preach at the sailor's funeral he finds himself faced with the problem of giving comfort to his bereaved gardener and of interpreting what has happened to the community as a whole. The vicar finally, but nevertheless uneasily, compromises, hastily mumbling a sermon 'which might have done as well for a baby cut off in a convulsion fit as for a strong man shot down with all his eager blood within him, by men as hot-blooded as himself'. In this case there is an inequality in death, and there is a discord between the Laws of Christ and the Laws of Man which Mrs Gaskell sees Wilson as incapable of resolving. The vicar's flock is sent away disappointed, but neither they nor the novelist condemn his weakness. The entire argument of the novel, however, presents a more complex and various approach to his dilemma, and its resolution of the argument in a statement of faith in the Laws of Christ is, in part, a final comment on Dr Wilson's earlier fallibility.

SUGGESTIONS FOR FURTHER READING

Biography and Criticism

There have been a number of important studies of Elizabeth Gaskell over the last twenty-five years or so. We give a selection below, with brief comments, and include one or two earlier studies which have some significance.

A. Stanton Whitfield, *Mrs Gaskell: Her Life and Work* (London: Routledge, 1929). Dated, but with some insightful comments.

A. B. Hopkins, *Elizabeth Gaskell: Her Life and Work* (London: John Lehmann, 1952). The major appraisal before expansive investigations; well-researched and documented, intelligent commentary.

J. G. Sharps, *Mrs Gaskell's Observation and Invention: A Study of Her Non-Biographic Works* (Arundell: Linden Press, 1970). An essential read for the Gaskell enthusiast. Introductions to each of the works, with factual, biographical, critical information, superbly researched. The detail is unsparingly provided, making it the complete companion to Gaskell studies.

Winifred Gérin, *Elizabeth Gaskell: A Biography* (Oxford: Clarendon Press, 1976). A sound, well-written life.

Arthur Pollard, *Mrs Gaskell: Novelist and Biographer* (Manchester: Manchester University Press, 1965). Sound, interesting.

Angus Easson, *Elizabeth Gaskell* (London: Routledge & Kegan Paul, 1979). A wide-ranging examination, with particular insights into the shorter works.

Patsy Stoneman, *Elizabeth Gaskell*, Key Women Writers (Brighton: Harvester Press, 1987). Gaskell seen in the light of feminist theory: a challenging and provocative study with some excellent closework.

Angus Easson (ed.), *Elizabeth Gaskell: The Critical Heritage* (London:

Routledge, 1991). A selection of contemporary reviews, with a useful extension of these in the form of comments and opinions up to 1910.

Hilary M. Schor, *Scheherazade in the Marketplace* (Oxford: Oxford University Press, 1992). Strong feminist emphasis on Victorian culture and Gaskell's coming to terms with her own identity as woman and writer.

Jenny Uglow, *Elizabeth Gaskell: A Habit of Stories* (London: Faber and Faber, 1993). Probably the definitive biography, as valuable for its close examination of the texts as for its focus on the writer in her domestic and literary context.

Letters

J. A. V. Chapple and A. Pollard (eds), *The Letters of Mrs Gaskell* (Manchester: Manchester University Press, 1966). The best possible introduction, showing Gaskell primarily in her domestic situation with her family worries and concerns but also as writer and reader. The letters indicate clearly the quality of her life and her wide-ranging interests.

J. A. V. Chapple with J. G. Sharps, *Elizabeth Gaskell: A Portrait in Letters* (Manchester: Manchester University Press, 1980). As above, stimulating and delightful.

The Gaskell Society (founded 1985) produces a newsletter and the *Gaskell Society Journal*, both of which are invaluable.

TEXT SUMMARY

Chapter 1: Monkshaven
The town and its history described – importance of the Greenland whaling trade – implementation of the press-gang – their local reception – their practice along the coast – the Randyvow-house.

Chapter 2: Home from Greenland
Introduction of Sylvia Robson and of Molly Corney – their conversation – their seeing the whaler home from Greenland – local excitement – Molly tells Sylvia of her specksioneer cousin Charley Kinraid – they set off for Foster's.

Chapter 3: Buying a New Cloak
The Foster brothers and their shopmen Philip Hepburn and William Coulson – Hester Rose and her mother – the purchase of the scarlet duffle – the press-gang seize sailors as they come ashore – anguish and anger of the populace – Sylvia breaks down hysterically – Philip offers to take her home – Hester's reactions.

Chapter 4: Philip Hepburn
The Robsons and Haytersbank farm – Philip's arrival with Sylvia – Daniel's account of his previous experience with the press-gang – his argument with Philip – Sylvia's gracefulness while spinning – debate with her mother about the cloak – Daniel more aggressive after drink.

Chapter 5: Story of the Press-Gang
Bad weather – Daniel kept at home – Sylvia conspires with Hester to get Harry Donkin to relieve Daniel's boredom – Harry tells the story of the press-gang in Monkshaven – the attack on the *Good Fortune* – Kinraid's heroism – his severe wounds – Sylvia determines to learn more of this from Molly.

Chapter 6: The Sailor's Funeral
The Corneys' house described – the slovenliness of it and its surroundings – Sylvia suspects a mutual attachment between Kinraid and Molly – news of Darley's funeral – Sylvia returns to find that Donkin and her

father have had a good argument – the Sunday of the funeral –
description of the old church – the vicar's sermon on the occasion – the
funeral procession – arrival of the wounded Kinraid – the burial and
the reactions of the mourners – Sylvia and Philip meet Kinraid – Sylvia
very taken with the latter.

Chapter 7: Tête-à-Tête – The Will

Philip's fears that Kinraid will be sought out by the gang – meeting
with Hester – Sylvia aware of Hester's goodness – gossip about Coulson
and Hester – later Sylvia questions Philip about the whaling trade and
Greenland – Philip offers to teach her – Bell's hope that Sylvia and
Philip will become attached to each other – switch to Alice Rose – her
simple making of her will – Coulson's hopes of Hester – talk of the
funeral with Philip absent – Coulson says that his sister's heart was
broken by her treatment in the past at the hands of Kinraid – Philip
late arriving back.

Chapter 8: Attraction and Repulsion

Activities at Haytersbank – Daniel and Sylvia set off to see Kinraid –
gift of sausages for him from Bell – Kinraid much recovered – agrees to
visit Daniel in return – Philip visits Haytersbank while they are at the
Corneys – has come to give Sylvia a lesson – returns the next night to
do so – Sylvia's irritation, frustration – Philip reads the war news to
Daniel – Sylvia resistant to Philip.

Chapter 9: The Specksioneer

Kinraid visits Haytersbank – clearly admires Sylvia – Kinraid and
Daniel talk of smuggling – then of Greenland adventures and the
whaling trade – graphic account of icebergs – individual anecdotes –
Kinraid's narrative flair – Daniel repeats his own stories – Bell suspects
Kinraid and Sylvia are attracted to each other – hastens their guest's
departure – Sylvia dreams of those distant seas.

Chapter 10: A Refractory Pupil

Philip's next lesson – Sylvia makes her interests clear – Kinraid arrives,
Philip offended – tries to outstay Kinraid but has to take his leave –
later Sylvia feels that Kinraid will marry Molly Corney – Philip
continues to visit during the winter months – Molly sees Sylvia and tells
her that she is to be married, but not to Kinraid.

Chapter 11: Visions of the Future

Molly, married, leaves for Newcastle – Sylvia noticed by Hester – the
latter in turn notes Philip's interest in Sylvia – Sylvia sells her market

produce – Daniel flattered by the attention she receives – Philip disapproves of her father's taking her to a public house – he tells Bell – Simpson pays Sylvia coarse compliments – the Foster brothers plans for Philip and Coulson.

Chapter 12: New Year's Fête

Bell taken ill – Sylvia invited to New Year's Eve party – mother urges her to go – Philip also decides to go – buys her a briar-rose pattern ribbon – Kinraid at the Corneys' party – Molly irritates Sylvia – couples her name with Philip's – Sylvia determines not to speak much to Philip – he notices her staid behaviour – Sylvia talks to Kinraid – the party described – Sylvia 'treated as the belle' – her refusal to pay the forfeit to Kinraid – he gets her alone and exacts the kiss – Philip realizes this – he is to escort her home – however, Daniel arrives to fetch her – friction with Kinraid avoided – Philip returns to his lodging at Alice Rose's.

Chapter 13: Perplexities

Coulson questions Philip about the party – next day Alice displeased with Philip because he did not attend the watch-night service with them – Philip tired and absorbed – forgets his promise to a customer's child – gives Hester a handkerchief from himself and Coulson – Philip criticized by Alice – she resents his constant trips to Haytersbank – Coulson reveals that he and Philip have been invited to supper at the Fosters – Kinraid and the Corney girls visit the shop.

Chapter 14: Partnership

Coulson and Philip at the Fosters' house – the brothers' proposals – outward sternness soon gives way to generous terms – financial details – partnership to be secret for the present – unofficial provision for Hester.

Chapter 15: A Difficult Question

Philip's prayers – Kinraid goes to Haytersbank – milking of the cows – Kinraid reveals that he is going to Shields next day – Kester praises Sylvia to Kinraid – the latter's courtship of Sylvia – Bell's intervention means Kinraid has to leave – the salutary story of Nancy Hartley – 'He once was here'.

Chapter 16: The Engagement

The winter – Bell the same – Philip's visits – milder weather – Kinraid purchases the ribbon – Coulson reveals to Philip the story of his sister's betrayal by Kinraid – the latter visits Sylvia – the courtship renewed –

Sylvia's shy withdrawal – Kinraid tells Daniel of his love for her –
Sylvia and Kinraid engaged.

Chapter 17: Rejected Warnings
John Foster gives Philip a commission to London – Philip tells Coulson,
Alice, Hester – the latter resents Coulson's resentment of Philip – Philip
goes to Haytersbank – meets Kinraid – the specksioneer leaves – Philip
tells Sylvia his news – then reveals the stories about Kinraid – Sylvia
angry – eventually says goodbye to Philip.

Chapter 18: Eddy in Love's Current
On a March morning Philip sets out for Hartlepool – sees Kinraid in
the distance leaving Haytersbank and signalling to Sylvia – Philip
follows him – sees him ambushed and taken by the press-gang – Kinraid
gives Philip his message for Sylvia – he is rowed away – Philip uncertain
whether he has promised to give the message to Sylvia or not.

Chapter 19: An Important Mission
Philip stays the night in Newcastle – writes to Daniel – does not
mention the impressment of Kinraid – hears sailors talking of Kinraid's
amatory and physical prowess – serves the Fosters well in London –
arrives back and sets off for Haytersbank.

Chapter 20: Loved and Lost
A May evening – Philip and Coulson now proclaimed as partners –
arrived at Haytersbank, Philip sees Sylvia standing alone in the garden
– Bell tells him that Kinraid dead – Sylvia deeply depressed – Philip
withholds his own good news – next day Daniel hears of it – Daniel
and Bell discuss Sylvia's state.

Chapter 21: A Rejected Suitor
The Fosters interest themselves in Philip's and Coulson's relationship
to Hester – Philip convinces himself (temporarily) that he was right not
to tell Sylvia what had happened to Kinraid – Hester meanwhile rejects
Coulson – the latter marries within the year.

Chapter 22: Deepening Shadows
Philip continues to visit Haytersbank – gossip that Kinraid was attached
to Bessy Corney – Philip makes progress in business – press-gang active
again in the area – some speculation that Kinraid was taken by them –
Daniel obsessed with the gang.

Chapter 23: Retaliation

The 'Randyvowse' and the gang – the resistance and Daniel's part in it – the attack and the firing of the place – Daniel's compassion towards Simpson – his contemplation of the night's work.

Chapter 24: Brief Rejoicing

Daniel late home, worn out – his account of what happened – Philip's arrival and his dismay at Daniel's part in the affair – threat of action – Kester decides to stay up on guard – atmosphere charged with fear.

Chapter 25: Coming Troubles

Warrant out for Daniel – he is taken – asks forgiveness of Sylvia as he leaves – Philip decides to get legal advice for Daniel – learns that Daniel will shortly be conveyed to York Castle – persuades Hester to go out to Haytersbank to bring Bell and Sylvia to see Daniel.

Chapter 26: A Dreary Vigil

Hester successful – Sylvia's praise for her – the journey to Monkshaven – Philip takes Daniel's comforter to him – on his return he tells Sylvia that her father is likely to be charged with felony – gradually she comes to realize that Daniel may be hanged – Philip reveals his love for her – she is in no condition to respond.

Chapter 27: Gloomy Days

Philip provides for Daniel's defence – Kester and the friction with Philip – Sylvia resents Kester's innuendo – Kester's apology – Philip in York – Sylvia and Bell awaiting the verdict – Bell's courage, Philip's support – Daniel is to be executed.

Chapter 28: The Ordeal

Kester has given Philip money to help Daniel – it is returned – Sylvia and Bell come home from York – Kester tells of Simpson's suffering at the hands of local sympathizers – mental deterioration of Bell – the Robsons to leave Haytersbank – Sylvia confides her feelings to Kester – asks his advice – but decides to marry Philip although she does not love him.

Chapter 29: Wedding Raiment

Philip and Sylvia engaged – she tells him that Kester believes that Kinraid may have been impressed – Philip still silent – Sylvia refuses to forgive the dying Simpson – thinks again – Simpson dies without her saying anything – she decides to wear mourning at her wedding – Hester refuses to be a bridesmaid, will stay with Bell – the latter hysterical on entering Philip's house – Sylvia's gratitude to Hester.

Chapter 30: Happy Days
Philip prospers – Sylvia cares for her mother – alterations at Hayters-bank – Kester's news and his feelings for Sylvia – Hester and the Fosters begin to love her – the visit to the Fosters – Sylvia loves Hester – Sylvia's baby, named Bella.

Chapter 31: Evil Omens
Philip hears Sylvia passionately call Charley's name – she is feverish – anger between them – Sylvia's obduracy – her regular churchgoing – she is happy on the seashore – Philip still prospers.

Chapter 32: Rescued from the Waves
Hester's feelings for Sylvia – her insight into the marriage – Philip's complaints – Bell reprimands Sylvia for not being a good wife – Sylvia tells Philip their marriage was a mistake – walks near sea – vessel nearly on the rocks – Sylvia helps with the rescue – she does not know it, but she has helped to save Kinraid.

Chapter 33: An Apparition
Bell ill but continues to nag Sylvia – the latter decides to go to Haytersbank to gather balm – does so and sees Kinraid by the stile – he follows her to her home – he reveals his message to Philip – Philip is summoned – Kinraid tells her she is not married – produces the ribbon – Sylvia swears not to forgive Philip – hysterically kisses Kinraid goodbye.

Chapter 34: A Reckless Recruit
Philip hears the news of the rescued ship and more of Kinraid, a commissioned officer – Philip leaves home – takes silhouette of Sylvia with him – comes to a small public house – joins the marines – calls himself Stephen Freeman.

Chapter 35: Things Unutterable
Sylvia exhausted – Bell is dying – Philip is missed – Bell dies – still no news of Philip – Sylvia rouses herself to attend her mother's funeral.

Chapter 36: Mysterious Tidings
Kester brings news to Sylvia – blesses her baby – Hester gets a letter from Philip – he begs her to look after Sylvia – Sylvia goes to Jeremiah Foster's – tells him her story about Philip and Kinraid – he promises not to tell his brother this.

Chapter 37: Bereavement
Jeremiah proposes that Hester and her mother share the market-place house with Sylvia and her child – little Bella the centre of attention –

Sylvia continues to confide in Kester – she learns that Hester loves Philip – Hester keeps her sufferings to herself.

Chapter 38: The Recognition
The siege of Acre – Sir Sidney Smith and Kinraid – Kinraid badly wounded – expects to die – saved by Philip – Kinraid recognizes him – Philip afterwards untraceable since he is wounded and scarred beyond recognition.

Chapter 39: Confidences
Molly Brunton (née Corney) returns to Monkshaven – tells Sylvia of Kinraid's marriage – Sylvia angry with Molly's lack of principle – Alice condemns Molly after she has gone – Hester confesses her feelings for Philip to Sylvia – Sylvia in turn confides that she will never forgive him for his concealment over Kinraid.

Chapter 40: An Unexpected Messenger
Kinraid's wife calls – gives an account of the siege – says that Philip saved her husband's life – Sylvia cannot believe that this is true – Hester accepts it.

Chapter 41: The Bedesman of St Sepulchre
Philip moved from ship to ship – arrives at Portsmouth – Kinraid passes him – does not recognize him but gives him money – Philip gives it to the wife of a dying fellow-marine – Philip arrives at the Hospital of St Sepulchre – taken in by the warden as a bedesman.

Chapter 42: A Fable at Fault
Philip broods about the past – reads about Sir Guy of Warwick – decides he must see Sylvia – takes two months to walk to Monkshaven – sees Sylvia with their child, apparently happy as a circus enters the town.

Chapter 43: The Unknown
Kester visits Sylvia – she tells him of Mrs Kinraid's visit – Sylvia unknown to Philip is softening towards him – Sylvia visits Kester's widowed sister – she has taken a lodger – this is Philip – thus Sylvia does not know how close to her husband she is.

Chapter 44: First Words
Philip somewhat stronger – little Bella gives him a piece of cake – Bella drops Hester's watch – Hester takes it for repair – recognizes Philip's watch among others there – thinks that Philip is near at hand.

Chapter 45: Saved and Lost

Sylvia broods about Philip – Kester brings the dramatic news that Philip has saved Bella from drowning – Sylvia goes to the dying Philip – she is moved to forgiveness – he is comforted – she begs him to forgive her – Hester takes charge of Bella – she is the great comfort to mother and child – Sylvia dies before Bella is grown up – Hester cares for Bella – Hester founds almshouses in memory of Philip.